AGENCY, PARTNERSHIP, AND THE LLC: THE LAW OF UNINCORPORATED BUSINESS ENTERPRISES

AGENCY, PARTNERSHIP, AND THE LLC: THE LAW OF UNINCORPORATED BUSINESS ENTERPRISES

Selected Statutes and Form Agreements

2008 Edition

J. Dennis Hynes
Nicholas A. Rosenbaum Professor of Law Emeritus
University of Colorado

Mark J. Loewenstein
Nicholas A. Rosenbaum Professor of Law
University of Colorado

ISBN#: 978-1-4224-1168-1

NOTE TO USERS
To ensure that you are using the latest materials available in this area, please be sure to periodically check the LexisNexis Law School web site for downloadable updates and supplements at www.lexisnexis.com/lawschool

Editorial Offices
744 Broad Street, Newark, NJ 07102 (973) 820-2000
201 Mission St., San Francisco, CA 94105-1831 (415) 908-3200
701 East Water Street, Charlottesville, VA 22902-7587 (434) 972-7600
www.lexis.com

PREFACE

This supplement makes available the complete text of the statutes essential for a study of the law of partnership, the limited liability partnership, and the limited liability company (LLC). It includes the Uniform Limited Partnership Act (2001); earlier iterations of uniform limited partnership acts (the 1916 act and the 1976 act with 1985 amendments); and the two versions of the uniform partnership acts, the Uniform Partnership Act (1914) and the Uniform Partnership Act (1997)("RUPA"). Also, the most recent amendments to the Uniform Limited Liability Company Act ("ULLCA") are included.

All of the comments to all of the statutes have been reproduced in their entirety, with the exception of the original Uniform Partnership Act (1914) ("UPA"). (The comments to UPA are reproduced in edited form, retaining the language that plays a material role in understanding UPA and its historical context without burdening the reader with the sometimes discursive quality of some of the UPA comments.) The comments to uniform acts are particularly helpful when substantial changes have been made to basic, nearly universally adopted legislation, which has happened in both the general and limited partnership areas of the law. They allow the reader to identify and trace the changes that have been made to the basic acts. Also, often the philosophy behind many of the changes is described, providing another reason for making comments available to the reader. There is no substitute, however, for first concentrating on and attempting to gain control over the statutes themselves for they, not the comments, are the primary source of law.

A sample LLC operating agreement and a sample partnership agreement usable in jurisdictions that have adopted RUPA are contained in the supplement. Also, a statutory short form power of attorney is included. The legislation underlying such powers makes available convenient, comprehensive, reliable powers of attorney for a variety of situations. Legislation enabling the use of such powers has been enacted in a number of states.

Finally, excerpts from the Restatement of Agency are included. Agency concepts play a significant role in the application and interpretation of the statutes reproduced below. This edition of the supplement includes numerous provisions from the recently adopted third edition of the Restatement.

Permission from the National Conference of Commissioners on Uniform State Laws to reprint the uniform acts and their comments, from West Publishing Company and Robert Keatinge to reproduce the sample LLC agreement and Professors Hillman, Weidner, and Vestal to reproduce the sample partnership agreement, and from the American Law Institute to reprint portions of the Restatement of Agency, is gratefully acknowledged.

September 2007

J. Dennis Hynes
Mark J. Loewenstein

TABLE OF CONTENTS

Page

PART SEVEN. SELECTED EXCERPTS FROM THE
RESTATEMENT OF AGENCY

PART ONE
PARTNERSHIP

UNIFORM PARTNERSHIP ACT (1914)[*]

Editor's note: The text and Comments of the Uniform Partnership Act (1914) ("UPA") contained below are taken from volume 6 of Uniform Laws Annotated, Master Edition (2001) and are reproduced with permission of the publishers. The Comments were prepared by Dr. Wm. Draper Lewis, the draftsman of the Act. They have been edited in the interest of keeping this supplement a manageable size, but all language in the Comments that contributes materially to an understanding of UPA has been retained. The information contained immediately below on adoptions of UPA is drawn from the 2006 Cumulative Annual Pocket Part to the 2001 revision of volume 6.

———

UPA was approved by the National Conference of Commissioners on Uniform State Laws in 1914 and until recently was the governing law in all states except Louisiana. It is still effective law in the following jurisdictions (the year noted immediately after each jurisdiction is the year it was adopted): Arkansas (1941), Colorado (1931), Georgia (1985), Illinois (1917), Indiana (1950), Kentucky (1954), Maine (1973), Massachusetts (1923), Michigan (1917), Mississippi (1977), Missouri (1949), Nevada (1931), New Hampshire (1973), New York (1919), North Carolina (1941), Ohio (1949), Pennsylvania (1915), Rhode Island (1957), South Carolina (1950), Utah (1921) and Wisconsin (1915).

Some of the above jurisdictions recently have adopted the revised Uniform Partnership Act ("RUPA"). A list of those jurisdictions is contained in the introduction to RUPA, which is set forth in these materials immediately following UPA and the conversion tables to UPA and RUPA.

PART I
PRELIMINARY PROVISIONS

§ 1.   Name of Act.

§ 2.   Definition of Terms.

PART I
PRELIMINARY PROVISIONS

§ 1. Name of Act

This act may be cited as Uniform Partnership Act.

§ 2. Definition of Terms

In this act, "Court" includes every court and judge having jurisdiction in the case.

"Business" includes every trade, occupation, or profession.

"Person" includes individuals, partnerships, corporations, and other associations.

"Bankrupt" includes bankrupt under the Federal Bankruptcy Act or insolvent under any state insolvent act.

"Conveyance" includes every assignment, lease, mortgage, or encumbrance.

"Real property" includes land and any interest or estate in land.

§ 3. Interpretation of Knowledge and Notice

(1) A person has "knowledge" of a fact within the meaning of this act not only when he has actual knowledge thereof, but also when he has knowledge of such other facts as in the circumstances shows bad faith.

(2) A person has "notice" of a fact within the meaning of this act when the person who claims the benefit of the notice:

(a) States the fact to such person, or

(b) Delivers through the mail, or by other means of communication, a written statement of the fact to such person or to a proper person at his place of business or residence.

§ 4. Rules of Construction

(1) The rule that statutes in derogation of the common law are to be strictly construed shall have no application to this act.

(2) The law of estoppel shall apply under this act.

(3) The law of agency shall apply under this act.

(4) This act shall be so interpreted and construed as to effect its general purpose to make uniform the law of those states which enact it.

(5) This act shall not be construed so as to impair the obligations of any contract existing when the act goes into effect, nor to affect any action or proceedings begun or right accrued before this act takes effect.

§ 5. Rules for Cases Not Provided for in This Act

In any case not provided for in this act the rules of law and equity, including the law merchant, shall govern.

PART II
NATURE OF PARTNERSHIP

§ 6. Partnership Defined

(1) A partnership is an association of two or more persons to carry on as co-owners a business for profit.

(2) But any association formed under any other statute of this state, or any statute adopted by authority, other than the authority of this state, is not a partnership under this act, unless such association would have been a partnership in this state prior to the adoption of this act; but this act shall apply to limited partnerships except in so far as the statutes relating to such partnerships are inconsistent herewith.

Comment

Subdivision (1). . . .

The words "to carry on as co-owners a business" remove any doubt in the following case: A and B sign partnership articles and make their agreed contributions to the common fund. A refuses to carry on business as agreed. Is there a partnership to be wound up in accordance with the provisions of Part VI "Dissolution and Winding-up"? The words quoted require an affirmative answer to this question. If the words "carrying on business" had been used, in the case given, no partnership would exist, and Part VI would not apply.

The definition asserts that the associates are "co-owners" of the business. This distinguishes a partnership from an agency -an association of principal and agent. A business is a series of acts directed toward an end. Ownership involves the power of ultimate control. To state that partners are co-owners of a business is to state that they each have the power of ultimate control.

Lastly, the definition asserts that the business is for profit. Partnership is a branch of our commercial law; it has developed in connection with a particular business association, and it is, therefore, essential that the operation of the act should be confined to associations organized for profit.

. . .

§ 7. Rules for Determining the Existence of a Partnership

In determining whether a partnership exists, these rules shall apply:

(1) Except as provided by section 16 persons who are not partners as to each other are not partners as to third persons.

(2) Joint tenancy, tenancy in common, tenancy by the entireties, joint property, common property, or part ownership does not of itself establish a partnership, whether such co-owners do or do not share any profits made by the use of the property.

(3) The sharing of gross returns does not of itself establish a partnership, whether or not the persons sharing them have a joint or common right or interest in any property from which the returns are derived.

(4) The receipt by a person of a share of the profits of a business is prima facie evidence that he is a partner in the business, but no such inference shall be drawn if such profits were received in payment:

(a) As a debt by installments or otherwise,

(b) As wages of an employee or rent to a landlord,

(c) As an annuity to a widow or representative of a deceased partner,

(d) As interest on a loan, though the amount of payment vary with the profits of the business,

(e) As the consideration for the sale of a good-will of a business or other property by installments or otherwise.

§ 8. Partnership Property

(1) All property originally brought into the partnership stock or subsequently acquired by purchase or otherwise, on account of the partnership, is partnership property.

(2) Unless the contrary intention appears, property acquired with partnership funds is partnership property.

(3) Any estate in real property may be acquired in the partnership name. Title so acquired can be conveyed only in the partnership name.

(4) A conveyance to a partnership in the partnership name, though without words of inheritance, passes the entire estate of the grantor unless a contrary intent appears.

Comment

Paragraphs (3), (4), in connection with section 10, infra, do away with existing confusions where there has been a conveyance to a partnership in the partnership name, or a conveyance by a partner in the partnership name. At present such conveyance may convey an equitable, but does not convey a legal title. To this extent paragraph (3) of this section and section 10(1), infra, change existing law.

PART III
RELATIONS OF PARTNERS TO PERSONS DEALING WITH THE PARTNERSHIP

§ 9. Partner Agent of Partnership as to Partnership Business

(1) Every partner is an agent of the partnership for the purpose of its business, and the act of every partner, including the execution in the partnership name of any instrument, for apparently carrying on in the usual way the business of the partnership of which he is a member binds the partnership, unless the partner so acting has in fact no authority to act for the partnership in the particular matter, and the person with whom he is dealing has knowledge of the fact that he has no such authority.

(2) An act of a partner which is not apparently for the carrying on of the business of the partnership in the usual way does not bind the partnership unless authorized by the other partners.

(3) Unless authorized by the other partners or unless they have abandoned the business, one or more but less than all the partners have no authority to:

(a) Assign the partnership property in trust for creditors or on the assignee's promise to pay the debts of the partnership,

(b) Dispose of the good-will of the business,

(c) Do any other act which would make it impossible to carry on the ordinary business of a partnership,

(d) Confess a judgment,

(e) Submit a partnership claim or liability to arbitration or reference.

(4) No act of a partner in contravention of a restriction on authority shall bind the partnership to persons having knowledge of the restriction.

§ 10. Conveyance of Real Property of the Partnership

(1) Where title to real property is in the partnership name, any partner may convey title to such property by a conveyance executed in the partnership name; but the partnership may recover such property unless the partner's act binds the partnership under the provisions of paragraph (1) of section 9, or unless such property has been conveyed by the grantee or a person claiming through such grantee to a holder for value without knowledge that the partner, in making the conveyance, has exceeded his authority.

(2) Where title to real property is in the name of the partnership, a conveyance executed by a partner, in his own name, passes the equitable interest of the partnership, provided the act is one within the authority of the partner under the provisions of paragraph (1) of section 9.

(3) Where title to real property is in the name of one or more but not all the partners, and the record does not disclose the right of the partnership, the partners in whose name the title stands may convey title to such property, but the partnership may recover such property if the partners' act does not bind the partnership under the provisions of paragraph (1) of section 9, unless the purchaser or his assignee, is a holder for value, without knowledge.

(4) Where the title to real property is in the name of one or more or all the partners, or in a third person in trust for the partnership, a conveyance executed by a partner in the partnership name, or in his own name, passes the equitable interest of the partnership, provided the act is one within the authority of the partner under the provisions of paragraph (1) of section 9.

(5) Where the title to real property is in the names of all the partners, a conveyance executed by all the partners passes all their rights in such property.

§ 11. Partnership Bound by Admission of Partner

An admission or representation made by any partner concerning partnership affairs within the scope of his authority as conferred by this act is evidence against the partnership.

§ 12. Partnership Charged with Knowledge of or Notice to Partner

Notice to any partner of any matter relating to partnership affairs, and the knowledge of the partner acting in the particular matter, acquired while a partner or then present to his mind, and the knowledge of any other partner who reasonably could and should have communicated it to the acting partner, operate as notice to or knowledge of the partnership, except in the case of a fraud on the partnership committed by or with the consent of that partner.

Comment

. . . .

It is not clear what the present law is when "knowledge," which is not the knowledge that may come from notice, has been obtained by a partner after the formation of the partnership, but the partner having such "knowledge" is not the one acting in the particular matter. It seems clear that in this case the partnership should be charged only when the partner having "knowledge" had reason to believe that the fact related to a matter which had some possibility of being the subject of partnership business, and then only if he was so situated that he could communicate it to the partner acting in the particular matter before such partner give binding effect to his act. The words "who reasonably could and should have communicated it to the acting partner" accomplish this result.

§ 13. Partnership Bound by Partner's Wrongful Act

Where, by any wrongful act or omission of any partner acting in the ordinary course of the business of the partnership or with the authority of his co-partners, loss or injury is caused to any person, not being a partner in the partnership, or any penalty is incurred, the partnership is liable therefor to the same extent as the partner so acting or omitting to act.

§ 14. Partnership Bound by Partner's Breach of Trust

The partnership is bound to make good the loss:

(a) Where one partner acting within the scope of his apparent authority receives money or property of a third person and misapplies it; and

(b) Where the partnership in the course of its business receives money or property of a third person and the money or property so received is misapplied by any partner while it is in the custody of the partnership.

§ 15. Nature of Partner's Liability

All partners are liable

(a) Jointly and severally for everything chargeable to the partnership under sections 13 and 14.

(b) Jointly for all other debts and obligations of the partnership; but any partner may enter into a separate obligation to perform a partnership contract.

§ 16. Partner by Estoppel

(1) When a person, by words spoken or written or by conduct, represents himself, or consents to another representing him to any one, as a partner

in an existing partnership or with one or more persons not actual partners, he is liable to any such person to whom such representation has been made, who has, on the faith of such representation, given credit to the actual or apparent partnership, and if he has made such representation or consented to its being made in a public manner he is liable to such person, whether the representation has or has not been made or communicated to such person so giving credit by or with the knowledge of the apparent partner making the representation or consenting to its being made.

(a) When a partnership liability results, he is liable as though he were an actual member of the partnership.

(b) When no partnership liability results, he is liable jointly with the other persons, if any, so consenting to the contract or representation as to incur liability, otherwise separately.

(2) When a person has been thus represented to be a partner in an existing partnership, or with one or more persons not actual partners, he is an agent of the persons consenting to such representation to bind them to the same extent and in the same manner as though he were a partner in fact, with respect to persons who rely upon the representation. Where all the members of the existing partnership consent to the representation, a partnership act or obligation results; but in all other cases it is the joint act or obligation of the person acting and the persons consenting to the representation.

Comment

The section clears several doubts and confusions of our existing case law. It has been held that a person is liable if he has been held out as a partner and knows that he is being held out, unless he prevents such holding out, even if to do so he has to take legal action. (Citations omitted.) On the other hand, the weight of authority is to the effect that to be held as a partner he must consent to the holding and that consent is a matter of fact. The act as drafted follows this weight of authority and better reasoning. (Citations omitted.)

§ 17. Liability of Incoming Partner

A person admitted as a partner into an existing partnership is liable for all the obligations of the partnership arising before his admission as though he had been a partner when such obligations were incurred, except that this liability shall be satisfied only out of partnership property.

Comment

The present section eliminates the difficulty which arises when a new partner is admitted without liquidation of firm debts. The present theory of the common law is that a new partnership is formed; all the property of the partnership which existed up to the moment of the entrance of the new partner being transferred to the new partnership. The result of this theory is that if the business fails, the creditors who have extended credit after the admission of the new partner have a prior claim on the assets in the business. The inequitable character of this result has led the courts, where no notice of the change of membership is had by the creditors, to be diligent in finding an assumption of liability on the part of the new partnership of the debts of the old partnership.

. . .

. . . There is no peculiar equity in the subsequent creditors giving them a right to be preferred, as against the property employed in the business, to the existing creditors. The incoming partner partakes of the benefit of the partnership property and an established business. He has every means of obtaining full knowledge and protecting himself, because he may insist on the liquidation or settlement of existing partnership debts. The creditors have no means of protecting themselves. So as to preserve the present law as nearly as possible it is declared that the liability of the incoming partner shall be satisfied only out of partnership property. It, therefore, results that existing and subsequent creditors have equal rights as against partnership property and the separate property of all the previously existing members of the partnership, while only the subsequent creditors have rights against the separate estate of the newly admitted partner.

The section should be read in connection with section 41, infra. Both sections are based on the principle that where there has been one continuous business the fact that A has been admitted to the business, or C ceased to be connected with it, should not be allowed to cause, as at present, endless confusion as to the claims of the creditors on the property employed in the business; but that all creditors of the business, irrespective of the times when they became creditors and the exact combinations of persons then owning the business, should have equal rights in such property. The recognition of this principle solves one of the most perplexing problems of present partnership law.

PART IV
RELATIONS OF PARTNERS TO ONE ANOTHER

§ 18. Rules Determining Rights and Duties of Partners

The rights and duties of the partners in relation to the partnership shall be determined, subject to any agreement between them, by the following rules:

(a) Each partner shall be repaid his contributions, whether by way of capital or advances to the partnership property and share equally in the profits and surplus remaining after all liabilities, including those to partners, are satisfied; and must contribute towards the losses, whether of capital or otherwise, sustained by the partnership according to his share in the profits.

(b) The partnership must indemnify every partner in respect of payments made and personal liabilities reasonably incurred by him in the ordinary and proper conduct of its business, or for the preservation of its business or property.

(c) A partner, who in aid of the partnership makes any payment or advance beyond the amount of capital which he agreed to contribute, shall be paid interest from the date of the payment or advance.

(d) A partner shall receive interest on the capital contributed by him only from the date when repayment should be made.

(e) All partners have equal rights in the management and conduct of the partnership business.

(f) No partner is entitled to remuneration for acting in the partnership business, except that a surviving partner is entitled to reasonable compensation for his services in winding up the partnership affairs.

(g) No person can become a member of a partnership without the consent of all the partners.

(h) Any difference arising as to ordinary matters connected with the partnership business may be decided by a majority of the partners; but no act in contravention of any agreement between the partners may be done rightfully without the consent of all the partners.

§ 19. Partnership Books

The partnership books shall be kept, subject to any agreement between the partners, at the principal place of business of the partnership, and every partner shall at all times have access to and may inspect and copy any of them.

§ 20. Duty of Partners to Render Information

Partners shall render on demand true and full information of all things affecting the partnership to any partner or the legal representative of any deceased partner or partner under legal disability.

§ 21. Partner Accountable as a Fiduciary

(1) Every partner must account to the partnership for any benefit, and hold as trustee for it any profits derived by him without the consent of the other partners from any transaction connected with the formation, conduct, or liquidation of the partnership or from any use by him of its property.

(2) This section applies also to the representatives of a deceased partner engaged in the liquidation of the affairs of the partnership as the personal representatives of the last surviving partner.

Comment

Subdivision (1) removes a doubt in the existing law. At present it is not clear whether the obligation to account where the partner has money or other property in his hands, is or is not an obligation in the nature of a trust. For instance: A, B and C are partners; A, as a result of a transaction connected with the conduct of the partnership, has in his hands, so that it may be traced, a specific sum of money or other property. A is insolvent. Is the claim of the partnership against A a claim against him as an ordinary creditor, or is it a claim to the specific property or money in his hands? The words "and hold as trustee for the partnership any profits" indicate clearly that the partnership can claim as their own any property or money that can be traced.

§ 22. Right to an Account

Any partner shall have the right to a formal account as to partnership affairs:

(a) If he is wrongfully excluded from the partnership business or possession of its property by his co-partners,

(b) If the right exists under the terms of any agreement,

(c) As provided by section 21,

(d) Whenever other circumstances render it just and reasonable.

Comment

Ordinarily a partner is not entitled to a formal account, except on dissolution. He has equal access with his partners to the partnership books, and there is no reason why they should constantly render to him accounts in the formal sense of that word, which is the sense in which it is here used. When, however, he is excluded from the business or the possession of partnership property, without any express agreement authorizing such exclusion, he should have the right to demand a formal account from his partners, without necessarily requiring him to dissolve the partnership.

The reason for clause (d) is that there frequently arise circumstances which impose on one or more of the partners the duty of rendering a formal account to the co-partner, as where one partner is traveling for a long period of time on partnership business, and the other partners are in possession of the partnership books. These various circumstances cannot be detailed in any act. In view of the wording of clause (d), the total effect of this section is to emphasize the fact that a partner, the partnership not being dissolved, has not necessarily the right to demand formal accounts, except at particular times and under particular circumstances.

§ 23. Continuation of Partnership Beyond Fixed Term

(1) When a partnership for a fixed term or particular undertaking is continued after the termination of such term or particular undertaking

without any express agreement, the rights and duties of the partners remain the same as they were at such termination, so far as is consistent with a partnership at will.

(2) A continuation of the business by the partners or such of them as habitually acted therein during the term, without any settlement or liquidation of the partnership affairs, is prima facie evidence of a continuation of the partnership.

PART V
PROPERTY RIGHTS OF A PARTNER

§ 24. Extent of Property Rights of a Partner

The property rights of a partner are (1) his rights in specific partnership property, (2) his interest in the partnership, and (3) his right to participate in the management.

§ 25. Nature of a Partner's Right in Specific Partnership Property

(1) A partner is co-owner with his partners of specific partnership property holding as a tenant in partnership.

(2) The incidents of this tenancy are such that:

(a) A partner, subject to the provisions of this act and to any agreement between the partners, has an equal right with his partners to possess specific partnership property for partnership purposes; but he has no right to possess such property for any other purpose without the consent of his partners.

(b) A partner's right in specific partnership property is not assignable except in connection with the assignment of rights of all the partners in the same property.

(c) A partner's right in specific partnership property is not subject to attachment or execution, except on a claim against the partnership. When partnership property is attached for a partnership debt the partners, or any of them, or the representatives of a deceased partner, cannot claim any right under the homestead or exemption laws.

(d) On the death of a partner his right in specific partnership property vests in the surviving partner or partners, except where the deceased was the last surviving partner, when his right in such property vests in his legal representative. Such surviving partner or partners, or the legal representative of the last surviving partner, has no right to possess the partnership property for any but a partnership purpose.

(e) A partner's right in specific partnership property is not subject to dower, curtesy, or allowances to widows, heirs, or next of kin.

Comment

Subdivision (1). One of the present principal difficulties in the adminis-tration of the law of partnerships arises out of the difficulty of determining the exact nature of the rights of a partner in specific partnership property. That the partners are co-owners of partnership property is clear; but the legal incidents attached to the right of each partner as co-owner are not clear. When the English courts in the seventeenth century first began to discuss the legal incidents of this co-ownership, they were already familiar with two other kinds of co-ownership, joint tenancy and tenancy in common. In joint tenancy on the death of one owner his right in the property passes to the other co-owners. This is known as the right of survivorship. The incident of survivorship fits in with the necessities of partnership. On the death of a partner, the other partners and not the executors of the deceased partner should have a right to wind up partnership affairs. (See clause (d), infra.) The early courts, therefore, declared that partners were joint tenants of partnership property, the consequence being that all the other legal incidents of joint tenancy were applied to partnership co-ownership. Many of these incidents, however, do not apply to the necessities of the partner-ship relation and produce most inequitable results. This is not to be wondered at because the legal incidents of joint tenancy grew out of a co-ownership of land not held for the purposes of business. The attempt of our courts to escape the inequitable results of applying the legal incidents of joint tenancy to partnership has produced very great confusion. Practically this confusion has had more unfortunate effect on substantive rights when the separate creditors of a partner attempt to attach and sell specific partnership property than when a partner attempts to assign specific partnership property not for a partnership purpose but for his own purposes.

The Commissioners, however, believe that the proper way to end the confusion which has arisen out of the attempt to treat partners as joint tenants, is to recognize the fact that the rights of a partner as co-owner with his partners of specific partnership property should depend on the necessities of the partnership relation. In short, that the legal incidents of the tenancy in partnership are not necessarily those of any other co-ownership.

. . . .

Subdivision (2-b). Clause (b) asserts that the right of a partner as co-owner in specific partnership property is not separately assignable. This peculiarity of tenancy in partnership is a necessary consequence of the partnership relation. If A and B are partners and A attempts to assign all his right in partnership property, say a particular chattel, to C, and the law recognizes the possibility of such a transfer, C would pro tanto become a partner with B; for the rights of A in the chattel are to possess the chattel for a partnership purpose. But partnership is a voluntary relation. B cannot have a partner thrust upon him by A without his, B's, consent.

A cannot confer on C his, A's, right to possess and deal with the chattel for a partnership purpose. Neither can he confer any other rights which he has in the property. A partner has a beneficial interest in partnership property considered as a whole. As profits accrue, he has a right to be paid his proportion, and on the winding up of the business, after the obligations due third persons have been met, he has a right to be paid in cash his share of what remains of the partnership property. These rights considered as a whole are his interest in the partnership; and this beneficial interest he may assign in whole or fractional part, as is indicated in section 27, infra. . . .

Subdivision (2-c). Compare this clause with section 28(1). The first sentence in this clause is similar to section 23(1) of the English Act. It is a logical consequence of clause (b). If a partner's right in specific partnership property is not assignable by voluntary assignment for a separate purpose of the assignment partner, his separate creditors should not be able to force an involuntary assignment. The beneficial rights of the separate creditors of a partner in partnership property should be no greater than the beneficial rights of their debtor. . . .

§ 26. Nature of Partner's Interest in the Partnership

A partner's interest in the partnership is his share of the profits and surplus, and the same is personal property.

§ 27. Assignment of Partner's Interest

(1) A conveyance by a partner of his interest in the partnership does not of itself dissolve the partnership, nor, as against the other partners in the absence of agreement, entitle the assignee, during the continuance of the partnership, to interfere in the management or administration of the partnership business or affairs, or to require any information or account of partnership transactions, or to inspect the partnership books; but it merely entitles the assignee to receive in accordance with his contract the profits to which the assigning partner would otherwise be entitled.

(2) In case of a dissolution of the partnership, the assignee is entitled to receive his assignor's interest and may require an account from the date only of the last account agreed to by all the partners.

Comment

In re the subject of this paragraph [subd. 1] see [citations omitted]. These authorities on the whole state that the mere assignment dissolves the partnership. Many such assignments, however, are merely by way of collateral security for a loan, the assigning partner in no wise intending to end the partnership relation. If he neglects his personal relation the other partners may dissolve the partnership under section 31 of this act. But the mere fact of assignment without more should not be said in all cases to be an act of dissolution. The change in the existing law follows a similar change of the English law embodied in section 31 of the English Partnership Act.

§ 28. Partner's Interest Subject to Charging Order

(1) On due application to a competent court by any judgment creditor of a partner, the court which entered the judgment, order, or decree, or any other court, may charge the interest of the debtor partner with payment of the unsatisfied amount of such judgment debt with interest thereon; and may then or later appoint a receiver of his share of the profits, and of any other money due or to fall due to him in respect of the partnership, and make all other orders, directions, accounts and inquiries which the debtor partner might have made, or which the circumstances of the case may require.

(2) The interest charged may be redeemed at any time before foreclosure, or in case of a sale being directed by the court may be purchased without thereby causing a dissolution:

(a) With separate property, by any one or more of the partners, or

(b) With partnership property, by any one or more of the partners with the consent of all the partners whose interests are not so charged or sold.

(3) Nothing in this act shall be held to deprive a partner of his right, if any, under the exemption laws, as regards his interest in the partnership.

PART VI
DISSOLUTION AND WINDING UP

§ 29. Dissolution Defined

The dissolution of a partnership is the change in the relation of the partners caused by any partner ceasing to be associated in the carrying on as distinguished from the winding up of the business.

Comment

As used by the legal profession the term "dissolution" designates, not only the single act of the termination of the actual conduct of the ordinary business, but also often the series of acts thereafter until the final settlement of all partnership affairs. It is also frequently said that dissolution, although the word is used to designate only the termination of ordinary business relations, terminates the partnership, it being at the same time explained that the partnership thereafter continues to exist for the purpose of suing and being sued in the process of winding up partnership affairs. Certainty demands that this confusion should be removed if possible. In this act dissolution designates the point in time when the partners cease to carry on the business together; termination is the point in time when all the partnership affairs are wound up; winding up, the process of settling partnership affairs after dissolution.

§ 30. Partnership Not Terminated by Dissolution

On dissolution the partnership is not terminated, but continues until the winding up of partnership affairs is completed.

§ 31. Causes of Dissolution

Dissolution is caused:

(1) Without violation of the agreement between the partners,

(a) By the termination of the definite term or particular undertaking specified in the agreement,

(b) By the express will of any partner when no definite term or particular undertaking is specified,

(c) By the express will of all the partners who have not assigned their interests or suffered them to be charged for their separate debts, either before or after the termination of any specified term or particular undertaking,

(d) By the expulsion of any partner from the business bona fide in accordance with such a power conferred by the agreement between the partners;

(2) In contravention of the agreement between the partners, where the circumstances do not permit a dissolution under any other provision of this section, by the express will of any partner at any time;

(3) By any event which makes it unlawful for the business of the partnership to be carried on or for the members to carry it on in partnership;

(4) By the death of any partner;

(5) By the bankruptcy of any partner or the partnership;

(6) By decree of court under section 32.

Comment

Paragraph (2) will settle a matter on which at present considerable confusion and uncertainty exists. The paragraph as drawn allows a partner to dissolve a partnership in contravention of the agreement between the partners. This is supported by the weight of authority. (Citations omitted.)

The relation of partners is one of agency. The agency is such a personal one that equity cannot enforce it even where the agreement provides that the partnership shall continue for a definite time. The power of any partner to terminate the relation, even though in doing so he breaks a contract, should, it is submitted, be recognized.

The rights of the parties upon a dissolution in contravention of the agreement are safeguarded by section 38(2), infra.

§ 32. Dissolution by Decree of Court

(1) On application by or for a partner the court shall decree a dissolution whenever:

(a) A partner has been declared a lunatic in any judicial proceeding or is shown to be of unsound mind,

(b) A partner becomes in any other way incapable of performing his part of the partnership contract,

(c) A partner has been guilty of such conduct as tends to affect prejudicially the carrying on of the business,

(d) A partner wilfully or persistently commits a breach of the partnership agreement, or otherwise so conducts himself in matters relating to the partnership business that it is not reasonably practicable to carry on the business in partnership with him,

(e) The business of the partnership can only be carried on at a loss,

(f) Other circumstances render a dissolution equitable.

(2) On the application of the purchaser of a partner's interest under sections 28 or 29 [should read 27 or 28]:

(a) After the termination of the specified term or particular undertaking,

(b) At any time if the partnership was a partnership at will when the interest was assigned or when the charging order was issued.

§ 33. General Effect of Dissolution on Authority of Partner

Except so far as may be necessary to wind up partnership affairs or to complete transactions begun but not then finished, dissolution terminates all authority of any partner to act for the partnership,

(1) With respect to the partners,

(a) When the dissolution is not by the act, bankruptcy or death of a partner; or

(b) When the dissolution is by such act, bankruptcy or death of a partner, in cases where section 34 so requires.

(2) With respect to persons not partners, as declared in section 35.

§ 34. Right of Partner to Contribution from Co-partners after Dissolution

Where the dissolution is caused by the act, death or bankruptcy of a partner, each partner is liable to his co-partners for his share of any liability created by any partner acting for the partnership as if the partnership had not been dissolved unless

(a) The dissolution being by act of any partner, the partner acting for the partnership had knowledge of the dissolution, or

(b) The dissolution being by the death or bankruptcy of a partner, the partner acting for the partnership had knowledge or notice of the death or bankruptcy.

Comment

. . . "Notice" should be, it is submitted, sufficient in all cases where the fact to be notified is an ordinary business fact, as notice to third persons of the dissolution of a partnership. But it is not customary for partners to dissolve a partnership at a time not previously specified, without consultation with their co-partners. Such dissolution may or may not amount to a breach of partnership contract; but in any event, if done without consultation, it is out of the ordinary course. This fact should not deprive the partner of a right to terminate a relationship which must necessarily depend on mutual good will and confidence; but if the partner so terminating wishes to show that he should not be required by his partners to be liable for his share of the loss due to a partnership contract thereafter made by them, he should be able to prove that they had "knowledge" that he had dissolved the partnership at the time they made the contract.

. . .

§ 35. Power of Partner to Bind Partnership to Third Persons after Dissolution

(1) After dissolution a partner can bind the partnership except as provided in Paragraph (3).

(a) By any act appropriate for winding up partnership affairs or completing transactions unfinished at dissolution;

(b) By any transaction which would bind the partnership if dissolution had not taken place, provided the other party to the transaction

(I) Had extended credit to the partnership prior to dissolution and had no knowledge or notice of the dissolution; or

(II) Though he had not so extended credit, had nevertheless known of the partnership prior to dissolution, and, having no knowledge or notice of dissolution, the fact of dissolution had not been advertised in a newspaper of general circulation in the place (or in each place if more than one) at which the partnership business was regularly carried on.

(2) The liability of a partner under Paragraph (1b) shall be satisfied out of partnership assets alone when such partner had been prior to dissolution

(a) Unknown as a partner to the person with whom the contract is made; and

(b) So far unknown and inactive in partnership affairs that the business reputation of the partnership could not be said to have been in any degree due to his connection with it.

(3) The partnership is in no case bound by any act of a partner after dissolution

(a) Where the partnership is dissolved because it is unlawful to carry on the business, unless the act is appropriate for winding up partnership affairs; or

(b) Where the partner has become bankrupt; or

(c) Where the partner has no authority to wind up partnership affairs; except by a transaction with one who

(I) Had extended credit to the partnership prior to dissolution and had no knowledge or notice of his want of authority; or

(II) Had not extended credit to the partnership prior to dissolution, and, having no knowledge or notice of his want of authority, the fact of his want of authority has not been advertised in the manner provided for advertising the fact of dissolution in Paragraph (1bII).

(4) Nothing in this section shall affect the liability under Section 16 of any person who after dissolution represents himself or consents to another representing him as a partner in a partnership engaged in carrying on business.

Comment

At present in most jurisdictions it is doubtful whether, under the circumstances set forth in (b), "the other party" can bind the partnership where such party has had no knowledge or notice of the dissolution and has had business transactions with the partnership before dissolution, but these business transactions have not involved any extension of credit to the partnership.

. . .

The practical impossibility of the partners knowing, by any feasible system of bookkeeping, all the persons with whom they have had dealings, unless credit has been extended, supports the wording adopted by the Commissioners.

§ 36. Effect of Dissolution on Partner's Existing Liability

(1) The dissolution of the partnership does not of itself discharge the existing liability of any partner.

(2) A partner is discharged from any existing liability upon dissolution of the partnership by an agreement to that effect between himself, the partnership creditor and the person or partnership continuing the business; and such agreement may be inferred from the course of dealing between the creditor having knowledge of the dissolution and the person or partnership continuing the business.

(3) Where a person agrees to assume the existing obligations of a dissolved partnership, the partners whose obligations have been assumed shall be discharged from any liability to any creditor of the partnership who, knowing of the agreement, consents to a material alteration in the nature or time of payment of such obligations.

(4) The individual property of a deceased partner shall be liable for all obligations of the partnership incurred while he was a partner but subject to the prior payment of his separate debts.

§ 37. Right to Wind Up

Unless otherwise agreed the partners who have not wrongfully dissolved the partnership or the legal representative of the last surviving partner, not bankrupt, has the right to wind up the partnership affairs; provided, however, that any partner, his legal representative or his assignee, upon cause shown, may obtain winding up by the court.

§ 38. Rights of Partners to Application of Partnership Property

(1) When dissolution is caused in any way, except in contravention of the partnership agreement, each partner, as against his co-partners and all persons claiming through them in respect of their interests in the partnership, unless otherwise agreed, may have the partnership property applied to discharge its liabilities, and the surplus applied to pay in cash the net amount owing to the respective partners. But if dissolution is caused by expulsion of a partner, bona fide under the partnership agreement and if the expelled partner is discharged from all partnership liabilities, either by payment or agreement under section 36(2), he shall receive in cash only the net amount due him from the partnership.

(2) When dissolution is caused in contravention of the partnership agreement the rights of the partners shall be as follows:

   (a) Each partner who has not caused dissolution wrongfully shall have,

      (I) All the rights specified in paragraph (1) of this section, and

(II) The right, as against each partner who has caused the dissolution wrongfully, to damages for breach of the agreement.

(b) The partners who have not caused the dissolution wrongfully, if they all desire to continue the business in the same name, either by themselves or jointly with others, may do so, during the agreed term for the partnership and for that purpose may possess the partnership property, provided they secure the payment by bond approved by the court, or pay to any partner who has caused the dissolution wrongfully, the value of his interest in the partnership at the dissolution, less any damages recoverable under clause (2a II) of this section, and in like manner indemnify him against all present or future partnership liabilities.

(c) A partner who has caused the dissolution wrongfully shall have:

(I) If the business is not continued under the provisions of paragraph (2b) all the rights of a partner under paragraph (1), subject to clause (2a II), of this section,

(II) If the business is continued under paragraph (2b) of this section the right as against his co-partners and all claiming through them in respect of their interests in the partnership, to have the value of his interest in the partnership, less any damages caused to his co-partners by the dissolution, ascertained and paid to him in cash, or the payment secured by bond approved by the court, and to be released from all existing liabilities of the partnership; but in ascertaining the value of the partner's interest the value of the goodwill of the business shall not be considered.

Comment

The right given to each partner, where no agreement to the contrary has been made, to have his share of the surplus paid to him in cash makes certain an existing uncertainty. At present it is not certain whether a partner may or may not insist on a physical partition of the property remaining after third persons have been paid.

§ 39. Rights Where Partnership Is Dissolved for Fraud or Misrepresentation

Where a partnership contract is rescinded on the ground of the fraud or misrepresentation of one of the parties thereto, the party entitled to rescind is, without prejudice to any other right, entitled,

(a) To a lien on, or a right of retention of, the surplus of the partnership property after satisfying the partnership liabilities to third persons for any sum of money paid by him for the purchase of an interest in the partnership and for any capital or advances contributed by him; and

(b) To stand, after all liabilities to third persons have been satisfied, in the place of the creditors of the partnership for any payments made by him in respect of the partnership liabilities; and

(c) To be indemnified by the person guilty of the fraud or making the representation against all debts and liabilities of the partnership.

§ 40. Rules for Distribution

In settling accounts between the partners after dissolution, the following rules shall be observed, subject to any agreement to the contrary:

(a) The assets of the partnership are:

(I) The partnership property,

(II) The contributions of the partners necessary for the payment of all the liabilities specified in clause (b) of this paragraph.

(b) The liabilities of the partnership shall rank in order of payment, as follows:

(I) Those owing to creditors other than partners,

(II) Those owing to partners other than for capital and profits,

(III) Those owing to partners in respect of capital,

(IV) Those owing to partners in respect of profits.

(c) The assets shall be applied in order of their declaration in clause (a) of this paragraph to the satisfaction of the liabilities.

(d) The partners shall contribute, as provided by section 18(a) the amount necessary to satisfy the liabilities; but if any, but not all, of the partners are insolvent, or, not being subject to process, refuse to contribute, the other partners shall contribute their share of the liabilities, and, in the relative proportions in which they share the profits, the additional amount necessary to pay the liabilities.

(e) An assignee for the benefit of creditors or any person appointed by the court shall have the right to enforce the contributions specified in clause (d) of this paragraph.

(f) Any partner or his legal representative shall have the right to enforce the contributions specified in clause (d) of this paragraph, to the extent of the amount which he has paid in excess of his share of the liability.

(g) The individual property of a deceased partner shall be liable for the contributions specified in clause (d) of this paragraph.

(h) When partnership property and the individual properties of the partners are in possession of a court for distribution, partnership creditors shall have priority on partnership property and separate creditors on individual property, saving the rights of lien or secured creditors as heretofore.

(i) Where a partner has become bankrupt or his estate is insolvent the claims against his separate property shall rank in the following order:

(I) Those owing to separate creditors,

(II) Those owing to partnership creditors,

(III) Those owing to partners by way of contribution.

§ 41. Liability of Persons Continuing the Business in Certain Cases

(1) When any new partner is admitted into an existing partnership, or when any partner retires and assigns (or the representative of the deceased partner assigns) his rights in partnership property to two or more of the partners, or to one or more of the partners and one or more third persons, if the business is continued without liquidation of the partnership affairs, creditors of the first or dissolved partnership are also creditors of the partnership so continuing the business.

(2) When all but one partner retire and assign (or the representative of a deceased partner assigns) their rights in partnership property to the remaining partner, who continues the business without liquidation of partnership affairs, either alone or with others, creditors of the dissolved partnership are also creditors of the person or partnership so continuing the business.

(3) When any partner retires or dies and the business of the dissolved partnership is continued as set forth in paragraphs (1) and (2) of this section, with the consent of the retired partners or the representative of the deceased partner, but without any assignment of his right in partnership property, rights of creditors of the dissolved partnership and of the creditors of the person or partnership continuing the business shall be as if such assignment had been made.

(4) When all the partners or their representatives assign their rights in partnership property to one or more third persons who promise to pay the debts and who continue the business of the dissolved partnership, creditors of the dissolved partnership are also creditors of the person or partnership continuing the business.

(5) When any partner wrongfully causes a dissolution and the remaining partners continue the business under the provisions of section 38(2b), either alone or with others, and without liquidation of the partnership affairs, creditors of the dissolved partnership are also creditors of the person or partnership continuing the business.

(6) When a partner is expelled and the remaining partners continue the business either alone or with others, without liquidation of the

partnership affairs, creditors of the dissolved partnership are also creditors of the person or partnership continuing the business.

(7) The liability of a third person becoming a partner in the partnership continuing the business, under this section, to the creditors of the dissolved partnership shall be satisfied out of partnership property only.

(8) When the business of a partnership after dissolution is continued under any conditions set forth in this section the creditors of the dissolved partnership, as against the separate creditors of the retiring or deceased partner or the representative of the deceased partner, have a prior right to any claim of the retired partner or the representative of the deceased partner against the person or partnership continuing the business, on account of the retired or deceased partner's interest in the dissolved partnership or on account of any consideration promised for such interest or for his right in partnership property.

(9) Nothing in this section shall be held to modify any right of creditors to set aside any assignment on the ground of fraud.

(10) The use by the person or partnership continuing the business of the partnership name, or the name of a deceased partner as part thereof, shall not of itself make the individual property of the deceased partner liable for any debts contracted by such person or partnership.

Comment

Subdivision (1). . . .

. . . It is universally admitted that any change in membership dissolves a partnership, and creates a new partnership. This section as drafted does not alter that rule. Neither does it alter the rule that on any change of personnel the property of the dissolved partnership becomes the property of the partnership continuing the business. At present, however, creditors of the dissolved partnership do not become creditors of the new partnership. . . .

The paragraph as drawn changes the law. . . . In every case the creditors of the first partnership become creditors of the second; though, of course, they do not cease to be creditors of the first partnership. As, however, the first partnership has assigned all its property, that is of little value to such creditors, unless the assignees have promised the retiring partner an additional consideration beyond the payment of the debts. The status of such additional consideration is treated in paragraph (8), infra.

The paragraph as a whole, as well as this entire section, is based on the opinion that when there is a continuous business carried on first by A, B and C, and then by A, B, C and D, or by B or C, or by B and C, by B and D, or by C and D, or by B, C and D, without any liquidation of the affairs of A, B, C, both justice and business convenience require that all the creditors of the business, irrespective of the exact grouping of the owners at the times their respective claims had their origin, should be treated alike, all being given an equal claim on the property embarked in the business. (Compare note to section 17, supra.)

Subdivision (2). Where all the partners assign to one partner, the partnership creditors are, under this paragraph, the separate creditors of the partner continuing the business, where he continues the business alone, whether such partner promises to pay the debts of the dissolved partnership or not. If he takes one or more new partners and they continue the business with the property of the dissolved partnership, the creditors of the dissolved partnership are the creditors of the partnership continuing the business. This paragraph changes the present law to the same extent as paragraph (1).

Subdivision (3). The paragraph extends the principle of the first and second paragraphs of the section to the case where the business is continued by two or more of the partners, alone or with others, after the retirement or death of a partner without any formal assignment to them of the retired or deceased partner's rights in partnership property. The neglect of the retiring partners or of the representatives of the deceased partner should not as at present create inexorable confusion between the creditors of the first and second partnership in regard to their respective rights in the property employed in the business. Both classes of creditors should be ahead of the claim of such retired partner or the representative of the deceased partner, and both classes of creditors should also have equal rights in the property. This paragraph probably effects a change in the present law, though the same result is often now brought about by implying a promise to pay the debts of the dissolved partnership on the part of the person or partnership continuing the business.

Subdivision (4). The existing law in relation to the subject matter covered by this paragraph is so uncertain that it is not possible to say whether its adoption would modify the law. The paragraph does not apply to the case where the third person or persons do not promise to pay the debts of the dissolved partnership. In that case the creditors of the dissolved partnership have no claim on the partnership continuing the business or its property unless the assignment can be set aside as a fraud on creditors, or is affected by a Sales in Bulk Act. Where, however, there has been a promise to pay the debts of the dissolved partnership, then, the creditors of the dissolved partnership are not only creditors of the promisor or promisors which, in the United States, they would be as beneficiaries but under this paragraph, if the business of the dissolved partnership is continued by a partnership, the creditors of the dissolved partnership become creditors of the partnership continuing the business, not merely the separate or joint creditors of the partners in such partnership.

. . .

§ 42. Rights of Retiring or Estate of Deceased Partner When the Business Is Continued

When any partner retires or dies, and the business is continued under any of the conditions set forth in section 41 (1, 2, 3, 5, 6), or section 38 (2b) without any settlement of accounts as between him or his estate and the person or partnership continuing the business, unless otherwise agreed, he or his legal representative as against such persons or partnership may have the value of his interest at the date of dissolution ascertained, and shall receive as an ordinary creditor an amount equal to the value of his interest in the dissolved partnership with interest, or, at his option or at the option of his legal representative, in lieu of interest, the profits attributable to the use of his right in the property of the dissolved partnership; provided that the creditors of the dissolved partnership as against the separate creditors, or the representative of the retired or deceased partner, shall have priority on any claim arising under this section, as provided by section 41(8) of this act.

§ 43. Accrual of Actions

The right to an account of his interest shall accrue to any partner, or his legal representative, as against the winding up partners or the surviving partners or the person or partnership continuing the business, at the date of dissolution, in the absence of any agreement to the contrary.

PART VII
MISCELLANEOUS PROVISIONS

§ 44. When Act Takes Effect

This act shall take effect on the _____ day of _____ one thousand nine hundred and _____.

§ 45. Legislation Repealed

All acts or parts of acts inconsistent with this act are hereby repealed.

CONVERSION TABLE
RUPA TO UPA

RUPA	UPA
101	2
102	3, 12
103	none
104	5
105	none
106	none
107	none
201	none
202	6, 7
203	8(1), 25
204	8
301	9
302	10
303	none
304	none
305	13,14
306	15, 17
307	none
308	16
401	18
402	38(1)
403	19, 20
404	21
405(a)	none
405(b)	22, 43
406	23
501	24, 25
502	26
503	27, 32(2)
504	28
601	See 31, 32
602	See 31(2), 38(2)
603	none
701	38, 42
702	34, 35
703	35, 36
704	none
705	41(10)
801	29, 31, 32
802	30

RUPA	UPA
803	37
804	33, 35
805	none
806	33(1), 34
807	38(1), 40
901	none
902	none
903	none
904	none
905	none
906	none
907	none
908	none
1001	4(4)
1002	1
1003	none
1004	44
1005	45
1006	none
1007	none

CONVERSION TABLE
UPA TO RUPA

UPA	RUPA
1	1002
2	101
3	102
4(2) and (3)	104(a)
4(4)	1001
4(5)	1007
5	104(a)
6	202
7	202
8	203, 204
9	301
10	302
11	none
12	102(f)
13	305(a)
14	305(b)
15	305(a)
16	308
17	306(b)
18	
401	
19	403(a) and (b)
20	403(c)
21	404
22	405(b)
23	406
24	none
25	501
26	502
27	503
28	504
29	801 (see also 601)
30	802
31	801 (see also 601, 602)
32	801 (5)(6) (see also 601(5)(7)(iii))
33	804 (see also 603(b)(i))
34	806 (see also 702(b))
35	804 (see also 702(a))
36	703
37	803

UPA	RUPA
38	602(c), 701, 807(a)
39	none
40	807
41	705 (re 41(10))
42	701(b) and (i)
43	405
44	1004
45	1005

UNIFORM PARTNERSHIP ACT (1997)[*]

Editor's note: The revised Uniform Partnership Act (1997) ("RUPA") and its comments are reproduced below. The text includes amendments enacted in 1996 incorporating limited liability partnership provisions and in 1997 modifying the dissolution provisions in response to the check-the-box regulations adopted by the Internal Revenue Service. The comments are reproduced in their entirety in order to assist the reader in tracing the many changes made by RUPA to the Uniform Partnership Act (1914) and in understanding the reasoning underlying the changes.

Based on the 2006 Cumulative Annual Pocket Part to 6 Pt, 1 Uniform Laws Annotated 1 (2001), RUPA has been adopted in 35 jurisdictions. (For the most recent adoptions, please check the web site of the National Conference of Commissioners on Uniform State Laws ("NCCUSL") at www.nccusl.org.) The date set forth immediately after each jurisdiction is the effective date of the Act. In some jurisdictions (e.g., Colorado), UPA remains effective law for all partnerships formed prior to the effective date of RUPA unless the partners elect to be governed by RUPA. In other jurisdictions UPA remains effective law until a certain date and then is repealed. In all other jurisdictions UPA is repealed upon the adoption of RUPA, although it will continue to govern disputes that arise prior to the effective date of RUPA.

RUPA has been adopted in the following jurisdictions: Alabama (1997), Alaska (2001), Arizona (1996), Arkansas (2000), California (1997), Colorado (1998), Connecticut (1997), Delaware (2000), District of Columbia (1997), Florida (1996), Hawaii (2000), Idaho (2001), Illinois (2003), Iowa (1999), Kansas (1999), Maryland (1998), Minnesota (1999), Mississippi (2005), Montana (1993), Nebraska (1998), Nevada (2006), New Jersey (2000), New Mexico (1997), North Dakota (1996); Oklahoma (1997), Oregon (1998), South Dakota (2001), Tennessee (2002), Texas (1994); Vermont (1999), Virgin Islands (1998), Virginia (1996), Washington (1999), West Virginia (1995); and Wyoming (1994).

UNIFORM PARTNERSHIP ACT — QUICK CHRONOLOGY

1914 — Original Uniform Partnership Act

1992 — Promulgation of Uniform Partnership Act (1992)

1993 — Amendments to 1992 Act, becomes Uniform Partnership Act (1993)

1994 — Amendments to 1993 Act, becomes Uniform Partnership Act (1994)

1996 — Amendments to 1994 act, becomes Uniform Partnership Act (1996)

1997 — Amendments to 1996 act, becomes Uniform Partnership Act (1997)

PREFATORY NOTE

The National Conference of Commissioners on Uniform State Laws first considered a uniform law of partnership in 1902. Although early drafts had proceeded along the mercantile or "entity" theory of partnerships, later drafts were based on the common-law "aggregate" theory. The resulting Uniform Partnership Act ("UPA"), which embodied certain aspects of each theory, was finally approved by the Conference in 1914. The UPA governs general partnerships, and also governs limited partnerships except where the limited partnership statute is inconsistent. The UPA has been adopted in every State other than Louisiana and has been the subject of remarkably few amendments in those States over the past 80 years.

In January of 1986, an American Bar Association subcommittee issued a detailed report that recommended extensive revisions to the UPA. *See* UPA Revision Subcommittee of the Committee on Partnerships and Unincorporated Business Organizations, Section of Business Law, American Bar Association, *Should the Uniform Partnership Act Be Revised?*, 43 Bus. Law. 121 (1987) ("ABA Report"). The ABA Report recommended that the entity theory *"should be incorporated into any revision of the UPA whenever possible." Id.* at 124.

In 1987, the Conference appointed a Drafting Committee to Revise the Uniform Partnership Act and named a Reporter. The Committee held its initial meeting in January of 1988 and a first reading of the Committee's draft was begun at the Conference's 1989 Annual Meeting in Kauai, Hawaii. The first reading was completed at the 1990 Annual Meeting in Milwaukee. The second reading was begun at Naples, Florida, in 1991 and completed at San Francisco in 1992. The Revised Uniform Partnership Act (1992) was adopted unanimously by a vote of the States on August 6, 1992. The following year, in response to suggestions from various groups, including an American Bar Association subcommittee and several state bar associations, the Drafting Committee recommended numerous revisions to the Act. Those were adopted at the Charleston, South Carolina, Annual Meeting in 1993, and the Act was restyled as the Uniform Partnership Act (1993). Subsequently, a final round of changes was incorporated, and the Conference unanimously adopted the Uniform Partnership Act (1994) at its 1994 Annual Meeting in Chicago. The Revised Act was approved by the American Bar Association House of Delegates in August, 1994.

The Uniform Partnership Act (1994) ("Revised Act" or "RUPA") gives supremacy to the partnership agreement in almost all situations. The Revised Act is, therefore, largely a series of "default rules" that govern the relations among partners in situations they have not addressed in a partnership agreement. The primary focus of RUPA is the small, often informal, partnership. Larger partnerships generally have a partnership agreement addressing, and often modifying, many of the provisions of the partnership act.

The Revised Act enhances the entity treatment of partnerships to achieve simplicity for state law purposes, particularly in matters concerning title to partnership property. RUPA does not, however, relentlessly apply the entity approach. The aggregate approach is retained for some purposes, such as partners' joint and several liability.

The Drafting Committee spent significant effort on the rules governing partnership breakups. RUPA's basic thrust is to provide stability for partnerships that have continuation agreements. Under the UPA, a partnership is dissolved every time a member leaves. The Revised Act provides that there are many departures or "dissociations" that do not result in a dissolution.

Under the Revised Act, the withdrawal of a partner is a "dissociation" that results in a dissolution of the partnership only in certain limited circumstances. Many dissociations result merely in a buyout of the withdrawing partner's interest rather than a winding up of the partnership's business. RUPA defines both the substance and procedure of the buyout right.

Article 6 of the Revised Act covers partner dissociations; Article 7 covers buyouts; and Article 8 covers dissolution and the winding up of the partnership business. *See generally* Donald J. Weidner & John W. Larson, *The Revised Uniform Partnership Act: The Reporters' Overview*, 49 Bus. Law. 1 (1993).

The Revised Act also includes a more extensive treatment of the fiduciary duties of partners. Although RUPA continues the traditional rule that a partner is a fiduciary, it also makes clear that a partner is not required to be a disinterested trustee. Provision is made for the legitimate pursuit of self-interest, with a counterbalancing irreducible core of fiduciary duties.

Another significant change introduced by RUPA is provision for the public filing of statements containing basic information about a partnership, such as the agency authority of its partners. Because of the informality of many partnerships, and the inadvertence of some, mandatory filings were eschewed in favor of a voluntary regime. It was the Drafting Committee's belief, however, that filings would become routine for sophisticated partnerships and would be required by lenders and others for major transactions.

Another innovation is found in Article 9. For the first time, the merger of two or more partnerships and the conversion of partnerships to limited partnerships (and the reverse) is expressly authorized, and a "safe harbor" procedure for effecting such transactions is provided.

One final change deserves mention. Partnership law no longer governs limited partnerships pursuant to the provisions of RUPA itself. First, limited partnerships are not "partnerships" within the RUPA definition. Second, UPA Section 6(2), which provides that the UPA governs limited partnerships in cases not provided for in the Uniform Limited Partnership Act (1976) (1985) ("RULPA") has been deleted. No substantive change in result is intended, however. Section 1105 of RULPA already provides that the UPA governs in any case not provided for in RULPA, and thus the express linkage in RUPA is unnecessary. *

Structurally, it is more appropriately left to RULPA to determine the applicability of RUPA to limited partnerships. It is contemplated that the Conference will review the linkage question carefully, although no changes in RULPA may be necessary despite the many changes in RUPA.

Addendum

In 1995, the Conference appointed a Drafting Committee to add provisions to RUPA authorizing the creation of a new form of general partnership called a limited liability partnership (LLP). At the time RUPA was first approved in 1992, only two states had adopted limited liability partnership legislation. By the time the LLP amendments to RUPA were approved by the Conference at the 1996 Annual Meeting, over forty states had adopted limited liability partnership provisions to their general partnership statute.

The LLP amendments to RUPA deal with four major issues: (1) scope of a partner's liability shield; (2) the voting requirement to become an LLP; (3) the effect of becoming an LLP on the partnership agreement; and (4) the annual filing requirement.

1. Scope of a Partner's Liability Shield

The amendments to add LLP provisions to RUPA include a new Section 306(c) providing for a corporate-styled liability shield which protects partners from vicarious personal liability for all partnership obligations incurred while a partnership is a limited liability partnership. The complete liability shield comports with the modern trend among the states. Most states, however, have adopted a partial liability shield protecting the partners only from vicarious personal liability for all partnership obligations arising from negligence, wrongful acts or misconduct, whether characterized as tort, contract, or otherwise, committed while the partnership is an LLP. The Act does not alter a partner's liability for personal misconduct and does not alter the normal partnership rules regarding a partner's right to indemnification from the partnership (Section 401(c)). Therefore, the primary effect of the new liability shield is to sever a partner's personal liability to make contributions to the partnership when partnership assets are insufficient to cover its indemnification obligation to a partner who incurs a partnership obligation in the ordinary course of the partnership's business. **

---

* Note that the Uniform Limited Partnership Act (2001) de-links the limited and general partnership laws and is a self-contained act. Eds.

** This statement is puzzling. In a full shield LLP individual partners are not liable for partnership obligations, whether contract or tort in nature. Individual

2. Voting Requirement to Become an LLP

The Act includes a new Section 1001(b) which provides that the decision to become an LLP is a major partnership event equivalent to an amendment to the partnership agreement. Therefore, the required vote equals the vote required to amend a partnership agreement. When the agreement is silent on these matters, the required vote would be unanimous. When the agreement includes several amendment votes depending on the nature of the amendment, the required vote is that which considers contribution obligations since those obligations are the most affected by the amendments. Many states currently consider the required vote to become a limited liability partnership to be an ordinary partnership decision requiring only a majority consent.

In becoming an LLP, each partner should consider a personal liability calculus. Where partnership assets are insufficient to indemnify a partner for an LLP obligation, each partner forfeits a right to receive contributions from other partners in exchange for being relieved of the obligation to contribute to the personal liability of other partners. This calculus will be different for each partner and will vary, for example, depending on the size and business of the partnership, the number of partners, the amount of insurance, and the relative risk of each partner's business practice compared to the other partners. * To adequately consider these varying

---

partners would not incur partnership obligations, any more than individual shareholders in a corporation incur business obligations. Instead, the acting partner would commit only the partnership as an entity. It seems more accurate to describe the primary effect of the LLP provisions as severing a partner's personal liability established in Section 306(a) for the obligations of the partnership, whether those obligations arise from the acts of partners or employees of the business. Individual liability would come about only as a result of personal wrongdoing, an event which presumably would be rare in the business and which may render questionable a claim for indemnification under some circumstances. For example, under UPA § 18(b), indemnification of individual partners exists only if the liability was "reasonably" incurred in the ordinary "and proper" conduct of the business. Under RUPA § 401(c), the counterpart provision to § 18(b), the words "reasonably" and "proper" are omitted, suggesting an obligation to indemnify wrongdoing partners. Also, on a related matter, the duty of care of partners toward their partnership is limited in RUPA § 404(c) "to refraining from grossly negligent or reckless conduct. . . ," reinforcing the reading of § 401(c) that RUPA contemplates indemnification of partners who are held liable for negligence while acting in the partnership business. Perhaps this is what the authors of the Addendum had in mind in the above text. Eds.

* Again, as suggested in the preceding footnote, it is difficult to follow the reasoning that seems to underlie this statement. If a partnership is an LLP, there is no personal liability for partnership obligations. A partner when conducting business instead is acting as an agent of the partnership, not as a co-owner personally liable for firm obligations. Thus, the "personal liability calculus" identified in the above text does not seem to exist. It is true that an issue would arise when a partner personally guarantees a partnership obligation, like a bank loan or a long-term lease for the partnership premises (this happens frequently with corporations, LLCs, and

interests, the Act adopts the vote required to amend the partnership agreement in special and general cases.

3. Effect of Becoming an LLP on the Partnership Agreement

The last sentence in new Section 306(c) provides that when a partnership becomes an LLP, the resulting liability shield applies notwithstanding inconsistent provisions of the partnership agreement existing immediately before the vote to become an LLP was taken. When the partners vote to become an LLP, they obviously intend to sever their personal responsibility to make contributions to the partnership when partnership assets are insufficient to cover partnership indemnification obligations to a partner. A partner's contribution obligation may be enforced not only by a partner (Sections 401 and 405) but also by a partner's creditors (Section 807(f)). In essence, the new Section 306(c) automatically "amends" the partnership agreement to remove personal liability for contribution obligations that may exist under the terms of the partnership agreement as it exists immediately before the vote. However, the partners are not prohibited from thereafter amending the partnership agreement again to reestablish contribution obligations (*see* Section 103(b)).

4. Annual Filing Requirement

The Act includes new Section 1001(d) which provides that a partnership's status as an LLP remains effective until it is revoked by a vote of the partners or is canceled by the Secretary of State under the new Section 1003(c) for the failure to file an annual report or pay the required annual fees. Most states provide that unless an LLP timely files an annual registration statement, its LLP status is "automatically" terminated, but may be resurrected prospectively only with a subsequent corrective filing. Under this view, an operating partnership may have significant "gaps" in its shield which is further complicated by sourcing rules necessary to determine when a partnership obligation belongs to the shielded LLP or the unshielded partnership. As with corporations and limited liability companies, the Act preserves the LLP status and the partners' liability shield unless the LLP status is revoked by the partners or canceled by the Secretary of State. In the latter case, potential gaps in the liability shield are cured with a retroactive resurrection of the LLP status if a corrective filing is made within two years (Section 1003(e)).

LLPs, where a bank or landlord will insist on the personal guaranty of the owners of a limited liability entity in a small business setting), but presumably contribution obligations will be separately negotiated at the time the guaranty is entered into or will be set forth in the underlying partnership agreement, or may exist by implication of law among the joint signers of a guaranty. Perhaps the text instead is addressing the point raised in the above note about indemnification of partners who have been negligent in the conduct of the business of the partnership. *See* Robert R. Keatinge, *Limited Liability Partnerships*, 51 Bus. Law. 147, 187-193 (1995). Eds.

ARTICLE 1. GENERAL PROVISIONS

ARTICLE 2. NATURE OF PARTNERSHIP

ARTICLE 3. RELATIONS OF PARTNERS TO PERSONS DEALING WITH PARTNERSHIP

ARTICLE 4. RELATIONS OF PARTNERS TO EACH OTHER AND TO PARTNERSHIP

[ARTICLE] 1
GENERAL PROVISIONS

Section 101. Definitions.

(1) "Business" includes every trade, occupation, and profession.

(2) "Debtor in bankruptcy" means a person who is the subject of:

  (i) an order for relief under Title 11 of the United States Code or a comparable order under a successor statute of general application; or

  (ii) a comparable order under federal, state, or foreign law governing insolvency.

(3) "Distribution" means a transfer of money or other property from a partnership to a partner in the partner's capacity as a partner or to the partner's transferee.

(4) "Foreign limited liability partnership" means a partnership that:

  (i) is formed under laws other than the laws of this State; and

  (ii) has the status of a limited liability partnership under those laws.

(5) "Limited liability partnership" means a partnership that has filed a statement of qualification under Section 1001 and does not have a similar statement in effect in any other jurisdiction.

(6) "Partnership" means an association of two or more persons to carry on as co-owners a business for profit formed under Section 202, predecessor law, or comparable law of another jurisdiction.

(7) "Partnership agreement" means the agreement, whether written, oral, or implied, among the partners concerning the partnership, including amendments to the partnership agreement.

(8) "Partnership at will" means a partnership in which the partners have not agreed to remain partners until the expiration of a definite term or the completion of a particular undertaking.

(9) "Partnership interest" or "partner's interest in the partnership" means all of a partner's interests in the partnership, including the partner's transferable interest and all management and other rights.

(10) "Person" means an individual, corporation, business trust, estate, trust, partnership, association, joint venture, government, governmental subdivision, agency, or instrumentality, or any other legal or commercial entity.

(11) "Property" means all property, real, personal, or mixed, tangible or intangible, or any interest therein.

(12) "State" means a State of the United States, the District of Columbia, the Commonwealth of Puerto Rico, or any territory or insular possession subject to the jurisdiction of the United States.

(13) "Statement" means a statement of partnership authority under Section 303, a statement of denial under Section 304, a statement of dissociation under Section 704, a statement of dissolution under Section 805, a statement of merger under Section 907, a statement of qualification under Section 1001, a statement of foreign qualification under Section 1102, or an amendment or cancellation of any of the foregoing.

(14) "Transfer" includes an assignment, conveyance, lease, mortgage, deed, and encumbrance.

Comment

These comments include the original comments to the Revised Uniform Partnership Act (RUPA or the Act) and the new comments to the Limited Liability Partnership Act Amendments to the Uniform Partnership Act (1994). The new comments regarding limited liability partnerships are integrated into the RUPA comments.

The RUPA continues the definition of "business" from Section 2 of the Uniform Partnership Act (UPA).

RUPA uses the more contemporary term "debtor in bankruptcy" instead of "bankrupt." The definition is adapted from the new Georgia Partnership Act, Ga. Code Ann. § 14-8-2(1). The definition does not distinguish between a debtor whose estate is being liquidated under Chapter 7 of the Bankruptcy Code and a debtor who is being rehabilitated under Chapter 11, 12, or 13 and includes both. The filing of a voluntary petition under Section 301 of the Bankruptcy Code constitutes an order for relief, but the debtor is entitled to notice and an opportunity to be heard before the entry of an order for relief in an involuntary case under Section 303 of the Code. The term also includes a debtor who is the subject of a comparable order under state or foreign law.

The definition of "distribution" is new and adds precision to the accounting rules established in Sections 401 and 807 and related sections. Transfers to a partner in the partner's capacity as a creditor, lessor, or employee of the partnership, for example, are not "distributions."

The definition of a "foreign limited liability partnership" includes a partnership formed under the laws of another state, foreign country, or other jurisdiction provided it has the status of a limited liability partnership in the other jurisdiction. Since the scope and nature of foreign limited liability partnership liability shields may vary in different jurisdictions, the definition avoids reference to similar or comparable laws. Rather, the definition incorporates the concept of a limited liability partnership in the foreign jurisdiction, however defined in that jurisdiction. The reference to formation "under laws other than the laws of this State" makes clear that the definition includes partnerships formed in foreign countries as well as in another state.

The definition of a "limited liability partnership" makes clear that a partnership may adopt the special liability shield characteristics of a limited liability partnership simply by filing a statement of qualification under Section 1001. A partnership may file the statement in this State regardless of where formed. When coupled with the governing law provisions of Section 106(b), this definition simplifies the choice of law issues applicable to partnership with multi-state activities and contacts. Once a statement of qualification is filed, a partnership's internal affairs and the liability of its partners are determined by the law of the State where the statement is filed. *See* Section 106(b). The partnership may not vary this particular requirement. *See* Section 103(b)(9).

The reference to a "partnership" in the definition of a limited liability partnership makes clear that the RUPA definition of the term rather than the UPA concept controls for purposes of a limited liability partnership. Section 101(6) defines a "partnership" as "an association of two or more persons to carry on as co-owners a business for profit formed under Section 202, predecessor law, or comparable law of another jurisdiction." Section 202(b) further provides that "an association formed under a statute other than this [Act], a predecessor statute, or a comparable statute of another jurisdiction is not a partnership under this [Act]." This language was intended to clarify that a limited partnership is not a RUPA general partnership. It was not intended to preclude the application of any RUPA general partnership rules to limited partnerships where limited partnership law otherwise adopts the RUPA rules. *See* Comments to Section 202(b) and Prefatory Note.

The effect of these definitions leaves the scope and applicability of RUPA to limited partnerships to limited partnership law, not to sever the linkage between the two Acts in all cases. Certain provisions of RUPA will continue to govern limited partnerships by virtue of Revised Uniform Limited Partnership Act (RULPA) Section 1105 which provides that "in any case not provided for in this [Act] the provisions of the Uniform Partnership Act govern." The RUPA partnership definition includes partnerships formed under the UPA. Therefore, the limited liability partnership rules will govern limited partnerships "in any case not provided for" in RULPA. Since RULPA does not provide for any rules applicable to a limited partnership becoming a limited liability partnership, the limited liability partnership rules should apply to limited partnerships that file a statement of qualification.

Partner liability deserves special mention. RULPA Section 403(b) provides that a general partner of a limited partnership "has the liabilities of a partner in a partnership without limited partners." Thus limited partnership law expressly references general partnership law for general partner liability and does not separately consider the liability of such partners. The liability of a general partner of a limited partnership that becomes a LLLP would therefore be the liability of a general partner in an LLP and would be governed by Section 306. The liability of a limited partner in a LLLP is a more complicated matter. RULPA Section 303(a) separately considers the liability of a limited partner. Unless also a general partner, a limited partner is not liable for the obligations of a limited partnership unless the partner participates in the control of the business and then only to persons reasonably believing the limited partner is a general partner. Therefore, arguably limited partners in a LLLP will have the specific RULPA Section 303(a) liability shield while general partners will have a superior Section 306(c) liability shield. In order to clarify limited partner liability and other linkage issues, states that have adopted RUPA, these limited liability partnership rules, and RULPA may wish to consider an amendment to RULPA. A suggested form of such an amendment is:

§ 1107. Limited Liability Limited Partnership.

(a) A limited partnership may become a limited liability partnership by:

(1) obtaining approval of the terms and conditions of the limited partnership becoming a limited liability limited partnership by the vote necessary to amend the limited partnership agreement except, in the case of a limited partnership agreement that expressly considers contribution obligations, the vote necessary to amend those provisions;

(2) filing a statement of qualification under Section 1001(c) of the Uniform Partnership Act (1994); and

(3) complying with the name requirements of Section 1002 of the Uniform Partnership Act (1994).

(b) A limited liability limited partnership continues to be the same entity that existed before the filing of a statement of qualification under Section 1001(c) of the Uniform Partnership Act (1994).

(c) Sections 306(c) and 307(f) [sic] of the Uniform Partnership Act (1994) apply to both general and limited partners of a limited liability limited partnership.

"Partnership" is defined to mean an association of two or more persons to carry on as co-owners a business for profit formed under Section 202 (or predecessor law or comparable law of another jurisdiction), that is, a general partnership. Thus, as used in RUPA, the term "partnership" does not encompass limited partnerships, contrary to the use of the term in the UPA. Section 901(3) defines "limited partnership" for the purpose of Article 9, which deals with conversions and mergers of general and limited partnerships.

The definition of "partnership agreement" is adapted from Section 101(9) of RULPA. The RUPA definition is intended to include the agreement among the partners, including amendments, concerning either the affairs of the partnership or the conduct of its business. It does not include other agreements between some or all of the partners, such as a lease or loan agreement. The partnership agreement need not be written; it may be oral or inferred from the conduct of the parties.

Any partnership in which the partners have not agreed to remain partners until the expiration of a definite term or the completion of a particular undertaking is a "partnership at will." The distinction between an "at-will" partnership and a partnership for "a definite term or the completion of a particular undertaking" is important in determining the rights of dissociating and continuing partners following the dissociation of a partner. *See* Sections 601, 602, 701(b), 801(a), 802(b), and 803.

It is sometimes difficult to determine whether a partnership is at will or is for a definite term or the completion of a particular undertaking. Presumptively, every partnership is an at-will partnership. *See, e.g., Stone v. Stone*, 292 So. 2d 686 (La. 1974); *Frey v. Hauke*, 171 Neb. 852, 108 N.W.2d 228 (1961). To constitute a partnership for a term or a particular undertaking, the partners must agree (i) that the partnership will continue for a definite term or until a particular undertaking is completed and (ii) that they will remain partners until the expiration of the term or the completion of the undertaking. Both are necessary for a term partnership; if the partners have the unrestricted right, as distinguished from the power, to withdraw from a partnership formed for a term or particular undertaking, the partnership is one at will, rather than a term partnership.

To find that the partnership is formed for a definite term or a particular undertaking, there must be clear evidence of an agreement among the partners that the partnership (i) has a minimum or maximum duration or (ii) terminates at the conclusion of a particular venture whose time is indefinite but certain to occur. *See, e.g., Stainton v. Tarantino*, 637 F. Supp. 1051 (E.D. Pa. 1986) (partnership to dissolve no later than December 30, 2020); *Abel v. American Art Analog, Inc.*, 838 F.2d 691 (3d Cir. 1988) (partnership purpose to market an art book); *68th Street Apts., Inc. v. Lauricella*, 362 A.2d 78 (N.J. Super. Ct. 1976) (partnership purpose to construct an apartment building). A partnership to conduct a business which may last indefinitely, however, is an at-will partnership, even though there may be an obligation of the partnership, such as a mortgage, which must be repaid by a certain date, absent a specific agreement that no partner can rightfully withdraw until the obligation is repaid. *See, e.g., Page v. Page*, 55 Cal. 2d. 192, 359 P.2d 41 (1961) (partnership purpose to operate a linen supply business); *Frey v. Hauke, supra* (partnership purpose to contract and operate a bowling alley); *Girard Bank v. Haley*, 460 Pa. 237, 332 A.2d 443 (1975) (partnership purpose to maintain and lease buildings).

"Partnership interest" or "partner's interest in the partnership" is defined to mean all of a partner's interests in the partnership, including the partner's transferable interest and all management and other rights. A partner's "transferable interest" is a more limited concept and means only his share of the profits and losses and right to receive distributions, that is, the partner's economic interests. *See* Section 502 and Comment. Compare RULPA § 101(10) ("partnership interest" includes partner's economic interests only).

The definition of "person" is the usual definition used by the National Conference of Commissioners on Uniform State Laws (NCCUSL or the Conference). The definition includes other legal or commercial entities such as limited liability companies.

"Property" is defined broadly to include all types of property, as well as any interest in property.

The definition of "State" is the Conference's usual definition.

The definition of "statement" is new and refers to one of the various statements authorized by RUPA to enhance or limit the agency authority of a partner, to deny the authority or status of a partner, or to give notice of certain events, such as the dissociation of a partner or the dissolution of the partnership. *See* Sections 303, 304, 704, 805, and 907. Generally, Section 105 governs the execution, filing, and recording of all statements. The definition also makes clear that a statement of qualification under Section 1001 and a statement of foreign qualification under Section 1102 are considered statements. Both qualification statements are therefore subject to the execution, filing, and recordation rules of Section 105.

"Transfer" is defined broadly to include all manner of conveyances, including leases and encumbrances.

Section 102. Knowledge and Notice.

(a) A person knows a fact if the person has actual knowledge of it.

(b) A person has notice of a fact if the person:

(1) knows of it;

(2) has received a notification of it; or

(3) has reason to know it exists from all of the facts known to the person at the time in question.

(c) A person notifies or gives a notification to another by taking steps reasonably required to inform the other person in ordinary course, whether or not the other person learns of it.

(d) A person receives a notification when the notification:

(1) comes to the person's attention; or

(2) is duly delivered at the person's place of business or at any other place held out by the person as a place for receiving communications.

(e) Except as otherwise provided in subsection (f), a person other than an individual knows, has notice, or receives a notification of a fact for purposes of a particular transaction when the individual conducting the transaction knows, has notice, or receives a notification of the fact, or in any event when the fact would have been brought to the individual's attention if the person had exercised reasonable diligence. The person exercises reasonable diligence if it maintains reasonable routines for communicating significant information to the individual conducting the transaction and there is reasonable compliance with the routines. Reasonable diligence does not require an individual acting for the person to communicate information unless the communication is part of the individual's regular duties or the individual has reason to know of the transaction and that the transaction would be materially affected by the information.

(f) A partner's knowledge, notice, or receipt of a notification of a fact relating to the partnership is effective immediately as knowledge by, notice to, or receipt of a notification by the partnership, except in the case of a fraud on the partnership committed by or with the consent of that partner.

Comment

The concepts and definitions of "knowledge," "notice," and "notification" draw heavily on Section 1-201(25) to (27) of the Uniform Commercial Code (UCC). The UCC text has been altered somewhat to improve clarity and style, but in general no substantive changes are intended from the UCC concepts. "A notification" replaces the UCC's redundant phrase, "a notice or notification," throughout the Act.

A person "knows" a fact only if that person has actual knowledge of it. Knowledge is cognitive awareness. That is solely an issue of fact. This is a change from the UPA Section 3(1) definition of "knowledge" which included the concept of "bad faith" knowledge arising from other known facts.

"Notice" is a lesser degree of awareness than "knows" and is based on a person's: (i) actual knowledge; (ii) receipt of a notification; or (iii) reason to know based on actual knowledge of other facts and the circumstances at the time. The latter is the traditional concept of inquiry notice.

Generally, under RUPA, statements filed pursuant to Section 105 do not constitute constructive knowledge or notice, except as expressly provided in the Act. *See* Section 301(1) (generally requiring knowledge of limitations on partner's apparent authority). Properly recorded statements of limitation on a partner's authority, on the other hand, generally constitute constructive knowledge with respect to the transfer of real property held in the partnership name. *See* Sections 303(d)(1), 303(e), 704(b), and 805(b). The other exceptions are Sections 704(c) (statement of dissociation effective 90 days after filing) and 805(c) (statement of dissolution effective 90 days after filing).

A person "receives" a notification when (i) the notification is delivered to the person's place of business (or other place for receiving communications) or (ii) the recipient otherwise actually learns of its existence.

The sender "notifies" or gives a notification by making an effort to inform the recipient, which is reasonably calculated to do so in ordinary course, even if the recipient does not actually learn of it.

The Official Comment to UCC Section 1-201(26), on which this subsection is based, explains that "notifies" is the word used when the essential fact is the proper dispatch of the notice, not its receipt. When the essential fact is the other party's receipt of the notice, that is stated.

A notification is not required to be in writing. That is a change from UPA Section 3(2)(b). As under the UCC, the time and circumstances under which a notification may cease to be effective are not determined by RUPA.

Subsection (e) determines when an agent's knowledge or notice is imputed to an organization, such as a corporation. In general, only the knowledge or notice of the agent conducting the particular transaction is imputed to the organization. Organizations are expected to maintain reasonable internal routines to insure that important information reaches the individual agent handling the transaction. If, in the exercise of reasonable diligence on the part of the organization, the agent should have known or had notice of a fact, or received a notification of it, the organization is bound. The Official Comment to UCC Section 1-201(27) explains:

> This makes clear that reason to know, knowledge, or a notification, although "received" for instance by a clerk in Department A of an organization, is effective for a transaction conducted in Department B only from the time when it was or should have been communicated to the individual conducting that transaction.

Subsection (e) uses the phrase "person other than an individual" in lieu of the UCC term "organization."

Subsection (f) continues the rule in UPA Section 12 that a partner's knowledge or notice of a fact relating to the partnership is imputed to the partnership, except in the case of fraud on the partnership. Limited partners, however, are not "partners" within the meaning of RUPA. *See* Comment 4 to Section 202. It is anticipated that RULPA will address the issue of whether notice to a limited partner is imputed to a limited partnership.

Section 103. Effect of Partnership Agreement; Nonwaivable Provisions.

(a) Except as otherwise provided in subsection (b), relations among the partners and between the partners and the partnership are governed by the partnership agreement. To the extent the partnership agreement does not otherwise provide, this [Act] governs relations among the partners and between the partners and the partnership.

(b) The partnership agreement may not:

(1) vary the rights and duties under Section 105 except to eliminate the duty to provide copies of statements to all of the partners;

(2) unreasonably restrict the right of access to books and records under Section 403(b);

(3) eliminate the duty of loyalty under Section 404(b) or 603(b)(3), but:

(i) the partnership agreement may identify specific types or categories of activities that do not violate the duty of loyalty, if not manifestly unreasonable; or

(ii) all of the partners or a number or percentage specified in the partnership agreement may authorize or ratify, after full disclosure of all material facts, a specific act or transaction that otherwise would violate the duty of loyalty;

(4) unreasonably reduce the duty of care under Section 404(c) or 603(b)(3);

(5) eliminate the obligation of good faith and fair dealing under Section 404(d), but the partnership agreement may prescribe the standards by which the performance of the obligation is to be measured, if the standards are not manifestly unreasonable;

(6) vary the power to dissociate as a partner under Section 602(a), except to require the notice under Section 601(1) to be in writing;

(7) vary the right of a court to expel a partner in the events specified in Section 601(5);

(8) vary the requirement to wind up the partnership business in cases specified in Section 801(4), (5), or (6); or

(9) vary the law applicable to a limited liability partnership under Section 106(b); or

(10) restrict rights of third parties under this [Act].

Comment

1. The general rule under Section 103(a) is that relations among the partners and between the partners and the partnership are governed by

the partnership agreement. *See* Section 101(5). To the extent that the partners fail to agree upon a contrary rule, RUPA provides the default rule. Only the right and duties listed in Section 103(b), and implicitly the corresponding liabilities and remedies under Section 405, are mandatory and cannot be waived or varied by agreement beyond what is authorized. Those are the only exceptions to the general principle that the provisions of RUPA with respect to the rights of the partners *inter se* are merely default rules, subject to modification by the partners. All modifications must also, of course, satisfy the general standards of contract validity. *See* Section 104.

2. Under subsection (b)(1), the partnership agreement may not vary the requirements for executing, filing, and recording statements under Section 105, except the duty to provide copies to all the partners. A statement that is not executed, filed, and recorded in accordance with the statutory requirements will not be accorded the effect prescribed in the Act, except as provided in Section 303(d).

3. Subsection (b)(2) provides that the partnership agreement may not unreasonably restrict a partner or former partner's access rights to books and records under Section 403(b). It is left to the courts to determine what restrictions are reasonable. *See* Comment 2 to Section 403. Other information rights in Section 403 can be varied or even eliminated by agreement.

4. Subsection (b)(3) through (5) are intended to ensure a fundamental core of fiduciary responsibility. Neither the fiduciary duties of loyalty or care, nor the obligation of good faith and fair dealing, may be eliminated entirely. However, the statutory requirements of each can be modified by agreement, subject to the limitation stated in subsection (b)(3) through (5).

There has always been a tension regarding the extent to which a partner's fiduciary duty of loyalty can be varied by agreement, as contrasted with the other partners' consent to a particular and known breach of duty. On the one hand, courts have been loathe to enforce agreements broadly "waiving" in advance a partner's fiduciary duty of loyalty, especially where there is unequal bargaining power information, or sophistication. For this reason, a very broad provision in a partnership agreement in effect negating any duty of loyalty, such as a provision giving a managing partner complete discretion to manage the business with no liability except for acts and omissions that constitute wilful misconduct, will not likely be enforced. *See, e.g., Labovitz v. Dolan*, 189 Ill. App. 3d 403, 136 Ill. Dec. 780, 545 N.E.2d 304 (1989). On the other hand, it is clear that the remaining partners can "consent" to a particular conflicting interest transaction or other breach of duty, after the fact, provided there is full disclosure.

RUPA attempts to provide a standard that partners can rely upon in drafting exculpatory agreements. It is not necessary that the agreement be restricted to a particular transaction. That would require bargaining over every transaction or opportunity, which would be excessively burdensome. The agreement may be drafted in terms of types or categories of activities or transactions, but it should be reasonably specific.

A provision in a real estate partnership agreement authorizing a partner who is a real estate agent to retain commissions on partnership property bought and sold by that partner would be an example of a "type or category" of activity that is not manifestly unreasonable and thus should be enforceable under the Act. Likewise, a provision authorizing that partner to buy or sell real property for his own account without prior disclosure to the other partners or without first offering it to the partnership would be enforceable as a valid category of partnership activity.

Ultimately, the courts must decide the outer limits of validity of such agreements, and context may be significant. It is intended that the risk of judicial refusal to enforce manifestly unreasonable exculpatory clauses will discourage sharp practices while accommodating the legitimate needs of the parties in structuring their relationship.

5. Subsection (b)(3)(i) permits the partners, in their partnership agreement, to identify specific types or categories of partnership activities that do not violate the duty of loyalty. A modification of the statutory standard must not, however, be manifestly unreasonable. This is intended to discourage overreaching by a partner with superior bargaining power since the courts may refuse to enforce an overly broad exculpatory clause. *See, e.g., Vlases v. Montgomery Ward & Co.*, 377 F.2d 846, 850 (3d Cir. 1967) (limitation prohibits unconscionable agreements); *PPG Industries, Inc. v. Shell Oil Co.*, 919 F.2d 17, 19 (5th Cir. 1990) (apply limitation deferentially to agreements of sophisticated parties).

Subsection (b)(3)(ii) is intended to clarify the right of partners, recognized under general law, to consent to a known past or anticipated violation of duty and to waive their legal remedies for redress of that violation. This is intended to cover situations where the conduct in question is not specifically authorized by the partnership agreement. It can also be used to validate conduct that might otherwise not satisfy the "manifestly unreasonable" standard. Clause (ii) provides that, after full disclosure of all material facts regarding a specific act or transaction that otherwise would violate the duty of loyalty, it may be authorized or ratified by the partners. That authorization or ratification must be unanimous unless a lesser number or percentage is specified for this purpose in the partnership agreement.

6. Under subsection (b)(4), the partners' duty of care may not be unreasonably reduced below the statutory standard set forth in Section 404(c), that is, to refrain from engaging in grossly negligent or reckless conduct, intentional misconduct, or a knowing violation of law.

For example, partnership agreements frequently contain provisions releasing a partner from liability for actions taken in good faith and in the honest belief that the actions are in the best interests of the partnership and indemnifying the partner against any liability incurred in connection with the business of the partnership if the partner acts in a good faith belief that he has authority to act. Many partnership agreements reach this same result by listing various activities and stating that the performance of these activities is deemed not to constitute gross negligence or wilful misconduct. These types of provisions are intended to come within the modifications authorized by subsection (b)(4). On the other hand, absolving partners of intentional misconduct is probably unreasonable. As with contractual standards of loyalty, determining the outer limit in reducing the standard of care is left to the courts.

The standard may, of course, be increased by agreement to one of ordinary care or an even higher standard of care.

7. Subsection (b)(5) authorizes the partners to determine the standards by which the performance of the obligation of good faith and fair dealing is to be measured. The language of subsection (b)(5) is based on UCC Section 1-102(3). The partners can negotiate and draft specific contract provisions tailored to their particular needs (e.g., five days notice of a partners' meeting is adequate notice), but blanket waivers of the obligation are unenforceable. *See, e.g., PPG Indus., Inc. v. Shell Oil Co.,* 919 F.2d 17 (5th Cir. 1990); *First Security Bank v. Mountain View Equip. Co.,* 112 Idaho 158, 730 P.2d 1078 (Ct. App. 1986), *aff'd,* 112 Idaho 1078, 739 P.2d 377 (1987); *American Bank of Commerce v. Covolo,* 88 N.M. 405, 540 P.2d 1294 (1975).

8. Section 602(a) continues the traditional UPA Section 31(2) rule that every partner has the power to withdraw from the partnership at any time, which power cannot be bargained away. Section 103(b)(6) provides that the partnership agreement may not vary the power to dissociate as a partner under Section 602(a), except to require that the notice of withdrawal under Section 601(1) be in writing. The UPA was silent with respect to requiring a written notice of withdrawal.

9. Under subsection (b)(7), the right of a partner to seek court expulsion of another partner under Section 601(5) cannot be waived or varied (e.g., requiring a 90-day notice) by agreement. Section 601(5) refers to judicial expulsion on such grounds as misconduct, breach of duty, or impracticability.

10. Under subsection (b)(8), the partnership agreement may not vary the right of partners to have the partnership dissolved and its business wound up under Section 801(4), (5), or (6). Section 801(4) provides that the partnership must be wound up if its business is unlawful. Section 801(5) provides for judicial winding up in such circumstances as frustration of the firm's economic purpose, partner misconduct, or impracticability. Section 801(6) accords standing to transferees of an interest in the partnership to seek judicial dissolution of the partnership in specified circumstances.

11. Subsection (b)(9) makes clear that a limited liability partnership may not designate the law of a State other than the State where it filed its statement of qualification to govern its internal affairs and the liability of its partners. *See* Sections 101(5), 106(b), and 202(a). Therefore, the selection of a state within which to file a statement of qualification has important choice of law ramifications, particularly where the partnership was formed in another state. *See* Comments to Section 106(b).

12. Although stating the obvious, subsection (b)(10) provides expressly that the rights of a third party under the Act may not be restricted by an agreement among the partners to which the third party has not agreed. A non-partner who is a party to an agreement among the partners is, of course, bound. *Cf.* Section 703(c) (creditor joins release).

13. The Article 9 rules regarding conversions and mergers are not listed in Section 103(b) as mandatory. Indeed Section 908 states expressly that partnerships may be converted and merged in any other manner provided by law. The effect of compliance with Article 9 is to provide a "safe harbor" assuring the legal validity of such conversions and mergers. Although not immune from variation in the partnership agreement, noncompliance with the requirements of Article 9 in effecting a conversion or merger is to deny that "safe harbor" validity to the transaction. In this regard, Sections 903(b) and 905(c)(2) require that the conversion or merger of a limited partnership be approved by all of the partners, notwithstanding a contrary provision in the limited partnership agreement. Thus, in effect, the agreement cannot vary the voting requirement without sacrificing the benefits of the "safe harbor."

Section 104. Supplemental Principles of Law.

(a) Unless displaced by particular provisions of this [Act], the principles of law and equity supplement this [Act].

(b) If an obligation to pay interest arises under this [Act] and the rate is not specified, the rate is that specified in [applicable statute].

Comment

The principles of law and equity supplement RUPA unless displaced by a particular provision of the Act. This broad statement combines the separate rules contained in UPA Sections 4(2), 4(3), and 5. These supplementary principles encompass not only the law of agency and estoppel and the law merchant mentioned in the UPA, but all of the other principles listed in UCC Section 1-103: the law, relative to capacity to contract, fraud, misrepresentation, duress, coercion, mistake, bankruptcy, and other common law validating or invalidating causes, such as unconscionability. No substantive change from either the UPA or the UCC is intended.

It was thought unnecessary to repeat the UPA Section 4(1) admonition that statutes in derogation of the common law are not to be strictly construed. This principle is now so well established that it is not necessary to so state in the Act. No change in the law is intended. *See* the Comment to RULPA Section 1101.

Subsection (b) is new. It is based on the definition of "interest" in Section 14-8-2(5) of the Georgia act and establishes the applicable rate of interest in the absence of an agreement among the partners. Adopting States can select the State's legal rate of interest or other statutory interest rate, such as the rate for judgments.

Section 105. Execution, Filing, and Recording of Statements.

(a) A statement may be filed in the office of [the Secretary of State]. A certified copy of a statement that is filed in an office in another State may be filed in the office of [the Secretary of State]. Either filing has the effect provided in this [Act] with respect to partnership property located in or transactions that occur in this State.

(b) A certified copy of a statement that has been filed in the office of the [Secretary of State] and recorded in the office for recording transfers of real property has the effect provided for recorded statements in this [Act]. A recorded statement that is not a certified copy of a statement filed in the office of the [Secretary of State] does not have the effect provided for recorded statements in this [Act].

(c) A statement filed by a partnership must be executed by at least two partners. Other statements must be executed by a partner or other person authorized by this [Act]. An individual who executes a statement as, or on behalf of, a partner or other person named as a partner in a statement shall personally declare under penalty of perjury that the contents of the statement are accurate.

(d) A person authorized by this [Act] to file a statement may amend or cancel the statement by filing an amendment or cancellation that names the partnership, identifies the statement, and states the substance of the amendment or cancellation.

(e) A person who files a statement pursuant to this section shall promptly send a copy of the statement to every nonfiling partner and to any other person named as a partner in the statement. Failure to send a copy of a statement to a partner or other person does not limit the effectiveness of the statement as to a person not a partner.

(f) The [Secretary of State] may collect a fee for filing or providing a certified copy of a statement. The [officer responsible for recording transfers of real property] may collect a fee for recording a statement.

Comment

1. Section 105 is new. It mandates the procedural rules for the execution, filing, and recording of the various "statements" (*see* Section 101(11))

authorized by RUPA. Section 101(13) makes clear that a statement of qualification filed by a partnership to become a limited liability partnership is included in the definition of a statement. Therefore, the execution, filing, and recording rules of this section must be followed except that the decision to file the statement of qualification must be approved by the vote of the partners necessary to amend the partnership agreement as to contribution requirements. *See* Section 1001(b) and comments.

No filings are mandatory under RUPA. In all cases, the filing of a statement is optional and voluntary. A system of mandatory filing and disclosure for partnerships, similar to that required for corporations and limited partnerships, was rejected for several reasons. First, RUPA is designed to accommodate the needs of small partnerships, which often have unwritten or sketchy agreements and limited resources. Furthermore, inadvertent partnerships are also governed by the Act, as the default form of business organization, in which case filing would be unlikely.

The RUPA filing provisions are, however, likely to encourage the voluntary use of partnership statements. There are a number of strong incentives for the partnership or the partners to file statements or for third parties, such as lenders or transferees of partnership property, to compel them to do so.

Only statements that are executed, filed, and, if appropriate (such as the authority to transfer real property), recorded in conformity with Section 105 have the legal consequences accorded statements by RUPA. The requirements of Section 105 cannot be varied in the partnership agreement, except the duty to provide copies of statements to all the partners. *See* Section 103(b)(1).

In most States today, the filing and recording of statements requires written documents. As technology advances, alternatives suitable for filing and recording may be developed. RUPA itself does not impose any requirement that statements be in writing. It is intended that the form or medium for filing and recording be left to the general law of adopting States.

2. Section 105(a) provides for a single, central filing of all statements, as is the case with corporations, limited partnerships, and limited liability companies. The expectation is that most States will assign to the Secretary of State the responsibility of maintaining the filing system for partnership statements. Since a partnership is an entity under RUPA, all statements should be indexed by partnership name, not by the names of the individual partners.

Partnerships transacting business in more than one State will want to file copies of statements in each State because subsection (a) limits the legal effect of filed statements to property located or transactions occurring within the state. The filing of a certified copy of a statement originally filed in another State is permitted, and indeed encouraged, in order to avoid inconsistencies between statements filed in different States.

3. Subsection (b), in effect, mandates the use of certified copies of filed statements for local recording in the real estate records by limiting the legal effect of recorded statements under the Act to those copies. The reason for recording only certified copies of filed statements is to eliminate the possibility of inconsistencies affecting the title to real property.

Subsection (c) requires that statements filed on behalf of a partnership, that is, the entity, be executed by at least two partners. Individual partners and other persons authorized by the Act to file a statement may execute it on their own behalf. To protect the partners and the partnership from unauthorized or improper filings, an individual who executes a statement as a partner must personally declare under penalty of perjury that the statement is accurate.

The amendment or cancellation of statements is authorized by subsection (d).

As a further safeguard against inaccurate or unauthorized filings, subsection (e) requires that a copy of every statement filed be sent to each partner, although the failure to do so does not limit the effectiveness of the statement. This requirement may, however, be eliminated in the partnership agreement. *See* Section 103(b)(1). Partners may also file a statement of denial under Section 304.

4. A filed statement may be amended or canceled by any person authorized by the Act to file an original statement. The amendment or cancellation must state the name of the partnership so that it can be properly indexed and found, identify the statement being amended or canceled, and the substance of the amendment or cancellation. An amendment generally has the same operative effect as an original statement. A cancellation of extraordinary authority terminates that authority. A cancellation of a limitation on authority revives a previous grant of authority. *See* Section 303(d). The subsequent filing of a statement similar in kind to a statement already of record is treated as an amendment, even if not so denominated. Any substantive conflict between filed statements operates as a cancellation of authority under Section 303.

Section 106. Governing Law.

(a) Except as otherwise provided in subsection (b), the law of the jurisdiction in which a partnership has its chief executive office governs relations among the partners and between the partners and the partnership.

(b) The law of this State governs relations among the partners and between the partners and the partnership and the liability of partners for an obligation of a limited liability partnership.

Comment

The subsection (a) internal relations rule is new. *Cf.* RULPA § 901 (internal affairs governed by law of State in which limited partnership organized).

RUPA looks to the jurisdiction in which a partnership's chief executive office is located to provide the law governing the internal relations among the partners and between the partners and the partnership. The concept of the partnership's "chief executive office" is drawn from UCC Section 9-103(3)(d). It was chosen in lieu of the State of organization because no filing is necessary to form a general partnership, and thus the situs of its organization is not always clear, unlike a limited partnership, which is organized in the State where its certificate is filed.

The term "chief executive office" is not defined in the Act, nor is it defined in the UCC. Paragraph 5 of the Official Comment to UCC Section 9-103(3)(d) explains:

> "Chief executive office" . . . means the place from which in fact the debtor manages the main part of his business operations. . . . Doubt may arise as to which is the "chief executive office" of a multistate enterprise, but it would be rare that there could be more than two possibilities. . . . [The rule] will be simple to apply in most cases. . . .

In the absence of any other clear rule for determining a partnership's legal situs, it seems convenient to use that rule for choice of law purposes as well.

The choice-of-law rule provided by subsection (a) is only a default rule, and the partners may by agreement select the law of another State to govern their internal affairs, subject to generally applicable conflict of laws requirements. For example, where the partners may not resolve a particular issue by an explicit provision of the partnership agreement, such as the rights and duties set forth in Section 103(b), the law chosen will not be applied if the partners or the partnership have no substantial relationship to the chosen State or other reasonable basis for their choice or if application of the law of the chosen State would be contrary to a fundamental policy of a State that has a materially greater interest than the chosen State. *See* Restatement (Second) of Conflict of Laws § 187(2) (1971). The partners must, however, select only one State to govern their internal relations. They cannot select one State for some aspects of their internal relations and another State for others.

Contrasted with the variable choice-of-law rule provided by subsection (a), the law of the State where a limited liability partnership files its statement of qualification applies to such a partnership and may not be varied by the agreement of the partners. *See* Section 103(b)(9). Also, a partnership that files a statement of qualification in another state is not defined as a limited liability partnership in this state. *See* Section 101(5).

Unlike a general partnership which may be formed without any filing, a partnership may only become a limited liability partnership by filing a statement of qualification. Therefore, the situs of its organization is clear. Because it is often unclear where a general partnership is actually formed, the decision to file a statement of qualification in a particular state constitutes a choice-of-law for the partnership which cannot be altered by the partnership agreement. *See* Comments to Section 103(b)(9). If the partnership agreement of an existing partnership specifies the law of a particular state as its governing law, and the partnership thereafter files a statement of qualification in another state, the partnership agreement choice is no longer controlling. In such cases, the filing of a statement of qualification "amends" the partnership agreement on this limited matter. Accordingly, if a statement of qualification is revoked or canceled for a limited liability partnership, the law of the state of filing would continue to apply unless the partnership agreement thereafter altered the applicable law rule.

Section 107. Partnership Subject to Amendment or Repeal of [Act].

A partnership governed by this [Act] is subject to any amendment to or repeal of this [Act].

Comment

The reservation of power provision is new. It is adapted from Section 1.02 of the Revised Model Business Corporation Act (RMBCA) and Section 1106 of RULPA.

As explained in the Official Comment to the RMBCA, the genesis of those provisions is *Trustees of Dartmouth College v. Woodward*, 17 U.S. (4 Wheat) 518 (1819), which held that the United States Constitution prohibits the application of newly enacted statutes to existing corporations, while suggesting the efficacy of a reservation of power provision. Its purpose is to avoid any possible argument that a legal entity created pursuant to statute or its members have a contractual or vested right in any specific statutory provision and to ensure that the State may in the future modify its enabling statute as it deems appropriate and require existing entities to comply with the statutes as modified.

[ARTICLE] 2
NATURE OF PARTNERSHIP

Section   201. Partnership As Entity.
Section   202. Formation of Partnership.
Section   203. Partnership Property.
Section   204. When Property Is Partnership Property.

Section 201. Partnership as Entity.

(a) A partnership is an entity distinct from its partners.

(b) A limited liability partnership continues to be the same entity that existed before the filing of a statement of qualification under Section 1001.

Comment

RUPA embraces the entity theory of the partnership. In light of the UPA's ambivalence on the nature of partnerships, the explicit statement provided by subsection (a) is deemed appropriate as an expression of the increased emphasis on the entity theory as the dominant model. *But see* Section 306 (partners' liability joint and several unless the partnership has filed a statement of qualification to become a limited liability partnership).

Giving clear expression to the entity nature of a partnership is intended to allay previous concerns stemming from the aggregate theory, such as the necessity of a deed to convey title from the "old" partnership to the "new" partnership every time there is a change of cast among the partners. Under RUPA, there is no "new" partnership just because of membership changes. That will avoid the result in cases such as *Fairway Development Co. v. Title Insurance Co.,* 621 F. Supp. 120 (N.D. Ohio 1985), which held that the "new" partnership resulting from a partner's death did not have standing to enforce a title insurance policy issued to the "old" partnership.

Subsection (b) makes clear that the explicit entity theory provided by subsection (a) applies to a partnership both before and after it files a statement of qualification to become a limited liability partnership. Thus, just as there is no "new" partnership resulting from membership changes, the filing of a statement of qualification does not create a "new" partnership. The filing partnership continues to be the same partnership entity that existed before the filing. Similarly, the amendment or cancellation of a statement of qualification under Section 105(d) or the revocation of a statement of qualification under Section 1003(c) does not terminate the partnership and create a "new" partnership. *See* Section 1003(d). Accordingly, a partnership remains the same entity regardless of a filing, cancellation, or revocation of a statement of qualification.

Section 202. Formation of Partnership.

(a) Except as otherwise provided in subsection (b), the association of two or more persons to carry on as co-owners a business for profit forms a partnership, whether or not the persons intend to form a partnership.

(b) An association formed under a statute other than this [Act], a predecessor statute, or a comparable statute of another jurisdiction is not a partnership under this [Act].

(c) In determining whether a partnership is formed, the following rules apply:

(1) Joint tenancy, tenancy in common, tenancy by the entireties, joint property, common property, or part ownership does not by itself establish a partnership, even if the co-owners share profits made by the use of the property.

(2) The sharing of gross returns does not by itself establish a partnership, even if the persons sharing them have a joint or common right or interest in property from which the returns are derived.

(3) A person who receives a share of the profits of a business is presumed to be a partner in the business, unless the profits were received in payment:

(i) of a debt by installments or otherwise;

(ii) for services as an independent contractor or of wages or other compensation to an employee;

(iii) of rent;

(iv) of an annuity or other retirement or health benefit to a beneficiary, representative, or designee of a deceased or retired partner;

(v) of interest or other charge on a loan, even if the amount of payment varies with the profits of the business, including a direct or indirect present or future ownership of the collateral, or rights to income, proceeds, or increase in value derived from the collateral; or

(vi) for the sale of the goodwill of a business or other property by installments or otherwise.

Comment

1. Section 202 combines UPA Sections 6 and 7. The traditional UPA Section 6(1) "definition" of a partnership is recast as an operative rule of law. No substantive change in the law is intended. The UPA "definition" has always been understood as an operative rule, as well as a definition. The addition of the phrase, "whether or not the persons intend to form a partnership," merely codifies the universal judicial construction of UPA Section 6(1) that a partnership is created by the association of persons whose intent is to carry on as co-owners a business for profit, regardless of their subjective intention to be "partners." Indeed, they may inadvertently create a partnership despite their expressed subjective intention not to do so. The new language alerts readers to this possibility.

As under the UPA, the attribute of co-ownership distinguishes a partnership from a mere agency relationship. A business is a series of acts directed toward an end. Ownership involves the power of ultimate control. To state that partners are co-owners of a business is to state that they each have the power of ultimate control. *See* Official Comment to UPA § 6(1). On the other hand, as subsection (c)(1) makes clear, passive co-ownership of property by itself, as distinguished from the carrying on of a business, does not establish a partnership.

2. Subsection (b) provides that business associations organized under other statutes are not partnerships. Those statutory associations include corporations, limited partnerships, and limited liability companies. That continues the UPA concept that general partnership is the residual form of for profit business association, existing only if another form does not.

A limited partnership is not a partnership under this definition. Nevertheless, certain provisions of RUPA will continue to govern limited partnerships because RULPA itself, in Section 1105, so requires "in any case not provided for" in RULPA. For example, the rules applicable to a limited liability partnership will generally apply to limited partnerships. *See* Comment to Section 101(5) (definition of a limited liability partnership). In light of RULPA Section 1105, UPA Section 6(2), which provides that limited partnerships are governed by the UPA, is redundant and has not been carried over to RUPA. It is also more appropriate that the applicability of RUPA to limited partnerships be governed exclusively by RULPA. For example, a RULPA amendment may clarify certain linkage questions regarding the application of the limited liability partnership rules to limited partnerships. See Comment to Section 101(5) for a suggested form of such an amendment.

It is not intended that RUPA change any common law rules concerning special types of associations, such as mining partnerships, which in some jurisdictions are not governed by the UPA.

Relationships that are called "joint ventures" are partnerships if they otherwise fit the definition of a partnership. An association is not classified as a partnership, however, simply because it is called a "joint venture."

An unincorporated nonprofit organization is not a partnership under RUPA, even if it qualifies as a business, because it is not a "for profit" organization.

3. Subsection (c) provides three rules of construction that apply in determining whether a partnership has been formed under subsection (a). They are largely derived from UPA Section 7, and to that extent no substantive change is intended. The sharing of profits is recast as a rebuttable presumption of a partnership, a more contemporary construction, rather than as prima facie evidence thereof. The protected categories, in which receipt of a share of the profits is not presumed to create a partnership, apply whether the profit share is a single flat percentage or a ratio which varies, for example, after reaching a dollar floor or different levels of profits.

Like its predecessor, RUPA makes no attempt to answer in every case whether a partnership is formed. Whether a relationship is more properly characterized as that of borrower and lender, employer and employee, or landlord and tenant is left to the trier of fact. As under the UPA, a person may function in both partner and nonpartner capacities.

Paragraph (3)(v) adds a new protected category to the list. It shields from the presumption a share of the profits received in payment of interest or other charges on a loan, "including a direct or indirect present or future ownership in the collateral, or rights to income, proceeds, or increase in value derived from the collateral." The quoted language is taken from Section 211 of the Uniform Land Security Interest Act. The purpose of the new language is to protect shared-appreciation mortgages, contingent or other variable or performance-related mortgages, and other equity participation arrangements by clarifying that contingent payments do not presumptively convert lending arrangements into partnerships.

4. Section 202(e) of the 1993 Act stated that partnerships formed under RUPA are general partnerships and that the partners are general partners. That section has been deleted as unnecessary. Limited partners are not "partners" within the meaning of RUPA, however.

Section 203. Partnership Property.

Property acquired by a partnership is property of the partnership and not of the partners individually.

Comment

All property acquired by a partnership, by transfer or otherwise, becomes partnership property and belongs to the partnership as an entity, rather than to the individual partners. This expresses the substantive result of UPA Sections 8(1) and 25.

Neither UPA Section 8(1) nor RUPA Section 203 provides any guidance concerning when property is "acquired by" the partnership. That problem is dealt with in Section 204.

UPA Sections 25(2)(c) and (e) also provide that partnership property is not subject to exemptions, allowances, or rights of a partner's spouse, heirs, or next of kin. Those provisions have been omitted as unnecessary. No substantive change is intended. Those exemptions and rights inure to the property of the partners, and not to partnership property.

Section 204. When Property Is Partnership Property.

(a) Property is partnership property if acquired in the name of:

(1) the partnership; or

(2) one or more partners with an indication in the instrument transferring title to the property of the person's capacity as a partner or

of the existence of a partnership but without an indication of the name of the partnership.

(b) Property is acquired in the name of the partnership by a transfer to:

(1) the partnership in its name; or

(2) one or more partners in their capacity as partners in the partnership, if the name of the partnership is indicated in the instrument transferring title to the property.

(c) Property is presumed to be partnership property if purchased with partnership assets, even if not acquired in the name of the partnership or of one or more partners with an indication in the instrument transferring title to the property of the person's capacity as a partner or of the existence of a partnership.

(d) Property acquired in the name of one or more of the partners, without an indication in the instrument transferring title to the property of the person's capacity as a partner or of the existence of a partnership and without use of partnership assets is presumed to be separate property, even if used for partnership purposes.

Comment

1. Section 204 sets forth the rules for determining when property is acquired by the partnership and, hence, becomes partnership property. It is based on UPA Section 8(3), as influenced by the recent Alabama and Georgia modifications. The rules govern the acquisition of personal property, as well as real property, that is held in the partnership name. *See* Section 101(9).

2. Subsection (a) governs the circumstances under which property becomes "partnership property," and subsection (b) clarifies the circumstances under which property is acquired "in the name of the partnership." The concept of record title is emphasized, although the term itself is not used. Titled personal property, as well as all transferable interests in real property acquired in the name of the partnership, are covered by this section.

Property becomes partnership property if acquired (1) in the name of the partnership or (2) in the name of one or more of the partners with an indication in the instrument transferring title of either (i) their capacity as partners or (ii) of the existence of a partnership, even if the name of the partnership is not indicated. Property acquired "in the name of the partnership" includes property acquired in the name of one or more partners in their capacity as partners, but only if the name of the partnership is indicated in the instrument transferring title.

Property transferred to a partner is partnership property, even though the name of the partnership is not indicated, if the instrument transferring title indicates either (i) the partner's capacity as a partner or (ii) the existence of a partnership. This is consonant with the entity theory of partnership and resolves the troublesome issue of a conveyance to fewer than all the partners but which nevertheless indicates their partner status.

3. Ultimately, it is the intention of the partners that controls whether property belongs to the partnership or to one or more of the partners in their individual capacities, at least as among the partners themselves. RUPA sets forth two rebuttable presumptions that apply when the partners have failed to express their intent.

First, under subsection (c), property purchased with partnership funds is presumed to be partnership property, notwithstanding the name in which title is held. The presumption is intended to apply if partnership credit is used to obtain financing, as well as the use of partnership cash or property for payment. Unlike the rule in subsection (b), under which property is **deemed** to be partnership property if the partnership's name or the partner's capacity as a partner is disclosed in the instrument of conveyance, subsection (c) raises only a **presumption** that the property is partnership property if it is purchased with partnership assets.

That presumption is also subject to an important caveat. Under Section 302(b), partnership property held in the name of individual partners, without an indication of their capacity as partners or of the existence of a partnership, that is transferred by the partners in whose name title is held to a purchaser without knowledge that it is partnership property is free of any claims of the partnership.

Second, under subsection (d), property acquired in the name of one or more of the partners, without an indication of their capacity as partners and without use of partnership funds or credit, is presumed to be the partners' separate property, even if used for partnership purposes. In effect, it is presumed in that case that only the use of the property is contributed to the partnership.

4. Generally, under RUPA, partners and third parties dealing with partnerships will be able to rely on the record to determine whether property is owned by the partnership. The exception is property purchased with partnership funds without any reference to the partnership in the title documents. The inference concerning the partners' intent from the use of partnership funds outweighs any inference from the state of the title, subject to the overriding reliance interest in the case of a purchaser without notice of the partnership's interest. This allocation of risk should encourage the partnership to eliminate doubt about ownership by putting title in the partnership.

5. UPA Section 8(4) provides, "A transfer to a partnership in the partnership name, even without words of inheritance, passes the entire estate or interest of the grantor unless a contrary intent appears." It has been

omitted from RUPA as unnecessary because modern conveyancing law deems all transfers to pass the entire estate or interest of the grantor unless a contrary intent appears.

[ARTICLE] 3
RELATIONS OF PARTNERS TO PERSONS DEALING WITH PARTNERSHIP

Section   301. Partner Agent of Partnership.

Section   302. Transfer of Partnership Property.

Section   303. Statement of Partnership Authority.

Section   304. Statement of Denial.

Section   305. Partnership Liable for Partner's Actionable Conduct.

Section   306. Partner's Liability.

Section   307. Actions By and Against Partnership and Partners.

Section   308. Liability of Purported Partner.

Section 301. Partner Agent of Partnership.

Subject to the effect of a statement of partnership authority under Section 303:

(1) Each partner is an agent of the partnership for the purpose of its business. An act of a partner, including the execution of an instrument in the partnership name, for apparently carrying on in the ordinary course the partnership business or business of the kind carried on by the partnership binds the partnership, unless the partner had no authority to act for the partnership in the particular matter and the person with whom the partner was dealing knew or had received a notification that the partner lacked authority.

(2) An act of a partner which is not apparently for carrying on in the ordinary course the partnership business or business of the kind carried on by the partnership binds the partnership only if the act was authorized by the other partners.

Comment

1. Section 301 sets forth a partner's power, as an agent of the firm, to bind the partnership entity to third parties. The rights of the partners among themselves, including the right to restrict a partner's authority, are governed by the partnership agreement and by Section 401.

The agency rules set forth in Section 301 are subject to an important qualification. They may be affected by the filing or recording of a statement of partnership authority. The legal effect of filing or recording a statement of partnership authority is set forth in Section 303.

2. Section 301(1) retains the basic principles reflected in UPA Section 9(1). It declares that each partner is an agent of the partnership and that, by virtue of partnership status, each partner has apparent authority to bind the partnership in ordinary course transactions. The effect of Section 301(1) is to characterize a partner as a general managerial agent having both actual and apparent authority co-extensive in scope with the firm's ordinary business, at least in the absence of a contrary partnership agreement.

Section 301(1) effects two changes from UPA Section 9(1). First, it clarifies that a partner's apparent authority includes acts for carrying on in the ordinary course "business of the kind carried on by the partnership," not just the business of the particular partnership in question. The UPA is ambiguous on this point, but there is some authority for an expanded construction in accordance with the so-called English rule. *See, e.g., Burns v. Gonzalez*, 439 S.W.2d 128, 131 (Tex. Civ. App. 1969) (dictum); *Commercial Hotel Co. v. Weeks*, 254 S.W. 521 (Tex. Civ. App. 1923). No substantive change is intended by use of the more customary phrase "carrying on in the ordinary course" in lieu of the UPA phrase "in the usual way." The UPA and the case law use both terms without apparent distinction.

The other change from the UPA concerns the allocation of risk of a partner's lack of authority. RUPA draws the line somewhat differently from the UPA.

Under UPA Section 9(1) and (4), only a person with knowledge of a restriction on a partner's authority is bound by it. Section 301(1) provides that a person who has received a notification of a partner's lack of authority is also bound. The meaning of "receives a notification" is explained in Section 102(d). Thus, the partnership may protect itself from unauthorized acts by giving a notification of a restriction on a partner's authority to a person dealing with that partner. A notification may be effective upon delivery, whether or not it actually comes to the other person's attention. To that extent, the risk of lack of authority is shifted to those dealing with partners.

On the other hand, as used in the UPA, the term "knowledge" embodies the concept of "bad faith" knowledge arising from other known facts. As used in RUPA, however, "knowledge" is limited to actual knowledge. *See* Section 102(a). Thus, RUPA does not expose persons dealing with a partner to the greater risk of being bound by a restriction based on their purported reason to know of the partner's lack of authority from all the facts they did know. Compare Section 102(b)(3) (notice).

With one exception, this result is not affected even if the partnership files a statement of partnership authority containing a limitation on a partner's authority. Section 303(f) makes clear that a person dealing with a partner is not deemed to know of such a limitation merely because it is contained in a filed statement of authority. Under Section 303(e), however, all persons are deemed to know of a limitation on the authority of a partner to transfer real property contained in a recorded statement. Thus, a recorded limitation on authority concerning real property constitutes constructive knowledge of the limitation to the whole world.

3. Section 301(2) is drawn directly from UPA Section 9(2), with conforming changes to mirror the new language of subsection (1). Subsection (2) makes it clear that the partnership is bound by a partner's actual authority, even if the partner has no apparent authority. Section 401(j) requires the unanimous consent of the partners for a grant of authority outside the ordinary course of business, unless the partnership agreement provides otherwise. Under general agency principles, the partners can subsequently ratify a partner's unauthorized act. *See* Section 104(a).

4. UPA Section 9(3) contains a list of five extraordinary acts that require unanimous consent of the partners before the partnership is bound. RUPA omits that section. That leaves it to the courts to decide the outer limits of the agency power of a partner. Most of the acts listed in UPA Section 9(3) probably remain outside the apparent authority of a partner under RUPA, such as disposing of the goodwill of the business, but elimination of a statutory rule will afford more flexibility in some situations specified in UPA Section 9(3). In particular, it seems archaic that the submission of a partnership claim to arbitration always requires unanimous consent. *See* UPA § 9(3)(e).

5. Section 301(1) fully reflects the principle embodied in UPA Section 9(4) that the partnership is not bound by an act of a partner in contravention of a restriction on his authority known to the other party.

Section 302. Transfer of Partnership Property.

(a) Partnership property may be transferred as follows:

(1) Subject to the effect of a statement of partnership authority under Section 303, partnership property held in the name of the partnership may be transferred by an instrument of transfer executed by a partner in the partnership name.

(2) Partnership property held in the name of one or more partners with an indication in the instrument transferring the property to them of their capacity as partners or of the existence of a partnership, but without an indication of the name of the partnership, may be transferred by an instrument of transfer executed by the persons in whose name the property is held.

(3) Partnership property held in the name of one or more persons other than the partnership, without an indication in the instrument transferring the property to them of their capacity as partners or of the existence of a partnership, may be transferred by an instrument of transfer executed by the persons in whose name the property is held.

(b) A partnership may recover partnership property from a transferee only if it proves that execution of the instrument of initial transfer did not bind the partnership under Section 301 and:

(1) as to a subsequent transferee who gave value for property transferred under subsection (a)(1) and (2), proves that the subsequent transferee knew or had received a notification that the person who executed the instrument of initial transfer lacked authority to bind the partnership; or

(2) as to a transferee who gave value for property transferred under subsection (a)(3), proves that the transferee knew or had received a notification that the property was partnership property and that the person who executed the instrument of initial transfer lacked authority to bind the partnership.

(c) A partnership may not recover partnership property from a subsequent transferee if the partnership would not have been entitled to recover the property, under subsection (b), from any earlier transferee of the property.

(d) If a person holds all of the partners' interests in the partnership, all of the partnership property vests in that person. The person may execute a document in the name of the partnership to evidence vesting of the property in that person and may file or record the document.

Comment

1. Section 302 replaces UPA Section 10 and provides rules for the transfer and recovery of partnership property. The language is adapted in part from Section 14-8-10 of the Georgia partnership statute.

2. Subsection (a)(1) deals with the transfer of partnership property held in the name of the partnership and subsection (a)(2) with property held in the name of one or more of the partners with an indication either of their capacity as partners or of the existence of a partnership. Subsection (a)(3) deals with partnership property held in the name of one or more of the partners without an indication of their capacity as partners or of the existence of a partnership. Like the general agency rules in Section 301, the power of a partner to transfer partnership property under subsection (a)(1) is subject to the effect under Section 303 of the filing or recording of a statement of partnership authority. These rules are intended to foster reliance on record title.

UPA Section 10 covers only real property. Section 302, however, also governs the transfer of partnership personal property acquired by instrument and held in the name of the partnership or one or more of the partners.

3. Subsection (b) deals with the right of the partnership to recover partnership property transferred by a partner without authority. Subsection (b)(1) deals with the recovery of property held in either the name of

the partnership or the name of one or more of the partners with an indication of their capacity as partners or of the existence of a partnership, while
subsection (b)(2) deals with the recovery of property held in the name of
one or more persons without an indication of their capacity as partners or
of the existence of a partnership.

In either case, a transfer of partnership property may be avoided only
if the partnership proves that it was not bound under Section 301 by the
execution of the instrument of initial transfer. Under Section 301, the
partnership is bound by a transfer in the ordinary course of business, unless
the transferee actually knew or had received a notification of the partner's
lack of authority. *See* Section 102(a) and (d). The reference to Section 301,
rather than Section 301(1), is intended to clarify that a partner's actual
authority is not revoked by Section 302. Compare UPA § 10(1) (refers to
partner's authority under Section 9(1)).

The burden of proof is on the partnership to prove the partner's lack of
authority and, in the case of a subsequent transferee, the transferee's
knowledge or notification thereof. Thus, even if the transfer to the initial
transferee could be avoided, the partnership may not recover the property
from a subsequent purchaser or other transferee for value unless it also
proves that the subsequent transferee knew or had received a notification
of the partner's lack of authority with respect to the initial transfer. Since
knowledge is required, rather than notice, a remote purchaser has no duty
to inquire as to the authority for the initial transfer, even if he knows it
was partnership property.

The burden of proof is on the transferee to show that value was given.
Value, as used in this context, is synonymous with valuable consideration
and means any consideration sufficient to support a simple contract.

The burden of proof on all other issues is allocated to the partnership
because it is generally in a better position than the transferee to produce
the evidence. Moreover, the partnership may protect itself against unauthorized transfers by ensuring that partnership real property is held in the
name of the partnership and that a statement of partnership authority is
recorded specifying any limitations on the partners' authority to convey real
property. Under Section 303(e), transferees of real property held in the
partnership name are conclusively bound by those limitations. On the other
hand, transferees can protect themselves by insisting that the partnership
record a statement specifying who is authorized to transfer partnership
property. Under Section 303(d), transferees for value, without actual
knowledge to the contrary, may rely on that grant of authority.

4. Subsection (b)(2) replaces UPA Section 10(3) and provides that partners who hold partnership property in their own names, without an
indication in the record of their capacity as partners or of the existence of
a partnership, may transfer good title to a transferee for value without
knowledge or a notification that it was partnership property. To recover

the property under this subsection, the partnership has the burden of proving that the transferee knew or had received a notification of the partnership's interest in the property, as well as of the partner's lack of authority for the initial transfer.

5. Subsection (c) is new and provides that property may not be recovered by the partnership from a remote transferee if any intermediate transferee of the property would have prevailed against the partnership. *Cf.* Uniform Fraudulent Transfer Act §§ 8(a) (subsequent transferee from bona fide purchaser protected), 8(b)(2) (same).

6. Subsection (d) is new. The UPA does not have a provision dealing with the situation in which all of the partners' interests in the partnership are held by one person, such as a surviving partner or a purchaser of all the other partners' interests. Subsection (d) allows for clear record title, even though the partnership no longer exists as a technical matter. When a partnership becomes a sole proprietorship by reason of the dissociation of all but one of the partners, title vests in the remaining "partner," although there is no "transfer" of the property. The remaining "partner" may execute a deed or other transfer of record in the name of the non-existent partnership to evidence vesting of the property in that person's individual capacity.

7. UPA Section 10(2) provides that, where title to real property is in the partnership name, a conveyance by a partner in his own name transfers the partnership's equitable interest in the property. It has been omitted as was done in Georgia and Florida. In this situation, the conveyance is clearly outside the chain of title and so should not pass title or any interest in the property. UPA Section 10(2) dilutes, albeit slightly, the effect of record title and is, therefore, inconsistent with RUPA's broad policy of fostering reliance on the record.

UPA Section 10(4) and (5) have also been omitted. Those situations are now adequately covered by Section 302(a).

Section 303. Statement of Partnership Authority.

(a) A partnership may file a statement of partnership authority, which:

(1) must include:

(i) the name of the partnership;

(ii) the street address of its chief executive office and of one office in this State, if there is one;

(iii) the names and mailing addresses of all of the partners or of an agent appointed and maintained by the partnership for the purpose of subsection (b); and

(iv) the names of the partners authorized to execute an instrument transferring real property held in the name of the partnership; and

(2) may state the authority, or limitations on the authority, of some or all of the partners to enter into other transactions on behalf of the partnership and any other matter.

(b) If a statement of partnership authority names an agent, the agent shall maintain a list of the names and mailing addresses of all of the partners and make it available to any person on request for good cause shown.

(c) If a filed statement of partnership authority is executed pursuant to Section 105(c) and states the name of the partnership but does not contain all of the other information required by subsection (a), the statement nevertheless operates with respect to a person not a partner as provided in subsections (d) and (e).

(d) Except as otherwise provided in subsection (g), a filed statement of partnership authority supplements the authority of a partner to enter into transactions on behalf of the partnership as follows:

(1) Except for transfers of real property, a grant of authority contained in a filed statement of partnership authority is conclusive in favor of a person who gives value without knowledge to the contrary, so long as and to the extent that a limitation on that authority is not then contained in another filed statement. A filed cancellation of a limitation on authority revives the previous grant of authority.

(2) A grant of authority to transfer real property held in the name of the partnership contained in a certified copy of a filed statement of partnership authority recorded in the office for recording transfers of that real property is conclusive in favor of a person who gives value without knowledge to the contrary, so long as and to the extent that a certified copy of a filed statement containing a limitation on that authority is not then of record in the office for recording transfers of that real property. The recording in the office for recording transfers of that real property of a certified copy of a filed cancellation of a limitation on authority revives the previous grant of authority.

(e) A person not a partner is deemed to know of a limitation on the authority of a partner to transfer real property held in the name of the partnership if a certified copy of the filed statement containing the limitation on authority is of record in the office for recording transfers of that real property.

(f) Except as otherwise provided in subsections (d) and (e) and Sections 704 and 805, a person not a partner is not deemed to know of a limitation on the authority of a partner merely because the limitation is contained in a filed statement.

(g) Unless earlier canceled, a filed statement of partnership authority is canceled by operation of law five years after the date on which the statement, or the most recent amendment, was filed with the [Secretary of State].

Comment

1. Section 303 is new. It provides for an optional statement of partnership authority specifying the names of the partners authorized to execute instruments transferring real property held in the name of the partnership. It may also grant supplementary authority to partners, or limit their authority, to enter into other transactions on behalf of the partnership. The execution, filing, and recording of statements is governed by Section 105.

RUPA follows the lead of California and Georgia in authorizing the optional filing of statements of authority. Filing a statement of partnership authority may be deemed to satisfy the disclosure required by a State's fictitious name statute, if the State so chooses.

Section 105 provides for the central filing of statements, rather than local filing. However, to be effective in connection with the transfer of real property, a statement of partnership authority must also be recorded locally with the land records.

2. The most important goal of the statement of authority is to facilitate the transfer of real property held in the name of the partnership. A statement must specify the names of the partners authorized to execute an instrument transferring that property.

Under subsection (d)(2), a recorded grant of authority to transfer real property held in the name of the partnership is conclusive in favor of a transferee for value without actual knowledge to the contrary. A partner's authority to transfer partnership real property is affected by a recorded statement only if the property is held in the name of the partnership. A recorded statement has no effect on the partners' authority to transfer partnership real property that is held other than in the name of the partnership. In that case, by definition, the record will not indicate the name of the partnership, and thus the partnership's interest would not be disclosed by a title search. *See* Section 204. To be effective, the statement recorded with the land records must be a certified copy of the original statement filed with the secretary of state. *See* Section 105(b).

The presumption of authority created by subsection (d)(2) operates only so long as and to the extent that a limitation on the partner's authority is not contained in another recorded statement. This is intended to condition reliance on the record to situations where there is no conflict among recorded statements, amendments, or denials of authority. *See* Section 304. If the record is in conflict regarding a partner's authority, transferees must go outside the record to determine the partners' actual authority. This rule is modified slightly in the case of a cancellation of a limitation on a partner's authority, which revives the previous grant of authority.

Under subsection (e), third parties are deemed to know of a recorded limitation on the authority of a partner to transfer real property held in the partnership name. Since transferees are bound under Section 301 by knowledge of a limitation on a partner's authority, they are bound by such a recorded limitation. Of course, a transferee with actual knowledge of a limitation on a partner's authority is bound under Section 301, whether or not there is a recorded statement of limitation.

3. A statement of partnership authority may have effect beyond the transfer of real property held in the name of the partnership. Under subsection (a)(2), a statement of authority may contain any other matter the partnership chooses, including a grant of authority, or a limitation on the authority, of some or all of the partners to enter into other transactions on behalf of the partnership. Since Section 301 confers authority on all partners to act for the partnership in ordinary matters, the real import of such a provision is to grant extraordinary authority, or to limit the ordinary authority, of some or all of the partners.

The effect given to such a provision is different from that accorded a provision regarding the transfer of real property. Under subsection (d)(1), a filed grant of authority is binding on the partnership, in favor of a person who gives value without actual knowledge to the contrary, unless limited by another filed statement. That is the same rule as for statements involving real property under subsection 301(d)(2). There is, however, no counterpart to subsection (e) regarding a filed limitation of authority. To the contrary, subsection (f) makes clear that filing a limitation of authority does not operate as constructive knowledge of a partner's lack of authority with respect to non-real property transactions.

Under Section 301, only a third party who knows or has received a notification of a partner's lack of authority in an ordinary course transaction is bound. Thus, a limitation on a partner's authority to transfer personal property or to enter into other non-real property transactions on behalf of the partnership, contained in a filed statement of partnership authority, is effective only against a third party who knows or has received a notification of it. The fact of the statement being filed has no legal significance in those transactions, although the filed statement is a potential source of actual knowledge to third parties.

4. It should be emphasized that Section 303 concerns the authority of partners to bind the partnership to third persons. As among the partners, the authority of a partner to take any action is governed by the partnership agreement, or by the provisions of RUPA governing the relations among partners, and is not affected by the filing or recording of a statement of partnership authority.

5. The exercise of the option to file a statement of partnership authority imposes a further disclosure obligation on the partnership. Under subsection (a)(1), a filed statement must include the street address of its chief

executive office and of an office in the State (if any), as well as the names and mailing addresses of all of the partners or, alternatively, of an agent appointed and maintained by the partnership for the purpose of maintaining such a list. If an agent is appointed, subsection (b) provides that the agent shall maintain a list of all of the partners and make it available to any person on request for good cause shown. Under subsection (c), the failure to make all of the required disclosures does not affect the statement's operative effect, however.

6. Under subsection (g), a statement of authority is canceled by operation of law five years after the date on which the statement, or the most recent amendment, was filed.

7. Section 308(c) makes clear that a person does not become a partner solely because he is named as a partner in a statement of partnership authority filed by another person. *See also* Section 304 ("person named as a partner" may file statement of denial).

Section 304. Statement of Denial.

A partner or other person named as a partner in a filed statement of partnership authority or in a list maintained by an agent pursuant to Section 303(b) may file a statement of denial stating the name of the partnership and the fact that is being denied, which may include denial of a person's authority or status as a partner. A statement of denial is a limitation on authority as provided in Section 303(d) and (e).

Comment

Section 304 is new and complements Section 303. It provides partners (and persons named as partners) an opportunity to deny any fact asserted in a statement of partnership authority, including denial of a person's status as a partner or of another person's authority as a partner. A statement of denial must be executed, filed, and recorded pursuant to the requirements of Section 105.

Section 304 does not address the consequences of a denial of partnership. No adverse inference should be drawn from the failure of a person named as a partner to deny such status, however. *See* Section 308(c) (person not liable as a partner merely because named in statement as a partner).

A statement of denial operates as a limitation on a partner's authority to the extent provided in Section 303. Section 303(d) provides that a filed or recorded statement of partnership authority is conclusive, in favor of purchasers without knowledge to the contrary, so long as and to the extent that a limitation on that authority is not contained in another filed or recorded statement. A filed or recorded statement of denial operates as such a limitation on authority, thereby precluding reliance on an inconsistent grant of authority. Under Section 303(d), a filed or recorded cancellation of a statement of denial that operates as a limitation on authority revives the previous grant of authority.

Under Section 303(e), a recorded statement of denial of a partner's authority to transfer partnership real property held in the partnership name constitutes constructive knowledge of that limitation.

Section 305. Partnership Liable for Partner's Actionable Conduct.

(a) A partnership is liable for loss or injury caused to a person, or for a penalty incurred, as a result of a wrongful act or omission, or other actionable conduct, of a partner acting in the ordinary course of business of the partnership or with authority of the partnership.

(b) If, in the course of the partnership's business or while acting with authority of the partnership, a partner receives or causes the partnership to receive money or property of a person not a partner, and the money or property is misapplied by a partner, the partnership is liable for the loss.

Comment

Section 305(a), which is derived from UPA Section 13, imposes liability on the partnership for the wrongful acts of a partner acting in the ordinary course of the partnership's business or otherwise within the partner's authority. The scope of the section has been expanded by deleting from UPA Section 13, "not being a partner in the partnership." This is intended to permit a partner to sue the partnership on a tort or other theory during the term of the partnership, rather than being limited to the remedies of dissolution and an accounting. *See also* Comment 2 to Section 405.

The section has also been broadened to cover no-fault torts by the addition of the phrase, "or other actionable conduct."

The partnership is liable for the actionable conduct or omission of a partner acting in the ordinary course of its business or "with the authority of the partnership." This is intended to include a partner's apparent, as well as actual, authority, thereby bringing within Section 305(a) the situation covered in UPA Section 14(a).

The phrase in UPA Section 13, "to the same extent as the partner so acting or omitting to act" has been deleted to prevent a partnership from asserting a partner's immunity from liability. This is consistent with the general agency rule that a principal is not entitled to its agent's immunities. *See* Restatement (Second) of Agency § 217(b) (1957). The deletion is not intended to limit a partnership's contractual rights.

Section 305(b) is drawn from UPA Section 14(b), but has been edited to improve clarity. It imposes strict liability on the partnership for the misapplication of money or property received by a partner in the course of the partnership's business or otherwise within the scope of the partner's actual authority.

Section 306. Partner's Liability.

(a) Except as otherwise provided in subsections (b) and (c), all partners are liable jointly and severally for all obligations of the partnership unless otherwise agreed by the claimant or provided by law.

(b) A person admitted as a partner into an existing partnership is not personally liable for any partnership obligation incurred before the person's admission as a partner.

(c) An obligation of a partnership incurred while the partnership is a limited liability partnership, whether arising in contract, tort, or otherwise, is solely the obligation of the partnership. A partner is not personally liable, directly or indirectly, by way of contribution or otherwise, for such a partnership obligation solely by reason of being or so acting as a partner. This subsection applies notwithstanding anything inconsistent in the partnership agreement that existed immediately before the vote required to become a limited liability partnership under Section 1001(b).

Comment

1. Section 306(a) changes the UPA rule by imposing joint and several liability on the partners for all partnership obligations where the partnership is not a limited liability partnership. Under UPA Section 15, partners' liability for torts is joint and several, while their liability for contracts is joint but not several. About ten States that have adopted the UPA already provide for joint and several liability. The UPA reference to "debts and obligations" is redundant and no change is intended by RUPA's reference solely to "obligations."

Joint and several liability under RUPA differs, however, from the classic model, which permits a judgment creditor to proceed immediately against any of the joint and several judgment debtors. Generally, Section 307(d) requires the judgment creditor to exhaust the partnership's assets before enforcing a judgment against the separate assets of a partner.

2. RUPA continues the UPA scheme of liability with respect to an incoming partner, but states the rule more clearly and simply. Under Section 306(a), an incoming partner becomes jointly and severally liable, as a partner, for all partnership obligations, except as otherwise provided in subsection (b). That subsection eliminates an incoming partner's personal liability for partnership obligations incurred before his admission as a partner. In effect, a new partner has no personal liability to existing creditors of the partnership, and only his investment in the firm is at risk for the satisfaction of existing partnership debts. That is presently the rule under UPA Sections 17 and 41(7), and no substantive change is intended.

As under the UPA, a new partner's personal assets are at risk with respect to partnership liabilities incurred after his admission as a partner.

3. Subsection (c) alters classic joint and several liability of general partners for obligations of a partnership that is a limited liability partnership. Like shareholders of a corporation and members of a limited liability company, partners of a limited liability partnership are not personally liable for partnership obligations incurred while the partnership liability shield is in place solely because they are partners. As with shareholders of a corporation and members of a limited liability company, partners remain personally liable for their personal misconduct.

In cases of partner misconduct, Section 401(c) sets forth a partnership's obligation to indemnify the culpable partner where the partner's liability was incurred in the ordinary course of the partnership's business. When indemnification occurs, the assets of both the partnership and the culpable partner are available to a creditor. However, Sections 306(c), 401(b), and 807(b) make clear that a partner who is not otherwise liable under Section 306(c) is not obligated to contribute assets to the partnership in excess of agreed contributions to share the loss with the culpable partner. (See Comments to Sections 401(b) and 807(b), regarding a slight variation in the context of priority of payment of partnership obligations.) Accordingly, Section 306(c) makes clear that an innocent partner is not personally liable for specified partnership obligations, directly or indirectly, by way of contribution or otherwise.

Although the liability shield protections of Section 306(c) may be modified in part or in full in a partnership agreement (and by way of private contractual guarantees), the modifications must constitute an intentional waiver of the liability protections. See Sections 103(b), 104(a), and 902(b). Since the mere act of filing a statement of qualification reflects the assumption that the partners intend to modify the otherwise applicable partner liability rules, the final sentence of subsection (c) makes clear that the filing negates inconsistent aspects of the partnership agreement that existed immediately before the vote to approve becoming a limited liability partnership. The negation only applies to a partner's personal liability for future partnership obligations. The filing however has no effect as to previously created partner obligations to the partnership in the form of specific capital contribution requirements.

Inter se contribution agreements may erode part or all of the effects of the liability shield. For example, Section 807(f) provides that an assignee for the benefit of creditors of a partnership or a partner may enforce a partner's obligation to contribute to the partnership. The ultimate effect of such contribution obligations may make each partner jointly and severally liable for all partnership obligations—even those incurred while the partnership is a limited liability partnership. Although the final sentence of subsection (c) negates such provisions existing before a statement of qualification is filed, it will have no effect on any amendments to the partnership agreement after the statement is filed.

The connection between partner status and personal liability for partnership obligations is severed only with respect to obligations incurred while the partnership is a limited liability partnership. Partnership obligations incurred before a partnership becomes a limited liability partnership or incurred after limited liability partnership status is revoked or canceled are treated as obligations of an ordinary partnership. *See* Sections 1001 (filing), 1003 (revocation), and 1006 (cancellation). Obligations incurred by a partnership during the period when its statement of qualification is administratively revoked will be considered as incurred by a limited liability partnership provided the partnership's status as such is reinstated within two years under Section 1003(e). *See* Section 1003(f).

When an obligation is incurred is determined by other law. *See* Section 104(a). Under that law, and for the limited purpose of determining when partnership contract obligations are incurred, the reasonable expectations of creditors and the partners are paramount. Therefore, partnership obligations under or relating to a note, contract, or other agreement generally are incurred when the note, contract, or other agreement is made. Also, an amendment, modification, extension, or renewal of a note, contract, or other agreement should not affect or otherwise reset the time at which a partnership obligation under or relating to that note, contract, or other agreement is incurred, even as to a claim that relates to the subject matter of the amendment, modification, extension, or renewal. A note, contract, or other agreement may expressly modify these rules and fix the time a partnership obligation is incurred thereunder.

For the limited purpose of determining when partnership tort obligations are incurred, a distinction is intended between injury and the conduct causing that injury. The purpose of the distinction is to prevent unjust results. Partnership obligations under or relating to a tort generally are incurred when the tort conduct occurs rather than at the time of the actual injury or harm. This interpretation prevents a culpable partnership from engaging in wrongful conduct and then filing a statement of qualification to sever the vicarious responsibility of its partners for future injury or harm caused by conduct that occurred prior to the filing.

Section 307. Actions By and Against Partnership and Partners.

(a) A partnership may sue and be sued in the name of the partnership.

(b) An action may be brought against the partnership and, to the extent not inconsistent with Section 306, any or all of the partners in the same action or in separate actions.

(c) A judgment against a partnership is not by itself a judgment against a partner. A judgment against a partnership may not be satisfied from a partner's assets unless there is also a judgment against the partner.

(d) A judgment creditor of a partner may not levy execution against the assets of the partner to satisfy a judgment based on a claim against the partnership unless the partner is personally liable for the claim under Section 306 and:

(1) a judgment based on the same claim has been obtained against the partnership and a writ of execution on the judgment has been returned unsatisfied in whole or in part;

(2) the partnership is a debtor in bankruptcy;

(3) the partner has agreed that the creditor need not exhaust partnership assets;

(4) a court grants permission to the judgment creditor to levy execution against the assets of a partner based on a finding that partnership assets subject to execution are clearly insufficient to satisfy the judgment, that exhaustion of partnership assets is excessively burdensome, or that the grant of permission is an appropriate exercise of the court's equitable powers; or

(5) liability is imposed on the partner by law or contract independent of the existence of the partnership.

(e) This section applies to any partnership liability or obligation resulting from a representation by a partner or purported partner under Section 308.

Comment

1. Section 307 is new. Subsection (a) provides that a partnership may sue and be sued in the partnership name. That entity approach is designed to simplify suits by and against a partnership.

At common law, a partnership, not being a legal entity, could not sue or be sued in the firm name. The UPA itself is silent on this point, so in the absence of another enabling statute, it is generally necessary to join all the partners in an action against the partnership.

Most States have statutes or rules authorizing partnerships to sue or be sued in the partnership name. Many of those statutes, however, are found in the state provisions dealing with civil procedure rather than in the partnership act.

2. Subsection (b) provides that suit generally may be brought against the partnership and any or all of the partners in the same action or in separate actions. It is intended to clarify that the partners need not be named in an action against the partnership. In particular, in an action against a partnership, it is not necessary to name a partner individually in addition to the partnership. This will simplify and reduce the cost of litigation, especially in cases of small claims where there are known to be significant

partnership assets and thus no necessity to collect the judgment out of the partners' assets.

Where the partnership is a limited liability partnership, the limited liability partnership rules clarify that a partner not liable for the alleged partnership obligation may not be named in the action against the partnership unless the action also seeks to establish personal liability of the partner for the obligation. *See* subsections (b) and (d).

3. Subsection (c) provides that a judgment against the partnership is not, standing alone, a judgment against the partners, and it cannot be satisfied from a partner's personal assets unless there is a judgment against the partner. Thus, a partner must be individually named and served, either in the action against the partnership or in a later suit, before his personal assets may be subject to levy for a claim against the partnership.

RUPA leaves it to the law of judgments, as did the UPA, to determine the collateral effects to be accorded a prior judgment for or against the partnership in a subsequent action against a partner individually. *See* Section 60 of the Second Restatement of Judgments (1982) and the Comments thereto.

4. Subsection (d) requires partnership creditors to exhaust the partnership's assets before levying on a judgment debtor partner's individual property where the partner is personally liable for the partnership obligation under Section 306. That rule respects the concept of the partnership as an entity and makes partners more in the nature of guarantors than principal debtors on every partnership debt. It is already the law in some States.

As a general rule, a final judgment against a partner cannot be enforced by a creditor against the partner's separate assets unless a writ of execution against the partnership has been returned unsatisfied. Under subsection (d), however, a creditor may proceed directly against the partner's assets if (i) the partnership is a debtor in bankruptcy (*see* Section 101(2)); (ii) the partner has consented; or (iii) the liability is imposed on the partner independently of the partnership. For example, a judgment creditor may proceed directly against the assets of a partner who is liable independently as the primary tortfeasor, but must exhaust the partnership's assets before proceeding against the separate assets of the other partners who are liable only as partners. There is also a judicial override provision in subsection (d)(4). A court may authorize execution against the partner's assets on the grounds that (i) the partnership's assets are clearly insufficient; (ii) exhaustion of the partnership's assets would be excessively burdensome; or (iii) it is otherwise equitable to do so. For example, if the partners who are parties to the action have assets located in the forum State, but the partnership does not, a court might find that exhaustion of the partnership's assets would be excessively burdensome.

5. Although subsection (d) is silent with respect to pre-judgment remedies, the law of pre-judgment remedies already adequately embodies the principle that partnership assets should be exhausted before partners' assets are attached or garnished. Attachment, for example, typically requires a showing that the partnership's assets are being secreted or fraudulently transferred or are otherwise inadequate to satisfy the plaintiff's claim. A showing of some exigent circumstance may also be required to satisfy due process. *See Connecticut v. Doehr*, 501 U.S. 1, 16 (1991).

6. Subsection (e) clarifies that actions against the partnership under Section 308, involving representations by partners or purported partners, are subject to Section 307.

Section 308. Liability of Purported Partner.

(a) If a person, by words or conduct, purports to be a partner, or consents to being represented by another as a partner, in a partnership or with one or more persons not partners, the purported partner is liable to a person to whom the representation is made, if that person, relying on the representation, enters into a transaction with the actual or purported partnership. If the representation, either by the purported partner or by a person with the purported partner's consent, is made in a public manner, the purported partner is liable to a person who relies upon the purported partnership even if the purported partner is not aware of being held out as a partner to the claimant. If partnership liability results, the purported partner is liable with respect to that liability as if the purported partner were a partner. If no partnership liability results, the purported partner is liable with respect to that liability jointly and severally with any other person consenting to the representation.

(b) If a person is thus represented to be a partner in an existing partnership, or with one or more persons not partners, the purported partner is an agent of persons consenting to the representation to bind them to the same extent and in the same manner as if the purported partner were a partner, with respect to persons who enter into transactions in reliance upon the representation. If all of the partners of the existing partnership consent to the representation, a partnership act or obligation results. If fewer than all of the partners of the existing partnership consent to the representation, the person acting and the partners consenting to the representation are jointly and severally liable.

(c) A person is not liable as a partner merely because the person is named by another in a statement of partnership authority.

(d) A person does not continue to be liable as a partner merely because of a failure to file a statement of dissociation or to amend a statement of partnership authority to indicate the partner's dissociation from the partnership.

(e) Except as otherwise provided in subsections (a) and (b), persons who are not partners as to each other are not liable as partners to other persons.

Comment

Section 308 continues the basic principles of partnership by estoppel from UPA Section 16, now more accurately entitled "Liability of Purported Partner." Subsection (a) continues the distinction between representations made to specific persons and those made in a public manner. It is the exclusive basis for imposing liability as a partner on persons who are not partners in fact. As under the UPA, there is no duty of denial, and thus a person held out by another as a partner is not liable unless he actually consents to the representation. *See* the Official Comment to UPA Section 16. Also see Section 308(c) (no duty to file statement of denial) and Section 308(d) (no duty to file statement of dissociation or to amend statement of partnership authority).

Subsection (b) emphasizes that the persons being protected by Section 308 are those who enter into transactions in reliance upon a representation. If all of the partners of an existing partnership consent to the representation, a partnership obligation results. Apart from Section 308, the firm may be bound in other situations under general principles of apparent authority or ratification.

If a partnership liability results under Section 308, the creditor must exhaust the partnership's assets before seeking to satisfy the claim from the partners. *See* Section 307.

Subsections (c) and (d) are new and deal with potential negative inferences to be drawn from a failure to correct inaccurate or outdated filed statements. Subsection (c) makes clear that an otherwise innocent person is not liable as a partner for failing to deny his partnership status as asserted by a third person in a statement of partnership authority. Under Subsection (d), a partner's liability as a partner does not continue after dissociation solely because of a failure to file a statement of dissociation.

Subsection (e) is derived from UPA Section 7(1). It means that only those persons who are partners as among themselves are liable as partners to third parties for the obligations of the partnership, except for liabilities incurred by purported partners under Section 308(a) and (b).

[ARTICLE] 4
RELATIONS OF PARTNERS TO EACH OTHER AND TO PARTNERSHIP

Section 401. Partner's Rights and Duties.
Section 402. Distributions in Kind.

Section 401. Partner's Rights and Duties.

(a) Each partner is deemed to have an account that is:

(1) credited with an amount equal to the money plus the value of any other property, net of the amount of any liabilities, the partner contributes to the partnership and the partner's share of the partnership profits; and

(2) charged with an amount equal to the money plus the value of any other property, net of the amount of any liabilities, distributed by the partnership to the partner and the partner's share of the partnership losses.

(b) Each partner is entitled to an equal share of the partnership profits and is chargeable with a share of the partnership losses in proportion to the partner's share of the profits.

(c) A partnership shall reimburse a partner for payments made and indemnify a partner for liabilities incurred by the partner in the ordinary course of the business of the partnership or for the preservation of its business or property.

(d) A partnership shall reimburse a partner for an advance to the partnership beyond the amount of capital the partner agreed to contribute.

(e) A payment or advance made by a partner which gives rise to a partnership obligation under subsection (c) or (d) constitutes a loan to the partnership which accrues interest from the date of the payment or advance.

(f) Each partner has equal rights in the management and conduct of the partnership business.

(g) A partner may use or possess partnership property only on behalf of the partnership.

(h) A partner is not entitled to remuneration for services performed for the partnership except for reasonable compensation for services rendered in winding up the business of the partnership.

(i) A person may become a partner only with the consent of all of the partners.

(j) A difference arising as to a matter in the ordinary course of business of a partnership may be decided by a majority of the partners. An act outside the ordinary course of business of a partnership and an amendment to the partnership agreement may be undertaken only with the consent of all of the partners.

(k) This section does not affect the obligations of a partnership to other persons under Section 301.

Comment

1. Section 401 is drawn substantially from UPA Section 18. It establishes many of the default rules that govern the relations among partners. All of these rules are, however, subject to contrary agreement of the partners as provided in Section 103.

2. Subsection (a) provides that each partner is deemed to have an account that is credited with the partner's contributions and share of the partnership profits and charged with distributions to the partner and the partner's share of partnership losses. In the absence of another system of partnership accounts, these rules establish a rudimentary system of accounts for the partnership. The rules regarding the settlement of the partners' accounts upon the dissolution and winding up of the partnership business are found in Section 807.

3. Subsection (b) establishes the default rules for the sharing of partnership profits and losses. The UPA Section 18(a) rules that profits are shared equally and that losses, whether capital or operating, are shared in proportion to each partner's share of the profits are continued. Thus, under the default rule, partners share profits per capita and not in proportion to capital contribution as do corporate shareholders or partners in limited partnerships. Compare RULPA Section 504. With respect to losses, the qualifying phrase, "whether capital or operating," has been deleted as inconsistent with contemporary partnership accounting practice and terminology; no substantive change is intended.

If partners agree to share profits other than equally, losses will be shared similarly to profits, absent agreement to do otherwise. That rule, carried over from the UPA, is predicated on the assumption that partners would likely agree to share losses on the same basis as profits, but may fail to say so. Of course, by agreement, they may share losses on a different basis from profits.

The default rules apply, as does UPA Section 18(a), where one or more of the partners contribute no capital, although there is case law to the contrary. See, e.g., Kovacik v. Reed, 49 Cal. 2d 166, 315 P.2d 314 (1957); Becker v. Killarney, 177 Ill. App. 3d 793, 523 N.E.2d 467 (1988). It may seem unfair that the contributor of services, who contributes little or no capital, should be obligated to contribute toward the capital loss of the large contributor who contributed no services. In entering a partnership with such a capital structure, the partners should foresee that application of the default rule may bring about unusual results and take advantage of their power to vary by agreement the allocation of capital losses.

Subsection (b) provides that each partner "is chargeable" with a share of the losses, rather than the UPA formulation that each partner shall "contribute" to losses. Losses are charged to each partner's account as provided in subsection (a)(2). It is intended to make clear that a partner is not obligated to contribute to partnership losses before his withdrawal or the liquidation of the partnership, unless the partners agree otherwise. In effect, unless related to an obligation for which the partner is not personally liable under Section 306(c), a partner's negative account represents a debt to the partnership unless the partners agree to the contrary. Similarly, each partner's share of the profits is credited to his account under subsection (a)(1). Absent an agreement to the contrary, however, a partner does not have a right to receive a current distribution of the profits credited to his account, the interim distribution of profits being a matter arising in the ordinary course of business to be decided by majority vote of the partners.

However, where a liability to contribute at dissolution and winding up relates to a partnership obligation governed by the limited liability rule of Section 306(c), a partner is not obligated to contribute additional assets even at dissolution and winding up. *See* Section 807(b). In such a case, although a partner is not personally liable for the partnership obligation, that partner's interest in the partnership remains at risk. See also Comment to Section 401(c) relating to indemnification.

In the case of an operating limited liability partnership, the Section 306 liability shield may be partially eroded where the limited liability partnership incurs both shielded and unshielded liabilities. Where the limited liability partnership uses its assets to pay shielded liabilities before paying unshielded liabilities, each partner's obligation to contribute to the limited liability partnership for that partner's share of the unpaid and unshielded obligations at dissolution and winding up remains intact. The same issue is less likely to occur in the context of the termination of a limited liability partnership since a partner's contribution obligation is based only on that partner's share of unshielded obligations and the partnership will ordinarily use the contributed assets to pay unshielded claims first as they were the basis of the contribution obligations. *See* Comments to Section 807(b).

4. Subsection (c) is derived from UPA Section 18(b) and provides that the partnership shall reimburse partners for payments made and indemnify them for liabilities incurred in the ordinary course of the partnership's business or for the preservation of its business or property. Reimbursement and indemnification is an obligation of the partnership. Indemnification may create a loss toward which the partners must contribute. Although the right to indemnification is usually enforced in the settlement of accounts among partners upon dissolution and winding up of the partnership business, the right accrues when the liability is incurred and thus may be

enforced during the term of the partnership in an appropriate case. *See* Section 405 and Comment. A partner's right to indemnification under this Act is not affected by the partnership becoming a limited liability partnership. Accordingly, partners continue to share partnership losses to the extent of partnership assets.

5. Subsection (d) is based on UPA Section 18(c). It makes explicit that the partnership must reimburse a partner for an advance of funds beyond the amount of the partner's agreed capital contribution, thereby treating the advance as a loan.

6. Subsection (e), which is also drawn from UPA Section 18(c), characterizes the partnership's obligation under subsections (c) or (d) as a loan to the partnership which accrues interest from the date of the payment or advance. *See* Section 104(b) (default rate of interest).

7. Under subsection (f), each partner has equal rights in the management and conduct of the business. It is based on UPA Section 18(e), which has been interpreted broadly to mean that, absent contrary agreement, each partner has a continuing right to participate in the management of the partnership and to be informed about the partnership business, even if his assent to partnership business decisions is not required. There are special rules regarding the partner vote necessary to approve a partnership becoming (or canceling its status as) a limited liability partnership. *See* Section 1001(b).

8. Subsection (g) provides that partners may use or possess partnership property only for partnership purposes. That is the edited remains of UPA Section 25(2)(a), which deals in detail with the incidents of tenancy in partnership. That tenancy is abolished as a consequence of the entity theory of partnerships. *See* Section 501 and Comments.

9. Subsection (h) continues the UPA Section 18(f) rule that a partner is not entitled to remuneration for services performed, except in winding up the partnership. Subsection (h) deletes the UPA reference to a "surviving" partner. That means any partner winding up the business is entitled to compensation, not just a surviving partner winding up after the death of another partner. The exception is not intended to apply in the hypothetical winding up that takes place if there is a buyout under Article 7.

10. Subsection (i) continues the substance of UPA Section 18(g) that no person can become a partner without the consent of all the partners.

11. Subsection (j) continues with one important clarification of the UPA Section 18(h) scheme of allocating management authority among the partners. In the absence of an agreement to the contrary, matters arising in the ordinary course of the business may be decided by a majority of the partners. Amendments to the partnership agreement and matters outside the ordinary course of the partnership business require unanimous consent

of the partners. Although the text of the UPA is silent regarding extraordinary matters, courts have generally required the consent of all partners for those matters. *See, e.g., Paciaroni v. Crane*, 408 A.2d 946 (Del. Ch. 1989); *Thomas v. Marvin E. Jewell & Co.*, 232 Neb. 261, 440 N.W.2d 437 (1989); *Duell v. Hancock*, 83 A.D.2d 762, 443 N.Y.S.2d 490 (1981).

It is not intended that subsection (j) embrace a claim for an objection to a partnership decision that is not discovered until after the fact. There is no cause of action based on that after-the-fact second-guessing.

12. Subsection (k) is new and was added to make it clear that Section 301 governs partners' agency power to bind the partnership to third persons, while Section 401 governs partners' rights among themselves.

Section 402. Distributions in Kind.

A partner has no right to receive, and may not be required to accept, a distribution in kind.

Comment

Section 402 provides that a partner has no right to demand and receive a distribution in kind and may not be required to take a distribution in kind. That continues the "in kind" rule of UPA Section 38(1). The new language is suggested by RULPA Section 605.

This section is complemented by Section 807(a) which provides that, in winding up the partnership business on dissolution, any surplus after the payment of partnership obligations must be applied to pay in cash the net amount distributable to each partner.

Section 403. Partner's Rights and Duties with Respect to Information.

(a) A partnership shall keep its books and records, if any, at its chief executive office.

(b) A partnership shall provide partners and their agents and attorneys access to its books and records. It shall provide former partners and their agents and attorneys access to books and records pertaining to the period during which they were partners. The right of access provides the opportunity to inspect and copy books and records during ordinary business hours. A partnership may impose a reasonable charge, covering the costs of labor and material, for copies of documents furnished.

(c) Each partner and the partnership shall furnish to a partner, and to the legal representative of a deceased partner or partner under legal disability:

(1) without demand, any information concerning the partnership's business and affairs reasonably required for the proper exercise of the

partner's rights and duties under the partnership agreement or this [Act]; and

(2) on demand, any other information concerning the partnership's business and affairs, except to the extent the demand or the information demanded is unreasonable or otherwise improper under the circumstances.

Comment

1. Subsection (a) provides that the partnership's books and records, if any shall be kept at its chief executive office. It continues the UPA Section 19 rule, modified to include partnership records other than its "books," i.e., financial records. The concept of "chief executive office" comes from UCC Section 9-103(3)(d). *See* the Comment to Section 106.

Since general partnerships are often informal or even inadvertent no books and records are enumerated as mandatory, such as that found in RULPA Section 105. Any requirement in UPA Section 19 that the partnership keep books is oblique at best, since it states merely where the books shall be kept, not that they shall be kept. Under RUPA, there is no liability to either partners or third parties for the failure to keep partnership books. A partner who undertakes to keep books, however, must do so accurately and adequately.

In general, a partnership should, at a minimum, keep those books and records necessary to enable the partners to determine their share of the profits and losses, as well as their rights on withdrawal. An action for an accounting provides an adequate remedy in the event adequate records are not kept. The partnership must also maintain any books and records required by state or federal taxing or other governmental authorities.

2. Under subsection (b), partners are entitled to access to the partnership books and records. Former partners are expressly given a similar right, although limited to the books and records pertaining to the period during which they were partners. The line between partners and former partners is not a bright one for this purpose, however, and should be drawn in light of the legitimate interests of a dissociated partner in the partnership. For example, a withdrawing partner's liability is ongoing for pre-withdrawal liabilities and will normally be extended to new liabilities for at least 90 days. It is intended that a former partner be accorded access to partnership books and records as reasonably necessary to protect that partner's legitimate interests during the period his rights and liabilities are being wound down.

The right of access is limited to ordinary business hours, and the right to inspect and copy by agent or attorney is made explicit. The partnership may impose a reasonable charge for furnishing copies of documents. *Accord*, RULPA § 105(b).

A partner's right to inspect and copy the partnership's books and records is not conditioned on the partner's purpose or motive. Compare RMBCA Section 16.02(c)(1) (shareholder must have proper purpose to inspect certain corporate records). A partner's unlimited personal liability justifies an unqualified right of access to the partnership books and records. An abuse of the right to inspect and copy might constitute a violation of the obligation of good faith and fair dealing for which the other partners would have a remedy. *See* Sections 404(d) and 405.

Under Section 103(b)(2), a partner's right of access to partnership books and records may not be unreasonably restricted by the partnership agreement. Thus, to preserve a partner's core information rights despite unequal bargaining power, an agreement limiting a partner's right to inspect and copy partnership books and records is subject to judicial review. Nevertheless, reasonable restrictions on access to partnership books and records by agreement are authorized. For example, a provision in a partnership agreement denying partners access to the compensation of other partners should be upheld, absent any abuse such as fraud or duress.

3. Subsection (c) is a significant revision of UPA Section 20 and provides a more comprehensive, although not exclusive, statement of partners' rights and duties with respect to partnership information other than books and records. Both the partnership and the other partners are obligated to furnish partnership information.

Paragraph (1) is new and imposes an affirmative disclosure obligation on the partnership and partners. There is no express UPA provision imposing an affirmative obligation to disclose any information other than the partnership books. Under some circumstances, however, an affirmative disclosure duty has been inferred from other sections of the Act, as well as from the common law, such as the fiduciary duty of good faith. Under UPA Section 18(e), for example, all partners enjoy an equal right in the management and conduct of the partnership business, absent contrary agreement. That right has been construed to require that every partner be provided with ongoing information concerning the partnership business. *See* Comment 7 to Section 401. Paragraph (1) provides expressly that partners must be furnished, without demand, partnership information reasonably needed for them to exercise their rights and duties as partners. In addition, a disclosure duty may, under some circumstances, also spring from the Section 404(d) obligation of good faith and fair dealing. *See* Comment 4 to Section 404.

Paragraph (2) continues the UPA rule that partners are entitled, on demand, to any other information concerning the partnership's business and affairs. The demand may be refused if either the demand or the information demanded is unreasonable or otherwise improper. That qualification is new to the statutory formulation. The burden is on the partnership or partner from whom the information is requested to show that the demand is unreasonable or improper. The UPA admonition that the information furnished be "true and full" has been deleted as unnecessary, and no substantive change is intended.

The Section 403(c) information rights can be waived or varied by agreement of the partners, since there is no Section 103(b) limitation on the variation of those rights as there is with respect to the Section 403(b) access rights to books and records. *See* Section 103(b)(2).

Section 404. General Standards of Partner's Conduct.

(a) The only fiduciary duties a partner owes to the partnership and the other partners are the duty of loyalty and the duty of care set forth in subsections (b) and (c).

(b) A partner's duty of loyalty to the partnership and the other partners is limited to the following:

(1) to account to the partnership and hold as trustee for it any property, profit, or benefit derived by the partner in the conduct and winding up of the partnership business or derived from a use by the partner of partnership property, including the appropriation of a partnership opportunity;

(2) to refrain from dealing with the partnership in the conduct or winding up of the partnership business as or on behalf of a party having an interest adverse to the partnership; and

(3) to refrain from competing with the partnership in the conduct of the partnership business before the dissolution of the partnership.

(c) A partner's duty of care to the partnership and the other partners in the conduct and winding up of the partnership business is limited to refraining from engaging in grossly negligent or reckless conduct, intentional misconduct, or a knowing violation of law.

(d) A partner shall discharge the duties to the partnership and the other partners under this [Act] or under the partnership agreement and exercise any rights consistently with the obligation of good faith and fair dealing.

(e) A partner does not violate a duty or obligation under this [Act] or under the partnership agreement merely because the partner's conduct furthers the partner's own interest.

(f) A partner may lend money to and transact other business with the partnership, and as to each loan or transaction the rights and obligations of the partner are the same as those of a person who is not a partner, subject to other applicable law.

(g) This section applies to a person winding up the partnership business as the personal or legal representative of the last surviving partner as if the person were a partner.

Comment

1. Section 404 is new. The title, "General Standards of Partner's Conduct," is drawn from RMBCA Section 8.30. Section 404 is both comprehensive and exclusive. In that regard, it is structurally different from the UPA which touches only sparingly on a partner's duty of loyalty and leaves any further development of the fiduciary duties of partners to the common law of agency. Compare UPA Sections 4(3) and 21.

Section 404 begins by stating that the **only** fiduciary duties a partner owes to the partnership and the other partners are the duties of loyalty and care set forth in subsections (b) and (c) of the Act. Those duties may not be waived or eliminated in the partnership agreement, but the agreement may identify activities and determine standards for measuring performance of the duties, if not manifestly unreasonable. *See* Sections 103(b)(3)-(5).

Section 404 continues the term "fiduciary" from UPA Section 21, which is entitled "Partner Accountable as a Fiduciary." Arguably, the term "fiduciary" is inappropriate when used to describe the duties of a partner because a partner may legitimately pursue self-interest (*see* Section 404(e)) and not solely the interest of the partnership and the other partners, as must a true trustee. Nevertheless, partners have long been characterized as fiduciaries. *See, e.g., Meinhard v. Salmon*, 249 N.Y. 458, 463, 164 N.E. 545, 546 (1928) (Cardozo, J.). Indeed, the law of partnership reflects the broader law of principal and agent, under which every agent is a fiduciary. *See* Restatement (Second) of Agency § 13 (1957).

2. Section 404(b) provides three specific rules that comprise a partner's duty of loyalty. Those rules are exclusive and encompass the entire duty of loyalty.

Subsection (b)(1) is based on UPA Section 21(1) and continues the rule that partnership property usurped by a partner, including the misappropriation of a partnership opportunity, is held in trust for the partnership. The express reference to the appropriation of a partnership opportunity is new, but merely codifies case law on the point. *See, e.g., Meinhard v. Salmon, supra; Fouchek v. Janicek*, 190 Ore. 251, 225 P.2d 783 (1950). Under a constructive trust theory, the partnership can recover any money or property in the partner's hands that can be traced to the partnership. *See, e.g., Yoder v. Hooper*, 695 P.2d 1182 (Colo. App. 1984), *aff'd*, 737 P.2d 852 (Colo. 1987); *Fortugno v. Hudson Manure Co.*, 51 N.J. Super. 482, 144 A.2d 207 (1958); *Harestad v. Weitzel*, 242 Or. 199, 536 P.2d 522 (1975). As a result, the partnership's claim is greater than that of an ordinary creditor. *See* Official Comment to UPA Section 21.

UPA Section 21(1) imposes the duty on partners to account for profits and benefits in all transactions connected with "the formation, conduct, or liquidation of the partnership." Reference to the "formation" of the partnership has been eliminated by RUPA because of concern that the duty of loyalty could be inappropriately extended to the pre-formation period when the parties are really negotiating at arm's length. *Compare Herring v. Offutt*, 295 A.2d 876 (Ct. App. Md. 1972), *with Phoenix Mutual Life Ins. Co. v. Shady Grove Plaza Limited Partnership*, 734 F. Supp. 1181 (D. Md. 1990), *aff'd*, 937 F.2d 603 (4th Cir. 1991). Once a partnership is agreed to, each partner becomes a fiduciary in the "conduct" of the business. Pre-formation negotiations are, of course, subject to the general contract obligation to deal honestly and without fraud.

Upon a partner's dissociation, Section 603(b)(3) limits the application of the duty to account for personal profits to those derived from matters arising or events occurring before the dissociation, unless the partner participates in winding up the partnership's business. Thus, after withdrawal, a partner is free to appropriate to his own benefit any new business opportunity thereafter coming to his attention, even if the partnership continues.

Subsection (b)(2) provides that a partner must refrain from dealing with the partnership as or on behalf of a party having an interest adverse to the partnership. This rule is derived from Sections 389 and 391 of the Restatement (Second) of Agency. Comment c to Section 389 explains that the rule is not based upon the harm caused to the principal, but upon avoiding a conflict of opposing interests in the mind of an agent whose duty is to act for the benefit of his principal.

Upon a partner's dissociation, Section 603(b)(3) limits the application of the duty to refrain from representing interests adverse to the partnership to the same extent as the duty to account. Thus, after withdrawal, a partner may deal with the partnership as an adversary with respect to new matters or events.

Section 404(b)(3) provides that a partner must refrain from competing with the partnership in the conduct of its business. This rule is derived from Section 393 of the Restatement (Second) of Agency and is an application of the general duty of an agent to act solely on his principal's behalf.

The duty not to compete applies only to the "conduct" of the partnership business; it does not extend to winding up the business, as do the other loyalty rules. Thus, a partner is free to compete immediately upon an event of dissolution under Section 801, unless the partnership agreement otherwise provides. A partner who dissociates without a winding up of the business resulting is also free to compete, because Section 603(b)(2) provides that the duty not to compete terminates upon dissociation. A dissociated partner is not, however, free to use confidential partnership information after dissociation. *See* Restatement (Second) of Agency § 393 cmt. e (1957). Trade secret law also may apply. *See* the Uniform Trade Secrets Act.

Under Section 103(b)(3), the partnership agreement may not "eliminate" the duty of loyalty. Section 103(b)(3)(i) expressly empowers the partners, however, to identify specific types or categories of activities that do not violate the duty of loyalty, if not manifestly unreasonable. As under UPA Section 21, the other partners may also consent to a specific act or transaction that otherwise violates one of the rules. For the consent to be effective under Section 103(b)(3)(ii), there must be full disclosure of all material facts regarding the act or transaction and the partner's conflict of interest. *See* Comment 5 to Section 103.

3. Subsection (c) is new and establishes the duty of care that partners owe to the partnership and to the other partners. There is no statutory duty of care under the UPA, although a common law duty of care is recognized by some courts. *See, e.g., Rosenthal v. Rosenthal*, 543 A.2d 348, 352 (Me. 1988) (duty of care limited to acting in a manner that does not constitute gross negligence or wilful misconduct).

The standard of care imposed by RUPA is that of gross negligence, which is the standard generally recognized by the courts. *See, e.g., Rosenthal v. Rosenthal, supra*. Section 103(b)(4) provides that the duty of care may not be eliminated entirely by agreement, but the standard may be reasonably reduced. *See* Comment 6 to Section 103.

4. Subsection (d) is also new. It provides that partners have an obligation of good faith and fair dealing in the discharge of all their duties, including those arising under the Act, such as their fiduciary duties of loyalty and care, and those arising under the partnership agreement. The exercise of any rights by a partner is also subject to the obligation of good faith and fair dealing. The obligation runs to the partnership and to the other partners in all matters related to the conduct and winding up of the partnership business.

The obligation of good faith and fair dealing is a contract concept, imposed on the partners because of the consensual nature of a partnership. *See* Restatement (Second) of Contracts § 205 (1981). It is not characterized, in RUPA, as a fiduciary duty arising out of the partners' special relationship. Nor is it a separate and independent obligation. It is an ancillary obligation that applies whenever a partner discharges a duty or exercises a right under the partnership agreement or the Act.

The meaning of "good faith and fair dealing" is not firmly fixed under present law. "Good faith" clearly suggests a subjective element, while "fair dealing" implies an objective component. It was decided to leave the terms undefined in the Act and allow the courts to develop their meaning based on the experience of real cases. Some commentators, moreover, believe that good faith is more properly understood by what it excludes than by what it includes. *See* Robert S. Summers, *"Good Faith" in General Contract Law and the Sales Provisions of the Uniform Commercial Code*, 54 Va. L. Rev. 195, 262 (1968):

> Good faith, as judges generally use the term in matters contractual, is best understood as an "excluder" a phrase with no general

meaning or meanings of its own. Instead, it functions to rule out many different forms of bad faith. It is hard to get this point across to persons used to thinking that every word must have one or more general meanings of its own must be either univocal or ambiguous.

The UCC definition of "good faith" is honesty in fact and, in the case of a merchant, the observance of reasonable commercial standards of fair dealing in the trade. *See* UCC §§ 1-201(19), 2-103(b). Those definitions were rejected as too narrow or not applicable.

In some situations the obligation of good faith includes a disclosure component. Depending on the circumstances, a partner may have an affirmative disclosure obligation that supplements the Section 403 duty to render information.

Under Section 103(b)(5), the obligation of good faith and fair dealing may not be eliminated by agreement, but the partners by agreement may determine the standards by which the performance of the obligation is to be measured, if the standards are not manifestly unreasonable. *See* Comment 7 to Section 103.

5. Subsection (e) is new and deals expressly with a very basic issue on which the UPA is silent. A partner as such is not a trustee and is not held to the same standards as a trustee. Subsection (e) makes clear that a partner's conduct is not deemed to be improper merely because it serves the partner's own individual interest.

That admonition has particular application to the duty of loyalty and the obligation of good faith and fair dealing. It underscores the partner's rights as an owner and principal in the enterprise, which must always be balanced against his duties and obligations as an agent and fiduciary. For example, a partner who, with consent, owns a shopping center may, under subsection (e), legitimately vote against a proposal by the partnership to open a competing shopping center.

6. Subsection (f) authorizes partners to lend money to and transact other business with the partnership and, in so doing, to enjoy the same rights and obligations as a nonpartner. That language is drawn from RULPA Section 107. The rights and obligations of a partner doing business with the partnership as an outsider are expressly made subject to the usual laws governing those transactions. They include, for example, rules limiting or qualifying the rights and remedies of inside creditors, such as fraudulent transfer law, equitable subordination, and the law of avoidable preferences, as well as general debtor-creditor law. The reference to "other applicable law" makes clear that subsection (f) is not intended to displace those laws, and thus they are preserved under Section 104(a).

It is unclear under the UPA whether a partner may, for the partner's own account, purchase the assets of the partnership at a foreclosure sale or upon the liquidation of the partnership. Those purchases are clearly within subsection (f)'s broad approval. It is also clear under that subsection that a partner may purchase partnership assets at a foreclosure sale, whether the partner is the mortgagee or the mortgagee is an unrelated third party. Similarly, a partner may purchase partnership property at a tax sale. The obligation of good faith requires disclosure of the partner's interest in the transaction, however.

7. Subsection (g) provides that the prescribed standards of conduct apply equally to a person engaged in winding up the partnership business as the personal or legal representative of the last surviving partner, as if the person were a partner. This is derived from UPA Section 21(2), but now embraces the duty of care and the obligation of good faith and fair dealing, as well as the duty of loyalty.

Section 405. Actions by Partnership and Partners.

(a) A partnership may maintain an action against a partner for a breach of the partnership agreement, or for the violation of a duty to the partnership, causing harm to the partnership.

(b) A partner may maintain an action against the partnership or another partner for legal or equitable relief, with or without an accounting as to partnership business, to:

(1) enforce the partner's rights under the partnership agreement;

(2) enforce the partner's rights under this [Act], including:

(i) the partner's rights under Sections 401, 403, or 404;

(ii) the partner's right on dissociation to have the partner's interest in the partnership purchased pursuant to Section 701 or enforce any other right under [Article] 6 or 7; or

(iii) the partner's right to compel a dissolution and winding up of the partnership business under Section 801 or enforce any other right under [Article] 8; or

(3) enforce the rights and otherwise protect the interests of the partner, including rights and interests arising independently of the partnership relationship.

(c) The accrual of, and any time limitation on, a right of action for a remedy under this section is governed by other law. A right to an accounting upon a dissolution and winding up does not revive a claim barred by law.

Comment

1. Section 405(a) is new and reflects the entity theory of partnership. It provides that the partnership itself may maintain an action against a partner for any breach of the partnership agreement or for the violation of any duty owed to the partnership, such as a breach of fiduciary duty.

2. Section 405(b) is the successor to UPA Section 22, but with significant changes. At common law, an accounting was generally not available before dissolution. That was modified by UPA Section 22 which specifies certain circumstances in which an accounting action is available without requiring a partner to dissolve the partnership. Section 405(b) goes far beyond the UPA rule. It provides that, during the term of the partnership, partners may maintain a variety of legal or equitable actions, including an action for an accounting, as well as a final action for an accounting upon dissolution and winding up. It reflects a new policy choice that partners should have access to the courts during the term of the partnership to resolve claims against the partnership and the other partners, leaving broad judicial discretion to fashion appropriate remedies.

Under RUPA, an accounting is not a prerequisite to the availability of the other remedies a partner may have against the partnership or the other partners. That change reflects the increased willingness courts have shown to grant relief without the requirement of an accounting, in derogation of the so-called "exclusivity rule." *See, e.g., Farney v. Hauser*, 109 Kan. 75, 79, 198 Pac. 178, 180 (1921) ("[F]or all practical purposes a partnership may be considered as a business entity"); *Auld v. Eastridge*, 86 Misc. 2d 895, 901, 382 N.Y.S.2d 897, 901 (1976) ("No purpose of justice is served by delaying the resolution here on empty procedural grounds").

Under subsection (b), a partner may bring a direct suit against the partnership or another partner for almost any cause of action arising out of the conduct of the partnership business. That eliminates the present procedural barriers to suits between partners filed independently of an accounting action. In addition to a formal account, the court may grant any other appropriate legal or equitable remedy. Since general partners are not passive investors like limited partners, RUPA does not authorize derivative actions, as does RULPA Section 1001.

Subsection (b)(3) makes it clear that a partner may recover against the partnership and the other partners for personal injuries or damage to the property of the partner caused by another partner. *See, e.g., Duffy v. Piazza Construction Co.*, 815 P.2d 267 (Wash. App. 1991); *Smith v. Hensley*, 354 S.W.2d 744 (Ky. App.). One partner's negligence is not imputed to bar another partner's action. *See, e.g., Reeves v. Harmon*, 475 P.2d 400 (Okla. 1970); *Eagle Star Ins. Co. v. Bean*, 134 F.2d 755 (9th Cir. 1943) (fire insurance company not subrogated to claim against partners who negligently caused fire that damaged partnership property).

3. Generally, partners may limit or contract away their Section 405 remedies. They may not, however, eliminate entirely the remedies for breach of those duties that are mandatory under Section 103(b). *See* Comment 1 to Section 103.

4. Section 405(c) replaces UPA Section 43 and provides that other (i.e., non-partnership) law governs the accrual of a cause of action for which

subsection (b) provides a remedy. The statute of limitations on such claims is also governed by other law, and claims barred by a statute of limitations are not revived by reason of the partner's right to an accounting upon dissolution, as they were under the UPA. The effect of those rules is to compel partners to litigate their claims during the life of the partnership or risk losing them. Because an accounting is an equitable proceeding, it may also be barred by laches where there is an undue delay in bringing the action. Under general law, the limitations periods may be tolled by a partner's fraud.

5. UPA Section 39 grants ancillary remedies to a person who rescinds his participation in a partnership because it was fraudulently induced, including the right to a lien on surplus partnership property for the amount of that person's interest in the partnership. RUPA has no counterpart provision to UPA Section 39, and leaves it to the general law of rescission to determine the rights of a person fraudulently induced to invest in a partnership. *See* Section 104(a).

Section 406. Continuation of Partnership Beyond Definite Term or Particular Undertaking.

(a) If a partnership for a definite term or particular undertaking is continued, without an express agreement, after the expiration of the term or completion of the undertaking, the rights and duties of the partners remain the same as they were at the expiration or completion, so far as is consistent with a partnership at will.

(b) If the partners, or those of them who habitually acted in the business during the term or undertaking, continue the business without any settlement or liquidation of the partnership, they are presumed to have agreed that the partnership will continue.

Comment

Section 406 continues UPA Section 23, with no substantive change. Subsection (a) provides that, if a term partnership is continued without an express agreement beyond the expiration of its term or the completion of the undertaking, the partners' rights and duties remain the same as they were, so far as is consistent with a partnership at will.

Subsection (b) provides that if the partnership is continued by the partners without any settlement or liquidation of the business, it is presumed that the partners have agreed not to wind up the business. The presumption is rebuttable. If the partnership is continued under this subsection, there is no dissolution under Section 801(2)(iii). As a partnership at will, however, the partnership may be dissolved under Section 801(1) at any time.

[ARTICLE] 5
TRANSFEREES AND CREDITORS OF PARTNER

Section 501. Partner Not Co-Owner of Partnership Property.

A partner is not a co-owner of partnership property and has no interest in partnership property which can be transferred, either voluntarily or involuntarily.

Comment

Section 501 provides that a partner is not a co-owner of partnership property and has no interest in partnership property that can be transferred, either voluntarily or involuntarily. Thus, the section abolishes the UPA Section 25(1) concept of tenants in partnership and reflects the adoption of the entity theory. Partnership property is owned by the entity and not by the individual partners. See also Section 203, which provides that property transferred to or otherwise acquired by the partnership is property of the partnership and not of the partners individually.

RUPA also deletes the references in UPA Sections 24 and 25 to a partner's "right in specific partnership property," although those rights are largely defined away by the detailed rules of UPA Section 25 itself. Thus, it is clear that a partner who misappropriates partnership property is guilty of embezzlement the same as a shareholder who misappropriates corporate property.

Adoption of the entity theory also has the effect of protecting partnership property from execution or other process by a partner's personal creditors. That continues the result under UPA Section 25(2)(c). Those creditors may seek a charging order under Section 504 to reach the partner's transferable interest in the partnership.

RUPA does not interfere with a partner's exemption claim in nonpartnership property. As under the UPA, disputes over whether specific property belongs to the partner or to the firm will likely arise in the context of an exemption claim by a partner.

A partner's spouse, heirs, or next of kin are not entitled to allowances or other rights in partnership property. That continues the result under UPA Section 25(2)(e).

Section 502. Partner's Transferable Interest in Partnership.

The only transferable interest of a partner in the partnership is the partner's share of the profits and losses of the partnership and the partner's right to receive distributions. The interest is personal property.

Comment

Section 502 continues the UPA Section 26 concept that a partner's only transferable interest in the partnership is the partner's share of profits and losses and right to receive distributions, that is, the partner's financial rights. The term "distribution" is defined in Section 101(3). Compare RULPA Section 101(10) ("partnership interest").

The partner's transferable interest is deemed to be personal property, regardless of the nature of the underlying partnership assets.

Under Section 503(b)(3), a transferee of a partner's transferable interest has standing to seek judicial dissolution of the partnership business.

A partner has other interests in the partnership that may not be transferred, such as the right to participate in the management of the business. Those rights are included in the broader concept of a "partner's interest in the partnership." *See* Section 101(9).

Section 503. Transfer of Partner's Transferable Interest.

(a) A transfer, in whole or in part, of a partner's transferable interest in the partnership:

(1) is permissible;

(2) does not by itself cause the partner's dissociation or a dissolution and winding up of the partnership business; and

(3) does not, as against the other partners or the partnership, entitle the transferee, during the continuance of the partnership, to participate in the management or conduct of the partnership business, to require access to information concerning partnership transactions, or to inspect or copy the partnership books or records.

(b) A transferee of a partner's transferable interest in the partnership has a right:

(1) to receive, in accordance with the transfer, distributions to which the transferor would otherwise be entitled;

(2) to receive upon the dissolution and winding up of the partnership business, in accordance with the transfer, the net amount otherwise distributable to the transferor; and

(3) to seek under Section 801(6) a judicial determination that it is equitable to wind up the partnership business.

(c) In a dissolution and winding up, a transferee is entitled to an account of partnership transactions only from the date of the latest account agreed to by all of the partners.

(d) Upon transfer, the transferor retains the rights and duties of a partner other than the interest in distributions transferred.

(e) A partnership need not give effect to a transferee's rights under this section until it has notice of the transfer.

(f) A transfer of a partner's transferable interest in the partnership in violation of a restriction on transfer contained in the partnership agreement is ineffective as to a person having notice of the restriction at the time of transfer.

Comment

1. Section 503 is derived from UPA Section 27. Subsection (a)(1) states explicitly that a partner has the right to transfer his transferable interest in the partnership. The term "transfer" is used throughout RUPA in lieu of the term "assignment." *See* Section 101(10).

Subsection (a)(2) continues the UPA Section 27(1) rule that an assignment of a partner's interest in the partnership does not of itself cause a winding up of the partnership business. Under Section 601(4)(ii), however, a partner who has transferred substantially all of his partnership interest may be expelled by the other partners.

Subsection (a)(3), which is also derived from UPA Section 27(1), provides that a transferee is not as against the other partners, entitled (i) to participate in the management or conduct of the partnership business; (ii) to inspect the partnership books or records; or (iii) to require any information concerning or an account of partnership transactions.

2. The rights of a transferee are set forth in subsection (b). Under subsection (b)(1), which is derived from UPA Section 27(1), a transferee is entitled to receive, in accordance with the terms of the assignment, any distributions to which the transferor would otherwise have been entitled under the partnership agreement before dissolution. After dissolution, the transferee is also entitled to receive, under subsection (b)(2), the net amount that would otherwise have been distributed to the transferor upon the winding up of the business.

Subsection (b)(3) confers standing on a transferee to seek a judicial dissolution and winding up of the partnership business as provided in Section 801(6), thus continuing the rule of UPA Section 32(2).

Section 504(b) accords the rights of a transferee to the purchaser at a sale foreclosing a charging order. The same rule should apply to creditors or other purchasers who acquire partnership interests by pursuing UCC remedies or statutory liens under federal or state law.

3. Subsection (c) is based on UPA Section 27(2). It grants to transferees the right to an account of partnership transactions, limited to the period since the date of the last account agreed to by all of the partners.

4. Subsection (d) is new. It makes clear that unless otherwise agreed the partner whose interest is transferred retains all of the rights and duties of a partner, other than the right to receive distributions. That means the transferor is entitled to participate in the management of the partnership and remains personally liable for all partnership obligations, unless and until he withdraws as a partner, is expelled under Section 601(4)(ii), or is otherwise dissociated under Section 601.

A divorced spouse of a partner who is awarded rights in the partner's partnership interest as part of a property settlement is entitled only to the rights of a transferee. The spouse may instead be granted a money judgment in the amount of the property award, enforceable by a charging order in the same manner as any other money judgment against a partner. In neither case, however, would the spouse become a partner by virtue of the property settlement or succeed to any of the partner's management rights. *See, e.g., Warren v. Warren*, 12 Ark. App. 260, 675 S.W.2d 371 (1984).

5. Subsection (e) is new and provides that the partnership has no duty to give effect to the transferee's rights until the partnership receives notice of the transfer. This is consistent with UCC Section 9-318(3), which provides that an "account debtor" is authorized to pay the assignor until the account debtor receives notification that the amount due or to become due has been assigned and that payment is to be made to the assignee. It further provides that the assignee, on request, must furnish reasonable proof of the assignment.

6. Subsection (f) is new and provides that a transfer of a partner's transferable interest in the partnership in violation of a restriction on transfer contained in a partnership agreement is ineffective as to a person with timely notice of the restriction. Under Section 103(a), the partners may agree among themselves to restrict the right to transfer their partnership interests. Subsection (f) makes explicit that a transfer in violation of such a restriction is ineffective as to a transferee with notice of the restriction. See Section 102(b) for the meaning of "notice." RUPA leaves to general law and the UCC the issue of whether a transfer in violation of a valid restriction is effective as to a transferee without notice of the restriction.

Whether a particular restriction will be enforceable, however, must be considered in light of other law. *See* 11 U.S.C. § 541(c)(1) (property owned by bankrupt passes to trustee regardless of restrictions on transfer); UCC § 9-318(4) (agreement between account debtor and assignor prohibiting creation of security interest in a general intangible or requiring account debtor's consent is ineffective); *Battista v. Carlo*, 57 Misc. 2d 495, 293 N.Y.S.2d 227 (1968) (restriction on transfer of partnership interest subject to rules against unreasonable restraints on alienation of property) (dictum); *Tupper v. Kroc*, 88 Nev. 146, 494 P.2d. 1275 (1972) (partnership interest subject to charging order even if partnership agreement prohibits assignments). *Cf. Tu-Vu Drive-In Corp. v. Ashkins*, 61 Cal. 2d 283, 38 Cal. Rptr. 348, 391 P.2d 828 (1964) (restraints on transfer of corporate stock must be reasonable). Even if a restriction on the transfer of a partner's transferable interest in a partnership were held to be unenforceable, the transfer might be grounds for expelling the partner-transferor from the partnership under Section 601(5)(ii).

7. Other rules that apply in the case of transfers include Section 601(4)(ii) (expulsion of partner who transfers substantially all of partnership interest); Section 601(6) (dissociation of partner who makes an assignment for benefit of creditors); and Section 801(6) (transferee has standing to seek judicial winding up).

Section 504. Partner's Transferable Interest Subject to Charging Order.

(a) On application by a judgment creditor of a partner or of a partner's transferee, a court having jurisdiction may charge the transferable interest of the judgment debtor to satisfy the judgment. The court may appoint a receiver of the share of the distributions due or to become due to the judgment debtor in respect of the partnership and make all other orders, directions, accounts, and inquiries the judgment debtor might have made or which the circumstances of the case may require.

(b) A charging order constitutes a lien on the judgment debtor's transferable interest in the partnership. The court may order a foreclosure of the interest subject to the charging order at any time. The purchaser at the foreclosure sale has the rights of a transferee.

(c) At any time before foreclosure, an interest charged may be redeemed:

(1) by the judgment debtor;

(2) with property other than partnership property, by one or more of the other partners; or

(3) with partnership property, by one or more of the other partners with the consent of all of the partners whose interests are not so charged.

(d) This [Act] does not deprive a partner of a right under exemption laws with respect to the partner's interest in the partnership.

(e) This section provides the exclusive remedy by which a judgment creditor of a partner or partner's transferee may satisfy a judgment out of the judgment debtor's transferable interest in the partnership.

Comment

1. Section 504 continues the UPA Section 28 charging order as the proper remedy by which a judgment creditor of a partner may reach the debtor's

transferable interest in a partnership to satisfy the judgment. Subsection (a) makes the charging order available to the judgment creditor of a transferee of a partnership interest. Under Section 503(b), the transferable interest of a partner or transferee is limited to the partner's right to receive distributions from the partnership and to seek judicial liquidation of the partnership. The court may appoint a receiver of the debtor's share of the distributions due or to become due and make all other orders that may be required.

2. Subsection (b) is new and codifies the case law under the UPA holding that a charging order constitutes a lien on the debtor's transferable interest. The lien may be foreclosed by the court at any time, and the purchaser at the foreclosure sale has the Section 503(b) rights of a transferee. For a general discussion of the charging order remedy, see I *Alan R. Bromberg & Larry E. Ribstein, Partnership* (1988), at 3:69.

3. Subsection (c) continues the UPA Section 28(2) right of the debtor or other partners to redeem the partnership interest before the foreclosure sale. Redemption by the partnership (i.e., with partnership property) requires the consent of all the remaining partners. Neither the UPA nor RUPA provide a statutory procedural framework for the redemption.

4. Subsection (d) provides that nothing in RUPA deprives a partner of his rights under the State's exemption laws. That is essentially the same as UPA Section 28(3).

5. Subsection (e) provides that the charging order is the judgment creditor's exclusive remedy. Although the UPA nowhere states that a charging order is the exclusive process for a partner's individual judgment creditor, the courts have generally so interpreted it. *See, e.g., Matter of Pischke*, 11 B.R. 913 (E.D. Va. 1981); *Baum v. Baum*, 51 Cal. 2d 610, 335 P.2d 481 (1959); *Atlantic Mobile Homes, Inc. v. LeFever*, 481 So. 2d 1002 (Fla. App. 1986).

Notwithstanding subsection (e), there may be an exception for the enforcement of family support orders. Some States have unique statutory procedures for the enforcement of support orders. In Florida, for example, a court may issue an "income deduction order" requiring any person or entity providing "income" to the obligor of a support order to remit to the obligee or a depository, as directed by the court, a specified portion of the income. Fla. Stat. § 61.1301 (1993). "Income" is broadly defined to include any form of payment to the obligor, including wages, salary, compensation as an independent contractor, dividends, interest, or other payment, regardless of source. Fla. Stat. § 61.046(4) (1993). That definition includes distributions payable to an obligor partner. A charging order under RUPA would still be necessary to reach the obligor's entire partnership interest, however.

[ARTICLE] 6
PARTNER'S DISSOCIATION

Section 601. Events Causing Partner's Dissociation.

A partner is dissociated from a partnership upon the occurrence of any of the following events:

(1) the partnership's having notice of the partner's express will to withdraw as a partner or on a later date specified by the partner;

(2) an event agreed to in the partnership agreement as causing the partner's dissociation;

(3) the partner's expulsion pursuant to the partnership agreement;

(4) the partner's expulsion by the unanimous vote of the other partners if:

(i) it is unlawful to carry on the partnership business with that partner;

(ii) there has been a transfer of all or substantially all of that partner's transferable interest in the partnership, other than a transfer for security purposes, or a court order charging the partner's interest, which has not been foreclosed;

(iii) within 90 days after the partnership notifies a corporate partner that it will be expelled because it has filed a certificate of dissolution or the equivalent, its charter has been revoked, or its right to conduct business has been suspended by the jurisdiction of its incorporation, there is no revocation of the certificate of dissolution or no reinstatement of its charter or its right to conduct business; or

(iv) a partnership that is a partner has been dissolved and its business is being wound up;

(5) on application by the partnership or another partner, the partner's expulsion by judicial determination because:

(i) the partner engaged in wrongful conduct that adversely and materially affected the partnership business;

(ii) the partner willfully or persistently committed a material breach of the partnership agreement or of a duty owed to the partnership or the other partners under Section 404; or

(iii) the partner engaged in conduct relating to the partnership business which makes it not reasonably practicable to carry on the business in partnership with the partner;

(6) the partner's:

(i) becoming a debtor in bankruptcy;

(ii) executing an assignment for the benefit of creditors;

(iii) seeking, consenting to, or acquiescing in the appointment of a trustee, receiver, or liquidator of that partner or of all or substantially all of that partner's property; or

(iv) failing, within 90 days after the appointment, to have vacated or stayed the appointment of a trustee, receiver, or liquidator of the partner or of all or substantially all of the partner's property obtained without the partner's consent or acquiescence, or failing within 90 days after the expiration of a stay to have the appointment vacated;

(7) in the case of a partner who is an individual:

(i) the partner's death;

(ii) the appointment of a guardian or general conservator for the partner; or

(iii) a judicial determination that the partner has otherwise become incapable of performing the partner's duties under the partnership agreement;

(8) in the case of a partner that is a trust or is acting as a partner by virtue of being a trustee of a trust, distribution of the trust's entire transferable interest in the partnership, but not merely by reason of the substitution of a successor trustee;

(9) in the case of a partner that is an estate or is acting as a partner by virtue of being a personal representative of an estate, distribution of the estate's entire transferable interest in the partnership, but not merely by reason of the substitution of a successor personal representative; or

(10) termination of a partner who is not an individual, partnership, corporation, trust, or estate.

Comment

1. RUPA dramatically changes the law governing partnership breakups and dissolution. An entirely new concept, "dissociation," is used in lieu of the UPA term "dissolution" to denote the change in the relationship caused by a partner's ceasing to be associated in the carrying on of the business. "Dissolution" is retained but with a different meaning. *See* Section 802. The entity theory of partnership provides a conceptual basis for continuing the firm itself despite a partner's withdrawal from the firm.

Under RUPA, unlike the UPA, the dissociation of a partner does not necessarily cause a dissolution and winding up of the business of the partnership. Section 801 identifies the situations in which the dissociation of a partner causes a winding up of the business. Section 701 provides that in all other situations there is a buyout of the partner's interest in the partnership, rather than a windup of the partnership business. In those other situations, the partnership entity continues, unaffected by the partner's dissociation.

A dissociated partner remains a partner for some purposes and still has some residual rights, duties, powers, and liabilities. Although Section 601 determines when a partner is dissociated from the partnership, the consequences of the partner's dissociation do not all occur at the same time. Thus, it is more useful to think of a dissociated partner as a partner for some purposes, but as a former partner for others. For example, see Section 403(b) (former partner's access to partnership books and records). The consequences of a partner's dissociation depend on whether the partnership continues or is wound up, as provided in Articles 6, 7, and 8.

Section 601 enumerates all of the events that cause a partner's dissociation. Section 601 is similar in approach to RULPA Section 402, which lists the events resulting in a general partner's withdrawal from a limited partnership.

2. Section 601(1) provides that a partner is dissociated when the partnership has notice of the partner's express will to withdraw as a partner, unless a later date is specified by the partner. If a future date is specified by the partner, other partners may dissociate before that date; specifying a future date does not bind the others to remain as partners until that date. *See also* Section 801(2)(i).

Section 602(a) provides that a partner has the power to withdraw at any time. The power to withdraw is immutable under Section 103(b)(6), with the exception that the partners may agree the notice must be in writing. This continues the present rule that a partner has the power to withdraw at will, even if not the right. *See* UPA Section 31(2). Since no writing is required to create a partner relationship, it was felt unnecessarily formalistic, and a trap for the unwary, to require a writing to end one. If a written notification is given, Section 102(d) clarifies when it is deemed received.

RUPA continues the UPA "express will" concept, thus preserving existing case law. Section 601(1) clarifies existing law by providing that the partnership must have notice of the partner's expression of will before the dissociation is effective. See Section 102(b) for the meaning of "notice."

3. Section 601(2) provides expressly that a partner is dissociated upon an event agreed to in the partnership agreement as causing dissociation. There is no such provision in the UPA, but that result has been assumed.

4. Section 601(3) provides that a partner may be expelled by the other partners pursuant to a power of expulsion contained in the partnership agreement. That continues the basic rule of UPA Section 31(1)(d). The

expulsion can be with or without cause. As under existing law, the obligation of good faith under Section 404(d) does not require prior notice, specification of cause, or an opportunity to be heard. *See Holman v. Coie*, 11 Wash. App. 195, 522 P.2d 515, *cert. denied*, 420 U.S. 984 (1974).

5. Section 601(4) empowers the partners, by unanimous vote, to expel a partner for specified causes, even if not authorized in the partnership agreement. This changes the UPA Section 31(1)(d) rule that authorizes expulsion only if provided in the partnership agreement. A partner may be expelled from a term partnership, as well as from a partnership at will. Under Section 103(a), the partnership agreement may change or abolish the partners' power of expulsion.

Subsection (4)(i) is derived from UPA Section 31(3). A partner may be expelled if it is unlawful to carry on the business with that partner. Section 801(4), on the other hand, provides that the partnership itself is dissolved and must be wound up if substantially all of the business is unlawful.

Subsection (4)(ii) provides that a partner may be expelled for transferring substantially all of his transferable interest in the partnership, other than as security for a loan. (He may, however, be expelled upon foreclosure.) This rule is derived from UPA Section 31(1)(c). To avoid the presence of an unwelcome transferee, the remaining partners may dissolve the partnership under Section 801(2)(ii), after first expelling the transferor partner. A transfer of a partner's entire interest may, in some circumstances, evidence the transferor's intention to withdraw under Section 601(1).

Subsection (4)(iii) provides for the expulsion of a corporate partner if it has filed a certificate of dissolution, its charter has been revoked, or its right to conduct business has been suspended, unless cured within 90 days after notice. This provision is derived from RULPA, Section 402(9). The cure proviso is important because charter revocation is very common in some States and partner status should not end merely because of a technical noncompliance with corporate law that can easily be cured. Withdrawal of a voluntarily filed notice of dissolution constitutes a cure.

Subsection (4)(iv) is the partnership analogue of paragraph (iii) and is suggested by RULPA Section 402(8). It provides that a partnership that is a partner may be expelled if it has been dissolved and its business is being wound up. It is intended that the right of expulsion not be triggered solely by the dissolution event, but only upon commencement of the liquidation process.

6. Section 601(5) empowers a court to expel a partner if it determines that the partner has engaged in specified misconduct. The enumerated grounds for judicial expulsion are based on the UPA Section 32(1) grounds for judicial dissolution. The application for expulsion may be brought by the partnership or any partner. The phrase "judicial determination" is intended to include an arbitration award, as well as any final court order or decree.

Subsection (5)(i) provides for the partner's expulsion if the court finds that the partner has engaged in wrongful conduct that adversely and materially affected the partnership business. That language is derived from UPA Section 32(1)(c).

Subsection (5)(ii) provides for expulsion if the court determines that the partner wilfully or persistently committed a material breach of the partnership agreement or of a duty owed to the partnership or to the other partners under Section 404. That would include a partner's breach of fiduciary duty. Paragraph (ii), together with paragraph (iii), carry forward the substance of UPA Section 32(1)(d).

Subsection (5)(iii) provides for judicial expulsion of a partner who engaged in conduct relating to the partnership business that makes it not reasonably practicable to carry on the business in partnership with that partner. Expulsion for such misconduct makes the partner's dissociation wrongful under Section 602(a)(ii) and may also support a judicial decree of dissolution under Section 801(5)(ii).

7. Section 601(6) provides that a partner is dissociated upon becoming a debtor in bankruptcy or upon taking or suffering other action evidencing the partner's insolvency or lack of financial responsibility.

Subsection (6)(i) is derived from UPA Section 31(5), which provides for dissolution upon a partner's bankruptcy. *Accord* RULPA § 402(4)(ii). There is some doubt as to whether UPA Section 31(1) is limited to so-called "straight bankruptcy" under Chapter 7 or includes other bankruptcy relief, such as Chapter 11. Under RUPA Section 101(2), however, "debtor in bankruptcy" includes a person who files a voluntary petition, or against whom relief is ordered in an involuntary case, under any chapter of the Bankruptcy Code.

Initially, upon the filing of the bankruptcy petition, the debtor partner's transferable interest in the partnership will pass to the bankruptcy trustee as property of the estate under Section 541(a)(1) of the Bankruptcy Code, notwithstanding any restrictions on transfer provided in the partnership agreement. In most Chapter 7 cases, that will result in the eventual buyout of the partner's interest.

The application of various provisions of the federal Bankruptcy Code to Section 601(6)(i) is unclear. In particular, there is uncertainty as to the validity of UPA Section 31(5), and thus its RUPA counterpart, under Sections 365(e) and 541(c)(1) of the Bankruptcy Code. Those sections generally invalidate so-called *ipso facto* laws that cause a termination or modification of the debtor's contract or property rights because of the bankruptcy filing. As a consequence, RUPA Section 601(6)(i), which provides for a partner's dissociation by operation of law upon becoming a debtor in bankruptcy, may be invalid under the Supremacy Clause. *See, e.g., In the Matter of Phillips*, 966 F.2d 926 (5th Cir. 1992); *In re Cardinal Industries, Inc.*, 105 B.R. 385 (Bankr. S.D. Ohio 1989), 116 B.R. 964 (Bankr.

S.D. Ohio 1990); *In re Corky Foods Corp.*, 85 B.R. 903 (Bankr. S.D. Fla. 1988). *But see, In re Catron*, 158 B.R. 629 (E.D. Va. 1993) (partnership agreement could not be assumed by debtor under Bankruptcy Code § 365(c)(1) because other partners excused by UPA from accepting performance by or rendering performance to party other than debtor and buyout option not invalid *ipso facto* clause under Code § 365 (e)), *aff'd per curiam*, 25 F.3d 1038 (4th Cir. 1994). RUPA reflects the policy choice, as a matter of state partnership law, that a partner be dissociated upon becoming a debtor in bankruptcy.

Subsection (6)(ii) is new and provides for dissociation upon a general assignment for the benefit of a partner's creditors. The UPA says nothing about an assignment for the benefit of creditors or the appointment of a trustee, receiver, or liquidator. Subsection (6)(iii) and (iv) cover the latter and are based substantially on RULPA Section 402(4) and (5).

8. UPA Section 31(4) provides for the dissolution of a partnership upon the death of any partner, although by agreement the remaining partners may continue the partnership business. RUPA Section 601(7)(i), on the other hand, provides for dissociation upon the death of a partner who is an individual, rather than dissolution of the partnership. That changes existing law, except in those States previously adopting a similar non-uniform provision, such as California, Georgia, and Texas. Normally, under RUPA, the deceased partner's transferable interest in the partnership will pass to his estate and be bought out under Article 7.

Section 601(7)(ii) replaces UPA Section 32(1)(a) and provides for dissociation upon the appointment of a guardian or general conservator for partner who is an individual. The appointment itself operates as the event of dissociation, and no further order of the court is necessary.

Section 601(7)(iii) is based on UPA Section 32(1)(b) and provides for dissociation upon a judicial determination that an individual partner has in any other way become incapable of performing his duties under the partnership agreement. The intent is to include physical incapacity.

9. Section 601(8) is new and provides for the dissociation of a partner that is a trust, or is acting as a partner by virtue of being a trustee of a trust, upon the distribution by the trust of its entire transferable interest in the partnership, but not merely upon the substitution of a successor trustee. The provision is inspired by RULPA Section 402(7).

10. Section 601(9) is new and provides for the dissociation of a partner that is an estate, or is acting as a partner by virtue of being a personal representative of an estate, upon the distribution of the estate's entire transferable interest in the partnership, but not merely the substitution of a successor personal representative. It is based on RULPA Section 402(10). Under Section 601(7), a partner is dissociated upon death, however, and the estate normally becomes a transferee, not a partner.

11. Section 601(10) is new and provides that a partner that is not an individual, partnership, corporation, trust, or estate is dissociated upon its termination. It is the comparable "death" analogue for other types of entity partners, such as a limited liability company.

Section 602. Partner's Power to Dissociate; Wrongful Dissociation.

(a) A partner has the power to dissociate at any time, rightfully or wrongfully, by express will pursuant to Section 601(1).

(b) A partner's dissociation is wrongful only if:

(1) it is in breach of an express provision of the partnership agreement; or

(2) in the case of a partnership for a definite term or particular undertaking, before the expiration of the term or the completion of the undertaking:

(i) the partner withdraws by express will, unless the withdrawal follows within 90 days after another partner's dissociation by death or otherwise under Section 601(6) through (10) or wrongful dissociation under this subsection;

(ii) the partner is expelled by judicial determination under Section 601(5);

(iii) the partner is dissociated by becoming a debtor in bankruptcy; or

(iv) in the case of a partner who is not an individual, trust other than a business trust, or estate, the partner is expelled or otherwise dissociated because it willfully dissolved or terminated.

(c) A partner who wrongfully dissociates is liable to the partnership and to the other partners for damages caused by the dissociation. The liability is in addition to any other obligation of the partner to the partnership or to the other partners.

Comment

1. Subsection (a) states explicitly what is implicit in UPA Section 31(2) and RUPA Section 601(1) that a partner has the power to dissociate at any time by expressing a will to withdraw, even in contravention of the partnership agreement. The phrase "rightfully or wrongfully" reflects the distinction between a partner's **power** to withdraw in contravention of the partnership agreement and a partner's **right** to do so. In this context, although a partner cannot be enjoined from exercising the power to dissociate, the dissociation may be wrongful under subsection (b).

2. Subsection (b) provides that a partner's dissociation is wrongful only if it results from one of the enumerated events. The significance of a

wrongful dissociation is that it may give rise to damages under subsection (c) and, if it results in the dissolution of the partnership, the wrongfully dissociating partner is not entitled to participate in winding up the business under Section 804.

Under subsection (b), a partner's dissociation is wrongful if (1) it breaches an express provision of the partnership agreement or (2), in a term partnership, before the expiration of the term or the completion of the undertaking (i) the partner voluntarily withdraws by express will, except a withdrawal following **another** partner's wrongful dissociation or dissociation by death or otherwise under Section 601(6) through (10); (ii) the partner is expelled for misconduct under Section 601(5); (iii) the partner becomes a debtor in bankruptcy (*see* Section 101(2)); or (iv) a partner that is an entity (other than a trust or estate) is expelled or otherwise dissociated because its dissolution or termination was willful. Since subsection (b) is merely a default rule, the partnership agreement may eliminate or expand the dissociations that are wrongful or modify the effects of wrongful dissociation.

The exception in subsection (b)(2)(i) is intended to protect a partner's reactive withdrawal from a term partnership after the premature departure of another partner, such as the partnership's rainmaker or main supplier of capital, under the same circumstances that may result in the dissolution of the partnership under Section 801(2)(i). Under that section, a term partnership is dissolved after the bankruptcy, incapacity, death (or similar dissociation of a partner that is an entity), or wrongful dissociation of any partner, if within 90 days after the dissociation at least half of the remaining partners express their will to dissolve the partnership. Under Section 602(b)(2)(i), a partner's exercise of the right of withdrawal by express will under those circumstances is rendered "rightful," even if the partnership is continued by others, and does not expose the withdrawing partner to damages for wrongful dissociation under Section 602(c).

A partner wishing to withdraw prematurely from a term partnership for any other reason, such as another partner's misconduct, can avoid being treated as a wrongfully dissociating partner by applying to a court under Section 601(5)(iii) to have the offending partner expelled. Then, the partnership could be dissolved under Section 801(2)(i) or the remaining partners could, by unanimous vote, dissolve the partnership under Section 801(2)(ii).

3. Subsection (c) provides that a wrongfully dissociating partner is liable to the partnership and to the other partners for any damages caused by the wrongful nature of the dissociation. That liability is in addition to any other obligation of the partner to the partnership or to the other partners. For example, the partner would be liable for any damage caused by breach of the partnership agreement or other misconduct. The partnership might also incur substantial expenses resulting from a partner's premature withdrawal from a term partnership, such as replacing the partner's expertise or obtaining new financing. The wrongfully dissociating partner

would be liable to the partnership for those and all other expenses and damages that are causally related to the wrongful dissociation.

Section 701(c) provides that any damages for wrongful dissociation may be offset against the amount of the buyout price due to the partner under Section 701(a), and Section 701(h) provides that a partner who wrongfully dissociates from a term partnership is not entitled to payment of the buyout price until the term expires.

Under UPA Section 38(2)(c)(II), in addition to an offset for damages, the goodwill value of the partnership is excluded in determining the value of a wrongfully dissociating partner's partnership interest. Under RUPA, however, unless the partnership's goodwill is damaged by the wrongful dissociation, the value of the wrongfully dissociating partner's interest will include any goodwill value of the partnership. If the firm's goodwill is damaged, the amount of the damages suffered by the partnership and the remaining partners will be offset against the buyout price. *See* Section 701 and Comments.

Section 603. Effect of Partner's Dissociation.

(a) If a partner's dissociation results in a dissolution and winding up of the partnership business, [Article] 8 applies; otherwise, [Article] 7 applies.

(b) Upon a partner's dissociation:

(1) the partner's right to participate in the management and conduct of the partnership business terminates, except as otherwise provided in Section 803;

(2) the partner's duty of loyalty under Section 404(b)(3) terminates; and

(3) the partner's duty of loyalty under Section 404(b)(1) and (2) and duty of care under Section 404(c) continue only with regard to matters arising and events occurring before the partner's dissociation, unless the partner participates in winding up the partnership's business pursuant to Section 803.

Comment

1. Section 603(a) is a "switching" provision. It provides that, after a partner's dissociation, the partner's interest in the partnership must be purchased pursuant to the buyout rules in Article 7 **unless** there is a dissolution and winding up of the partnership business under Article 8. Thus, a partner's dissociation will always result in either a buyout of the dissociated partner's interest or a dissolution and winding up of the business.

By contrast, under the UPA, every partner dissociation results in the dissolution of the partnership, most of which trigger a right to have the business wound up unless the partnership agreement provides otherwise. *See* UPA § 38. The only exception in which the remaining partners have a statutory right to continue the business is when a partner wrongfully dissolves the partnership in breach of the partnership agreement. *See* UPA § 38(2)(b).

2. Section 603(b) is new and deals with some of the internal effects of a partner's dissociation. Subsection (b)(1) makes it clear that one of the consequences of a partner's dissociation is the immediate loss of the right to participate in the management of the business, unless it results in a dissolution and winding up of the business. In that case, Section 804(a) provides that all of the partners who have not wrongfully dissociated may participate in winding up the business.

Subsection (b)(2) and (3) clarify a partner's fiduciary duties upon dissociation. No change from current law is intended. With respect to the duty of loyalty, the Section 404(b)(3) duty not to compete terminates upon dissociation, and the dissociated partner is free immediately to engage in a competitive business, without any further consent. With respect to the partner's remaining loyalty duties under Section 404(b) and duty of care under Section 404(c), a withdrawing partner has a continuing duty after dissociation, but it is limited to matters that arose or events that occurred before the partner dissociated. For example, a partner who leaves a brokerage firm may immediately compete with the firm for new clients, but must exercise care in completing on-going client transactions and must account to the firm for any fees received from the old clients on account of those transactions. As the last clause makes clear, there is no contraction of a dissociated partner's duties under subsection (b)(3) if the partner thereafter participates in the dissolution and winding up the partnership's business.

[ARTICLE] 7
PARTNER'S DISSOCIATION WHEN BUSINESS NOT WOUND UP

Section   701. Purchase of Dissociated Partner's Interest.

Section   702. Dissociated Partner's Power to Bind and Liability to Partnership.

Section   703. Dissociated Partner's Liability to Other Persons.

Section   704. Statement of Dissociation.

Section   705. Continued Use of Partnership Name.

Section 701. Purchase of Dissociated Partner's Interest.

(a) If a partner is dissociated from a partnership without resulting in a dissolution and winding up of the partnership business under Section 801, the partnership shall cause the dissociated partner's interest in the partnership to be purchased for a buyout price determined pursuant to subsection (b).

(b) The buyout price of a dissociated partner's interest is the amount that would have been distributable to the dissociating partner under Section 807(b) if, on the date of dissociation, the assets of the partnership were sold at a price equal to the greater of the liquidation value or the value based on a sale of the entire business as a going concern without the dissociated partner and the partnership were wound up as of that date. Interest must be paid from the date of dissociation to the date of payment.

(c) Damages for wrongful dissociation under Section 602(b), and all other amounts owing, whether or not presently due, from the dissociated partner to the partnership, must be offset against the buyout price. Interest must be paid from the date the amount owed becomes due to the date of payment.

(d) A partnership shall indemnify a dissociated partner whose interest is being purchased against all partnership liabilities, whether incurred before or after the dissociation, except liabilities incurred by an act of the dissociated partner under Section 702.

(e) If no agreement for the purchase of a dissociated partner's interest is reached within 120 days after a written demand for payment, the partnership shall pay, or cause to be paid, in cash to the dissociated partner the amount the partnership estimates to be the buyout price and accrued interest, reduced by any offsets and accrued interest under subsection (c).

(f) If a deferred payment is authorized under subsection (h), the partnership may tender a written offer to pay the amount it estimates to be the buyout price and accrued interest, reduced by any offsets under subsection (c), stating the time of payment, the amount and type of security for payment, and the other terms and conditions of the obligation.

(g) The payment or tender required by subsection (e) or (f) must be accompanied by the following:

(1) a statement of partnership assets and liabilities as of the date of dissociation;

(2) the latest available partnership balance sheet and income statement, if any;

(3) an explanation of how the estimated amount of the payment was calculated; and

(4) written notice that the payment is in full satisfaction of the obligation to purchase unless, within 120 days after the written notice, the dissociated partner commences an action to determine the buyout price, any offsets under subsection (c), or other terms of the obligation to purchase.

(h) A partner who wrongfully dissociates before the expiration of a definite term or the completion of a particular undertaking is not entitled to payment of any portion of the buyout price until the expiration of the term or completion of the undertaking, unless the partner establishes to the satisfaction of the court that earlier payment will not cause undue hardship to the business of the partnership. A deferred payment must be adequately secured and bear interest.

(i) A dissociated partner may maintain an action against the partnership, pursuant to Section 405(b)(2)(ii), to determine the buyout price of that partner's interest, any offsets under subsection (c), or other terms of the obligation to purchase. The action must be commenced within 120 days after the partnership has tendered payment or an offer to pay or within one year after written demand for payment if no payment or offer to pay is tendered. The court shall determine the buyout price of the dissociated partner's interest, any offset due under subsection (c), and accrued interest, and enter judgment for any additional payment or refund. If deferred payment is authorized under subsection (h), the court shall also determine the security for payment and other terms of the obligation to purchase. The court may assess reasonable attorney's fees and the fees and expenses of appraisers or other experts for a party to the action, in amounts the court finds equitable, against a party that the court finds acted arbitrarily, vexatiously, or not in good faith. The finding may be based on the partnership's failure to tender payment or an offer to pay or to comply with subsection (g).

Comment

1. Article 7 is new and provides for the buyout of a dissociated partner's interest in the partnership when the partner's dissociation does not result in a dissolution and winding up of its business under Article 8. *See* Section 603(a). If there is no dissolution, the remaining partners have a right to continue the business and the dissociated partner has a right to be paid the value of his partnership interest. These rights can, of course, be varied in the partnership agreement. *See* Section 103. A dissociated partner has a continuing relationship with the partnership and third parties as provided in Sections 603(b), 702, and 703. *See also* Section 403(b) (former partner's access to partnership books and records).

2. Subsection (a) provides that, if a partner's dissociation does not result in a windup of the business, the partnership shall cause the interest of the dissociating partner to be purchased for a buyout price determined pursuant to subsection (b). The buyout is mandatory. The "cause to be purchased" language is intended to accommodate a purchase by the partnership, one or more of the remaining partners, or a third party.

For federal income tax purposes, a payment to a partner for his interest can be characterized either as a purchase of the partner's interest or as a liquidating distribution. The two have different tax consequences. RUPA permits either option by providing that the payment may come from either the partnership, some or all of the continuing partners, or a third party purchaser.

3. Subsection (b) provides how the "buyout price" is to be determined. The terms "fair market value" or "fair value" were not used because they are often considered terms of art having a special meaning depending on the context, such as in tax or corporate law. "Buyout price" is a new term. It is intended that the term be developed as an independent concept appropriate to the partnership buyout situation, while drawing on valuation principles developed elsewhere.

Under subsection (b), the buyout price is the amount that would have been distributable to the dissociating partner under Section 807(b) if, on the date of dissociation, the assets of the partnership were sold at a price equal to the greater of liquidation value or going concern value without the departing partner. Liquidation value is not intended to mean distress sale value. Under general principles of valuation, the hypothetical selling price in either case should be the price that a willing and informed buyer would pay a willing and informed seller, with neither being under any compulsion to deal. The notion of a minority discount in determining the buyout price is negated by valuing the business as a going concern. Other discounts, such as for a lack of marketability or the loss of a key partner, may be appropriate, however.

Since the buyout price is based on the value of the business at the time of dissociation, the partnership must pay interest on the amount due from the date of dissociation until payment to compensate the dissociating partner for the use of his interest in the firm. Section 104(b) provides that interest shall be at the legal rate unless otherwise provided in the partnership agreement. The UPA Section 42 option of electing a share of the profits in lieu of interest has been eliminated.

UPA Section 38(2)(c)(II) provides that the good will of the business not be considered in valuing a wrongfully dissociating partner's interest. The forfeiture of good will rule is implicitly rejected by RUPA. See Section 602(c) and Comment 3.

The Section 701 rules are merely default rules. The partners may, in the partnership agreement, fix the method or formula for determining the buyout price and all of the other terms and conditions of the buyout right. Indeed, the very right to a buyout itself may be modified, although a provision providing for a complete forfeiture would probably not be enforceable. See Section 104(a).

4. Subsection (c) provides that the partnership may offset against the buyout price all amounts owing by the dissociated partner to the partnership, whether or not presently due, including any damages for wrongful dissociation under Section 602(c). This has the effect of accelerating

payment of amounts not yet due from the departing partner to the partner-ship, including a long-term loan by the partnership to the dissociated partner. Where appropriate, the amounts not yet due should be discounted to present value. A dissociating partner, on the other hand, is not entitled to an add-on for amounts owing to him by the partnership. Thus, a departing partner who has made a long-term loan to the partnership must wait for repayment, unless the terms of the loan agreement provide for acceleration upon dissociation.

It is not intended that the partnership's right of setoff be construed to limit the amount of the damages for the partner's wrongful dissociation and any other amounts owing to the partnership to the value of the dissociated partner's interest. Those amounts may result in a net sum due to the partnership from the dissociated partner.

5. Subsection (d) follows the UPA Section 38 rule and provides that the partnership must indemnify a dissociated partner against all partnership liabilities, whether incurred before or after the dissociation, except those incurred by the dissociated partner under Section 702.

6. Subsection (e) provides that, if no agreement for the purchase of the dissociated partner's interest is reached within 120 days after the dissoci-ated partner's written demand for payment, the partnership must pay, or cause to be paid, in cash the amount it estimates to be the buyout price, adjusted for any offsets allowed and accrued interest. Thus, the dissociating partner will receive in cash within 120 days of dissociation the undisputed minimum value of the partner's partnership interest. If the dissociated partner claims that the buyout price should be higher, suit may thereafter be brought as provided in subsection (i) to have the amount of the buyout price determined by the court. This is similar to the procedure for determin-ing the value of dissenting shareholders' shares under RMBCA Sections 13.20-13.28.

The "cause to be paid" language of subsection (a) is repeated here to permit either the partnership, one or more of the continuing partners, or a third-party purchaser to tender payment of the estimated amount due.

7. Subsection (f) provides that, when deferred payment is authorized in the case of a wrongfully dissociating partner, a written offer stating the amount the partnership estimates to be the purchase price should be tendered within the 120-day period, even though actual payment of the amount may be deferred, possibly for many years. See Comment 8. The dissociated partner is entitled to know at the time of dissociation what amount the remaining partners think is due, including the estimated amount of any damages allegedly caused by the partner's wrongful dissocia-tion that may be offset against the buyout price.

8. Subsection (g) provides that the payment of the estimated price (or tender of a written offer under subsection (f)) by the partnership must be

accompanied by (1) a statement of the partnership's assets and liabilities as of the date of the partner's dissociation; (2) the latest available balance sheet and income statement, if the partnership maintains such financial statements; (3) an explanation of how the estimated amount of the payment was calculated; and (4) a written notice that the payment will be in full satisfaction of the partnership's buyout obligation unless the dissociated partner commences an action to determine the price within 120 days of the notice. Subsection (g) is based in past on the dissenters' rights provisions of RMBCA Section 13.25(b).

Those disclosures should serve to identify and narrow substantially the items of dispute between the dissociated partner and the partnership over the valuation of the partnership interest. They will also serve to pin down the parties as to their claims of partnership assets and values and as to the existence and amount of all known liabilities. *See* Comment 4. Lastly, it will force the remaining partners to consider thoughtfully the difficult and important questions as to the appropriate method of valuation under the circumstances, and in particular, whether they should use going concern or liquidation value. Simply getting that information on the record in a timely fashion should increase the likelihood of a negotiated resolution of the parties' differences during the 120-day period within which the dissociated partner must bring suit.

9. Subsection (h) replaces UPA Section 38(2)(c) and provides a somewhat different rule for payment to a partner whose dissociation before the expiration of a definite term or the completion of a particular undertaking is wrongful under Section 602(b). Under subsection (h), a wrongfully dissociating partner is not entitled to receive any portion of the buyout price before the expiration of the term or completion of the undertaking, unless the dissociated partner establishes to the satisfaction of the court that earlier payment will not cause undue hardship to the business of the partnership. In all other cases, there must be an immediate payment in cash.

10. Subsection (i) provides that a dissociated partner may maintain an action against the partnership to determine the buyout price, any offsets, or other terms of the purchase obligation. The action must be commenced within 120 days after the partnership tenders payment of the amount it estimates to be due or, if deferred payment is authorized, its written offer. This provision creates a 120-day "cooling off" period. It also allows the parties an opportunity to negotiate their differences after disclosure by the partnership of its financial statements and other required information.

If the partnership fails to tender payment of the estimated amount due (or a written offer, if deferred payment is authorized), the dissociated partner has one year after written demand for payment in which to commence suit.

If the parties fail to reach agreement, the court must determine the buyout price of the partner's interest, any offsets, including damages for wrongful dissociation, and the amount of interest accrued. If payment to a wrongfully dissociated partner is deferred, the court may also require security for payment and determine the other terms of the obligation.

Under subsection (i), attorney's fees and other costs may be assessed against any party found to have acted arbitrarily, vexatiously, or not in good faith in connection with the valuation dispute, including the partnership's failure to tender payment of the estimated price or to make the required disclosures. This provision is based in part on RMBCA Section 13.31(b).

Section 702. Dissociated Partner's Power to Bind and Liability to Partnership.

(a) For two years after a partner dissociates without resulting in a dissolution and winding up of the partnership business, the partnership, including a surviving partnership under [Article] 9, is bound by an act of the dissociated partner which would have bound the partnership under Section 301 before dissociation only if at the time of entering into the transaction the other party:

(1) reasonably believed that the dissociated partner was then a partner;

(2) did not have notice of the partner's dissociation; and

(3) is not deemed to have had knowledge under Section 303(e) or notice under Section 704(c).

(b) A dissociated partner is liable to the partnership for any damage caused to the partnership arising from an obligation incurred by the dissociated partner after dissociation for which the partnership is liable under subsection (a).

Comment

1. Section 702 deals with a dissociated partner's lingering apparent authority to bind the partnership in ordinary course partnership transactions and the partner's liability to the partnership for any loss caused thereby. It also applies to partners who withdraw incident to a merger under Article 9. *See* Section 906(e).

A dissociated partner has no **actual** authority to act for the partnership. *See* Section 603(b)(1). Nevertheless, in order to protect innocent third parties, Section 702(a) provides that the partnership remains bound, for two years after a partner's dissociation, by that partner's acts that would, before his dissociation, have bound the partnership under Section 301 if, and only if, the other party to the transaction reasonably believed that he was still a partner, did not have notice of the partner's dissociation, and is not deemed to have had knowledge of the dissociation under Section 303(e) or notice thereof under Section 704(c).

Under Section 301, every partner has **apparent** authority to bind the partnership by any act for carrying on the partnership business in the ordinary course, unless the other party knows that the partner has no actual authority to act for the partnership or has received a notification of the partner's lack of authority. Section 702(a) continues that general rule for two years after a partner's dissociation, subject to three modifications.

After a partner's dissociation, the general rule is modified, first, by requiring the other party to show reasonable reliance on the partner's status as a partner. Section 301 has no explicit reliance requirement, although the partnership is bound only if the partner purports to act on its behalf. Thus, the other party will normally be aware of the partnership and presumably the partner's status as such.

The second modification is that, under Section 702(a), the partnership is not bound if the third party has **notice** of the partner's dissociation, while under the general rule of Section 301 the partnership is bound unless the third party **knows** of the partner's lack of authority. Under Section 102(b), a person has "notice" of a fact if he knows or has reason to know it exists from all the facts that are known to him or he has received a notification of it. Thus, the partnership may protect itself by sending a notification of the dissociation to a third party, and a third party may, in any event, have a duty to inquire further based on what is known. That provides the partnership with greater protection from the unauthorized acts of a dissociated partner than from those of partners generally.

The third modification of the general apparent authority rule under Section 702(a) involves the effect of a statement of dissociation. Section 704(c) provides that, for the purposes of Sections 702(a)(3) and 703(b)(3), third parties are deemed to have notice of a partner's dissociation 90 days after the filing of a statement of dissociation. Thus, the filing of a statement operates as constructive notice of the dissociated partner's lack of authority after 90 days, conclusively terminating the dissociated partner's Section 702 apparent authority.

With respect to a dissociated partner's authority to transfer partnership real property, Section 303(e) provides that third parties are deemed to have knowledge of a limitation on a partner's authority to transfer real property held in the partnership name upon the proper recording of a statement containing such a limitation. Section 704(b) provides that a statement of dissociation operates as a limitation on the dissociated partner's authority for the purposes of Section 303(e). Thus, a properly recorded statement of dissociation operates as constructive knowledge of a dissociated partner's lack of authority to transfer real property held in the partnership name, effective immediately upon recording,

Under RUPA, therefore, a partnership should notify all known creditors of a partner's dissociation and may, by filing a statement of dissociation, conclusively limit to 90 days a dissociated partner's lingering agency power.

Moreover, under Section 703(b), a dissociated partner's lingering liability for post-dissociation partnership liabilities may be limited to 90 days by filing a statement of dissociation. These incentives should encourage both partnerships and dissociating partners to file statements routinely. Those transacting substantial business with partnerships can protect themselves from the risk of dealing with dissociated partners, or relying on their credit, by checking the partnership records at least every 90 days.

2. Section 702(b) is a corollary to subsection (a) and provides that a dissociated partner is liable to the partnership for any loss resulting from an obligation improperly incurred by the partner under subsection (a). In effect, the dissociated partner must indemnify the partnership for any loss, meaning a loss net of any gain from the transaction. The dissociated partner is also personally liable to the third party for the unauthorized obligation.

Section 703. Dissociated Partner's Liability to Other Persons.

(a) A partner's dissociation does not of itself discharge the partner's liability for a partnership obligation incurred before dissociation. A dissociated partner is not liable for a partnership obligation incurred after dissociation, except as otherwise provided in subsection (b).

(b) A partner who dissociates without resulting in a dissolution and winding up of the partnership business is liable as a partner to the other party in a transaction entered into by the partnership, or a surviving partnership under [Article] 9, within two years after the partner's dissociation, only if the partner is liable for the obligation under Section 306 and at the time of entering into the transaction the other party:

(1) reasonably believed that the dissociated partner was then a partner;

(2) did not have notice of the partner's dissociation; and

(3) is not deemed to have had knowledge under Section 303(e) or notice under Section 704(c).

(c) By agreement with the partnership creditor and the partners continuing the business, a dissociated partner may be released from liability for a partnership obligation.

(d) A dissociated partner is released from liability for a partnership obligation if a partnership creditor, with notice of the partner's dissociation but without the partner's consent, agrees to a material alteration in the nature or time of payment of a partnership obligation.

Comment

Section 703(a) is based on UPA Section 36(1) and continues the basic rule that the departure of a partner does not of itself discharge the partner's liability to third parties for any partnership obligation incurred before dissociation. The word "obligation" is used instead of "liability" and is intended to include broadly both tort and contract liability incurred before dissociation. The second sentence states affirmatively that a dissociating partner is not liable for any partnership obligation incurred after dissociation except as expressly provided in subsection (b).

Section 703(b) is new and deals with the problem of protecting third parties who extend credit to the partnership after a partner's dissociation, believing that he is still a partner. It provides that the dissociated partner remains liable as a partner for transactions entered into by the partnership within two years after departure, if the other party does not have notice of the partner's dissociation and reasonably believes when entering the transaction that the dissociated partner is still a partner. The dissociated partner is not personally liable, however, if the other party is deemed to know of the dissociation under Section 303(e) or to have notice thereof under Section 704(c). Also, a dissociated partner is not personally liable for limited liability partnership obligations for which the partner is not personally liable under Section 306.

Section 703(b) operates similarly to Section 702(a) in that it requires reliance on the departed partner's continued partnership status, as well as lack of notice. Under Section 704(c), a statement of dissociation operates conclusively as constructive notice 90 days after filing for the purposes Section 703(b)(3) and, under Section 704(b), as constructive knowledge when recorded for the purposes of Section 303(d) and (e).

Section 703(c) continues the rule of UPA Section 36(2) that a departing partner can bargain for a contractual release from personal liability for a partnership obligation, but it requires the consent of both the creditor and the remaining partners.

Section 703(d) continues the rule of UPA Section 36(3) that a dissociated partner is released from liability for a partnership obligation if the creditor, with notice of the partner's departure, agrees to a material alteration in the nature or time of payment, without that partner's consent. This rule covers all partner dissociations and is not limited, as is the UPA rule, to situations in which a third party "agrees to assume the existing obligations of a dissolved partnership."

In general under RUPA, as a result of the adoption of the entity theory, relationships between a partnership and its creditors are not affected by the dissociation of a partner or by the addition of a new partner, unless otherwise agreed. Therefore, there is no need under RUPA, as there is under the UPA, for an elaborate provision deeming the new partnership to assume the liabilities of the old partnership. *See* UPA Section 41.

The "dual priority" rule in UPA Section 36(4) is eliminated to reflect the abolition of the "jingle rule," providing that separate debts have first claim on separate property, in order to conform to the Bankruptcy Code. *See* Comment 2 to Section 807. A deceased partner's estate, and thus all of his individual property, remains liable for partnership obligations incurred while he was a partner, however.

Section 704. Statement of Dissociation.

(a) A dissociated partner or the partnership may file a statement of dissociation stating the name of the partnership and that the partner is dissociated from the partnership.

(b) A statement of dissociation is a limitation on the authority of a dissociated partner for the purposes of Section 303(d) and (e).

(c) For the purposes of Sections 702(a)(3) and 703(b)(3), a person not a partner is deemed to have notice of the dissociation 90 days after the statement of dissociation is filed.

Comment

Section 704 is new and provides for a statement of dissociation and its effects. Subsection (a) authorizes either a dissociated partner or the partnership to file a statement of dissociation. Like other RUPA filings, the statement of dissociation is voluntary. Both the partnership and the departing partner have an incentive to file, however, and it is anticipated that those filings will become routine upon a partner's dissociation. The execution, filing, and recording of the statement is governed by Section 105.

Filing or recording a statement of dissociation has threefold significance:

(1) It is a statement of limitation on the dissociated partner's authority to the extent provided in Section 303(d) and (e). Under Section 303(d), a filed or recorded limitation on the authority of a partner destroys the conclusive effect of a prior grant of authority to the extent it contradicts the prior grant. Under Section 303(e), nonpartners are conclusively bound by a limitation on the authority of a partner to transfer real property held in the partnership name, if the statement is properly recorded in the real property records.

(2) Ninety days after the statement is filed, nonpartners are deemed to have notice of the dissociation and thus conclusively bound for purposes of cutting off the partner's apparent authority under Sections 301 and 702(a)(3).

(3) Ninety days after the statement is filed, third parties are conclusively bound for purposes of cutting off the dissociated partner's continuing liability under Section 703(b)(3) for transactions entered into by the partnership after dissociation.

Section 705. Continued Use of Partnership.

Continued use of a partnership name, or a dissociated partner's name as part thereof, by partners continuing the business does not of itself make the dissociated partner liable for an obligation of the partners or the partnership continuing the business.

Comment

Section 705 is an edited version of UPA Section 41(10) and provides that a dissociated partner is not liable for the debts of the continuing business simply because of continued use of the partnership name or the dissociated partner's name as a part thereof. That prevents forcing the business to forego the good will associated with its name.

[ARTICLE] 8
WINDING UP PARTNERSHIP BUSINESS

Section 801. Events Causing Dissolution and Winding Up of Partnership Business.

A partnership is dissolved, and its business must be wound up, only upon the occurrence of any of the following events:

(1) in a partnership at will, the partnership's having notice from a partner, other than a partner who is dissociated under Section 601(2) through (10), of that partner's express will to withdraw as a partner, or on a later date specified by the partner;

(2) in a partnership for a definite term or particular undertaking:

(i) within 90 days after a partner's dissociation by death or otherwise under Section 601(6) through (10) or wrongful dissociation under Section 602(b), the express will of at least half of the remaining partners to wind up the partnership business, for which purpose a partner's rightful dissociation pursuant to Section 602(b)(2)(i) constitutes the expression of that partner's will to wind up the partnership business;

(ii) the express will of all of the partners to wind up the partnership business; or

(iii) the expiration of the term or the completion of the undertaking;

(3) an event agreed to in the partnership agreement resulting in the winding up of the partnership business;

(4) an event that makes it unlawful for all or substantially all of the business of the partnership to be continued, but a cure of illegality within 90 days after notice to the partnership of the event is effective retroactively to the date of the event for purposes of this section;

(5) on application by a partner, a judicial determination that:

(i) the economic purpose of the partnership is likely to be unreasonably frustrated;

(ii) another partner has engaged in conduct relating to the partnership business which makes it not reasonably practicable to carry on the business in partnership with that partner; or

(iii) it is not otherwise reasonably practicable to carry on the partnership business in conformity with the partnership agreement; or

(6) on application by a transferee of a partner's transferable interest, a judicial determination that it is equitable to wind up the partnership business:

(i) after the expiration of the term or completion of the undertaking, if the partnership was for a definite term or particular undertaking at the time of the transfer or entry of the charging order that gave rise to the transfer; or

(ii) at any time, if the partnership was a partnership at will at the time of the transfer or entry of the charging order that gave rise to the transfer.

Comment

1. Under UPA Section 29, a partnership is dissolved every time a partner leaves. That reflects the aggregate nature of the partnership under the UPA. Even if the business of the partnership is continued by some of the partners, it is technically a new partnership. The dissolution of the old partnership and creation of a new partnership causes many unnecessary problems.

Under RULPA, limited partnerships dissolve far less readily than do general partnerships under the UPA. A limited partnership does not dissolve on the withdrawal of a limited partner, nor does it necessarily dissolve on the withdrawal of a general partner. *See* RULPA § 801(4).

RUPA's move to the entity theory is driven in part by the need to prevent a technical dissolution or its consequences. Under RUPA, not every partner dissociation causes a dissolution of the partnership. Only certain departures trigger a dissolution. The basic rule is that a partnership is dissolved, and its business must be wound up, only upon the occurrence of one of the events listed in Section 801. All other dissociations result in a buyout of the partner's interest under Article 7 and a continuation of the partnership entity and business by the remaining partners. *See* Section 603(a).

With only three exceptions, the provisions of Section 801 are merely default rules and may by agreement be varied or eliminated as grounds for dissolution. The first exception is dissolution under Section 801(4) resulting from carrying on an illegal business. The other two exceptions cover the power of a court to dissolve a partnership under Section 801(5) on application of a partner and under Section 801(6) on application of a transferee. See Comments 6-8 for further explanation of these provisions.

2. Under RUPA, "dissolution" is merely the commencement of the winding up process. The partnership continues for the limited purpose of winding up the business. In effect, that means the scope of the partnership business contracts to completing work in process and taking such other actions as may be necessary to wind up the business. Winding up the partnership business entails selling its assets, paying its debts, and distributing the net balance, if any, to the partners in cash according to their interests. The partnership entity continues, and the partners are associated in the winding up of the business until winding up is completed. When the winding up is completed, the partnership entity terminates.

3. Section 801 continues two basic rules from the UPA. First, it continues the rule that any member of an **at-will** partnership has the right to force a liquidation. Second, by negative implication, it continues the rule that the partners who wish to continue the business of a **term** partnership cannot be forced to liquidate the business by a partner who withdraws prematurely in violation of the partnership agreement.

Those rules are gleaned from the separate UPA provisions governing dissolution and its consequences. Under UPA Section 31(1)(b), dissolution is caused by the express will of any partner when no definite term or particular undertaking is specified. UPA Section 38(1) provides that upon dissolution any partner has the right to have the business wound up. That is a default rule and applies only in the absence of an agreement affording the other partners a right to continue the business.

UPA Section 31(2) provides that a term partnership may be dissolved at any time, in contravention of the partnership agreement, by the express will of any partner. In that case, however, UPA Section 38(2)(b) provides that the nonbreaching partners may by unanimous consent continue the business. If the business is continued, they must buy out the breaching partner.

4. Section 801(1) provides that a partnership at will is dissolved and its business must be wound up upon the partnership's having notice of a partner's express will to withdraw as a partner, unless a later effective date is specified by the partner. A partner at will who has already been dissociated in some other manner, such as a partner who has been expelled, does not thereafter have a right to cause the partnership to be dissolved and its business wound up.

If, after dissolution, none of the partners wants the partnership wound up, Section 802(b) provides that, with the consent of all the partners, including the withdrawing partner, the remaining partners may continue the business. In that event, although there is a technical dissolution of the partnership and, at least in theory, a temporary contraction of the scope of the business, the partnership entity continues and the scope of its business is restored. *See* Section 802(b) and Comment 2.

5. Section 801(2) provides three ways in which a term partnership may be dissolved before the expiration of the term:

(i) Subsection (2)(i) provides for dissolution after a partner's dissociation by death or otherwise under Section 601(6) to (10) or wrongful dissociation under Section 602(b), if within 90 days after the dissociation at least half of the remaining partners express their will to dissolve the partnership. *
Thus if a term partnership had six partners and one of the partners dies or wrongfully dissociates before the end of the term, the partnership will, as a result of the dissociation, be dissolved only if three of the remaining five partners affirmatively vote in favor of dissolution within 90 days after the dissociation. On the other hand, if the partnership had seven partners and one dissociates, the partnership will be dissolved if three of the remaining partners vote in favor of dissolution within 90 days after the dissociation because they are equal to half of the remaining partners. This reactive dissolution of a term partnership protects the remaining partners where the dissociating partner is crucial to the successful continuation of the business. The corresponding UPA Section 38(2)(b) rule requires unanimous consent of the remaining partners to continue the business, thus giving each partner an absolute right to a reactive liquidation. Under RUPA, if the partnership is continued by the majority, any dissenting partner who wants to withdraw may do so rightfully under the exception to Section 602(b)(2)(i), in which case his interest in the partnership will be bought out under Article 7. By itself, however, a partner's vote not to continue the business is not necessarily an expression of the partner's will to withdraw, and a dissenting partner may still elect to remain a partner and continue in the business.

The Section 601 dissociations giving rise to a reactive dissolution are: (6) a partner's bankruptcy or similar financial impairment; (7) a partner's

---

* Prior to August 1997, Section 801(2)(i) provided that upon the dissociation of a partner in a term partnership by death or otherwise under Section 601(6) through (10) or wrongful dissociation under 602(b) the partnership would dissolve unless "a majority in interest of the remaining partners (including partners who have rightfully dissociated pursuant to section 602(b)(2)(i) agree to continue the partnership." This language was thought to be necessary for a term partnership to lack continuity of life under the Internal Revenue Act tax classification regulations. Those regulations were repealed effective January 1, 1997. The current language, approved at the 1997 annual meeting of the National Conference of Commissioners on Uniform State Laws, allows greater continuity in a term partnership than the prior version of this subsection and UPA Section 38(2)(b). [footnote by NCCUSL.]

death or incapacity; (8) the distribution by a trust-partner of its entire partnership interest; (9) the distribution by an estate-partner of its entire partnership interest; and (10) the termination of an entity-partner. Any dissociation during the term of the partnership that is wrongful under Section 602(b), including a partner's voluntary withdrawal, expulsion or bankruptcy, also gives rise to a reactive dissolution. Those statutory grounds may be varied by agreement or the reactive dissolution may be abolished entirely.

Under Section 601(6)(i), a partner is dissociated upon becoming a debtor in bankruptcy. The bankruptcy of a partner or of the partnership is not, however, an event of dissolution under Section 801. That is a change from UPA Section 31(5). A partner's bankruptcy does, however, cause dissolution of a term partnership under Section 801(2)(i), if within 90 days after the dissociation at least half of the remaining partners express their will to dissolve the partnership. Affording the other partners the option of buying out the bankrupt partner's interest avoids the necessity of winding up a term partnership every time a partner becomes a debtor in bankruptcy.

Similarly, under Section 801(2)(i), the death of any partner will result in the dissolution of a term partnership only if at least half of the remaining partners express their will to wind up the partnership's business. If dissolution does occur, the deceased partner's transferable interest in the partnership passes to his estate and must be bought out under Article 7. *See* Comment 8 to Section 601.

(ii) Section 801(2)(ii) provides that a term partnership may be dissolved and wound up at any time by the express will of all the partners. That is merely an expression of the general rule that the partnership agreement may override the statutory default rules and that the partnership agreement, like any contract, can be amended at any time by unanimous consent.

UPA Section 31(1)(c) provides that a term partnership may be wound up by the express will of all the partners whose transferable interests have not been assigned or charged for a partner's separate debts. That rule reflects the belief that the remaining partners may find transferees very intrusive. This provision has been deleted, however, because the liquidation is easily accomplished under Section 801(2)(ii) by first expelling the transferor partner under Section 601(4)(ii).

(iii) Section 801(2)(iii) is based on UPA Section 31(1)(a) and provides for winding up a term partnership upon the expiration of the term or the completion of the undertaking.

Subsection (2)(iii) must be read in conjunction with Section 406(a), if the partners continue the business after the expiration of the term or the completion of the undertaking, the partnership will be treated as a partnership at will. Moreover, if the partners continue the business without any settlement or liquidation of the partnership, under Section 406(b) they are presumed to have agreed that the partnership will continue, despite the lack of a formal agreement. The partners may also agree to ratify all acts taken since the end of the partnership's term.

6. Section 801(3) provides for dissolution upon the occurrence of an event specified in the partnership agreement as resulting in the winding up of the partnership business. The partners may, however, agree to continue the business and to ratify all acts taken since dissolution.

7. Section 801(4) continues the basic rule in UPA Section 31(3) and provides for dissolution if it is unlawful to continue the business of the partnership, unless cured. The "all or substantially all" proviso is intended to avoid dissolution for insubstantial or innocent regulatory violations. If the illegality is cured within 90 days after notice to the partnership, it is effective retroactively for purposes of this section. The requirement that an uncured illegal business be wound up cannot be varied in the partnership agreement. *See* Section 103(b)(8).

8. Section 801(5) provides for judicial dissolution on application by a partner. It is based in part on UPA Section 32(1), and the language comes in part from RULPA Section 802. A court may order a partnership dissolved upon a judicial determination that: (i) the economic purpose of the partnership is likely to be unreasonably frustrated; (ii) another partner has engaged in conduct relating to the partnership business which makes it not reasonably practicable to carry on the business in partnership with that partner; or (iii) it is not otherwise reasonably practicable to carry on the partnership business in conformity with the partnership agreement. The court's power to wind up the partnership under Section 801(5) cannot be varied in the partnership agreement. *See* Section 103(b)(8).

RUPA deletes UPA Section 32(1)(e) which provides for dissolution when the business can only be carried on at a loss. That provision might result in a dissolution contrary to the partners' expectations in a start-up or tax shelter situation, in which case "book" or "tax" losses do not signify business failure. Truly poor financial performance may justify dissolution under subsection (5)(i) as a frustration of the partnership's economic purpose.

RUPA also deletes UPA Section 32(1)(f) which authorizes a court to order dissolution of a partnership when "other circumstances render a dissolution equitable." That provision was regarded as too open-ended and, given RUPA's expanded remedies for partners, unnecessary. No significant change in result is intended, however, since the interpretation of UPA Section 32(1)(f) is comparable to the specific grounds expressed in subsection (5). *See, e.g., Karber v. Karber*, 145 Ariz. 293, 701 P.2d 1 (Ct. App. 1985) (partnership dissolved on basis of suspicion and ill will, citing UPA §§ 32(1)(d) and (f)); *Fuller v. Brough*, 159 Colo. 147, 411 P.2d 18 (1966) (not equitable to dissolve partnership for trifling causes or temporary grievances that do not render it impracticable to carry on partnership business); *Lau v. Wong*, 1 Haw. App. 217, 616 P.2d 1031 (1980) (partnership dissolved where business operated solely for benefit of managing partner).

9. Section 801(6) provides for judicial dissolution on application by a transferee of a partner's transferable interest in the partnership, including the purchaser of a partner's interest upon foreclosure of a charging order. It is based on UPA Section 32(2) and authorizes dissolution upon a judicial determination that it is equitable to wind up the partnership business (i) after the expiration of the partnership term or completion of the undertaking or (ii) at any time, if the partnership were a partnership at will at the time of the transfer or when the charging order was issued. The requirement that the court determine that it is equitable to wind up the business is new. The rights of a transferee under this section cannot be varied in the partnership agreement. *See* Section 103(b)(8).

Section 802. Partnership Continues After Dissolution.

(a) Subject to subsection (b), a partnership continues after dissolution only for the purpose of winding up its business. The partnership is terminated when the winding up of its business is completed.

(b) At any time after the dissolution of a partnership and before the winding up of its business is completed, all of the partners, including any dissociating partner other than a wrongfully dissociating partner, may waive the right to have the partnership's business wound up and the partnership terminated. In that event:

(1) the partnership resumes carrying on its business as if dissolution had never occurred, and any liability incurred by the partnership or a partner after the dissolution and before the waiver is determined as if dissolution had never occurred; and

(2) the rights of a third party accruing under Section 804(1) or arising out of conduct in reliance on the dissolution before the third party knew or received a notification of the waiver may not be adversely affected.

Comment

1. Section 802(a) is derived from UPA Section 30 and provides that a partnership continues after dissolution only for the purpose of winding up its business, after which it is terminated. RUPA continues the concept of "termination" to mark the completion of the winding up process. Since no filing or other formality is required, the date will often be determined only by hindsight. No legal rights turn on the partnership's termination or the date thereof. Even after termination, if a previously unknown liability is asserted, all of the partners are still liable.

2. Section 802(b) makes explicit the right of the remaining partners to continue the business after an event of dissolution if all of the partners, including the dissociating partner or partners, waive the right to have the business wound up and the partnership terminated. Only those "dissociating" partners whose dissociation was the immediate cause of the dissolution

must waive the right to have the business wound up. The consent of wrongfully dissociating partners is not required.

3. Upon waiver of the right to have the business wound up, Paragraph (1) of the subsection provides that the partnership entity may resume carrying on its business as if dissolution had never occurred, thereby restoring the scope of its business to normal. "Resumes" is intended to mean that acts appropriate to winding up, authorized when taken, are in effect ratified, and the partnership remains liable for those acts, as provided explicitly in paragraph (2).

If the business is continued following a waiver of the right to dissolution, any liability incurred by the partnership or a partner after the dissolution and before the waiver is to be determined as if dissolution had never occurred. That has the effect of validating transactions entered into after dissolution that might not have been appropriate for winding up the business, because, upon waiver, any liability incurred by either the partnership or a partner in those transactions will be determined under Sections 702 and 703, rather than Sections 804 and 806.

As to the liability for those transactions among the partners themselves, the partners by agreement may provide otherwise. Thus, a partner who, after dissolution, incurred an obligation appropriate for winding up, but not appropriate for continuing the business, may protect himself by conditioning his consent to the continuation of the business on the ratification of the transaction by the continuing partners.

Paragraph (2) of the subsection provides that the rights of third parties accruing under Section 804(1) before they knew (or were notified) of the waiver may not be adversely affected by the waiver. That is intended to mean the partnership is bound, notwithstanding a subsequent waiver of dissolution and resumption of its business, by a transaction entered into after dissolution that was appropriate for winding up the partnership business, even if not appropriate for continuing the business. Similarly, any rights of a third party arising out of conduct in reliance on the dissolution are protected, absent knowledge (or notification) of the waiver. Thus, for example, a partnership loan, callable upon dissolution, that has been called is not reinstated by a subsequent waiver. If the loan has not been called before the lender learns (or is notified) of the waiver, however, it may not thereafter be called because of the dissolution. On the other hand, a waiver does not reinstate a lease that is terminated by the dissolution itself.

Section 803. Right to Wind Up Partnership Business.

(a) After dissolution, a partner who has not wrongfully dissociated may participate in winding up the partnership's business, but on application of any partner, partner's legal representative, or transferee, the [designate the appropriate court], for good cause shown, may order judicial supervision of the winding up.

(b) The legal representative of the last surviving partner may wind up a partnership's business.

(c) A person winding up a partnership's business may preserve the partnership business or property as a going concern for a reasonable time, prosecute and defend actions and proceedings, whether civil, criminal, or administrative, settle and close the partnership's business, dispose of and transfer the partnership's property, discharge the partnership's liabilities, distribute the assets of the partnership pursuant to Section 807, settle disputes by mediation or arbitration, and perform other necessary acts.

Comment

Section 803(a) is drawn from UPA Section 37. It provides that the partners who have not wrongfully dissociated may participate in winding up the partnership business. Wrongful dissociation is defined in Section 602. On application of any partner, a court may for good cause judicially supervise the winding up.

Section 803(b) continues the rule of UPA Section 25(2)(d) that the legal representative of the last surviving partner may wind up the business. It makes clear that the representative of the last surviving partner will not be forced to go to court for authority to wind up the business. On the other hand, the legal representative of a deceased partner, other than the last surviving partner, has only the rights of a transferee of the deceased partner's transferable interest. *See* Comment 8 to Section 601.

Section 803(c) is new and provides further guidance on the powers of a person who is winding up the business. It is based on Delaware Laws, Title 6, Section 17-803. The powers enumerated are not intended to be exclusive.

Subsection (c) expressly authorizes the preservation of the partnership's business or property as a going concern for a reasonable time. Some courts have reached that result without benefit of statutory authority. *See, e.g., Paciaroni v. Crane*, 408 A.2d 946 (Del. Ch. 1979). An agreement to continue the partnership business in order to preserve its going-concern value until sale is not a waiver of a partner's right to have the business liquidated.

The authorization of mediation and arbitration implements Conference policy to encourage alternative dispute resolution.

A partner's fiduciary duties of care and loyalty under Section 404 extend to winding up the business, except as modified by Section 603(b).

Section 804. Partner's Power to Bind Partnership After Dissolution.

Subject to Section 805, a partnership is bound by a partner's act after dissolution that:

(1) is appropriate for winding up the partnership business; or

(2) would have bound the partnership under Section 301 before dissolution, if the other party to the transaction did not have notice of the dissolution.

Comment

Section 804 is the successor to UPA Sections 33(2) and 35, which wind down the authority of partners to bind the partnership to third persons.

Section 804(1) provides that partners have the authority to bind the partnership after dissolution in transactions that are appropriate for winding-up the partnership business. Section 804(2) provides that partners also have the power after dissolution to bind the partnership in transactions that are inconsistent with winding up. The partnership is bound in a transaction not appropriate for winding up, however, only if the partner's act would have bound the partnership under Section 301 before dissolution and the other party to the transaction did not have notice of the dissolution. *See* Section 102(b) (notice). Compare Section 301(1) (partner has apparent authority unless other party knows or has received a notification of lack of authority).

Section 804(2) attempts to balance the interests of the partners to terminate their mutual agency authority against the interests of outside creditors who have no notice of the partnership's dissolution. Even if the partnership is not bound under Section 804, the faithless partner who purports to act for the partnership after dissolution may be liable individually to an innocent third party under the law of agency. *See* Section 330 of the Restatement (Second) of Agency (agent liable for misrepresentation of authority), applicable under RUPA as provided in Section 104(a).

RUPA eliminates the special and confusing UPA rules limiting the authority of partners after dissolution. The special protection afforded by UPA Section 35(1)(b)(I) to former creditors and the lesser special protection afforded by UPA Section 35(1)(b)(II) to other parties who knew of the partnership before dissolution are both abolished. RUPA eschews these cumbersome notice provisions in favor of the general apparent authority rules of Section 301, subject to the effect of a filed or recorded statement of dissolution under Section 805. This enhances the protection of innocent third parties and imposes liability on the partnership and the partners who choose their fellow partner-agents and are in the best position to protect others by providing notice of the dissolution.

Also deleted are the special rules for unknown partners in UPA Section 35(2) and for certain causes of dissolution in UPA Section 35(3). Those, too, are inconsistent with RUPA's policy of adhering more closely to the general agency rules of Section 301.

Section 804 should be contrasted with Section 702, which winds down the power of a partner being bought out. The power of a dissociating partner is limited to transactions entered into within two years after the partner's dissociation. Section 804 has no time limitation. However, the apparent authority of partners in both situations is now subject to the filing of a statement of dissociation or dissolution, as the case may be, which operates to cut off such authority after 90 days.

Section 805. Statement of Dissolution.

(a) After dissolution, a partner who has not wrongfully dissociated may file a statement of dissolution stating the name of the partnership and that the partnership has dissolved and is winding up its business.

(b) A statement of dissolution cancels a filed statement of partnership authority for the purposes of Section 303(d) and is a limitation on authority for the purposes of Section 303(e).

(c) For the purposes of Sections 301 and 804, a person not a partner is deemed to have notice of the dissolution and the limitation on the partners' authority as a result of the statement of dissolution 90 days after it is filed.

(d) After filing and, if appropriate, recording a statement of dissolution, a dissolved partnership may file and, if appropriate, record a statement of partnership authority which will operate with respect to a person not a partner as provided in Section 303(d) and (e) in any transaction, whether or not the transaction is appropriate for winding up the partnership business.

Comment

1. Section 805 is new. Subsection (a) provides that, after an event of dissolution, any partner who has not wrongfully dissociated may file a statement of dissolution on behalf of the partnership. The filing and recording of a statement of dissolution is optional. The execution, filing, and recording of the statement is governed by Section 105. The legal consequences of filing a statement of dissolution are similar to those of a statement of dissociation under Section 704.

2. Subsection (b) provides that a statement of dissolution cancels a filed statement of partnership authority for the purposes of Section 303(d), thereby terminating any extraordinary grant of authority contained in that statement.

A statement of dissolution also operates as a limitation on authority for the purposes of Section 303(e). That section provides that third parties are deemed to know of a limitation on the authority of a partner to transfer real property held in the name of the partnership if a certified copy of the statement containing the limitation is recorded with the real estate records. In effect, a properly recorded statement of dissolution restricts the authority of all partners to real property transfers that are appropriate for winding up the business. Thus, third parties must inquire of the partnership whether a contemplated real property transfer is appropriate for winding up. After dissolution, the partnership may, however, file and record a new statement of authority that will bind the partnership under Section 303(d).

3. Subsection (c) operates in conjunction with Sections 301 and 804 to wind down partners' apparent authority after dissolution. It provides that, for purposes of those sections, 90 days after the filing of a statement of dissolution nonpartners are deemed to have notice of the dissolution and the corresponding limitation on the authority of all partners. Sections 301 and 804 provide that a partner's lack of authority is binding on persons with notice thereof. Thus, after 90 days the statement of dissolution operates as constructive notice conclusively limiting the apparent authority of partners to transactions that are appropriate for winding up the business.

4. Subsection (d) provides that, after filing and, if appropriate, recording a statement of dissolution, the partnership may file and record a new statement of partnership authority that will operate as provided in Section 303(d). A grant of authority contained in that statement is conclusive and may be relied upon by a person who gives value without knowledge to the contrary, whether or not the transaction is appropriate for winding up the partnership business. That makes the partners' record authority conclusive after dissolution, and precludes going behind the record to inquire into whether or not the transaction was appropriate for winding up.

Section 806. Partner's Liability to Other Partners After Dissolution.

(a) Except as otherwise provided in subsection (b) and Section 306, after dissolution a partner is liable to the other partners for the partner's share of any partnership liability incurred under Section 804.

(b) A partner who, with knowledge of the dissolution, incurs a partnership liability under Section 804(2) by an act that is not appropriate for winding up the partnership business is liable to the partnership for any damage caused to the partnership arising from the liability.

Comment

Section 806 is the successor to UPA Sections 33(1) and 34, which govern the rights of partners among themselves with respect to post-dissolution liability.

Subsection (a) provides that, except as provided in Section 306(a) and subsection (b), after dissolution each partner is liable to the other partners by way of contribution for his share of any partnership liability incurred under Section 804. That includes not only obligations that are appropriate for winding up the business, but also obligations that are inappropriate if within the partner's apparent authority. Consistent with other provisions of this Act, Section 806(a) makes clear that a partner does not have a contribution obligation with regard to limited liability partnership obligations for which the partner is not liable under Section 306. *See* Comments to Section 401(b).

Subsection (a) draws no distinction as to the cause of dissolution. Thus, as among the partners, their liability is treated alike in all events of dissolution. That is a change from UPA Section 33(1).

Subsection (b) creates an exception to the general rule in subsection (a). It provides that a partner, who with knowledge of the winding up nevertheless incurs a liability binding on the partnership by an act that is inappropriate for winding up the business, is liable to the partnership for any loss caused thereby.

Section 806 is merely a default rule and may be varied in the partnership agreement. *See* Section 103(a).

Section 807. Settlement of Accounts and Contributions Among Partners.

(a) In winding up a partnership's business, the assets of the partnership, including the contributions of the partners required by this section, must be applied to discharge its obligations to creditors, including, to the extent permitted by law, partners who are creditors. Any surplus must be applied to pay in cash the net amount distributable to partners in accordance with their right to distributions under subsection (b).

(b) Each partner is entitled to a settlement of all partnership accounts upon winding up the partnership business. In settling accounts among the partners, the profits and losses that result from the liquidation of the partnership assets must be credited and charged to the partners' accounts. The partnership shall make a distribution to a partner in an amount equal to any excess of the credits over the charges in the partner's account. A partner shall contribute to the partnership an amount equal to any excess of the charges over the credits in the partner's account but excluding from the calculation charges attributable to an obligation for which the partner is not personally liable under Section 306.

(c) If a partner fails to contribute the full amount required under subsection (b), all of the other partners shall contribute, in the proportions in which those partners share partnership losses, the additional amount necessary to satisfy the partnership obligations for which they are personally liable under Section 306. A partner or partner's legal representative may recover from the other partners any contributions the partner makes to the extent the amount contributed exceeds that partner's share of the partnership obligations for which the partner is personally liable under Section 306.

(d) After the settlement of accounts, each partner shall contribute, in the proportion in which the partner shares partnership losses, the amount necessary to satisfy partnership obligations that were not known at the time of the settlement and for which the partner is personally liable under Section 306.

(e) The estate of a deceased partner is liable for the partner's obligation to contribute to the partnership.

(f) An assignee for the benefit of creditors of a partnership or a partner, or a person appointed by a court to represent creditors of a partnership or a partner, may enforce a partner's obligation to contribute to the partnership.

Comment

1. Section 807 provides the default rules for the settlement of accounts and contributions among the partners in winding up the business. It is derived in part from UPA Sections 38(1) and 40.

2. Subsection (a) continues the rule in UPA Section 38(1) that, in winding up the business, the partnership assets must first be applied to discharge partnership liabilities to creditors. For this purpose, any required contribution by the partners is treated as an asset of the partnership. After the payment of all partnership liabilities, any surplus must be applied to pay in cash the net amount due the partners under subsection (b) by way of a liquidating distribution.

RUPA continues the "in-cash" rule of UPA Section 38(1) and is consistent with Section 402, which provides that a partner has no right to receive, and may not be required to accept, a distribution in kind, unless otherwise agreed. The in-cash rule avoids the valuation problems that afflict unwanted in-kind distributions.

The partnership must apply its assets to discharge the obligations of partners who are creditors on a parity with other creditors. *See* Section 404(f) and Comment 6. In effect, that abolishes the priority rules in UPA Section 40(b) and (c) which subordinate the payment of inside debt to outside debt. Both RULPA and the RMBCA do likewise. *See* RULPA § 804; RMBCA §§ 6.40(f), 14.05(a). Ultimately, however, a partner whose "debt" has been repaid by the partnership is personally liable, as a partner, for any outside debt remaining unsatisfied, unlike a limited partner or corporate shareholder. Accordingly, the obligation to contribute sufficient funds to satisfy the claims of outside creditors may result in the equitable subordination of inside debt when partnership assets are insufficient to satisfy all obligations to non-partners.

RUPA in effect abolishes the "dual priority" or "jingle" rule of UPA Section 40(h) and (i). Those sections gave partnership creditors priority as to partnership property and separate creditors priority as to separate property. The jingle rule has already been preempted by the Bankruptcy Code, at least as to Chapter 7 partnership liquidation proceedings. Under

Section 723(c) of the Bankruptcy Code, and under RUPA, partnership creditors share pro rata with the partners' individual creditors in the assets of the partners' estates.

3. Subsection (b) provides that each partner is entitled to a settlement of all partnership accounts upon winding up. It also establishes the default rules for closing out the partners' accounts. First, the profits and losses resulting from the liquidation of the partnership assets must be credited or charged to the partners' accounts, according to their respective shares of profits and losses. Then, the partnership must make a final liquidating distribution to those partners with a positive account balance. That distribution should be in the amount of the excess of credits over the charges in the account. Any partner with a negative account balance must contribute to the partnership an amount equal to the excess of charges over the credits in the account provided the excess relates to an obligation for which the partner is personally liable under Section 306. The partners may, however, agree that a negative account does not reflect a debt to the partnership and need not be repaid in settling the partners' accounts.

Section 807(d) makes clear that a partner's contribution obligation to a partnership in dissolution only considers the partner's share of obligations for which the partner was personally liable under Section 306 ("unshielded obligations"). *See* Comments to Section 401(b) (partner contribution obligation to an operating partnership). Properly determined under this Section, the total required partner contributions will be sufficient to satisfy the partnership's total unshielded obligations. In special circumstances where a partnership has both shielded and unshielded obligations and the partner required contributions are used to first pay shielded partnership obligations, the partners may be required to make further contributions to satisfy the partnership unpaid unshielded obligations. The proper resolution of this matter is left to debtor-creditor law as well as the law governing the fiduciary obligations of the partners. *See* Section 104(a).

RUPA eliminates the distinction in UPA Section 40(b) between the liability owing to a partner in respect of capital and the liability owing in respect of profits. Section 807(b) speaks simply of the right of a partner to a liquidating distribution. That implements the logic of RUPA Sections 401(a) and 502 under which contributions to capital and shares in profits and losses combine to determine the right to distributions. The partners may, however, agree to share "operating" losses differently from "capital" losses, thereby continuing the UPA distinction.

4. Subsection (c) continues the UPA Section 40(d) rule that solvent partners share proportionately in the shortfall caused by insolvent partners who fail to contribute their proportionate share. The partnership may enforce a partner's obligation to contribute. *See* Section 405(a). A partner is entitled to recover from the other partners any contributions in excess of that partner's share of the partnership's liabilities. *See* Section 405(b)(iii).

5. Subsection (d) provides that after settling the partners' accounts, each partner must contribute, in the proportion in which he shares losses, the amount necessary to satisfy partnership obligations that were not known at the time of the settlement. That continues the basic rule of UPA Section 40(d) and underscores that the obligation to contribute exists independently of the partnership's books of account. It specifically covers the situation of a partnership liability that was unknown when the partnership books were closed.

6. Under subsection (e), the estate of a deceased partner is liable for the partner's obligation to contribute to partnership losses. That continues the rule of UPA Section 40(g).

7. Subsection (f) provides that an assignee for the benefit of creditors of the partnership or of a partner (or other court appointed creditor representative) may enforce any partner's obligation to contribute to the partnership. That continues the rules of UPA Sections 36(4) and 40(e).

[ARTICLE] 9
CONVERSIONS AND MERGERS

Section 901. Definitions.

In this [article]:

(1) "General partner" means a partner in a partnership and a general partner in a limited partnership.

(2) "Limited partner" means a limited partner in a limited partnership.

(3) "Limited partnership" means a limited partnership created under the [State Limited Partnership Act], predecessor law, or comparable law of another jurisdiction.

(4) "Partner" includes both a general partner and a limited partner.

Comment

1. Article 9 is new. The UPA is silent with respect to the conversion or merger of partnerships, and thus it is necessary under the UPA to structure

those types of transactions as asset transfers. RUPA provides specific statutory authority for conversions and mergers. It provides for continuation of the partnership entity, thereby simplifying those transactions and adding certainty to the legal consequences.

A number of States currently authorize the merger of limited partnerships, and some authorize them to merge with other business entities such as corporations and limited liability companies. A few States currently authorize the merger of a general and a limited partnership or the conversion of a general to a limited partnership.

2. As Section 908 makes clear, the requirements of Article 9 are not mandatory, and a partnership may convert or merge in any other manner provided by law. Article 9 is merely a "safe harbor." If the requirements of the article are followed, the conversion or merger is legally valid. Since most States have no other established procedure for the conversion or merger of partnerships, it is likely that the Article 9 procedures will be used in virtually all cases.

3. Article 9 does not restrict the provisions authorizing conversions and mergers to domestic partnerships. Since no filing is required for the creation of a partnership under RUPA, it is often unclear where a partnership is domiciled. Moreover, a partnership doing business in the State satisfies the definition of a partnership created under this Act since it is an association of two or more co-owners carrying on a business for profit. Even a partnership clearly domiciled in another State could easily amend its partnership agreement to provide that its internal affairs are to be governed by the laws of a jurisdiction that has enacted Article 9 of RUPA. No harm is likely to result from extending to foreign partnerships the right to convert or merge under local law.

4. Because Article 9 deals with the conversion and merger of both general and limited partnerships, Section 901 sets forth four definitions distinguishing between the two types of partnerships solely for the purposes of Article 9. "Partner" includes both general and limited partners, and "general partner" includes general partners in both general and limited partnerships.

Section 902. Conversion of Partnership to Limited Partnership.

(a) A partnership may be converted to a limited partnership pursuant to this section.

(b) The terms and conditions of a conversion of a partnership to a limited partnership must be approved by all of the partners or by a number or percentage specified for conversion in the partnership agreement.

(c) After the conversion is approved by the partners, the partnership shall file a certificate of limited partnership in the jurisdiction in which the limited partnership is to be formed. The certificate must include:

(1) a statement that the partnership was converted to a limited partnership from a partnership;

(2) its former name; and

(3) a statement of the number of votes cast by the partners for and against the conversion and, if the vote is less than unanimous, the number or percentage required to approve the conversion under the partnership agreement.

(d) The conversion takes effect when the certificate of limited partnership is filed or at any later date specified in the certificate.

(e) A general partner who becomes a limited partner as a result of the conversion remains liable as a general partner for an obligation incurred by the partnership before the conversion takes effect. If the other party to a transaction with the limited partnership reasonably believes when entering the transaction that the limited partner is a general partner, the limited partner is liable for an obligation incurred by the limited partnership within 90 days after the conversion takes effect. The limited partner's liability for all other obligations of the limited partnership incurred after the conversion takes effect is that of a limited partner as provided in the [State Limited Partnership Act].

Comment

Section 902(a) authorizes the conversion of a "partnership" to a "limited partnership." Section 202(b) limits the usual RUPA definition of "partnership" to general partnerships. That definition is applicable to Article 9. If a limited partnership is contemplated, Article 9 uses the term "limited partnership." *See* Section 901(3).

Subsection (b) provides that the terms and conditions of the conversion must be approved by all the partners, unless the partnership agreement specifies otherwise for a conversion.

Subsection (c) provides that, after approval, the partnership must file a certificate of limited partnership which includes the requisite information concerning the conversion.

Subsection (d) provides that the conversion takes effect when the certificate is filed, unless a later effective date is specified.

Subsection (e) establishes the partners' liabilities following a conversion. A partner who becomes a limited partner as a result of the conversion remains fully liable as a general partner for any obligation arising before the effective date of the conversion, both to third parties and to other partners for contribution. Third parties who transact business with the converted partnership unaware of a partner's new status as a limited partner are protected for 90 days after the conversion. Since RULPA Section 201(a)(3) requires the certificate of limited partnership to name all of the general partners, and under RUPA Section 902(c) the certificate must also include a statement of the conversion, parties transacting business with the converted partnership can protect themselves by checking the record of the State where the limited partnership is formed (the State where the conversion takes place). A former general partner who becomes a limited partner as a result of the conversion can avoid the lingering 90-day exposure to liability as a general partner by notifying those transacting business with the partnership of his limited partner status.

Although Section 902 does not expressly provide that a partner's withdrawal upon a term partnership's conversion to a limited partnership is rightful, it was assumed that the unanimity requirement for the approval of a conversion would afford a withdrawing partner adequate opportunity to protect his interest as a condition of approval. This question is left to the partnership agreement if it provides for conversion without the approval of all the partners.

Section 903. Conversion of Limited Partnership to Partnership.

(a) A limited partnership may be converted to a partnership pursuant to this section.

(b) Notwithstanding a provision to the contrary in a limited partnership agreement, the terms and conditions of a conversion of a limited partnership to a partnership must be approved by all of the partners.

(c) After the conversion is approved by the partners, the limited partnership shall cancel its certificate of limited partnership.

(d) The conversion takes effect when the certificate of limited partnership is canceled.

(e) A limited partner who becomes a general partner as a result of the conversion remains liable only as a limited partner for an obligation incurred by the limited partnership before the conversion takes effect. Except as otherwise provided in Section 306, the partner is liable as a general partner for an obligation of the partnership incurred after the conversion takes effect.

Comment

Section 903(a) authorizes the conversion of a limited partnership to a general partnership.

Subsection (b) provides that the conversion must be approved by all of the partners, even if the partnership agreement provides to the contrary. That includes all of the general and limited partners. *See* Section 901(4). The purpose of the unanimity requirement is to protect a limited partner from exposure to personal liability as a general partner without clear and knowing consent at the time of conversion. Despite a general voting provision to the contrary in the partnership agreement, conversion to a general partnership may never have been contemplated by the limited partner when the partnership investment was made.

Subsection (c) provides that, after approval of the conversion, the converted partnership must cancel its certificate of limited partnership. *See* RULPA § 203.

Subsection (d) provides that the conversion takes effect when the certificate of limited partnership is canceled.

Subsection (e) provides that a limited partner who becomes a general partner is liable as a general partner for all partnership obligations for which a general partner would otherwise be personally liable for if incurred after the effective date of the conversion, but still has only limited liability for obligations incurred before the conversion.

Section 904. Effect of Conversion; Entity Unchanged.

(a) A partnership or limited partnership that has been converted pursuant to this [article] is for all purposes the same entity that existed before the conversion.

(b) When a conversion takes effect:

(1) all property owned by the converting partnership or limited partnership remains vested in the converted entity;

(2) all obligations of the converting partnership or limited partnership continue as obligations of the converted entity; and

(3) an action or proceeding pending against the converting partnership or limited partnership may be continued as if the conversion had not occurred.

Comment

Section 904 sets forth the effect of a conversion on the partnership. Subsection (a) provides that the converted partnership is for all purposes the same entity as before the conversion.

Subsection (b) provides that upon conversion: (1) all partnership property remains vested in the converted entity; (2) all obligations remain the obligations of the converted entity; and (3) all pending legal actions may be continued as if the conversion had not occurred. The term "entity" as used in Article 9 refers to either or both general and limited partnerships as the context requires.

Under subsection (b)(1), title to partnership property remains vested in the converted partnership. As a matter of general property law, title remains vested without further act or deed and without reversion or impairment.

Section 905. Merger of Partnerships.

(a) Pursuant to a plan of merger approved as provided in subsection (c), a partnership may be merged with one or more partnerships or limited partnerships.

(b) The plan of merger must set forth:

(1) the name of each partnership or limited partnership that is a party to the merger;

(2) the name of the surviving entity into which the other partnerships or limited partnerships will merge;

(3) whether the surviving entity is a partnership or a limited partnership and the status of each partner;

(4) the terms and conditions of the merger;

(5) the manner and basis of converting the interests of each party to the merger into interests or obligations of the surviving entity, or into money or other property in whole or part; and

(6) the street address of the surviving entity's chief executive office.

(c) The plan of merger must be approved:

(1) in the case of a partnership that is a party to the merger, by all of the partners, or a number or percentage specified for merger in the partnership agreement; and

(2) in the case of a limited partnership that is a party to the merger, by the vote required for approval of a merger by the law of the State or foreign jurisdiction in which the limited partnership is organized and, in the absence of such a specifically applicable law, by all of the partners, notwithstanding a provision to the contrary in the partnership agreement.

(d) After a plan of merger is approved and before the merger takes effect, the plan may be amended or abandoned as provided in the plan.

(e) The merger takes effect on the later of:

(1) the approval of the plan of merger by all parties to the merger, as provided in subsection (c);

(2) the filing of all documents required by law to be filed as a condition to the effectiveness of the merger; or

(3) any effective date specified in the plan of merger.

Comment

Section 905 provides a "safe harbor" for the merger of a general partnership and one or more general or limited partnerships. The surviving entity may be either a general or a limited partnership.

The plan of merger must set forth the information required by subsection (b), including the status of each partner and the manner and basis of converting the interests of each party to the merger into interests or obligations of the surviving entity.

Subsection (c) provides that the plan of merger must be approved: (1) by all the partners of each general partnership that is a party to the merger, unless its partnership agreement specifically provides otherwise for mergers; and (2) by all the partners, including both general and limited partners, of each limited partnership that is a party to the merger, notwithstanding a contrary provision in its partnership agreement, unless specifically authorized by the law of the jurisdiction in which that limited partnership is organized. Like Section 903(b), the purpose of the unanimity requirement is to protect limited partners from exposure to liability as general partners without their clear and knowing consent.

Subsection (d) provides that the plan of merger may be amended or abandoned at any time before the merger takes effect, if the plan so provides.

Subsection (e) provides that the merger takes effect on the later of: (1) approval by all parties to the merger; (2) filing of all required documents; or (3) the effective date specified in the plan. The surviving entity must file all notices and documents relating to the merger required by other applicable statutes governing the entities that are parties to the merger, such as articles of merger or a certificate of limited partnership. It may also amend or cancel a statement of partnership authority previously filed by any party to the merger.

Section 906. Effect of Merger.

(a) When a merger takes effect:

(1) the separate existence of every partnership or limited partnership that is a party to the merger, other than the surviving entity, ceases;

(2) all property owned by each of the merged partnerships or limited partnerships vests in the surviving entity;

(3) all obligations of every partnership or limited partnership that is a party to the merger become the obligations of the surviving entity; and

(4) an action or proceeding pending against a partnership or limited partnership that is a party to the merger may be continued as if the merger had not occurred, or the surviving entity may be substituted as a party to the action or proceeding.

(b) The [Secretary of State] of this State is the agent for service of process in an action or proceeding against a surviving foreign partnership or limited partnership to enforce an obligation of a domestic partnership or limited partnership that is a party to a merger. The surviving entity shall promptly notify the [Secretary of State] of the mailing address of its chief executive office and of any change of address. Upon receipt of process, the [Secretary of State] shall mail a copy of the process to the surviving foreign partnership or limited partnership.

(c) A partner of the surviving partnership or limited partnership is liable for:

(1) all obligations of a party to the merger for which the partner was personally liable before the merger;

(2) all other obligations of the surviving entity incurred before the merger by a party to the merger, but those obligations may be satisfied only out of property of the entity; and

(3) except as otherwise provided in Section 306, all obligations of the surviving entity incurred after the merger takes effect, but those obligations may be satisfied only out of property of the entity if the partner is a limited partner.

(d) If the obligations incurred before the merger by a party to the merger are not satisfied out of the property of the surviving partnership or limited partnership, the general partners of that party immediately before the effective date of the merger shall contribute the amount necessary to satisfy that party's obligations to the surviving entity, in the manner provided in Section 807 or in the [Limited Partnership Act] of the jurisdiction in which the party was formed, as the case may be, as if the merged party were dissolved.

(e) A partner of a party to a merger who does not become a partner of the surviving partnership or limited partnership is dissociated from the entity, of which that partner was a partner, as of the date the merger takes effect. The surviving entity shall cause the partner's interest in the entity to be purchased under Section 701 or another statute specifically applicable to that partner's interest with respect to a merger. The surviving entity is bound under Section 702 by an act of a general partner dissociated under this subsection, and the partner is liable under Section 703 for transactions entered into by the surviving entity after the merger takes effect.

Comment

Section 906 states the effect of a merger on the partnerships that are parties to the merger and on the individual partners.

Subsection (a) provides that when the merger takes effect: (1) the separate existence of every partnership that is a party to the merger (other than the surviving entity) ceases; (2) all property owned by the parties to the merger vests in the surviving entity; (3) all obligations of every party to the merger become the obligations of the surviving entity; and (4) all legal actions pending against a party to the merger may be continued as if the merger had not occurred or the surviving entity may be substituted as a party. Title to partnership property vests in the surviving entity without further act or deed and without reversion or impairment.

Subsection (b) makes the secretary of state the agent for service of process in any action against the surviving entity, if it is a foreign entity, to enforce an obligation of a domestic partnership that is a party to the merger. The purpose of this rule is to make it more convenient for local creditors to sue a foreign surviving entity when the credit was extended to a domestic partnership that has disappeared as a result of the merger.

Subsection (c) provides that a general partner of the surviving entity is liable for (1) all obligations for which the partner was personally liable before the merger; (2) all other obligations of the surviving entity incurred before the merger by a party to the merger, which obligations may be satisfied only out of the surviving entity's partnership property; and (3) all obligations incurred by the surviving entity after the merger, limited to the surviving entity's property in the case of limited partners and also limited to obligations of the partnership for which the partner was personally liable under Section 306.

This scheme of liability is similar to that of an incoming partner under Section 306(b). Only the surviving partnership itself is liable for all obligations, including obligations incurred by every constituent party before the merger. A general partner of the surviving entity is personally liable for obligations of the surviving entity incurred before the merger by the partnership of which he was a partner and those incurred by the surviving entity after the merger. Thus, a general partner of the surviving entity is liable only to the extent of his partnership interest for obligations incurred before the merger by a constituent party of which he was not a general partner.

Subsection (d) requires general partners to contribute the amount necessary to satisfy all obligations for which they were personally liable before the merger, if such obligations are not satisfied out of the partnership property of the surviving entity, in the same manner as provided in Section 807 or the limited partnership act of the applicable jurisdiction, as if the merged party were then dissolved. See RULPA §§ 502, 608.

Subsection (e) provides for the dissociation of a partner of a party to the merger who does not become a partner in the surviving entity. The surviving entity must buy out that partner's interest in the partnership under Section 701 or other specifically applicable statute. If the state limited partnership act has a dissenter's rights provision providing a different method of determining the amount due a dissociating limited partner, it would apply, rather than Section 701, since the two statutes should be read in pari materia.

Although subsection (e) does not expressly provide that a partner's withdrawal upon the merger of a term partnership is rightful, it was assumed that the unanimity requirement for the approval of a merger would afford a withdrawing partner adequate opportunity to protect his interest as a condition of approval. This question is left to the partnership agreement if it provides for merger without the approval of all the partners.

Under subsection (e), a dissociating general partner's lingering agency power is wound down, pursuant to Section 702, the same as in any other dissociation. Moreover, a dissociating general partner may be liable, under Section 703, for obligations incurred by the surviving entity for up to two years after the merger. A dissociating general partner can, however, limit to 90 days his exposure to liability by filing a statement of dissociation under Section 704.

Section 907. Statement of Merger.

(a) After a merger, the surviving partnership or limited partnership may file a statement that one or more partnerships or limited partnerships have merged into the surviving entity.

(b) A statement of merger must contain:

(1) the name of each partnership or limited partnership that is a party to the merger;

(2) the name of the surviving entity into which the other partnerships or limited partnership were merged;

(3) the street address of the surviving entity's chief executive office and of an office in this State, if any; and

(4) whether the surviving entity is a partnership or a limited partnership.

(c) Except as otherwise provided in subsection (d), for the purposes of Section 302, property of the surviving partnership or limited partnership which before the merger was held in the name of another party to the merger is property held in the name of the surviving entity upon filing a statement of merger.

(d) For the purposes of Section 302 real property of the surviving partnership or limited partnership which before the merger was held in the name of another party to the merger is property held in the name of the surviving entity upon recording a certified copy of the statement of merger in the office for recording transfers of that real property.

(e) A filed and, if appropriate, recorded statement of merger, executed and declared to be accurate pursuant to Section 105(c), stating the name of a partnership or limited partnership that is a party to the merger in whose name property was held before the merger and the name of the surviving entity, but not containing all of the other information required by subsection (b), operates with respect to the partnerships or limited partnerships named to the extent provided in subsections (c) and (d).

Comment

Section 907(a) provides that the surviving entity may file a statement of merger. The execution, filing, and recording of the statement are governed by Section 105.

Subsection (b) requires the statement to contain the name of each party to the merger, the name and address of the surviving entity, and whether it is a general or limited partnership.

Subsection (c) provides that, for the purpose of the Section 302 rules regarding the transfer of partnership property, all personal and intangible property which before the merger was held in the name of a party to the merger becomes, upon the filing of the statement of merger with the secretary of state, property held in the name of the surviving entity.

Subsection (d) provides a similar rule for real property, except that real property does not become property held in the name of the surviving entity until a certified copy of the statement of merger is recorded in the office for recording transfers of that real property under local law.

Subsection (e) is a savings provision in the event a statement of merger fails to contain all of the information required by subsection (b). The statement will have the operative effect provided in subsections (c) and (d) if it is executed and declared to be accurate pursuant to Section 105(e) and correctly states the name of the party to the merger in whose name the property was held before the merger, so that it would be found by someone searching the record. Compare Section 303(c) (statement of partnership authority).

Section 908. Nonexclusive.

This [article] is not exclusive. Partnerships or limited partnerships may be converted or merged in any other manner provided by law.

Comment

Section 908 provides that Article 9 is not exclusive. It is merely a "safe harbor." Partnerships may be converted or merged in any other manner provided by statute or common law. Existing statutes in a few States already authorize the conversion or merger of general partnerships and limited partnerships. *See* Comment 1 to Section 901. Those procedures may be followed in lieu of Article 9.

[ARTICLE] 10
LIMITED LIABILITY PARTNERSHIP

Section 1001. Statement of Qualification.

(a) A partnership may become a limited liability partnership pursuant to this section.

(b) The terms and conditions on which a partnership becomes a limited liability partnership must be approved by the vote necessary to amend the partnership agreement except, in the case of a partnership agreement that expressly considers contribution obligations, the vote necessary to amend those provisions.

(c) After the approval required by subsection (b), a partnership may become a limited liability partnership by filing a statement of qualification. The statement must contain:

(1) the name of the partnership;

(2) the street address of the partnership's chief executive office and, if different, the street address of an office in this State, if any;

(3) if there is no office in this State, the name and street address of the partnership's agent for service of process who must be an individual resident of this State or any other person authorized to do business in this State;

(4) a statement that the partnership elects to be a limited liability partnership; and

(5) a deferred effective date, if any.

(d) The status of a partnership as a limited liability partnership is effective on the later of the filing of the statement or a date specified in the statement. The status remains effective, regardless of changes in the partnership, until it is canceled pursuant to Section 105(d) or revoked pursuant to Section 1003.

(e) The status of a partnership as a limited liability partnership and the liability of its partners is not affected by errors or later changes in the information required to be contained in the statement of qualification under subsection (c).

(f) The filing of a statement of qualification establishes that a partnership has satisfied all conditions precedent to the qualification of the partnership as a limited liability partnership.

(g) An amendment or cancellation of a statement of qualification is effective when it is filed or on a deferred effective date specified in the amendment or cancellation.

Comment

Any partnership may become a limited liability partnership by filing a statement of qualification. See Comments to Sections 101(6) and 202(b) regarding a limited partnership filing a statement of qualification to become a limited liability limited partnership. Section 1001 sets forth the required contents of a statement of qualification. The section also sets forth requirements for the approval of a statement of qualification, establishes the effective date of the filing (and any amendments) which remains effective until canceled or revoked, and provides that the liability of the partners of a limited liability partnership is not affected by errors or later changes in the statement information.

Subsection (b) provides that the terms and conditions on which a partnership becomes a limited liability partnership must generally be approved by the vote necessary to amend the partnership agreement. This means that the act of becoming a limited liability partnership is equivalent to an amendment of the partnership agreement. Where the partnership agreement is silent as to how it may be amended, the subsection (b) vote requires the approval of every partner. Since the limited liability partnership rules are not intended to increase the vote necessary to amend the partnership agreement, where the partnership agreement specifically sets forth an amendment process, that process may be used. Where a partnership agreement sets forth several amendment procedures depending upon the nature of the amendment, the required vote will be that necessary to amend the contribution obligations of the partners. The specific "contribution" vote is preferred because the filing of the statement directly affects partner contribution obligations. Therefore, the language "considers contribution" should be broadly interpreted to include any amendment vote that indirectly affects any partner's contribution obligation such as a partner's obligation to "indemnify" other partners.

The unanimous vote default rule reflects the significance of a partnership becoming a limited liability partnership. In general, upon such a filing each partner is released from the personal contribution obligation imposed under this Act in exchange for relinquishing the right to enforce the contribution obligations of other partners under this Act. See Comments to Sections 306(c) and 401(b). The wisdom of this bargain will depend on many factors including the relative risks of the partners' duties and the assets of the partnership.

Subsection (c) sets forth the information required in a statement of qualification. It must include the name of the partnership which must comply with Section 1002 to identify the partnership as a limited liability partnership. The statement must also include the address of the partnership's chief executive office and, if different, the street address of any other office in this State. A statement must include the name and street address of an agent for service of process only if it does not have any office in this State.

As with other statements, a statement of qualification must be filed in the office of the Secretary of State. *See* Sections 101(13) and 105(a). Accordingly, a statement of qualification is executed, filed, and otherwise regarded as a statement under this Act. For example, a copy of a filed statement must be sent to every nonfiling partner unless otherwise provided in the partnership agreement. *See* Sections 105(e) and 103(b)(1). A statement of qualification must be executed by at least two partners under penalties of perjury that the contents of the statement are accurate. *See* Section 105(c). A person who files the statement must promptly send a copy of the statement to every nonfiling partner but failure to send the copy does not limit the effectiveness of the filed statement to a nonpartner. Section 105(e). The filing must be accompanied by the fee required by the Secretary of State. Section 105(f).

Subsection (d) makes clear that once a statement is filed and effective, the status of the partnership as a limited liability partnership remains effective until the partnership status is either canceled or revoked "regardless of changes in the partnership." Accordingly, a partnership that dissolves but whose business is continued under a business continuation agreement retains its status as a limited liability partnership without the need to refile a new statement. Also, limited liability partnership status remains even though a partnership may be dissolved, wound up, and terminated. Even after the termination of the partnership, the former partners of a terminated partnership would not be personally liable for partnership obligations incurred while the partnership was a limited liability partnership.

Subsection (d) also makes clear that limited liability partnership status remains effective until actual cancellation under Section 1003 or revocation under Section 105(d). Ordinarily the terms and conditions of becoming a limited liability partnership must be approved by the vote necessary to amend the partnership agreement. *See* Sections 1001(b), 306(c), and 401(j). Since the statement of cancellation may be filed by a person authorized to file the original statement of qualification, the same vote necessary to approve the filing of the statement of qualification must be obtained to file the statement of cancellation. *See* Section 105(d).

Subsection (f) provides that once a statement of qualification is executed and filed under subsection (c) and Section 105, the partnership assumes the status of a limited liability partnership. This status is intended to be conclusive with regard to third parties dealing with the partnership. It is not intended to affect the rights of partners. For example, a properly executed and filed statement of qualification conclusively establishes the limited liability shield described in Section 306(c). If the partners executing and filing the statement exceed their authority, the internal abuse of authority has no effect on the liability shield with regard to third parties. Partners may challenge the abuse of authority for purposes of establishing the liability of the culpable partners but may not effect the liability shield as to third parties. Likewise, third parties may not challenge the existence of the liability shield because the decision to file the statement lacked the proper vote. As a result, the filing of the statement creates the liability shield even when the required subsection (b) vote is not obtained.

Section 1002. Name.

The name of a limited liability partnership must end with "Registered Limited Liability Partnership", "Limited Liability Partnership", "R.L.L.P.", "L.L.P.", "RLLP", or "LLP".

Comment

The name provisions are intended to alert persons dealing with a limited liability partnership of the presence of the liability shield. Because many jurisdictions have adopted the naming concept of a "registered" limited liability partnership, this aspect has been retained. These name requirements also distinguish limited partnerships and general partnerships that become limited liability partnerships because the new name must be at the end of and in addition to the general or limited partnership's regular name. *See* Comments to Section 101(6). Since the name identification rules of this section do not alter the regular name of the partnership, they do not disturb historic notions of apparent authority of partners in both general and limited partnerships.

Section 1003. Annual Report.

(a) A limited liability partnership, and a foreign limited liability partnership authorized to transact business in this State, shall file an annual report in the office of the [Secretary of State] which contains:

(1) the name of the limited liability partnership and the State or other jurisdiction under whose laws the foreign limited liability partnership is formed;

(2) the current street address of the partnership's chief executive office and, if different, the current street address of an office in this State, if any; and

(3) if there is no current office in this State, the name and street address of the partnership's current agent for service of process who must be an individual resident of this State or any other person authorized to do business in this State.

(b) An annual report must be filed between [January 1 and April 1] of each year following the calendar year in which a partnership files a statement of qualification or a foreign partnership becomes authorized to transact business in this State.

(c) The [Secretary of State] may administratively revoke the statement of qualification of a partnership that fails to file an annual report when due or to pay the required filing fee. The [Secretary of State] shall provide the partnership at least 60 days' written notice of intent to revoke the statement. The notice must be mailed to the partnership at its chief executive office set forth in the last filed statement of qualification or annual report. The notice must specify the annual report that has not been filed, the fee that has not been paid, and the effective date of the revocation. The revocation is not effective if the annual report is filed and the fee is paid before the effective date of the revocation.

(d) A revocation under subsection (c) only affects a partnership's status as a limited liability partnership and is not an event of dissolution of the partnership.

(e) A partnership whose statement of qualification has been administratively revoked may apply to the [Secretary of State] for reinstatement within two years after the effective date of the revocation. The application must state:

(1) the name of the partnership and the effective date of the revocation; and

(2) that the ground for revocation either did not exist or has been corrected.

(f) A reinstatement under subsection (e) relates back to and takes effect as of the effective date of the revocation, and the partnership's status as a limited liability partnership continues as if the revocation had never occurred.

Comment

Section 1003 sets forth the requirements of an annual report that must be filed by all limited liability partnerships and any foreign limited liability partnership authorized to transact business in this State. *See* Sections 101(5) (definition of a limited liability partnership) and 101(4) (definition of a foreign limited liability partnership). The failure of a limited liability partnership to file an annual report is a basis for the Secretary of State to administratively revoke its statement of qualification. *See* Section 1003(c). A foreign limited liability partnership that fails to file an annual report may not maintain an action or proceeding in this State. *See* Section 1103(a).

Subsection (a) generally requires that an annual report contain the same information required in a statement of qualification. Compare Sections 1001(a) and 1003(a). The differences are that the annual report requires disclosure of the state of formation of a foreign limited liability partnership but deletes the delayed effective date and limited liability partnership election statement provisions of a statement of qualification. As such, the annual report serves to update the information required in a statement of qualification. Under subsection (b), the annual report must be filed between January 1 and April 1 of each calendar year following the year in which a statement of qualification was filed or a foreign limited liability partnership becomes authorized to transact business. This timing requirement means that a limited liability partnership must make an annual filing and may not prefile multiple annual reports in a single year.

Subsection (c) sets forth the procedure for the Secretary of State to administratively revoke a partnership's statement of qualification for the failure to file an annual report when due or pay the required filing fee. The Secretary of State must provide a partnership at least 60 days' written notice of the intent to revoke the statement. The notice must be mailed to the partnership at the address of its chief executive office set forth in the last filed statement or annual report and must state the grounds for revocation as well as the effective date of revocation. The revocation is not effective if the stated problem is cured before the stated effective date.

Under subsection (d), a revocation only terminates the partnership's status as a limited liability partnership but is not an event of dissolution of the partnership itself. Where revocation occurs, a partnership may apply for reinstatement under subsection (e) within two years after the effective date of the revocation. The application must state that the grounds for revocation either did not exist or have been corrected. The Secretary of State may grant the application on the basis of the statements alone or require proof of correction. Under subsection (f), when the application is granted, the reinstatement relates back to and takes effect as of the effective date of the revocation. The relation back doctrine prevents gaps in a reinstated partner's liability shield. *See* Comments to Section 306(c).

[ARTICLE] 11
FOREIGN LIMITED LIABILITY PARTNERSHIP

Section   1101. Law Governing Foreign Limited Liability Partnership.

Section   1102. Statement of Foreign Qualification.

Section   1103. Effect of Failure to Qualify.

Section   1104. Activities Not Constituting Transacting Business.

Section   1105. Acton by [Attorney General].

Section 1101. Law Governing Foreign Limited Liability Partnership.

(a) The laws under which a foreign limited liability partnership is formed govern relations among the partners and between the partners and the partnership and the liability of partners for obligations of the partnership.

(b) A foreign limited liability partnership may not be denied a statement of foreign qualification by reason of any difference between the laws under which the partnership was formed and the laws of this State.

(c) A statement of foreign qualification does not authorize a foreign limited liability partnership to engage in any business or exercise any power that a partnership may not engage in or exercise in this State as a limited liability partnership.

Comment

Section 1101 provides that the laws where a foreign limited liability partnership is formed rather than the laws of this State govern both the internal relations of the partnership and liability of its partners for the obligations of the partnership. *See* Section 101(4) (definition of a foreign limited liability partnership). Section 106(b) provides that the laws of this State govern the internal relations of a domestic limited liability partnership and the liability of its partners for the obligations of the partnership. *See* Section 101(5) (definition of a domestic limited liability partnership). A partnership may therefore choose the laws of a particular jurisdiction by filing a statement of qualification in that jurisdiction. But there are limitations on this choice.

Subsections (b) and (c) together make clear that although a foreign limited liability partnership may not be denied a statement of foreign qualification simply because of a difference between the laws of its foreign jurisdiction and the laws of this State, it may not engage in any business or exercise any power in this State that a domestic limited liability partnership may not engage in or exercise. Under subsection (e), a foreign limited liability partnership that engages in a business or exercises a power in this State that a domestic may not engage in or exercise, does so only as an ordinary partnership without the benefit of the limited liability partnership liability shield set forth in Section 306(c). In this sense, a foreign limited liability partnership is treated the same as a domestic limited liability partnership. Also, the Attorney General may maintain an action to restrain a foreign limited liability partnership from transacting an unauthorized business in this State. *See* Section 1105.

Section 1102. Statement of Foreign Qualification.

(a) Before transacting business in this State, a foreign limited liability partnership must file a statement of foreign qualification. The statement must contain:

(1) the name of the foreign limited liability partnership which satisfies the requirements of the State or other jurisdiction under whose laws it is formed and ends with "Registered Limited Liability Partnership", "Limited Liability Partnership", "R.L.L.P.", "L.L.P.", "RLLP", or "LLP";

(2) the street address of the partnership's chief executive office and, if different, the street address of an office in this State, if any;

(3) if there is no office in this State, the name and street address of the partnership's agent for service of process who must be an individual resident of this State or any other person authorized to do business in this State; and

(4) a deferred effective date, if any.

(b) The agent of a foreign limited liability partnership for service of process must be an individual who is a resident of this State or other person authorized to do business in this State.

(c) The status of a partnership as a foreign limited liability partnership is effective on the later of the filing of the statement of foreign qualification or a date specified in the statement. The status remains effective, regardless of changes in the partnership, until it is canceled pursuant to Section 105(d) or revoked pursuant to Section 1003.

(d) An amendment or cancellation of a statement of foreign qualification is effective when it is filed or on a deferred effective date specified in the amendment or cancellation.

Comment

Section 1102 provides that a foreign limited liability partnership must file a statement of foreign qualification before transacting business in this State. The section also sets forth the information required in the statement. As with other statements, a statement of foreign qualification must be filed in the office of the Secretary of State. *See* Sections 101(13), 105(a), and 1001(c). Accordingly, a statement of foreign qualification is executed, filed, and otherwise regarded as a statement under this Act. *See* Section 101(13) (definition of a statement includes a statement of foreign qualification).

Subsection (a) generally requires the same information in a statement of foreign qualification as is required in a statement of qualification. The statement of foreign qualification must include a name that complies with the requirements for domestic limited liability partnership under Section 1002 and must include the address of the partnership's chief executive office and, if different, the street address of any other office in this State. If a foreign limited liability partnership does not have any office in this State, the statement of foreign qualification must include the name and street address of an agent for service of process.

As with a statement of qualification, a statement of foreign qualification (and amendments) is effective when filed or at a later specified filing date. Compare Sections 1102(b) and (c) with Sections 1001(e) and (h). Likewise, a statement of foreign qualification remains effective until canceled by the partnership or revoked by the Secretary of State, regardless of changes in the partnership. See Section 105(d) (statement cancellation) and Section 1003 (revocation for failure to file annual report or pay annual filing fee) and compare Sections 1102(b) and 1001(e). Statement of qualification provisions regarding the relationship or the status of a foreign partnership relative to its initial filing of a statement are governed by foreign law and are therefore omitted from this section. *See* Sections 1001(f) (effect of errors and omissions) and (g) (filing establishes all conditions precedent to qualification).

Section 1103. Effect of Failure to Qualify.

(a) A foreign limited liability partnership transacting business in this State may not maintain an action or proceeding in this State unless it has in effect a statement of foreign qualification.

(b) The failure of a foreign limited liability partnership to have in effect a statement of foreign qualification does not impair the validity of a contract or act of the foreign limited liability partnership or preclude it from defending an action or proceeding in this State.

(c) Limitations on personal liability of partners are not waived solely by transacting business in this State without a statement of foreign qualification.

(d) If a foreign limited liability partnership transacts business in this State without a statement of foreign qualification, the [Secretary of State] is its agent for service of process with respect to [claims for relief] arising out of the transaction of business in this State.

Comment

Section 1103 makes clear that the only consequence of a failure to file a statement of foreign qualification is that the foreign limited liability partnership will not be able to maintain an action or proceeding in this State. The partnership's contracts remain valid, it may defend an action or proceeding, personal liability of the partners is not waived, and the Secretary of State is the agent for service of process with respect to claims arising out of transacting business in this State. Sections 1103(b)-(d). Once a statement of foreign qualification is filed, the Secretary of State may revoke the statement for failure to file an annual report but the partnership has the right to cure the failure for two years. *See* Section 1003(c) and (e). Since the failure to file a statement of foreign qualification has no impact on the liability shield of the partners, a revocation of a statement of foreign qualification also has no impact on the liability shield created under foreign laws. Compare Sections 1103(c) and 1003(f) (revocation of the statement of qualification of a domestic limited liability partnership removes partner liability shield unless filing problems cured within two years).

Section 1104. Activities   Not   Constituting   Transacting Business.

(a) Activities of a foreign limited liability partnership which do not constitute transacting business within the meaning of this [article] include:

(1) maintaining, defending, or settling an action or proceeding;

(2) holding meetings of its partners or carrying on any other activity concerning its internal affairs;

(3) maintaining bank accounts;

(4) maintaining offices or agencies for the transfer, exchange, and registration of the partnership's own securities or maintaining trustees or depositories with respect to those securities;

(5) selling through independent contractors;

(6) soliciting or obtaining orders, whether by mail or through employees or agents or otherwise, if the orders require acceptance outside this State before they become contracts;

(7) creating or acquiring indebtedness, mortgages, or security interests in real or personal property;

(8) securing or collecting debts or foreclosing mortgages or other security interests in property securing the debts, and holding, protecting, and maintaining property so acquired;

(9) conducting an isolated transaction that is completed within 30 days and is not one in the course of similar transactions of like nature; and

(10) transacting business in interstate commerce.

(b) For purposes of this [article], the ownership in this State of income-producing real property or tangible personal property, other than property excluded under subsection (a), constitutes transacting business in this State.

(c) This section does not apply in determining the contacts or activities that may subject a foreign limited liability partnership to service of process, taxation, or regulation under any other law of this State.

Comment

Because the Attorney General may restrain a foreign limited liability partnership from transacting an unauthorized business in this State and a foreign partnership may not maintain an action or proceeding in this State, the concept of "transacting business" in this State is important. To provide more certainty, subsection (a) sets forth ten separate categories of activities that do not constitute transacting business. Subsection (c) makes clear that the section only considers the definition of "transacting business" and has no impact on whether a foreign limited liability partnership's activities in this State subject it to service of process, taxation, or regulation under any other law of this State.

Section 1105. Action by [Attorney General].

The [Attorney General] may maintain an action to restrain a foreign limited liability partnership from transacting business in this State in violation of this [article].

Comment

Section 1105 makes clear that the Attorney General may restrain a foreign limited liability partnership from transacting an unauthorized business in this State. As a threshold matter, a foreign limited liability partnership must be "transacting business" in this State within the meaning of Section 1104. Secondly, the business transacted in this State must be that which could not be engaged in by a domestic limited liability partnership. *See* Section 1101(c). The fact that a foreign limited liability partnership has a statement of foreign qualification does not permit it to engage in any unauthorized business in this State or impair the power of the Attorney General to restrain the foreign partnership from engaging in the unauthorized business. *See* Section 1101(c).

[ARTICLE] 12
MISCELLANEOUS PROVISIONS

Section 1201. Uniformity of Application and Construction.

This [Act] shall be applied and construed to effectuate its general purpose to make uniform the law with respect to the subject of this [Act] among States enacting it.

Section 1202. Short Title.

This [Act] may be cited as the Uniform Partnership Act (1997).

Section 1203. Severability Clause.

If any provision of this [Act] or its application to any person or circumstance is held invalid, the invalidity does not affect other provisions or applications of this [Act] which can be given effect without the invalid provision or application, and to this end the provisions of this [Act] are severable.

Section 1204. Effective Date.

This [Act] takes effect. . . .

Comment

The effective date of the Act established by an adopting State has operative effects under Section 1206, which defers mandatory application of the Act to existing partnerships.

Section 1205. Repeals.

Effective January 1, 199_____, the following acts and parts of acts are repeated: [the State Partnership Act as amended and in effect immediately before the effective date of this Act].

Comment

This section repeals the adopting State's present general partnership act. The effective date of the repealer should not be any earlier than the date selected by that State in Section 1206(b) for the application of the Act to all partnerships.

Section 1206. Applicability.

(a) Before January 1, 199_____, this [Act] governs only a partnership formed:

(1) after the effective date of this [Act], unless that partnership is continuing the business of a dissolved partnership under [Section 41 of the prior Uniform Partnership Act]; and

(2) before the effective date of this [Act], that elects, as provided by subsection (c), to be governed by this [Act].

(b) On or after January 1, 199_____, this [Act] governs all partnerships.

(c) Before January 1, 199_____, a partnership voluntarily may elect, in the manner provided in its partnership agreement or by law for amending the partnership agreement, to be governed by this [Act]. The provisions of this [Act] relating to the liability of the partnership's partners to third parties apply to limit those partners' liability to a third party who had done business with the partnership within one year preceding the partnership's election to be governed by this [Act], only if the third party knows or has received a notification of the partnership's election to be governed by this [Act].

Comment

This section provides for a transition period in the applicability of the Act to existing partnerships, similar to that provided in the revised Texas partnership act. *See* Tex. Rev. Civ. Stat. Ann. art. 6132b-10.03 (Vernon Supp. 1994). Subsection (a) makes application of the Act mandatory for all partnerships formed after the effective date of the Act and permissive, by election, for existing partnerships. That affords existing partnerships and partners an opportunity to consider the changes effected by RUPA and to amend their partnership agreements, if appropriate.

Under subsection (b), application of the Act becomes mandatory for all partnerships, including existing partnerships that did not previously elect to be governed by it, upon a future date to be established by the adopting State. Texas, for example, deferred for five years mandatory compliance by existing partnerships.

Subsection (c) provides that an existing partnership may voluntarily elect to be governed by RUPA in the manner provided for amending its partnership agreement. Under UPA Section 18(h), that requires the consent of all the partners, unless otherwise agreed. Third parties doing business with the partnership must know or be notified of the election before RUPA's rules limiting a partner's liability become effective as to them. Those rules would include, for example, the provisions of Section 704 limiting the liability of a partner 90 days after the filing of a statement of dissociation. Without knowledge of the partnership's election, third parties would not be aware that they must check the record to ascertain the extent of a dissociated partner's personal liability.

Section 1207. Savings Clause.

This [Act] does not affect an action or proceeding commenced or right accrued before this [Act] takes effect.

Comment

This section continues the prior law after the effective date of the Act with respect to a pending action or proceeding or a right accrued at the time of the effective date. Since courts generally apply the law that exists at the time an action is commenced, in many circumstances the new law of this Act would displace the old law, but for this section.

Almost all States have general savings statutes, usually as part of their statutory construction acts. These are often very broad. Compare Uniform Statute and Rule Construction Act § 16(a) (narrow savings clause). As RUPA is remedial, the more limited savings provisions in Section 1207 are more appropriate than the broad savings provisions of the usual general savings clause. *See generally*, Comment to Uniform Statute and Rule Construction Act § 16.

Pending "action" refers to a judicial proceeding, while "proceeding" is broader and includes administrative proceedings. Although it is not always clear whether a right has "accrued," the term generally means that a cause of action has matured and is ripe for legal redress. *See, e.g., Estate of Hoover v. Iowa Dept. of Social Services,* 299 Iowa 702, 251 N.W.2d 529 (1977); *Nielsen v. State of Wisconsin,* 258 Wis. 1110, 141 N.W.2d 194 (1966). An inchoate right is not enough, and thus, for example, there is no accrued right under a contract until it is breached.

Section 1208. Effective Date.

These [Amendments] take effect. . . .

Section 1209. Repeals.

Effective January 1, 199_____, the following acts and parts of acts are repealed: [the Limited Liability Partnership amendments to the State Partnership Act as amended and in effect immediately before the effective date of these [Amendments]].

Section 1210. Applicability.

(a) Before January 1, 199_____, these [Amendments] govern only a limited liability partnership formed:

(1) on or after the effective date of these [Amendments], unless that partnership is continuing the business of a dissolved limited liability partnership; and

(2) before the effective date of these [Amendments], that elects, as provided by subsection (c), to be governed by these [Amendments].

(b) On and after January 1, 199_____, these [Amendments] govern all partnerships.

(c) Before January 1, 199_____, a partnership voluntarily may elect, in the manner provided in its partnership agreement or by law for amending the partnership agreement, to be governed by these [Amendments]. The provisions of these [Amendments] relating to the liability of the partnership's partners to third parties apply to limit those partners' liability to a third party who had done business with the partnership within one year preceding the partnership's election to be governed by these [Amendments], only if the third party knows or has received a notification of the partnership's election to be governed by these [Amendments].

(d) The existing provisions for execution and filing a statement of qualification of a limited liability partnership continue until either the limited liability partnership elects to have this [Act] apply or January 1, 199_____.

Section 1211. Savings Clause.

These [Amendments] do not affect an action or proceeding commenced or right accrued before these [Amendments] take effect.

PART TWO
LIMITED PARTNERSHIP

UNIFORM LIMITED PARTNERSHIP ACT (1916)[*]

Editor's note: The text and Official Comments of the Uniform Limited Partnership Act (1916) ("ULPA") are taken from volume 6A of Uniform Laws Annotated (1995) and reproduced by permission. All of the Official Comments to ULPA are reproduced below.

The reader should be alert to the fact that all jurisdictions other than Louisiana have now adopted the Revised Uniform Limited Partnership Act ("RULPA"). The effect on ULPA of the adoption of RULPA varies from state to state. In Colorado, for example, ULPA remains in effect for limited partnerships formed prior to the effective date of RULPA, unless the general partner or partners of the firm elect to be governed by RULPA and file evidence of that election. Other states have repealed ULPA upon adoption of RULPA. For information about particular states, see the section entitled Action in Adopting Jurisdictions immediately following § 1104 of RULPA in 6A U.L.A. (1995).

―――――

ULPA was approved by the National Conference of Commissioners on Uniform State Laws on August 28, 1916, and adopted at one time in all states except Louisiana. At the present time it is still governing law in the following jurisdictions: Colorado, Georgia, Minnesota, New York, and Oklahoma. All of these jurisdictions have adopted RULPA, with ULPA applying only to limited partnerships formed prior to the enactment of RULPA.

§ 1. Limited Partnership Defined

A limited partnership is a partnership formed by two or more persons under the provisions of Section 2, having as members one or more general partners and one or more limited partners. The limited partners as such shall not be bound by the obligations of the partnership.

Official Comment

The business reason for the adoption of acts making provisions for limited or special partners is that men in business often desire to secure capital from others. There are at least three classes of contracts which can be made with those from whom the capital is secured: One, the ordinary loan on interest; another, the loan where the lender, in lieu of interest, takes a share in the profits of the business; third, those cases in which the person advancing the capital secures, besides a share in the profits, some measure of control over the business.

At first, in the absence of statutes the courts, both in this country and in England, assumed that one who is interested in a business is bound by its obligations, carrying the application of this principle so far, that a contract where the only evidence of interest was a share in the profits made one who supposed himself a lender, and who was probably unknown to the creditors at the times they extended their credits, unlimitedly liable as a partner for the obligations of those actually conducting the business.

Later decisions have much modified the earlier cases. The lender who takes a share in the profits, except possibly in one or two of our jurisdictions, does not by reason of that fact run a risk of being held as a partner. If, however, his contract falls within the third class mentioned, and he has any measure of control over the business, he at once runs serious risk of being held liable for the debts of the business as a partner; the risk increasing as he increases the amount of his control.

The first Limited Partnership Act was adopted by New York in 1822; the other commercial states, during the ensuing 30 years, following her example. Most of the statutes follow the language of the New York statute with little material alteration. These statutes were adopted, and to a considerable degree interpreted by the courts, during that period when it was generally held that any interest in a business should make the person holding the interest liable for its obligations. As a result the courts usually assume in the interpretation of these statutes two principles as fundamental.

First: That a limited (or as he is also called a special) partner is a partner in all respects like any other partner, except that to obtain the privilege of a limitation on his liability, he has conformed to the statutory requirements in respect to filing a certificate and refraining from participation in the conduct of the business.

Second: The limited partner, on any failure to follow the requirements in regard to the certificate or any participation in the conduct of his business, loses his privilege of limited liability and becomes, as far as those dealing with the business are concerned, in all respects a partner.

The courts in thus interpreting the statutes, although they made an American partnership with limited members something very different from the French Societe en Commandite from which the idea of the original statutes was derived, unquestionably carried out the intent of those responsible for their adoption. This is shown by the very wording of the statutes themselves. For instance, all the statutes require that all partners, limited and general, shall sign the certificate, and nearly all state that: "If any false statement be made in such certificate all the persons interested in such partnership shall be liable for all the engagements thereof as general partners."

The practical result of the spirit shown in the language and in the interpretation of existing statutes, coupled with the fact that a man may now lend money to a partnership and take a share in the profits in lieu of interest without running serious danger of becoming bound for partnership obligations, has, to a very great extent, deprived the existing statutory provisions for limited partners of any practical usefulness. Indeed, apparently their use is largely confined to associations in which those who conduct the business have not more than one limited partner.

One of the causes forcing business into the corporate form, in spite of the fact that the corporate form is ill suited to many business conditions, is the failure of the existing limited partnership acts to meet the desire of the owners of a business to secure necessary capital under the existing limited partnership form of business association.

The draft herewith submitted proceeds on the following assumptions:

First: No public policy requires a person who contributes to the capital of a business, acquires an interest in the profits, and some degree of control over the conduct of the business, to become bound for the obligations of the business; provided creditors have no reason to believe at the times their credits were extended that such person was so bound.

Second: That persons in business should be able, while remaining themselves liable without limit for the obligations contracted in its conduct, to associate with themselves others who contribute to the capital and acquire rights of ownership, provided that such contributors do not compete with creditors for the assets of the partnership.

The attempt to carry out these ideas has led to the incorporation into the draft submitted of certain features, not found in, or differing from, existing limited partnership acts.

First: In the draft the person who contributes the capital, though in accordance with custom called a limited partner, is not in any sense a partner. He is, however, a member of the association (see Sec. 1.).

Second: As limited partners are not partners securing limited liability by filing a certificate, the association is formed when substantial compliance, in good faith, is had with the requirements for a certificate (Sec. 2(2)). This provision eliminates the difficulties which arise from the recognition of de facto associations, made necessary by the assumption that the association is not formed unless a strict compliance with the requirements of the act is had.

Third: The limited partner not being in any sense a principal in the business, failure to comply with the requirements of the act in respect to the certificate, while it may result in the nonformation of the association, does not make him a partner or liable as such. The exact nature of his liability in such cases is set forth in Sec. 11.

Fourth: The limited partner, while not as such in any sense a partner, may become a partner as any person not a member of the association may become a partner; and, becoming a partner, may nevertheless retain his rights as limited partner; this last provision enabling the entire capital embraced in the business to be divided between the limited partners, all the general partners being also limited partners (Sec. 12).

Fifth: The limited partner is not debarred from loaning money or transacting other business with the partnership as any other non-member; provided he does not, in respect to such transactions, accept from the partnership collateral security, or receive from any partner or the partnership any payment, conveyance, or release from liability, if at the time the assets of the partnership are not sufficient to discharge its obligations to persons not general or limited partners. (Sec. 13).

Sixth: The substitution of a person as limited partner in place of an existing limited partner, or the withdrawal of a limited partner, or the addition of new limited partners, does not necessarily dissolve the association (Secs. 8, 16(2b)); no limited partner, however, can withdraw his contribution until all liabilities to creditors are paid (Sec. 16(1a)).

Seventh: As limited partners are not principals in transactions of the partnership, their liability, except for known false statements in the certificate (Sec. 6), is to the partnership, not to creditors of the partnership (Sec. 17). The general partners cannot, however, waive any liability of the limited partners to the prejudice of such creditors (Sec. 17(3)).

§ 2. Formation

(1) Two or more persons desiring to form a limited partnership shall

(a) Sign and swear to a certificate, which shall state

[I.] The name of the partnership,

[II.] The character of the business,

[III.] The location of the principal place of business,

[IV.] The name and place of residence of each member; general and limited partners being respectively designated,

[V.] The term for which the partnership is to exist,

[VI.] The amount of cash and a description of and the agreed value of the other property contributed by each limited partner,

[VII.] The additional contributions, if any, agreed to be made by each limited partner and the times at which or events on the happening of which they shall be made,

[VIII.] The time, if agreed upon, when the contribution of each limited partner is to be returned,

[IX.] The share of the profits or the other compensation by way of income which each limited partner shall receive by reason of his contribution,

[X.] The right, if given, of a limited partner to substitute an assignee as contributor in his place, and the terms and conditions of the substitution,

[XI.] The right, if given, of the partners to admit additional limited partners,

[XII.] The right, if given, of one or more of the limited partners to priority over other limited partners, as to contributions or as to compensation by way of income, and the nature of such priority,

[XIII.] The right, if given, of the remaining general partner or partners to continue the business on the death, retirement or insanity of a general partner, and

[XIV.] The right, if given, of a limited partner to demand and receive property other than cash in return for his contribution.

(b) File for record the certificate in the office of [here designate the proper office].

(2) A limited partnership is formed if there has been substantial compliance in good faith with the requirements of paragraph (1).

§ 3. Business Which May Be Carried On

A limited partnership may carry on any business which a partnership without limited partners may carry on, except [here designate the business to be prohibited].

§ 4. Character of Limited Partner's Contribution

The contributions of a limited partner may be cash or other property, but not services.

§ 5. A Name Not to Contain Surname of Limited Partner; Exceptions

(1) The surname of a limited partner shall not appear in the partnership name, unless

(a) It is also the surname of a general partner, or

(b) Prior to the time when the limited partner became such the business had been carried on under a name in which his surname appeared.

(2) A limited partner whose name appears in a partnership name contrary to the provisions of paragraph (1) is liable as a general partner to partnership creditors who extend credit to the partnership without actual knowledge that he is not a general partner.

§ 6. Liability for False Statements in Certificate

If the certificate contains a false statement, one who suffers loss by reliance on such statement may hold liable any party to the certificate who knew the statement to be false.

(a) At the time he signed the certificate, or

(b) Subsequently, but within a sufficient time before the statement was relied upon to enable him to cancel or amend the certificate, or to file a petition for its cancellation or amendment as provided in Section 25(3).

§ 7. Limited Partner Not Liable to Creditors

A limited partner shall not become liable as a general partner unless, in addition to the exercise of his rights and powers as a limited partner, he takes part in the control of the business.

§ 8. Admission of Additional Limited Partners

After the formation of a limited partnership, additional limited partners may be admitted upon filing an amendment to the original certificate in accordance with the requirements of Section 25.

§ 9. Rights, Powers and Liabilities of a General Partner

(1) A general partner shall have all the rights and powers and be subject to all the restrictions and liabilities of a partner in a partnership without limited partners, except that without the written consent or ratification of the specific act by all the limited partners, a general partner or all of the general partners have no authority to

(a) Do any act in contravention of the certificate,

(b) Do any act which would make it impossible to carry on the ordinary business of the partnership,

(c) Confess a judgment against the partnership,

(d) Possess partnership property, or assign their rights in specific partnership property, for other than a partnership purpose,

(e) Admit a person as a general partner,

(f) Admit a person as a limited partner, unless the right so to do is given in the certificate,

(g) Continue the business with partnership property on the death, retirement or insanity of a general partner, unless the right so to do is given in the certificate.

§ 10. Rights of a Limited Partner

(1) A limited partner shall have the same rights as a general partner to

(a) Have the partnership books kept at the principal place of business of the partnership, and at all times to inspect and copy any of them.

(b) Have on demand true and full information of all things affecting the partnership, and a formal account of partnership affairs whenever circumstances render it just and reasonable, and

(c) Have dissolution and winding up by decree of court.

(2) A limited partner shall have the right to receive a share of the profits or other compensation by way of income, and to the return of his contribution as provided in Sections 15 and 16.

§ 11. Status of Person Erroneously Believing Himself a Limited Partner

A person who has contributed to the capital of a business conducted by a person or partnership erroneously believing that he has become a limited partner in a limited partnership, is not, by reason of his exercise of the rights of a limited partner, a general partner with the person or in the partnership carrying on the business, or bound by the obligations of such person or partnership; provided that on ascertaining the mistake he promptly renounces his interest in the profits of the business, or other compensation by way of income.

§ 12. One Person Both General and Limited Partner

(1) A person may be a general partner and a limited partner in the same partnership at the same time.

(2) A person who is a general, and also at the same time a limited partner, shall have all the rights and powers and be subject to all the restrictions of a general partner; except that, in respect to his contribution, he shall have the rights against the other members which he would have had if he were not also a general partner.

§ 13. Loans and Other Business Transactions with Limited Partner

(1) A limited partner also may loan money to and transact other business with the partnership, and, unless he is also a general partner, receive on account of resulting claims against the partnership, with general creditors, a pro rata share of the assets. No limited partner shall in respect to any such claim

(a) Receive or hold as collateral security any partnership property, or

(b) Receive from a general partner or the partnership any payment, conveyance, or release from liability, if at the time the assets of the partnership are not sufficient to discharge partnership liabilities to persons not claiming as general or limited partners,

(2) The receiving of collateral security, or a payment, conveyance, or release in violation of the provisions of paragraph (1) is a fraud on the creditors of the partnership.

§ 14. Relation of Limited Partners Inter Se

Where there are several limited partners the members may agree that one or more of the limited partners shall have a priority over other limited partners as to the return of their contributions, as to their compensation by way of income, or as to any other matter. If such an agreement is made it shall be stated in the certificate, and in the absence of such a statement all the limited partners shall stand upon equal footing.

§ 15. Compensation of Limited Partner

A limited partner may receive from the partnership the share of the profits or the compensation by way of income stipulated for in the certificate; provided, that after such payment is made, whether from the property of the partnership or that of a general partner, the partnership assets are in excess of all liabilities of the partnership except liabilities to limited partners on account of their contributions and to general partners.

§ 16. Withdrawal or Reduction of Limited Partner's Contribution

(1) A limited partner shall not receive from a general partner or out of partnership property any part of his contribution until

(a) All liabilities of the partnership, except liabilities to general partners and to limited partners on account of their contributions, have been paid or there remains property of the partnership sufficient to pay them,

(b) The consent of all members is had, unless the return of the contribution may be rightfully demanded under the provisions of paragraph (2), and

(c) The certificate is cancelled or so amended as to set forth the withdrawal or reduction.

(2) Subject to the provisions of paragraph (1) a limited partner may rightfully demand the return of his contribution

(a) On the dissolution of a partnership, or

(b) When the date specified in the certificate for its return has arrived, or

(c) After he has given six months' notice in writing to all other members, if no time is specified in the certificate either for the return of the contribution or for the dissolution of the partnership,

(3) In the absence of any statement in the certificate to the contrary or the consent of all members, a limited partner, irrespective of the nature

of his contribution, has only the right to demand and receive cash in return for his contribution.

(4) A limited partner may have the partnership dissolved and its affairs wound up when

(a) He rightfully but unsuccessfully demands the return of his contribution, or

(b) The other liabilities of the partnership have not been paid, or the partnership property is insufficient for their payment as required by paragraph (1a) and the limited partner would otherwise be entitled to the return of his contribution.

§ 17. Liability of Limited Partner to Partnership

(1) A limited partner is liable to the partnership

(a) For the difference between his contribution as actually made and that stated in the certificate as having been made, and

(b) For any unpaid contribution which he agreed in the certificate to make in the future at the time and on the conditions stated in the certificate.

(2) A limited partner holds as trustee for the partnership

(a) Specific property stated in the certificate as contributed by him, but which was not contributed or which has been wrongfully returned, and

(b) Money or other property wrongfully paid or conveyed to him on account of his contribution.

(3) The liabilities of a limited partner as set forth in this section can be waived or compromised only by the consent of all members; but a waiver or compromise shall not affect the right of a creditor of a partnership who extended credit or whose claim arose after the filing and before a cancellation or amendment of the certificate, to enforce such liabilities.

(4) When a contributor has rightfully received the return in whole or in part of the capital of his contribution, he is nevertheless liable to the partnership for any sum, not in excess of such return with interest, necessary to discharge its liabilities to all creditors who extended credit or whose claims arose before such return.

§ 18. Nature of Limited Partner's Interest in Partnership

A limited partner's interest in the partnership is personal property.

§ 19. Assignment of Limited Partner's Interest

(1) A limited partner's interest is assignable.

(2) A substituted limited partner is a person admitted to all the rights of a limited partner who has died or has assigned his interest in a partnership.

(3) An assignee, who does not become a substituted limited partner, has no right to require any information or account of the partnership transactions or to inspect the partnership books; he is only entitled to receive the share of the profits or other compensation by way of income, or the return of his contribution, to which his assignor would otherwise be entitled.

(4) An assignee shall have the right to become a substituted limited partner if all the members (except the assignor) consent thereto or if the assignor, being thereunto empowered by the certificate, gives the assignee that right.

(5) An assignee becomes a substituted limited partner when the certificate is appropriately amended in accordance with Section 25.

(6) The substituted limited partner has all the rights and powers, and is subject to all the restrictions and liabilities of his assignor, except those liabilities of which he was ignorant at the time he became a limited partner and which could not be ascertained from the certificate.

(7) The substitution of the assignee as a limited partner does not release the assignor from liability to the partnership under Sections 6 and 17.

§ 20. Effect of Retirement, Death or Insanity of a General Partner

The retirement, death or insanity of a general partner dissolves the partnership, unless the business is continued by the remaining general partners

(a) Under a right so to do stated in the certificate, or

(b) With the consent of all members.

§ 21. Death of Limited Partner

(1) On the death of a limited partner his executor or administrator shall have all the rights of a limited partner for the purpose of settling his estate, and such power as the deceased had to constitute his assignee a substituted limited partner.

(2) The estate of a deceased limited partner shall be liable for all his liabilities as a limited partner.

§ 22. Rights of Creditors of Limited Partner

(1) On due application to a court of competent jurisdiction by any judgment creditor of a limited partner, the court may charge the interest of the indebted limited partner with payment of the unsatisfied amount

of the judgment debt; and may appoint a receiver, and make all other orders, directions, and inquiries which the circumstances of the case may require.

(2) The interest may be redeemed with the separate property of any general partner, but may not be redeemed with partnership property.

(3) The remedies conferred by paragraph (1) shall not be deemed exclusive of others which may exist.

(4) Nothing in this act shall be held to deprive a limited partner of his statutory exemption.

Official Comment

In those states where a creditor on beginning an action can attach debts due the defendant before he has obtained a judgment against the defendant it is recommended that paragraph (1) of this section read as follows:

"On due application to a court of competent jurisdiction by any creditor of a limited partner, the court may charge the interest of the indebted limited partner with payment of the unsatisfied amount of such claim; and may appoint a receiver, and make all other orders, directions, and inquiries which the circumstances of the case may require."

§ 23. Distribution of Assets

(1) In settling accounts after dissolution the liabilities of the partnership shall be entitled to payment in the following order:

(a) Those to creditors, in the order of priority as provided by law, except those to limited partners on account of their contributions, and to general partners,

(b) Those to limited partners in respect to their share of the profits and other compensation by way of income on their contributions,

(c) Those to limited partners in respect to the capital of their contributions,

(d) Those to general partners other than for capital and profits,

(e) Those to general partners in respect to profits,

(f) Those to general partners in respect to capital.

(2) Subject to any statement in the certificate or to subsequent agreement, limited partners share in the partnership assets in respect to their claims for capital, and in respect to their claims for profits or for compensation by way of income on their contributions respectively, in proportion to the respective amounts of such claims.

§ 24. When Certificate Shall Be Cancelled or Amended

(1) The certificate shall be cancelled when the partnership is dissolved or all limited partners cease to be such.

(2) A certificate shall be amended when

(a) There is a change in the name of the partnership or in the amount or character of the contribution of any limited partner,

(b) A person is substituted as a limited partner,

(c) An additional limited partner is admitted,

(d) A person is admitted as a general partner,

(e) A general partner retires, dies or becomes insane, and the business is continued under Section 20,

(f) There is a change in the character of the business of the partnership,

(g) There is a false or erroneous statement in the certificate,

(h) There is a change in the time as stated in the certificate for the dissolution of the partnership or for the return of a contribution,

(i) A time is fixed for the dissolution of the partnership, or the return of a contribution, no time having been specified in the certificate, or

(j) The members desire to make a change in any other statement in the certificate in order that it shall accurately represent the agreement between them.

§ 25. Requirements for Amendment and for Cancellation of Certificate

(1) The writing to amend a certificate shall

(a) Conform to the requirements of Section 2(1a) as far as necessary to set forth clearly the change in the certificate which it is desired to make, and

(b) Be signed and sworn to by all members, and an amendment substituting a limited partner or adding a limited or general partner shall be signed also by the member to be substituted or added, and when a limited partner is to be substituted, the amendment shall also be signed by the assigning limited partner.

(2) The writing to cancel a certificate shall be signed by all members.

(3) A person desiring the cancellation or amendment of a certificate, if any person designated in paragraphs (1) and (2) as a person who must execute the writing refuses to do so, may petition the [here designate the proper court] to direct a cancellation or amendment thereof.

(4) If the court finds that the petitioner has a right to have the writing executed by a person who refuses to do so, it shall order the [here designate the responsible official in the office designated in Section 2] in the office where the certificate is recorded to record the cancellation or amendment of the certificate; and where the certificate is to be amended, the court shall also cause to be filed for record in said office a certified copy of its decree setting forth the amendment.

(5) A certificate is amended or cancelled when there is filed for record in the office [here designate the office designated in Section 2] where the certificate is recorded

(a) A writing in accordance with the provisions of paragraph (1), or (2) or

(b) A certified copy of the order of court in accordance with the provisions of paragraph (4).

(6) After the certificate is duly amended in accordance with this section, the amended certificate shall thereafter be for all purposes the certificate provided for by this act.

§ 26. Parties to Actions

A contributor, unless he is a general partner, is not a proper party to proceedings by or against a partnership, except where the object is to enforce a limited partner's right against or liability to the partnership.

§ 27. Name of Act

This act may be cited as The Uniform Limited Partnership Act.

§ 28. Rules of Construction

(1) The rule that statutes in derogation of the common law are to be strictly construed shall have no application to this act.

(2) This act shall be so interpreted and construed as to effect its general purpose to make uniform the law of those states which enact it.

(3) This act shall not be so construed as to impair the obligations of any contract existing when the act goes into effect, nor to affect any action or proceedings begun or right accrued before this act takes effect.

§ 29. Rules for Cases Not Provided for in This Act

In any case not provided for in this act the rules of law and equity, including the law merchant, shall govern.

§ 30. Provisions for Existing Limited Partnerships

(1) A limited partnership formed under any statute of this state prior to the adoption of this act, may become a limited partnership under this act by complying with the provisions of Section 2; provided the certificate set forth

(a) The amount of the original contribution of each limited partner, and the time when the contribution was made, and

(b) That the property of the partnership exceeds the amount sufficient to discharge its liabilities to persons not claiming as general or limited partners by an amount greater than the sum of the contributions of its limited partners.

(2) A limited partnership formed under any statute of this state prior to the adoption of this act, until or unless it becomes a limited partnership under this act, shall continue to be governed by the provisions of [here insert proper reference to the existing limited partnership act or acts], except that such partnership shall not be renewed unless so provided in the original agreement.

Official Comment

Section 30 will be omitted in any state which has not a limited partnership act.

§ 31. Act (Acts) Repealed

Except as affecting existing limited partnerships to the extent set forth in Section 30, the act (acts) of [here designate the existing limited partnership act or acts] is (are) hereby repealed.

Official Comment

Section 31 will be omitted in any state which has not a limited partnership act.

REVISED UNIFORM LIMITED PARTNERSHIP ACT (1976) WITH 1985 AMENDMENTS (SHOWN BY DELETION AND ADDITION)*

Historical Notes

The Revised Uniform Limited Partnership Act was approved by the National Conference of Commissioners on Uniform State Laws (NCCUSL) in 1976. It supersedes the original Uniform Limited Partnership Act approved by NCCUSL in 1916.

In 1985 NCCUSL initially approved a separate new Uniform Limited Partnership Act (1985). Subsequently, however, the Conference determined that the separate new act should be eliminated and that the changes made therein be incorporated instead into the existing Revised Uniform Limited Partnership Act of 1976. Accordingly, the changes have been incorporated here into the 1976 Act together with the revised prefatory note and comments. Changes in the text, prefatory note, and comments are indicated by Text for additions, T̶e̶x̶t̶ for deletions.

Editor's notes: The format described above in the Historical Notes to the Act, showing the 1985 amendments by deletion and addition to the 1976 Act, is the format utilized in volume 6A, Uniform Laws Annotated (1995). It is used in these materials. As noted below, nearly all states have adopted both the 1976 Act and the 1985 amendments to the Act.

The Revised Uniform Limited Partnership Act with the 1985 amendments, although called a uniform act, has been treated more like a model act by many of the adopting states. As a result, many states have made substantial amendments to their acts. 6A Uniform Laws Annotated (1995, as supplemented by 2006 Pocket Part) describes the amendments, state by state, in notes following each section.

The 2006 Cumulative Annual Pocket Part to 6A Uniform Laws Annotated (1995) contains a list of the jurisdictions that have adopted the 1976 Act and the effective date of adoption. All states, other than Louisiana, adopted the 1976 Act. Six of those states (Florida, Hawaii, Illinois, Iowa, Minnesota, North Dakota), however, have since repealed the 1976 Act and adopted Re-RULPA (the Uniform Limited Partnership Act (2001) -see below). All adopting states, other than Michigan and North Carolina, have adopted the 1985 amendments, albeit with fairly substantial revisions in many cases.

The limited liability limited partnership

The limited liability limited partnership ("LLLP") is a limited partnership in which not only the limited partners but also the general partners have limited liability. It is a very recent addition to the law. Once authorized by statute, a certificate can be filed with the state to provide limited liability for general partners of a limited partnership, similar to the limited liability enjoyed by the partners in an LLP. In all other respects, the LLLP is like a regular limited partnership. To date, at least 18 jurisdictions allow limited liability limited partnerships.

Re-RULPA. In 2001, NCCUSL approved a new revised limited partnership act (referred to as "Re-RULPA" or the Uniform Limited Partnership Act (2001), which is set forth elsewhere in this book).

REVISED UNIFORM LIMITED PARTNERSHIP ACT (1976) WITH THE 1985 AMENDMENTS (SHOWN BY DELETION AND ADDITION)

Prefatory Note

~~The Revised Uniform Limited Partnership Act adopted by the National Conference of Commissioners on Uniform State Laws in August, 1976,~~ In 1976, the National Conference of Commissioners on Uniform State Laws adopted the first revision of the Uniform Limited Partnership Act, originally promulgated in 1916. The 1976 Act was intended to modernize the prior uniform law while retaining the special character of limited partnerships as compared with corporations. The draftsman of a limited partnership agreement has a degree of flexibility in defining the relations among the partners that is not available in the corporate form. Moreover, the relationship among partners is consensual, and ~~requires a degree of privity that forces the~~ under some circumstances may require a general partner to seek approval of the other partners (sometimes unanimous approval) under circumstances that corporate management would find unthinkable. The limited partnership was not intended to be an alternative in all cases where the corporate form is undesirable for tax or other reasons, and the ~~new~~ 1976 Act was not intended to make it so. The ~~new~~ 1976 Act ~~clarifies~~ clarified many ambiguities and ~~fills~~ filled interstices in the ~~prior uniform law~~ 1916 Act by adding more detailed language and mechanics. In addition, it effected some important substantive changes and additions ~~have been made~~ from the prior uniform law.

The Uniform Limited Partnership Act (1976) with the 1985 Amendments (the 1985 Act) follows the 1976 Act very closely in most respects. It makes almost no change in the basic structure of the 1976 Act. It does, however, differ from the 1976 Act in certain significant respects for the purpose of more effectively modernizing, improving, and establishing uniformity in the law of limited partnerships. The 1985 Act accomplishes this, without impairing the basic philosophy or values underlying the 1976 Act, by incorporating into the structure, framework, and text of the 1976 Act the best and most important improvements that have emerged in the limited partnership acts enacted recently by certain states. Most of those improvements were considered by the draftsmen of the 1976 Act but were not included in it because of uncertainties as to the possible consequences of such inclusion under applicable Federal income tax laws. Those uncertainties have since been resolved satisfactorily, and no impediment to incorporating them in the 1985 Act remains at this time.

Article 1 provides a list of all of the definitions used in the Act, integrates the use of limited partnership names with corporate names and provides for an office and agent for service of process in the state of organization. All of these provisions ~~are new~~ were innovations in the 1976 Act and were carried over from the 1976 Act to the 1985 Act. Article 2 collects in one place all provisions dealing with execution and filing of certificates of limited partnership and certificates of amendment and cancellation. When adopted in 1976, Articles 1 and 2 ~~reflect~~ reflected an important change in the prior statutory scheme: recognition that the basic document in any partnership, including a limited partnership, is the partnership agreement. The certificate of limited partnership is not a constitutive document (except in the sense that it is a statutory prerequisite to creation of the limited partnership), and merely reflects the most basic matters as to which government officials, creditors , and others dealing or considering dealing with the partnership should be put on notice. This principle is further implemented by the 1985 Act's elimination of the requirement, carried from the original 1916 Act into the 1976 Act, that the certificate of limited partnership set out the name, address, and capital contribution of each limited partner and certain other details relating to the operation of the partnership and the respective rights of the partners. The former requirement served no significant practical purpose while it imposed on limited partnerships (particularly those having large numbers of partners or doing business in more than one state) inordinate administrative and logistical burdens and expenses connected with filing and amending their certificates of limited partnership. Many of the other changes made by the 1985 Act merely reflect the elimination of that requirement.

Article 3 deals with the single most difficult issue facing lawyers who use the limited partnership form of organization: the powers and potential liabilities of limited partners. Section 303 lists a number of activities in which a limited partner may engage without being held to have so significantly participated in the control of the business that he ~~assumes~~ acquires the liability of a general partner. Moreover, it goes on to confine the liability

of a limited partner who merely ~~steps over the line of participation~~ partici-
pates in control to situations in which persons who actually know of that
participation in control are misled thereby to their detriment into reason-
ably believing the limited partner to be a general partner. ~~General liability
for partnership debts is imposed only on those limited partners who are,
in effect, "silent general partners." With that exception, the provisions of
the new Act that impose liability on a limited partner who has somehow
permitted third parties to be misled to their detriment as to the limited
partner's true status confine that liability to those who have actually been
misled.~~ This "detrimental reliance" test, together with an expansion of the
"laundry list" of specific activities in which limited partners may participate
without incurring liability, are among the principal innovations in the 1985
Act.

The provisions relating to general partners are collected in Article 4. It
differs little from the corresponding article in the 1976 Act, except that some
of the 1976 Act's references to the certificate of limited partnership have
been changed to refer instead to the partnership agreement. This is in
recognition of the principle that the limited partnership agreement, not the
certificate of limited partnership, is the primary constitutive, organizational, and governing document of a limited partnership.

Article 5, ~~the~~ dealing with finance ~~section, makes~~ , differs in some
important respects from Article 5 of the 1976 Act, which itself made some
important changes from the ~~prior uniform law~~ 1916 Act. The 1976 Act
explicitly permitted contributions to the partnership to be made in the form
of the contribution of services and promises to contribute cash, property,
or services ~~are now explicitly permitted as contributions. And~~ , and provided
that those who ~~fail~~ failed to perform promised services ~~are~~ were required,
in the absence of an agreement to the contrary, to pay the value of the
services as stated in the certificate of limited partnership. These important
innovations of the 1976 Act are retained in substance in the 1985 Act.
However, the 1985 Act substitutes the partnership agreement and the
records of the limited partnership for the certificate of limited partnership
as the place such agreements are to be set out and such information is to
be kept. ~~A~~

Article 6 of the 1976 Act, dealing with distributions and with the
withdrawal of partners from the partnership, made a number of changes
from the ~~prior uniform law are made in Article 6, dealing with distributions
from and the withdrawal of partners from the partnership~~ 1916 Act. For
example, Section 608 ~~creates~~ created a statute of limitations ~~on~~ applicable
to the right of a limited partnership to recover all or part of a contribution
that ~~has~~ had been returned to a limited partner, whether to satisfy creditors
or otherwise. The 1985 Act retains these features of the 1976 Act without
substantive change.

~~The~~ In both the 1976 and the 1985 Acts, the assignability of partnership
interests is dealt with in considerable detail in Article 7~~. The~~ , and the
provisions relating to dissolution appear in Article 8~~, which, among other~~

~~things, imposes~~. Article 8 of the 1976 Act established a new standard for seeking judicial dissolution of a limited partnership , which standard is carried forward into the 1985 Act.

~~One~~ Article 9 of the 1976 and 1985 Acts deals with one of the thorniest questions for those who operate limited partnerships in more than one state ~~has been~~ , i.e., the status of the partnership in a state other than the state of its organization. Neither ~~existing~~ case law under the 1916 Act nor administrative practice ~~makes~~ made it clear which state's law governed the partnership or whether , in that other state, the limited partners ~~continue~~ continued to possess ~~their~~ limited liability ~~and which law governs the partnership~~. Article 9 ~~deals~~ of the 1976 Act dealt with this problem by providing for registration of foreign limited partnerships and specifying choice-of-law rules. Article 9 of the 1985 Act retains all of those basic provisions and innovations of the 1976 Act.

~~Finally,~~ Article 10 of the ~~new~~ 1976 Act ~~authorizes~~ represented another significant innovation, by authorizing derivative actions to be brought by limited partners. The 1916 Act failed to address this entire concept. Article 10 of the 1985 Act clarifies certain provisions of the 1976 Act but does not make any substantive changes in the corresponding provisions of the 1976 Act.

Finally, Article 11 sets out a number of miscellaneous provisions, not the least of which are those dealing with the application of the new statute to limited partnerships in existence at the time of its enactment. Those provisions in the 1976 Act were expanded upon by the 1985 Act to give greater deference to the possible expectations, some of which may have constitutionally protected status, of partners in such limited partnerships concerning the continuing applicability to their partnerships of the law in effect when they were organized.

REVISED UNIFORM LIMITED PARTNERSHIP ACT (1976) WITH 1985 AMENDMENTS (SHOWN BY DELETION AND ADDITION)

ARTICLE 1 GENERAL PROVISIONS

ARTICLE 11 MISCELLANEOUS

ARTICLE 1
GENERAL PROVISIONS

§ 101. Definitions.

As used in this [Act], unless the context otherwise requires:

(1) "Certificate of limited partnership" means the certificate referred to in Section 201, and the certificate as amended or restated.

(2) "Contribution" means any cash, property, services rendered, or a promissory note or other binding obligation to contribute cash or property or to perform services, which a partner contributes to a limited partnership in his capacity as a partner.

(3) "Event of withdrawal of a general partner" means an event that causes a person to cease to be a general partner as provided in Section 402.

(4) "Foreign limited partnership" means a partnership formed under the laws of any ~~State~~ state other than this State and having as partners one or more general partners and one or more limited partners.

(5) "General partner" means a person who has been admitted to a limited partnership as a general partner in accordance with the partnership agreement and named in the certificate of limited partnership as a general partner.

(6) "Limited partner" means a person who has been admitted to a limited partnership as a limited partner in accordance with the partnership agreement ~~and named in the certificate of limited partnership as a limited partner~~.

(7) "Limited partnership" and "domestic limited partnership" mean a partnership formed by two or more persons under the laws of this State

and having one or more general partners and one or more limited partners.

(8) "Partner" means a limited or general partner.

(9) "Partnership agreement" means any valid agreement, written or oral, of the partners as to the affairs of a limited partnership and the conduct of its business.

(10) "Partnership interest" means a partner's share of the profits and losses of a limited partnership and the right to receive distributions of partnership assets.

(11) "Person" means a natural person, partnership, limited partnership (domestic or foreign), trust, estate, association, or corporation.

(12) "State" means a state, territory, or possession of the United States, the District of Columbia, or the Commonwealth of Puerto Rico.

Comment

The definitions in this section clarify a number of uncertainties in the law existing ~~law~~ prior to the 1976 Act, and also make certain changes in such prior law. The 1985 Act makes very few additional changes in Section 101.

Contribution: this definition makes it clear that a present contribution of services and a promise to make a future payment of cash, contribution of property or performance of services are permissible forms for a contribution. ~~Accordingly, the present~~ Section 502 of the 1985 Act provides that a limited partner's promise to make a contribution is enforceable only when set out in a writing signed by the limited partner. (This result is not dissimilar from that under the 1976 Act, which required all promises of future contributions to be described in the certificate of limited partnership, which was to be signed by, among others, the partners making such promises.) The property or services contributed presently or ~~promise~~ promised to be contributed in the future must be accorded a value in the ~~certificate of limited partnership (Section 201(5))~~ partnership agreement or the partnership records required to be kept pursuant to Section 105, and, in the case of a promise, that value may determine the liability of a partner who fails to honor his agreement (Section 502). Section 3 of the ~~prior uniform law~~ 1916 Act did not permit a limited partner's contribution to be in the form of services, although that inhibition did not apply to general partners.

Foreign limited partnership: the Act only deals with foreign limited partnerships formed under the laws of another ~~"State"~~ "state" of the United States (see subdivision 12 of Section 101), and any adopting ~~State~~ state that desires to deal by statute with the status of entities formed under the laws of foreign countries must make appropriate changes throughout the Act.

The exclusion of such entities from the Act was not intended to suggest that their "limited partners" should not be accorded limited liability by the courts of a ~~State~~ state adopting the Act. That question would be resolved by the choice-of-law rules of the forum ~~State~~ state.

General partner: this definition recognizes the separate functions of the partnership agreement and the certificate of limited partnership. The partnership agreement establishes the basic grant of management power to the persons named as general partners; but because of the passive role played by the limited partners, the separate, formal step of ~~embodying~~ memorializing that grant of power in the certificate of limited partnership has been preserved to emphasize its importance and to provide notice of the identity of the partnership's general partners to persons dealing with the partnership.

Limited partner: ~~as in~~ unlike the ~~case of~~ definition of general partners, this definition provides for admission of limited partners through the partnership agreement ~~and solemnization in the certificate of limited partnership. In addition, the definition makes it clear that being named in the certificate of limited partnership is a prerequisite to limited partner status. Failure to file does not, however, mean that the participant is a general partner or that he has general liability. See Sections 202(c) and 303~~ alone and does not require identification of any limited partner in the certificate of limited partnership (Section 201). Under the 1916 and the 1976 Acts, being named as a limited partner in the certificate of limited partnership was a statutory requirement and, in most if not all cases, probably also a prerequisite to limited partner status. By eliminating the requirement that the certificate of limited partnership contain the name, address, and capital contribution of each limited partner, the 1985 Act all but eliminates any risk that a person intended to be a limited partner may be exposed to liability as a general partner as a result of the inadvertent omission of any of that information from the certificate of limited partnership, and also dispenses with the need to amend the certificate of limited partnership upon the admission or withdrawal of, transfer of an interest by, or change in the address or capital contribution of, any limited partner.

Partnership agreement: the ~~prior uniform law~~ 1916 Act did not refer to the partnership agreement, assuming that all important matters affecting limited partners would be set forth in the certificate of limited partnership. Under modern practice, however, it has been common for the partners to enter into a comprehensive partnership agreement, only part of which was required to be included or summarized in the certificate of limited partnership. As reflected in Section 201 of the 1985 Act, the certificate of limited partnership is confined principally to matters respecting the partnership itself and the ~~addition and withdrawal~~ identity of general partners ~~and of capital~~, and other important issues are left to the partnership agreement. Most of the information formerly provided by, but no longer required to be included in, the certificate of limited partnership is now required to be kept in the partnership records (Section 105).

Partnership interest: this definition ~~is new~~ first appeared in the 1976 Act and is intended to define what it is that is transferred when a partnership interest is assigned.

§ 102. Name.

The name of each limited partnership as set forth in its certificate of limited partnership:

(1) shall contain without abbreviation the words "limited partnership";

(2) may not contain the name of a limited partner unless (i) it is also the name of a general partner or the corporate name of a corporate general partner, or (ii) the business of the limited partnership had been carried on under that name before the admission of that limited partner;

[~~(3)~~] may not contain any word or phrase indicating or implying that it is organized other than for a purpose stated in its certificate of limited partnership;

[~~(4)~~ (3)] may not be the same as, or deceptively similar to, the name of any corporation or limited partnership organized under the laws of this State or licensed or registered as a foreign corporation or limited partnership in this State; and

[~~(5)~~ (4)] may not contain the following words [here insert prohibited words].

Comment

Subdivision (2) of Section 102 has been carried over from Section 5 of the ~~prior uniform law~~ 1916 Act with certain editorial changes. The remainder of Section 102 ~~is new~~ first appeared in the 1976 Act and primarily reflects the intention to integrate the registration of limited partnership names with that of corporate names. Accordingly, Section 201 provides for central, ~~State-wide~~ state-wide filing of certificates of limited partnership, and subdivisions (3)~~,~~ and (4) ~~and (5)~~ of Section 102 contain standards to be applied by the filing officer in determining whether the certificate should be filed. Subdivision (1) requires that the proper name of a limited partnership contain the words "limited partnership" in full. Subdivision (3) of the 1976 Act has been deleted, to reflect the deletion from Section 201 of any requirement that the certificate of limited partnership describe the partnership's purposes or the character of its business.

§ 103. Reservation of Name.

(a) The exclusive right to the use of a name may be reserved by:

(1) any person intending to organize a limited partnership under this [Act] and to adopt that name;

(2) any domestic limited partnership or any foreign limited partner-ship registered in this State which, in either case, intends to adopt that name;

(3) any foreign limited partnership intending to register in this State and adopt that name; and

(4) any person intending to organize a foreign limited partnership and intending to have it register in this State and adopt that name.

(b) The reservation shall be made by filing with the Secretary of State an application, executed by the applicant, to reserve a specified name. If the Secretary of State finds that the name is available for use by a domestic or foreign limited partnership, he [or she] shall reserve the name for the exclusive use of the applicant for a period of 120 days. Once having so reserved a name, the same applicant may not again reserve the same name until more than 60 days after the expiration of the last 120-day period for which that applicant reserved that name. The right to the exclusive use of a reserved name may be transferred to any other person by filing in the office of the Secretary of State a notice of the transfer, executed by the applicant for whom the name was reserved and specifying the name and address of the transferee.

Comment

Section 103 is new first appeared in the 1976 Act. The prior uniform law 1916 Act did not provide for registration of names.

§ 104. Specified Office and Agent.

Each limited partnership shall continuously maintain in this State:

(1) an office, which may but need not be a place of its business in this State, at which shall be kept the records required by Section 105 to be maintained; and

(2) an agent for service of process on the limited partnership, which agent must be an individual resident of this State, a domestic corpora-tion, or a foreign corporation authorized to do business in this State.

Comment

Section 104 is new first appeared in the 1976 Act. It requires that a limited partnership have certain minimum contacts with its State of organization, i.e., an office at which the constitutive documents and basic financial information is kept and an agent for service of process.

§ 105. Records to be Kept.

[(a)] Each limited partnership shall keep at the office referred to in Section 104(1) the following:

(1) a current list of the full name and last known business address of each partner ~~set forth~~, separately identifying the general partners (in alphabetical order) and the limited partners (in alphabetical order~~;~~);

(2) a copy of the certificate of limited partnership and all certificates of amendment thereto, together with executed copies of any powers of attorney pursuant to which any certificate has been executed~~;~~;

(3) copies of the limited partnership's federal, state and local income tax returns and reports, if any, for the three most recent years~~; and~~;

(4) copies of any then effective written partnership agreements and of any financial statements of the limited partnership for the three most recent years; and

[(5)] unless contained in a written partnership agreement, a writing setting out: (i) the amount of cash and a description and statement of the agreed value of the other property or services contributed by each partner and which each partner has agreed to contribute; (ii) the times at which or events on the happening of which any additional contributions agreed to be made by each partner are to be made; (iii) any right of a partner to receive, or of a general partner to make, distributions to a partner which include a return of all or any part of the partner's contribution; and (iv) any events upon the happening of which the limited partnership is to be dissolved and its affairs wound up.

[(b)] ~~Those records~~ Records kept under this section are subject to inspection and copying at the reasonable request and at the expense of any partner during ordinary business hours.

Comment

Section 105 ~~is new~~ first appeared in the 1976 Act. In view of the passive nature of the limited partner's position, it has been widely felt that limited partners are entitled to access to certain basic documents and information, including the certificate of limited partnership ~~and~~, any partnership agreement , and a writing setting out certain important matters which, under the 1916 and 1976 Acts, were required to be set out in the certificate of limited partnership. In view of the great diversity among limited partnerships, it was thought inappropriate to require a standard form of financial report, and Section 105 does no more than require retention of tax returns and any other financial statements that are prepared. The names and addresses of the general partners are made available to the general public in the certificate of limited partnership.

§ 106. Nature of Business.

A limited partnership may carry on any business that a partnership without limited partners may carry on except [here designate prohibited activities].

Comment

Section 106 is identical to Section 3 of the ~~prior uniform law.~~ 1916 Act. Many states require that certain regulated industries, such as banking, may be carried on only by entities organized pursuant to special statutes, and it is contemplated that the prohibited activities would be confined to the matters covered by those statutes.

§ 107. Business Transactions of Partner with Partnership.

Except as provided in the partnership agreement, a partner may lend money to and transact other business with the limited partnership and, subject to other applicable law, has the same rights and obligations with respect thereto as a person who is not a partner.

Comment

Section 107 makes a number of important changes in Section 13 of the ~~prior uniform law.~~ 1916 Act. Section 13, in effect, created a special fraudulent conveyance provision applicable to the making of secured loans by limited partners and the repayment by limited partnerships of loans from limited partners. Section 107 leaves that question to a ~~State's~~ state's general fraudulent conveyance statute. In addition, Section 107 eliminates the prohibition in ~~former~~ Section 13 against a general ~~partner (as opposed to a limited partner)~~ partner's sharing pro rata with general creditors in the case of an unsecured loan. Of course, other doctrines developed under bankruptcy and insolvency laws may require the subordination of loans by partners under appropriate circumstances.

ARTICLE 2
FORMATION; CERTIFICATE OF LIMITED PARTNERSHIP

§ 201. Certificate of Limited Partnership.

(a) In order to form a limited partnership, ~~two or more persons must execute~~ a certificate of limited partnership. ~~The certificate shall be~~ must be executed and filed in the office of the Secretary of State. ~~and~~ The certificate shall set forth:

(1) the name of the limited partnership;

[~~(2)~~] ~~the general character of its business;~~

[~~(3)~~ (2)] the address of the office and the name and address of the agent for service of process required to be maintained by Section 104;

[~~(4)~~ (3)] the name and the business address of each general partner ~~(specifying separately the general partners and limited partners)~~;

[~~(5)~~] ~~the amount of cash and a description and statement of the agreed value of the other property or services contributed by each partner and which each partner has agreed to contribute in the future;~~

[(6)] ~~the times at which or events on the happening of which any additional contributions agreed to be made by each partner are to be made;~~

[(7)] ~~any power of a limited partner to grant the right to become a limited partner to an assignee of any part of his partnership interest, and the terms and conditions of the power;~~

[(8)] ~~if agreed upon, the time at which or the events on the happening of which a partner may terminate his membership in the limited partnership and the amount of, or the method of determining, the distribution to which he may be entitled respecting his partnership interest, and the terms and conditions of the termination and distribution;~~

[(9)] ~~any right of a partner to receive distributions of property, including cash from the limited partnership;~~

[(10)] ~~any right of a partner to receive, or of a general partner to make, distributions to a partner which include a return of all or any part of the partner's contribution;~~

[(11)] ~~any time at which or events upon the happening of which the limited partnership is to be dissolved and its affairs wound-up;~~

[(12)] ~~any right of the remaining general partners to continue the business on the happening of an event of withdrawal of a general partner;~~

[(4)] the latest date upon which the limited partnership is to dissolve; and

[~~(13)~~ (5)] any other matters the general partners determine to include therein.

(b) A limited partnership is formed at the time of the filing of the certificate of limited partnership in the office of the Secretary of State or at any later time specified in the certificate of limited partnership if, in either case, there has been substantial compliance with the requirements of this section.

Comment

The 1985 Act requires far fewer matters ~~required~~ to be set forth in the certificate of limited partnership ~~are not different in kind from those required by~~ than did Section 2 of the ~~prior uniform law, although certain additions and deletions have been made and the description has been revised to conform with the rest of the Act. In general, the certificate is intended to serve two functions: first, to place creditors on notice of the~~ 1916 Act and Section 201 of the 1976 Act. This is in recognition of the fact that the partnership agreement, not the certificate of limited partnership, has become the authoritative and comprehensive document for most limited partnerships, and that creditors and potential creditors of the partnership do and should refer to the partnership agreement and to other information furnished to them directly by the partnership and by others, not to the certificate of limited partnership, to obtain facts concerning the capital and finances of the partnership and ~~the rules regarding additional contributions to and withdrawals from the partnership; second, to clearly delineate the time at which persons become general partners and limited partners~~ other matters of concern. Subparagraph (b), which is based upon the ~~prior uniform law~~ 1916 Act, has been retained to make it clear that the existence of the limited partnership depends only upon compliance with this section. Its continued existence is not dependent upon compliance with other provisions of this Act.

§ 202. Amendment to Certificate.

(a) A certificate of limited partnership is amended by filing a certificate of amendment thereto in the office of the Secretary of State. The certificate shall set forth:

(1) the name of the limited partnership;

(2) the date of filing the certificate; and

(3) the amendment to the certificate.

(b) Within 30 days after the happening of any of the following events, an amendment to a certificate of limited partnership reflecting the occurrence of the event or events shall be filed:

[(1)] ~~a change in the amount or character of the contribution of any partner, or in any partner's obligation to make a contribution;~~

[(2) (1)] the admission of a new general partner;

[(3) (2)] the withdrawal of a general partner; or

[(4) (3)] the continuation of the business under Section 801 after an event of withdrawal of a general partner.

(c) A general partner who becomes aware that any statement in a certificate of limited partnership was false when made or that any arrangements or other facts described have changed, making the certificate inaccurate in any respect, shall promptly amend the certificate~~, but an amendment to show a change of address of a limited partner need be filed only once every 12 months~~.

(d) A certificate of limited partnership may be amended at any time for any other proper purpose the general partners determine.

(e) No person has any liability because an amendment to a certificate of limited partnership has not been filed to reflect the occurrence of any event referred to in subsection (b) of this ~~Section~~ section if the amendment is filed within the 30-day period specified in subsection (b).

[(f)] A restated certificate of limited partnership may be executed and filed in the same manner as a certificate of amendment.

Comment

Section 202 ~~makes~~ of the 1976 Act made substantial changes in Section 24 of the ~~prior uniform law~~ 1916 Act. Further changes in this section are made by the 1985 Act. Paragraph (b) lists the basic events the addition or withdrawal of ~~partners or capital or capital obligations~~ a general partner that are so central to the function of the certificate of limited partnership that they require prompt amendment. With the elimination of the requirement that the certificate of limited partnership include the names of all limited partners and the amount and character of all capital contributions, the requirement of the 1916 and 1976 Acts that the certificate be amended upon the admission or withdrawal of limited partners or on any change in the partnership capital must also be eliminated. This change should greatly reduce the frequency and complexity of amendments to the certificate of limited partnership. Paragraph (c) makes it clear, as it was not clear under ~~subdivision (2)(g) of former~~ Section ~~24~~ 24(2)(g) of the 1916 Act, that the certificate of limited partnership is intended to be an accurate description of the facts to which it relates at all times and does not speak merely as of the date it is executed.

Paragraph (e) provides a "safe harbor" against claims of creditors or others who assert that they have been misled by the failure to amend the certificate of limited partnership to reflect changes in any of the important facts referred to in paragraph (b); if the certificate of limited partnership is amended within 30 days of the occurrence of the event, no creditor or other person can recover for damages sustained during the interim. Additional protection is afforded by the provisions of Section 304. The elimination of the requirement that the certificate of limited partnership identify all limited partners and their respective capital contributions may have rendered paragraph (e) an obsolete and unnecessary vestige. The principal, if not the sole, purpose of paragraph (e) in the 1976 Act was to protect limited partners newly admitted to a partnership from being held liable as general partners when an amendment to the certificate identifying them as limited partners and describing their contributions was not filed contemporaneously with their admission to the partnership. Such liability cannot arise under the 1985 Act because such information is not required to be stated in the certificate. Nevertheless, the 1985 Act retains paragraph (e) because it is protective of partners, shielding them from liability to the extent its provisions apply, and does not create or impose any liability.

Paragraph (f) is added in the 1985 Act to provide explicit statutory recognition of the common practice of restating an amended certificate of limited partnership. While a limited partnership seeking to amend its certificate of limited partnership may do so by recording a restated certificate which incorporates the amendment, that is by no means the only purpose or function of a restated certificate, which may be filed for the sole purpose of restating in a single integrated instrument all the provisions of a limited partnership's certificate of limited partnership which are then in effect.

§ 203. Cancellation of Certificate.

A certificate of limited partnership shall be cancelled upon the dissolution and the commencement of winding up of the partnership or at any other time there are no limited partners. A certificate of cancellation shall be filed in the office of the Secretary of State and set forth:

(1) the name of the limited partnership;

(2) the date of filing of its certificate of limited partnership;

(3) the reason for filing the certificate of cancellation;

(4) the effective date (which shall be a date certain) of cancellation if it is not to be effective upon the filing of the certificate; and

(5) any other information the general partners filing the certificate determine.

Comment

Section 203 changes Section 24 of the ~~prior uniform law~~ 1916 Act by making it clear that the certificate of cancellation should be filed upon the commencement of winding up of the limited partnership. Section 24 provided for cancellation "when the partnership is dissolved."

§ 204. Execution of Certificates.

(a) Each certificate required by this Article to be filed in the office of the Secretary of State shall be executed in the following manner:

(1) an original certificate of limited partnership must be signed by all general partners ~~named therein~~;

(2) a certificate of amendment must be signed by at least one general partner and by each other general partner designated in the certificate as a new general partner ~~or whose contribution is described as having been increased~~; and

(3) a certificate of cancellation must be signed by all general partners~~;~~.

(b) Any person may sign a certificate by an attorney-in-fact, but a power of attorney to sign a certificate relating to the admission~~, or increased contribution,~~ of a general partner must specifically describe the admission ~~or increase~~.

(c) The execution of a certificate by a general partner constitutes an affirmation under the penalties of perjury that the facts stated therein are true.

Comment

Section 204 collects in one place the formal requirements for the execution of certificates which were set forth in Sections 2 and 25 of the ~~prior uniform law~~ 1916 Act. Those sections required that each certificate be signed by all partners, and there developed an unnecessarily cumbersome practice of having each limited partner sign powers of attorney to authorize the general partners to execute certificates of amendment on their behalf. ~~Section 204 insures that each partner must sign a certificate obligation to make contributions.~~ The 1976 Act, while simplifying the execution requirements, nevertheless required that an original certificate of limited partnership be signed by all partners and a certificate of amendment by all new partners being admitted to the limited partnership. However, the certificate of limited partnership is no longer required to include the name or capital contribution of any limited partner. Therefore, while the 1985 Act still requires all general partners to sign the original certificate of limited partnership, no limited partner is required to sign any certificate. Certificates of amendment are required to be signed by only one general partner and all general partners must sign certificates of cancellation. ~~Section 204 prohibits blanket powers of attorney for the execution of certificates in many cases, since those conditions under which a partner is required to sign have been narrowed to circumstances of special importance to that partner.~~ The ~~former~~ requirement in the 1916 Act that all certificates be sworn ~~has been confined to statements by the general partners, recognizing that the limited partner's role is a limited one~~ was deleted in the 1976 and 1985 Acts as potentially an unfair trap for the unwary (*see, e.g., Wisniewski v. Johnson*, 223 Va. 141, 286 S.E.2d 223 (1982)); in its place, paragraph (c) now provides, as a matter of law, that the execution of a certificate by a general partner subjects him to the penalties of perjury for inaccuracies in the certificate.

§ 205. ~~Amendment or Cancellation~~ Execution by Judicial Act.

If a person required by Section 204 to execute ~~a~~ any certificate ~~of amendment or cancellation~~ fails or refuses to do so, any other ~~partner, and any assignee of a partnership interest,~~ person who is adversely affected by the failure or refusal~~;~~ may petition the [designate the appropriate court] to direct the ~~amendment or cancellation~~ execution of the certificate. If the court finds that ~~the amendment or cancellation is proper~~ it is proper for the certificate to be executed and that any person so designated has failed or refused to execute the certificate, it shall order the Secretary of State to record an appropriate certificate ~~of amendment or cancellation~~.

Comment

Section 205 ~~changes~~ of the 1976 Act changed subdivisions (3) and (4) of Section 25 of the ~~prior uniform law~~ 1916 Act by confining the persons who have standing to seek judicial intervention to partners and to those assignees who ~~are~~ were adversely affected by the failure or refusal of the appropriate persons to file a certificate of amendment or cancellation. Section 205 of the 1985 Act reverses that restriction, and provides that any person adversely affected by a failure or refusal to file any certificate (not only a certificate of cancellation or amendment) has standing to seek judicial intervention.

§ 206. Filing in Office of Secretary of State.

(a) Two signed copies of the certificate of limited partnership and of any certificates of amendment or cancellation (or of any judicial decree of amendment or cancellation) shall be delivered to the Secretary of State. A person who executes a certificate as an agent or fiduciary need not exhibit evidence of his [or her] authority as a prerequisite to filing. Unless the Secretary of State finds that any certificate does not conform to law, upon receipt of all filing fees required by law he [or she] shall:

(1) endorse on each duplicate original the word "Filed" and the day, month, and year of the filing thereof;

(2) file one duplicate original in his [or her] office; and

(3) return the other duplicate original to the person who filed it or his [or her] representative.

(b) Upon the filing of a certificate of amendment (or judicial decree of amendment) in the office of the Secretary of State, the certificate of limited partnership shall be amended as set forth therein, and upon the effective date of a certificate of cancellation (or a judicial decree thereof), the certificate of limited partnership is cancelled.

Comment

Section 206 ~~is new.~~ first appeared in the 1976 Act. In addition to providing mechanics for the central filing system, the second sentence of this section does away with the requirement, formerly imposed by some local filing officers, that persons who have executed certificates under a power of attorney exhibit executed copies of the power of attorney itself. Paragraph (b) changes subdivision (5) of Section 25 of the ~~prior uniform law~~ 1916 Act by providing that certificates of cancellation are effective upon their effective date under Section 203.

§ 207. Liability for False Statement in Certificate.

If any certificate of limited partnership or certificate of amendment or cancellation contains a false statement, one who suffers loss by reliance on the statement may recover damages for the loss from:

(1) any person who executes the certificate, or causes another to execute it on his behalf, and knew, and any general partner who knew or should have known, the statement to be false at the time the certificate was executed; and

(2) any general partner who thereafter knows or should have known that any arrangement or other fact described in the certificate has changed, making the statement inaccurate in any respect within a sufficient time before the statement was relied upon reasonably to have enabled that general partner to cancel or amend the certificate, or to file a petition for its cancellation or amendment under Section 205.

Comment

Section 207 changes Section 6 of the ~~prior uniform law~~ 1916 Act by providing explicitly for the liability of persons who sign a certificate as agent under a power of attorney and by confining the obligation to amend a certificate of limited partnership in light of future events to general partners.

§ 208. Scope of Notice.

The fact that a certificate of limited partnership is on file in the office of the Secretary of State is notice that the partnership is a limited partnership and the persons designated therein as ~~limited~~ general partners are ~~limited~~ general partners, but it is not notice of any other fact.

Comment

Section 208 ~~is new~~ first appeared in the 1976 Act, and referred to the certificate's providing constructive notice of the status as limited partners of those so identified therein. The 1985 Act's deletion of any requirement that the certificate name limited partners required that Section 208 be modified accordingly.

By stating that the filing of a certificate of limited partnership only results in notice of the ~~limited~~ general liability of the ~~limited~~ general partners, ~~it~~ Section 208 obviates the concern that third parties may be held to have notice of special provisions set forth in the certificate. While this section is designed to preserve by implication the limited liability of limited partners, the ~~notice~~ implicit protection provided is not intended to change any liability of a limited partner which may be created by his action or inaction under the law of estoppel, agency, fraud, or the like.

§ 209. Delivery of Certificates to Limited Partners.

Upon the return by the Secretary of State pursuant to Section 206 of a certificate marked "Filed," the general partners shall promptly deliver or mail a copy of the certificate of limited partnership and each certificate of amendment or cancellation to each limited partner unless the partnership agreement provides otherwise.

Comment

This section is new. first appeared in the 1976 Act.

ARTICLE 3
LIMITED PARTNERS

§ 301. Admission of ~~Additional~~ Limited Partners.

[(a)] A person becomes a limited partner:

[(1)] at the time the limited partnership is formed; or

[(2)] at any later time specified in the records of the limited partnership for becoming a limited partner.

[~~(a)~~(b)] After the filing of a limited partnership's original certificate of limited partnership, a person may be admitted as an additional limited partner:

(1) in the case of a person acquiring a partnership interest directly from the limited partnership, upon compliance with the partnership agreement or, if the partnership agreement does not so provide, upon the written consent of all partners; and

(2) in the case of an assignee of a partnership interest of a partner who has the power, as provided in Section 704, to grant the assignee the right to become a limited partner, upon the exercise of that power and compliance with any conditions limiting the grant or exercise of the power.

[~~(b)~~] ~~In each case under subsection (a), the person acquiring the partnership interest becomes a limited partner only upon amendment of the certificate of limited partnership reflecting that fact.~~

Comment

Section 301(a) is new; no counterpart was found in the 1916 or 1976 Acts. This section imposes on the partnership an obligation to maintain in its records the date each limited partner becomes a limited partner. Under the 1976 Act, one could not become a limited partner until an appropriate certificate reflecting his status as such was filed with the Secretary of State. Because the 1985 Act eliminates the need to name limited partners in the certificate of limited partnership, an alternative mechanism had to be established to evidence the fact and date of a limited partner's admission. The partnership records required to be maintained under Section 105 now serve that function, subject to the limitation that no person may become a limited partner before the partnership is formed (Section 201(b)).

Subdivision (1) of Section ~~301(a)~~ 301(b) adds to Section 8 of the ~~prior uniform law~~ 1916 Act an explicit recognition of the fact that unanimous consent of all partners is required for admission of new limited partners unless the partnership agreement provides otherwise. Subdivision (2) is derived from Section 19 of the ~~prior uniform law~~ 1916 Act but abandons the former terminology of "substituted limited partner."

§ 302. Voting.

Subject to Section 303, the partnership agreement may grant to all or a specified group of the limited partners the right to vote (on a per capita or other basis) upon any matter.

Comment

Section 302 ~~is new~~ first appeared in the 1976 Act, and must be read together with subdivision ~~(b)(5)~~ (b)(6) of Section 303. Although the ~~prior uniform law~~ 1916 Act did not speak specifically of the voting powers of limited partners, it ~~is~~ was not uncommon for partnership agreements to grant such ~~power~~ powers to limited partners. Section 302 is designed only to make it clear that the partnership agreement may grant such power to limited partners. If such powers are granted to limited partners beyond the "safe harbor" of subdivision (6) or (8) of Section ~~303(b)(5)~~ 303(b), a court may (but of course need not) hold that, under the circumstances, the limited partners have participated in "control of the business" within the meaning of Section 303(a). Section 303(c) ~~simply means~~ makes clear that the exercise of powers beyond the ambit of Section 303(b) is not ipso facto to be taken as taking part in the control of the business.

§ 303. Liability to Third Parties.

(a) Except as provided in subsection (d), a limited partner is not liable for the obligations of a limited partnership unless he [or she] is also a general partner or, in addition to the exercise of his [or her] rights and powers as a limited partner, he [or she] ~~takes part~~ participates in the control of the business. However, if the limited ~~partner's participation~~ partner participates in the control of the business ~~is not substantially the same as the exercise of the powers of a general partner~~, he [or she] is liable only to persons who transact business with the limited partnership ~~with actual knowledge of his participation in control~~ reasonably believing, based upon the limited partner's conduct, that the limited partner is a general partner.

(b) A limited partner does not participate in the control of the business within the meaning of subsection (a) solely by doing one or more of the following:

(1) being a contractor for or an agent or employee of the limited partnership or of a general partner or being an officer, director, or shareholder of a general partner that is a corporation;

(2) consulting with and advising a general partner with respect to the business of the limited partnership;

(3) acting as surety for the limited partnership or guaranteeing or assuming one or more specific obligations of the limited partnership;

(4) ~~approving or disapproving an amendment to the partnership agreement~~ taking any action required or permitted by law to bring or pursue a derivative action in the right of the limited partnership; ~~or~~

[(5)] ~~voting on one or more of the following matters:~~

[(5)] requesting or attending a meeting of partners;

[(6)] proposing, approving, or disapproving, by voting or otherwise, one or more of the following matters:

(i) the dissolution and winding up of the limited partnership;

(ii) the sale, exchange, lease, mortgage, pledge, or other transfer of all or substantially all of the assets of the limited partnership ~~other than in the ordinary course of its business~~;

(iii) the incurrence of indebtedness by the limited partnership other than in the ordinary course of its business;

(iv) a change in the nature of the business; ~~or~~

(v) the admission or removal of a general partner~~:~~;

[(vi)] the admission or removal of a limited partner;

[(vii)] a transaction involving an actual or potential conflict of interest between a general partner and the limited partnership or the limited partners;

[(viii)] an amendment to the partnership agreement or certificate of limited partnership; or

[(ix)] matters related to the business of the limited partnership not otherwise enumerated in this subsection (b), which the partnership agreement states in writing may be subject to the approval or disapproval of limited partners;

[(7)] winding up the limited partnership pursuant to Section 803; or

[(8)] exercising any right or power permitted to limited partners under this [Act] and not specifically enumerated in this subsection (b).

(c) The enumeration in subsection (b) does not mean that the possession or exercise of any other powers by a limited partner constitutes participation by him [or her] in the business of the limited partnership.

(d) A limited partner who knowingly permits his [or her] name to be used in the name of the limited partnership, except under circumstances permitted by Section 102(2), is liable to creditors who extend credit to the limited partnership without actual knowledge that the limited partner is not a general partner.

Comment

Section 303 makes several important changes in Section 7 of the ~~prior uniform law~~ 1916 Act. The first sentence of Section 303(a) ~~carries over the basic test from former Section 7 whether the limited partner "takes part in the control of the business" in order to insure that judicial decisions under the prior uniform law remain applicable to the extent not expressly changed~~ differs from the text of Section 7 of the 1916 Act in that it speaks of participating (rather than taking part) in the control of the business; this was done for the sake of consistency with the second sentence of Section 303(a), not to change the meaning of the text. It is intended that judicial decisions interpreting the phrase "takes part in the control of the business" under the prior uniform law will remain applicable to the extent that a different result is not called for by other provisions of Section 303 and other provisions of the Act. The second sentence of Section 303(a) reflects a wholly new concept~~. Because~~ in the 1976 Act that has been further modified in the 1985 Act. It was adopted partly because of the difficulty of determining when the "control" line has been overstepped, ~~it was thought it unfair to impose general partner's liability on a limited partner except to the extent that a third party had knowledge of his participation in control of the business. On the other hand, in order to avoid permitting a limited partner to exercise all of the powers of a general partner while avoiding any direct dealings with third parties, the "is not substantially the same as" test was introduced~~ but also (and more importantly) because of a determination that it is not sound public policy to hold a limited partner who is not also a general partner liable for the obligations of the partnership except to persons who have done business with the limited partnership reasonably believing, based on the limited partner's conduct, that he is a general partner. Paragraph (b) is intended to provide a "safe harbor" by enumerating certain activities which a limited partner may carry on for the partnership without being deemed to have taken part in control of the business. This "safe harbor" list has been expanded beyond that set out in the 1976 Act to reflect case law and statutory developments and more clearly to assure that limited partners are not subjected to general liability where such liability is inappropriate. Paragraph (d) is derived from Section 5 of the ~~prior uniform law~~ 1916 Act, but adds as a condition to the limited partner's liability the ~~fact~~ requirement that a limited partner must have knowingly permitted his name to be used in the name of the limited partnership.

§ 304. Person Erroneously Believing Himself [or Herself] Limited Partner.

(a) Except as provided in subsection (b), a person who makes a contribution to a business enterprise and erroneously but in good faith believes that he [or she] has become a limited partner in the enterprise is not a general partner in the enterprise and is not bound by its obligations by reason of making the contribution, receiving distributions from the enterprise, or exercising any rights of a limited partner, if, on ascertaining the mistake, he [or she]:

(1) causes an appropriate certificate of limited partnership or a certificate of amendment to be executed and filed; or

(2) withdraws from future equity participation in the enterprise by executing and filing in the office of the Secretary of State a certificate declaring withdrawal under this section.

(b) A person who makes a contribution of the kind described in subsection (a) is liable as a general partner to any third party who transacts business with the enterprise (i) before the person withdraws and an appropriate certificate is filed to show withdrawal, or (ii) before an appropriate certificate is filed to show ~~his status as a limited partner and, in the case of an amendment, after expiration of the 30-day period for filing an amendment relating to the person as a limited partner under Section 202~~ that he [or she] is not a general partner, but in either case only if the third party actually believed in good faith that the person was a general partner at the time of the transaction.

Comment

Section 304 is derived from Section 11 of the ~~prior uniform law.~~ 1916 Act. The "good faith" requirement has been added in the first sentence of Section 304(a). The provisions of subdivision (2) of Section 304(a) are intended to clarify an ambiguity in the prior law by providing that a person who chooses to withdraw from the enterprise in order to protect himself from liability is not required to renounce any of his then current interest in the enterprise so long as he has no further participation as an equity participant. Paragraph (b) preserves the liability of the equity participant prior to withdrawal ~~(and after the time for appropriate amendment in the case of a limited partnership)~~ by such person from the limited partnership or amendment to the certificate demonstrating that such person is not a general partner to any third party who has transacted business with the person believing in good faith that he was a general partner.

Evidence strongly suggests that Section 11 of the 1916 Act and Section 304 of the 1976 Act were rarely used, and one might expect that Section 304 of the 1985 Act may never have to be used. Section 11 of the 1916 Act and Section 304 of the 1976 Act could have been used by a person who invested in a limited partnership believing he would be a limited partner but who was not identified as a limited partner in the certificate of limited partnership. However, because the 1985 Act does not require limited partners to be named in the certificate, the only situation to which Section 304 would now appear to be applicable is one in which a person intending to be a limited partner was erroneously identified as a general partner in the certificate.

§ 305. Information.

Each limited partner has the right to:

(1) inspect and copy any of the partnership records required to be maintained by Section 105; and

(2) obtain from the general partners from time to time upon reasonable demand (i) true and full information regarding the state of the business and financial condition of the limited partnership, (ii) promptly after becoming available, a copy of the limited partnership's federal, state, and local income tax returns for each year, and (iii) other information regarding the affairs of the limited partnership as is just and reasonable.

Comment

Section 305 changes and restates the rights of limited partners to information about the partnership formerly provided by Section 10 of the prior uniform law. 1916 Act. Its importance has increased as a result of the 1985 Act's substituting the records of the partnership for the certificate of limited partnership as the place where certain categories of information are to be kept.

Section 305, which should be read together with Section 105(b), provides a mechanism for limited partners to obtain information about the partnership useful to them in making decisions concerning the partnership and their investments in it. Its purpose is not to provide a mechanism for competitors of the partnership or others having interests or agendas adverse to the partnership's to subvert the partnership's business. It is assumed that courts will protect limited partnerships from abuses and attempts to misuse Section 305 for improper purposes.

ARTICLE 4
GENERAL PARTNERS

§ 401. Admission of Additional General Partners.

After the filing of a limited partnership's original certificate of limited partnership, additional general partners may be admitted only as provided in writing in the partnership agreement or, if the partnership agreement does not provide in writing for the admission of additional general partners, with the specific written consent of each partner all partners.

Comment

Section 401 is derived from, but represents a significant departure from, Section 9(1)(e) of the prior law and carries over the unwaivable requirement that all limited partners must consent 1916 Act and Section 401 of the 1976 Act, which required, as a condition to the admission of an additional general partner, that all limited partners consent and that such consent must specifically identify the general partner involved. Section 401 of the 1985 Act provides that the written partnership agreement determines the procedure for authorizing the admission of additional general partners, and that the written consent of all partners is required only when the partnership agreement fails to address the question.

§ 402. Events of Withdrawal.

Except as approved by the specific written consent of all partners at the time, a person ceases to be a general partner of a limited partnership upon the happening of any of the following events:

(1) the general partner withdraws from the limited partnership as provided in Section 602;

(2) the general partner ceases to be a member of the limited partnership as provided in Section 702;

(3) the general partner is removed as a general partner in accordance with the partnership agreement;

(4) unless otherwise provided in writing in the ~~certificate of limited~~ partnership agreement, the general partner: (i) makes an assignment for the benefit of creditors; (ii) files a voluntary petition in bankruptcy; (iii) is adjudicated a bankrupt or insolvent; (iv) files a petition or answer seeking for himself [or herself] any reorganization, arrangement, composition, readjustment, liquidation, dissolution or similar relief under any statute, law, or regulation; (v) files an answer or other pleading admitting or failing to contest the material allegations of a petition filed against him [or her] in any proceeding of this nature; or (vi) seeks, consents to, or acquiesces in the appointment of a trustee, receiver, or liquidator of the general partner or of all or any substantial part of his [or her] properties;

(5) unless otherwise provided in writing in the ~~certificate of limited~~ partnership agreement, [120] days after the commencement of any proceeding against the general partner seeking reorganization, arrangement, composition, readjustment, liquidation, dissolution or similar relief under any statute, law, or regulation, the proceeding has not been dismissed, or if within [90] days after the appointment without his [or her] consent or acquiescence of a trustee, receiver, or liquidator of the general partner or of all or any substantial part of his [or her] properties, the appointment is not vacated or stayed or within [90] days after the expiration of any such stay, the appointment is not vacated;

(6) in the case of a general partner who is a natural person,

  (i) his [or her] death; or

  (ii) the entry of an order by a court of competent jurisdiction adjudicating him [or her] incompetent to manage his [or her] person or his [or her] estate;

(7) in the case of a general partner who is acting as a general partner by virtue of being a trustee of a trust, the termination of the trust (but not merely the substitution of a new trustee);

(8) in the case of a general partner that is a separate partnership, the dissolution and commencement of winding up of the separate partnership;

(9) in the case of a general partner that is a corporation, the filing of a certificate of dissolution, or its equivalent, for the corporation or the revocation of its charter; or

(10) in the case of an estate, the distribution by the fiduciary of the estate's entire interest in the partnership.

Comment

Section 402 expands considerably the provisions of Section 20 of the ~~prior uniform law~~ 1916 Act, which provided for dissolution in the event of the retirement, death or insanity of a general partner. Subdivisions (1), (2) and (3) recognize that the general partner's agency relationship is terminable at will, although it may result in a breach of the partnership agreement giving rise to an action for damages. Subdivisions (4) and (5) reflect a judgment that, unless the limited partners agree otherwise, they ought to have the power to rid themselves of a general partner who is in such dire financial straits that he is the subject of proceedings under the National Bankruptcy ~~Act~~ Code or a similar provision of law. Subdivisions (6) through (10) simply elaborate on the notion of death in the case of a general partner who is not a natural person. ~~Of course, the addition of the words "and in the partnership agreement" was not intended to suggest that liabilities to third parties could be affected by provisions in the partnership agreement.~~ Subdivisions (4) and (5) differ from their counterparts in the 1976 Act, reflecting the policy underlying the 1985 revision of Section 201, that the partnership agreement, not the certificate of limited partnership, is the appropriate document for setting out most provisions relating to the respective powers, rights and obligations of the partners inter se. Although the partnership agreement need not be written, the 1985 Act provides that, to protect the partners from fraud, these and certain other particularly significant provisions must be set out in a written partnership agreement to be effective for the purposes described in the Act.

§ 403. General Powers and Liabilities.

(a) Except as provided in this [Act] or in the partnership agreement, a general partner of a limited partnership has the rights and powers and is subject to the restrictions of a partner in a partnership without limited partners.

(b) Except as provided in this [Act], a general partner of a limited partnership has the liabilities of a partner in a partnership without limited partners to persons other than the partnership and the other partners. Except as provided in this [Act] or in the partnership agreement, a general partner of a limited partnership has the liabilities of a partner in a partnership without limited partners to the partnership and to the other partners.

Comment

Section 403 is derived from Section 9(1) of the ~~prior uniform law.~~ 1916 Act.

§ 404. Contributions by General Partner.

A general partner of a limited partnership may make contributions to the partnership and share in the profits and losses of, and in distributions from, the limited partnership as a general partner. A general partner also may make contributions to and share in profits, losses, and distributions as a limited partner. A person who is both a general partner and a limited partner has the rights and powers, and is subject to the restrictions and liabilities, of a general partner and, except as provided in the partnership agreement, also has the powers, and is subject to the restrictions, of a limited partner to the extent of his [or her] participation in the partnership as a limited partner.

Comment

Section 404 is derived from Section 12 of the ~~prior uniform law~~ 1916 Act and makes clear that the partnership agreement may provide that a general partner who is also a limited partner may exercise all of the powers of a limited partner.

§ 405. Voting.

The partnership agreement may grant to all or certain identified general partners the right to vote (on a per capita or any other basis), separately or with all or any class of the limited partners, on any matter.

Comment

Section 405 ~~is new~~ first appeared in the 1976 Act and is intended to make it clear that the Act does not require that the limited partners have any right to vote on matters as a separate class.

ARTICLE 5
FINANCE

§ 501. Form of Contribution.

The contribution of a partner may be in cash, property, or services rendered, or a promissory note or other obligation to contribute cash or property or to perform services.

Comment

As noted in the comment to Section 101, the explicit permission to make contributions of services expands Section 4 of the ~~prior uniform law.~~ 1916 Act.

§ 502. Liability for Contribution.

[(a)] A promise by a limited partner to contribute to the limited partnership is not enforceable unless set out in a writing signed by the limited partner.

[~~(a)~~ (b)] Except as provided in the certificate of limited partnership agreement, a partner is obligated to the limited partnership to perform any enforceable promise to contribute cash or property or to perform services, even if he [or she] is unable to perform because of death, disability, or any other reason. If a partner does not make the required contribution of property or services, he [or she] is obligated at the option of the limited partnership to contribute cash equal to that portion of the value, as stated in the ~~certificate of limited~~ partnership records required to be kept pursuant to Section 105, of the stated contribution which has not been made.

[~~(b)~~ (c)] Unless otherwise provided in the partnership agreement, the obligation of a partner to make a contribution or return money or other property paid or distributed in violation of this [Act] may be compromised only by consent of all partners. Notwithstanding the compromise, a creditor of a limited partnership who extends credit, or ~~whose claim arises~~, otherwise acts in reliance on that obligation after the ~~filing of the certificate of limited partnership or an amendment thereto~~ partner signs a writing which~~, in either case,~~ reflects the obligation~~,~~ and before the amendment or cancellation thereof to reflect the compromise~~,~~ may enforce the original obligation.

Comment

Section 502(a) is new: it has no counterpart in the 1916 or 1976 Acts. Because, unlike the prior uniform acts, the 1985 Act does not require that promises to contribute cash, property, or services be described in the limited partnership certificate, to protect against fraud it requires instead that such important promises be in a signed writing.

Although Section 17(1) of the ~~prior uniform law~~ 1916 Act required a partner to fulfill his promise to make contributions, the addition of contributions in the form of a promise to render services means that a partner who is unable to perform those services because of death or disability as well as because of an intentional default is required to pay the cash value of the services unless the ~~certificate of limited partnership~~ partnership agreement provides otherwise.

Subdivision (b) (c) is derived from, but expands upon, Section 17(3) of the prior uniform law 1916 Act.

§ 503. Sharing of Profits and Losses.

The profits and losses of a limited partnership shall be allocated among the partners, and among classes of partners, in the manner provided in writing in the partnership agreement. If the partnership agreement does not so provide in writing, profits and losses shall be allocated on the basis of the value, as stated in the certificate of limited partnership records required to be kept pursuant to Section 105, of the contributions made by each partner to the extent they have been received by the partnership and have not been returned.

Comment

Section 503 is new first appeared in the 1976 Act. The prior uniform law 1916 Act did not provide for the basis on which partners would share profits and losses in the absence of agreement. The 1985 Act differs from its counterpart in the 1976 Act by requiring that, to be effective, the partnership agreement provisions concerning allocation of profits and losses be in writing, and by its reference to records required to be kept pursuant to Section 105, the latter reflecting the 1985 changes in Section 201.

§ 504. Sharing of Distributions.

Distributions of cash or other assets of a limited partnership shall be allocated among the partners and among classes of partners in the manner provided in writing in the partnership agreement. If the partnership agreement does not so provide in writing, distributions shall be made on the basis of the value, as stated in the certificate of limited partnership records required to be kept pursuant to Section 105, of the contributions made by each partner to the extent they have been received by the partnership and have not been returned.

Comment

Section 504 is new first appeared in the 1976 Act. The prior uniform law 1916 Act did not provide for the basis on which partners would share distributions in the absence of agreement. Section 504 also differs from its counterpart in the 1976 Act by requiring that, to be effective, the partnership agreement provisions concerning allocation of distributions be in writing, and in its reference to records required to be kept pursuant to Section 105, the latter reflecting the 1985 changes in Section 201. This section also recognizes that partners may choose to share in distribution distributions on a different basis than different from that on which they share in profits and losses.

ARTICLE 6
DISTRIBUTIONS AND WITHDRAWAL

§ 601. Interim Distributions.

Except as provided in this Article, a partner is entitled to receive distributions from a limited partnership before his [or her] withdrawal from the limited partnership and before the dissolution and winding up thereof:

[(1)] ~~to the extent and at the times or upon the happening of the events specified in the partnership agreement; and~~

[(2)] ~~if any distribution constitutes a return of any part of his contribution under Section 608(c), to the extent and at the times or upon the happening of the events specified in the certificate of limited partnership.~~

Comment

Section 601 ~~is new~~ first appeared in the 1976 Act. The 1976 Act provisions have been modified to reflect the 1985 changes made in Section 201.

§ 602. Withdrawal of General Partner.

A general partner may withdraw from a limited partnership at any time by giving written notice to the other partners, but if the withdrawal violates the partnership agreement, the limited partnership may recover from the withdrawing general partner damages for breach of the partnership agreement and offset the damages against the amount otherwise distributable to him [or her].

Comment

Section 602 ~~is new~~ first appeared in the 1976 Act, but is generally derived from Section 38 of the Uniform Partnership Act.

§ 603. Withdrawal of Limited Partner.

A limited partner may withdraw from a limited partnership at the time or upon the happening of events specified ~~in the certificate of limited partnership and in accordance with~~ in writing in the partnership agreement. If the ~~certificate~~ agreement does not specify in writing the time or the events upon the happening of which a limited partner may withdraw or a definite time for the dissolution and winding up of the limited partnership, a limited partner may withdraw upon not less than six months' prior written notice to each general partner at his [or her] address on the books of the limited partnership at its office in this State.

Comment

Section 603 is derived from Section ~~16(c)~~ 16 of the ~~prior uniform law~~ 1916 Act. The 1976 Act provision has been modified to reflect the 1985 changes made in Section 201. This section additionally reflects the policy determination, also embodied in certain other sections of the 1985 Act, that to avoid fraud, agreements concerning certain matters of substantial importance to the partners will be enforceable only if in writing. If the partnership agreement does provide, in writing, whether a limited partner may withdraw and, if he may, when and on what terms and conditions, those provisions will control.

§ 604. Distribution Upon Withdrawal.

Except as provided in this Article, upon withdrawal any withdrawing partner is entitled to receive any distribution to which he [or she] is entitled under the partnership agreement and, if not otherwise provided in the agreement, he [or she] is entitled to receive, within a reasonable time after withdrawal, the fair value of his [or her] interest in the limited partnership as of the date of withdrawal based upon his [or her] right to share in distributions from the limited partnership.

Comment

Section 604 is new first appeared in the 1976 Act. It fixes the distributive share of a withdrawing partner in the absence of an agreement among the partners.

§ 605. Distribution in Kind.

Except as provided in writing in the certificate of limited partnership agreement, a partner, regardless of the nature of his [or her] contribution, has no right to demand and receive any distribution from a limited partnership in any form other than cash. Except as provided in writing in the partnership agreement, a partner may not be compelled to accept a distribution of any asset in kind from a limited partnership to the extent that the percentage of the asset distributed to him [or her] exceeds a percentage of that asset which is equal to the percentage in which he [or she] shares in distributions from the limited partnership.

Comment

The first sentence of Section 605 is derived from Section 16(3) of the prior uniform law; 1916 Act; it also differs from its counterpart in the 1976 Act, reflecting the 1985 changes made in Section 201. The second sentence is new first appeared in the 1976 Act, and is intended to protect a limited partner (and the remaining partners) against a distribution in kind of more than his share of particular assets.

§ 606. Right to Distribution.

At the time a partner becomes entitled to receive a distribution, he [or she] has the status of, and is entitled to all remedies available to, a creditor of the limited partnership with respect to the distribution.

Comment

Section 606 ~~is new~~ first appeared in the 1976 Act, and is intended to make it clear that the right of a partner to receive a distribution, as between the partners, is not subject to the equity risks of the enterprise. On the other hand, since partners entitled to distributions have creditor status, there did not seem to be a need for the extraordinary remedy of Section 16(4)(a) of the ~~prior uniform law.~~ 1916 Act, which granted a limited partner the right to seek dissolution of the partnership if he was unsuccessful in demanding the return of his contribution. It is more appropriate for the partner to simply sue as an ordinary creditor and obtain a judgment.

§ 607. Limitations on Distribution.

A partner may not receive a distribution from a limited partnership to the extent that, after giving effect to the distribution, all liabilities of the limited partnership, other than liabilities to partners on account of their partnership interests, exceed the fair value of the partnership assets.

Comment

Section 607 is derived from Section 16(1)(a) of the ~~prior uniform law.~~ 1916 Act.

§ 608. Liability Upon Return of Contribution.

(a) If a partner has received the return of any part of his [or her] contribution without violation of the partnership agreement or this [Act], he [or she] is liable to the limited partnership for a period of one year thereafter for the amount of the returned contribution, but only to the extent necessary to discharge the limited partnership's liabilities to creditors who extended credit to the limited partnership during the period the contribution was held by the partnership.

(b) If a partner has received the return of any part of his [or her] contribution in violation of the partnership agreement or this [Act], he [or she] is liable to the limited partnership for a period of six years thereafter for the amount of the contribution wrongfully returned.

(c) A partner receives a return of his [or her] contribution to the extent that a distribution to him [or her] reduces his [or her] share of the fair value of the net assets of the limited partnership below the value, as set forth in the ~~certificate of limited~~ partnership records required to be kept pursuant to Section 105, of his [or her] contribution which has not been distributed to him [or her].

Comment

Paragraph (a) is derived from Section 17(4) of the ~~prior uniform law~~ 1916 Act, but the one year statute of limitations has been added. Paragraph (b) is derived from Section 17(2)(b) of the ~~prior uniform law~~ 1916 Act but, again, a statute of limitations has been added.

Paragraph (c) ~~is new~~ first appeared in the 1976 Act. The provisions of former Section 17(2) that referred to the partner holding as "trustee" any money or specific property wrongfully returned to him have been eliminated. Paragraph (c) in the 1985 Act also differs from its counterpart in the 1976 Act to reflect the 1985 changes made in Sections 105 and 201.

ARTICLE 7
ASSIGNMENT OF PARTNERSHIP INTERESTS

§ 701. Nature of Partnership Interest.

A partnership interest is personal property.

Comment

This section is derived from Section 18 of the ~~prior uniform law.~~ 1916 Act.

§ 702. Assignment of Partnership Interest.

Except as provided in the partnership agreement, a partnership interest is assignable in whole or in part. An assignment of a partnership interest does not dissolve a limited partnership or entitle the assignee to become or to exercise any rights of a partner. An assignment entitles the assignee to receive, to the extent assigned, only the distribution to which the assignor would be entitled. Except as provided in the partnership agreement, a partner ceases to be a partner upon assignment of all his [or her] partnership interest.

Comment

Section 19(1) of the ~~prior uniform law~~ 1916 Act provided simply that "a limited partner's interest is assignable," raising a question whether any limitations on the right of assignment were permitted. While the first sentence of Section 702 recognizes that the power to assign may be restricted in the partnership agreement, there was no intention to affect in any way the usual rules regarding restraints on alienation of personal property. The second and third sentences of Section 702 are derived from Section 19(3) of the ~~prior uniform law.~~ 1916 Act. The last sentence ~~is new.~~ first appeared in the 1976 Act.

§ 703. Rights of Creditor.

On application to a court of competent jurisdiction by any judgment creditor of a partner, the court may charge the partnership interest of the partner with payment of the unsatisfied amount of the judgment with interest. To the extent so charged, the judgment creditor has only the rights of an assignee of the partnership interest. This [Act] does not deprive any partner of the benefit of any exemption laws applicable to his [or her] partnership interest.

Comment

Section 703 is derived from Section 22 of the ~~prior uniform law~~ 1916 Act but has not carried over some provisions that were thought to be superfluous. For example, references in Section 22(1) to specific remedies have been omitted, as has a prohibition in Section 22(2) against discharge of the lien with partnership property. Ordinary rules governing the remedies available to a creditor and the fiduciary obligations of general partners will determine those matters.

§ 704. Right of Assignee to Become Limited Partner.

(a) An assignee of a partnership interest, including an assignee of a general partner, may become a limited partner if and to the extent that ~~(1)~~ (i) the assignor gives the assignee that right in accordance with authority described in the ~~certificate of limited partnership~~ agreement, or ~~(2)~~ (ii) all other partners consent.

(b) An assignee who has become a limited partner has, to the extent assigned, the rights and powers, and is subject to the restrictions and liabilities, of a limited partner under the partnership agreement and this [Act]. An assignee who becomes a limited partner also is liable for the obligations of his [or her] assignor to make and return contributions as provided in ~~Article~~ Articles 5 and 6. However, the assignee is not obligated for liabilities unknown to the assignee at the time he [or she] became a limited partner ~~and which could not be ascertained from the certificate of limited partnership~~.

(c) If an assignee of a partnership interest becomes a limited partner, the assignor is not released from his [or her] liability to the limited partnership under Sections 207 and 502.

Comment

Section 704 is derived from Section 19 of the ~~prior uniform law,~~ 1916 Act, but paragraph (b) defines more narrowly than Section 19 the obligations of the assignor that are automatically assumed by the assignee. Section 704 of the 1985 Act also differs from the 1976 Act to reflect the 1985 changes made in Section 201.

§ 705. Power of Estate of Deceased or Incompetent Partner.

If a partner who is an individual dies or a court of competent jurisdiction adjudges him [or her] to be incompetent to manage his [or her] person or his [or her] property, the partner's executor, administrator, guardian, conservator, or other legal representative may exercise all the partner's rights for the purpose of settling his [or her] estate or administering his [or her] property, including any power the partner had to give an assignee the right to become a limited partner. If a partner is a corporation, trust, or other entity and is dissolved or terminated, the powers of that partner may be exercised by its legal representative or successor.

Comment

Section 705 is derived from Section 21(1) of the ~~prior uniform law.~~ 1916 Act. Former Section 21(2), making a deceased limited partner's estate liable for his liabilities as a limited partner was deleted as superfluous, with no intention of changing the liability of the estate.

ARTICLE 8
DISSOLUTION

§ 801. Nonjudicial Dissolution.

A limited partnership is dissolved and its affairs shall be wound up upon the happening of the first to occur of the following:

(1) at the time specified in the certificate of limited partnership;

[(2)] ~~or~~ upon the happening of events specified in writing in the ~~certificate of limited~~ partnership agreement;

[~~(2)~~ (3)] written consent of all partners;

[~~(3)~~ (4)] an event of withdrawal of a general partner unless at the time there is at least one other general partner and the ~~certificate of limited~~ written provisions of the partnership agreement ~~permits~~ permit the business of the limited partnership to be carried on by the remaining general partner and that partner does so, but the limited partnership is not dissolved and is not required to be wound up by reason of any event of withdrawal; if, within 90 days after the withdrawal, all partners agree in writing to continue the business of the limited partnership and to the appointment of one or more additional general partners if necessary or desired; or

[~~(4)~~ (5)] entry of a decree of judicial dissolution under Section 802.

Comment

Section 801 merely collects in one place all of the events causing dissolution. Paragraph (3) is derived from Sections 9(1)(g) and 20 of the ~~prior uniform law,~~ 1916 Act, but adds the 90-day grace period. Section 801 also differs from its counterpart in the 1976 Act to reflect the 1985 changes made in Section 201.

§ 802. Judicial Dissolution.

On application by or for a partner the [designate the appropriate court] court may decree dissolution of a limited partnership whenever it is not reasonably practicable to carry on the business in conformity with the partnership agreement.

Comment

Section 802 ~~is new~~ first appeared in the 1976 Act.

§ 803. Winding Up.

Except as provided in the partnership agreement, the general partners who have not wrongfully dissolved a limited partnership or, if none, the limited partners, may wind up the limited partnership's affairs; but the [designate the appropriate court] court may wind up the limited partnership's affairs upon application of any partner, his [or her] legal representative, or assignee.

Comment

Section 803 ~~is new~~ first appeared in the 1976 Act, and is derived in part from Section 37 of the Uniform ~~General~~ Partnership Act.

§ 804. Distribution of Assets.

Upon the winding up of a limited partnership, the assets shall be distributed as follows:

(1) to creditors, including partners who are creditors, to the extent permitted by law, in satisfaction of liabilities of the limited partnership other than liabilities for distributions to partners under Section 601 or 604;

(2) except as provided in the partnership agreement, to partners and former partners in satisfaction of liabilities for distributions under Section 601 or 604; and

(3) except as provided in the partnership agreement, to partners first for the return of their contributions and secondly respecting their partnership interests, in the proportions in which the partners share in distributions.

Comment

Section 804 revises Section 23 of the ~~prior uniform law~~ 1916 Act by providing that (1) to the extent partners are also creditors, other than in respect of their interests in the partnership, they share with other creditors, (2) once the partnership's obligation to make a distribution accrues, it must be paid before any other distributions of an "equity" nature are made, and

(3) general and limited partners rank on the same level except as otherwise provided in the partnership agreement.

ARTICLE 9
FOREIGN LIMITED PARTNERSHIPS

§ 901. Law Governing.

Subject to the Constitution of this State, (i) the laws of the state under which a foreign limited partnership is organized govern its organization and internal affairs and the liability of its limited partners, and (ii) a foreign limited partnership may not be denied registration by reason of any difference between those laws and the laws of this State.

Comment

Section 901 ~~is new.~~ first appeared in the 1976 Act.

§ 902. Registration.

Before transacting business in this State, a foreign limited partnership shall register with the Secretary of State. In order to register, a foreign limited partnership shall submit to the Secretary of State, in duplicate, an application for registration as a foreign limited partnership, signed and sworn to by a general partner and setting forth:

(1) the name of the foreign limited partnership and, if different, the name under which it proposes to register and transact business in this State;

(2) the ~~state~~ State and date of its formation;

[~~(3)~~] ~~the general character of the business it proposes to transact in this State;~~

[~~(4)~~ (3)] the name and address of any agent for service of process on the foreign limited partnership whom the foreign limited partnership elects to appoint; the agent must be an individual resident of this ~~state~~ State, a domestic corporation, or a foreign corporation having a place of business in, and authorized to do business in, this State;

[~~(5)~~ (4)] a statement that the Secretary of State is appointed the agent of the foreign limited partnership for service of process if no agent has been appointed under paragraph ~~(4)~~ (3) or, if appointed, the agent's authority has been revoked or if the agent cannot be found or served with the exercise of reasonable diligence;

[~~(6)~~ (5)] the address of the office required to be maintained in the ~~State~~ state of its organization by the laws of that ~~State~~ state or, if not so required, of the principal office of the foreign limited partnership; ~~and~~

[(7)] ~~if the certificate of limited partnership filed in the foreign limited partnership's state of organization is not required to include the names and business addresses of the partners, a list of the names and addresses.~~

[(6)] the name and business address of each general partner; and

[(7)] the address of the office at which is kept a list of the names and addresses of the limited partners and their capital contributions, together with an undertaking by the foreign limited partnership to keep those records until the foreign limited partnership's registration in this State is cancelled or withdrawn.

Comment

Section 902 ~~is new~~ first appeared in the 1976 Act. It was thought that requiring a full copy of the certificate of limited partnership and all amendments thereto to be filed in each state in which the partnership does business would impose an unreasonable burden on interstate limited partnerships and that the information ~~on file was~~ Section 902 required to be filed would be sufficient to tell interested persons where they could write to obtain copies of those basic documents. Subdivision (3) of the 1976 Act has been omitted, and subdivisions (6) and (7) differ from their counterparts in the 1976 Act, to conform these provisions relating to the registration of foreign limited partnerships to the corresponding changes made by the Act in the provisions relating to domestic limited partnerships. The requirement that an application for registration be sworn to by a general partner is simply intended to produce the same result as is provided for in Section 204(c) with respect to certificates of domestic limited partnerships; the acceptance and endorsement by the Secretary of State (or equivalent authority) of an application which was not sworn by a general partner should be deemed a mere technical and insubstantial shortcoming, and should not result in the limited partners' being subjected to general liability for the obligations of the foreign limited partnership (See Section 907(c)).

§ 903. Issuance of Registration.

(a) If the Secretary of State finds that an application for registration conforms to law and all requisite fees have been paid, he [or she] shall:

(1) endorse on the application the word "Filed," and the month, day and year of the filing thereof;

(2) file in his [or her] office a duplicate original of the application; and

(3) issue a certificate of registration to transact business in this State.

(b) The certificate of registration, together with a duplicate original of the application, shall be returned to the person who filed the application or his [or her] representative.

Comment

Section 903 first appeared in the 1976 Act.

§ 904. Name.

A foreign limited partnership may register with the Secretary of State under any name, whether or not it is the name under which it is registered in its state of organization, that includes without abbreviation the words "limited partnership" and that could be registered by a domestic limited partnership.

Comment

Section 904 is new: first appeared in the 1976 Act.

§ 905. Changes and Amendments.

If any statement in the application for registration of a foreign limited partnership was false when made or any arrangements or other facts described have changed, making the application inaccurate in any respect, the foreign limited partnership shall promptly file in the office of the Secretary of State a certificate, signed and sworn to by a general partner, correcting such statement.

Comment

Section 905 is new: first appeared in the 1976 Act. It corresponds to the provisions of Section 202(c) relating to domestic limited partnerships.

§ 906. Cancellation of Registration.

A foreign limited partnership may cancel its registration by filing with the Secretary of State a certificate of cancellation signed and sworn to by a general partner. A cancellation does not terminate the authority of the Secretary of State to accept service of process on the foreign limited partnership with respect to [claims for relief] [causes of action] arising out of the transactions of business in this State.

Comment

Section 906 is new: first appeared in the 1976 Act.

§ 907. Transaction of Business Without Registration.

(a) A foreign limited partnership transacting business in this State may not maintain any action, suit, or proceeding in any court of this State until it has registered in this State.

(b) The failure of a foreign limited partnership to register in this State does not impair the validity of any contract or act of the foreign limited partnership or prevent the foreign limited partnership from defending any action, suit, or proceeding in any court of this State.

(c) A limited partner of a foreign limited partnership is not liable as a general partner of the foreign limited partnership solely by reason of having transacted business in this State without registration.

(d) A foreign limited partnership, by transacting business in this State without registration, appoints the Secretary of State as its agent for service of process with respect to [claims for relief] [causes of action] arising out of the transaction of business in this State.

Comment

Section 907 is new. first appeared in the 1976 Act.

§ 908. Action by [Appropriate Official].

The [designate the appropriate official] may bring an action to restrain a foreign limited partnership from transacting business in this State in violation of this Article.

Comment

Section 908 is new. first appeared in the 1976 Act.

ARTICLE 10
DERIVATIVE ACTIONS

§ 1001. Right of Action.

A limited partner may bring an action in the right of a limited partnership to recover a judgment in its favor if general partners with authority to do so have refused to bring the action or if an effort to cause those general partners to bring the action is not likely to succeed.

Comment

Section 1001 is new. first appeared in the 1976 Act.

§ 1002. Proper Plaintiff.

In a derivative action, the plaintiff must be a partner at the time of bringing the action and (i) must have been a partner at the time of the transaction of which he [or she] complains or (ii) his [or her] status as a partner had must have devolved upon him [or her] by operation of law or pursuant to the terms of the partnership agreement from a person who was a partner at the time of the transaction.

Comment

Section 1002 is new. first appeared in the 1976 Act.

§ 1003. Pleading.

In a derivative action, the complaint shall set forth with particularity the effort of the plaintiff to secure initiation of the action by a general partner or the reasons for not making the effort.

Comment

Section 1003 ~~is new.~~ first appeared in the 1976 Act.

§ 1004. Expenses.

If a derivative action is successful, in whole or in part, or if anything is received by the plaintiff as a result of a judgment, compromise or settlement of an action or claim, the court may award the plaintiff reasonable expenses, including reasonable attorney's fees, and shall direct him [or her] to remit to the limited partnership the remainder of those proceeds received by him [or her].

Comment

Section 1004 ~~is new.~~ first appeared in the 1976 Act.

ARTICLE 11
MISCELLANEOUS

§ 1101. Construction and Application.

This [Act] shall be so applied and construed to effectuate its general purpose to make uniform the law with respect to the subject of this [Act] among states enacting it.

Comment

Because the principles set out in Sections 28(1) and 29 of the 1916 Act have become so universally established, it was felt that the 1976 and 1985 Acts need not contain express provisions to the same effect. However, it is intended that the principles enunciated in those provisions of the 1916 Act also apply to this Act.

§ 1102. Short Title.

This [Act] may be cited as the Uniform Limited Partnership Act.

§ 1103. Severability.

If any provision of this [Act] or its application to any person or circumstance is held invalid, the invalidity does not affect other provisions or applications of the [Act] which can be given effect without the invalid provision or application, and to this end the provisions of this [Act] are severable.

§ 1104. Effective Date, Extended Effective Date and Repeal.

Except as set forth below, the effective date of this [Act] is _____ and the following acts [list ~~prior~~ existing limited partnership acts] are hereby repealed:

(1) The existing provisions for execution and filing of certificates of limited partnerships and amendments thereunder and cancellations

thereof continue in effect until [specify time required to create central filing system], the extended effective date, and Sections 102, 103, 104, 105, 201, 202, 203, 204 and 206 are not effective until the extended effective date.

(2) Section 402, specifying the conditions under which a general partner ceases to be a member of a limited partnership, is not effective until the extended effective date, and the applicable provisions of existing law continue to govern until the extended effective date.

(3) Sections 501, 502 and 608 apply only to contributions and distributions made after the effective date of this [Act].

(4) Section 704 applies only to assignments made after the effective date of this [Act].

(5) Article 9, dealing with registration of foreign limited partnerships, is not effective until the extended effective date.

[(6)] Unless otherwise agreed by the partners, the applicable provisions of existing law governing allocation of profits and losses (rather than the provisions of Section 503), distributions to a withdrawing partner (rather than the provisions of Section 604), and distribution of assets upon the winding up of a limited partnership (rather than the provisions of Section 804) govern limited partnerships formed before the effective date of this [Act].

Comment

Subdivisions (6) and (7) did not appear in Section 1104 of the 1976 Act. They are included in the 1985 Act to ensure that the application of the Act to limited partnerships formed and existing before the Act becomes effective would not violate constitutional prohibitions against the impairment of contracts. [There is no subdivision (7) in 6A Uniform Laws Annotated 293 (1995), from which this language was taken. *Eds.*]

§ 1105. Rules for Cases Not Provided for in This [Act].

In any case not provided for in this [Act] the provisions of the Uniform Partnership Act govern.

Comment

The result provided for in Section 1105 would obtain even in its absence in a jurisdiction which had adopted the Uniform Partnership Act, by operation of Section 6 of that act.

§ 1106. Savings Clause.

The repeal of any statutory provision by this [Act] does not impair, or otherwise affect, the organization or the continued existence of a limited partnership existing at the effective date of this [Act], nor does the repeal of any existing statutory provision by this [Act] impair any contract or affect any right accrued before the effective date of this [Act].

Comment

Section 1106 did not appear in the 1976 Act. It was included in the 1985 Act to ensure that the application of the Act to limited partnerships formed and existing before the Act becomes effective would not violate constitutional prohibitions against the impairment of contracts.

UNIFORM LIMITED PARTNERSHIP ACT (2001)*

Editor's note: Based on the 2006 Cumulative Annual Pocket Part to 6 Pt, 1 Uniform Laws Annotated 1 (2001), ULPA (2001) has been adopted in 6 jurisdictions. (For the most recent adoptions, please check the website of the National Conference of Commissioners on Uniform State Laws ("NCCUSL") at www.nccusl.org.) The date set forth immediately after each jurisdiction is the effective date of the Act: Florida (2006), Hawaii (2004), Illinois (2005), Iowa (2005), Minnesota (2004), and North Dakota (2005).

PREFATORY NOTE

The Act's Overall Approach

The new Limited Partnership Act is a "stand alone" act, "de-linked" from both the original general partnership act ("UPA") and the Revised Uniform Partnership Act ("RUPA"). To be able to stand alone, the Limited Partnership incorporates many provisions from RUPA and some from the Uniform Limited Liability Company Act ("ULLCA"). As a result, the new Act is far longer and more complex than its immediate predecessor, the Revised Uniform Limited Partnership Act ("RULPA").

The new Act has been drafted for a world in which limited liability partnerships and limited liability companies can meet many of the needs formerly met by limited partnerships. This Act therefore targets two types of enterprises that seem largely beyond the scope of LLPs and LLCs: (i) sophisticated, manager-entrenched commercial deals whose participants commit for the long term, and (ii) estate planning arrangements (family limited partnerships). This Act accordingly assumes that, more often than not, people utilizing it will want:

- strong centralized management, strongly entrenched, and

- passive investors with little control over or right to exit the entity

The Act's rules, and particularly its default rules, have been designed to reflect these assumptions.

The Decision to "De-Link" and Create a Stand Alone Act

Unlike this Act, RULPA is not a stand alone statute. RULPA was drafted to rest on and link to the UPA. RULPA Section 1105 states that "In any case not provided for in this [Act] the provisions of the Uniform Partnership Act govern." UPA Section 6(2) in turn provides that "this Act shall apply to limited partnerships except in so far as the statutes relating to such partnerships are inconsistent herewith." More particularly, RULPA Section 403 defines the rights, powers, restrictions and liabilities of a "general partner of a limited partnership" by equating them to the rights, powers, restrictions and liabilities of "a partner in a partnership without limited partners."

This arrangement has not been completely satisfactory, because the consequences of linkage are not always clear. *See, e.g., Frye v. Manacare Ltd.*, 431 So. 2d 181, 183–84 (Fla. Dist. Ct. App. 1983) (applying UPA Section 42 in favor of a limited partner), *Porter v. Barnhouse*, 354 N.W.2d 227, 232–33 (Iowa 1984) (declining to apply UPA Section 42 in favor of a limited partner) and *Baltzell-Wolfe Agencies, Inc. v. Car Wash Investments No. 1, Ltd.*, 389 N.E.2d 517, 518–20 (Ohio App. 1978) (holding that neither the specific provisions of the general partnership statute nor those of the limited partnership statute determined the liability of a person who had withdrawn as general partner of a limited partnership). Moreover, in some instances the "not inconsistent" rules of the UPA can be inappropriate for the fundamentally different relations involved in a limited partnership.

In any event, the promulgation of RUPA unsettled matters. RUPA differs substantially from the UPA, and the drafters of RUPA expressly declined to decide whether RUPA provides a suitable base and link for the limited partnership statute. According to RUPA's Prefatory Note:

> Partnership law no longer governs limited partnerships pursuant to the provisions of RUPA itself. First, limited partnerships are not "partnerships" within the RUPA definition. Second, UPA Section 6(2), which provides that the UPA governs limited partnerships in cases not provided for in the Uniform Limited Partnership Act (1976) (1985) ("RULPA") has been deleted. No substantive change in result is intended, however. Section 1105 of RULPA already provides that the UPA governs in any case not provided for in RULPA, and thus the express linkage in RUPA is unnecessary. Structurally, it is more appropriately left to RULPA to determine the applicability of RUPA to limited partnerships. It is contemplated that the Conference will review the linkage question carefully, although no changes in RULPA may be necessary despite the many changes in RUPA.

The linkage question was the first major issue considered and decided by this Act's Drafting Committee. Since the Conference has recommended the repeal of the UPA, it made no sense to recommend retaining the UPA as the base and link for a revised or new limited partnership act. The

Drafting Committee therefore had to choose between recommending link-age to the new general partnership act (i.e., RUPA) or recommending de-linking and a stand alone act.

The Committee saw several substantial advantages to de-linking. A stand alone statute would:

- be more convenient, providing a single, self-contained source of statutory authority for issues pertaining to limited partnerships;

- eliminate confusion as to which issues were solely subject to the limited partnership act and which required reference (i.e., linkage) to the general partnership act; and

- rationalize future case law, by ending the automatic link between the cases concerning partners in a general partnership and issues pertaining to general partners in a limited partnership.

Thus, a stand alone act seemed likely to promote efficiency, clarity, and coherence in the law of limited partnerships.

In contrast, recommending linkage would have required the Drafting Committee to (1) consider each provision of RUPA and determine whether the provision addressed a matter provided for in RULPA; (2) for each RUPA provision which addressed a matter not provided for in RULPA, determine whether the provision stated an appropriate rule for limited partnerships; and (3) for each matter addressed both by RUPA and RULPA, determine whether RUPA or RULPA stated the better rule for limited partnerships.

That approach was unsatisfactory for at least two reasons. No matter how exhaustive the Drafting Committee's analysis might be, the Committee could not guarantee that courts and practitioners would reach the same conclusions. Therefore, in at least some situations linkage would have produced ambiguity. In addition, the Drafting Committee could not guarantee that all currently appropriate links would remain appropriate as courts begin to apply and interpret RUPA. Even if the Committee recommended linkage, RUPA was destined to be interpreted primarily in the context of general partnerships. Those interpretations might not make sense for limited partnership law, because the modern limited partnership involves fundamentally different relations than those involved in "the small, often informal, partnership" that is "[t]he primary focus of RUPA." RUPA, Prefatory Note.

The Drafting Committee therefore decided to draft and recommend a stand alone act.

Availability of LLLP Status

Following the example of a growing number of States, this Act provides for limited liability limited partnerships. In a limited liability limited partnership ("LLLP"), no partner — whether general or limited — is liable on account of partner status for the limited partnership's obligations. Both general and limited partners benefit from a full, status-based liability shield that is equivalent to the shield enjoyed by corporate shareholders, LLC members, and partners in an LLP.

This Act is designed to serve preexisting limited partnerships as well as limited partnerships formed after the Act's enactment. Most of those preexisting limited partnership will not be LLLPs, and accordingly the Act does not prefer or presume LLLP status. Instead, the Act makes LLLP status available through a simple statement in the certificate of limited partnership. *See* Sections 102(9), 201(a)(4) and 404(c).

Liability Shield for Limited Partners

RULPA provides only a restricted liability shield for limited partners. The shield is at risk for any limited partner who "participates in the control of the business." RULPA Section 303(a). Although this "control rule" is subject to a lengthy list of safe harbors, RULPA Section 303(b), in a world with LLPs, LLCs and, most importantly, LLLPs, the rule is an anachronism. This Act therefore eliminates the control rule and provides a full, status-based shield against limited partner liability for entity obligations. The shield applies whether or not the limited partnership is an LLLP. *See* Section 303.

Transition Issues

Following RUPA's example, this Act provides (i) an effective date, after which all newly formed limited partnerships are subject to this Act; (ii) an optional period, during which limited partnerships formed under a predecessor statute may elect to become subject to this Act; and (iii) a mandatory date, on which all preexisting limited partnerships become subject to this Act by operation of law.

A few provisions of this Act differ so substantially from prior law that they should not apply automatically to a preexisting limited partnership. Section 1206(c) lists these provisions and states that each remains inapplicable to a preexisting limited partnership, unless the limited partnership elects for the provision to apply.

Comparison of RULPA and this Act

The following table compares some of the major characteristics of RULPA and this Act. In most instances, the rules involved are "default" rules — i.e., subject to change by the partnership agreement.

Characteristic	RULPA	this Act
relationship to general partnership act	linked, Sections 1105, 403; UPA Section 6(2)	de-linked (but many RUPA provisions incorporated)

Characteristic	RULPA	this Act
permitted purposes	subject to any specified exceptions, "any business that a partnership without limited partners may carry on," Section 106	any lawful purpose, Section 104(b)
constructive notice via publicly filed documents	only that limited partnership exists and that designated general partners are general partners, Section 208	RULPA constructive notice provisions carried forward, Section 103(c), plus constructive notice, 90 days after appropriate filing, of: general partner dissociation and of limited partnership dissolution, termination, merger and conversion, Section 103(d)
duration	specified in certificate of limited partnership, Section 201(a)(4)	perpetual, Section 104(c); subject to change in partnership agreement
use of limited partner name in entity name	prohibited, except in unusual circumstances, Section 102(2)	permitted, Section108(a)
annual report	none	required, Section 210
limited partner liability for entity debts	none unless limited partner "participates in the control of the business" and person "transact[s] business with the limited partnership reasonably believing . . . that the limited partner is a general partner," Section 303(a); safe harbor lists many activities that do not constitute participating in the control of the business, Section 303(b)	none, regardless of whether the limited partnership is an LLLP, "even if the limited partner participates in the management and control of the limited partnership," Section 303

Characteristic	RULPA	this Act
limited partner duties	none specified	no fiduciary duties "solely by reason of being a limited partner," Section 305(a); each limited partner is obliged to "discharge duties . . . and exercise rights consistently with the obligation of good faith and fair dealing," Section 305(b)
partner access to information — required records/ information	all partners have right of access; no requirement of good cause; Act does not state whether partnership agreement may limit access; Sections 105(b) and 305(1)	list of required information expanded slightly; Act expressly states that partner does not have to show good cause; Sections 304(a), 407(a); however, the partnership agreement may set reasonable restrictions on access to and use of required information, Section 110(b)(4), and limited partnership may impose reasonable restrictions on the use of information, Sections 304(g) and 407(f)
partner access to information — other information	limited partners have the right to obtain other relevant information "upon reasonable demand," Section 305(2); general partner rights linked to general partnership act, Section 403	for limited partners, RULPA approach essentially carried forward, with procedures and standards for making a reasonable demand stated in greater detail, plus requirement that limited partnership supply known material information when limited partner consent sought, Section 304; general partner access rights made explicit, following ULLCA and RUPA, including obligation of limited partnership and general partners to volunteer certain information, Section 407; access rights provided for former partners, Sections 304 and 407

Characteristic	RULPA	this Act
general partner liability for entity debts	complete, automatic and formally inescapable, Section 403(b) (*n.b.* — in practice, most modern limited partnerships have used a general partner that has its own liability shield; *e.g.*, a corporation or limited liability company)	LLLP status available via a simple statement in the certificate of limited partnership, Sections 102(9), 201(a)(4); LLLP status provides a full liability shield to all general partners, Section 404(c); if the limited partnership is not an LLLP, general partners are liable just as under RULPA, Section 404(a)
general partner duties	linked to duties of partners in a general partnership, Section 403	RUPA general partner duties imported, Section 408; general partner's non-compete duty continues during winding up, Section 408(b)(3)
allocation of profits, losses and distributions	provides separately for sharing of profits and losses, Section 503, and for sharing of distributions, Section 504; allocates each according to contributions made and not returned	eliminates as unnecessary the allocation rule for profits and losses; allocates distributions according to contributions made, Section 503 (*n.b.* — in the default mode, the Act's formulation produces the same result as RULPA formulation)
partner liability for distributions	recapture liability if distribution involved "the return of . . . contribution"; one year recapture liability if distribution rightful, Section 608(a); six year recapture liability if wrongful, Section 608(b)	following ULLCA Sections 406 and 407, the Act adopts the RMBCA approach to improper distributions, Sections 508 and 509

Characteristic	RULPA	this Act
limited partner voluntary dissociation	theoretically, limited partner may withdraw on six months notice unless partnership agreement specifies a term for the limited partnership or withdrawal events for limited partner, Section 603; practically, virtually every partnership agreement specifies a term, thereby eliminating the right to withdraw (*n.b.* — due to estate planning concerns, several States have amended RULPA to prohibit limited partner withdrawal unless otherwise provided in the partnership agreement)	no "right to dissociate as a limited partner before the termination of the limited partnership," Section 601(a); power to dissociate expressly recognized, Section 601(b)(1), but can be eliminated by the partnership agreement
limited partner involuntary dissociation	not addressed	lengthy list of causes, Section 601(b), taken with some modification from RUPA
limited partner dissociation — payout	"fair value . . . based upon [the partner's] right to share in distributions," Section 604	no payout; person becomes transferee of its own transferable interest, Section 602(3)
general partner voluntary dissociation	right exists unless otherwise provided in partnership agreement, Section 602; power exists regardless of partnership agreement, Section 602	RULPA rule carried forward, although phrased differently, Section 604(a); dissociation before termination of the limited partnership is defined as wrongful, Section 604(b)(2)
general partner involuntary dissociation	Section 402 lists causes	following RUPA, Section 603 expands the list of causes, including expulsion by court order, Section 603(5)

Characteristic	RULPA	this Act
general partner dissociation — payout	"fair value . . . based upon [the partner's] right to share in distributions," Section 604, subject to offset for damages caused by wrongful withdrawal, Section 602	no payout; person becomes transferee of its own transferable interest, Section 605(5)
transfer of partner interest — nomenclature	"Assignment of Partnership Interest," Section 702	"Transfer of Partner's Transferable Interest," Section 702
transfer of partner interest — substance	economic rights fully transferable, but management rights and partner status are not transferable, Section 702	same rule, but Sections 701 and 702 follow RUPA's more detailed and less oblique formulation
rights of creditor of partner	limited to charging order, Section 703	essentially the same rule, but, following RUPA and ULLCA, the Act has a more elaborate provision that expressly extends to creditors of transferees, Section 703
dissolution by partner consent	requires unanimous written consent, Section 801(3)	requires consent of "all general partners and of limited partners owning a majority of the rights to receive distributions as limited partners at the time the consent is to be effective," Section 801(2)

Characteristic	RULPA	this Act
dissolution following dissociation of a general partner	occurs automatically unless all partners agree to continue the business and, if there is no remaining general partner, to appoint a replacement general partner, Section 801(4)	if at least one general partner remains, no dissolution unless "within 90 days after the dissociation . . . partners owning a majority of the rights to receive distributions as partners" consent to dissolve the limited partnership; Section 801(3)(A); if no general partner remains, dissolution occurs upon the passage of 90 days after the dissociation, unless before that deadline limited partners owning a majority of the rights to receive distributions owned by limited partners consent to continue the business and admit at least one new general partner and a new general partner is admitted, Section 801(3)(B)
filings related to entity termination	certificate of limited partnership to be cancelled when limited partnership dissolves and begins winding up, Section 203	limited partnership may amend certificate to indicate dissolution, Section 803(b)(1), and may file statement of termination indicating that winding up has been completed and the limited partnership is terminated, Section 203
procedures for barring claims against dissolved limited partnership	none	following ULLCA Sections 807 and 808, the Act adopts the RMBCA approach providing for giving notice and barring claims, Sections 806 and 807

Characteristic	RULPA	this Act
conversions and mergers	no provision	Article 11 permits conversions to and from and mergers with any "organization," defined as "a general partnership, including a limited liability partnership; limited partnership, including a limited liability limited partnership; limited liability company; business trust; corporation; or any other entity having a governing statute . . . [including] domestic and foreign entities regardless of whether organized for profit." Section 1101(8)
writing requirements	some provisions pertain only to written understandings; *see, e.g.,* Sections 401 (partnership agreement may "provide in writing for the admission of additional general partners"; such admission also permitted "with the written consent of all partners"), 502(a) (limited partner's promise to contribute "is not enforceable unless set out in a writing signed by the limited partner"), 801(2) and (3) (dissolution occurs "upon the happening of events specified in writing in the partnership agreement" and upon "written consent of all partners"), 801(4) (dissolution avoided following withdrawal of a general partner if "all partners agree in writing")	removes virtually all writing requirements; but does require that certain information be maintained in record form, Section 111

UNIFORM LIMITED PARTNERSHIP ACT (2001)

[ARTICLE] 1 GENERAL PROVISIONS

[ARTICLE] 2 FORMATION; CERTIFICATE OF LIMITED PARTNERSHIP AND OTHER FILINGS

[ARTICLE] 3 LIMITED PARTNERS

[ARTICLE] 4 GENERAL PARTNERS

[ARTICLE] 5 CONTRIBUTIONS AND DISTRIBUTIONS

[ARTICLE] 6 DISSOCIATION

[ARTICLE] 7 TRANSFERABLE INTERESTS AND RIGHTS OF TRANSFEREES AND CREDITORS

[ARTICLE] 8 DISSOLUTION

[ARTICLE] 9 FOREIGN LIMITED PARTNERSHIPS

Section   1207. Savings Clause

ARTICLE 1
GENERAL PROVISIONS

Section 101. Short Title

This [Act] may be cited as the Uniform Limited Partnership Act [year of enactment].

Section 102. Definitions

In this [Act]:

(1) "Certificate of limited partnership" means the certificate required by Section 201. The term includes the certificate as amended or restated.

(2) "Contribution", except in the phrase "right of contribution," means any benefit provided by a person to a limited partnership in order to become a partner or in the person's capacity as a partner.

(3) "Debtor in bankruptcy" means a person that is the subject of:

   (A) an order for relief under Title 11 of the United States Code or a comparable order under a successor statute of general application; or

   (B) a comparable order under federal, state, or foreign law governing insolvency.

(4) "Designated office" means:

   (A) with respect to a limited partnership, the office that the limited partnership is required to designate and maintain under Section 114; and

   (B) with respect to a foreign limited partnership, its principal office.

(5) "Distribution" means a transfer of money or other property from a limited partnership to a partner in the partner's capacity as a partner or to a transferee on account of a transferable interest owned by the transferee.

(6) "Foreign limited liability limited partnership" means a foreign limited partnership whose general partners have limited liability for the obligations of the foreign limited partnership under a provision similar to Section 404(c).

(7) "Foreign limited partnership" means a partnership formed under the laws of a jurisdiction other than this State and required by those laws to have one or more general partners and one or more limited partners. The term includes a foreign limited liability limited partnership.

(8) "General partner" means:

(A) with respect to a limited partnership, a person that:

(i) becomes a general partner under Section 401; or

(ii) was a general partner in a limited partnership when the limited partnership became subject to this [Act] under Section 1206(a) or (b); and

(B) with respect to a foreign limited partnership, a person that has rights, powers, and obligations similar to those of a general partner in a limited partnership.

(9) "Limited liability limited partnership", except in the phrase "foreign limited liability limited partnership", means a limited partnership whose certificate of limited partnership states that the limited partnership is a limited liability limited partnership.

(10) "Limited partner" means:

(A) with respect to a limited partnership, a person that:

(i) becomes a limited partner under Section 301; or

(ii) was a limited partner in a limited partnership when the limited partnership became subject to this [Act] under Section 1206(a) or (b); and

(B) with respect to a foreign limited partnership, a person that has rights, powers, and obligations similar to those of a limited partner in a limited partnership.

(11) "Limited partnership", except in the phrases "foreign limited partnership" and "foreign limited liability limited partnership", means an entity, having one or more general partners and one or more limited partners, which is formed under this [Act] by two or more persons or becomes subject to this [Act] under [Article] 11 or Section 1206(a) or (b). The term includes a limited liability limited partnership.

(12) "Partner" means a limited partner or general partner.

(13) "Partnership agreement" means the partners' agreement, whether oral, implied, in a record, or in any combination, concerning the limited partnership. The term includes the agreement as amended.

(14) "Person" means an individual, corporation, business trust, estate, trust, partnership, limited liability company, association, joint venture, government; governmental subdivision, agency, or instrumentality; public corporation, or any other legal or commercial entity.

(15) "Person dissociated as a general partner" means a person dissociated as a general partner of a limited partnership.

(16) "Principal office" means the office where the principal executive office of a limited partnership or foreign limited partnership is located, whether or not the office is located in this State.

(17) "Record" means information that is inscribed on a tangible medium or that is stored in an electronic or other medium and is retrievable in perceivable form.

(18) "Required information" means the information that a limited partnership is required to maintain under Section 111.

(19) "Sign" means:

(A) to execute or adopt a tangible symbol with the present intent to authenticate a record; or

(B) to attach or logically associate an electronic symbol, sound, or process to or with a record with the present intent to authenticate the record.

(20) "State" means a State of the United States, the District of Columbia, Puerto Rico, the United States Virgin Islands, or any territory or insular possession subject to the jurisdiction of the United States.

(21) "Transfer" includes an assignment, conveyance, deed, bill of sale, lease, mortgage, security interest, encumbrance, gift, and transfer by operation of law.

(22) "Transferable interest" means a partner's right to receive distributions.

(23) "Transferee" means a person to which all or part of a transferable interest has been transferred, whether or not the transferor is a partner.

Comment

This section contains definitions applicable throughout the Act. Section 1101 provides additional definitions applicable within Article 11.

Paragraph 8(A)(i) [General partner] — A partnership agreement may vary Section 401 and provide a process or mechanism for becoming a general partner which is different from or additional to the rules stated in that section. For the purposes of this definition, a person who becomes a general partner pursuant to a provision of the partnership agreement "becomes a general partner under Section 401."

Paragraph 10(A)(i) [Limited partner] — The Comment to Paragraph 8(A)(i) applies here as well. For the purposes of this definition, a person who becomes a limited partner pursuant to a provision of the partnership agreement "becomes a limited partner under Section 301."

Paragraph (11) [Limited partnership] — This definition pertains to what is commonly termed a "domestic" limited partnership. The definition encompasses: (i) limited partnerships originally formed under this Act, including limited partnerships formed under Section 1101(11) to be the surviving organization in a merger; (ii) any entity that becomes subject to this Act by converting into a limited partnership under Article 11; (iii) any preexisting domestic limited partnership that elects pursuant to Section 1206(a) to become subject to this Act; and (iv) all other preexisting domestic limited partnerships when they become subject to this Act under Section 1206(b).

Following the approach of predecessor law, RULPA Section 101(7), this definition contains two substantive requirements. First, it is of the essence of a limited partnership to have two classes of partners. Accordingly, under Section 101(11) a limited partnership must have at least one general and one limited partner. Section 801(3)(B) and (4) provide that a limited partnership dissolves if its sole general partner or sole limited partner dissociates and the limited partnership fails to admit a replacement within 90 days of the dissociation. The 90 day limitation is a default rule, but, in light of Section 101(11), a limited partnership may not indefinitely delay "having one or more general partners and one or more limited partners."

It is also of the essence of a limited partnership to have at least two partners. Section 101(11) codifies this requirement by referring to a limited partnership as "an entity . . . which is formed under this [Act] by two or more persons." Thus, while the same person may be both a general and limited partner, Section 113 (Dual Capacity), one person alone cannot be the "two persons" contemplated by this definition. However, nothing in this definition prevents two closely affiliated persons from satisfying the two person requirement.

Paragraph (13) [Partnership agreement] — Section 110 is essential to understanding the significance of the partnership agreement. *See also* Section 201(d) (resolving inconsistencies between the certificate of limited partnership and the partnership agreement).

Paragraph (21) [Transfer] — Following RUPA, this Act uses the words "transfer" and "transferee" rather than the words "assignment" and "assignee." *See* RUPA Section 503.

The reference to "transfer by operation of law" is significant in connection with Section 702 (Transfer of Partner's Transferable Interest). That section severely restricts a transferee's rights (absent the consent of the partners), and this definition makes those restrictions applicable, for example, to transfers ordered by a family court as part of a divorce proceeding and transfers resulting from the death of a partner.

Paragraph (23) [Transferee] — See comment to Paragraph 21 for an explanation of why this Act refers to "transferee" rather than "assignee."

Section 103. Knowledge and Notice

(a) A person knows a fact if the person has actual knowledge of it.

(b) A person has notice of a fact if the person:

(1) knows of it;

(2) has received a notification of it;

(3) has reason to know it exists from all of the facts known to the person at the time in question; or

(4) has notice of it under subsection (c) or (d).

(c) A certificate of limited partnership on file in the [office of the Secretary of State] is notice that the partnership is a limited partnership and the persons designated in the certificate as general partners are general partners. Except as otherwise provided in subsection (d), the certificate is not notice of any other fact.

(d) A person has notice of:

(1) another person's dissociation as a general partner, 90 days after the effective date of an amendment to the certificate of limited partnership which states that the other person has dissociated or 90 days after the effective date of a statement of dissociation pertaining to the other person, whichever occurs first;

(2) a limited partnership's dissolution, 90 days after the effective date of an amendment to the certificate of limited partnership stating that the limited partnership is dissolved;

(3) a limited partnership's termination, 90 days after the effective date of a statement of termination;

(4) a limited partnership's conversion under [Article] 11, 90 days after the effective date of the articles of conversion; or

(5) a merger under [Article] 11, 90 days after the effective date of the articles of merger.

(e) A person notifies or gives a notification to another person by taking steps reasonably required to inform the other person in ordinary course, whether or not the other person learns of it.

(f) A person receives a notification when the notification:

(1) comes to the person's attention; or

(2) is delivered at the person's place of business or at any other place held out by the person as a place for receiving communications.

(g) Except as otherwise provided in subsection (h), a person other than an individual knows, has notice, or receives a notification of a fact for purposes of a particular transaction when the individual conducting the transaction for the person knows, has notice, or receives a notification of the fact, or in any event when the fact would have been brought to the individual's attention if the person had exercised reasonable diligence. A person other than an individual exercises reasonable diligence if it maintains reasonable routines for communicating significant information to the individual conducting the transaction for the person and there is reasonable compliance with the routines. Reasonable diligence does not require an individual acting for the person to communicate information unless the communication is part of the individual's regular duties or the individual has reason to know of the transaction and that the transaction would be materially affected by the information.

(h) A general partner's knowledge, notice, or receipt of a notification of a fact relating to the limited partnership is effective immediately as knowledge of, notice to, or receipt of a notification by the limited partnership, except in the case of a fraud on the limited partnership committed by or with the consent of the general partner. A limited partner's knowledge, notice, or receipt of a notification of a fact relating to the limited partnership is not effective as knowledge of, notice to, or receipt of a notification by the limited partnership.

Comment

Source — RUPA Section 102; RULPA Section 208.

Notice and the relationship among subsections (b), (c) and (d) — These subsections provide separate and independent avenues through which a person can have notice of a fact. A person has notice of a fact as soon as any of the avenues applies.

> **Example:** A limited partnership dissolves and amends its certificate of limited partnership to indicate dissolution. The amendment is effective on March 1. On March 15, Person #1 has reason to know of the dissolution and therefore has "notice" of the dissolution under Section 103(b)(3) even though Section 103(d)(2) does not yet apply. Person #2 does not have actual knowledge of the dissolution until June 15. Nonetheless, under Section 103(d)(2) Person #2 has "notice" of the dissolution on May 30.

Subsection (c) — This subsection provides what is commonly called constructive notice and comes essentially verbatim from RULPA Section 208. As for the significance of constructive notice "that the partnership is a limited partnership," *see Water, Waste & Land, Inc. v. Lanham*, 955 P.2d 997, 1001–1003 (Colo. 1998) (interpreting a comparable provision of the Colorado LLC statute and holding the provision ineffective to change common law agency principles, including the rules relating to the liability of an agent that transacts business for an undisclosed principal).

As for constructive notice that "the persons designated in the certificate as general partners are general partners," Section 201(a)(3) requires the initial certificate of limited partnership to name each general partner, and Section 202(b) requires a limited partnership to promptly amend its certificate of limited partnership to reflect any change in the identity of its general partners. Nonetheless, it will be possible, albeit improper, for a person to be designated in the certificate of limited partnership as a general partner without having become a general partner as contemplated by Section 401. Likewise, it will be possible for a person to have become a general partner under Section 401 without being designated as a general partner in the certificate of limited partnership. According to the last clause of this subsection, the fact that a person is **not** listed as in the certificate as a general partner is **not** notice that the person is **not** a general partner. For further discussion of this point, see the Comment to Section 401.

If the partnership agreement and the public record are inconsistent, Section 201(d) applies (partnership agreement controls *inter se*; public record controls as to third parties who have relied). *See also* Section 202(b) (requiring the limited partnership to amend its certificate of limited partnership to keep accurate the listing of general partners), 202(c) (requiring a general partner to take corrective action when the general partner knows that the certificate of limited partnership contains false information), and 208 (imposing liability for false information in *inter alia* the certificate of limited partnership).

Subsection (d) — This subsection also provides what is commonly called constructive notice and works in conjunction with other sections of this Act to curtail the power to bind and personal liability of general partners and persons dissociated as general partners. *See* Sections 402, 606, 607, 804, 805, 1111, and 1112. Following RUPA (in substance, although not in form), the constructive notice begins 90 days after the effective date of the filed record. For the Act's rules on delayed effective dates, see Section 206(c).

The 90-day delay applies only to the constructive notice and not to the event described in the filed record.

> **Example:** On March 15 X dissociates as a general partner from XYZ Limited Partnership by giving notice to XYZ. *See* Section 603(1). On March 20, XYZ amends its certificate of limited partnership to remove X's name from the list of general partners. *See* Section 202(b)(2).
>
> X's **dissociation** is effective March 15. If on March 16 X purports to be a general partner of XYZ and under Section 606(a) binds XYZ to some obligation, X will be liable under Section 606(b) as a "person dissociated as a general partner."
>
> On June 13 (90 days after March 15), the world has constructive notice of X's dissociation as a general partner. Beginning on that date, X will lack the power to bind XYZ. *See* Section 606(a)(2)(B) (person dissociated as a general partner can bind the limited partnership only if, *inter alia*, "at the time the other party enters into the transaction . . . the other party does not have notice of the dissociation").
>
> Constructive notice under this subsection applies to partners and transferees as well as other persons.

Subsection (e) — The phrase "person learns of it" in this subsection is equivalent to the phrase "knows of it" in subsection (b)(1).

Subsection (h) — Under this subsection and Section 302, information possessed by a person that is only a limited partner is not attributable to the limited partnership. However, information possessed by a person that is both a general partner and a limited partner is attributable to the limited partnership. *See* Section 113 (Dual Capacity).

Section 104. Nature, Purpose, and Duration of Entity

(a) A limited partnership is an entity distinct from its partners. A limited partnership is the same entity regardless of whether its certificate states that the limited partnership is a limited liability limited partnership.

(b) A limited partnership may be organized under this [Act] for any lawful purpose.

(c) A limited partnership has a perpetual duration.

Comment

Subsection (a) — Acquiring or relinquishing an LLLP shield changes only the rules governing a general partner's liability for subsequently incurred obligations of the limited partnership. The underlying entity is unaffected.

Subsection (b) — In contrast with RULPA Section 106, this Act does not require a limited partnership to have a business purpose. However, many of the Act's default rules presuppose at least a profit-making purpose. *See, e.g.*, Section 503 (providing for the sharing of distributions in proportion to the value of contributions), 701 (defining a transferable interest in terms of the right to receive distributions), 801 (allocating the right to consent to cause or avoid dissolution in proportion to partners' rights to receive distributions), and 812 (providing that, after a dissolved limited partnership has paid its creditors, "[a]ny surplus remaining . . . must be paid in cash as a distribution" to partners and transferees). If a limited partnership is organized for an essentially non-pecuniary purpose, the organizers should carefully review the Act's default rules and override them as necessary via the partnership agreement.

Subsection (c) — The partnership agreement has the power to vary this subsection, either by stating a definite term or by specifying an event or events which cause dissolution. Sections 110(a) and 801(1). Section 801 also recognizes several other occurrences that cause dissolution. Thus, the public record pertaining to a limited partnership will not necessarily reveal whether the limited partnership actually has a perpetual duration.

The public record might also fail to reveal whether the limited partnership has in fact dissolved. A dissolved limited partnership may amend its certificate of limited partnership to indicate dissolution but is not required to do so. Section 803(b)(1).

Predecessor law took a somewhat different approach. RULPA Section 201(4) required the certificate of limited partnership to state "the latest date upon which the limited partnership is to dissolve." Although RULPA Section 801(2) provided for a limited partnership to dissolve "upon the happening of events specified in writing in the partnership agreement," RULPA Section 203 required the limited partnership to file a certificate of cancellation to indicate that dissolution had occurred.

Section 105. Powers

A limited partnership has the powers to do all things necessary or convenient to carry on its activities, including the power to sue, be sued, and defend in its own name and to maintain an action against a partner for harm caused to the limited partnership by a breach of the partnership agreement or violation of a duty to the partnership.

Comment

This Act omits as unnecessary any detailed list of specific powers. The power to sue and be sued is mentioned specifically so that Section 110(b)(1) can prohibit the partnership agreement from varying that power. The power to maintain an action against a partner is mentioned specifically to establish that the limited partnership itself has standing to enforce the partnership agreement.

Section 106. Governing Law

The law of this State governs relations among the partners of a limited partnership and between the partners and the limited partnership and the liability of partners as partners for an obligation of the limited partnership.

Comment

To partially define its scope, this section uses the phrase "relations among the partners of a limited partnership and between the partners and the limited partnership." Section 110(a) uses essentially identical language in defining the proper realm of the partnership agreement: "relations among the partners and between the partners and the partnership."

Despite the similarity of language, this section has no bearing on the power of a partnership agreement to vary other provisions of this Act. It is quite possible for a provision of this Act to involve "relations among the partners of a limited partnership and between the partners and the limited partnership" and thus come within this section, and yet not be subject to variation by the partnership agreement. Although Section 110(a) grants plenary authority to the partnership agreement to regulate "relations among the partners and between the partners and the partnership," that authority is subject to Section 110(b).

For example, Section 408 (General Standards of General Partners's Conduct) certainly involves "relations among the partners of a limited partnership and between the partners and the limited partnership." Therefore, according to this section, Section 408 applies to a limited partnership formed or otherwise subject to this Act. Just as certainly, Section 408 pertains to "relations among the partners and between the partners and the partnership" for the purposes of Section 110(a), and therefore the partnership agreement may properly address matters covered by Section 408. However, Section 110(b)(5), (6), and (7) limit the power of the partnership agreement to vary the rules stated in Section 408. *See also, e.g.*, Section 502(c) (stating creditor's rights, which are protected under Section 110(b)(13) from being restricted by the partnership agreement) and Comment to Section 509.

This section also applies to "the liability of partners as partners for an obligation of a limited partnership." The phrase "as partners" contemplates the liability shield for limited partners under Section 303 and the rules for general partner liability stated in Section 404. Other grounds for liability can be supplied by other law, including the law of some other jurisdiction. For example, a partner's contractual guaranty of a limited partnership obligation might well be governed by the law of some other jurisdiction.

Transferees derive their rights and status under this Act from partners and accordingly this section applies to the relations of a transferee to the limited partnership.

The partnership agreement may not vary the rule stated in this section. *See* Section 110(b)(2).

Section 107. Supplemental Principles of Law; Rate of Interest

(a) Unless displaced by particular provisions of this [Act], the principles of law and equity supplement this [Act].

(b) If an obligation to pay interest arises under this [Act] and the rate is not specified, the rate is that specified in [applicable statute].

Comment

Subsection (a) — This language comes from RUPA Section 104 and does not address an important question raised by the de-linking of this Act from the UPA and RUPA — namely, to what extent is the case law of general partnerships relevant to limited partnerships governed by this Act?

Predecessor law, RULPA Section 403, expressly equated the rights, powers, restrictions, and liabilities of a general partner in a limited partnership with the rights, powers, restrictions, and liabilities of a partner in a general partnership. This Act has no comparable provision. *See* Prefatory Note. Therefore, a court should not assume that a case concerning a general partnership is automatically relevant to a limited partnership governed by this Act. A general partnership case may be relevant by analogy, especially if (1) the issue in dispute involves a provision of this Act for which a comparable provision exists under the law of general partnerships; and (2) the fundamental differences between a general partnership and limited partnership are immaterial to the disputed issue.

Section 108. Name

(a) The name of a limited partnership may contain the name of any partner.

(b) The name of a limited partnership that is not a limited liability limited partnership must contain the phrase "limited partnership" or the abbreviation "L.P."or "LP" and may not contain the phrase "limited liability limited partnership" or the abbreviation "LLLP" or "L.L.L.P.".

(c) The name of a limited liability limited partnership must contain the phrase "limited liability limited partnership" or the abbreviation "LLLP" or "L.L.L.P." and must not contain the abbreviation "L.P."or "LP."

(d) Unless authorized by subsection (e), the name of a limited partnership must be distinguishable in the records of the [Secretary of State] from:

(1) the name of each person other than an individual incorporated, organized, or authorized to transact business in this State; and

(2) each name reserved under Section 109 [or other state laws allowing the reservation or registration of business names, including fictitious name statutes].

(e) A limited partnership may apply to the [Secretary of State] for authorization to use a name that does not comply with subsection (d). The [Secretary of State] shall authorize use of the name applied for if, as to each conflicting name:

(1) the present user, registrant, or owner of the conflicting name consents in a signed record to the use and submits an undertaking in a form satisfactory to the [Secretary of State] to change the conflicting name to a name that complies with subsection (d) and is distinguishable in the records of the [Secretary of State] from the name applied for;

(2) the applicant delivers to the [Secretary of State] a certified copy of the final judgment of a court of competent jurisdiction establishing the applicant's right to use in this State the name applied for; or

(3) the applicant delivers to the [Secretary of State] proof satisfactory to the [Secretary of State] that the present user, registrant, or owner of the conflicting name:

(A) has merged into the applicant;

(B) has been converted into the applicant; or

(C) has transferred substantially all of its assets, including the conflicting name, to the applicant.

(f) Subject to Section 905, this section applies to any foreign limited partnership transacting business in this State, having a certificate of authority to transact business in this State, or applying for a certificate of authority.

Comment

Subsection (a) — Predecessor law, RULPA Section 102, prohibited the use of a limited partner's name in the name of a limited partnership except in unusual circumstances. That approach derived from the 1916 Uniform Limited Partnership Act and has become antiquated. In 1916, most business organizations were either unshielded (*e.g.*, general partnerships) or partially shielded (*e.g.*, limited partnerships), and it was reasonable for third parties to believe that an individual whose own name appeared in the name of a business would "stand behind" the business. Today most businesses have a full shield (*e.g.*, corporations, limited liability companies, most limited liability partnerships), and corporate, LLC and LLP statutes generally pose no barrier to the use of an owner's name in the name of the entity. This Act eliminates RULPA's restriction and puts limited partnerships on equal footing with these other "shielded" entities.

Subsection (d)(1) — If a sole proprietor registers or reserves a business name under a fictitious name statute, that name comes within this provision. For the purposes of this provision, a sole proprietor doing business under a registered or reserved name is a "person other than an individual."

Subsection (f) — Section 905 permits a foreign limited partnership to obtain a certificate of authority under an alternate name if the foreign limited partnership's actual name does not comply with this section.

Section 109. Reservation of Name

(a) The exclusive right to the use of a name that complies with Section 108 may be reserved by:

(1) a person intending to organize a limited partnership under this [Act] and to adopt the name;

(2) a limited partnership or a foreign limited partnership authorized to transact business in this State intending to adopt the name;

(3) a foreign limited partnership intending to obtain a certificate of authority to transact business in this State and adopt the name;

(4) a person intending to organize a foreign limited partnership and intending to have it obtain a certificate of authority to transact business in this State and adopt the name;

(5) a foreign limited partnership formed under the name; or

(6) a foreign limited partnership formed under a name that does not comply with Section 108(b) or (c), but the name reserved under this paragraph may differ from the foreign limited partnership's name only to the extent necessary to comply with Section 108(b) and (c).

(b) A person may apply to reserve a name under subsection (a) by delivering to the [Secretary of State] for filing an application that states the name to be reserved and the paragraph of subsection (a) which applies. If the [Secretary of State] finds that the name is available for use by the applicant, the [Secretary of State] shall file a statement of name reservation and thereby reserve the name for the exclusive use of the applicant for a 120 days.

(c) An applicant that has reserved a name pursuant to subsection (b) may reserve the same name for additional 120-day periods. A person having a current reservation for a name may not apply for another 120-day period for the same name until 90 days have elapsed in the current reservation.

(d) A person that has reserved a name under this section may deliver to the [Secretary of State] for filing a notice of transfer that states the reserved name, the name and street and mailing address of some other person to which the reservation is to be transferred, and the paragraph of subsection (a) which applies to the other person. Subject to Section 206(c), the transfer is effective when the [Secretary of State] files the notice of transfer.

Section 110. Effect of Partnership Agreement; Nonwaivable Provisions

(a) Except as otherwise provided in subsection (b), the partnership agreement governs relations among the partners and between the partners and the partnership. To the extent the partnership agreement does not otherwise provide, this [Act] governs relations among the partners and between the partners and the partnership.

(b) A partnership agreement may not:

(1) vary a limited partnership's power under Section 105 to sue, be sued, and defend in its own name;

(2) vary the law applicable to a limited partnership under Section 106;

(3) vary the requirements of Section 204;

(4) vary the information required under Section 111 or unreasonably restrict the right to information under Sections 304 or 407, but the partnership agreement may impose reasonable restrictions on the availability and use of information obtained under those sections and may define appropriate remedies, including liquidated damages, for a breach of any reasonable restriction on use;

(5) eliminate the duty of loyalty under Section 408, but the partnership agreement may:

(A) identify specific types or categories of activities that do not violate the duty of loyalty, if not manifestly unreasonable; and

(B) specify the number or percentage of partners which may authorize or ratify, after full disclosure to all partners of all material facts, a specific act or transaction that otherwise would violate the duty of loyalty;

(6) unreasonably reduce the duty of care under Section 408(c);

(7) eliminate the obligation of good faith and fair dealing under Sections 305(b) and 408(d), but the partnership agreement may prescribe the standards by which the performance of the obligation is to be measured, if the standards are not manifestly unreasonable;

(8) vary the power of a person to dissociate as a general partner under Section 604(a) except to require that the notice under Section 603(1) be in a record;

(9) vary the power of a court to decree dissolution in the circumstances specified in Section 802;

(10) vary the requirement to wind up the partnership's business as specified in Section 803;

(11) unreasonably restrict the right to maintain an action under [Article] 10;

(12) restrict the right of a partner under Section 1110(a) to approve a conversion or merger or the right of a general partner under Section 1110(b) to consent to an amendment to the certificate of limited partnership which deletes a statement that the limited partnership is a limited liability limited partnership; or

(13) restrict rights under this [Act] of a person other than a partner or a transferee.

Comment

Source — RUPA Section 103.

Subject only to subsection (b), the partnership agreement has plenary power to structure and regulate the relations of the partners *inter se*. Although the certificate of limited partnership is a limited partnership's foundational document, among the partners the partnership agreement controls. *See* Section 201(d).

The partnership agreement has the power to control the manner of its own amendment. In particular, a provision of the agreement prohibiting oral modifications is enforceable, despite any common law antagonism to "no oral modification" provisions. Likewise, a partnership agreement can impose "made in a record" requirements on other aspects of the partners' relationship, such as requiring consents to be made in a record and signed, or rendering unenforceable oral promises to make contributions or oral understandings as to "events upon the happening of which the limited partnership is to be dissolved," Section 111(9)(D). *See also* Section 801(1).

Subsection (b)(3) — The referenced section states who must sign various documents.

Subsection (b)(4) — In determining whether a restriction is reasonable, a court might consider: (i) the danger or other problem the restriction seeks to avoid; (ii) the purpose for which the information is sought; and (iii) whether, in light of both the problem and the purpose, the restriction is reasonably tailored. Restricting access to or use of the names and addresses of limited partners is not per se unreasonable.

Under this Act, general and limited partners have sharply different roles. A restriction that is reasonable as to a limited partner is not necessarily reasonable as to a general partner.

Sections 304(g) and 407(f) authorize the limited partnership (as distinguished from the partnership agreement) to impose restrictions on the use of information. For a comparison of restrictions contained in the partnership agreement and restrictions imposed unilaterally by the limited partnership, see the Comment to Section 304(g).

Subsection (b)(5)(A) — It is not per se manifestly unreasonable for the partnership agreement to permit a general partner to compete with the limited partnership.

Subsection (b)(5)(B) — The Act does not require that the authorization or ratification be by **disinterested** partners, although the partnership agreement may so provide. The Act does require that the disclosure be made to all partners, even if the partnership agreement excludes some partners from the authorization or ratification process. An interested partner that participates in the authorization or ratification process is subject to the obligation of good faith and fair dealing. Sections 305(b) and 408(d).

Subsection (b)(8) — This restriction applies only to the power of a person to dissociate as a general partner. The partnership agreement may eliminate the power of a person to dissociate as a limited partner.

Subsection (b)(9) — This provision should not be read to limit a partnership agreement's power to provide for arbitration. For example, an agreement to arbitrate all disputes — including dissolution disputes — is enforceable. Any other interpretation would put this Act at odds with federal law. *See Southland Corp. v. Keating*, 465 U.S. 1 (1984) (holding that the Federal Arbitration Act preempts state statutes that seek to invalidate agreements to arbitrate) and *Allied-Bruce Terminix Cos., Inc. v. Dobson*,

513 U.S. 265 (1995) (same). This provision does prohibit any narrowing of the substantive grounds for judicial dissolution as stated in Section 802.

> **Example:** A provision of a partnership agreement states that no partner may obtain judicial dissolution without showing that a general partner is in material breach of the partnership agreement. The provision is ineffective to prevent a court from ordering dissolution under Section 802.

Subsection (b)(11) — Section 1001 codifies a partner's right to bring a direct action, and the rest of Article 10 provides for derivative actions. The partnership agreement may not restrict a partner's right to bring either type of action if the effect is to undercut or frustrate the duties and rights protected by Section 110(b).

The reasonableness of a restriction on derivative actions should be judged in light of the history and purpose of derivative actions. They originated as an equitable remedy, intended to protect passive owners against management abuses. A partnership agreement may not provide that all derivative claims will be subject to final determination by a special litigation committee appointed by the limited partnership, because that provision would eliminate, not merely restrict, a partner's right to bring a derivative *action*.

Subsection (b)(12) — Section 1110 imposes special consent requirements with regard to transactions that might make a partner personally liable for entity debts.

Subsection (b)(13) — The partnership agreement is a contract, and this provision reflects a basic notion of contract law — namely, that a contract can directly restrict rights only of parties to the contract and of persons who derive their rights from the contract. A provision of a partnership agreement can be determined to be unenforceable against third parties under paragraph (b)(13) without therefore and automatically being unenforceable *inter se* the partners and any transferees. How the former determination affects the latter question is a matter of other law.

Section 111. Required Information

A limited partnership shall maintain at its designated office the following information:

(1) a current list showing the full name and last known street and mailing address of each partner, separately identifying the general partners, in alphabetical order, and the limited partners, in alphabetical order;

(2) a copy of the initial certificate of limited partnership and all amendments to and restatements of the certificate, together with signed copies of any powers of attorney under which any certificate, amendment, or restatement has been signed;

(3) a copy of any filed articles of conversion or merger;

(4) a copy of the limited partnership's federal, state, and local income tax returns and reports, if any, for the three most recent years;

(5) a copy of any partnership agreement made in a record and any amendment made in a record to any partnership agreement;

(6) a copy of any financial statement of the limited partnership for the three most recent years;

(7) a copy of the three most recent annual reports delivered by the limited partnership to the [Secretary of State] pursuant to Section 210;

(8) a copy of any record made by the limited partnership during the past three years of any consent given by or vote taken of any partner pursuant to this [Act] or the partnership agreement; and

(9) unless contained in a partnership agreement made in a record, a record stating:

(A) the amount of cash, and a description and statement of the agreed value of the other benefits, contributed and agreed to be contributed by each partner;

(B) the times at which, or events on the happening of which, any additional contributions agreed to be made by each partner are to be made;

(C) for any person that is both a general partner and a limited partner, a specification of what transferable interest the person owns in each capacity; and

(D) any events upon the happening of which the limited partnership is to be dissolved and its activities wound up.

Comment

Source — RULPA Section 105.

Sections 304 and 407 govern access to the information required by this section, as well as to other information pertaining to a limited partnership.

Paragraph (5) — This requirement applies to superseded as well as current agreements and amendments. An agreement or amendment is "made in a record" to the extent the agreement is "integrated" into a record and consented to in that memorialized form. It is possible for a partnership agreement to be made in part in a record and in part otherwise. *See* Comment to Section 110. An oral agreement that is subsequently inscribed in a record (but not consented to as such) was not "made in a record" and is not covered by paragraph (5). However, if the limited partnership happens to have such a record, Section 304(b) might and Section 407(a)(2) will provide a right of access.

Paragraph (8) — This paragraph does not require a limited partnership to make a record of consents given and votes taken. However, if the limited partnership has made such a record, this paragraph requires that the limited partnership maintain the record for three years. The requirement applies to any record made by the limited partnership, not just to records made contemporaneously with the giving of consent or voting. The three year period runs from when the record was made and not from when the consent was given or vote taken.

Paragraph (9) — Information is "contained in a partnership agreement made in a record" only to the extent that the information is "integrated" into a record and, in that memorialized form, has been consented to as part of the partnership agreement.

This paragraph is not a statute of frauds provision. For example, failure to comply with paragraph (9)(A) or (B) does not render unenforceable an oral promise to make a contribution. Likewise, failure to comply with paragraph (9)(D) does not invalidate an oral term of the partnership specifying "events upon the happening of which the limited partnership is to be dissolved and its activities wound up." *See also* Section 801(1).

Obversely, the mere fact that a limited partnership maintains a record in purported compliance with paragraph (9)(A) or (B) does not prove that a person has actually promised to make a contribution. Likewise, the mere fact that a limited partnership maintains a record in purported compliance with paragraph (9)(D) does not prove that the partnership agreement actually includes the specified events as causes of dissolution.

Consistent with the partnership agreement's plenary power to structure and regulate the relations of the partners *inter se*, a partnership agreement can impose "made in a record" requirements which render unenforceable oral promises to make contributions or oral understandings as to "events upon the happening of which the limited partnership is to be dissolved." *See* Comment to Section 110.

Paragraph (9)(A) and (B) — Often the partnership agreement will state in record form the value of contributions made and promised to be made. If not, these provisions require that the value be stated in a record maintained as part of the limited partnership's required information. The Act does not authorize the limited partnership or the general partners to set the value of a contribution without the concurrence of the person who has made or promised the contribution, although the partnership agreement itself can grant that authority.

Paragraph (9)(C) — The information required by this provision is essential for determining what happens to the transferable interests of a person that is both a general partner and a limited partner and that dissociates in one of those capacities but not the other. *See* Sections 602(3) and 605(5).

Section 112. Business Transactions of Partner with Partnership

A partner may lend money to and transact other business with the limited partnership and has the same rights and obligations with respect to the loan or other transaction as a person that is not a partner.

Comment

Source — RULPA Section 107. *See also* RUPA Section 404(f) and ULLCA Section 409(f).

This section has no impact on a general partner's duty under Section 408(b)(2) (duty of loyalty includes refraining from acting as or for an adverse party) and means rather that this Act does not discriminate against a creditor of a limited partnership that happens also to be a partner. *See, e.g., BT-I v. Equitable Life Assurance Society of the United States,* 75 Cal. App. 4th 1406, 1415, 89 Cal. Rptr. 2d 811, 814 (Cal. App. 4 Dist.1999). and *SEC v. DuPont, Homsey & Co.*, 204 F. Supp. 944, 946 (D. Mass. 1962), vacated and remanded on other grounds, 334 F.2d 704 (1st Cir. 1964). This section does not, however, override other law, such as fraudulent transfer or conveyance acts.

Section 113. Dual Capacity

A person may be both a general partner and a limited partner. A person that is both a general and limited partner has the rights, powers, duties, and obligations provided by this [Act] and the partnership agreement in each of those capacities. When the person acts as a general partner, the person is subject to the obligations, duties and restrictions under this [Act] and the partnership agreement for general partners. When the person acts as a limited partner, the person is subject to the obligations, duties and restrictions under this [Act] and the partnership agreement for limited partners.

Comment

Source — RULPA Section 404, redrafted for reasons of style.

Section 114. Office and Agent for Service of Process

(a) A limited partnership shall designate and continuously maintain in this State:

(1) an office, which need not be a place of its activity in this State; and

(2) an agent for service of process.

(b) A foreign limited partnership shall designate and continuously maintain in this State an agent for service of process.

(c) An agent for service of process of a limited partnership or foreign limited partnership must be an individual who is a resident of this State or other person authorized to do business in this State.

Comment

Subsection (a) — The initial designation occurs in the original certificate of limited partnership. Section 201(a)(2). A limited partnership may change the designation in any of three ways: a statement of change, Section 115, an amendment to the certificate, Section 202, and the annual report, Section 210(e). If a limited partnership fails to maintain an agent for service of process, substituted service may be made on the Secretary of State. Section 117(b). Although a limited partnership's failure to maintain an agent for service of process is not immediate grounds for administrative dissolution, Section 809(a), the failure will prevent the limited partnership from delivering to the Secretary of State for filing an annual report that complies with Section 210(a)(2). Failure to deliver a proper annual report is grounds for administrative dissolution. Section 809(a)(2).

Subsection (b) — The initial designation occurs in the application for a certificate of authority. *See* Section 902(a)(4). A foreign limited partnership may change the designation in either of two ways: a statement of change, Section 115, and the annual report, Section 210(e). If a foreign limited partnership fails to maintain an agent for service of process, substituted service may be made on the Secretary of State. Section 117(b). A foreign limited partnership's failure to maintain an agent for service of process is grounds for administrative revocation of the certificate of authority. Section 906(a)(3).

A foreign limited partnership need not maintain an office in this State.

Section 115. Change of Designated Office or Agent for Service of Process

(a) In order to change its designated office, agent for service of process, or the address of its agent for service of process, a limited partnership or a foreign limited partnership may deliver to the [Secretary of State] for filing a statement of change containing:

(1) the name of the limited partnership or foreign limited partnership;

(2) the street and mailing address of its current designated office;

(3) if the current designated office is to be changed, the street and mailing address of the new designated office;

(4) the name and street and mailing address of its current agent for service of process; and

(5) if the current agent for service of process or an address of the agent is to be changed, the new information.

(b) Subject to Section 206(c), a statement of change is effective when filed by the [Secretary of State].

Comment

Source — ULLCA Section 109.

Subsection (a) — The Act uses "may" rather than "shall" here because other avenues exist. A limited partnership may also change the information by an amendment to its certificate of limited partnership, Section 202, or through its annual report. Section 210(e). A foreign limited partnership may use its annual report. Section 210(e). However, neither a limited partnership nor a foreign limited partnership may wait for the annual report if the information described in the public record becomes inaccurate. *See* Sections 208 (imposing liability for false information in record) and 117(b) (providing for substitute service).

Section 116. Resignation of Agent for Service of Process

(a) In order to resign as an agent for service of process of a limited partnership or foreign limited partnership, the agent must deliver to the [Secretary of State] for filing a statement of resignation containing the name of the limited partnership or foreign limited partnership.

(b) After receiving a statement of resignation, the [Secretary of State] shall file it and mail a copy to the designated office of the limited partnership or foreign limited partnership and another copy to the principal office if the address of the office appears in the records of the [Secretary of State] and is different from the address of the designated office.

(c) An agency for service of process is terminated on the 31st day after the [Secretary of State] files the statement of resignation.

Comment

Source — ULLCA Section 110.

This section provides the only way an agent can resign without cooperation from the limited partnership or foreign limited partnership and the only way the agent, rather than the limited partnership or foreign limited partnership, can effect a change in the public record. *See* Sections 115(a) (Statement of Change), 202 (Amendment or Restatement of Certificate), and 210(e) (Annual Report), all of which involve the limited partnership or foreign limited partnership designating a replacement agent for service of process.

Subsection (c) — In contrast to most records authorized or required to be delivered to the filing officer for filing under this Act, a statement of resignation may not provide for a delayed effective date. This subsection mandates the effective date, and an effective date included in a statement of resignation is disregarded. *See also* Section 206(c).

Section 117. Service of Process

(a) An agent for service of process appointed by a limited partnership or foreign limited partnership is an agent of the limited partnership or foreign limited partnership for service of any process, notice, or demand required or permitted by law to be served upon the limited partnership or foreign limited partnership.

(b) If a limited partnership or foreign limited partnership does not appoint or maintain an agent for service of process in this State or the agent for service of process cannot with reasonable diligence be found at the agent's address, the [Secretary of State] is an agent of the limited partnership or foreign limited partnership upon whom process, notice, or demand may be served.

(c) Service of any process, notice, or demand on the [Secretary of State] may be made by delivering to and leaving with the [Secretary of State] duplicate copies of the process, notice, or demand. If a process, notice, or demand is served on the [Secretary of State], the [Secretary of State] shall forward one of the copies by registered or certified mail, return receipt requested, to the limited partnership or foreign limited partnership at its designated office.

(d) Service is effected under subsection (c) at the earliest of:

(1) the date the limited partnership or foreign limited partnership receives the process, notice, or demand;

(2) the date shown on the return receipt, if signed on behalf of the limited partnership or foreign limited partnership; or

(3) five days after the process, notice, or demand is deposited in the mail, if mailed postpaid and correctly addressed.

(e) The [Secretary of State] shall keep a record of each process, notice, and demand served pursuant to this section and record the time of, and the action taken regarding, the service.

(f) This section does not affect the right to serve process, notice, or demand in any other manner provided by law.

Comment

Source — ULLCA Section 111.

Requiring a foreign limited partnership to name an agent for service of process is a change from RULPA. *See* RULPA Section 902(3).

Section 118. Consent and Proxies of Partners

Action requiring the consent of partners under this [Act] may be taken without a meeting, and a partner may appoint a proxy to consent or otherwise act for the partner by signing an appointment record, either personally or by the partner's attorney in fact.

Comment

Source — ULLCA Section 404(d) and (e).

This Act imposes no meeting requirement and does not distinguish among oral, record, express and tacit consent. The partnership agreement may establish such requirements and make such distinctions.

ARTICLE 2
FORMATION; CERTIFICATE OF LIMITED PARTNERSHIP AND OTHER FILINGS

Section 201. Formation of Limited Partnership; Certificate of Limited Partnership

(a) In order for a limited partnership to be formed, a certificate of limited partnership must be delivered to the [Secretary of State] for filing. The certificate must state:

(1) the name of the limited partnership, which must comply with Section 108;

(2) the street and mailing address of the initial designated office and the name and street and mailing address of the initial agent for service of process;

(3) the name and the street and mailing address of each general partner;

(4) whether the limited partnership is a limited liability limited partnership; and

(5) any additional information required by [Article] 11.

(b) A certificate of limited partnership may also contain any other matters but may not vary or otherwise affect the provisions specified in Section 110(b) in a manner inconsistent with that section.

(c) If there has been substantial compliance with subsection (a), subject to Section 206(c) a limited partnership is formed when the [Secretary of State] files the certificate of limited partnership.

(d) Subject to subsection (b), if any provision of a partnership agreement is inconsistent with the filed certificate of limited partnership or with a filed statement of dissociation, termination, or change or filed articles of conversion or merger:

(1) the partnership agreement prevails as to partners and transferees; and

(2) the filed certificate of limited partnership, statement of dissociation, termination, or change or articles of conversion or merger prevail
as to persons, other than partners and transferees, that reasonably
rely on the filed record to their detriment.

Comment

Source — RULPA Section 201.

A limited partnership is a creature of statute, and this section governs
how a limited partnership comes into existence. A limited partnership is
formed only if (i) a certificate of limited partnership is prepared and
delivered to the specified public official for filing, (ii) the public official files
the certificate, and (iii) the certificate, delivery and filing are in "substantial
compliance" with the requirements of subsection (a). Section 206(c) governs
when a limited partnership comes into existence.

Despite its foundational importance, a certificate of limited partnership
is far less powerful than a corporation's articles of incorporation. Among
partners and transferees, for example, the partnership agreement is
paramount. *See* Section 201(d).

Subsection (a)(1) — Section 108 contains name requirements. To be
acceptable for filing, a certificate of limited partnership must state a name
for the limited partnership which complies with Section 108.

Subsection (a)(3) — This provision should be read in conjunction with
Section 103(c) and Section 401. See the Comment to those sections.

Subsection (a)(4) — This Act permits a limited partnership to be a
limited liability limited partnership ("LLLP"), and this provision requires
the certificate of limited partnership to state whether the limited partnership is an LLLP. The requirement is intended to force the organizers of
a limited partnership to decide whether the limited partnership is to be
an LLLP.

Subject to Sections 406(b)(2) and 1110, a limited partnership may amend
its certificate of limited partnership to add or delete a statement that the
limited partnership is a limited liability limited partnership. An amendment deleting such a statement must be accompanied by an amendment
stating that the limited partnership is **not** a limited liability limited partnership. Section 201(a)(4) does not permit a certificate of limited partnership to be silent on this point, except for pre-existing partnerships that
become subject to this Act under Section 1206. *See* Section 1206(c)(2).

Subsection (d) — Source: ULLCA Section 203(c).

A limited partnership is a creature of contract as well as a creature of
statute. It will be possible, albeit improper, for the partnership agreement
to be inconsistent with the certificate of limited partnership or other

specified public filings relating to the limited partnership. For those circumstances, this subsection provides the rule for determining which source of information prevails.

For partners and transferees, the partnership agreement is paramount. For third parties seeking to invoke the public record, actual knowledge of that record is necessary and notice under Section 103(c) or (d) is irrelevant. A third party wishing to enforce the public record over the partnership agreement must show reasonable reliance on the public record, and reliance presupposes knowledge.

This subsection does not expressly cover a situation in which (i) one of the specified filed records contains information in addition to, but not inconsistent with, the partnership agreement, and (ii) a person, other than a partner or transferee, detrimentally relies on the additional information. However, the policy reflected in this subsection seems equally applicable to that situation.

Responsibility for maintaining a limited partnership's public record rests with the general partner or partners. Section 202(c). A general partner's failure to meet that responsibility can expose the general partner to liability to third parties under Section 208(a)(2) and might constitute a breach of the general partner's duties under Section 408. In addition, an aggrieved person may seek a remedy under Section 205 (Signing and Filing Pursuant to Judicial Order).

Section 202. Amendment or Restatement of Certificate

(a) In order to amend its certificate of limited partnership, a limited partnership must deliver to the [Secretary of State] for filing an amendment or, pursuant to [Article] 11, articles of merger stating:

(1) the name of the limited partnership;

(2) the date of filing of its initial certificate; and

(3) the changes the amendment makes to the certificate as most recently amended or restated.

(b) A limited partnership shall promptly deliver to the [Secretary of State] for filing an amendment to a certificate of limited partnership to reflect:

(1) the admission of a new general partner;

(2) the dissociation of a person as a general partner; or

(3) the appointment of a person to wind up the limited partnership's activities under Section 803(c) or (d).

(c) A general partner that knows that any information in a filed certificate of limited partnership was false when the certificate was filed or has become false due to changed circumstances shall promptly:

(1) cause the certificate to be amended; or

(2) if appropriate, deliver to the [Secretary of State] for filing a statement of change pursuant to Section 115 or a statement of correction pursuant to Section 207.

(d) A certificate of limited partnership may be amended at any time for any other proper purpose as determined by the limited partnership.

(e) A restated certificate of limited partnership may be delivered to the [Secretary of State] for filing in the same manner as an amendment.

(f) Subject to Section 206(c), an amendment or restated certificate is effective when filed by the [Secretary of State].

Comment

Source — RULPA Section 202.

Subsection (b) — This subsection lists changes in circumstances which require an amendment to the certificate. Neither a statement of change, Section 115, nor the annual report, Section 210(e), suffice to report the addition or deletion of a general partner or the appointment of a person to wind up a limited partnership that has no general partner.

This subsection states an obligation of the limited partnership. However, so long as the limited partnership has at least one general partner, the general partner or partners are responsible for managing the limited partnership's activities. Section 406(a). That management responsibility includes maintaining accuracy in the limited partnership's public record. Moreover, subsection (c) imposes direct responsibility on any general partner that knows that the filed certificate of limited partnership contains false information.

Acquiring or relinquishing LLLP status also requires an amendment to the certificate. *See* Sections 201(a)(4), 406(b)(2), and 1110(b)(2).

Subsection (c) — This provision imposes an obligation directly on the general partners rather than on the limited partnership. A general partner's failure to meet that responsibility can expose the general partner to liability to third parties under Section 208(a)(2) and might constitute a breach of the general partner's duties under Section 408. In addition, an aggrieved person may seek a remedy under Section 205 (Signing and Filing Pursuant to Judicial Order).

Subsection (d) — A limited partnership that desires to change its name will have to amend its certificate of limited partnership. The new name will have to comply with Section 108. *See* Section 201(a)(1).

Section 203. Statement of Termination

A dissolved limited partnership that has completed winding up may deliver to the [Secretary of State] for filing a statement of termination that states:

(1) the name of the limited partnership;

(2) the date of filing of its initial certificate of limited partnership; and

(3) any other information as determined by the general partners filing the statement or by a person appointed pursuant to Section 803(c) or (d).

Comment

Under Section 103(d)(3), a filed statement of termination provides constructive notice, 90 days after the statement's effective date, that the limited partnership is terminated. That notice effectively terminates any apparent authority to bind the limited partnership.

However, this section is permissive. Therefore, it is not possible to use Section 205 (Signing and Filing Pursuant to Judicial Order) to cause a statement of termination to be filed.

This section differs from predecessor law, RULPA Section 203, which required the filing of a certificate of cancellation when a limited partnership dissolved.

Section 204. Signing of Records

(a) Each record delivered to the [Secretary of State] for filing pursuant to this [Act] must be signed in the following manner:

(1) An initial certificate of limited partnership must be signed by all general partners listed in the certificate.

(2) An amendment adding or deleting a statement that the limited partnership is a limited liability limited partnership must be signed by all general partners listed in the certificate.

(3) An amendment designating as general partner a person admitted under Section 801(3)(B) following the dissociation of a limited partnership's last general partner must be signed by that person.

(4) An amendment required by Section 803(c) following the appointment of a person to wind up the dissolved limited partnership's activities must be signed by that person.

(5) Any other amendment must be signed by:

(A) at least one general partner listed in the certificate;

(B) each other person designated in the amendment as a new general partner; and

(C) each person that the amendment indicates has dissociated as a general partner, unless:

(i) the person is deceased or a guardian or general conservator has been appointed for the person and the amendment so states; or

(ii) the person has previously delivered to the [Secretary of State] for filing a statement of dissociation.

(6) A restated certificate of limited partnership must be signed by at least one general partner listed in the certificate, and, to the extent the restated certificate effects a change under any other paragraph of this subsection, the certificate must be signed in a manner that satisfies that paragraph.

(7) A statement of termination must be signed by all general partners listed in the certificate or, if the certificate of a dissolved limited partnership lists no general partners, by the person appointed pursuant to Section 803(c) or (d) to wind up the dissolved limited partnership's activities.

(8) Articles of conversion must be signed by each general partner listed in the certificate of limited partnership.

(9) Articles of merger must be signed as provided in Section 1108(a).

(10) Any other record delivered on behalf of a limited partnership to the [Secretary of State] for filing must be signed by at least one general partner listed in the certificate.

(11) A statement by a person pursuant to Section 605(a)(4) stating that the person has dissociated as a general partner must be signed by that person.

(12) A statement of withdrawal by a person pursuant to Section 306 must be signed by that person.

(13) A record delivered on behalf of a foreign limited partnership to the [Secretary of State] for filing must be signed by at least one general partner of the foreign limited partnership.

(14) Any other record delivered on behalf of any person to the [Secretary of State] for filing must be signed by that person.

(b) Any person may sign by an attorney in fact any record to be filed pursuant to this [Act].

Comment

Source — ULLCA Section 205.

This section pertains only to signing requirements and implies nothing about approval requirements. For example, Section 204(a)(2) requires that an amendment changing a limited partnership's LLLP status be signed by all **general** partners listed in the certificate, but under Section 406(b)(2) **all** partners must consent to that change unless otherwise provided in the partnership agreement.

A person who signs a record without ascertaining that the record has been properly authorized risks liability under Section 208.

Subsection (a) — The recurring reference to general partners "listed in the certificate" recognizes that a person might be admitted as a general partner under Section 401 without immediately being listed in the certificate of limited partnership. Such persons may have rights, powers and obligations despite their unlisted status, but they cannot act as general partners for the purpose of affecting the limited partnership's public record. *See* the Comment to Section 103(c) and the Comment to Section 401.

Section 205. Signing and Filing Pursuant to Judicial Order

(a) If a person required by this [Act] to sign a record or deliver a record to the [Secretary of State] for filing does not do so, any other person that is aggrieved may petition the [appropriate court] to order:

(1) the person to sign the record;

(2) deliver the record to the [Secretary of State] for filing; or

(3) the [Secretary of State] to file the record unsigned.

(b) If the person aggrieved under subsection (a) is not the limited partnership or foreign limited partnership to which the record pertains, the aggrieved person shall make the limited partnership or foreign limited partnership a party to the action. A person aggrieved under subsection (a) may seek the remedies provided in subsection (a) in the same action in combination or in the alternative.

(c) A record filed unsigned pursuant to this section is effective without being signed.

Comment

Source — RULPA Section 205.

Section 206. Delivery to and Filing of Records by [Secretary of State]; Effective Time and Date

(a) A record authorized or required to be delivered to the [Secretary of State] for filing under this [Act] must be captioned to describe the record's purpose, be in a medium permitted by the [Secretary of State], and be delivered to the [Secretary of State]. Unless the [Secretary of State] determines that a record does not comply with the filing requirements of this [Act], and if all filing fees have been paid, the [Secretary of State] shall file the record and:

(1) for a statement of dissociation, send:

(A) a copy of the filed statement and a receipt for the fees to the person which the statement indicates has dissociated as a general partner; and

(B) a copy of the filed statement and receipt to the limited partnership;

(2) for a statement of withdrawal, send:

(A) a copy of the filed statement and a receipt for the fees to the person on whose behalf the record was filed; and

(B) if the statement refers to an existing limited partnership, a copy of the filed statement and receipt to the limited partnership; and

(3) for all other records, send a copy of the filed record and a receipt for the fees to the person on whose behalf the record was filed.

(b) Upon request and payment of a fee, the [Secretary of State] shall send to the requester a certified copy of the requested record.

(c) Except as otherwise provided in Sections 116 and 207, a record delivered to the [Secretary of State] for filing under this [Act] may specify an effective time and a delayed effective date. Except as otherwise provided in this [Act], a record filed by the [Secretary of State] is effective:

(1) if the record does not specify an effective time and does not specify a delayed effective date, on the date and at the time the record is filed as evidenced by the [Secretary of State's] endorsement of the date and time on the record;

(2) if the record specifies an effective time but not a delayed effective date, on the date the record is filed at the time specified in the record;

(3) if the record specifies a delayed effective date but not an effective time, at 12:01 a.m. on the earlier of:

(A) the specified date; or

(B) the 90th day after the record is filed; or

(4) if the record specifies an effective time and a delayed effective date, at the specified time on the earlier of:

(A) the specified date; or

(B) the 90th day after the record is filed.

Comment

Source — ULLCA Section 206.

In order for a record prepared by a private person to become part of the public record under this Act, (i) someone must put a properly prepared version of the record into the possession of the public official specified in the Act as the appropriate filing officer, and (ii) that filing officer must determine that the record complies with the filing requirements of this Act and then officially make the record part of the public record. This Act refers to the first step as *delivery to the [Secretary of State] for filing* and refers to the second step as *filing*. Thus, under this Act "filing" is an official act.

Subsection (a) — The caption need only indicate the title of the record; *e.g.*, Certificate of Limited Partnership, Statement of Change for Limited Partnership.

Filing officers typically note on a filed record the fact, date and time of filing. The copies provided by the filing officer under this subsection should contain that notation.

This Act does not provide a remedy if the filing officer wrongfully fails or refuses to file a record.

Subsection (c) — This subsection allows most records to have a delayed effective date, up to 90 days after the date the record is filed by the filing officer. A record specifying a longer delay will **not** be rejected. Instead, under paragraph (c)(3) and (4), the delayed effective date is adjusted by operation of law to the "90th day after the record is filed." The Act does not require the filing officer to notify anyone of the adjustment.

Section 207. Correcting Filed Record

(a) A limited partnership or foreign limited partnership may deliver to the [Secretary of State] for filing a statement of correction to correct a record previously delivered by the limited partnership or foreign limited partnership to the [Secretary of State] and filed by the [Secretary of State], if at the time of filing the record contained false or erroneous information or was defectively signed.

(b) A statement of correction may not state a delayed effective date and must:

(1) describe the record to be corrected, including its filing date, or attach a copy of the record as filed;

(2) specify the incorrect information and the reason it is incorrect or the manner in which the signing was defective; and

(3) correct the incorrect information or defective signature.

(c) When filed by the [Secretary of State], a statement of correction is effective retroactively as of the effective date of the record the statement corrects, but the statement is effective when filed:

(1) for the purposes of Section 103(c) and (d); and

(2) as to persons relying on the uncorrected record and adversely affected by the correction.

Comment

Source — ULLCA Section 207.

A statement of correction is appropriate only to correct inaccuracies that existed or signatures that were defective "at the time of filing." A statement of correction may not be used to correct a record that was accurate when filed but has become inaccurate due to subsequent events.

Subsection (c) — Generally, a statement of correction "relates back." However, there is no retroactive effect: (1) for the purposes of constructive notice under Section 103(c) and (d); and (2) against persons who have relied on the uncorrected record and would be adversely affected if the correction related back.

Section 208. Liability for False Information in Filed Record

(a) If a record delivered to the [Secretary of State] for filing under this [Act] and filed by the [Secretary of State] contains false information, a person that suffers loss by reliance on the information may recover damages for the loss from:

(1) a person that signed the record, or caused another to sign it on the person's behalf, and knew the information to be false at the time the record was signed; and

(2) a general partner that has notice that the information was false when the record was filed or has become false because of changed circumstances, if the general partner has notice for a reasonably sufficient time before the information is relied upon to enable the general partner to effect an amendment under Section 202, file a petition pursuant to Section 205, or deliver to the [Secretary of State] for filing a statement of change pursuant to Section 115 or a statement of correction pursuant to Section 207.

(b) Signing a record authorized or required to be filed under this [Act] constitutes an affirmation under the penalties of perjury that the facts stated in the record are true.

Comment

This section pertains to both limited partnerships and foreign limited partnerships.

LLLP status is irrelevant to this section. The LLLP shield protects only to the extent that (i) the obligation involved is an obligation of the limited partnership or foreign limited partnership, and (ii) a partner is claimed to be liable for that obligation by reason of being a partner. This section does not address the obligations of a limited partnership or foreign limited partnership and instead imposes direct liability on signers and general partners.

Subsection (a) — This subsection's liability rules apply only to records (i) created by private persons ("delivered to the [Secretary of State] for filing"), (ii) which actually become part of the public record ("filed by the [Secretary of State]"). This subsection does not preempt other law, which might provide remedies for misleading information contained, for example, in a record that is delivered to the filing officer for filing but withdrawn before the filing officer takes the official action of filing the record.

Records filed under this Act are signed subject to the penalties for perjury. *See* subsection (b). This subsection therefore does not require a party who relies on a record to demonstrate that the reliance was reasonable. Contrast Section 201(d)(2), which provides that, if the partnership agreement is inconsistent with the public record, the public record prevails in favor of a person that is neither a partner nor a transferee and that reasonably relied on the record.

Section 209. Certificate of Existence or Authorization

(a) The [Secretary of State], upon request and payment of the requisite fee, shall furnish a certificate of existence for a limited partnership if the records filed in the [office of the Secretary of State] show that the [Secretary of State] has filed a certificate of limited partnership and has not filed a statement of termination. A certificate of existence must state:

(1) the limited partnership's name;

(2) that it was duly formed under the laws of this State and the date of formation;

(3) whether all fees, taxes, and penalties due to the [Secretary of State] under this [Act] or other law have been paid;

(4) whether the limited partnership's most recent annual report required by Section 210 has been filed by the [Secretary of State];

(5) whether the [Secretary of State] has administratively dissolved the limited partnership;

(6) whether the limited partnership's certificate of limited partnership has been amended to state that the limited partnership is dissolved;

(7) that a statement of termination has not been filed by the [Secretary of State]; and

(8) other facts of record in the [office of the Secretary of State] which may be requested by the applicant.

(b) The [Secretary of State], upon request and payment of the requisite fee, shall furnish a certificate of authorization for a foreign limited partnership if the records filed in the [office of the Secretary of State] show that the [Secretary of State] has filed a certificate of authority, has not revoked the certificate of authority, and has not filed a notice of cancellation. A certificate of authorization must state:

(1) the foreign limited partnership's name and any alternate name adopted under Section 905(a) for use in this State;

(2) that it is authorized to transact business in this State;

(3) whether all fees, taxes, and penalties due to the [Secretary of State] under this [Act] or other law have been paid;

(4) whether the foreign limited partnership's most recent annual report required by Section 210 has been filed by the [Secretary of State];

(5) that the [Secretary of State] has not revoked its certificate of authority and has not filed a notice of cancellation; and

(6) other facts of record in the [office of the Secretary of State] which may be requested by the applicant.

(c) Subject to any qualification stated in the certificate, a certificate of existence or authorization issued by the [Secretary of State] may be relied upon as conclusive evidence that the limited partnership or foreign limited partnership is in existence or is authorized to transact business in this State.

Comment

Source — ULLCA Section 208.

A certificate of existence can reveal only information present in the public record, and under this Act significant information bearing on the status of a limited partnership may be outside the public record. For example, while this Act provides for a limited partnership to have a perpetual duration, Section 104(c), the partnership agreement may set a definite term or designate particular events whose occurrence will cause dissolution. Section 801(1). Dissolution is also possible by consent, Section 801(2), and, absent a contrary provision in the partnership agreement, will at least be at issue whenever a general partner dissociates. Section 801(3). Nothing in this Act requires a limited partnership to deliver to the filing officer for filing a record indicating that the limited partnership has dissolved.

A certificate of authorization furnished under this section is different than a certificate of authority filed under Section 904.

Section 210. Annual Report for [Secretary of State]

(a) A limited partnership or a foreign limited partnership authorized to transact business in this State shall deliver to the [Secretary of State] for filing an annual report that states:

(1) the name of the limited partnership or foreign limited partnership;

(2) the street and mailing address of its designated office and the name and street and mailing address of its agent for service of process in this State;

(3) in the case of a limited partnership, the street and mailing address of its principal office; and

(4) in the case of a foreign limited partnership, the State or other jurisdiction under whose law the foreign limited partnership is formed and any alternate name adopted under Section 905(a).

(b) Information in an annual report must be current as of the date the annual report is delivered to the [Secretary of State] for filing.

(c) The first annual report must be delivered to the [Secretary of State] between [January 1 and April 1] of the year following the calendar year in which a limited partnership was formed or a foreign limited partnership was authorized to transact business. An annual report must be delivered to the [Secretary of State] between [January 1 and April 1] of each subsequent calendar year.

(d) If an annual report does not contain the information required in subsection (a), the [Secretary of State] shall promptly notify the reporting limited partnership or foreign limited partnership and return the report to it for correction. If the report is corrected to contain the information required in subsection (a) and delivered to the [Secretary of State] within 30 days after the effective date of the notice, it is timely delivered.

(e) If a filed annual report contains an address of a designated office or the name or address of an agent for service of process which differs from the information shown in the records of the [Secretary of State] immediately before the filing, the differing information in the annual report is considered a statement of change under Section 115.

Comment

Source — ULLCA Section 211.

Subsection (d) — This subsection's rule affects only Section 809(a)(2) (late filing of annual report grounds for administrative dissolution) and any late fees that the filing officer might have the right to impose. For the purposes of subsection (e), the annual report functions as a statement of change only when "filed" by the filing officer. Likewise, a person cannot rely on subsection (d) to escape liability arising under Section 208.

ARTICLE 3
LIMITED PARTNERS

Section 301. Becoming Limited Partner

A person becomes a limited partner:

(1) as provided in the partnership agreement;

(2) as the result of a conversion or merger under [Article] 11; or

(3) with the consent of all the partners.

Comment

Source — RULPA Section 301.

Although Section 801(4) contemplates the admission of a limited partner to avoid dissolution, that provision does not itself authorize the admission. Instead, this section controls. Contrast Section 801(3)(B), which itself authorizes the admission of a general partner in order to avoid dissolution.

Section 302. No Right or Power as Limited Partner to Bind Limited Partnership

A limited partner does not have the right or the power as a limited partner to act for or bind the limited partnership.

Comment

In this respect a limited partner is analogous to a shareholder in a corporation; status as owner provides neither the right to manage nor a reasonable appearance of that right.

The phrase "as a limited partner" is intended to recognize that: (i) this section does not disable a general partner that also owns a limited partner interest, (ii) the partnership agreement may as a matter of contract allocate managerial rights to one or more limited partners; and (iii) a separate agreement can empower and entitle a person that is a limited partner to act for the limited partnership in another capacity; *e.g.*, as an agent. *See* Comment to Section 305

The fact that a limited partner *qua* limited partner has no power to bind the limited partnership means that, subject to Section 113 (Dual Capacity), information possessed by a limited partner is not attributed to the limited partnership. *See* Section 103(h).

This Act specifies various circumstances in which limited partners have consent rights, including:

- admission of a limited partner, Section 301(3)
- admission of a general partner, Section 401(4)
- amendment of the partnership agreement, Section 406(b)(1)
- the decision to amend the certificate of limited partnership so as to obtain or relinquish LLLP status, Section 406(b)(2)
- the disposition of all or substantially all of the limited partnership's property, outside the ordinary course, Section 406(b)(3)
- the compromise of a partner's obligation to make a contribution or return an improper distribution, Section 502(c)

- expulsion of a limited partner by consent of the other partners, Section 601(b)(4)

- expulsion of a general partner by consent of the other partners, Section 603(4)

- redemption of a transferable interest subject to charging order, using limited partnership property, Section 703(c)(3)

- causing dissolution by consent, Section 801(2)

- causing dissolution by consent following the dissociation of a general partner, when at least one general partner remains, Section 801(3)(A)

- avoiding dissolution and appointing a successor general partner, following the dissociation of the sole general partner, Section 801(3)(B)

- appointing a person to wind up the limited partnership when there is no general partner, Section 803(C)

- approving, amending or abandoning a plan of conversion, Section 1103(a) and (b)(2)

- approving, amending or abandoning a plan of merger, Section 1107(a) and (b)(2).

Section 303. No Liability as Limited Partner for Limited Partnership Obligations

An obligation of a limited partnership, whether arising in contract, tort, or otherwise, is not the obligation of a limited partner. A limited partner is not personally liable, directly or indirectly, by way of contribution or otherwise, for an obligation of the limited partnership solely by reason of being a limited partner, even if the limited partner participates in the management and control of the limited partnership.

Comment

This section provides a full, status-based liability shield for each limited partner, "even if the limited partner participates in the management and control of the limited partnership." The section thus eliminates the so-called "control rule" with respect to personal liability for entity obligations and brings limited partners into parity with LLC members, LLP partners and corporate shareholders.

The "control rule" first appeared in an uniform act in 1916, although the concept is much older. Section 7 of the original Uniform Limited Partnership Act provided that "A limited partner shall not become liable as a general partner [i.e., for the obligations of the limited partnership] unless . . . he takes part in the control of the business." The 1976 Uniform Limited Partnership Act (ULPA — 1976) "carrie[d] over the basic test from former Section 7," but recognized "the difficulty of determining when the'control' line has been overstepped." Comment to ULPA-1976, Section 303. Accordingly, ULPA-1976 tried to buttress the limited partner's shield by (i) providing a safe harbor for a lengthy list of activities deemed not to constitute participating in control, ULPA-1976, Section 303(b), and (ii) limiting a limited partner's "control rule" liability "only to persons who transact business with the limited partnership with actual knowledge of [the limited partner's] participation in control." ULPA-1976, Section 303(a). However, these protections were complicated by a countervailing rule which made a limited partner generally liable for the limited partnership's obligations "if the limited partner's participation in the control of the business is . . . substantially the same as the exercise of the powers of a general partner." ULPA-1976, Section 303(a).

The 1985 amendments to ULPA-1976 (i.e., RULPA) further buttressed the limited partner's shield, removing the "substantially the same" rule, expanding the list of safe harbor activities and limiting "control rule" liability "only to persons who transact business with the limited partnership reasonably believing, based upon the limited partner's conduct, that the limited partner is a general partner."

In a world with LLPs, LLCs and, most importantly, LLLPs, the control rule has become an anachronism. This Act therefore takes the next logical step in the evolution of the limited partner's liability shield and renders the control rule extinct.

The shield established by this section protects only against liability for the limited partnership's obligations and only to the extent that the limited partner is claimed to be liable on account of being a limited partner. Thus, a person that is both a general and limited partner will be liable as a general partner for the limited partnership's obligations. Moreover, this section does not prevent a limited partner from being liable as a result of the limited partner's own conduct and is therefore inapplicable when a third party asserts that a limited partner's own wrongful conduct has injured the third party. This section is likewise inapplicable to claims by the limited partnership or another partner that a limited partner has breached a duty under this Act or the partnership agreement.

This section does not eliminate a limited partner's liability for promised contributions, Section 502 or improper distributions. Section 509. That liability pertains to a person's status as a limited partner but is **not** liability for an obligation of the limited partnership.

The shield provided by this section applies whether or not a limited partnership is a limited liability limited partnership.

Section 304. Right of Limited Partner and Former Limited Partner to Information

(a) On 10 days' demand, made in a record received by the limited partnership, a limited partner may inspect and copy required information during regular business hours in the limited partnership's designated office. The limited partner need not have any particular purpose for seeking the information.

(b) During regular business hours and at a reasonable location specified by the limited partnership, a limited partner may obtain from the limited partnership and inspect and copy true and full information regarding the state of the activities and financial condition of the limited partnership and other information regarding the activities of the limited partnership as is just and reasonable if:

(1) the limited partner seeks the information for a purpose reasonably related to the partner's interest as a limited partner;

(2) the limited partner makes a demand in a record received by the limited partnership, describing with reasonable particularity the information sought and the purpose for seeking the information; and

(3) the information sought is directly connected to the limited partner's purpose.

(c) Within 10 days after receiving a demand pursuant to subsection (b), the limited partnership in a record shall inform the limited partner that made the demand:

(1) what information the limited partnership will provide in response to the demand;

(2) when and where the limited partnership will provide the information; and

(3) if the limited partnership declines to provide any demanded information, the limited partnership's reasons for declining.

(d) Subject to subsection (f), a person dissociated as a limited partner may inspect and copy required information during regular business hours in the limited partnership's designated office if:

(1) the information pertains to the period during which the person was a limited partner;

(2) the person seeks the information in good faith; and

(3) the person meets the requirements of subsection (b).

(e) The limited partnership shall respond to a demand made pursuant to subsection (d) in the same manner as provided in subsection (c).

(f) If a limited partner dies, Section 704 applies.

(g) The limited partnership may impose reasonable restrictions on the use of information obtained under this section. In a dispute concerning the reasonableness of a restriction under this subsection, the limited partnership has the burden of proving reasonableness.

(h) A limited partnership may charge a person that makes a demand under this section reasonable costs of copying, limited to the costs of labor and material.

(i) Whenever this [Act] or a partnership agreement provides for a limited partner to give or withhold consent to a matter, before the consent is given or withheld, the limited partnership shall, without demand, provide the limited partner with all information material to the limited partner's decision that the limited partnership knows.

(j) A limited partner or person dissociated as a limited partner may exercise the rights under this section through an attorney or other agent. Any restriction imposed under subsection (g) or by the partnership agreement applies both to the attorney or other agent and to the limited partner or person dissociated as a limited partner.

(k) The rights stated in this section do not extend to a person as transferee, but may be exercised by the legal representative of an individual under legal disability who is a limited partner or person dissociated as a limited partner.

Comment

This section balances two countervailing concerns relating to information: the need of limited partners and former limited partners for access versus the limited partnership's need to protect confidential business data and other intellectual property. The balance must be understood in the context of fiduciary duties. The general partners are obliged through their duties of care and loyalty to protect information whose confidentiality is important to the limited partnership or otherwise inappropriate for dissemination. *See* Section 408 (general standards of general partner conduct). A limited partner, in contrast, "does not have any fiduciary duty to the limited partnership or to any other partner solely by reason of being a limited partner." Section 305(a). (Both general partners and limited partners are subject to a duty of good faith and fair dealing. Section 305(b) and 408(d).)

Like predecessor law, this Act divides limited partner access rights into two categories — required information and other information. However, this Act builds on predecessor law by:

- expanding slightly the category of required information and stating explicitly that a limited partner may have access to that information without having to show cause

- specifying a procedure for limited partners to follow when demanding access to other information

- specifying how a limited partnership must respond to such a demand and setting a time limit for the response

- retaining predecessor law's "just and reasonable" standard for determining a limited partner's right to other information, while recognizing that, to be "just and reasonable," a limited partner's demand for other information must meet at minimum standards of relatedness and particularity

- expressly requiring the limited partnership to volunteer known, material information when seeking or obtaining consent from limited partners

- codifying (while limiting) the power of the partnership agreement to vary limited partner access rights

- permitting the limited partnership to establish other reasonable limits on access

- providing access rights for former limited partners.

The access rights stated in this section are personal to each limited partner and are enforceable through a direct action under Section 1001(a). These access rights are in addition to whatever discovery rights a party has in a civil suit.

Subsection (a) — The phrase "required information" is a defined term. *See.* Sections 102(18) and 111. This subsection's broad right of access is subject not only to reasonable limitations in the partnership agreement, Section 110(b)(4), but also to the power of the limited partnership to impose reasonable limitations on use. Unless the partnership agreement provides otherwise, it will be the general partner or partners that have the authority to use that power. *See* Section 406(a).

Subsection (b) — The language describing the information to be provided comes essentially verbatim from RULPA Section 305(a)(2)(i) and (iii). The procedural requirements derive from RMBCA Section 16.02(c). This subsection does not impose a requirement of good faith, because Section 305(b) contains a generally applicable obligation of good faith and fair dealing for limited partners.

Subsection (d) — The notion that former owners should have information rights comes from RUPA Section 403(b) and ULLCA Section 408(a). The access is limited to the required information and is subject to certain conditions.

Example: A person dissociated as a limited partner seeks data which the limited partnership has compiled, which relates to the period when the person was a limited partner, but which is beyond the scope of the information required by Section 111. No matter how reasonable the person's purpose and how well drafted the person's demand, the limited partnership is not obliged to provide the data.

Example: A person dissociated as a limited partner seeks access to required information pertaining to the period during which the person was a limited partner. The person makes a bald demand, merely stating a desire to review the required information at the limited partnership's designated office. In particular, the demand does not describe "with reasonable particularity the information sought and the purpose for seeking the information." *See* subsection (b)(2). The limited partnership is not obliged to allow access. The person must first comply with subsection (d), which incorporates by reference the requirements of subsection (b).

Subsection (f) and Section 704 provide greater access rights for the estate of a deceased limited partner.

Subsection (d)(2) — A duty of good faith is needed here, because a person claiming access under this subsection is no longer a limited partner and is no longer subject to Section 305(b). *See* Section 602(a)(2) (dissociation as a limited partner terminates duty of good faith as to subsequent events).

Subsection (g) — This subsection permits the limited partnership — as distinguished from the partnership agreement — to impose use limitations. Contrast Section 110(b)(4). Under Section 406(a), it will be the general partner or partners that decide whether the limited partnership will impose use restrictions.

The limited partnership bears the burden of proving the reasonableness of any restriction imposed under this subsection. In determining whether a restriction is reasonable, a court might consider: (i) the danger or other problem the restriction seeks to avoid; (ii) the purpose for which the information is sought; and (iii) whether, in light of both the problem and the purpose, the restriction is reasonably tailored. Restricting use of the names and addresses of limited partners is not per se unreasonable.

The following table compares the limitations available through the partnership agreement with those available under this subsection.

	Partnership agreement	Section 304(g)
how restrictions adopted	by the consent of partners when they adopt or amend the partnership agreement, unless the partnership agreement provides another method of amendment	by the general partners, acting under Section 406(a)
what restrictions may be imposed	"reasonable restrictions on the availability and use of information obtained," Section 110(b)(4)	"reasonable restrictions on the use of information obtained"

	Partnership agreement	Section 304(g)
burden of proof	the person challenging the restriction must prove that the restriction will "unreasonably restrict the right of information," Section 110(b)(4)	"the limited partnership has the burden of proving reasonableness"

Subsection (h) — Source: RUPA Section 403(b) and ULLCA Section 408(a).

Subsection (i) — Source: ULLCA Section 408(b).

The duty stated in this subsection is at the core of the duties owed the limited partners by a limited partnership and its general partners. This subsection imposes an affirmative duty to volunteer information, but that obligation is limited to information which is both material and known by the limited partnership. The duty applies to known, material information, even if the limited partnership does not know that the information is material.

A limited partnership will "know" what its general partners know. Section 103(h). A limited partnership may also know information known by the "individual conducting the transaction for the [limited partnership]." Section 103(g).

A limited partner's right to information under this subsection is enforceable through the full panoply of "legal or equitable relief" provided by Section 1001(a), including in appropriate circumstances the withdrawal or invalidation of improperly obtained consent and the invalidation or rescission of action taken pursuant to that consent.

Subsection (k) — Section 304 provides no information rights to a transferee as transferee. Transferee status brings only the very limited information rights stated in Section 702(c).

It is nonetheless possible for a person that happens to be a transferee to have rights under this section. For example, under Section 602(a)(3) a person dissociated as a limited partner becomes a "mere transferee" of its own transferable interest. While that status provides the person no rights under this section, the status of person dissociated as a limited partner triggers rights under subsection (d).

Section 305. Limited Duties of Limited Partners

(a) A limited partner does not have any fiduciary duty to the limited partnership or to any other partner solely by reason of being a limited partner.

(b) A limited partner shall discharge the duties to the partnership and the other partners under this [Act] or under the partnership agreement and exercise any rights consistently with the obligation of good faith and fair dealing.

(c) A limited partner does not violate a duty or obligation under this [Act] or under the partnership agreement merely because the limited partner's conduct furthers the limited partner's own interest.

Comment

Subsection (a) — Fiduciary duty typically attaches to a person whose status or role creates significant power for that person over the interests of another person. Under this Act, limited partners have very limited power of any sort in the regular activities of the limited partnership and no power whatsoever justifying the imposition of fiduciary duties either to the limited partnership or fellow partners. It is possible for a partnership agreement to allocate significant managerial authority and power to a limited partner, but in that case the power exists not as a matter of status or role but rather as a matter of contract. The proper limit on such contract-based power is the obligation of good faith and fair dealing, not fiduciary duty, unless the partnership agreement itself expressly imposes a fiduciary duty or creates a role for a limited partner which, as a matter of other law, gives rise to a fiduciary duty. For example, if the partnership agreement makes a limited partner an agent for the limited partnership as to particular matters, the law of agency will impose fiduciary duties on the limited partner with respect to the limited partner's role as agent.

Subsection (b) — Source: RUPA Section 404 (d). The same language appears in Section 408(d), pertaining to general partners.

The obligation of good faith and fair dealing is *not* a fiduciary duty, does not command altruism or self-abnegation, and does not prevent a partner from acting in the partner's own self-interest. Courts should not use the obligation to change *ex post facto* the parties' or this Act's allocation of risk and power. To the contrary, in light of the nature of a limited partnership, the obligation should be used only to protect agreed-upon arrangements from conduct that is manifestly beyond what a reasonable person could have contemplated when the arrangements were made.

The partnership agreement or this Act may grant discretion to a partner, and that partner may properly exercise that discretion even though another partner suffers as a consequence. Conduct does not violate the obligation of good faith and fair dealing merely because that conduct substantially prejudices a party. Indeed, parties allocate risk precisely because prejudice may occur. The exercise of discretion constitutes a breach of the obligation of good faith and fair dealing only when the party claiming breach shows that the conduct has no honestly-held purpose that legitimately comports with the parties' agreed-upon arrangements. Once such a purpose appears, courts should not second guess a party's choice of method in serving that purpose, unless the party invoking the obligation of good faith and fair dealing shows that the choice of method itself lacks any honestly-held purpose that legitimately comports with the parties' agreed-upon arrangements.

In sum, the purpose of the obligation of good faith and fair dealing is to protect the arrangement the partners have chosen for themselves, not to restructure that arrangement under the guise of safeguarding it.

Section 306. Person Erroneously Believing Self to Be Limited Partner

(a) Except as otherwise provided in subsection (b), a person that makes an investment in a business enterprise and erroneously but in good faith believes that the person has become a limited partner in the enterprise is not liable for the enterprise's obligations by reason of making the investment, receiving distributions from the enterprise, or exercising any rights of or appropriate to a limited partner, if, on ascertaining the mistake, the person:

(1) causes an appropriate certificate of limited partnership, amendment, or statement of correction to be signed and delivered to the [Secretary of State] for filing; or

(2) withdraws from future participation as an owner in the enterprise by signing and delivering to the [Secretary of State] for filing a statement of withdrawal under this section.

(b) A person that makes an investment described in subsection (a) is liable to the same extent as a general partner to any third party that enters into a transaction with the enterprise, believing in good faith that the person is a general partner, before the [Secretary of State] files a statement of withdrawal, certificate of limited partnership, amendment, or statement of correction to show that the person is not a general partner.

(c) If a person makes a diligent effort in good faith to comply with subsection (a)(1) and is unable to cause the appropriate certificate of limited partnership, amendment, or statement of correction to be signed and delivered to the [Secretary of State] for filing, the person has the right to withdraw from the enterprise pursuant to subsection (a)(2) even if the withdrawal would otherwise breach an agreement with others that are or have agreed to become co-owners of the enterprise.

Comment

Source — RULPA Section 304, substantially redrafted for reasons of style.

Subsection (a)(2) — The requirement that a person "withdraw[] from future participation as an owner in the enterprise" means, in part, that the person refrain from taking any further profit from the enterprise. The requirement does not mean, however, that the person is required to return previously obtained profits or forfeit any investment.

ARTICLE 4
GENERAL PARTNERS

Section 401. Becoming General Partner

A person becomes a general partner:

(1) as provided in the partnership agreement:

(2) under Section 801(3)(B) following the dissociation of a limited partnership's last general partner;

(3) as the result of a conversion or merger under [Article] 11; or

(4) with the consent of all the partners.

Comment

This section does not make a person's status as a general partner dependent on the person being so designated in the certificate of limited partnership. If a person does become a general partner under this section without being so designated:

- the limited partnership is obligated to promptly and appropriately amend the certificate of limited partnership, Section 202(b)(1);

- each general partner that knows of the anomaly is personally obligated to cause the certificate to be promptly and appropriately amended, Section 202(c)(1), and is subject to liability for failing to do so, Section 208(a)(2);

- the "non-designated" general partner has:

~ all the rights and duties of a general partner to the limited partnership and the other partners, and

~ the powers of a general partner to bind the limited partnership under Sections 402 and 403, but

~ no power to sign records which are to be filed on behalf of the limited partnership under this Act

Example: By consent of the partners of XYZ Limited Partnership, G is admitted as a general partner. However, XYZ's certificate of limited partnership is not amended accordingly. Later, G — acting without actual authority — purports to bind XYZ to a transaction with Third Party. Third Party does not review the filed certificate of limited partnership before entering into the transaction. XYZ might be bound under Section 402.

Section 402 attributes to a limited partnership "[a]n act of a general partner . . . for apparently carrying on in the ordinary course the limited partnership's activities or activities of the kind carried on by the limited partnership." The limited partnership's liability under **Section 402** does not depend on the "act of a general partner" being the act of a general partner designated in the certificate of limited partnership. Moreover, the notice provided by Section 103(c) does not undercut G's appearance of authority. Section 402 refers only to notice under Section 103(d) and, in any event, according to the second sentence of Section 103(c), the fact that a person is **not** listed as in the certificate as a general partner is **not** notice that the person is **not** a general partner. *See* Comment to Section 103(c).

Example: Same facts, except that Third Party does review the certificate of limited partnership before entering into the transaction. The result might still be the same.

The omission of a person's name from the certificate's list of general partners is **not** notice that the person is **not** a general partner. Therefore, Third Party's review of the certificate does not mean that Third Party knew, had received a notification or had notice that G lacked authority. At most, XYZ could argue that, because Third Party knew that G was not listed in the certificate, a transaction entered into by G could not appear to Third Party to be for apparently carrying on the limited partnership's activities in the ordinary course.

Section 402. General Partner Agent of Limited Partnership

(a) Each general partner is an agent of the limited partnership for the purposes of its activities. An act of a general partner, including the signing of a record in the partnership's name, for apparently carrying on in the ordinary course the limited partnership's activities or activities of the kind carried on by the limited partnership binds the limited partnership, unless the general partner did not have authority to act for the limited partnership in the particular matter and the person with which the general partner was dealing knew, had received a notification, or had notice under Section 103(d) that the general partner lacked authority.

(b) An act of a general partner which is not apparently for carrying on in the ordinary course the limited partnership's activities or activities of the kind carried on by the limited partnership binds the limited partnership only if the act was actually authorized by all the other partners.

Comment

Source — RUPA Section 301. For the meaning of "authority" in subsection (a) and "authorized" in subsection (b), see RUPA Section 301, Comment 3 (stating that "Subsection (2) [of RUPA Section 301] makes it clear that the partnership is bound by a partner's *actual* authority, even if the partner has no apparent authority"; emphasis added).

The fact that a person is not listed in the certificate of limited partnership as a general partner is **not** notice that the person is **not** a partner and is **not** notice that the person lacks authority to act for the limited partnership. *See* Comment to Section 103(c) and Comment to Section 401.

Section 103(f) defines receipt of notification. Section 103(d) lists various public filings, each of which provides notice 90 days after its effective date.

> **Example:** For the past ten years, X has been a general partner of XYZ Limited Partnership and has regularly conducted the limited partnership's business with Third Party. However, 100 days ago the limited partnership expelled X as a general partner and the next day delivered for filing an amendment to XYZ's certificate of limited partnership which stated that X was no longer a general partner. On that same day, the filing officer filed the amendment.
>
> Today X approaches Third Party, purports still be to a general partner of XYZ and purports to enter into a transaction with Third Party on XYZ's behalf. Third Party is unaware that X has been expelled and has no reason to doubt that X's bona fides. Nonetheless, XYZ is not liable on the transaction. Under Section 103(d), Third Party has notice that X is dissociated and perforce has notice that X is not a general partner authorized to bind XYZ.

Section 403. Limited Partnership Liable for General Partner's Actionable Conduct

(a) A limited partnership is liable for loss or injury caused to a person, or for a penalty incurred, as a result of a wrongful act or omission, or other actionable conduct, of a general partner acting in the ordinary course of activities of the limited partnership or with authority of the limited partnership.

(b) If, in the course of the limited partnership's activities or while acting with authority of the limited partnership, a general partner receives or causes the limited partnership to receive money or property of a person not a partner, and the money or property is misapplied by a general partner, the limited partnership is liable for the loss.

Comment

Source — RUPA Section 305. For the meaning of "authority" in subsections (a) and (b), see RUPA Section 305, Comment. The third-to-last paragraph of that Comment states:

> The partnership is liable for the actionable conduct or omission of a partner acting in the ordinary course of its business or "with the authority of the partnership." This is intended to include a

partner's apparent, as well as actual, authority, thereby bringing within Section 305(a) the situation covered in UPA Section 14(a).

The last paragraph of that Comment states:

Section 305(b) is drawn from UPA Section 14(b), but has been edited to improve clarity. It imposes strict liability on the partnership for the misapplication of money or property received by a partner in the course of the partnership's business or otherwise within the scope of the partner's actual authority.

Section 403(a) of this Act is taken essentially verbatim from RUPA Section 305(a), and Section 403(b) of this Act is taken essentially verbatim from RUPA Section 305(b).

This section makes the limited partnership vicariously liable for a partner's misconduct. That vicariously liability in no way discharges or diminishes the partner's direct liability for the partner's own misconduct.

A general partner can cause a limited partnership to be liable under this section, even if the general partner is not designated as a general partner in the certificate of limited partnership. *See* Comment to Section 401.

Section 404. General Partner's Liability

(a) Except as otherwise provided in subsections (b) and (c), all general partners are liable jointly and severally for all obligations of the limited partnership unless otherwise agreed by the claimant or provided by law.

(b) A person that becomes a general partner of an existing limited partnership is not personally liable for an obligation of a limited partnership incurred before the person became a general partner.

(c) An obligation of a limited partnership incurred while the limited partnership is a limited liability limited partnership, whether arising in contract, tort, or otherwise, is solely the obligation of the limited partnership. A general partner is not personally liable, directly or indirectly, by way of contribution or otherwise, for such an obligation solely by reason of being or acting as a general partner. This subsection applies despite anything inconsistent in the partnership agreement that existed immediately before the consent required to become a limited liability limited partnership under Section 406(b)(2).

Comment

Source — RUPA Section 306.

Following RUPA and the UPA, this Act leaves to other law the question of when a limited partnership obligation is incurred.

Subsection (c) — For an explanation of the decision to provide for limited liability limited partnerships, see the Prefatory Note.

Section 405. Actions by and Against Partnership and Partners

(a) To the extent not inconsistent with Section 404, a general partner may be joined in an action against the limited partnership or named in a separate action.

(b) A judgment against a limited partnership is not by itself a judgment against a general partner. A judgment against a limited partnership may not be satisfied from a general partner's assets unless there is also a judgment against the general partner.

(c) A judgment creditor of a general partner may not levy execution against the assets of the general partner to satisfy a judgment based on a claim against the limited partnership, unless the partner is personally liable for the claim under Section 404 and:

(1) a judgment based on the same claim has been obtained against the limited partnership and a writ of execution on the judgment has been returned unsatisfied in whole or in part;

(2) the limited partnership is a debtor in bankruptcy;

(3) the general partner has agreed that the creditor need not exhaust limited partnership assets;

(4) a court grants permission to the judgment creditor to levy execution against the assets of a general partner based on a finding that limited partnership assets subject to execution are clearly insufficient to satisfy the judgment, that exhaustion of limited partnership assets is excessively burdensome, or that the grant of permission is an appropriate exercise of the court's equitable powers; or

(5) liability is imposed on the general partner by law or contract independent of the existence of the limited partnership.

Comment

Source — RUPA Section 307.

If a limited partnership is a limited liability limited partnership throughout its existence, this section will bar a creditor of a limited partnership from impleading, suing or reaching the assets of a general partner unless the creditor can satisfy subsection (c)(5).

Section 406. Management Rights of General Partner

(a) Each general partner has equal rights in the management and conduct of the limited partnership's activities. Except as expressly provided in this [Act], any matter relating to the activities of the limited partnership may be exclusively decided by the general partner or, if there is more than one general partner, by a majority of the general partners.

(b) The consent of each partner is necessary to:

(1) amend the partnership agreement;

(2) amend the certificate of limited partnership to add or, subject to Section 1110, delete a statement that the limited partnership is a limited liability limited partnership; and

(3) sell, lease, exchange, or otherwise dispose of all, or substantially all, of the limited partnership's property, with or without the good will, other than in the usual and regular course of the limited partnership's activities.

(c) A limited partnership shall reimburse a general partner for payments made and indemnify a general partner for liabilities incurred by the general partner in the ordinary course of the activities of the partnership or for the preservation of its activities or property.

(d) A limited partnership shall reimburse a general partner for an advance to the limited partnership beyond the amount of capital the general partner agreed to contribute.

(e) A payment or advance made by a general partner which gives rise to an obligation of the limited partnership under subsection (c) or (d) constitutes a loan to the limited partnership which accrues interest from the date of the payment or advance.

(f) A general partner is not entitled to remuneration for services performed for the partnership.

Comment

Source — RUPA Section 401 and ULLCA Section 404.

Subsection (a) — As explained in the Prefatory Note, this Act assumes that, more often than not, people utilizing the Act will want (i) strong centralized management, strongly entrenched, and (ii) passive investors with little control over the entity. Section 302 essentially excludes limited partners from the ordinary management of a limited partnership's activities. This subsection states affirmatively the general partners' commanding role. Only the partnership agreement and the express provisions of this Act can limit that role.

The authority granted by this subsection includes the authority to delegate. Delegation does not relieve the delegating general partner or partners of their duties under Section 408. However, the fact of delegation is a fact relevant to any breach of duty analysis.

Example: A sole general partner personally handles all "important paperwork" for a limited partnership. The general partner neglects to renew the fire insurance coverage on the a building owned by the limited partnership, despite having received and read a warning notice from the insurance company. The building subsequently burns to the ground and is a total loss. The general partner might be liable for breach of the duty of care under Section 408(c) (gross negligence).

Example: A sole general partner delegates responsibility for insurance renewals to the limited partnership's office manager, and that manager neglects to renew the fire insurance coverage on the building. Even assuming that the office manager has been grossly negligent, the general partner is not necessarily liable under Section 408(c). The office manager's gross negligence is not automatically attributed to the general partner. Under Section 408(c), the question is whether the general partner was grossly negligent (or worse) in selecting the general manager, delegating insurance renewal matters to the general manager and supervising the general manager after the delegation.

For the consequences of delegating authority to a person that is a limited partner, see the Comment to Section 305.

The partnership agreement may also provide for delegation and, subject to Section 110(b)(5) — (7), may modify a general partner's Section 408 duties.

Subsection (b) — This subsection limits the managerial rights of the general partners, requiring the consent of each general and limited partner for the specified actions. The subsection is subject to change by the partnership agreement, except as provided in Section 110(b)(12) (pertaining to consent rights established by Section 1110).

Subsection (c) — This Act does not include any parallel provision for limited partners, because they are assumed to be passive. To the extent that by contract or other arrangement a limited partner has authority to act on behalf of the limited partnership, agency law principles will create an indemnity obligation. In other situations, principles of restitution might apply.

Subsection (f) — Unlike RUPA Section 401(h), this subsection provides no compensation for winding up efforts. In a limited partnership, winding up is one of the tasks for which the limited partners depend on the general partner. There is no reason for the Act to single out this particular task as giving rise to compensation.

Section 407. Right of General Partner and Former General Partner to Information

(a) A general partner, without having any particular purpose for seeking the information, may inspect and copy during regular business hours:

(1) in the limited partnership's designated office, required information; and

(2) at a reasonable location specified by the limited partnership, any other records maintained by the limited partnership regarding the limited partnership's activities and financial condition.

(b) Each general partner and the limited partnership shall furnish to a general partner:

(1) without demand, any information concerning the limited partnership's activities and activities reasonably required for the proper exercise of the general partner's rights and duties under the partnership agreement or this [Act]; and

(2) on demand, any other information concerning the limited partnership's activities, except to the extent the demand or the information demanded is unreasonable or otherwise improper under the circumstances.

(c) Subject to subsection (e), on 10 days' demand made in a record received by the limited partnership, a person dissociated as a general partner may have access to the information and records described in subsection (a) at the location specified in subsection (a) if:

(1) the information or record pertains to the period during which the person was a general partner;

(2) the person seeks the information or record in good faith; and

(3) the person satisfies the requirements imposed on a limited partner by Section 304(b).

(d) The limited partnership shall respond to a demand made pursuant to subsection (c) in the same manner as provided in Section 304(c).

(e) If a general partner dies, Section 704 applies.

(f) The limited partnership may impose reasonable restrictions on the use of information under this section. In any dispute concerning the reasonableness of a restriction under this subsection, the limited partnership has the burden of proving reasonableness.

(g) A limited partnership may charge a person dissociated as a general partner that makes a demand under this section reasonable costs of copying, limited to the costs of labor and material.

(h) A general partner or person dissociated as a general partner may exercise the rights under this section through an attorney or other agent. Any restriction imposed under subsection (f) or by the partnership agreement applies both to the attorney or other agent and to the general partner or person dissociated as a general partner.

(i) The rights under this section do not extend to a person as transferee, but the rights under subsection (c) of a person dissociated as a general may be exercised by the legal representative of an individual who dissociated as a general partner under Section 603(7)(B) or (C).

Comment

This section's structure parallels the structure of Section 304 and the Comment to that section may be helpful in understanding this section.

Subsection (b) — Source: RUPA Section 403(c).

Subsection (b)(1) — If a particular item of material information is apparent in the limited partnership's records, whether a general partner is obliged to disseminate that information to fellow general partners depends on the circumstances.

> **Example:** A limited partnership has two general partners: each of which is regularly engaged in conducting the limited partnership's activities; both of which are aware of and have regular access to all significant limited partnership records; and neither of which has special responsibility for or knowledge about any particular aspect of those activities or the partnership records pertaining to any particular aspect of those activities. Most likely, neither general partner is obliged to draw the other general partner's attention to information apparent in the limited partnership's records.

> **Example:** Although a limited partnership has three general partners, one is the managing partner with day-to-day responsibility for running the limited partnership's activities. The other two meet periodically with the managing general partner, and together with that partner function in a manner analogous to a corporate board of directors. Most likely, the managing general partner has a duty to draw the attention of the other general partners to important information, even if that information would be apparent from a review of the limited partnership's records.

In all events under subsection (b)(1), the question is whether the disclosure by one general partner is "reasonably required for the proper exercise" of the other general partner's rights and duties.

Subsection (f) — This provision is identical to Section 304(g) and the Comment to Section 304(g) is applicable here. Under this Act, general and limited partners have sharply different roles. A restriction that is reasonable as to a limited partner is not necessarily reasonable as to a general partner.

Subsection (g) — No charge is allowed for current general partners, because in almost all cases they would be entitled to reimbursement under Section 406(c). Contrast Section 304(h), which authorizes charges to current limited partners.

Subsection (i) — The Comment to Section 304(k) is applicable here.

Section 408. General Standards of General Partner's Conduct

(a) The only fiduciary duties that a general partner has to the limited partnership and the other partners are the duties of loyalty and care under subsections (b) and (c).

(b) A general partner's duty of loyalty to the limited partnership and the other partners is limited to the following:

(1) to account to the limited partnership and hold as trustee for it any property, profit, or benefit derived by the general partner in the conduct and winding up of the limited partnership's activities or derived from a use by the general partner of limited partnership property, including the appropriation of a limited partnership opportunity;

(2) to refrain from dealing with the limited partnership in the conduct or winding up of the limited partnership's activities as or on behalf of a party having an interest adverse to the limited partnership; and

(3) to refrain from competing with the limited partnership in the conduct or winding up of the limited partnership's activities.

(c) A general partner's duty of care to the limited partnership and the other partners in the conduct and winding up of the limited partnership's activities is limited to refraining from engaging in grossly negligent or reckless conduct, intentional misconduct, or a knowing violation of law.

(d) A general partner shall discharge the duties to the partnership and the other partners under this [Act] or under the partnership agreement and exercise any rights consistently with the obligation of good faith and fair dealing.

(e) A general partner does not violate a duty or obligation under this [Act] or under the partnership agreement merely because the general partner's conduct furthers the general partner's own interest.

Comment

Source — RUPA Section 404.

This section does not prevent a general partner from delegating one or more duties, but delegation does not discharge the duty. For further discussion, see the Comment to Section 406(a).

If the partnership agreement removes a particular responsibility from a general partner, that general partner's fiduciary duty must be judged according to the rights and powers the general partner retains. For example, if the partnership agreement denies a general partner the right to act in a particular matter, the general partner's compliance with the partnership agreement cannot be a breach of fiduciary duty. However, the general partner may still have a duty to provide advice with regard to the matter. That duty could arise from the fiduciary duty of care under Section 408(c) and the duty to provide information under Sections 304(i) and 407(b).

For the partnership agreement's power directly to circumscribe a general partner's fiduciary duty, see Section 110(b)(5) and (6).

Subsection (a) — The reference to "the other partners" does not affect the distinction between direct and derivative claims. *See* Section 1001(b) (prerequisites for a partner bringing a direct claim).

Subsection (b) — A general partner's duty under this subsection continues through winding up, since the limited partners' dependence on the general partner does not end at dissolution. *See* Comment to Section 406(f) (explaining why this Act provides no remuneration for a general partner's winding up efforts).

Subsection (d) — This provision is identical to Section 305(b) and the Comment to Section 305(b) is applicable here.

ARTICLE 5
CONTRIBUTIONS AND DISTRIBUTIONS

Section 501. Form of Contribution

A contribution of a partner may consist of tangible or intangible property or other benefit to the limited partnership, including money, services performed, promissory notes, other agreements to contribute cash or property, and contracts for services to be performed.

Comment

Source — ULLCA Section 401.

Section 502. Liability for Contribution

(a) A partner's obligation to contribute money or other property or other benefit to, or to perform services for, a limited partnership is not excused by the partner's death, disability, or other inability to perform personally.

(b) If a partner does not make a promised non-monetary contribution, the partner is obligated at the option of the limited partnership to contribute money equal to that portion of the value, as stated in the required information, of the stated contribution which has not been made.

(c) The obligation of a partner to make a contribution or return money or other property paid or distributed in violation of this [Act] may be compromised only by consent of all partners. A creditor of a limited partnership which extends credit or otherwise acts in reliance on an obligation described in subsection (a), without notice of any compromise under this subsection, may enforce the original obligation.

Comment

In contrast with predecessor law, RULPA Section 502(a), this Act does not include a statute of frauds provision covering promised contributions. Section 111(9)(A) does require that the value of a promised contribution be memorialized, but that requirement does not affect enforceability. *See* Comment to Section 111(9).

Subsection (a) — Source: RULPA Section 502(b).

Under common law principles of impracticability, an individual's death or incapacity will sometimes discharge a duty to render performance. Restatement (Second) of Contracts, Sections 261 and 262. This subsection overrides those principles.

Subsection (b) — RULPA Section 502(b).

This subsection is a statutory liquidated damage provision, exercisable at the option of the limited partnership, with the damage amount set according to the value of the promised, non-monetary contribution as stated in the required information.

> **Example:** In order to become a limited partner, a person promises to contribute to the limited partnership various assets which the partnership agreement values at $150,000. In return for the person's promise, and in light of the agreed value, the limited partnership admits the person as a limited partner with a right to receive 25% of the limited partnership's distributions.
>
> The promised assets are subject to a security agreement, but the limited partner promises to contribute them "free and clear." Before the limited partner can contribute the assets, the secured party forecloses on the security interest and sells the assets at a public sale for $75,000. Even if the $75,000 reflects the actual fair market value of the assets, under this subsection the limited partnership has a claim against the limited partner for "the value, as stated in the required information, of the stated contribution which has not been made" — i.e, $150,000.

This section applies "at the option of the limited partnership" and does not affect other remedies which the limited partnership may have under other law.

> **Example:** Same facts as the previous example, except that the public sale brings $225,000. The limited partnership is not obliged to invoke this subsection and may instead sue for breach of the promise to make the contribution, asserting the $225,000 figure as evidence of the actual loss suffered as a result of the breach.

Subsection (c) — Source: ULLCA Section 402(b); RULPA Section 502(c). The first sentence of this subsection applies not only to promised contributions but also to improper distributions. *See* Sections 508 and 509. The second sentence, pertaining to creditor's rights, applies only to promised contributions.

Section 503. Sharing of Distributions

A distribution by a limited partnership must be shared among the partners on the basis of the value, as stated in the required records when the limited partnership decides to make the distribution, of the contributions the limited partnership has received from each partner.

Comment

This Act has no provision allocating profits and losses among the partners. Instead, the Act directly apportions the right to receive distributions.

Nearly all limited partnerships will choose to allocate profits and losses in order to comply with applicable tax, accounting and other regulatory requirements. Those requirements, rather than this Act, are the proper source of guidance for that profit and loss allocation.

Unlike predecessor law, this section apportions distributions in relation to the value of contributions received from each partner without regard to whether the limited partnership has returned any of those contributions. Compare RULPA Sections 503 and 504. This Act's approach produces the same result as predecessor law, so long as the limited partnership does not vary this section's approach to apportioning distributions.

This section's rule for sharing distributions is subject to change under Section 110. A limited partnership that does vary the rule should be careful to consider not only the tax and accounting consequences but also the "ripple" effect on other provisions of this Act. *See, e.g.*, Sections 801 and 803(c) (apportioning consent power in relation to the right to receive distributions).

Section 504. Interim Distributions

A partner does not have a right to any distribution before the dissolution and winding up of the limited partnership unless the limited partnership decides to make an interim distribution.

Comment

Under Section 406(a), the general partner or partners make this decision for the limited partnership.

Section 505. No Distribution on Account of Dissociation

A person does not have a right to receive a distribution on account of dissociation.

Comment

This section varies substantially from predecessor law. RULPA Sections 603 and 604 permitted a limited partner to withdraw on six months notice and receive the fair value of the limited partnership interest, unless the partnership agreement provided the limited partner with some exit right or stated a definite duration for the limited partnership.

Under this Act, a partner that dissociates becomes a transferee of its own transferable interest. *See* Sections 602(a)(3) (person dissociated as a limited partner) and 605(a)(5) (person dissociated as a general partner).

Section 506. Distribution in Kind

A partner does not have a right to demand or receive any distribution from a limited partnership in any form other than cash. Subject to Section 812(b), a limited partnership may distribute an asset in kind to the extent each partner receives a percentage of the asset equal to the partner's share of distributions.

Comment

Source — RULPA Section 605.

Section 507. Right to Distribution

When a partner or transferee becomes entitled to receive a distribution, the partner or transferee has the status of, and is entitled to all remedies available to, a creditor of the limited partnership with respect to the distribution. However, the limited partnership's obligation to make a distribution is subject to offset for any amount owed to the limited partnership by the partner or dissociated partner on whose account the distribution is made.

Comment

Source — RULPA Section 606.

This section's first sentence refers to distributions generally. Contrast Section 508(e), which refers to indebtedness issued as a distribution.

The reference in the second sentence to "dissociated partner" encompasses circumstances in which the partner is gone and the dissociated partner's transferable interest is all that remains.

Section 508. Limitations on Distribution

(a) A limited partnership may not make a distribution in violation of the partnership agreement.

(b) A limited partnership may not make a distribution if after the distribution:

(1) the limited partnership would not be able to pay its debts as they become due in the ordinary course of the limited partnership's activities; or

(2) the limited partnership's total assets would be less than the sum of its total liabilities plus the amount that would be needed, if the limited partnership were to be dissolved, wound up, and terminated at the time of the distribution, to satisfy the preferential rights upon dissolution, winding up, and termination of partners whose preferential rights are superior to those of persons receiving the distribution.

(c) A limited partnership may base a determination that a distribution is not prohibited under subsection (b) on financial statements prepared on the basis of accounting practices and principles that are reasonable in the circumstances or on a fair valuation or other method that is reasonable in the circumstances.

(d) Except as otherwise provided in subsection (g), the effect of a distribution under subsection (b) is measured:

(1) in the case of distribution by purchase, redemption, or other acquisition of a transferable interest in the limited partnership, as of the date money or other property is transferred or debt incurred by the limited partnership; and

(2) in all other cases, as of the date:

(A) the distribution is authorized, if the payment occurs within 120 days after that date; or

(B) the payment is made, if payment occurs more than 120 days after the distribution is authorized.

(e) A limited partnership's indebtedness to a partner incurred by reason of a distribution made in accordance with this section is at parity with the limited partnership's indebtedness to its general, unsecured creditors.

(f) A limited partnership's indebtedness, including indebtedness issued in connection with or as part of a distribution, is not considered a liability for purposes of subsection (b) if the terms of the indebtedness provide that payment of principal and interest are made only to the extent that a distribution could then be made to partners under this section.

(g) If indebtedness is issued as a distribution, each payment of principal or interest on the indebtedness is treated as a distribution, the effect of which is measured on the date the payment is made.

Comment

Source — ULLCA Section 406. *See also* RMBCA Section 6.40.

Subsection (c) — This subsection appears to impose a standard of ordinary care, in contrast with the general duty of care stated in Section 408(c). For a reconciliation of these two provisions, see Comment to Section 509(a).

Section 509. Liability for Improper Distributions

(a) A general partner that consents to a distribution made in violation of Section 508 is personally liable to the limited partnership for the amount of the distribution which exceeds the amount that could have been distributed without the violation if it is established that in consenting to the distribution the general partner failed to comply with Section 408.

(b) A partner or transferee that received a distribution knowing that the distribution to that partner or transferee was made in violation of Section 508 is personally liable to the limited partnership but only to the extent that the distribution received by the partner or transferee exceeded the amount that could have been properly paid under Section 508.

(c) A general partner against which an action is commenced under subsection (a) may:

(1) implead in the action any other person that is liable under subsection (a) and compel contribution from the person; and

(2) implead in the action any person that received a distribution in violation of subsection (b) and compel contribution from the person in the amount the person received in violation of subsection (b).

(d) An action under this section is barred if it is not commenced within two years after the distribution.

Comment

Source — ULLCA Section 407. *See also* RMBCA Section 8.33.

In substance and effect this section protects the interests of creditors of the limited partnership. Therefore, according to Section 110(b)(13), the partnership agreement may not change this section in a way that restricts the rights of those creditors. As for a limited partnership's power to compromise a claim under this section, see Section 502(c).

Subsection (a) — This subsection refers both to Section 508, which includes in its subsection (c) a standard of ordinary care ("reasonable in the circumstances"), and to Section 408, which includes in its subsection (c) a general duty of care that is limited to "refraining from engaging in grossly negligent or reckless conduct, intentional misconduct, or a knowing violation of law."

A limited partnership's failure to meet the standard of Section 508(c) cannot by itself cause a general partner to be liable under Section 509(a).

Both of the following would have to occur before a failure to satisfy Section 508(c) could occasion personal liability for a general partner under Section 509(a):

- the limited partnership "base[s] a determination that a distribution is not prohibited . . . on financial statements prepared on the basis of accounting practices and principles that are [not] reasonable in the circumstances or on a [not] fair valuation or other method that is [not] reasonable in the circumstances" [Section 508(c)]

AND

- the general partner's decision to rely on the improper methodology in consenting to the distribution constitutes "grossly negligent or reckless conduct, intentional misconduct, or a knowing violation of law" [Section 408(c)] or breaches some other duty under Section 408.

To serve the protective purpose of Sections 508 and 509, in this subsection "consent" must be understood as encompassing any form of approval, assent or acquiescence, whether formal or informal, express or tacit.

Subsection (d) — The subsection's limitation applies to the commencement of an action under subsection (a) or (b) and not to subsection (c), under which a general partner may implead other persons.

ARTICLE 6
DISSOCIATION

Section 601. Dissociation as Limited Partner

(a) A person does not have a right to dissociate as a limited partner before the termination of the limited partnership.

(b) A person is dissociated from a limited partnership as a limited partner upon the occurrence of any of the following events:

(1) the limited partnership's having notice of the person's express will to withdraw as a limited partner or on a later date specified by the person;

(2) an event agreed to in the partnership agreement as causing the person's dissociation as a limited partner;

(3) the person's expulsion as a limited partner pursuant to the partnership agreement;

(4) the person's expulsion as a limited partner by the unanimous consent of the other partners if:

(A) it is unlawful to carry on the limited partnership's activities with the person as a limited partner;

(B) there has been a transfer of all of the person's transferable interest in the limited partnership, other than a transfer for security purposes, or a court order charging the person's interest, which has not been foreclosed;

(C) the person is a corporation and, within 90 days after the limited partnership notifies the person that it will be expelled as a limited partner because it has filed a certificate of dissolution or the equivalent, its charter has been revoked, or its right to conduct business has been suspended by the jurisdiction of its incorporation, there is no revocation of the certificate of dissolution or no reinstatement of its charter or its right to conduct business; or

(D) the person is a limited liability company or partnership that has been dissolved and whose business is being wound up;

(5) on application by the limited partnership, the person's expulsion as a limited partner by judicial order because:

(A) the person engaged in wrongful conduct that adversely and materially affected the limited partnership's activities;

(B) the person willfully or persistently committed a material breach of the partnership agreement or of the obligation of good faith and fair dealing under Section 305(b); or

(C) the person engaged in conduct relating to the limited partnership's activities which makes it not reasonably practicable to carry on the activities with the person as limited partner;

(6) in the case of a person who is an individual, the person's death;

(7) in the case of a person that is a trust or is acting as a limited partner by virtue of being a trustee of a trust, distribution of the trust's entire transferable interest in the limited partnership, but not merely by reason of the substitution of a successor trustee;

(8) in the case of a person that is an estate or is acting as a limited partner by virtue of being a personal representative of an estate, distribution of the estate's entire transferable interest in the limited partnership, but not merely by reason of the substitution of a successor personal representative;

(9) termination of a limited partner that is not an individual, partnership, limited liability company, corporation, trust, or estate;

(10) the limited partnership's participation in a conversion or merger under [Article] 11, if the limited partnership:

(A) is not the converted or surviving entity; or

(B) is the converted or surviving entity but, as a result of the conversion or merger, the person ceases to be a limited partner.

Comment

Source — RUPA Section 601.

This section adopts RUPA's dissociation provision essentially verbatim, except for provisions inappropriate to limited partners. For example, this section does not provide for the dissociation of a person as a limited partner on account of bankruptcy, insolvency or incompetency.

This Act refers to *a person's dissociation as a limited partner* rather than to the *dissociation of a limited partner*, because the same person may be both a general and a limited partner. *See* Section 113 (Dual Capacity). It is possible for a dual capacity partner to dissociate in one capacity and not in the other.

Subsection (a) — This section varies substantially from predecessor law. *See* Comment to Section 505.

Subsection (b)(1) — This provision gives a person the power to dissociate as a limited partner even though the dissociation is wrongful under subsection (a). See, however, Section 110(b)(8) (prohibiting the partnership agreement from eliminating the power of a person to dissociate as a *general* partner but imposing no comparable restriction with regard to a person's dissociation as a *limited* partner).

Subsection (b)(5) — In contrast to RUPA, this provision may be varied or even eliminated by the partnership agreement.

Section 602. Effect of Dissociation as Limited Partner

(a) Upon a person's dissociation as a limited partner:

(1) subject to Section 704, the person does not have further rights as a limited partner;

(2) the person's obligation of good faith and fair dealing as a limited partner under Section 305(b) continues only as to matters arising and events occurring before the dissociation; and

(3) subject to Section 704 and [Article] 11, any transferable interest owned by the person in the person's capacity as a limited partner immediately before dissociation is owned by the person as a mere transferee.

(b) A person's dissociation as a limited partner does not of itself discharge the person from any obligation to the limited partnership or the other partners which the person incurred while a limited partner.

Comment

Source — RUPA Section 603(b).

Subsection (a)(1) — In general, when a person dissociates as a limited partner, the person's rights as a limited partner disappear and, subject to Section 113 (Dual Status), the person's status degrades to that of a mere transferee. However, Section 704 provides some special rights when dissociation is caused by an individual's death.

Subsection (a)(3) — For any person that is both a general partner and a limited partner, the required records must state which transferable interest is owned in which capacity. Section 111(9)(C).

Article 11 provides for conversions and mergers. A plan of conversion or merger may provide for the dissociation of a person as a limited partner and may override the rule stated in this paragraph.

Section 603. Dissociation as General Partner.

A person is dissociated from a limited partnership as a general partner upon the occurrence of any of the following events:

(1) the limited partnership's having notice of the person's express will to withdraw as a general partner or on a later date specified by the person;

(2) an event agreed to in the partnership agreement as causing the person's dissociation as a general partner;

(3) the person's expulsion as a general partner pursuant to the partnership agreement;

(4) the person's expulsion as a general partner by the unanimous consent of the other partners if:

(A) it is unlawful to carry on the limited partnership's activities with the person as a general partner;

(B) there has been a transfer of all or substantially all of the person's transferable interest in the limited partnership, other than a transfer for security purposes, or a court order charging the person's interest, which has not been foreclosed;

(C) the person is a corporation and, within 90 days after the limited partnership notifies the person that it will be expelled as a general partner because it has filed a certificate of dissolution or the equivalent, its charter has been revoked, or its right to conduct business has been suspended by the jurisdiction of its incorporation, there is no revocation of the certificate of dissolution or no reinstatement of its charter or its right to conduct business; or

(D) the person is a limited liability company or partnership that has been dissolved and whose business is being wound up;

(5) on application by the limited partnership, the person's expulsion as a general partner by judicial determination because:

(A) the person engaged in wrongful conduct that adversely and materially affected the limited partnership activities;

(B) the person willfully or persistently committed a material breach of the partnership agreement or of a duty owed to the partnership or the other partners under Section 408; or

(C) the person engaged in conduct relating to the limited partnership's activities which makes it not reasonably practicable to carry on the activities of the limited partnership with the person as a general partner;

(6) the person's:

(A) becoming a debtor in bankruptcy;

(B) execution of an assignment for the benefit of creditors;

(C) seeking, consenting to, or acquiescing in the appointment of a trustee, receiver, or liquidator of the person or of all or substantially all of the person's property; or

(D) failure, within 90 days after the appointment, to have vacated or stayed the appointment of a trustee, receiver, or liquidator of the general partner or of all or substantially all of the person's property obtained without the person's consent or acquiescence, or failing within 90 days after the expiration of a stay to have the appointment vacated;

(7) in the case of a person who is an individual:

(A) the person's death;

(B) the appointment of a guardian or general conservator for the person; or

(C) a judicial determination that the person has otherwise become incapable of performing the person's duties as a general partner under the partnership agreement;

(8) in the case of a person that is a trust or is acting as a general partner by virtue of being a trustee of a trust, distribution of the trust's entire transferable interest in the limited partnership, but not merely by reason of the substitution of a successor trustee;

(9) in the case of a person that is an estate or is acting as a general partner by virtue of being a personal representative of an estate, distribution of the estate's entire transferable interest in the limited partnership,

but not merely by reason of the substitution of a successor personal representative;

(10) termination of a general partner that is not an individual, partnership, limited liability company, corporation, trust, or estate; or

(11) the limited partnership's participation in a conversion or merger under [Article] 11, if the limited partnership:

(A) is not the converted or surviving entity; or

(B) is the converted or surviving entity but, as a result of the conversion or merger, the person ceases to be a general partner.

Comment

Source — RUPA Section 601.

This section adopts RUPA's dissociation provision essentially verbatim. This Act refers to *a person's dissociation as a general partner* rather than to the *dissociation of a general partner*, because the same person may be both a general and a limited partner. *See* Section 113 (Dual Capacity). It is possible for a dual capacity partner to dissociate in one capacity and not in the other.

Paragraph (1) — The partnership agreement may not eliminate this power to dissociate. *See* Section 110(b)(8).

Paragraph (5) — In contrast to RUPA, this provision may be varied or even eliminated by the partnership agreement.

Section 604. Person's Power to Dissociate as General Partner; Wrongful Dissociation.

(a) A person has the power to dissociate as a general partner at any time, rightfully or wrongfully, by express will pursuant to Section 603(1).

(b) A person's dissociation as a general partner is wrongful only if:

(1) it is in breach of an express provision of the partnership agreement; or

(2) it occurs before the termination of the limited partnership, and:

(A) the person withdraws as a general partner by express will;

(B) the person is expelled as a general partner by judicial determination under Section 603(5);

(C) the person is dissociated as a general partner by becoming a debtor in bankruptcy; or

(D) in the case of a person that is not an individual, trust other than a business trust, or estate, the person is expelled or otherwise

Section 606. Power to Bind and Liability to Limited Partnership Before Dissolution of Partnership of Person Dissociated as General Partner

(a) After a person is dissociated as a general partner and before the limited partnership is dissolved, converted under [Article] 11, or merged out of existence under [Article 11], the limited partnership is bound by an act of the person only if:

(1) the act would have bound the limited partnership under Section 402 before the dissociation; and

(2) at the time the other party enters into the transaction:

(A) less than two years has passed since the dissociation; and

(B) the other party does not have notice of the dissociation and reasonably believes that the person is a general partner.

(b) If a limited partnership is bound under subsection (a), the person dissociated as a general partner which caused the limited partnership to be bound is liable:

(1) to the limited partnership for any damage caused to the limited partnership arising from the obligation incurred under subsection (a); and

(2) if a general partner or another person dissociated as a general partner is liable for the obligation, to the general partner or other person for any damage caused to the general partner or other person arising from the liability.

Comment

Source — RUPA Section 702.

This Act contains three sections pertaining to the lingering power to bind of a person dissociated as a general partner:

- this section, which applies until the limited partnership dissolves, converts to another form of organization under Article 11, or is merged out of existence under Article 11;
- Section 804(b), which applies after a limited partnership dissolves; and
- Section 1112(b), which applies after a conversion or merger.

Subsection (a)(2)(B) — A person might have notice under Section 103(d)(1) as well as under Section 103(b).

Subsection (b) — The liability provided by this subsection is not exhaustive. For example, if a person dissociated as a general partner causes a limited partnership to be bound under subsection (a) and, due to a guaranty, some other person is liable on the resulting obligation, that other person may have a claim under other law against the person dissociated as a general partner.

Section 607. Liability to Other Persons of Person Dissociated as General Partner

(a) A person's dissociation as a general partner does not of itself discharge the person's liability as a general partner for an obligation of the limited partnership incurred before dissociation. Except as otherwise provided in subsections (b) and (c), the person is not liable for a limited partnership's obligation incurred after dissociation.

(b) A person whose dissociation as a general partner resulted in a dissolution and winding up of the limited partnership's activities is liable to the same extent as a general partner under Section 404 on an obligation incurred by the limited partnership under Section 804.

(c) A person that has dissociated as a general partner but whose dissociation did not result in a dissolution and winding up of the limited partnership's activities is liable on a transaction entered into by the limited partnership after the dissociation only if:

(1) a general partner would be liable on the transaction; and

(2) at the time the other party enters into the transaction:

(A) less than two years has passed since the dissociation; and

(B) the other party does not have notice of the dissociation and reasonably believes that the person is a general partner.

(d) By agreement with a creditor of a limited partnership and the limited partnership, a person dissociated as a general partner may be released from liability for an obligation of the limited partnership.

(e) A person dissociated as a general partner is released from liability for an obligation of the limited partnership if the limited partnership's creditor, with notice of the person's dissociation as a general partner but without the person's consent, agrees to a material alteration in the nature or time of payment of the obligation.

Comment

Source — RUPA Section 703.

A person's dissociation as a general partner does not categorically prevent the person from being liable as a general partner for subsequently incurred obligations of the limited partnership. If the dissociation results in dissolution, subsection (b) applies and the person will be liable as a general partner on any partnership obligation incurred under Section 804. In these circumstances, neither filing a statement of dissociation nor amending the certificate of limited partnership to state that the person has dissociated as a general partner will curtail the person's lingering exposure to liability.

If the dissociation does not result in dissolution, subsection (c) applies. In this context, filing a statement of dissociation or amending the certificate of limited partnership to state that the person has dissociated as a general partner will curtail the person's lingering liability. *See* subsection (c)(2)(B).

If the limited partnership subsequently dissolves as the result of some other occurrence (i.e., not a result of the person's dissociation as a general partner), subsection (c) continues to apply. In that situation, Section 804 will determine whether, for the purposes of subsection (c), the limited partnership has entered into a transaction after dissolution.

If the limited partnership is a limited liability limited partnership, these liability rules are moot.

Subsection (a) — The phrase "liability as a general partner for an obligation of the limited partnership" refers to liability under Section 404. Following RUPA and the UPA, this Act leaves to other law the question of when a limited partnership obligation is incurred.

Subsection (c)(2)(B) — A person might have notice under Section 103(d)(1) as well as under Section 103(b).

ARTICLE 7
TRANSFERABLE INTERESTS AND RIGHTS OF TRANSFEREES AND CREDITORS

Section 701. Partner's Transferable Interest

The only interest of a partner which is transferable is the partner's transferable interest. A transferable interest is personal property.

Comment

Source — RUPA Section 502.

Like all other partnership statutes, this Act dichotomizes each partner's rights into economic rights and other rights. The former are freely transferable, as provided in Section 702. The latter are not transferable at all, unless the partnership agreement so provides.

Although a partner or transferee owns a transferable interest as a present right, that right only entitles the owner to distributions if and when made. *See* Sections 504 (subject to any contrary provision in the partnership agreement, no right to interim distribution unless the limited partnership decides to make an interim distribution) and the Comment to Section 812 (subject to any contrary provision in the partnership agreement, no partner obligated to contribute for the purpose of equalizing or otherwise allocating capital losses).

Section 702. Transfer of Partner's Transferable Interest

(a) A transfer, in whole or in part, of a partner's transferable interest:

(1) is permissible;

(2) does not by itself cause the partner's dissociation or a dissolution and winding up of the limited partnership's activities; and

(3) does not, as against the other partners or the limited partnership, entitle the transferee to participate in the management or conduct of the limited partnership's activities, to require access to information concerning the limited partnership's transactions except as otherwise provided in subsection (c), or to inspect or copy the required information or the limited partnership's other records.

(b) A transferee has a right to receive, in accordance with the transfer:

(1) distributions to which the transferor would otherwise be entitled; and

(2) upon the dissolution and winding up of the limited partnership's activities the net amount otherwise distributable to the transferor.

(c) In a dissolution and winding up, a transferee is entitled to an account of the limited partnership's transactions only from the date of dissolution.

(d) Upon transfer, the transferor retains the rights of a partner other than the interest in distributions transferred and retains all duties and obligations of a partner.

(e) A limited partnership need not give effect to a transferee's rights under this section until the limited partnership has notice of the transfer.

(f) A transfer of a partner's transferable interest in the limited partnership in violation of a restriction on transfer contained in the partnership agreement is ineffective as to a person having notice of the restriction at the time of transfer.

(g) A transferee that becomes a partner with respect to a transferable interest is liable for the transferor's obligations under Sections 502 and 509. However, the transferee is not obligated for liabilities unknown to the transferee at the time the transferee became a partner.

Comment

Source — RUPA Section 503, except for subsection (g), which derives from RULPA Section 704(b). Following RUPA, this Act uses the words "transfer" and "transferee" rather than the words "assignment" and "assignee." *See* RUPA Section 503.

Subsection (a)(2) — The phrase "by itself" is significant. A transfer of all of a person's transferable interest could lead to dissociation via expulsion, Sections 601(b)(4)(B) and 603(4)(B).

Subsection (a)(3) — Mere transferees have no right to intrude as the partners carry on their activities as partners. Moreover, a partner's obligation of good faith and fair dealing under Sections 305(b) and 408(d) is framed in reference to "the limited partnership and the other partners." *See also* Comment to Section 1102(b)(3) and Comment to Section 1106(b)(3).

Section 703. Rights of Creditor of Partner or Transferee

(a) On application to a court of competent jurisdiction by any judgment creditor of a partner or transferee, the court may charge the transferable interest of the judgment debtor with payment of the unsatisfied amount of the judgment with interest. To the extent so charged, the judgment creditor has only the rights of a transferee. The court may appoint a receiver of the share of the distributions due or to become due to the judgment debtor in respect of the partnership and make all other orders, directions, accounts, and inquiries the judgment debtor might have made or which the circumstances of the case may require to give effect to the charging order.

(b) A charging order constitutes a lien on the judgment debtor's transferable interest. The court may order a foreclosure upon the interest subject to the charging order at any time. The purchaser at the foreclosure sale has the rights of a transferee.

(c) At any time before foreclosure, an interest charged may be redeemed:

(1) by the judgment debtor;

(2) with property other than limited partnership property, by one or more of the other partners; or

(3) with limited partnership property, by the limited partnership with the consent of all partners whose interests are not so charged.

(d) This [Act] does not deprive any partner or transferee of the benefit of any exemption laws applicable to the partner's or transferee's transferable interest.

(e) This section provides the exclusive remedy by which a judgment creditor of a partner or transferee may satisfy a judgment out of the judgment debtor's transferable interest.

Comment

Source — RUPA Section 504 and ULLCA Section 504.

This section balances the needs of a judgment creditor of a partner or transferee with the needs of the limited partnership and non-debtor partners and transferees. The section achieves that balance by allowing the judgment creditor to collect on the judgment through the transferable interest of the judgment debtor while prohibiting interference in the management and activities of the limited partnership.

Under this section, the judgment creditor of a partner or transferee is entitled to a charging order against the relevant transferable interest. While in effect, that order entitles the judgment creditor to whatever distributions would otherwise be due to the partner or transferee whose interest is subject to the order. The creditor has no say in the timing or amount of those distributions. The charging order does not entitle the creditor to accelerate any distributions or to otherwise interfere with the management and activities of the limited partnership.

Foreclosure of a charging order effects a permanent transfer of the charged transferable interest to the purchaser. The foreclosure does not, however, create any rights to participate in the management and conduct of the limited partnership's activities. The purchaser obtains nothing more than the status of a transferee.

Subsection (a) — The court's power to appoint a receiver and "make all other orders, directions, accounts, and inquiries the judgment debtor might have made or which the circumstances of the case may require" must be understood in the context of the balance described above. In particular, the court's power to make orders "which the circumstances may require" is limited to "giv[ing] effect to the charging order."

> **Example:** A judgment creditor with a charging order believes that the limited partnership should invest less of its surplus in operations, leaving more funds for distributions. The creditor moves the court for an order directing the general partners to restrict reinvestment. This section does not authorize the court to grant the motion.

> **Example:** A judgment creditor with a judgment for $10,000 against a partner obtains a charging order against the partner's transferable interest. The limited partnership is duly served with the order. However, the limited partnership subsequently fails to comply with the order and makes a $3000 distribution to the partner. The court has the power to order the limited partnership to turn over $3000 to the judgment creditor to "give effect to the charging order."

The court also has the power to decide whether a particular payment is a distribution, because this decision determines whether the payment is part of a transferable interest subject to a charging order. (To the extent a payment is not a distribution, it is not part of the transferable interest and is not subject to subsection (e). The payment is therefore subject to whatever other creditor remedies may apply.)

Subsection (c)(3) — This provision requires the consent of all the limited as well as general partners.

Section 704. Power of Estate of Deceased Partner

If a partner dies, the deceased partner's personal representative or other legal representative may exercise the rights of a transferee as provided in Section 702 and, for the purposes of settling the estate, may exercise the rights of a current limited partner under Section 304.

Comment

Section 702 strictly limits the rights of transferees. In particular, a transferee has no right to participate in management in any way, no voting rights and, except following dissolution, no information rights. Even after dissolution, a transferee's information rights are limited. *See* Section 702(c).

This section provides special informational rights for a deceased partner's legal representative for the purposes of settling the estate. For those purposes, the legal representative may exercise the informational rights of a current limited partner under Section 304. Those rights are of course subject to the limitations and obligations stated in that section — *e.g.*, Section 304 (g) (restrictions on use) and (h) (charges for copies) — as well as any generally applicable limitations stated in the partnership agreement.

ARTICLE 8
DISSOLUTION

Section 801. Nonjudicial Dissolution

Except as otherwise provided in Section 802, a limited partnership is dissolved, and its activities must be wound up, only upon the occurrence of any of the following:

(1) the happening of an event specified in the partnership agreement;

(2) the consent of all general partners and of limited partners owning a majority of the rights to receive distributions as limited partners at the time the consent is to be effective;

(3) after the dissociation of a person as a general partner:

(A) if the limited partnership has at least one remaining general partner, the consent to dissolve the limited partnership given within 90 days after the dissociation by partners owning a majority of the rights to receive distributions as partners at the time the consent is to be effective; or

(B) if the limited partnership does not have a remaining general partner, the passage of 90 days after the dissociation, unless before the end of the period:

(i) consent to continue the activities of the limited partnership and admit at least one general partner is given by limited partners owning a majority of the rights to receive distributions as limited partners at the time the consent is to be effective; and

(ii) at least one person is admitted as a general partner in accordance with the consent;

(4) the passage of 90 days after the dissociation of the limited partnership's last limited partner, unless before the end of the period the limited partnership admits at least one limited partner; or

(5) the signing and filing of a declaration of dissolution by the [Secretary of State] under Section 809(c).

Comment

This Act does not require that any of the consents referred to in this section be given in the form of a signed record. The partnership agreement has the power to impose that requirement. *See* Comment to Section 110.

In several provisions, this section provides for consent in terms of rights to receive distributions. Distribution rights of non-partner transferees are not relevant. Mere transferees have no consent rights, and their distribution rights are not counted in determining whether majority consent has been obtained.

Paragraph (1) — There is no requirement that the relevant provision of the partnership agreement be made in a record, unless the partnership agreement creates that requirement. However, if the relevant provision is not "contained in a partnership agreement made in a record," Section 111(9)(D) includes among the limited partnership's required information "a record stating . . . any events upon the happening of which the limited partnership is to be dissolved and its activities wound up."

Paragraph (2) — Rights to receive distributions owned by a person that is both a general and a limited partner figure into the limited partner determination only to the extent those rights are owned in the person's capacity as a limited partner. *See* Section 111(9)(C).

Example: XYZ is a limited partnership with three general partners, each of whom is also a limited partner, and 5 other limited partners. Rights to receive distributions are allocated as follows:

Partner #1 as general partner — 3%

Partner #2 as general partner — 2%

Partner #3 as general partner — 1%

Partner #1 as limited partner — 7%

Partner #2 as limited partner — 3%

Partner #3 as limited partner — 4%

Partner #4 as limited partner — 5%

Partner #5 as limited partner — 5%

Partner #6 as limited partner — 5%

Partner #7 as limited partner — 5%

Partner #8 as limited partner — 5%

Several non-partner transferees, in the aggregate — 55%

Distribution rights owned by persons as limited partners amount to 39% of total distribution rights. A majority is therefore anything greater than 19.5%. If only Partners 1,2, 3 and 4 consent to dissolve, the limited partnership is not dissolved. Together these partners own as limited partners 19% of the distribution rights owned by persons as limited partners — just short of the necessary majority. For purposes of this calculation, distribution rights owned by non-partner transferees are irrelevant. So, too, are distribution rights owned by persons as general partners. (However, dissolution under this provision requires "the consent of all general partners.")

Paragraph (3)(A) — Unlike paragraph (2), this paragraph makes no distinction between distribution rights owned by persons as general partners and distribution rights owned by persons as limited partners. Distribution rights owned by non-partner transferees are irrelevant.

Section 802. Judicial Dissolution

On application by a partner the [appropriate court] may order dissolution of a limited partnership if it is not reasonably practicable to carry on the activities of the limited partnership in conformity with the partnership agreement.

Comment

Source — RULPA Section 802.

Section 110(b)(9) limits the power of the partnership agreement with regard to this section.

Section 803. Winding Up

(a) A limited partnership continues after dissolution only for the purpose of winding up its activities.

(b) In winding up its activities, the limited partnership:

(1) may amend its certificate of limited partnership to state that the limited partnership is dissolved, preserve the limited partnership business or property as a going concern for a reasonable time, prosecute and defend actions and proceedings, whether civil, criminal, or administrative, transfer the limited partnership's property, settle disputes by mediation or arbitration, file a statement of termination as provided in Section 203, and perform other necessary acts; and

(2) shall discharge the limited partnership's liabilities, settle and close the limited partnership's activities, and marshal and distribute the assets of the partnership.

(c) If a dissolved limited partnership does not have a general partner, a person to wind up the dissolved limited partnership's activities may be appointed by the consent of limited partners owning a majority of the rights to receive distributions as limited partners at the time the consent is to be effective. A person appointed under this subsection:

(1) has the powers of a general partner under Section 804; and

(2) shall promptly amend the certificate of limited partnership to state:

(A) that the limited partnership does not have a general partner;

(B) the name of the person that has been appointed to wind up the limited partnership; and

(C) the street and mailing address of the person.

(d) On the application of any partner, the [appropriate court] may order judicial supervision of the winding up, including the appointment of a person to wind up the dissolved limited partnership's activities, if:

(1) a limited partnership does not have a general partner and within a reasonable time following the dissolution no person has been appointed pursuant to subsection (c); or

(2) the applicant establishes other good cause.

Comment

Source — RUPA Sections 802 and 803.

Subsection (b)(2) — A limited partnership may satisfy its duty to "discharge" a liability either by paying or by making an alternative arrangement satisfactory to the creditor.

Subsection (c) — The method for determining majority consent is analogous to the method applicable under Section 801(2). See the Comment to that paragraph.

A person appointed under this subsection is not a general partner and therefore is not subject to Section 408.

Section 804. Power of General Partner and Person Dissociated as General Partner to Bind Partnership after Dissolution

(a) A limited partnership is bound by a general partner's act after dissolution which:

(1) is appropriate for winding up the limited partnership's activities; or

(2) would have bound the limited partnership under Section 402 before dissolution, if, at the time the other party enters into the transaction, the other party does not have notice of the dissolution.

(b) A person dissociated as a general partner binds a limited partnership through an act occurring after dissolution if:

(1) at the time the other party enters into the transaction:

(A) less than two years has passed since the dissociation; and

(B) the other party does not have notice of the dissociation and reasonably believes that the person is a general partner; and

(2) the act:

(A) is appropriate for winding up the limited partnership's activities; or

(B) would have bound the limited partnership under Section 402 before dissolution and at the time the other party enters into the transaction the other party does not have notice of the dissolution.

Comment

Subsection (a) — Source: RUPA Section 804.

Subsection (a)(2) — A person might have notice under Section 103(d)(2) (amendment of certificate of limited partnership to indicate dissolution) as well as under Section 103(b).

Subsection (b) — This subsection deals with the post-dissolution power to bind of a person dissociated as a general partner. Paragraph (1) replicates the provisions of Section 606, pertaining to the pre-dissolution power to bind of a person dissociated as a general partner. Paragraph (2) replicates the provisions of subsection (a), which state the post-dissolution power to bind of a general partner. For a person dissociated as a general partner to bind a dissolved limited partnership, the person's act will have to satisfy both paragraph (1) and paragraph (2).

Subsection (b)(1)(B) — A person might have notice under Section 103(d)(1) as well as under Section 103(b).

Subsection (b)(2)(B) — A person might have notice under Section 103(d)(2) (amendment of certificate of limited partnership to indicate dissolution) as well as under Section 103(b).

Section 805. Liability after Dissolution of General Partner and Person Dissociated as General Partner to Limited Partnership, Other General Partners, and Persons Dissociated as General Partner

(a) If a general partner having knowledge of the dissolution causes a limited partnership to incur an obligation under Section 804(a) by an act that is not appropriate for winding up the partnership's activities, the general partner is liable:

(1) to the limited partnership for any damage caused to the limited partnership arising from the obligation; and

(2) if another general partner or a person dissociated as a general partner is liable for the obligation, to that other general partner or person for any damage caused to that other general partner or person arising from the liability.

(b) If a person dissociated as a general partner causes a limited partnership to incur an obligation under Section 804(b), the person is liable:

(1) to the limited partnership for any damage caused to the limited partnership arising from the obligation; and

(2) if a general partner or another person dissociated as a general partner is liable for the obligation, to the general partner or other person for any damage caused to the general partner or other person arising from the liability.

Comment

Source — RUPA Section 806.

It is possible for more than one person to be liable under this section on account of the same limited partnership obligation. This Act does not provide any rule for apportioning liability in that circumstance.

Subsection (a)(2) — If the limited partnership is not a limited liability limited partnership, the liability created by this paragraph includes liability under Sections 404(a), 607(b), and 607(c). The paragraph also applies when a partner or person dissociated as a general partner suffers damage due to a contract of guaranty.

Section 806. Known Claims Against Dissolved Limited Partnership

(a) A dissolved limited partnership may dispose of the known claims against it by following the procedure described in subsection (b).

(b) A dissolved limited partnership may notify its known claimants of the dissolution in a record. The notice must:

(1) specify the information required to be included in a claim;

(2) provide a mailing address to which the claim is to be sent;

(3) state the deadline for receipt of the claim, which may not be less than 120 days after the date the notice is received by the claimant;

(4) state that the claim will be barred if not received by the deadline; and

(5) unless the limited partnership has been throughout its existence a limited liability limited partnership, state that the barring of a claim against the limited partnership will also bar any corresponding claim against any general partner or person dissociated as a general partner which is based on Section 404.

(c) A claim against a dissolved limited partnership is barred if the requirements of subsection (b) are met and:

(1) the claim is not received by the specified deadline; or

(2) in the case of a claim that is timely received but rejected by the dissolved limited partnership, the claimant does not commence an action to enforce the claim against the limited partnership within 90 days after the receipt of the notice of the rejection.

(d) This section does not apply to a claim based on an event occurring after the effective date of dissolution or a liability that is contingent on that date.

Comment

Source — ULLCA Section 807. *See also* RMBCA Section 14.06.

Paragraph (b)(5) — If the limited partnership has always been a limited liability limited partnership, there can be no liability under Section 404 for any general partner or person dissociated as a general partner.

Section 807. Other Claims Against Dissolved Limited Partnership

(a) A dissolved limited partnership may publish notice of its dissolution and request persons having claims against the limited partnership to present them in accordance with the notice.

(b) The notice must:

(1) be published at least once in a newspaper of general circulation in the [county] in which the dissolved limited partnership's principal office is located or, if it has none in this State, in the [county] in which the limited partnership's designated office is or was last located;

(2) describe the information required to be contained in a claim and provide a mailing address to which the claim is to be sent;

(3) state that a claim against the limited partnership is barred unless an action to enforce the claim is commenced within five years after publication of the notice; and

(4) unless the limited partnership has been throughout its existence a limited liability limited partnership, state that the barring of a claim against the limited partnership will also bar any corresponding claim against any general partner or person dissociated as a general partner which is based on Section 404.

(c) If a dissolved limited partnership publishes a notice in accordance with subsection (b), the claim of each of the following claimants is barred unless the claimant commences an action to enforce the claim against the dissolved limited partnership within five years after the publication date of the notice:

(1) a claimant that did not receive notice in a record under Section 806;

(2) a claimant whose claim was timely sent to the dissolved limited partnership but not acted on; and

(3) a claimant whose claim is contingent or based on an event occurring after the effective date of dissolution.

(d) A claim not barred under this section may be enforced:

(1) against the dissolved limited partnership, to the extent of its undistributed assets;

(2) if the assets have been distributed in liquidation, against a partner or transferee to the extent of that person's proportionate share of the claim or the limited partnership's assets distributed to the partner or transferee in liquidation, whichever is less, but a person's total liability for all claims under this paragraph does not exceed the total amount of assets distributed to the person as part of the winding up of the dissolved limited partnership; or

(3) against any person liable on the claim under Section 404.

Comment

Source — ULLCA Section 808. *See also* RMBCA Section 14.07.

Paragraph (b)(4) — If the limited partnership has always been a limited liability limited partnership, there can be no liability under Section 404 for any general partner or person dissociated as a general partner.

Section 808. Liability of General Partner and Person Dissociated as General Partner When Claim Against Limited Partnership Barred

If a claim against a dissolved limited partnership is barred under Section 806 or 807, any corresponding claim under Section 404 is also barred.

Comment

The liability under Section 404 of a general partner or person dissociated as a general partner is merely liability for the obligations of the limited partnership.

Section 809. Administrative Dissolution

(a) The [Secretary of State] may dissolve a limited partnership administratively if the limited partnership does not, within 60 days after the due date:

(1) pay any fee, tax, or penalty due to the [Secretary of State] under this [Act] or other law; or

(2) deliver its annual report to the [Secretary of State].

(b) If the [Secretary of State] determines that a ground exists for administratively dissolving a limited partnership, the [Secretary of State] shall file a record of the determination and serve the limited partnership with a copy of the filed record.

(c) If within 60 days after service of the copy the limited partnership does not correct each ground for dissolution or demonstrate to the reasonable satisfaction of the [Secretary of State] that each ground determined by the [Secretary of State] does not exist, the [Secretary of State] shall administratively dissolve the limited partnership by preparing, signing and filing a declaration of dissolution that states the grounds for dissolution. The [Secretary of State] shall serve the limited partnership with a copy of the filed declaration.

(d) A limited partnership administratively dissolved continues its existence but may carry on only activities necessary to wind up its activities and liquidate its assets under Sections 803 and 812 and to notify claimants under Sections 806 and 807.

(e) The administrative dissolution of a limited partnership does not terminate the authority of its agent for service of process.

Comment

Source — ULLCA Sections 809 and 810. *See also* RMBCA Sections 14.20 and 14.21.

Subsection (a)(1) — This provision refers solely to money due the specified filing officer and does not apply to other money due to the State.

Subsection (c) — The filing of a declaration of dissolution does not provide notice under Section 103(d).

Section 810. Reinstatement   Following   Administrative Dissolution

(a) A limited partnership that has been administratively dissolved may apply to the [Secretary of State] for reinstatement within two years after the effective date of dissolution. The application must be delivered to the [Secretary of State] for filing and state:

(1) the name of the limited partnership and the effective date of its administrative dissolution;

(2) that the grounds for dissolution either did not exist or have been eliminated; and

(3) that the limited partnership's name satisfies the requirements of Section 108.

(b) If the [Secretary of State] determines that an application contains the information required by subsection (a) and that the information is correct, the [Secretary of State] shall prepare a declaration of reinstatement that states this determination, sign, and file the original of the declaration of reinstatement, and serve the limited partnership with a copy.

(c) When reinstatement becomes effective, it relates back to and takes effect as of the effective date of the administrative dissolution and the limited partnership may resume its activities as if the administrative dissolution had never occurred.

Comment

Source — ULLCA Section 811. *See also* RMBCA Section 14.22.

Section 811. Appeal from Denial of Reinstatement

(a) If the [Secretary of State] denies a limited partnership's application for reinstatement following administrative dissolution, the [Secretary of State] shall prepare, sign and file a notice that explains the reason or reasons for denial and serve the limited partnership with a copy of the notice.

(b) Within 30 days after service of the notice of denial, the limited partnership may appeal from the denial of reinstatement by petitioning the [appropriate court] to set aside the dissolution. The petition must be served on the [Secretary of State] and contain a copy of the [Secretary of State's] declaration of dissolution, the limited partnership's application for reinstatement, and the [Secretary of State's] notice of denial.

(c) The court may summarily order the [Secretary of State] to reinstate the dissolved limited partnership or may take other action the court considers appropriate.

Comment

Source — ULLCA Section 812.

Section 812. Disposition of Assets; When Contributions Required

(a) In winding up a limited partnership's activities, the assets of the limited partnership, including the contributions required by this section, must be applied to satisfy the limited partnership's obligations to creditors, including, to the extent permitted by law, partners that are creditors.

(b) Any surplus remaining after the limited partnership complies with subsection (a) must be paid in cash as a distribution.

(c) If a limited partnership's assets are insufficient to satisfy all of its obligations under subsection (a), with respect to each unsatisfied obligation incurred when the limited partnership was not a limited liability limited partnership, the following rules apply:

(1) Each person that was a general partner when the obligation was incurred and that has not been released from the obligation under Section 607 shall contribute to the limited partnership for the purpose of enabling the limited partnership to satisfy the obligation. The contribution due from each of those persons is in proportion to the right to receive distributions in the capacity of general partner in effect for each of those persons when the obligation was incurred.

(2) If a person does not contribute the full amount required under paragraph (1) with respect to an unsatisfied obligation of the limited partnership, the other persons required to contribute by paragraph (1) on account of the obligation shall contribute the additional amount necessary to discharge the obligation. The additional contribution due from each of those other persons is in proportion to the right to receive distributions in the capacity of general partner in effect for each of those other persons when the obligation was incurred.

(3) If a person does not make the additional contribution required by paragraph (2), further additional contributions are determined and due in the same manner as provided in that paragraph.

(d) A person that makes an additional contribution under subsection (c)(2) or (3) may recover from any person whose failure to contribute under subsection (c)(1) or (2) necessitated the additional contribution. A person may not recover under this subsection more than the amount additionally contributed. A person's liability under this subsection may not exceed the amount the person failed to contribute.

(e) The estate of a deceased individual is liable for the person's obligations under this section.

(f) An assignee for the benefit of creditors of a limited partnership or a partner, or a person appointed by a court to represent creditors of a limited partnership or a partner, may enforce a person's obligation to contribute under subsection (c).

Comment

In some circumstances, this Act requires a partner to make payments to the limited partnership. *See, e.g.*, Sections 502(b), 509(a), 509(b), and 812(c). In other circumstances, this Act requires a partner to make payments to other partners. *See, e.g.*, Sections 509(c) and 812(d). In no circumstances does this Act require a partner to make a payment for the purpose of equalizing or otherwise reallocating capital losses incurred by partners.

Example: XYZ Limited Partnership ("XYZ") has one general partner and four limited partners. According to XYZ's required information, the value of each partner's contributions to XYZ are:

General partner — $5,000

Limited partner #1 — $10,000

Limited partner #2 — $15,000

Limited partner #3 — $20,000

Limited partner #4 — $25,000

XYZ is unsuccessful and eventually dissolves without ever having made a distribution to its partners. XYZ lacks any assets with which to return to the partners the value of their respective contributions. No partner is obliged to make any payment either to the limited partnership or to fellow partners to adjust these capital losses. These losses are not part of "the limited partnership's obligations to creditors." Section 812(a).

Example: Same facts, except that Limited Partner #4 loaned $25,000 to XYZ when XYZ was not a limited liability limited partnership, and XYZ lacks the assets to repay the loan. The general partner must contribute to the limited partnership whatever funds are necessary to enable XYZ to satisfy the obligation owned to Limited Partner #4 on account of the loan. Section 812(a) and (c).

Subsection (c) — Following RUPA and the UPA, this Act leaves to other law the question of when a limited partnership obligation is incurred.

ARTICLE 9
FOREIGN LIMITED PARTNERSHIPS

Section 901. Governing Law

(a) The laws of the State or other jurisdiction under which a foreign limited partnership is organized govern relations among the partners of the foreign limited partnership and between the partners and the foreign limited partnership and the liability of partners as partners for an obligation of the foreign limited partnership.

(b) A foreign limited partnership may not be denied a certificate of authority by reason of any difference between the laws of the jurisdiction under which the foreign limited partnership is organized and the laws of this State.

(c) A certificate of authority does not authorize a foreign limited partnership to engage in any business or exercise any power that a limited partnership may not engage in or exercise in this State.

Comment

Source — ULLCA Section 1001 for subsections (b) and (c).

Subsection (a) — This subsection parallels and is analogous in scope and effect to Section 106 (choice of law for domestic limited partnerships).

Section 902. Application for Certificate of Authority

(a) A foreign limited partnership may apply for a certificate of authority to transact business in this State by delivering an application to the [Secretary of State] for filing. The application must state:

(1) the name of the foreign limited partnership and, if the name does not comply with Section 108, an alternate name adopted pursuant to Section 905(a).

(2) the name of the State or other jurisdiction under whose law the foreign limited partnership is organized;

(3) the street and mailing address of the foreign limited partnership's principal office and, if the laws of the jurisdiction under which the foreign limited partnership is organized require the foreign limited partnership to maintain an office in that jurisdiction, the street and mailing address of the required office;

(4) the name and street and mailing address of the foreign limited partnership's initial agent for service of process in this State;

(5) the name and street and mailing address of each of the foreign limited partnership's general partners; and

(6) whether the foreign limited partnership is a foreign limited liability limited partnership.

(b) A foreign limited partnership shall deliver with the completed application a certificate of existence or a record of similar import signed by the [Secretary of State] or other official having custody of the foreign limited partnership's publicly filed records in the State or other jurisdiction under whose law the foreign limited partnership is organized.

Comment

Source — ULLCA Section 1002.

A certificate of authority applied for under this section is different than a certificate of authorization furnished under Section 209.

Section 903. Activities Not Constituting Transacting Business

(a) Activities of a foreign limited partnership which do not constitute transacting business in this State within the meaning of this [article] include:

(1) maintaining, defending, and settling an action or proceeding;

(2) holding meetings of its partners or carrying on any other activity concerning its internal affairs;

(3) maintaining accounts in financial institutions;

(4) maintaining offices or agencies for the transfer, exchange, and registration of the foreign limited partnership's own securities or maintaining trustees or depositories with respect to those securities;

(5) selling through independent contractors;

(6) soliciting or obtaining orders, whether by mail or electronic means or through employees or agents or otherwise, if the orders require acceptance outside this State before they become contracts;

(7) creating or acquiring indebtedness, mortgages, or security interests in real or personal property;

(8) securing or collecting debts or enforcing mortgages or other security interests in property securing the debts, and holding, protecting, and maintaining property so acquired;

(9) conducting an isolated transaction that is completed within 30 days and is not one in the course of similar transactions of a like manner; and

(10) transacting business in interstate commerce.

(b) For purposes of this [article], the ownership in this State of income-producing real property or tangible personal property, other than property excluded under subsection (a), constitutes transacting business in this State.

(c) This section does not apply in determining the contacts or activities that may subject a foreign limited partnership to service of process, taxation, or regulation under any other law of this State.

Comment

Source — ULLCA Section 1003.

Section 904. Filing of Certificate of Authority

Unless the [Secretary of State] determines that an application for a certificate of authority does not comply with the filing requirements of this [Act], the [Secretary of State], upon payment of all filing fees, shall file the application, prepare, sign and file a certificate of authority to transact business in this State, and send a copy of the filed certificate, together with a receipt for the fees, to the foreign limited partnership or its representative.

Comment

Source — ULLCA Section 1004 and RULPA Section 903.

A certificate of authority filed under this section is different than a certificate of authorization furnished under Section 209.

Section 905. Noncomplying Name of Foreign Limited Partnership

(a) A foreign limited partnership whose name does not comply with Section 108 may not obtain a certificate of authority until it adopts, for the purpose of transacting business in this State, an alternate name that complies with Section 108. A foreign limited partnership that adopts an alternate name under this subsection and then obtains a certificate of authority with the name need not comply with [fictitious name statute]. After obtaining a certificate of authority with an alternate name, a foreign limited partnership shall transact business in this State under the name unless the foreign limited partnership is authorized under [fictitious name statute] to transact business in this State under another name.

(b) If a foreign limited partnership authorized to transact business in this State changes its name to one that does not comply with Section 108, it may not thereafter transact business in this State until it complies with subsection (a) and obtains an amended certificate of authority.

Comment

Source — ULLCA Section 1005.

Section 906. Revocation of Certificate of Authority

(a) A certificate of authority of a foreign limited partnership to transact business in this State may be revoked by the [Secretary of State] in the manner provided in subsections (b) and (c) if the foreign limited partnership does not:

(1) pay, within 60 days after the due date, any fee, tax or penalty due to the [Secretary of State] under this [Act] or other law;

(2) deliver, within 60 days after the due date, its annual report required under Section 210;

(3) appoint and maintain an agent for service of process as required by Section 114(b); or

(4) deliver for filing a statement of a change under Section 115 within 30 days after a change has occurred in the name or address of the agent.

(b) In order to revoke a certificate of authority, the [Secretary of State] must prepare, sign, and file a notice of revocation and send a copy to the foreign limited partnership's agent for service of process in this State, or if the foreign limited partnership does not appoint and maintain a proper agent in this State, to the foreign limited partnership's designated office. The notice must state:

(1) the revocation's effective date, which must be at least 60 days after the date the [Secretary of State] sends the copy; and

(2) the foreign limited partnership's failures to comply with subsection (a) which are the reason for the revocation.

(c) The authority of the foreign limited partnership to transact business in this State ceases on the effective date of the notice of revocation unless before that date the foreign limited partnership cures each failure to comply with subsection (a) stated in the notice. If the foreign limited partnership cures the failures, the [Secretary of State] shall so indicate on the filed notice.

Comment

Source — ULLCA Section 1006.

Section 907. Cancellation of Certificate of Authority; Effect of Failure to Have Certificate

(a) In order to cancel its certificate of authority to transact business in this State, a foreign limited partnership must deliver to the [Secretary of State] for filing a notice of cancellation. The certificate is canceled when the notice becomes effective under Section 206.

(b) A foreign limited partnership transacting business in this State may not maintain an action or proceeding in this State unless it has a certificate of authority to transact business in this State.

(c) The failure of a foreign limited partnership to have a certificate of authority to transact business in this State does not impair the validity of a contract or act of the foreign limited partnership or prevent the foreign limited partnership from defending an action or proceeding in this State.

(d) A partner of a foreign limited partnership is not liable for the obligations of the foreign limited partnership solely by reason of the foreign limited partnership's having transacted business in this State without a certificate of authority.

(e) If a foreign limited partnership transacts business in this State without a certificate of authority or cancels its certificate of authority, it appoints the [Secretary of State] as its agent for service of process for rights of action arising out of the transaction of business in this State.

Comment

Source — RULPA Section 907(d); ULLCA Section 1008.

Section 908. Action by [Attorney General]

The [Attorney General] may maintain an action to restrain a foreign limited partnership from transacting business in this State in violation of this [article].

Comment

Source — RULPA Section 908; ULLCA Section 1009.

ARTICLE 10
ACTIONS BY PARTNERS

Section 1001. Direct Action by Partner

(a) Subject to subsection (b), a partner may maintain a direct action against the limited partnership or another partner for legal or equitable relief, with or without an accounting as to the partnership's activities, to enforce the rights and otherwise protect the interests of the partner, including rights and interests under the partnership agreement or this [Act] or arising independently of the partnership relationship.

(b) A partner commencing a direct action under this section is required to plead and prove an actual or threatened injury that is not solely the result of an injury suffered or threatened to be suffered by the limited partnership.

(c) The accrual of, and any time limitation on, a right of action for a remedy under this section is governed by other law. A right to an accounting upon a dissolution and winding up does not revive a claim barred by law.

Comment

Subsection (a) — Source: RUPA Section 405(b).

Subsection (b) — In ordinary contractual situations it is axiomatic that each party to a contract has standing to sue for breach of that contract. Within a limited partnership, however, different circumstances may exist. A partner does not have a direct claim against another partner merely because the other partner has breached the partnership agreement. Likewise a partner's violation of this Act does not automatically create a direct claim for every other partner. To have standing in his, her, or its own right, a partner plaintiff must be able to show a harm that occurs independently of the harm caused or threatened to be caused to the limited partnership.

The reference to "threatened" harm is intended to encompass claims for injunctive relief and does not relax standards for proving injury.

Section 1002. Derivative Action

A partner may maintain a derivative action to enforce a right of a limited partnership if:

(1) the partner first makes a demand on the general partners, requesting that they cause the limited partnership to bring an action to enforce the right, and the general partners do not bring the action within a reasonable time; or

(2) a demand would be futile.

Comment

Source — RULPA Section 1001.

Section 1003. Proper Plaintiff

A derivative action may be maintained only by a person that is a partner at the time the action is commenced and:

(1) that was a partner when the conduct giving rise to the action occurred; or

(2) whose status as a partner devolved upon the person by operation of law or pursuant to the terms of the partnership agreement from a person that was a partner at the time of the conduct.

Comment

Source — RULPA Section 1002.

Section 1004. Pleading

In a derivative action, the complaint must state with particularity:

(1) the date and content of plaintiff's demand and the general partners' response to the demand; or

(2) why demand should be excused as futile.

Comment

Source — RULPA Section 1003.

Section 1005. Proceeds and Expenses

(a) Except as otherwise provided in subsection (b):

(1) any proceeds or other benefits of a derivative action, whether by judgment, compromise, or settlement, belong to the limited partnership and not to the derivative plaintiff;

(2) if the derivative plaintiff receives any proceeds, the derivative plaintiff shall immediately remit them to the limited partnership.

(b) If a derivative action is successful in whole or in part, the court may award the plaintiff reasonable expenses, including reasonable attorney's fees, from the recovery of the limited partnership.

Comment

Source — RULPA Section 1004.

ARTICLE 11
CONVERSION AND MERGER

Section 1101. Definitions

In this [article]:

(1) "Constituent limited partnership" means a constituent organization that is a limited partnership.

(2) "Constituent organization" means an organization that is party to a merger.

(3) "Converted organization" means the organization into which a converting organization converts pursuant to Sections 1102 through 1105.

(4) "Converting limited partnership" means a converting organization that is a limited partnership.

(5) "Converting organization" means an organization that converts into another organization pursuant to Section 1102.

(6) "General partner" means a general partner of a limited partnership.

(7) "Governing statute" of an organization means the statute that governs the organization's internal affairs.

(8) "Organization" means a general partnership, including a limited liability partnership; limited partnership, including a limited liability

limited partnership; limited liability company; business trust; corporation; or any other person having a governing statute. The term includes domestic and foreign organizations whether or not organized for profit.

(9) "Organizational documents" means:

(A) for a domestic or foreign general partnership, its partnership agreement;

(B) for a limited partnership or foreign limited partnership, its certificate of limited partnership and partnership agreement;

(C) for a domestic or foreign limited liability company, its articles of organization and operating agreement, or comparable records as provided in its governing statute;

(D) for a business trust, its agreement of trust and declaration of trust;

(E) for a domestic or foreign corporation for profit, its articles of incorporation, bylaws, and other agreements among its shareholders which are authorized by its governing statute, or comparable records as provided in its governing statute; and

(F) for any other organization, the basic records that create the organization and determine its internal governance and the relations among the persons that own it, have an interest in it, or are members of it.

(10) "Personal liability" means personal liability for a debt, liability, or other obligation of an organization which is imposed on a person that co-owns, has an interest in, or is a member of the organization:

(A) by the organization's governing statute solely by reason of the person co-owning, having an interest in, or being a member of the organization; or

(B) by the organization's organizational documents under a provision of the organization's governing statute authorizing those documents to make one or more specified persons liable for all or specified debts, liabilities, and other obligations of the organization solely by reason of the person or persons co-owning, having an interest in, or being a member of the organization.

(11) "Surviving organization" means an organization into which one or more other organizations are merged. A surviving organization may preexist the merger or be created by the merger.

Comment

This section contains definitions specific to this Article.

Section 1102. Conversion

(a) An organization other than a limited partnership may convert to a limited partnership, and a limited partnership may convert to another organization pursuant to this section and Sections 1103 through 1105 and a plan of conversion, if:

(1) the other organization's governing statute authorizes the conversion;

(2) the conversion is not prohibited by the law of the jurisdiction that enacted the governing statute; and

(3) the other organization complies with its governing statute in effecting the conversion.

(b) A plan of conversion must be in a record and must include:

(1) the name and form of the organization before conversion;

(2) the name and form of the organization after conversion; and

(3) the terms and conditions of the conversion, including the manner and basis for converting interests in the converting organization into any combination of money, interests in the converted organization, and other consideration; and

(4) the organizational documents of the converted organization.

Comment

In a statutory conversion an existing entity changes its form, the jurisdiction of its governing statute or both. For example, a limited partnership organized under the laws of one jurisdiction might convert to:

- a limited liability company (or other form of entity) organized under the laws of the same jurisdiction,

- a limited liability company (or other form of entity) organized under the laws of another jurisdiction, or

- a limited partnership organized under the laws of another jurisdiction (referred to in some statutes as "domestication").

In contrast to a merger, which involves at least two entities, a conversion involves only one. The converting and converted organization are the same entity. *See* Section 1105(a). For this Act to apply to a conversion, either the converting or converted organization must be a limited partnership subject to this Act. If the converting organization is a limited partnership subject to this Act, the partners of the converting organization are subject to the duties and obligations stated in this Act, including Sections 304 (informational rights of limited partners), 305(b) (limited partner's obligation of good faith and fair dealing), 407 (informational rights of general partners), and 408 (general partner duties).

Subsection (a)(2) — Given the very broad definition of "organization," Section 1101(8), this Act authorizes conversions involving non-profit organizations. This provision is intended as an additional safeguard for that context.

Subsection (b)(3) — A plan of conversion may provide that some persons with interests in the converting organization will receive interests in the converted organization while other persons with interests in the converting organization will receive some other form of consideration. Thus, a "squeeze out" conversion is possible. As noted above, if the converting organization is a limited partnership subject to this Act, the partners of the converting organization are subject to the duties and obligations stated in this Act. Those duties would apply to the process and terms under which a squeeze out conversion occurs.

If the converting organization is a limited partnership, the plan of conversion will determine the fate of any interests held by mere transferees. This Act does not state any duty or obligation owed by a converting limited partnership or its partners to mere transferees. That issue is a matter for other law.

Section 1103. Action on Plan of Conversion by Converting Limited Partnership

(a) Subject to Section 1110, a plan of conversion must be consented to by all the partners of a converting limited partnership.

(b) Subject to Section 1110 and any contractual rights, after a conversion is approved, and at any time before a filing is made under Section 1104, a converting limited partnership may amend the plan or abandon the planned conversion:

(1) as provided in the plan; and

(2) except as prohibited by the plan, by the same consent as was required to approve the plan.

Comment

Section 1110 imposes special consent requirements for transactions which might cause a partner to have "personal liability," as defined in

Section 1101 (10) for entity debts. The partnership agreement may not restrict the rights provided by Section 1110. *See* Section 110(b)(12).

Subsection (a) — Like many of the rules stated in this Act, this subsection's requirement of unanimous consent is a default rule. Subject only to Section 1110, the partnership agreement may state a different quantum of consent or provide a completely different approval mechanism. Varying this subsection's rule means that a partner might be subject to a conversion (including a "squeeze out" conversion) without consent and with no appraisal remedy. If the converting organization is a limited partnership subject to this Act, the partners of the converting organization are subject to the duties and obligations stated in this Act. Those duties would apply to the process and terms under which the conversion occurs. However, if the partnership agreement allows for a conversion with less than unanimous consent, the mere fact a partner objects to a conversion does not mean that the partners favoring, arranging, consenting to or effecting the conversation have breached a duty under this Act.

Section 1104. Filings Required for Conversion; Effective Date

(a) After a plan of conversion is approved:

(1) a converting limited partnership shall deliver to the [Secretary of State] for filing articles of conversion, which must include:

(A) a statement that the limited partnership has been converted into another organization;

(B) the name and form of the organization and the jurisdiction of its governing statute;

(C) the date the conversion is effective under the governing statute of the converted organization;

(D) a statement that the conversion was approved as required by this [Act];

(E) a statement that the conversion was approved as required by the governing statute of the converted organization; and

(F) if the converted organization is a foreign organization not authorized to transact business in this State, the street and mailing address of an office which the [Secretary of State] may use for the purposes of Section 1105(c); and

(2) if the converting organization is not a converting limited partnership, the converting organization shall deliver to the [Secretary of State] for filing a certificate of limited partnership, which must include, in addition to the information required by Section 201:

(A) a statement that the limited partnership was converted from another organization;

(B) the name and form of the organization and the jurisdiction of its governing statute; and

(C) a statement that the conversion was approved in a manner that complied with the organization's governing statute.

(b) A conversion becomes effective:

(1) if the converted organization is a limited partnership, when the certificate of limited partnership takes effect; and

(2) if the converted organization is not a limited partnership, as provided by the governing statute of the converted organization.

Comment

Subsection (b) — The effective date of a conversion is determined under the governing statute of the converted organization.

Section 1105. Effect of Conversion

(a) An organization that has been converted pursuant to this [article] is for all purposes the same entity that existed before the conversion.

(b) When a conversion takes effect:

(1) all property owned by the converting organization remains vested in the converted organization;

(2) all debts, liabilities, and other obligations of the converting organization continue as obligations of the converted organization;

(3) an action or proceeding pending by or against the converting organization may be continued as if the conversion had not occurred;

(4) except as prohibited by other law, all of the rights, privileges, immunities, powers, and purposes of the converting organization remain vested in the converted organization;

(5) except as otherwise provided in the plan of conversion, the terms and conditions of the plan of conversion take effect; and

(6) except as otherwise agreed, the conversion does not dissolve a converting limited partnership for the purposes of [Article] 8.

(c) A converted organization that is a foreign organization consents to the jurisdiction of the courts of this State to enforce any obligation owed by the converting limited partnership, if before the conversion the converting limited partnership was subject to suit in this State on the obligation. A converted organization that is a foreign organization and not authorized to transact business in this State appoints the [Secretary of State] as its agent for service of process for purposes of enforcing an obligation under this subsection. Service on the [Secretary of State] under this subsection is made in the same manner and with the same consequences as in Section 117(c) and (d).

Comment

Subsection (a) — A conversion changes an entity's legal type, but does not create a new entity.

Subsection (b) — Unlike a merger, a conversion involves a single entity, and the conversion therefore does not transfer any of the entity's rights or obligations.

Section 1106. Merger

(a) A limited partnership may merge with one or more other constituent organizations pursuant to this section and Sections 1107 through 1109 and a plan of merger, if:

(1) the governing statute of each the other organizations authorizes the merger;

(2) the merger is not prohibited by the law of a jurisdiction that enacted any of those governing statutes; and

(3) each of the other organizations complies with its governing statute in effecting the merger.

(b) A plan of merger must be in a record and must include:

(1) the name and form of each constituent organization;

(2) the name and form of the surviving organization and, if the surviving organization is to be created by the merger, a statement to that effect;

(3) the terms and conditions of the merger, including the manner and basis for converting the interests in each constituent organization into any combination of money, interests in the surviving organization, and other consideration;

(4) if the surviving organization is to be created by the merger, the surviving organization's organizational documents; and

(5) if the surviving organization is not to be created by the merger, any amendments to be made by the merger to the surviving organization's organizational documents.

Comment

For this Act to apply to a merger, at least one of the constituent organizations must be a limited partnership subject to this Act. The partners of any such limited partnership are subject to the duties and obligations stated in this Act, including Sections 304 (informational rights of limited partners), 305(b) (limited partner's obligation of good faith and fair dealing), 407 (informational rights of general partners), and 408 (general partner duties).

Subsection (a)(2) — Given the very broad definition of "organization," Section 1101(8), this Act authorizes mergers involving non-profit organizations. This provision is intended as an additional safeguard for that context.

Subsection (b)(3) — A plan of merger may provide that some persons with interests in a constituent organization will receive interests in the surviving organization, while other persons with interests in the same constituent organization will receive some other form of consideration. Thus, a "squeeze out" merger is possible. As noted above, the duties and obligations stated in this Act apply to the partners of a constituent organization that is a limited partnership subject to this Act. Those duties would apply to the process and terms under which a squeeze out merger occurs.

If a constituent organization is a limited partnership, the plan of merger will determine the fate of any interests held by mere transferees. This Act does not state any duty or obligation owed by a constituent limited partnership or its partners to mere transferees. That issue is a matter for other law.

Section 1107. Action on Plan of Merger by Constituent Limited Partnership

(a) Subject to Section 1110, a plan of merger must be consented to by all the partners of a constituent limited partnership.

(b) Subject to Section 1110 and any contractual rights, after a merger is approved, and at any time before a filing is made under Section 1108, a constituent limited partnership may amend the plan or abandon the planned merger:

(1) as provided in the plan; and

(2) except as prohibited by the plan, with the same consent as was required to approve the plan.

Comment

Section 1110 imposes special consent requirements for transactions which might make a partner personally liable for entity debts. The partnership agreement may not restrict the rights provided by Section 1110. *See* Section 110(b)(12).

Subsection (a) — Like many of the rules stated in this Act, this subsection's requirement of unanimous consent is a default rule. Subject only to Section 1110, the partnership agreement may state a different quantum of consent or provide a completely different approval mechanism. Varying this subsection's rule means that a partner might be subject to a merger (including a "squeeze out" merger) without consent and with no appraisal remedy. The partners of a constituent limited partnership are subject to the duties and obligations stated in this Act, and those duties would apply to the process and terms under which the merger occurs. However, if the partnership agreement allows for a merger with less than unanimous consent, the mere fact a partner objects to a merger does not mean that the partners favoring, arranging, consenting to or effecting the merger have breached a duty under this Act.

Section 1108. Filings Required for Merger; Effective Date

(a) After each constituent organization has approved a merger, articles of merger must be signed on behalf of:

(1) each preexisting constituent limited partnership, by each general partner listed in the certificate of limited partnership; and

(2) each other preexisting constituent organization, by an authorized representative.

(b) The articles of merger must include:

(1) the name and form of each constituent organization and the jurisdiction of its governing statute;

(2) the name and form of the surviving organization, the jurisdiction of its governing statute, and, if the surviving organization is created by the merger, a statement to that effect;

(3) the date the merger is effective under the governing statute of the surviving organization;

(4) if the surviving organization is to be created by the merger:

(A) if it will be a limited partnership, the limited partnership's certificate of limited partnership; or

(B) if it will be an organization other than a limited partnership, the organizational document that creates the organization;

(5) if the surviving organization preexists the merger, any amendments provided for in the plan of merger for the organizational document that created the organization;

(6) a statement as to each constituent organization that the merger was approved as required by the organization's governing statute;

(7) if the surviving organization is a foreign organization not authorized to transact business in this State, the street and mailing address of an office which the [Secretary of State] may use for the purposes of Section 1109(b); and

(8) any additional information required by the governing statute of any constituent organization.

(c) Each constituent limited partnership shall deliver the articles of merger for filing in the [office of the Secretary of State].

(d) A merger becomes effective under this [article]:

(1) if the surviving organization is a limited partnership, upon the later of:

(i) compliance with subsection (c); or

(ii) subject to Section 206(c), as specified in the articles of merger; or

(2) if the surviving organization is not a limited partnership, as provided by the governing statute of the surviving organization.

Comment

Subsection (b) — The effective date of a merger is determined under the governing statute of the surviving organization.

Section 1109. Effect of Merger

(a) When a merger becomes effective:

(1) the surviving organization continues or comes into existence;

(2) each constituent organization that merges into the surviving organization ceases to exist as a separate entity;

(3) all property owned by each constituent organization that ceases to exist vests in the surviving organization;

(4) all debts, liabilities, and other obligations of each constituent organization that ceases to exist continue as obligations of the surviving organization;

(5) an action or proceeding pending by or against any constituent organization that ceases to exist may be continued as if the merger had not occurred;

(6) except as prohibited by other law, all of the rights, privileges, immunities, powers, and purposes of each constituent organization that ceases to exist vest in the surviving organization;

(7) except as otherwise provided in the plan of merger, the terms and conditions of the plan of merger take effect; and

(8) except as otherwise agreed, if a constituent limited partnership ceases to exist, the merger does not dissolve the limited partnership for the purposes of [Article] 8;

(9) if the surviving organization is created by the merger:

(A) if it is a limited partnership, the certificate of limited partnership becomes effective; or

(B) if it is an organization other than a limited partnership, the organizational document that creates the organization becomes effective; and

(10) if the surviving organization preexists the merger, any amendments provided for in the articles of merger for the organizational document that created the organization become effective.

(b) A surviving organization that is a foreign organization consents to the jurisdiction of the courts of this State to enforce any obligation owed by a constituent organization, if before the merger the constituent organization was subject to suit in this State on the obligation. A surviving organization that is a foreign organization and not authorized to transact business in this State appoints the [Secretary of State] as its agent for service of process for the purposes of enforcing an obligation under this subsection. Service on the [Secretary of State] under this subsection is made in the same manner and with the same consequences as in Section 117(c) and (d).

Section 1110. Restrictions on Approval of Conversions and Mergers and on Relinquishing LLLP Status

(a) If a partner of a converting or constituent limited partnership will have personal liability with respect to a converted or surviving organization, approval and amendment of a plan of conversion or merger are ineffective without the consent of the partner, unless:

(1) the limited partnership's partnership agreement provides for the approval of the conversion or merger with the consent of fewer than all the partners; and

(2) the partner has consented to the provision of the partnership agreement.

(b) An amendment to a certificate of limited partnership which deletes a statement that the limited partnership is a limited liability limited partnership is ineffective without the consent of each general partner unless:

(1) the limited partnership's partnership agreement provides for the amendment with the consent of less than all the general partners; and

(2) each general partner that does not consent to the amendment has consented to the provision of the partnership agreement.

(c) A partner does not give the consent required by subsection (a) or (b) merely by consenting to a provision of the partnership agreement which permits the partnership agreement to be amended with the consent of fewer than all the partners.

Comment

This section imposes special consent requirements for transactions that might make a partner personally liable for entity debts. The partnership agreement may not restrict the rights provided by this section. *See* Section 110(b)(12).

Subsection (c) — This subsection prevents circumvention of the consent requirements of subsections (a) and (b).

> **Example:** As initially a [sic] consented to, the partnership agreement of a limited partnership leaves in place the Act's rule requiring unanimous consent for a conversion or merger. The partnership agreement does provide, however, that the agreement may be amended with the affirmative vote of general partners owning 2/3 of the rights to receive distributions as general partners and of limited partners owning 2/3 of the rights to receive distributions as limited partners. The required vote is obtained for an amendment that permits approval of a conversion or merger by the same vote necessary to amend the partnership agreement. Partner X votes for the amendment. Partner Y votes against. Partner Z does not vote.

Subsequently the limited partnership proposes to convert to a limited partnership (not an LLLP) organized under the laws of another state, with Partners X, Y and Z each receiving interests as general partners. Under the amended partnership agreement, approval of the conversion does not require unanimous consent. However, since after the conversion, Partners X, Y and Z will each have "personal liability with respect to [the] converted . . . organization," Section 1110(a) applies.

As a result, the approval of the plan of conversion will require the consent of Partner Y and Partner Z. They did not consent to the amendment that provided for non-unanimous approval of a conversion or merger. Their initial consent to the partnership agreement, with its provision permitting non-unanimous consent for amendments, does not satisfy the consent requirement of Subsection 1110(a)(2).

In contrast, Partner X's consent is not required. Partner X lost its Section 1110(a) veto right by consenting directly to the amendment to the partnership agreement which permitted non-unanimous consent to a conversion or merger.

Section 1111. Liability of General Partner after Conversion or Merger

(a) A conversion or merger under this [article] does not discharge any liability under Sections 404 and 607 of a person that was a general partner in or dissociated as a general partner from a converting or constituent limited partnership, but:

(1) the provisions of this [Act] pertaining to the collection or discharge of the liability continue to apply to the liability;

(2) for the purposes of applying those provisions, the converted or surviving organization is deemed to be the converting or constituent limited partnership; and

(3) if a person is required to pay any amount under this subsection:

(A) the person has a right of contribution from each other person that was liable as a general partner under Section 404 when the obligation was incurred and has not been released from the obligation under Section 607; and

(B) the contribution due from each of those persons is in proportion to the right to receive distributions in the capacity of general partner in effect for each of those persons when the obligation was incurred.

(b) In addition to any other liability provided by law:

(1) a person that immediately before a conversion or merger became effective was a general partner in a converting or constituent limited partnership that was not a limited liability limited partnership is personally liable for each obligation of the converted or surviving organization arising from a transaction with a third party after the conversion or merger becomes effective, if, at the time the third party enters into the transaction, the third party:

(A) does not have notice of the conversion or merger; and

(B) reasonably believes that:

(i) the converted or surviving business is the converting or constituent limited partnership;

(ii) the converting or constituent limited partnership is not a limited liability limited partnership; and

(iii) the person is a general partner in the converting or constituent limited partnership; and

(2) a person that was dissociated as a general partner from a converting or constituent limited partnership before the conversion or merger became effective is personally liable for each obligation of the converted or surviving organization arising from a transaction with a third party after the conversion or merger becomes effective, if:

(A) immediately before the conversion or merger became effective the converting or surviving limited partnership was a not a limited liability limited partnership; and

(B) at the time the third party enters into the transaction less than two years have passed since the person dissociated as a general partner and the third party:

(i) does not have notice of the dissociation;

(ii) does not have notice of the conversion or merger; and

(iii) reasonably believes that the converted or surviving organization is the converting or constituent limited partnership, the converting or constituent limited partnership is not a limited liability limited partnership, and the person is a general partner in the converting or constituent limited partnership.

Comment

This section extrapolates the approach of Section 607 into the context of a conversion or merger involving a limited partnership.

Subsection (a) — This subsection pertains to general partner liability for obligations which a limited partnership incurred before a conversion or merger. Following RUPA and the UPA, this Act leaves to other law the question of when a limited partnership obligation is incurred.

If the converting or constituent limited partnership was a limited liability limited partnership at all times before the conversion or merger, this subsection will not apply because no person will have any liability under Section 404 or 607.

Subsection (b) — This subsection pertains to entity obligations incurred after a conversion or merger and creates lingering exposure to personal liability for general partners and persons previously dissociated as general partners. In contrast to subsection (a)(3), this subsection does not provide for contribution among persons personally liable under this section for the same entity obligation. That issue is left for other law.

Subsection (b)(1) — If the converting or constituent limited partnership was a limited liability limited partnership immediately before the conversion or merger, there is no lingering exposure to personal liability under this subsection.

Subsection (b)(1)(A) — A person might have notice under Section 103(d)(4) or (5) as well as under Section 103(b).

Subsection (b)(2)(B)(i) — A person might have notice under Section 103(d)(1) as well as under Section 103(b).

Subsection (b)(2)(B)(ii) — A person might have notice under Section 103(d)(4) or (5) as well as under Section 103(b).

Section 1112. Power of General Partners and Persons Dissociated as General Partners to Bind Organization after Conversion or Merger

(a) An act of a person that immediately before a conversion or merger became effective was a general partner in a converting or constituent limited partnership binds the converted or surviving organization after the conversion or merger becomes effective, if:

(1) before the conversion or merger became effective, the act would have bound the converting or constituent limited partnership under Section 402; and

(2) at the time the third party enters into the transaction, the third party:

(A) does not have notice of the conversion or merger; and

(B) reasonably believes that the converted or surviving business is the converting or constituent limited partnership and that the person is a general partner in the converting or constituent limited partnership.

(b) An act of a person that before a conversion or merger became effective was dissociated as a general partner from a converting or constituent limited partnership binds the converted or surviving organization after the conversion or merger becomes effective, if:

(1) before the conversion or merger became effective, the act would have bound the converting or constituent limited partnership under Section 402 if the person had been a general partner; and

(2) at the time the third party enters into the transaction, less than two years have passed since the person dissociated as a general partner and the third party:

(A) does not have notice of the dissociation;

(B) does not have notice of the conversion or merger; and

(C) reasonably believes that the converted or surviving organization is the converting or constituent limited partnership and that the person is a general partner in the converting or constituent limited partnership.

(c) If a person having knowledge of the conversion or merger causes a converted or surviving organization to incur an obligation under subsection (a) or (b), the person is liable:

(1) to the converted or surviving organization for any damage caused to the organization arising from the obligation; and

(2) if another person is liable for the obligation, to that other person for any damage caused to that other person arising from the liability.

Comment

This section extrapolates the approach of Section 606 into the context of a conversion or merger involving a limited partnership.

Subsection (a)(2)(A) — A person might have notice under Section 103(d)(4) or (5) as well as under Section 103(b).

Subsection (b)(2)(A) — A person might have notice under Section 103(d)(1) as well as under Section 103(b).

Subsection (b)(2)(B) — A person might have notice under Section 103(d)(4) or (5) as well as under Section 103(b).

Section 1113. [Article] Not Exclusive

This [article] does not preclude an entity from being converted or merged under other law.

ARTICLE 12
MISCELLANEOUS PROVISIONS

Section 1201. Uniformity of Application and Construction

In applying and construing this Uniform Act, consideration must be given to the need to promote uniformity of the law with respect to its subject matter among States that enact it.

Section 1202. Severability Clause

If any provision of this [Act] or its application to any person or circumstance is held invalid, the invalidity does not affect other provisions or applications of this [Act] which can be given effect without the invalid provision or application, and to this end the provisions of this [Act] are severable.

Section 1203. Relation to Electronic Signatures in Global and National Commerce Act

This [Act] modifies, limits, or supersedes the federal Electronic Signatures in Global and National Commerce Act, 15 U.S.C. Section 7001 et seq., but this [Act] does not modify, limit, or supersede Section 101(c) of that Act or authorize electronic delivery of any of the notices described in Section 103(b) of that Act.

Section 1204. Effective Date

This [Act] takes effect [effective date].

Comment

Section 1206 specifies how this Act affects domestic limited partnerships, with special provisions pertaining to domestic limited partnerships formed before the Act's effective date. Section 1206 contains no comparable provisions for foreign limited partnerships. Therefore, once this Act is effective, it applies immediately to all foreign limited partnerships, whether formed before or after the Act's effective date.

Section 1205. Repeals

Effective [all-inclusive date], the following acts and parts of acts are repealed: [the State Limited Partnership Act as amended and in effect immediately before the effective date of this [Act]].

Section 1206. Application to Existing Relationships

(a) Before [all-inclusive date], this [Act] governs only:

(1) a limited partnership formed on or after [the effective date of this [Act]]; and

(2) except as otherwise provided in subsections (c) and (d), a limited partnership formed before [the effective date of this [Act]] which elects, in the manner provided in its partnership agreement or by law for amending the partnership agreement, to be subject to this [Act].

(b) Except as otherwise provided in subsection (c), on and after [all-inclusive date] this [Act] governs all limited partnerships.

(c) With respect to a limited partnership formed before [the effective date of this [Act]], the following rules apply except as the partners otherwise elect in the manner provided in the partnership agreement or by law for amending the partnership agreement:

(1) Section 104(c) does not apply and the limited partnership has whatever duration it had under the law applicable immediately before [the effective date of this [Act]].

(2) the limited partnership is not required to amend its certificate of limited partnership to comply with Section 201(a)(4).

(3) Sections 601 and 602 do not apply and a limited partner has the same right and power to dissociate from the limited partnership, with the same consequences, as existed immediately before [the effective date of this [Act].

(4) Section 603(4) does not apply.

(5) Section 603(5) does not apply and a court has the same power to expel a general partner as the court had immediately before [the effective date of this [Act]].

(6) Section 801(3) does not apply and the connection between a person's dissociation as a general partner and the dissolution of the limited partnership is the same as existed immediately before [the effective date of this [Act]].

(d) With respect to a limited partnership that elects pursuant to subsection (a)(2) to be subject to this [Act], after the election takes effect the provisions of this [Act] relating to the liability of the limited partnership's general partners to third parties apply:

(1) before [all-inclusive date], to:

(A) a third party that had not done business with the limited partnership in the year before the election took effect; and

(B) a third party that had done business with the limited partnership in the year before the election took effect only if the third party knows or has received a notification of the election; and

(2) on and after [all-inclusive date], to all third parties, but those provisions remain inapplicable to any obligation incurred while those provisions were inapplicable under paragraph (1)(B).

Comment

Source: RUPA Section 1206.

This section pertains exclusively to domestic limited partnerships — i.e., to limited partnerships formed under this Act or a predecessor statute enacted by the same jurisdiction. For foreign limited partnerships, see the Comment to Section 1204.

This Act governs all limited partnerships formed on or after the Act's effective date. As for pre-existing limited partnerships, this section establishes an optional "elect in" period and a mandatory, all-inclusive date. The "elect in" period runs from the effective date, stated in Section 1204, until the all-inclusive date, stated in both subsection(a) and (b).

During the "elect in" period, a pre-existing limited partnership may elect to become subject to this Act. Subsection (d) states certain important consequences for a limited partnership that elects in. Beginning on the all-inclusive date, each pre-existing limited partnership that has not previously elected in becomes subject to this Act by operation of law.

Subsection (c) — This subsection specifies six provisions of this Act which never automatically apply to any pre-existing limited partnership. Except for subsection (c)(2), the list refers to provisions governing the relationship of the partners *inter se* and considered too different than predecessor law to be fairly applied to a preexisting limited partnership without the consent of its partners. Each of these *inter se* provisions is subject to change in the partnership agreement. However, many pre-existing limited partnerships may have taken for granted the analogous provisions of predecessor law and may therefore not have addressed the issues in their partnership agreements.

Subsection (c)(1) — Section 104(c) provides that a limited partnership has a perpetual duration.

Subsection (c)(2) — Section 201(a)(4) requires the certificate of limited partnership to state "whether the limited partnership is a limited liability limited partnership." The requirement is intended to force the organizers of a limited partnership to decide whether the limited partnership is to be an LLLP and therefore is inapposite to pre-existing limited partnerships. Moreover, applying the requirement to pre-existing limited partnerships would create a significant administrative burden both for limited partnerships and the filing officer and probably would result in many preexisting limited partnerships being in violation of the requirement.

Subsection (c)(3) — Section 601 and 602 concern a person's dissociation as a limited partner.

Subsection (c)(4) — Section 603(4) provides for the expulsion of a general partner by the unanimous consent of the other partners in specified circumstances.

Subsection (c)(5) — Section 603(5) provides for the expulsion of a general partner by a court in specified circumstances.

Subsection (c)(6) — Section 801(3) concerns the continuance or dissolution of a limited partnership following a person's dissociation as a general partner.

Subsection (d) — Following RUPA Section 1206(c), this subsection limits the efficacy of the Act's liability protections for partners of an "electing in" limited partnership. The limitation:

- applies only to the benefit of "a third party that had done business with the limited partnership in the year before the election took effect," and

- ceases to apply when "the third party knows or has received a notification of the election" or on the "all-inclusive" date, whichever occurs first.

If the limitation causes a provision of this Act to be inapplicable with regard to a third party, the comparable provision of predecessor law applies.

> **Example:** A pre-existing limited partnership elects to be governed by this Act before the "all-inclusive" date. Two months before the election, Third Party provided services to the limited partnership. Third Party neither knows nor has received a notification of the election. Until the "all inclusive" date, with regard to Third Party, Section 303's full liability shield does not apply to each limited partner. Instead, each limited partner has the liability shield applicable under predecessor law.

Subsection (d)(2) — To the extent subsection (d) causes a provision of this Act to be inapplicable when an obligation is incurred, the inapplicability continues as to that obligation even after the "all inclusive" date.

Legislative Note: In a State that has previously amended its existing limited partnership statute to provide for limited liability limited partnerships (LLLPs), this Act should include transition provisions specifically applicable to preexisting limited liability limited partnerships. The precise wording of those provisions must depend on the wording of the State's previously enacted LLLP provisions. However, the following principles apply generally:

1. *In Sections 806(b)(5) and 807(b)(4) (notice by dissolved limited partnership to claimants), the phrase "the limited partnership has been throughout its existence a limited liability limited partnership" should be revised to encompass a limited partnership that was a limited liability limited partnership under the State's previously enacted LLLP provisions.*

2. *Section 1206(d) should provide that, if a preexisting limited liability limited partnership elects to be subject to this Act, this Act's provisions relating to the liability of general partners to third parties apply immediately to all third parties, regardless of whether a third party has previously done business with the limited liability limited partnership.*

3. *A preexisting limited liability limited partnership that elects to be subject to this Act should have to comply with Sections 201(a)(4) (requiring the certificate of limited partnership to state whether the limited partnership is a limited liability limited partnership) and 108(c) (establishing name requirements for a limited liability limited partnership).*

4. *As for Section 1206(b) (providing that, after a transition period, this Act applies to all preexisting limited partnerships):*

   a. *if a State's previously enacted LLLP provisions have require-ments essentially the same as Sections 201(a)(4) and 108(c), preexisting limited liability limited partnerships should auto-matically retain LLLP status under this Act.*

   b. *if a State's previously enacted LLLP provisions have name requirements essentially the same as Section 108(c) and pro-vide that a public filing other than the certificate of limited partnership establishes a limited partnership's status as a lim-ited liability limited partnership:*

      i. *that filing can be deemed to an amendment to the certifi-cate of limited partnership to comply with Section 201(a)(4), and*

      ii. *preexisting limited liability limited partnerships should automatically retain LLLP status under this Act.*

   c. *if a State's previously enacted LLLP provisions do not have name requirements essentially the same as Section 108(c), it will be impossible both to enforce Section 108(c) and provide for automatic transition to LLLP status under this Act.*

Section 1207. Savings Clause

This [Act] does not affect an action commenced, proceeding brought, or right accrued before this [Act] takes effect.

PART THREE
THE LIMITED LIABILITY COMPANY

UNIFORM LIMITED
LIABILITY COMPANY ACT (1996)[*]

Historical Notes

The Uniform Limited Liability Company Act (1995) ("ULLCA") was approved by the National Conference of Commissioners on Uniform State Laws in 1995.

Editor's note: ULLCA and all of its Comments are reproduced below. ULLCA is contained in volume 6A of Uniform Laws Annotated (2001). The 2006 Cumulative Annual Pocket Part to volume 6A lists the following jurisdictions that have adopted ULLCA and the effective date of adoption: Alabama (1998), Hawaii (1997), Illinois (1998), Montana (1999), South Carolina (1996), South Dakota (1998), Vermont (1996), Virgin Islands (1998) and West Virginia (1996). In addition, a number of other states have redrafted their limited liability company acts to incorporate provisions from ULLCA. The version of ULLCA reproduced below incorporates the amendments made to ULLCA in 1996 in response to the check-the-box changes made by the Internal Revenue Service.

Prefatory Note

Borrowing from abroad, Wyoming initiated a national movement in 1977 by enacting this country's first limited liability company act. The movement started slowly as the Internal Revenue Service took more than ten years to announce finally that a Wyoming limited liability company would be taxed like a partnership. Since that time, every State has adopted a limited liability company act, many of which have already been amended one or more times.

The allure of the limited liability company is its unique ability to bring together in a single business organization the best features of all other business forms -properly structured, its owners obtain both a corporate-styled liability shield and the pass-through tax benefits of a partnership. General and limited partnerships do not offer their partners a

---

corporate-styled liability shield. Corporations, including those having made a Subchapter S election, do not offer their shareholders all the pass-through tax benefits of a partnership. All state limited liability company acts contain provisions for a liability shield and partnership tax status.

Despite these two common themes, state limited liability company acts display a dazzling array of diversity. Multistate activities of businesses are widespread. Recognition of out-of-state limited liability companies varies. Unfortunately, this lack of uniformity manifests itself in basic but fundamentally important questions, such as: may a company be formed and operated by only one owner; may it be formed for purposes other than to make a profit; whether owners have the power and right to withdraw from a company and receive a distribution of the fair value of their interests; who has the apparent authority to bind the company and the limits of that authority; what are the fiduciary duties of owners and managers to a company and each other; how are the rights to manage a company allocated among its owners and managers; do the owners have the right to sue a company and its other owners in their own right as well as derivatively on behalf of the company; may general and limited partnerships be converted to limited liability companies and may limited liability companies merge with other limited liability companies and other business organizations; what is the law governing foreign limited liability companies; and are any or all of these and other rules simply default rules that may be modified by agreement or are they nonwaivable.

Practitioners and entrepreneurs struggle to understand the law governing limited liability companies organized in their own State and to understand the burgeoning law of other States. Simple questions concerning where to organize are increasingly complex. Since most state limited liability company acts are in their infancy, little if any interpretative case law exists. Even when case law develops, it will have limited precedential value because of the diversity of the state acts.

Accordingly, uniform legislation in this area of the law appeared to have become urgent.

After a Study Committee appointed by the National Conference of Commissioners in late 1991 recommended that a comprehensive project be undertaken, the Conference appointed a Drafting Committee which worked on a Uniform Limited Liability Company Act (ULLCA) from early 1992 until its adoption by the Conference at its Annual Meeting in August 1994. The Drafting Committee was assisted by a blue ribbon panel of national experts and other interested and affected parties and organizations. Many, if not all, of those assisting the Committee brought substantial experience from drafting limited liability company legislation in their own States. Many are also authors of leading treatises and articles in the field. Those represented in the drafting process included an American Bar Association (ABA) liaison, four advisors representing the three separate ABA Sections of Business Law, Taxation, and Real Property, Trust and Probate, the United States Treasury Department, the Internal Revenue Service, and many observers representing several other organizations, including the California Bar Association, the New York City Bar Association, the American College of Real Estate Lawyer., the National Association of Certified Public Accountants, the National Association of Secretaries of State, the Chicago and Lawyers Title Companies, the American Land Title Association, and several university law and business school faculty members.

The Committee met nine times and engaged in numerous national telephonic conferences to discuss policies, review over fifteen drafts, evaluate legal developments and consider comments by our many knowledgeable advisers and observers, as well as an ABA subcommittee's earlier work on a prototype. In examining virtually every aspect of each state limited liability company act, the Committee maintained a single policy vision -to draft a flexible act with a comprehensive set of default rules designed to substitute as the essence of the bargain for small entrepreneurs and others.

This Act is flexible in the sense that the vast majority of its provisions may be modified by the owners in a private agreement. To simplify, those nonwaivable provisions are set forth in a single subsection. Helped thereby, sophisticated parties will negotiate their own deal with the benefit of counsel.

The Committee also recognized that small entrepreneurs without the benefit of counsel should also have access to the Act. To that end, the great bulk of the Act sets forth default rules designed to operate a limited liability company without sophisticated agreements and to recognize that members may also modify the default rules by oral agreements defined in part by their own conduct. Uniquely, the Act combines two simple defau.it structures which depend upon the presence of designations in the articles of organization. All default rules under the Act flow from these two designations.

First, unless the articles reflect that a limited liability company is a term company and the duration of that term, the company will be an at-will company. Generally, an at-will company dissolves more easily than a term company and its owners may demand a payment of the fair value of their interests at any time. Owners of a term company must generally wait until the expiration of the term to obtain the value of their interests. Secondly, unless the articles reflect that a company will be managed by managers, the company will be managed by its members. This designation controls whether the members or managers have apparent agency authority, management authority, the nature of fiduciary duties in the company, and important dissolution characteristics.

In January of 1995 the Executive Committee of the Conference adopted an amendment to harmonize the Act with new and important Internal Revenue Service announcements, and the amendment was ratified by the National Conference at its Annual Meeting in August of 1995. The amendment modifies the Act's dissolution provision. NCCUSL has since embarked on a comprehensive re-working of ULLCA and, while approved by the Commissioners, has not been adopted by any states and may be subject to further revision. The most recent draft may viewed on the NCCUSL Web site: www.law.upenn.edu/bll/ulc/ullca/2006act_final.htm

UNIFORM LIMITED LIABILITY COMPANY ACT (1995)
(AS AMENDED 1996)

[ARTICLE] 1 GENERAL PROVISIONS

[ARTICLE] 2 ORGANIZATION

[ARTICLE] 11 DERIVATIVE ACTIONS

[ARTICLE] 12 MISCELLANEOUS PROVISIONS

ARTICLE 1
GENERAL PROVISIONS

§ 101. Definitions.

In this [Act]:

(1) "Articles of organization" means initial, amended, and restated articles of organization and articles of merger. In the case of a foreign limited liability company, the term includes all records serving a similar function required to be filed in the office of the [Secretary of State] or other official having custody of company records in the State or country under whose law it is organized.

(2) "At-will company" means a limited liability company other than a term company.

(3) "Business" includes every trade, occupation, profession, and other lawful purpose, whether or not carried on for profit.

(4) "Debtor in bankruptcy" means a person who is the subject of an order for relief under Title 11 of the United States Code or a comparable order

under a successor statute of general application or a comparable order under federal, state, or foreign law governing insolvency.

(5) "Distribution" means a transfer of money, property, or other benefit from a limited liability company to a member in the member's capacity as a member or to a transferee of the member's distributional interest.

(6) "Distributional interest" means all of a member's interest in distributions by the limited liability company.

(7) "Entity" means a person other than an individual.

(8) "Foreign limited liability company" means an unincorporated entity organized under laws other than the laws of this State which afford limited liability to its owners comparable to the liability under Section 303 and is not required to obtain a certificate of authority to transact business under any law of this State other than this [Act].

(9) "Limited liability company" means a limited liability company organized under this [Act].

(10) "Manager" means a person, whether or not a member of a manager-managed company, who is vested with authority under Section 301.

(11) "Manager-managed company" means a limited liability company which is so designated in its articles of organization.

(12) "Member-managed company" means a limited liability company other than a manager-managed company.

(13) "Operating agreement" means the agreement under Section 103 concerning the relations among the members, managers, and limited liability company. The term includes amendments to the agreement.

(14) "Person" means an individual, corporation, business trust, estate, trust, partnership, limited liability company, association, joint venture, government, governmental subdivision, agency, or instrumentality, or any other legal or commercial entity.

(15) "Principal office" means the office, whether or not in this State, where the principal executive office of a domestic or foreign limited liability company is located.

(16) "Record" means information that is inscribed on a tangible medium or that is stored in an electronic or other medium and is retrievable in perceivable form.

(17) "Sign" means to identify a record by means of a signature, mark, or other symbol, with intent to authenticate it.

(18) "State" means a State of the United States, the District of Columbia, the Commonwealth of Puerto Rico, or any territory or insular possession subject to the jurisdiction of the United States.

(19) "Term company" means a limited liability company in which its members have agreed to remain members until the expiration of a term specified in the articles of organization.

(20) "Transfer" includes an assignment, conveyance, deed, bill of sale, lease, mortgage, security interest, encumbrance, and gift.

Comment

Uniform Limited Liability Company Act ("ULLCA") definitions, like the rest of the Act, are a blend of terms and concepts derived from the Uniform Partnership Act ("UPA"), the Uniform Partnership Act (1994) ("UPA 1994", also previously known as the Revised Uniform Partnership Act or "RUPA"), the Revised Uniform Limited Partnership Act ("RULPA"), the Uniform Commercial Code ("UCC"), and the Model Business Corporation Act ("MBCA"), or their revisions from time to time; some are tailored specially for this Act.

"Business." A limited liability company may be organized to engage in an activity either for or not for profit. The extent to which contributions to a nonprofit company may be deductible for Federal income tax purposes is determined by federal law. Other state law determines the extent of exemptions from state and local income and property taxes.

"Debtor in bankruptcy." The filing of a voluntary petition operates immediately as an "order for relief." *See* Sections 601(7)(i) and 602(b)(2)(iii).

"Distribution." This term includes all sources of a member's distributions including the member's capital contributions, undistributed profits, and residual interest in the assets of the company after all claims, including those of third parties and debts to members, have been paid.

"Distributional interest." The term does not include a member's broader rights to participate in the management of the company. *See* Comments to Article 5.

"Foreign limited liability company." The term is not restricted to companies formed in the United States.

"Manager." The rules of agency apply to limited liability companies. Therefore, managers may designate agents with whatever titles, qualifications, and responsibilities they desire. For example, managers may designate an agent as "President."

"Manager-managed company." The term includes only a company designated as such in the articles of organization. In a manager-managed company agency authority is vested exclusively in one or more managers and not in the members. *See* Sections 101(10) (manager), 203(a)(6) (articles designation), and 301(b) (agency authority of members and managers).

"Member-managed limited liability company." The term includes every company not designated as "manager-managed" under Section 203(a)(6) in its articles of organization.

"Operating agreement." This agreement may be oral. Members may agree upon the extent to which their relationships are to be governed by writings.

"Principal office." The address of the principal office must be set forth in the annual report required under Section 211(a)(3).

"Record." This Act is the first Uniform Act promulgated with a definition of this term. The definition brings this Act in conformity with the present state of technology and accommodates prospective future technology in the communication and storage of information other than by human memory. Modern methods of communicating and storing information employed in commercial practices are no longer confined to physical documents.

The term includes any writing. A record need not be permanent or indestructible, but an oral or other unwritten communication must be stored or preserved on some medium to qualify as a record. Information that has not been retained other than through human memory does not qualify as a record. A record may be signed or may be created without the knowledge or intent of a particular person. Other law must be consulted to determine admissibility in evidence, the applicability of statute of frauds, and other questions regarding the use of records. Under Section 206(a), electronic filings may be permitted and even encouraged.

§ 102. Knowledge and notice.

(a) A person knows a fact if the person has actual knowledge of it.

(b) A person has notice of a fact if the person:

(1) knows the fact;

(2) has received a notification of the fact; or

(3) has reason to know the fact exists from all of the facts known to the person at the time in question.

(c) A person notifies or gives a notification of a fact to another by taking steps reasonably required to inform the other person in ordinary course, whether or not the other person knows the fact.

(d) A person receives a notification when the notification:

(1) comes to the person's attention; or

(2) is duly delivered at the person's place of business or at any other place held out by the person as a place for receiving communications.

(e) An entity knows, has notice, or receives a notification of a fact for purposes of a particular transaction when the individual conducting the transaction for the entity knows, has notice, or receives a notification of the fact, or in any event when the fact would have been brought to the individual's attention had the entity exercised reasonable diligence. An entity exercises reasonable diligence if it maintains reasonable routines for communicating significant information to the individual conducting the transaction for the entity and there is reasonable compliance with the routines. Reasonable diligence does not require an individual acting for the entity to communicate information unless the communication is part of the individual's regular duties or the individual has reason to know of the transaction and that the transaction would be materially affected by the information.

Comment

Knowledge requires cognitive awareness of a fact, whereas notice is based on a lesser degree of awareness. The Act imposes constructive knowledge under limited circumstances. *See* Comments to Sections 301(c), 703, and 704.

§ 103. Effect of operating agreement; nonwaivable provisions.

(a) Except as otherwise provided in subsection (b), all members of a limited liability company may enter into an operating agreement, which need not be in writing, to regulate the affairs of the company and the conduct of its business, and to govern relations among the members, managers, and company. To the extent the operating agreement does not otherwise provide, this [Act] governs relations among the members, managers, and company.

(b) The operating agreement may not:

(1) unreasonably restrict a right to information or access to records under Section 408;

(2) eliminate the duty of loyalty under Section 409(b) or 603(b)(3), but the agreement may:

(i) identify specific types or categories of activities that do not violate the duty of loyalty, if not manifestly unreasonable; and

(ii) specify the number or percentage of members or disinterested managers that may authorize or ratify, after full disclosure of all material facts, a specific act or transaction that otherwise would violate the duty of loyalty;

(3) unreasonably reduce the duty of care under Section 409(c) or 603(b)(3);

(4) eliminate the obligation of good faith and fair dealing under Section 409(d), but the operating agreement may determine the standards by which the performance of the obligation is to be measured, if the standards are not manifestly unreasonable;

(5) vary the right to expel a member in an event specified in Section 601(6);

(6) vary the requirement to wind up the limited liability company's business in a case specified in Section 801(3) or (4); or

(7) restrict rights of a person, other than a manager, member, and transferee of a member's distributional interest, under this [Act].

Comment

The operating agreement is the essential contract that governs the affairs of a limited liability company. Since it is binding on all members, amendments must be approved by all members unless otherwise provided in the agreement. Although many agreements will be in writing, the agreement and any amendments may be oral or may be in the form of a record. Course of dealing, course of performance and usage of trade are relevant to determine the meaning of the agreement unless the agreement provides that all amendments must be in writing.

This section makes clear that the only matters an operating agreement may not control are specified in subsection (b). Accordingly, an operating agreement may modify or eliminate any rule specified in any section of this Act except matters specified in subsection (b). To the extent not otherwise mentioned in subsection (b), every section of this Act is simply a default rule, regardless of whether the language of the section appears to be otherwise mandatory. This approach eliminates the necessity of repeating the phrase "unless otherwise agreed" in each section and its commentary.

Under subsection (b)(1), an operating agreement may not unreasonably restrict the right to information or access to any records under Section 408. This does not create an independent obligation beyond Section 408 to maintain any specific records. Under subsections (b)(2) to (4), an irreducible core of fiduciary responsibilities survive any contrary provision in the operating agreement. Subsection (b)(2)(i) authorizes an operating agreement to modify, but not eliminate, the three specific duties of loyalty set forth in Section 409(b)(1) to (3) provided the modification itself is not manifestly unreasonable, a question of fact. Subsection (b)(2)(ii) preserves the common law right of the members to authorize future or ratify past violations of the duty of loyalty provided there has been a full disclosure of all material facts. The authorization or ratification must be unanimous unless otherwise provided in an operating agreement, because the authorization or ratification itself constitutes an amendment to the agreement. The authorization or ratification of specific past or future conduct may sanction conduct that would have been manifestly unreasonable under subsection (b)(2)(i).

§ 104. Supplemental principles of law.

(a) Unless displaced by particular provisions of this [Act], the principles of law and equity supplement this [Act].

(b) If an obligation to pay interest arises under this [Act] and the rate is not specified, the rate is that specified in [applicable statute].

Comment

Supplementary principles include, but are not limited to, the law of agency, estoppel, law merchant, and all other principles listed in UCC Section 1-103, including the law relative to the capacity to contract, fraud, misrepresentation, duress, coercion, mistake, bankruptcy, and other validating and invalidating clauses. Other principles such as those mentioned in UCC Section 1-205 (Course of Dealing and Usage of Trade) apply as well as course of performance. As with UPA 1994 Section 104, upon which this provision is based, no substantive change from either the UPA or the UCC is intended. Section 104(b) establishes the applicable rate of interest in the absence of an agreement among the members.

§ 105. Name.

(a) The name of a limited liability company must contain "limited liability company" or "limited company" or the abbreviation "L.L.C.", "LLC", "L.C.", or "LC". "Limited" may be abbreviated as "Ltd.", and "company" may be abbreviated as "Co.".

(b) Except as authorized by subsections (c) and (d), the name of a limited liability company must be distinguishable upon the records of the [Secretary of State] from:

(1) the name of any corporation, limited partnership, or company incorporated, organized or authorized to transact business, in this State;

(2) a name reserved or registered under Section 106 or 107;

(3) a fictitious name approved under Section 1005 for a foreign company authorized to transact business in this State because its real name is unavailable.

(c) A limited liability company may apply to the [Secretary of State] for authorization to use a name that is not distinguishable upon the records of the [Secretary of State] from one or more of the names described in subsection (b). The [Secretary of State] shall authorize use of the name applied for if:

(1) the present user, registrant, or owner of a reserved name consents to the use in a record and submits an undertaking in form satisfactory to the [Secretary of State] to change the name to a name that is distinguishable upon the records of the [Secretary of State] from the name applied for; or

(2) the applicant delivers to the [Secretary of State] a certified copy of the final judgment of a court of competent jurisdiction establishing the applicant's right to use the name applied for in this State.

(d) A limited liability company may use the name, including a fictitious name, of another domestic or foreign company which is used in this State if the other company is organized or authorized to transact business in this State and the company proposing to use the name has:

(1) merged with the other company;

(2) been formed by reorganization with the other company; or

(3) acquired substantially all of the assets, including the name, of the other company.

§ 106. Reserved name.

(a) A person may reserve the exclusive use of the name of a limited liability company, including a fictitious name for a foreign company whose name is not available, by delivering an application to the [Secretary of State] for filing. The application must set forth the name and address of the applicant and the name proposed to be reserved. If the [Secretary of State] finds that the name applied for is available, it must be reserved for the applicant's exclusive use for a nonrenewable 120-day period.

(b) The owner of a name reserved for a limited liability company may transfer the reservation to another person by delivering to the [Secretary of State] a signed notice of the transfer which states the name and address of the transferee.

Comment

A foreign limited liability company that is not presently authorized to transact business in the State may reserve a fictitious name for a nonrenewable 120-day period. When its actual name is available, a company will generally register that name under Section 107 because the registration is valid for a year and may be extended indefinitely.

§ 107. Registered name.

(a) A foreign limited liability company may register its name subject to the requirements of Section 1005, if the name is distinguishable upon the records of the [Secretary of State] from names that are not available under Section 105(b).

(b) A foreign limited liability company registers its name, or its name with any addition required by Section 1005, by delivering to the [Secretary of State] for filing an application:

(1) setting forth its name, or its name with any addition required by Section 1005, the State or country and date of its organization, and a brief description of the nature of the business in which it is engaged; and

(2) accompanied by a certificate of existence, or a record of similar import, from the State or country of organization.

(c) A foreign limited liability company whose registration is effective may renew it for successive years by delivering for filing in the office of the [Secretary of State] a renewal application complying with subsection (b) between October 1 and December 31 of the preceding year. The renewal application renews the registration for the following calendar year.

(d) A foreign limited liability company whose registration is effective may qualify as a foreign company under its name or consent in writing to the use of its name by a limited liability company later organized under this [Act] or by another foreign company later authorized to transact business in this State. The registered name terminates when the limited liability company is organized or the foreign company qualifies or consents to the qualification of another foreign company under the registered name.

§ 108. Designated office and agent for service of process.

(a) A limited liability company and a foreign limited liability company authorized to do business in this State shall designate and continuously maintain in this State:

(1) an office, which need not be a place of its business in this State; and

(2) an agent and street address of the agent for service of process on the company.

(b) An agent must be an individual resident of this State, a domestic corporation, another limited liability company, or a foreign corporation or foreign company authorized to do business in this State.

Comment

Limited liability companies organized under Section 202 or authorized to transact business under Section 1004 are required to designate and continuously maintain an office in the State. Although the designated office need not be a place of business, it most often will be the only place of business of the company. The company must also designate an agent for service of process within the State and the agent's street address. The agent's address need not be the same as the company's designated office address. The initial office and agent designations must be set forth in the articles of organization, including the address of the designated office. *See* Section 203(a)(2) to (3). The current office and agent designations must be set forth in the company's annual report. *See* Section 211(a)(2). *See also* Section 109 (procedure for changing the office or agent designations), Section 110 (procedure for an agent to resign), and Section 111(b) (the filing officer is the service agent for the company if it fails to maintain its own service agent).

§ 109. Change of designated office or agent for service of process.

A limited liability company may change its designated office or agent for service of process by delivering to the [Secretary of State] for filing a statement of change which sets forth:

(1) the name of the company;

(2) the street address of its current designated office;

(3) if the current designated office is to be changed, the street address of the new designated office;

(4) the name and address of its current agent for service of process; and

(5) if the current agent for service of process or street address of that agent is to be changed, the new address or the name and street address of the new agent for service of process.

§ 110. Resignation of agent for service of process.

(a) An agent for service of process of a limited liability company may resign by delivering to the [Secretary of State] for filing a record of the statement of resignation.

(b) After filing a statement of resignation, the [Secretary of State] shall mail a copy to the designated office and another copy to the limited liability company at its principal office.

(c) An agency is terminated on the 31st day after the statement is filed in the office of the [Secretary of State].

§ 111. Service of process.

(a) An agent for service of process appointed by a limited liability company or a foreign limited liability company is an agent of the company for service of any process, notice, or demand required or permitted by law to be served upon the company.

(b) If a limited liability company or foreign limited liability company fails to appoint or maintain an agent for service of process in this State or the agent for service of process cannot with reasonable diligence be found at the agent's address, the [Secretary of State] is an agent of the company upon whom process, notice, or demand may be served.

(c) Service of any process, notice, or demand on the [Secretary of State] may be made by delivering to and leaving with the [Secretary of State], the [Assistant Secretary of State], or clerk having charge of the limited liability company department of the [Secretary of State's] office duplicate copies of the process, notice, or demand. If the process, notice, or demand is served on the [Secretary of State], the [Secretary of State] shall forward one of the copies by registered or certified mail, return receipt requested, to the company at its designated office. Service is effected under this subsection at the earliest of:

(1) the date the company receives the process, notice, or demand;

(2) the date shown on the return receipt, if signed on behalf of the company; or

(3) five days after its deposit in the mail, if mailed postpaid and correctly addressed.

(d) The [Secretary of State] shall keep a record of all processes, notices, and demands served pursuant to this section and record the time of and the action taken regarding the service.

(e) This section does not affect the right to serve process, notice, or demand in any manner otherwise provided by law.

Comment

Service of process on a limited liability company and a foreign company authorized to transact business in the State must be made on the company's agent for service of process whose name and address should be on file with the filing office. If for any reason a company fails to appoint or maintain an agent for service of process or the agent cannot be found with reasonable diligence at the agent's address, the filing officer will be deemed the proper agent.

§ 112. Nature of business and powers.

(a) A limited liability company may be organized under this [Act] for any lawful purpose, subject to any law of this State governing or regulating business.

(b) Unless its articles of organization provide otherwise, a limited liability company has the same powers as an individual to do all things necessary or convenient to carry on its business or affairs, including power to:

(1) sue and be sued, and defend in its name;

(2) purchase, receive, lease, or otherwise acquire, and own, hold, improve, use, and otherwise deal with real or personal property, or any legal or equitable interest in property, wherever located;

(3) sell, convey, mortgage, grant a security interest in, lease, exchange, and otherwise encumber or dispose of all or any part of its property;

(4) purchase, receive, subscribe for, or otherwise acquire, own, hold, vote, use, sell, mortgage, lend, grant a security interest in, or otherwise dispose of and deal in and with, shares or other interests in or obligations of any other entity;

(5) make contracts and guarantees, incur liabilities, borrow money, issue its notes, bonds, and other obligations, which may be convertible into or include the option to purchase other securities of the limited liability company, and secure any of its obligations by a mortgage on or a security interest in any of its property, franchises, or income;

(6) lend money, invest and reinvest its funds, and receive and hold real and personal property as security for repayment;

(7) be a promoter, partner, member, associate, or manager of any partnership, joint venture, trust, or other entity;

(8) conduct its business, locate offices, and exercise the powers granted by this [Act] within or without this State;

(9) elect managers and appoint officers, employees, and agents of the limited liability company, define their duties, fix their compensation, and lend them money and credit;

(10) pay pensions and establish pension plans, pension trusts, profit sharing plans, bonus plans, option plans, and benefit or incentive plans for any or all of its current or former members, managers, officers, employees, and agents;

(11) make donations for the public welfare or for charitable, scientific, or educational purposes; and

(12) make payments or donations, or do any other act, not inconsistent with law, that furthers the business of the limited liability company.

Comment

A limited liability company may be organized for any lawful purpose unless the State has specifically prohibited a company from engaging in a specific activity. For example, many States require that certain regulated industries, such as banking and insurance, be conducted only by organizations that meet the special requirements. Also, many States impose restrictions on activities in which a limited liability company may engage. For example, the practice of certain professionals is often subject to special conditions. A limited liability company has the power to engage in and perform important and necessary acts related to its operation and function. A company's power to enter into a transaction is distinguishable from the authority of an agent to enter into the transaction. *See* Section 301 (agency rules).

ARTICLE 2
ORGANIZATION

§ 201. Limited liability company as legal entity.

A limited liability company is a legal entity distinct from its members.

Comment

A limited liability company is legally distinct from its members who are not normally liable for the debts, obligations, and liabilities of the company. *See* Section 303. Accordingly, members are not proper parties to suits against the company unless an object of the proceeding is to enforce members' rights against the company or to enforce their liability to the company.

§ 202. Organization.

(a) One or more persons may organize a limited liability company, consisting of one or more members, by delivering articles of organization to the office of the [Secretary of State] for filing.

(b) Unless a delayed effective date is specified, the existence of a limited liability company begins when the articles of organization are filed.

(c) The filing of the articles of organization by the [Secretary of State] is conclusive proof that the organizers satisfied all conditions precedent to the creation of a limited liability company.

Comment

Any person may organize a limited liability company by performing the ministerial act of signing and filing the articles of organization. The person need not be a member. As a matter of flexibility, a company may be organized and operated with only one member to enable sole proprietors to obtain the benefit of a liability shield. The effect of organizing or operating a company with one member on the Federal tax classification of the company is determined by federal law.

The existence of a company begins when the articles are filed. Therefore, the filing of the articles of organization is conclusive as to the existence of the limited liability shield for persons who enter into transactions on behalf of the company. Until the articles are filed, a firm is not organized under this Act and is not a "limited liability company" as defined in Section 101(9). In that case, the parties' relationships are not governed by this Act unless they have expressed a contractual intent to be bound by the provisions of the Act. Third parties would also not be governed by the provisions of this Act unless they have expressed a contractual intent to extend a limited liability shield to the members of the would-be limited liability company.

§ 203. Articles of organization.

(a) Articles of organization of a limited liability company must set forth:

(1) the name of the company;

(2) the address of the initial designated office;

(3) the name and street address of the initial agent for service of process;

(4) the name and address of each organizer;

(5) whether the company is to be a term company and, if so, the term specified;

(6) whether the company is to be manager-managed, and, if so, the name and address of each initial manager; and

(7) whether one or more of the members of the company are to be liable for its debts and obligations under Section 303(c).

(b) Articles of organization of a limited liability company may set forth:

(1) provisions permitted to be set forth in an operating agreement; or

(2) other matters not inconsistent with law.

(c) Articles of organization of a limited liability company may not vary the nonwaivable provisions of Section 103(b). As to all other matters, if any provision of an operating agreement is inconsistent with the articles of organization:

(1) the operating agreement controls as to managers, members, and members' transferees; and

(2) the articles of organization control as to persons, other than managers, members and their transferees, who reasonably rely on the articles to their detriment.

Comment

The articles serve primarily a notice function and generally do not reflect the substantive agreement of the members regarding the business affairs of the company. Those matters are generally reserved for an operating agreement which may be unwritten. Under Section 203(b), the articles may contain provisions permitted to be set forth in an operating agreement. Where the articles and operating agreement conflict, the operating agreement controls as to members but the articles control as to third parties. The articles may also contain any other matter not inconsistent with law. The most important is a Section 301(c) limitation on the authority of a member or manager to transfer interests in the company's real property.

A company will be at-will unless it is designated as a term company and the duration of its term is specified in its articles under Section 203(a)(5).

The duration of a term company may be specified in any manner which sets forth a specific and final date for the dissolution of the company. For example, the period specified may be in the form of "50 years from the date of filing of the articles" or "the period ending on January 1, 2020." Mere specification of a particular undertaking of an uncertain business duration is not sufficient unless the particular undertaking is within a longer fixed period. An example of this type of designation would include "2020 or until the building is completed, whichever occurs first." When the specified period is incorrectly specified, the company will be an at-will company. Notwithstanding the correct specification of a term in the articles, a company will be an at-will company among the members under Section 203(c)(1) if an operating agreement so provides. A term company that continues after the expiration of its term specified in its articles will also be an at-will company.

A term company possesses several important default rule characteristics that differentiate it dramatically from an at-will company. An operating agreement may alter any of these rules. Any dissociation of an at-will member dissolves a member-managed company unless a specified percentage of the remaining members agree to continue the business of the company. Before the expiration of its term, only specified dissociation events (excluding voluntary withdrawal) of a term member will dissolve a member-managed company unless a specified percentage of the remaining members agree to continue the business of the company. *See* Comments to Sections 601 and 801(b)(3). Also, even if the dissociation of an at-will member does not result in a dissolution of a member-managed company, the dissociated member is entitled to have the company purchase that member's interest for its fair value. Unless the company earlier dissolves, a term member must generally await the expiration of the agreed term to withdraw the fair value of the interest. *See* Comments to Section 701(a).

A company will be member-managed unless it is designated as manager-managed under Section 203(a)(6). Absent further designation in the articles, a company will be a member-managed at-will company. The designation of a limited liability company as either member or manager-managed is important because it defines who are agents and have the apparent authority to bind the company under Section 301 and determines whether the dissociation of members who are not managers will threaten dissolution of the company. In a member-managed company, the members have the agency authority to bind the company. In a manager-managed company only the managers have that authority. The effect of the agency structure of a company on the Federal tax classification of the company is determined by federal law. The agency designation relates only to agency and does not preclude members of a manager-managed company from participating in the actual management of company business. *See* Comments to Section 404(b).

In a member-managed company, the dissociation of any member will cause the company to dissolve unless a specified percentage of the remaining members agree to continue the business of the company. In a manager-managed company, only the dissociation of any member who is also a manager threatens dissolution of the company. Only where there are no members who are also managers will the dissociation of members who are not managers threaten dissolution of a manager-managed company. *See* Comments to Section 801.

§ 204. Amendment or restatement of articles of organization.

(a) Articles of organization of a limited liability company may be amended at any time by delivering articles of amendment to the [Secretary of State] for filing. The articles of amendment must set forth the:

(1) name of the limited liability company;

(2) date of filing of the articles of organization; and

(3) amendment to the articles.

(b) A limited liability company may restate its articles of organization at any time. Restated articles of organization must be signed and filed in the same manner as articles of amendment. Restated articles of organization must be designated as such in the heading and state in the heading or in an introductory paragraph the limited liability company's present name and, if it has been changed, all of its former names and the date of the filing of its initial articles of organization.

Comment

An amendment to the articles requires the consent of all the members unless an operating agreement provides for a lesser number. *See* Section 404(c)(3).

§ 205. Signing of records.

(a) Except as otherwise provided in this [Act], a record to be filed by or on behalf of a limited liability company in the office of the [Secretary of State] must be signed in the name of the company by a:

(1) manager of a manager-managed company;

(2) member of a member-managed company;

(3) person organizing the company, if the company has not been formed; or

(4) fiduciary, if the company is in the hands of a receiver, trustee, or other court-appointed fiduciary.

(b) A record signed under subsection (a) must state adjacent to the signature the name and capacity of the signer.

(c) Any person may sign a record to be filed under subsection (a) by an attorney-in-fact. Powers of attorney relating to the signing of records to be filed under subsection (a) by an attorney-in-fact need not be filed in the office of the [Secretary of State] as evidence of authority by the person filing but must be retained by the company.

Comment

Both a writing and a record may be signed. An electronic record is signed when a person adds a name to the record with the intention to authenticate the record. *See* Sections 101(16) ("record" definition) and 10l(17) ("signed" definition). Other provisions of this Act also provide for the filing of records with the filing office but do not require signing by the persons specified in clauses (1) to (3). Those specific sections prevail.

§ 206. Filing in office of [Secretary of State].

(a) Articles of organization or any other record authorized to be filed under this [Act] must be in a medium permitted by the [Secretary of State] and must be delivered to the office of the [Secretary of State]. Unless the [Secretary of State] determines that a record fails to comply as to form with the filing requirements of this [Act], and if all filing fees have been paid, the [Secretary of State] shall file the record and send a receipt for the record and the fees to the limited liability company or its representative.

(b) Upon request and payment of a fee, the [Secretary of State] shall send to the requester a certified copy of the requested record.

(c) Except as otherwise provided in subsection (d) and Section 207(c), a record accepted for filing by the [Secretary of State] is effective:

(1) at the time of filing on the date it is filed, as evidenced by the [Secretary of State's] date and time endorsement on the original record; or

(2) at the time specified in the record as its effective time on the date it is filed.

(d) A record may specify a delayed effective time and date, and if it does so the record becomes effective at the time and date specified. If a delayed effective date but no time is specified, the record is effective at the close of business on that date. If a delayed effective date is later than the 90th day after the record is filed, the record is effective on the 90th day.

Comment

The definition and use of the term "record" permits filings with the filing office under this Act to conform to technological advances that have been adopted by the filing office. However, since Section 206(a) provides that the filing "must be in a medium permitted by the [Secretary of State]", the Act simply conforms to filing changes as they are adopted.

§ 207. Correcting filed record.

(a) A limited liability company or foreign limited liability company may correct a record filed by the [Secretary of State] if the record contains a false or erroneous statement or was defectively signed.

(b) A record is corrected:

(1) by preparing articles of correction that:

(i) describe the record, including its filing date, or attach a copy of it to the articles of correction;

(ii) specify the incorrect statement and the reason it is incorrect or the manner in which the signing was defective; and

(iii) correct the incorrect statement or defective signing; and

(2) by delivering the corrected record to the [Secretary of State] for filing.

(c) Articles of correction are effective retroactively on the effective date of the record they correct except as to persons relying on the uncorrected record and adversely affected by the correction. As to those persons, articles of correction are effective when filed.

§ 208. Certificate of existence or authorization.

(a) A person may request the [Secretary of State] to furnish a certificate of existence for a limited liability company or a certificate of authorization for a foreign limited liability company.

(b) A certificate of existence for a limited liability company must set forth:

(1) the company's name;

(2) that it is duly organized under the laws of this State, the date of organization, whether its duration is at-will or for a specified term, and, if the latter, the period specified;

(3) if payment is reflected in the records of the [Secretary of State] and if nonpayment affects the existence of the company, that all fees, taxes, and penalties owed to this State have been paid;

(4) whether its most recent annual report required by Section 211 has been filed with the [Secretary of State];

(5) that articles of termination have not been filed; and

(6) other facts of record in the office of the [Secretary of State] which may be requested by the applicant.

(c) A certificate of authorization for a foreign limited liability company must set forth:

(1) the company's name used in this State;

(2) that it is authorized to transact business in this State;

(3) if payment is reflected in the records of the [Secretary of State] and if nonpayment affects the authorization of the company, that all fees, taxes, and penalties owed to this State have been paid;

(4) whether its most recent annual report required by Section 211 has been filed with the [Secretary of State];

(5) that a certificate of cancellation has not been filed; and

(6) other facts of record in the office of the [Secretary of State] which may be requested by the applicant.

(d) Subject to any qualification stated in the certificate, a certificate of existence or authorization issued by the [Secretary of State] may be relied upon as conclusive evidence that the domestic or foreign limited liability company is in existence or is authorized to transact business in this State.

§ 209. Liability for false statement in filed record.

If a record authorized or required to be filed under this [Act] contains a false statement, one who suffers loss by reliance on the statement may recover damages for the loss from a person who signed the record or caused another to sign it on the person's behalf and knew the statement to be false at the time the record was signed.

§ 210. Filing by judicial act.

If a person required by Section 205 to sign any record fails or refuses to do so, any other person who is adversely affected by the failure or refusal may petition the [designate the appropriate court] to direct the signing of the record. If the court finds that it is proper for the record to be signed and that a person so designated has failed or refused to sign the record, it shall order the [Secretary of State] to sign and file an appropriate record.

§ 211. Annual report for [Secretary of State].

(a) A limited liability company, and a foreign limited liability company authorized to transact business in this State, shall deliver to the [Secretary of State] for filing an annual report that sets forth:

(1) the name of the company and the State or country under whose law it is organized;

(2) the address of its designated office and the name and address of its agent for service of process in this State;

(3) the address of its principal office; and

(4) the names and business addresses of any managers.

(b) Information in an annual report must be current as of the date the annual report is signed on behalf of the limited liability company.

(c) The first annual report must be delivered to the [Secretary of State] between [January 1 and April 1] of the year following the calendar year in which a limited liability company was organized or a foreign company was authorized to transact business. Subsequent annual reports must be delivered to the [Secretary of State] between [January 1 and April 1] of the ensuing calendar years.

(d) If an annual report does not contain the information required in subsection (a), the [Secretary of State] shall promptly notify the reporting limited liability company or foreign limited liability company and return the report to it for correction. If the report is corrected to contain the information required in subsection (a) and delivered to the [Secretary of State] within 30 days after the effective date of the notice, it is timely filed.

Comment

Failure to deliver the annual report within 60 days after its due date is a primary ground for administrative dissolution of the company under Section 809. *See* Comments to Sections 809 to 812.

ARTICLE 3
RELATIONS OF MEMBERS AND MANAGERS TO PERSONS DEALING WITH LIMITED LIABILITY COMPANY

§ 301. Agency of members and managers.

(a) Subject to subsections (b) and (c):

(1) Each member is an agent of the limited liability company for the purpose of its business, and an act of a member, including the signing of an instrument in the company's name, for apparently carrying on in the ordinary course the company's business or business of the kind carried on by the company binds the company, unless the member had no authority to act for the company in the particular matter and the person with whom the member was dealing knew or had notice that the member lacked authority.

(2) An act of a member which is not apparently for carrying on in the ordinary course the company's business or business of the kind carried on by the company binds the company only if the act was authorized by the other members.

(b) Subject to subsection (c), in a manager-managed company:

(1) A member is not an agent of the company for the purpose of its business solely by reason of being a member. Each manager is an agent

of the company for the purpose of its business, and an act of a manager, including the signing of an instrument in the company's name, for apparently carrying on in the ordinary course the company's business or business of the kind carried on by the company binds the company, unless the manager had no authority to act for the company in the particular matter and the person with whom the manager was dealing knew or had notice that the manager lacked authority.

(2) An act of a manager which is not apparently for carrying on in the ordinary course the company's business or business of the kind carried on by the company binds the company only if the act was authorized under Section 404.

(c) Unless the articles of organization limit their authority, any member of a member-managed company or manager of a manager-managed company may sign and deliver any instrument transferring or affecting the company's interest in real property. The instrument is conclusive in favor of a person who gives value without knowledge of the lack of the authority of the person signing and delivering the instrument.

Comment

Members of a member-managed and managers of manager-managed company, as agents of the firm, have the apparent authority to bind a company to third parties. Members of a manager-managed company are not as such agents of the firm and do not have the apparent authority, as members, to bind a company. Members and managers with apparent authority possess actual authority by implication unless the actual authority is restricted in an operating agreement. Apparent authority extends to acts for carrying on in the ordinary course the company's business and business of the kind carried on by the company. Acts beyond this scope bind the company only where supported by actual authority created before the act or ratified after the act.

Ordinarily, restrictions on authority in an operating agreement do not affect the apparent authority of members and managers to bind the company to third parties without notice of the restriction. However, the restriction may make a member or manager's conduct wrongful and create liability to the company for the breach. This rule is subject to three important exceptions. First, under Section 301(c), a limitation reflected in the articles of organization on the authority of any member or manager to sign and deliver an instrument affecting an interest in company real property is effective when filed, even to persons without knowledge of the agent's lack of authority. The effect of such a limitation on authority on the Federal tax classification of the company is determined by federal law. Secondly, under Section 703, a dissociated member's apparent authority terminates two years after dissociation, even to persons without knowledge of the dissociation. Thirdly, under Section 704, a dissociated member's apparent authority may be terminated earlier than the two years by filing a statement of dissociation. The statement is effective 90 days after filing, even to persons without knowledge of the filing. Together, these three provisions provide constructive knowledge to the world of the lack of apparent authority of an agent to bind the company.

§ 302. Limited liability company liable for member's or manager's actionable conduct.

A limited liability company is liable for loss or injury caused to a person, or for a penalty incurred, as a result of a wrongful act or omission, or other actionable conduct, of a member or manager acting in the ordinary course of business of the company or with authority of the company.

Comment

Since a member of a manager-managed company is not as such an agent, the acts of the member are not imputed to the company unless the member is acting under actual or apparent authority created by circumstances other than membership status.

§ 303. Liability of members and managers.

(a) Except as otherwise provided in subsection (c), the debts, obligations, and liabilities of a limited liability company, whether arising in contract, tort, or otherwise, are solely the debts, obligations, and liabilities of the company. A member or manager is not personally liable for a debt, obligation, or liability of the company solely by reason of being or acting as a member or manager.

(b) The failure of a limited liability company to observe the usual company formalities or requirements relating to the exercise of its company powers or management of its business is not a ground for imposing personal liability on the members or managers for liabilities of the company.

(c) All or specified members of a limited liability company are liable in their capacity as members for all or specified debts, obligations, or liabilities of the company if:

(1) a provision to that effect is contained in the articles of organization; and

(2) a member so liable has consented in writing to the adoption of the provision or to be bound by the provision.

Comment

A member or manager, as an agent of the company, is not liable for the debts, obligations, and liabilities of the company simply because of the agency. A member or manager is responsible for acts or omissions to the extent those acts or omissions would be actionable in contract or tort against the member or manager if that person were acting in an individual capacity. Where a member or manager delegates or assigns the authority or duty to exercise appropriate company functions, the member or manager is ordinarily not personally liable for the acts or omissions of the officer, employee, or agent if the member or manager has complied with the duty of care set forth in Section 409(c).

Under Section 303(c), the usual liability shield may be waived, in whole or in part, provided the waiver is reflected in the articles of organization and the member has consented in writing to be bound by the waiver. The importance and unusual nature of the waiver consent requires that the consent be evidenced by a writing and not merely an unwritten record. *See* Comments to Section 205. The effect of a waiver on the Federal tax classification of the company is determined by federal law.

ARTICLE 4
RELATIONS OF MEMBERS TO EACH OTHER AND TO LIMITED LIABILITY COMPANY

§ 401. Form of contribution.

A contribution of a member of a limited liability company may consist of tangible or intangible property or other benefit to the company, including money, promissory notes, services performed, or other agreements to contribute cash or property, or contracts for services to be performed.

Comment

Unless otherwise provided in an operating agreement, admission of a member and the nature and valuation of a would-be member's contribution are matters requiring the consent of all of the other members. *See* Section 404(c)(7). An agreement to contribute to a company is controlled by the operating agreement and therefore may not be created or modified without amending that agreement through the unanimous consent of all the members, including the member to be bound by the new contribution terms. *See* 404(c)(1).

§ 402. Member's liability for contributions.

(a) A member's obligation to contribute money, property, or other benefit to, or to perform services for, a limited liability company is not excused by the member's death, disability, or other inability to perform personally. If a member does not make the required contribution of property or services, the member is obligated at the option of the company to contribute money equal to the value of that portion of the stated contribution which has not been made.

(b) A creditor of a limited liability company who extends credit or otherwise acts in reliance on an obligation described in subsection (a), and without notice of any compromise under Section 404(c)(5), may enforce the original obligation.

Comment

An obligation need not be in writing to be enforceable. Given the informality of some companies, a writing requirement may frustrate reasonable expectations of members based on a clear oral agreement. Obligations may be compromised with the consent of all of the members under Section 404(c)(5), but the compromise is generally effective only among the consenting members. Company creditors are bound by the compromise only as provided in Section 402(b).

§ 403. Member's and manager's rights to payments and reimbursement.

(a) A limited liability company shall reimburse a member or manager for payments made and indemnify a member or manager for liabilities incurred by the member or manager in the ordinary course of the business of the company or for the preservation of its business or property.

(b) A limited liability company shall reimburse a member for an advance to the company beyond the amount of contribution the member agreed to make.

(c) A payment or advance made by a member which gives rise to an obligation of a limited liability company under subsection (a) or (b) constitutes a loan to the company upon which interest accrues from the date of the payment or advance.

(d) A member is not entitled to remuneration for services performed for a limited liability company, except for reasonable compensation for services rendered in winding up the business of the company.

Comment

The presence of a liability shield will ordinarily prevent a member or manager from incurring personal liability on behalf of the company in the ordinary course of the company's business. Where a member of a member-managed or a manager of a manager-managed company incurs such liabilities, Section 403(a) provides that the company must indemnify the member or manager where that person acted in the ordinary course of the company's business or the preservation of its property. A member or manager is therefore entitled to indemnification only if the act was within the member or manager's actual authority, a member or manager is therefore not entitled to indemnification for conduct that violates the duty of care set forth in Section 409(c) or for tortious conduct against a third party. Since members of a manager-managed company do not possess the apparent authority to bind the company, it would be more unusual for such a member to incur a liability for indemnification in the ordinary course of the company's business.

§ 404. Management of limited liability company.

(a) In a member-managed company:

(1) each member has equal rights in the management and conduct of the company's business; and

(2) except as otherwise provided in subsection (c), any matter relating to the business of the company may be decided by a majority of the members.

(b) In a manager-managed company:

(1) each manager has equal rights in the management and conduct of the company's business;

(2) except as otherwise provided in subsection (c), any matter relating to the business of the company may be exclusively decided by the manager or, if there is more than one manager, by a majority of the managers; and

(3) a manager:

(i) must be designated, appointed, elected, removed, or replaced by a vote, approval, or consent of a majority of the members; and

(ii) holds office until a successor has been elected and qualified, unless the manager sooner resigns or is removed.

(c) The only matters of a member or manager-managed company's business requiring the consent of all of the members are:

(1) the amendment of the operating agreement under Section 103;

(2) the authorization or ratification of acts or transactions under Section 103(b)(2)(ii) which would otherwise violate the duty of loyalty;

(3) an amendment to the articles of organization under Section 204;

(4) the compromise of an obligation to make a contribution under Section 402(b);

(5) the compromise, as among members, of an obligation of a member to make a contribution or return money or other property paid or distributed in violation of this [Act];

(6) the making of interim distributions under Section 405(a), including the redemption of an interest;

(7) the admission of a new member;

(8) the use of the company's property to redeem an interest subject to a charging order;

(9) the consent to dissolve the company under Section 801(2);

(10) a waiver of the right to have the company's business wound up and the company terminated under Section 802(b);

(11) the consent of members to merge with another entity under Section 904(c)(1); and

(12) the sale, lease, exchange, or other disposal of all, or substantially all, of the company's property with or without goodwill.

(d) Action requiring the consent of members or managers under this [Act] may be taken without a meeting.

(e) A member or manager may appoint a proxy to vote or otherwise act for the member or manager by signing an appointment instrument, either personally or by the member's or manager's attorney-in-fact.

Comment

In a member-managed company, each member has equal rights in the management and conduct of the company's business unless otherwise provided in an operating agreement. For example, an operating agreement may allocate voting rights based upon capital contributions rather than the subsection (a) per capita rule. Also, member disputes as to any matter relating to the company's business may be resolved by a majority of the members unless the matter relates to a matter specified in subsection (c) (unanimous consent required). Regardless of how the members allocate management rights, each member is an agent of the company with the apparent authority to bind the company in the ordinary course of its business. *See* Comments to Section 301(a). A member's right to participate in management terminates upon dissociation. *See* Section 603(b)(1).

In a manager-managed company, the members, unless also managers, have no rights in the management and conduct of the company's business unless otherwise provided in an operating agreement. If there is more than one manager, manager disputes as to any matter relating to the company's business may be resolved by a majority of the managers unless the matter relates to a matter specified in subsection (c) (unanimous member consent required). Managers must be designated, appointed, or elected by a majority of the members. A manager need not be a member and is an agent of the company with the apparent authority to bind the company in the ordinary course of its business. *See* Sections 101(10) and 301(b).

To promote clarity and certainty, subsection (c) specifies those exclusive matters requiring the unanimous consent of the members, whether the company is member-or manager-managed. For example, interim distributions, including redemptions, may not be made without the unanimous consent of all the members. Unless otherwise agreed, all other company matters are to be determined under the majority of members or managers rules of subsections (a) and (b).

§ 405. Sharing of and right to distributions.

(a) Any distributions made by a limited liability company before its dissolution and winding up must be in equal shares.

(b) A member has no right to receive, and may not be required to accept, a distribution in kind.

(c) If a member becomes entitled to receive a distribution, the member has the status of, and is entitled to all remedies available to, a creditor of the limited liability company with respect to the distribution.

Comment

Recognizing the informality of many limited liability companies, this section creates a simple default rule regarding interim distributions. Any interim distributions made must be in equal shares and approved by all members. See Section 404(c)(6). The rule assumes that: profits will be shared equally; some distributions will constitute a return of contributions that should be shared equally rather than a distribution of profits; and property contributors should have the right to veto any distribution that threatens their return of contributions on liquidation. In the simple case where the members make equal contributions of property or equal contributions of services, those assumptions avoid the necessity of maintaining a complex capital account or determining profits. Where some members contribute services and others property, the unanimous vote necessary to approve interim distributions protects against unwanted distributions of contributions to service contributors. Consistently, Section 408(a) does not require the company to maintain a separate account for each member, the Act does not contain a default rule for allocating profits and losses, and Section 806(b) requires that liquidating distributions to members be made in equal shares after the return of contributions not previously returned. See Comments to Section 806(b).

Section 405(c) governs distributions declared or made when the company was solvent. Section 406 governs distributions declared or made when the company is insolvent.

§ 406. Limitations on distributions.

(a) A distribution may not be made if:

(1) the limited liability company would not be able to pay its debts as they become due in the ordinary course of business; or

(2) the company's total assets would be less than the sum of its total liabilities plus the amount that would be needed, if the company were to be dissolved, wound up, and terminated at the time of the distribution to satisfy the preferential rights upon dissolution, winding up, and termination of members whose preferential rights are superior to those receiving the distribution.

(b) A limited liability company may base a determination that a distribution is not prohibited under subsection (a) on financial statements prepared on the basis of accounting practices and principles that are reasonable in the circumstances or on a fair valuation or other method that is reasonable in the circumstances.

(c) Except as otherwise provided in subsection (e), the effect of a distribution under subsection (a) is measured:

(1) in the case of distribution by purchase, redemption, or other acquisition of a distributional interest in a limited liability company, as of the date money or other property is transferred or debt incurred by the company; and

(2) in all other cases, as of the date the:

(i) distribution is authorized if the payment occurs within 120 days after the date of authorization; or

(ii) payment is made if it occurs more than 120 days after the date of authorization.

(d) A limited liability company's indebtedness to a member incurred by reason of a distribution made in accordance with this section is at parity with the company's indebtedness to its general, unsecured creditors.

(e) Indebtedness of a limited liability company, including indebtedness issued in connection with or as part of a distribution, is not considered a liability for purposes of determinations under subsection (a) if its terms provide that payment of principal and interest are made only if and to the extent that payment of a distribution to members could then be made under this section. If the indebtedness is issued as a distribution, each payment of principal or interest on the indebtedness is treated as a distribution, the effect of which is measured on the date the payment is made.

Comment

This section establishes the validity of company distributions, which in turn determines the potential liability of members and managers for improper distributions under Section 407. Distributions are improper if the company is insolvent under subsection (a) at the time the distribution is measured under subsection (c). In recognition of the informality of many limited liability companies, the solvency determination under subsection (b) may be made on the basis of a fair valuation or other method reasonable under the circumstances.

The application of the equity insolvency and balance sheet tests present special problems in the context of the purchase, redemption, or other acquisition of a company's distributional interests. Special rules establish the time of measurement of such transfers. Under Section 406(c)(1), the time for measuring the effect of a distribution to purchase a distributional interest is the date of payment. The company may make payment either by transferring property or incurring a debt to transfer property in the future. In the latter case, subsection (c)(1) establishes a clear rule that the legality of the distribution is tested when the debt is actually incurred, not later when the debt is actually paid. Under Section 406(e), indebtedness is not considered a liability for purposes of subsection (a) if the terms of the indebtedness itself provide that payments can be made only if and to the extent that a payment of a distribution could then be made under this section. The effect makes the holder of the indebtedness junior to all other creditors but senior to members in their capacity as members.

§ 407. Liability for unlawful distributions.

(a) A member of a member-managed company or a member or manager of a manager-managed company who votes for or assents to a distribution made in violation of Section 406, the articles of organization, or the operating agreement is personally liable to the company for the amount of the distribution which exceeds the amount that could have been distributed without violating Section 406, the articles of organization, or the operating agreement if it is established that the member or manager did not perform the member's or manager's duties in compliance with Section 409.

(b) A member of a manager-managed company who knew a distribution was made in violation of Section 406, the articles of organization, or the operating agreement is personally liable to the company, but only to the extent that the distribution received by the member exceeded the amount that could have been properly paid under Section 406.

(c) A member or manager against whom an action is brought under this section may implead in the action all:

(1) other members or managers who voted for or assented to the distribution in violation of subsection (a) and may compel contribution from them; and

(2) members who received a distribution in violation of subsection (b) and may compel contribution from the member in the amount received in violation of subsection (b).

(d) A proceeding under this section is barred unless it is commenced within two years after the distribution.

Comment

Whenever members or managers fail to meet the standards of conduct of Section 409 and vote for or assent to an unlawful distribution, they are personally liable to the company for the portion of the distribution that exceeds the maximum amount that could have been lawfully distributed.

The recovery remedy under this section extends only to the company, not the company's creditors. Under subsection (a), members and managers are not liable for an unlawful distribution provided their vote in favor of the distribution satisfies the duty of care of Section 409(c).

Subsection (a) creates personal liability in favor of the company against members or managers who approve an unlawful distribution for the entire amount of a distribution that could not be lawfully distributed. Subsection (b) creates personal liability against only members who knowingly received the unlawful distribution, but only in the amount measured by the portion of the actual distribution received that was not lawfully made. Members who both vote for or assent to an unlawful distribution and receive a portion or all of the distribution will be liable, at the election of the company, under either but not both subsections.

A member or manager who is liable under subsection (a) may seek contribution under subsection (c)(1) from other members and managers who also voted for or assented to the same distribution and may also seek recoupment under subsection (c)(2) from members who received the distribution, but only if they accepted the payments knowing they were unlawful.

The two-year statute of limitations of subsection (d) is measured from the date of the distribution. The date of the distribution is determined under Section 406(c).

§ 408. Member's right to information.

(a) A limited liability company shall provide members and their agents and attorneys access to its records, if any, at the company's principal office or other reasonable locations specified in the operating agreement. The company shall provide former members and their agents and attorneys access for proper purposes to records pertaining to the period during which they were members. The right of access provides the opportunity to inspect and copy records during ordinary business hours. The company may impose a reasonable charge, limited to the costs of labor and material, for copies of records furnished.

(b) A limited liability company shall furnish to a member, and to the legal representative of a deceased member or member under legal disability:

(1) without demand, information concerning the company's business or affairs reasonably required for the proper exercise of the member's rights and performance of the member's duties under the operating agreement or this [Act]; and

(2) on demand, other information concerning the company's business or affairs, except to the extent the demand or the information demanded is unreasonable or otherwise improper under the circumstances.

(c) A member has the right upon written demand given to the limited liability company to obtain at the company's expense a copy of any written operating agreement.

Comment

Recognizing the informality of many limited liability companies, subsection (a) does not require a company to maintain any records. In general, a company should maintain records necessary to enable members to determine their share of profits and losses and their rights on dissociation. If inadequate records are maintained to determine those and other critical rights, a member may maintain an action for an accounting under Section 410(a). Normally, a company will maintain at least records required by state or federal authorities regarding tax and other filings.

The obligation to furnish access includes the obligation to insure that all records, if any, are accessible in intelligible form. For example, a company that switches computer systems has an obligation either to convert the records from the old system or retain at least one computer capable of accessing the records from the old system.

The right to inspect and copy records maintained is not conditioned on a member or former member's purpose or motive. However, an abuse of the access and copy right may create a remedy in favor of the other members as a violation of the requesting member or former member's obligation of good faith and fair dealing. See Section 409(d).

Although a company is not required to maintain any records under subsection (a), it is nevertheless subject to a disclosure duty to furnish specified information under subsection (b)(1). A company must therefore furnish to members, without demand, information reasonably needed for members to exercise their rights and duties as members. A member's exercise of these duties justifies an unqualified right of access to the company's records. The member's right to company records may not be unreasonably restricted by the operating agreement. See Section 103(b)(1).

§ 409. General standards of member's and manager's conduct.

(a) The only fiduciary duties a member owes to a member-managed company and its other members are the duty of loyalty and the duty of care imposed by subsections (b) and (c).

(b) A member's duty of loyalty to a member-managed company and its other members is limited to the following:

(1) to account to the company and to hold as trustee for it any property, profit, or benefit derived by the member in the conduct or winding up of the company's business or derived from a use by the member of the company's property, including the appropriation of a company's opportunity;

(2) to refrain from dealing with the company in the conduct or winding up of the company's business as or on behalf of a party having an interest adverse to the company; and

(3) to refrain from competing with the company in the conduct of the company's business before the dissolution of the company.

(c) A member's duty of care to a member-managed company and its other members in the conduct of and winding up of the company's business is limited to refraining from engaging in grossly negligent or reckless conduct, intentional misconduct, or a knowing violation of law.

(d) A member shall discharge the duties to a member-managed company and its other members under this [Act] or under the operating agreement and exercise any rights consistently with the obligation of good faith and fair dealing.

(e) A member of a member-managed company does not violate a duty or obligation under this [Act] or under the operating agreement merely because the member's conduct furthers the member's own interest.

(f) A member of a member-managed company may lend money to and transact other business with the company. As to each loan or transaction, the rights and obligations of the member are the same as those of a person who is not a member, subject to other applicable law.

(g) This section applies to a person winding up the limited liability company's business as the personal or legal representative of the last surviving member as if the person were a member.

(h) In a manager-managed company:

(1) a member who is not also a manager owes no duties to the company or to the other members solely by reason of being a member;

(2) a manager is held to the same standards of conduct prescribed for members in subsections (b) through (f);

(3) a member who pursuant to the operating agreement exercises some or all of the rights of a manager in the management and conduct of the company's business is held to the standards of conduct in subsections (b) through (f) to the extent that the member exercises the managerial authority vested in a manager by this [Act]; and

(4) a manager is relieved of liability imposed by law for violation of the standards prescribed by subsections (b) through (f) to the extent of the managerial authority delegated to the members by the operating agreement.

Comment

Under subsections (a), (c), and (h), members and managers, and their delegatees, owe to the company and to the other members and managers only the fiduciary duties of loyalty and care set forth in subsections (b) and (c) and the obligation of good faith and fair dealing set forth in subsection (d). An operating agreement may not waive or eliminate the duties or obligation, but may, if not manifestly unreasonable, identify activities and determine standards for measuring the performance of them. *See* Section 103(b)(2) to (4).

Upon a member's dissociation, the duty to account for personal profits under subsection (b)(1), the duty to refrain from acting as or representing adverse interests under subsection (b)(2), and the duty of care under subsection (c) are limited to those derived from matters arising or events occurring before the dissociation unless the member participates in winding up the company's business. Also, the duty not to compete terminates upon dissociation. *See* Section 603(b)(3) and (b)(2). However, a dissociated member is not free to use confidential company information after dissociation. For example, a dissociated member of a company may immediately compete with the company for new clients but must exercise care in completing on-going client transactions and must account to the company for any fees from the old clients on account of those transactions. Subsection (c) adopts a gross negligence standard for the duty of care, the standard actually used in most partnerships and corporations.

Subsection (b)(2) prohibits a member from acting adversely or representing an adverse party to the company. The rule is based on agency principles and seeks to avoid the conflict of opposing interests in the mind of the member agent whose duty is to act for the benefit of the principal company. As reflected in subsection (f), the rule does not prohibit the member from dealing with the company other than as an adversary. A member may generally deal with the company under subsection (f) when the transaction is approved by the company.

Subsection (e) makes clear that a member does not violate the obligation of good faith under subsection (d) merely because the member's conduct furthers that member's own interest. For example, a member's refusal to vote for an interim distribution because of negative tax implications to that member does not violate that member's obligation of good faith to the other members. Likewise, a member may vote against a proposal by the company to open a shopping center that would directly compete with another shopping center in which the member owns an interest.

§ 410. Actions by members.

(a) A member may maintain an action against a limited liability company or another member for legal or equitable relief, with or without an accounting as to the company's business, to enforce:

(1) the member's rights under the operating agreement;

(2) the member's rights under this [Act]; and

(3) the rights and otherwise protect the interests of the member, including rights and interests arising independently of the member's relationship to the company.

(b) The accrual, and any time limited for the assertion, of a right of action for a remedy under this section is governed by other law. A right to an accounting upon a dissolution and winding up does not revive a claim barred by law.

Comment

During the existence of the company, members have under this section access to the courts to resolve claims against the company and other members, leaving broad judicial discretion to fashion appropriate legal remedies. A member pursues only that member's claim against the company or another member under this section. Article 11 governs a member's derivative pursuit of a claim on behalf of the company.

A member may recover against the company and the other members under subsection (a)(3) for personal injuries or damage to the member's property caused by another member. One member's negligence is therefore not imputed to bar another member's action.

§ 411. Continuation of term company after expiration of specified term.

(a) If a term company is continued after the expiration of the specified term, the rights and duties of the members and managers remain the same as they were at the expiration of the term except to the extent inconsistent with rights and duties of members and managers of an at-will company.

(b) If the members in a member-managed company or the managers in a manager-managed company continue the business without any winding up of the business of the company, it continues as an at-will company.

Comment

A term company will generally dissolve upon the expiration of its term unless either its articles are amended before the expiration of the original specified term to provide for an additional specified term or the members or managers simply continue the company as an at-will company under this section. Amendment of the articles specifying an additional term requires the unanimous consent of the members. *See* Section 404(c)(3). Therefore, any member has the right to block the amendment. Absent an amendment to the articles, a company may only be continued under subsection (b) as an at-will company. The decision to continue a term company as an at-will company does not require the unanimous consent of the members and is treated as an ordinary business matter with disputes resolved by a simple majority vote of either the members or managers. *See* Section 404. In that case, subsection (b) provides that the members' conduct amends or becomes part of an operating agreement to "continue" the company as an at-will company. The amendment to the operating agreement does not alter the rights of creditors who suffer detrimental reliance because the company does not liquidate after the expiration of its specified term. *See* Section 203(c)(2).

Preexisting operating-agreement provisions continue to control the relationship of the members under subsection (a) except to the extent inconsistent with the rights and duties of members of an at-will company with an operating agreement containing the same provisions. However, the members could agree in advance that, if the company's business continues after the expiration of its specified term, the company continues as a company with a new specified term or that the provisions of its operating agreement survive the expiration of the specified term.

ARTICLE 5
TRANSFEREES AND CREDITORS OF MEMBER

§ 501. Member's distributional interest.

(a) A member is not a co-owner of, and has no transferable interest in, property of a limited liability company.

(b) A distributional interest in a limited liability company is personal property and, subject to Sections 502 and 503, may be transferred in whole or in part.

(c) An operating agreement may provide that a distributional interest may be evidenced by a certificate of the interest issued by the limited liability company and, subject to Section 503, may also provide for the transfer of any interest represented by the certificate.

Comment

Members have no property interest in property owned by a limited liability company. A distributional interest is personal property and is defined under Section 101(6) as a member's interest in distributions only and does not include the member's broader rights to participate in management under Section 404 and to inspect company records under Section 408.

Under Section 405(a), distributions are allocated in equal shares unless otherwise provided in an operating agreement. Whenever it is desirable to allocate distributions in proportion to contributions rather than per capita, certification may be useful to reduce valuation issues. The effect of certification on the Federal tax classification of the company is determined by federal law.

§ 502. Transfer of distributional interest.

A transfer of a distributional interest does not entitle the transferee to become or to exercise any rights of a member. A transfer entitles the transferee to receive, to the extent transferred, only the distributions to which the transferor would be entitled.

Comment

Under Sections 501(b) and 502, the only interest a member may freely transfer is that member's distributional interest. Only the transfer of all or substantially all of a member's distributional interest constitutes or may constitute a member dissociation. A transfer of less than substantially all of a member's distributional interest is not an event of dissociation. A member ceases to be a member upon the transfer of all that member's distributional interest and that transfer is also an event of dissociation under Section 601(3). Relating the event of dissociation to the member's transfer of all of the member's distributional interest avoids the need for the company to track potential future dissociation events associated with a member no longer financially interested in the company. Also, all the remaining members may expel a member upon the transfer of "substantially all" the member's distributional interest. The expulsion is an event of dissociation under Section 601(5)(ii).

§ 503. Rights of transferee.

(a) A transferee of a distributional interest may become a member of a limited liability company if and to the extent that the transferor gives the transferee the right in accordance with authority described in the operating agreement or all other members consent.

(b) A transferee who has become a member, to the extent transferred, has the rights and powers, and is subject to the restrictions and liabilities, of a member under the operating agreement of a limited liability company and this [Act]. A transferee who becomes a member also is liable for the transferor member's obligations to make contributions under Section 402 and for obligations under Section 407 to return unlawful distributions, but the transferee is not obligated for the transferor member's liabilities unknown to the transferee at the time the transferee becomes a member.

(c) Whether or not a transferee of a distributional interest becomes a member under subsection (a), the transferor is not released from liability to the limited liability company under the operating agreement or this [Act].

(d) A transferee who does not become a member is not entitled to participate in the management or conduct of the limited liability company's business, require access to information concerning the company's transactions, or inspect or copy any of the company's records.

(e) A transferee who does not become a member is entitled to:

(1) receive, in accordance with the transfer, distributions to which the transferor would otherwise be entitled;

(2) receive, upon dissolution and winding up of the limited liability company's business:

(i) in accordance with the transfer, the net amount otherwise distributable to the transferor;

(ii) a statement of account only from the date of the latest statement of account agreed to by all the members;

(3) seek under Section 801(5) a judicial determination that it is equitable to dissolve and wind up the company's business.

(f) A limited liability company need not give effect to a transfer until it has notice of the transfer.

Comment

The only interest a member may freely transfer is the member's distributional interest. A transferee may acquire the remaining rights of a member only by being admitted as a member of the company by all of the remaining members. The effect of these default rules and any modifications on the Federal tax classification of the company is determined by federal law.

A transferee not admitted as a member is not entitled to participate in management, require access to information, or inspect or copy company records. The only rights of a transferee are to receive the distributions the transferor would otherwise be entitled, receive a limited statement of account, and seek a judicial dissolution under Section 801(5).

Subsection (e) sets forth the rights of a transferee of an existing member. Although the rights of a dissociated member to participate in the future management of the company parallel the rights of a transferee, a dissociated member retains additional rights that accrued from that person's membership such as the right to enforce Article 7 purchase rights. See and compare Sections 603(b)(1) and 801(4) and Comments.

§ 504. Rights of creditor.

(a) On application by a judgment creditor of a member of a limited liability company or of a member's transferee, a court having jurisdiction may charge the distributional interest of the judgment debtor to satisfy the judgment. The court may appoint a receiver of the share of the distributions due or to become due to the judgment debtor and make all other orders, directions, accounts, and inquiries the judgment debtor might have made or which the circumstances may require to give effect to the charging order.

(b) A charging order constitutes a lien on the judgment debtor's distributional interest. The court may order a foreclosure of a lien on a distributional interest subject to the charging order at any time. A purchaser at the foreclosure sale has the rights of a transferee.

(c) At any time before foreclosure, a distributional interest in a limited liability company which is charged may be redeemed:

(1) by the judgment debtor;

(2) with property other than the company's property, by one or more of the other members; or

(3) with the company's property, but only if permitted by the operating agreement.

(d) This [Act] does not affect a member's right under exemption laws with respect to the member's distributional interest in a limited liability company.

(e) This section provides the exclusive remedy by which a judgment creditor of a member or a transferee may satisfy a judgment out of the judgment debtor's distributional interest in a limited liability company.

Comment

A charging order is the only remedy by which a judgment creditor of a member or a member's transferee may reach the distributional interest of a member or member's transferee. Under Section 503(e), the distributional interest of a member or transferee is limited to the member's right to receive distributions from the company and to seek judicial liquidation of the company.

ARTICLE 6
MEMBER'S DISSOCIATION

§ 601. Events causing member's dissociation.

A member is dissociated from a limited liability company upon the occurrence of any of the following events:

(1) the company's having notice of the member's express will to withdraw upon the date of notice or on a later date specified by the member;

(2) an event agreed to in the operating agreement as causing the member's dissociation;

(3) upon transfer of all of a member's distributional interest, other than a transfer for security purposes or a court order charging the member's distributional interest which has not been foreclosed;

(4) the member's expulsion pursuant to the operating agreement;

(5) the member's expulsion by unanimous vote of the other members if:

(i) it is unlawful to carry on the company's business with the member;

(ii) there has been a transfer of substantially all of the member's distributional interest, other than a transfer for security purposes or a court order charging the member's distributional interest which has not been foreclosed;

(iii) within 90 days after the company notifies a corporate member that it will be expelled because it has filed a certificate of dissolution or the equivalent, its charter has been revoked, or its right to conduct business has been suspended by the jurisdiction of its incorporation, the member fails to obtain a revocation of the certificate of dissolution or a reinstatement of its charter or its right to conduct business; or

(iv) a partnership or a limited liability company that is a member has been dissolved and its business is being wound up;

(6) on application by the company or another member, the member's expulsion by judicial determination because the member:

(i) engaged in wrongful conduct that adversely and materially affected the company's business;

(ii) willfully or persistently committed a material breach of the operating agreement or of a duty owed to the company or the other members under Section 409; or

(iii) engaged in conduct relating to the company's business which makes it not reasonably practicable to carry on the business with the member;

(7) the member's:

(i) becoming a debtor in bankruptcy;

(ii) executing an assignment for the benefit of creditors;

(iii) seeking, consenting to, or acquiescing in the appointment of a trustee, receiver, or liquidator of the member or of all or substantially all of the member's property; or

(iv) failing, within 90 days after the appointment, to have vacated or stayed the appointment of a trustee, receiver, or liquidator of the member or of all or substantially all of the member's property obtained without the member's consent or acquiescence, or failing within 90 days after the expiration of a stay to have the appointment vacated;

(8) in the case of a member who is an individual:

(i) the member's death;

(ii) the appointment of a guardian or general conservator for the member; or

(iii) a judicial determination that the member has otherwise become incapable of performing the member's duties under the operating agreement;

(9) in the case of a member that is a trust or is acting as a member by virtue of being a trustee of a trust, distribution of the trust's entire rights to receive distributions from the company, but not merely by reason of the substitution of a successor trustee;

(10) in the case of a member that is an estate or is acting as a member by virtue of being a personal representative of an estate, distribution of the estate's entire rights to receive distributions from the company, but not merely the substitution of a successor personal representative; or

(11) termination of the existence of a member if the member is not an individual, estate, or trust other than a business trust.

Comment

The term "dissociation" refers to the change in the relationships among the dissociated member, the company and the other members caused by a member's ceasing to be associated in the carrying on of the company's business.

A member may be expelled from the company under paragraph (5)(ii) by the unanimous vote of the other members upon a transfer of "substantially all" of the member's distributional interest other than for a transfer as security for a loan. A transfer of "all" of the member's distributional interest is an event of dissociation under paragraph (3).

Although a member is dissociated upon death, the effect of the dissociation where the company does not dissolve depends upon whether the company is at-will or term and whether manager-managed. Only the decedent's distributional interest transfers to the decedent's estate which does not acquire the decedent member's management rights. See Section 603(b)(1). Unless otherwise agreed, if the company was at-will, the estate's distributional interest must be purchased by the company at fair value determined at the date of death. However, if a term company, the estate and its transferees continue only as the owner of the distributional interest with no management rights until the expiration of the specified term that existed on the date of death. At the expiration of that term, the company must purchase the interest of a dissociated member if the company continues for an additional term by amending its articles or simply continues as an at-will company. See Sections 411 and 701(a)(2) and Comments. Before that time, the estate and its transferees have the right to make application for a judicial dissolution of the company under Section 801(4) as successors in interest to a dissociated member. See Comments to Sections 801, 411, and 701. Where the members have allocated management rights on the basis of contributions rather than simply the number of members, a member's death will result in a transfer of management rights to the remaining members on a proportionate basis. This transfer of rights may be avoided by a provision in an operating agreement extending the Section 701(a)(1) at-will purchase right to a decedent member of a term company.

§ 602. Member's power to dissociate; wrongful dissociation.

(a) Unless otherwise provided in the operating agreement, a member has the power to dissociate from a limited liability company at any time, rightfully or wrongfully, by express will pursuant to Section 601(1).

(b) If the operating agreement has not eliminated a member's power to dissociate, the member's dissociation from a limited liability company is wrongful only if:

(1) it is in breach of an express provision of the agreement; or

(2) before the expiration of the specified term of a term company:

(i) the member withdraws by express will;

(ii) the member is expelled by judicial determination under Section 601(6);

(iii) the member is dissociated by becoming a debtor in bankruptcy; or

(iv) in the case of a member who is not an individual, trust other than a business trust, or estate, the member is expelled or otherwise dissociated because it willfully dissolved or terminated its existence.

(c) A member who wrongfully dissociates from a limited liability company is liable to the company and to the other members for damages caused by the dissociation. The liability is in addition to any other obligation of the member to the company or to the other members.

(d) If a limited liability company does not dissolve and wind up its business as a result of a member's wrongful dissociation under subsection (b), damages sustained by the company for the wrongful dissociation must be offset against distributions otherwise due the member after the dissociation.

Comment

A member has the power to withdraw from both an at-will company and a term company although the effects of the withdrawal are remarkably different. *See* Comments to Section 601. At a minimum, the exercise of a power to withdraw enables members to terminate their continuing duties of loyalty and care. *See* Section 603(b)(2) to (3).

A member's power to withdraw by express will may be eliminated by an operating agreement. An operating agreement may eliminate a member's power to withdraw by express will to promote the business continuity of an at-will company by removing the threat of dissolution and to eliminate the member's right to force the company to purchase the member's distributional interest. *See* Sections 801(b)(3) and 701(a)(1). However, such a member retains the ability to seek a judicial dissolution of the company. *See* Section 801(4).

If a member's power to withdraw by express will is not eliminated in an operating agreement, the withdrawal may nevertheless be made wrongful under subsection (b). All dissociations, including withdrawal by express will, may be made wrongful under subsection (b)(l) in both an at-will and term company by the inclusion of a provision in an operating agreement. Even where an operating agreement does not eliminate the power to withdraw by express will or make any dissociation wrongful, the dissociation of a member of a term company for the reasons specified under subsection (b)(2) is wrongful. The member is liable to the company and other members for damages caused by a wrongful dissociation under subsection (c) and, under subsection (d), the damages may be offset against all distributions otherwise due the member after the dissociation. Section 701(f) provides a similar rule permitting damages for wrongful dissociation to be offset against any company purchase of the member's distributional interest.

§ 603. Effect of member's dissociation.

(a) Upon a member's dissociation:

(1) in an at-will company, the company must cause the dissociated member's distributional interest to be purchased under [Article] 7; and

(2) in a term company:

(i) if the company dissolves and winds up its business on or before the expiration of its specified term, [Article] 8 applies to determine the dissociated member's rights to distributions; and

(ii) if the company does not dissolve and wind up its business on or before the expiration of its specified term, the company must cause the dissociated member's distributional interest to be purchased under [Article] 7 on the date of the expiration of the term specified at the time of the member's dissociation.

(b) Upon a member's dissociation from a limited liability company:

(1) the member's right to participate in the management and conduct of the company's business terminates, except as otherwise provided in Section 803, and the member ceases to be a member and is treated the same as a transferee of a member;

(2) the member's duty of loyalty under Section 409(b)(3) terminates; and

(3) the member's duty of loyalty under Section 409(b)(1) and (2) and duty of care under Section 409(c) continue only with regard to matters

arising and events occurring before the member's dissociation, unless the member participates in winding up the company's business pursuant to Section 803.

Comment

Dissociation from an at-will company that does not dissolve the company causes the dissociated member's distributional interest to be immediately purchased under Article 7. *See* Comments to Sections 602 and 603. Dissociation from a term company that does not dissolve the company does not cause the dissociated member's distributional interest to be purchased under Article 7 until the expiration of the specified term that existed on the date of dissociation.

Subsection (b)(1) provides that a dissociated member forfeits the right to participate in the future conduct of the company's business. Dissociation does not however forfeit that member's right to enforce the Article 7 rights that accrue by reason of the dissociation. Similarly, where dissociation occurs by death, the decedent member's successors in interest may enforce that member's Article 7 rights. See and compare Comments to Section 503(e).

Dissociation terminates the member's right to participate in management, including the member's actual authority to act for the company under Section 301, and begins the two-year period after which a member's apparent authority conclusively ends. *See* Comments to Section 703. Dissociation also terminates a member's continuing duties of loyalty and care, except with regard to continuing transactions, to the company and other members unless the member participates in winding up the company's business. *See* Comments to Section 409.

ARTICLE 7
MEMBER'S DISSOCIATION WHEN BUSINESS NOT WOUND UP

§ 701. Company purchase of distributional interest.

(a) A limited liability company shall purchase a distributional interest of a:

(1) member of an at-will company for its fair value determined as of the date of the member's dissociation if the member's dissociation does not result in a dissolution and winding up of the company's business under Section 801; or

(2) member of a term company for its fair value determined as of the date of the expiration of the specified term that existed on the date of the member's dissociation if the expiration of the specified term does

not result in a dissolution and winding up of the company's business under Section 801.

(b) A limited liability company must deliver a purchase offer to the dissociated member whose distributional interest is entitled to be purchased not later than 30 days after the date determined under subsection (a). The purchase offer must be accompanied by:

(1) a statement of the company's assets and liabilities as of the date determined under subsection (a);

(2) the latest available balance sheet and income statement, if any; and

(3) an explanation of how the estimated amount of the payment was calculated.

(c) If the price and other terms of a purchase of a distributional interest are fixed or are to be determined by the operating agreement, the price and terms so fixed or determined govern the purchase unless the purchaser defaults. If a default occurs, the dissociated member is entitled to commence a proceeding to have the company dissolved under Section 801(4)(iv).

(d) If an agreement to purchase the distributional interest is not made within 120 days after the date determined under subsection (a), the dissociated member, within another 120 days, may commence a proceeding against the limited liability company to enforce the purchase. The company at its expense shall notify in writing all of the remaining members, and any other person the court directs, of the commencement of the proceeding. The jurisdiction of the court in which the proceeding is commenced under this subsection is plenary and exclusive.

(e) The court shall determine the fair value of the distributional interest in accordance with the standards set forth in Section 702 together with the terms for the purchase. Upon making these determinations, the court shall order the limited liability company to purchase or cause the purchase of the interest.

(f) Damages for wrongful dissociation under Section 602(b), and all other amounts owing, whether or not currently due, from the dissociated member to a limited liability company, must be offset against the purchase price.

Comment

This section sets forth default rules regarding an otherwise mandatory company purchase of a distributional interest. Even though a dissociated member's rights to participate in the future management of the company are equivalent to those of a transferee of a member, the dissociation does not forfeit that member's right to enforce the Article 7 purchase right.

Similarly, if the dissociation occurs by reason of death, the decedent member's successors in interest may enforce the Article 7 rights. *See* Comments to Sections 503(e) and 603(b)(1).

An at-will company must purchase a dissociated member's distributional interest under subsection (a)(l) when that member's dissociation does not result in a dissolution of the company. The purchase price is equal to the fair value of the interest determined as of the date of dissociation. Any damages for wrongful dissociation must be offset against the purchase price.

Dissociation from a term company does not require an immediate purchase of the member's interest. A term company must only purchase the dissociated member's distributional interest under subsection (a)(2) on the expiration of the specified term that existed on the date of the member's dissociation. The purchase price is equal to the fair value of the interest determined as of the date of the expiration of that specified term. Any damages for wrongful dissociation must be offset against the purchase price.

The valuation dates differ between subsections (a)(l) and (a)(2) purchases. The former is valued on the date of member dissociation whereas the latter is valued on the date of the expiration of the specified term that existed on the date of dissociation. A subsection (a)(2) dissociated member therefore assumes the risk of loss between the date of dissociation and the expiration of the then stated specified term. *See* Comments to Section 801 (dissociated member may file application to dissolve company under Section 801 (5).

The default valuation standard is fair value. *See* Comments to Section 702. An operating agreement may fix a method or formula for determining the purchase price and the terms of payment. The purchase right may be modified. For example, an operating agreement may eliminate a member's power to withdraw from an at-will company which narrows the dissociation events contemplated under subsection (a)(l). *See* Comments to Section 602(a). However, a provision in an operating agreement providing for complete forfeiture of the purchase right may be unenforceable where the power to dissociate has not also been eliminated. *See* Section 104(a).

The company must deliver a purchase offer to the dissociated member within 30 days after the date determined under subsection (a). The offer must be accompanied by information designed to enable the dissociated member to evaluate the fairness of the offer. The subsection (b)(3) explanation of how the offer price was calculated need not be elaborate. For example, a mere statement of the basis of the calculation, such as "book value," may be sufficient.

The company and the dissociated member must reach an agreement on the purchase price and terms within 120 days after the date determined under subsection (a). Otherwise, the dissociated member may file suit within another 120 days to enforce the purchase under subsection (d). The court will then determine the fair value and terms of purchase under subsection (e). *See* Section 702. The member's lawsuit is not available under subsection (c) if the parties have previously agreed to price and terms in an operating agreement.

§ 702. Court action to determine fair value of distributional interest.

(a) In an action brought to determine the fair value of a distributional interest in a limited liability company, the court shall:

(1) determine the fair value of the interest, considering among other relevant evidence the going concern value of the company, any agreement among some or all of the members fixing the price or specifying a formula for determining value of distributional interests for any other purpose, the recommendations of any appraiser appointed by the court, and any legal constraints on the company's ability to purchase the interest;

(2) specify the terms of the purchase, including, if appropriate, terms for installment payments, subordination of the purchase obligation to the rights of the company's other creditors, security for a deferred purchase price, and a covenant not to compete or other restriction on a dissociated member; and

(3) require the dissociated member to deliver an assignment of the interest to the purchaser upon receipt of the purchase price or the first installment of the purchase price.

(b) After the dissociated member delivers the assignment, the dissociated member has no further claim against the company, its members, officers, or managers, if any, other than a claim to any unpaid balance of the purchase price and a claim under any agreement with the company or the remaining members that is not terminated by the court.

(c) If the purchase is not completed in accordance with the specified terms, the company is to be dissolved upon application under Section 801(4)(iv). If a limited liability company is so dissolved, the dissociated member has the same rights and priorities in the company's assets as if the sale had not been ordered.

(d) If the court finds that a party to the proceeding acted arbitrarily, vexatiously, or not in good faith, it may award one or more other parties their reasonable expenses, including attorney's fees and the expenses of appraisers or other experts, incurred in the proceeding. The finding may be based on the company's failure to make an offer to pay or to comply with Section 701(b).

(e) Interest must be paid on the amount awarded from the date determined under Section 701(a) to the date of payment.

Comment

The default valuation standard is fair value. Under this broad standard, a court is free to determine the fair value of a distributional interest on a fair market, liquidation, or any other method deemed appropriate under the circumstances. A fair market value standard is not used because it is too narrow, often inappropriate, and assumes a fact not contemplated by this section -a willing buyer and a willing seller.

The court has discretion under subsection (a)(2) to include in its order any conditions the court deems necessary to safeguard the interests of the company and the dissociated member or transferee. The discretion may be based on the financial and other needs of the parties.

If the purchase is not consummated or the purchaser defaults, the dissociated member or transferee may make application for dissolution of the company under subsection (c). The court may deny the petition for good cause but the proceeding affords the company an opportunity to be heard on the matter and avoid dissolution. *See* Comments to Section 801(b)(5).

The power of the court to award all costs and attorney's fees incurred in the suit under subsection (d) is an incentive for both parties to act in good faith. *See* Section 701(c).

§ 703. Dissociated member's power to bind limited liability company.

For two years after a member dissociates without the dissociation resulting in a dissolution and winding up of a limited liability company's business, the company, including a surviving company under [Article] 9, is bound by an act of the dissociated member which would have bound the company under Section 301 before dissociation only if at the time of entering into the transaction the other party:

(1) reasonably believed that the dissociated member was then a member;

(2) did not have notice of the member's dissociation; and

(3) is not deemed to have had notice under Section 704.

Comment

A dissociated member of a member-managed company does not have actual authority to act for the company. *See* Section 603(b)(1). Under Section 301(a), a dissociated member of a member-managed company has apparent authority to bind the company in ordinary course transactions except as to persons who knew or had notice of the dissociation. This section modifies that rule by requiring the person to show reasonable reliance on the member's status as a member provided a Section 704 statement has not been filed within the previous 90 days. *See also* Section 804 (power to bind after dissolution).

§ 704. Statement of dissociation.

(a) A dissociated member or a limited liability company may file in the office of the [Secretary of State] a statement of dissociation stating the name of the company and that the member is dissociated from the company.

(b) For the purposes of Sections 301 and 703, a person not a member is deemed to have notice of the dissociation 90 days after the statement of dissociation is filed.

ARTICLE 8
WINDING UP COMPANY'S BUSINESS

§ 801. Events causing dissolution and winding up of company's business.

A limited liability company is dissolved, and its business must be wound up, upon the occurrence of any of the following events:

(1) an event specified in the operating agreement;

(2) consent of the number or percentage of members specified in the operating agreement;

(3) an event that makes it unlawful for all or substantially all of the business of the company to be continued, but any cure of illegality within 90 days after notice to the company of the event is effective retroactively to the date of the event for purposes of this section;

(4) on application by a member or a dissociated member, upon entry of a judicial decree that:

(i) the economic purpose of the company is likely to be unreasonably frustrated;

(ii) another member has engaged in conduct relating to the company's business that makes it not reasonably practicable to carry on the company's business with that member;

(iii) it is not otherwise reasonably practicable to carry on the company's business in conformity with the articles of organization and the operating agreement;

(iv) the company failed to purchase the petitioner's distributional interest as required by Section 701; or

(v) the managers or members in control of the company have acted, are acting, or will act in a manner that is illegal, oppressive, fraudulent, or unfairly prejudicial to the petitioner; or

(5) on application by a transferee of a member's interest, a judicial determination that it is equitable to wind up the company's business:

(i) after the expiration of the specified term, if the company was for a specified term at the time the applicant became a transferee by member dissociation, transfer, or entry of a charging order that gave rise to the transfer; or

(ii) at any time, if the company was at will at the time the applicant became a transferee by member dissociation, transfer, or entry of a charging order that gave rise to the transfer.

Comment

The dissolution rules of this section are mostly default rules and may be modified by an operating agreement. However, an operating agreement may not modify or eliminate the dissolution events specified in subsection (3) (illegal business) or subsection (4) (member application). *See* Section 103(b)(6).

A member or dissociated member whose interest is not required to be purchased by the company under Section 701 may make application under subsection (4) for the involuntary dissolution of both an at-will company and a term company. A transferee may make application under subsection (5). A transferee's application right, but not that of a member or dissociated member, may be modified by an operating agreement. *See* Section 103(b)(6). A dissociated member is not treated as a transferee for purposes of an application under subsections (4) and (5). *See* Section 603(b)(1). For example, this affords reasonable protection to a dissociated member of a term company to make application under subsection (4) before the expiration of the term that existed at the time of dissociation. For purposes of a subsection (4) application, a dissociated member includes a successor in interest, e.g., surviving spouse. *See* Comments to Section 601.

In the case of applications under subsections (4) and (5), the applicant has the burden of proving either the existence of one or more of the circumstances listed under subsection (4) or that it is equitable to wind up the company's business under subsection (5). Proof of the existence of one or more of the circumstances in subsection (4), may be the basis of a subsection (5) application. Even where the burden of proof is met, the court has the discretion to order relief other than the dissolution of the company. Examples include an accounting, a declaratory judgment, a distribution, the purchase of the distributional interest of the applicant or another member, or the appointment of a receiver. *See* Section 410.

A court has the discretion to dissolve a company under subsection (4)(i) when the company has a very poor financial record that is not likely to improve. In this instance, dissolution is an alternative to placing the company in bankruptcy. A court may dissolve a company under subsections (4)(ii), (4)(iii), and (4)(iv) for serious and protracted misconduct by one or more members. Subsection (4)(v) provides a specific remedy for an improper squeeze-out of a member.

In determining whether and what type of relief to order under subsections (4) and (5) involuntary dissolution suits, a court should take into account other rights and remedies of the applicant. For example, a court should not grant involuntary dissolution of an at-will company if the applicant member has the right to dissociate and force the company to purchase that member's distributional interest under Sections 701 and 702. In other cases, involuntary dissolution or some other remedy such as a buy-out might be appropriate where, for example, one or more members have (i) engaged in fraudulent or unconscionable conduct, (ii) improperly expelled a member seeking an unfair advantage of a provision in an operating agreement that provides for a significantly lower price on expulsion than would be payable in the event of voluntary dissociation, or (iii) engaged in serious misconduct and the applicant member is a member of a term company and would not have a right to have the company purchase that member's distributional interest upon dissociation until the expiration of the company's specified term.

§ 802. Limited liability company continues after dissolution.

(a) Subject to subsection (b), a limited liability company continues after dissolution only for the purpose of winding up its business.

(b) At any time after the dissolution of a limited liability company and before the winding up of its business is completed, the members, including a dissociated member whose dissociation caused the dissolution, may unanimously waive the right to have the company's business wound up and the company terminated. In that case:

(1) the limited liability company resumes carrying on its business as if dissolution had never occurred and any liability incurred by the company or a member after the dissolution and before the waiver is determined as if the dissolution had never occurred; and

(2) the rights of a third party accruing under Section 804(a) or arising out of conduct in reliance on the dissolution before the third party knew or received a notification of the waiver are not adversely affected.

Comment

The liability shield continues in effect for the winding up period because the legal existence of the company continues under subsection (a). The company is terminated on the filing of articles of termination. *See* Section 805.

§ 803. Right to wind up limited liability company's business.

(a) After dissolution, a member who has not wrongfully dissociated may participate in winding up a limited liability company's business, but on application of any member, member's legal representative, or transferee, the [designate the appropriate court], for good cause shown, may order judicial supervision of the winding up.

(b) A legal representative of the last surviving member may wind up a limited liability company's business.

(c) A person winding up a limited liability company's business may preserve the company's business or property as a going concern for a reasonable time, prosecute and defend actions and proceedings, whether civil, criminal, or administrative, settle and close the company's business, dispose of and transfer the company's property, discharge the company's liabilities, distribute the assets of the company pursuant to Section 806, settle disputes by mediation or arbitration, and perform other necessary acts.

§ 804. Member's or manager's power and liability as agent after dissolution.

(a) A limited liability company is bound by a member's or manager's act after dissolution that:

(1) is appropriate for winding up the company's business; or

(2) would have bound the company under Section 301 before dissolution, if the other party to the transaction did not have notice of the dissolution.

(b) A member or manager who, with knowledge of the dissolution, subjects a limited liability company to liability by an act that is not appropriate for winding up the company's business is liable to the company for any damage caused to the company arising from the liability.

Comment

After dissolution, members and managers continue to have the authority to bind the company that they had prior to dissolution provided that the third party did not have notice of the dissolution. *See* Section 102(b) (notice defined). Otherwise, they have only the authority appropriate for winding up the company's business. *See* Section 703 (agency power of member after dissociation).

§ 805. Articles of termination.

(a) At any time after dissolution and winding up, a limited liability company may terminate its existence by filing with the [Secretary of State] articles of termination stating:

(1) the name of the company;

(2) the date of the dissolution; and

(3) that the company's business has been wound up and the legal existence of the company has been terminated.

(b) The existence of a limited liability company is terminated upon the filing of the articles of termination, or upon a later effective date, if specified in the articles of termination.

Comment

The termination of legal existence also terminates the company's liability shield. *See* Comments to Section 802 (liability shield continues in effect during winding up). It also ends the company's responsibility to file an annual report. *See* Section 211.

§ 806. Distribution of assets in winding up limited liability company's business.

(a) In winding up a limited liability company's business, the assets of the company must be applied to discharge its obligations to creditors, including members who are creditors. Any surplus must be applied to pay in money the net amount distributable to members in accordance with their right to distributions under subsection (b).

(b) Each member is entitled to a distribution upon the winding up of the limited liability company's business consisting of a return of all contributions which have not previously been returned and a distribution of any remainder in equal shares.

§ 807. Known claims against dissolved limited liability company.

(a) A dissolved limited liability company may dispose of the known claims against it by following the procedure described in this section.

(b) A dissolved limited liability company shall notify its known claimants in writing of the dissolution. The notice must:

(1) specify the information required to be included in a claim;

(2) provide a mailing address where the claim is to be sent;

(3) state the deadline for receipt of the claim, which may not be less than 120 days after the date the written notice is received by the claimant; and

(4) state that the claim will be barred if not received by the deadline.

(c) A claim against a dissolved limited liability company is barred if the requirements of subsection (b) are met, and:

(1) the claim is not received by the specified deadline; or

(2) in the case of a claim that is timely received but rejected by the dissolved company, the claimant does not commence a proceeding to enforce the claim within 90 days after the receipt of the notice of the rejection.

(d) For purposes of this section, "claim" does not include a contingent liability or a claim based on an event occurring after the effective date of dissolution.

Comment

A known claim will be barred when the company provides written notice to a claimant that a claim must be filed with the company no later than at least 120 days after receipt of the written notice and the claimant fails to file the claim. If the claim is timely received but is rejected by the company, the claim is nevertheless barred unless the claimant files suit to enforce the claim within 90 days after the receipt of the notice of rejection. A claim described in subsection (d) is not a "known" claim and is governed by Section 808. This section does not extend any other applicable statutes of limitation. *See* Section 104. Depending on the management of the company, members or managers must discharge or make provision for discharging all of the company's known liabilities before distributing the remaining assets to the members. *See* Sections 806(a), 406, and 407.

§ 808. Other claims against dissolved limited liability company.

(a) A dissolved limited liability company may publish notice of its dissolution and request persons having claims against the company to present them in accordance with the notice.

(b) The notice must:

(1) be published at least once in a newspaper of general circulation in the [county] in which the dissolved limited liability company's principal office is located or, if none in this State, in which its designated office is or was last located;

(2) describe the information required to be contained in a claim and provide a mailing address where the claim is to be sent; and

(3) state that a claim against the limited liability company is barred unless a proceeding to enforce the claim is commenced within five years after publication of the notice.

(c) If a dissolved limited liability company publishes a notice in accordance with subsection (b), the claim of each of the following claimants is barred unless the claimant commences a proceeding to enforce the claim against the dissolved company within five years after the publication date of the notice:

(1) a claimant who did not receive written notice under Section 807;

(2) a claimant whose claim was timely sent to the dissolved company but not acted on; and

(3) a claimant whose claim is contingent or based on an event occurring after the effective date of dissolution.

(d) A claim not barred under this section may be enforced:

(1) against the dissolved limited liability company, to the extent of its undistributed assets; or

(2) if the assets have been distributed in liquidation, against a member of the dissolved company to the extent of the member's proportionate share of the claim or the company's assets distributed to the member in liquidation, whichever is less, but a member's total liability for all claims under this section may not exceed the total amount of assets distributed to the member.

Comment

An unknown claim will be barred when the company publishes notice requesting claimants to file claims with the company and stating that claims will be barred unless the claimant files suit to enforce the claim within five years after the date of publication. The procedure also bars known claims where the claimant either did not receive written notice described in Section 807 or received notice, mailed a claim, but the company did not act on the claim.

Depending on the management of the company, members or managers must discharge or make provision for discharging all of the company's known liabilities before distributing the remaining assets to the members. *See* Comment to Section 807. This section does not contemplate that a company will postpone member distributions until all unknown claims are barred under this section. In appropriate cases, the company may purchase insurance or set aside funds permitting a distribution of the remaining assets. Where winding up distributions have been made to members, subsection (d)(2) authorizes recovery against those members. However, a claimant's recovery against a member is limited to the lesser of the member's proportionate share of the claim or the amount received in the distribution. This section does not extend any other applicable statutes of limitation. *See* Section 104.

§ 809. Grounds for administrative dissolution.

The [Secretary of State] may commence a proceeding to dissolve a limited liability company administratively if the company does not:

(1) pay any fees, taxes, or penalties imposed by this [Act] or other law within 60 days after they are due; or

(2) deliver its annual report to the [Secretary of State] within 60 days after it is due.

Comment

Administrative dissolution is an effective enforcement mechanism for a variety of statutory obligations under this Act and it avoids the more expensive judicial dissolution process. When applicable, administrative dissolution avoids wasteful attempts to compel compliance by a company abandoned by its members.

§ 810. Procedure for and effect of administrative dissolution.

(a) If the [Secretary of State] determines that a ground exists for administratively dissolving a limited liability company, the [Secretary of State] shall enter a record of the determination and serve the company with a copy of the record.

(b) If the company does not correct each ground for dissolution or demonstrate to the reasonable satisfaction of the [Secretary of State] that each ground determined by the [Secretary of State] does not exist within 60 days after service of the notice, the [Secretary of State] shall administratively dissolve the company by signing a certification of the dissolution that recites the ground for dissolution and its effective date. The [Secretary of State] shall file the original of the certificate and serve the company with a copy of the certificate.

(c) A company administratively dissolved continues its existence but may carry on only business necessary to wind up and liquidate its business and affairs under Section 802 and to notify claimants under Sections 807 and 808.

(d) The administrative dissolution of a company does not terminate the authority of its agent for service of process.

Comment

A company's failure to comply with a ground for administrative dissolution may simply occur because of oversight. Therefore, subsections (a) and (b) set forth a mandatory notice by the filing officer to the company of the ground for dissolution and a 60 day grace period for correcting the ground.

§ 811. Reinstatement following administrative dissolution.

(a) A limited liability company administratively dissolved may apply to the [Secretary of State] for reinstatement within two years after the effective date of dissolution. The application must:

(1) recite the name of the company and the effective date of its administrative dissolution;

(2) state that the ground for dissolution either did not exist or have [sic] been eliminated;

(3) state that the company's name satisfies the requirements of Section 105; and

(4) contain a certificate from the [taxing authority] reciting that all taxes owed by the company have been paid.

(b) If the [Secretary of State] determines that the application contains the information required by subsection (a) and that the information is correct, the [Secretary of State] shall cancel the certificate of dissolution and prepare a certificate of reinstatement that recites this determination and the effective date of reinstatement, file the original of the certificate, and serve the company with a copy of the certificate.

(c) When reinstatement is effective, it relates back to and takes effect as of the effective date of the administrative dissolution and the company may resume its business as if the administrative dissolution had never occurred.

§ 812. Appeal from denial of reinstatement.

(a) If the [Secretary of State] denies a limited liability company's application for reinstatement following administrative dissolution, the [Secretary of State] shall serve the company with a record that explains the reason or reasons for denial.

(b) The company may appeal the denial of reinstatement to the [name appropriate] court within 30 days after service of the notice of denial is perfected. The company appeals by petitioning the court to set aside the dissolution and attaching to the petition copies of the [Secretary of State's] certificate of dissolution, the company's application for reinstatement, and the [Secretary of State's] notice of denial.

(c) The court may summarily order the [Secretary of State] to reinstate the dissolved company or may take other action the court considers appropriate.

(d) The court's final decision may be appealed as in other civil proceedings.

ARTICLE 9
CONVERSIONS AND MERGERS

§ 901. Definitions.

In this [article]:

(1) "Corporation" means a corporation under [the State Corporation Act], a predecessor law, or comparable law of another jurisdiction.

(2) "General partner" means a partner in a partnership and a general partner in a limited partnership.

(3) "Limited partner" means a limited partner in a limited partnership.

(4) "Limited partnership" means a limited partnership created under [the State Limited Partnership Act], a predecessor law, or comparable law of another jurisdiction.

(5) "Partner" includes a general partner and a limited partner.

(6) "Partnership" means a general partnership under [the State Partnership Act], a predecessor law, or comparable law of another jurisdiction.

(7) "Partnership agreement" means an agreement among the partners concerning the partnership or limited partnership.

(8) "Shareholder" means a shareholder in a corporation.

Comment

Section 907 makes clear that the provisions of Article 9 are not mandatory. Therefore, a partnership or a limited liability company may convert or merge in any other manner provided by law. However, if the requirements of Article 9 are followed, the conversion or merger is legally valid. Article 9 is not restricted to domestic business entities.

§ 902. Conversion of partnership or limited partnership to limited liability company.

(a) A partnership or limited partnership may be converted to a limited liability company pursuant to this section.

(b) The terms and conditions of a conversion of a partnership or limited partnership to a limited liability company must be approved by all of the partners or by a number or percentage of the partners required for conversion in the partnership agreement.

(c) An agreement of conversion must set forth the terms and conditions of the conversion of the interests of partners of a partnership or of a limited partnership, as the case may be, into interests in the converted limited liability company or the cash or other consideration to be paid or delivered as a result of the conversion of the interests of the partners, or a combination thereof.

(d) After a conversion is approved under subsection (b), the partnership or limited partnership shall file articles of organization in the office of the [Secretary of State] which satisfy the requirements of Section 203 and contain:

(1) a statement that the partnership or limited partnership was converted to a limited liability company from a partnership or limited partnership, as the case may be;

(2) its former name;

(3) a statement of the number of votes cast by the partners entitled to vote for and against the conversion and, if the vote is less than unanimous, the number or percentage required to approve the conversion under subsection (b); and

(4) in the case of a limited partnership, a statement that the certificate of limited partnership is to be canceled as of the date the conversion took effect.

(e) In the case of a limited partnership, the filing of articles of organization under subsection (d) cancels its certificate of limited partnership as of the date the conversion took effect.

(f) A conversion takes effect when the articles of organization are filed in the office of the [Secretary of State] or at any later date specified in the articles of organization.

(g) A general partner who becomes a member of a limited liability company as a result of a conversion remains liable as a partner for an obligation incurred by the partnership or limited partnership before the conversion takes effect.

(h) A general partner's liability for all obligations of the limited liability company incurred after the conversion takes effect is that of a member of the company. A limited partner who becomes a member as a result of a conversion remains liable only to the extent the limited partner was liable for an obligation incurred by the limited partnership before the conversion takes effect.

Comment

Subsection (b) makes clear that the terms and conditions of the conversion of a general or limited partnership to a limited liability company must be approved by all of the partners unless the partnership agreement specifies otherwise.

§ 903. Effect of conversion; entity unchanged.

(a) A partnership or limited partnership that has been converted pursuant to this [article] is for all purposes the same entity that existed before the conversion.

(b) When a conversion takes effect:

(1) all property owned by the converting partnership or limited partnership vests in the limited liability company;

(2) all debts, liabilities, and other obligations of the converting partnership or limited partnership continue as obligations of the limited liability company;

(3) an action or proceeding pending by or against the converting partnership or limited partnership may be continued as if the conversion had not occurred;

(4) except as prohibited by other law, all of the rights, privileges, immunities, powers, and purposes of the converting partnership or limited partnership vest in the limited liability company; and

(5) except as otherwise provided in the agreement of conversion under Section 902(c), all of the partners of the converting partnership continue as members of the limited liability company.

Comment

A conversion is not a conveyance or transfer and does not give rise to claims of reverter or impairment of title based on a prohibited conveyance or transfer. Under subsection (b)(1), title to all partnership property, including real estate, vests in the limited liability company as a matter of law without reversion or impairment.

§ 904. Merger of entities.

(a) Pursuant to a plan of merger approved under subsection (c), a limited liability company may be merged with or into one or more limited liability companies, foreign limited liability companies, corporations, foreign corporations, partnerships, foreign partnerships, limited partnerships, foreign limited partnerships, or other domestic or foreign entities.

(b) A plan of merger must set forth:

(1) the name of each entity that is a party to the merger;

(2) the name of the surviving entity into which the other entities will merge;

(3) the type of organization of the surviving entity;

(4) the terms and conditions of the merger;

(5) the manner and basis for converting the interests of each party to the merger into interests or obligations of the surviving entity, or into money or other property in whole or in part; and

(6) the street address of the surviving entity's principal place of business.

(c) A plan of merger must be approved:

(1) in the case of a limited liability company that is a party to the merger, by all of the members or by a number or percentage of members specified in the operating agreement;

(2) in the case of a foreign limited liability company that is a party to the merger, by the vote required for approval of a merger by the law of the State or foreign jurisdiction in which the foreign limited liability company is organized;

(3) in the case of a partnership or domestic limited partnership that is a party to the merger, by the vote required for approval of a conversion under Section 902(b); and

(4) in the case of any other entities that are parties to the merger, by the vote required for approval of a merger by the law of this State or of the State or foreign jurisdiction in which the entity is organized and, in the absence of such a requirement, by all the owners of interests in the entity.

(d) After a plan of merger is approved and before the merger takes effect, the plan may be amended or abandoned as provided in the plan.

(e) The merger is effective upon the filing of the articles of merger with the [Secretary of State], or at such later date as the articles may provide.

Comment

This section sets forth a "safe harbor" for cross-entity mergers of limited liability companies with both domestic and foreign: corporations, general and limited partnerships, and other limited liability companies. Subsection (c) makes clear that the terms and conditions of the plan of merger must be approved by all of the partners unless applicable state law specifies otherwise for the merger.

§ 905. Articles of merger.

(a) After approval of the plan of merger under Section 904(c), unless the merger is abandoned under Section 904(d), articles of merger must be signed on behalf of each limited liability company and other entity that is a party to the merger and delivered to the [Secretary of State] for filing. The articles must set forth:

(1) the name and jurisdiction of formation or organization of each of the limited liability companies and other entities that are parties to the merger;

(2) for each limited liability company that is to merge, the date its articles of organization were filed with the [Secretary of State];

(3) that a plan of merger has been approved and signed by each limited liability company and other entity that is to merge;

(4) the name and address of the surviving limited liability company or other surviving entity;

(5) the effective date of the merger;

(6) if a limited liability company is the surviving entity, such changes in its articles of organization as are necessary by reason of the merger;

(7) if a party to a merger is a foreign limited liability company, the jurisdiction and date of filing of its initial articles of organization and the date when its application for authority was filed by the [Secretary of State] or, if an application has not been filed, a statement to that effect; and

(8) if the surviving entity is not a limited liability company, an agreement that the surviving entity may be served with process in this State and is subject to liability in any action or proceeding for the enforcement of any liability or obligation of any limited liability company previously subject to suit in this State which is to merge, and for the enforcement, as provided in this [Act], of the right of members of any limited liability company to receive payment for their interest against the surviving entity.

(b) If a foreign limited liability company is the surviving entity of a merger, it may not do business in this State until an application for that authority is filed with the [Secretary of State].

(c) The surviving limited liability company or other entity shall furnish a copy of the plan of merger, on request and without cost, to any member of any limited liability company or any person holding an interest in any other entity that is to merge.

(d) Articles of merger operate as an amendment to the limited liability company's articles of organization.

§ 906. Effect of merger.

(a) When a merger takes effect:

(1) the separate existence of each limited liability company and other entity that is a party to the merger, other than the surviving entity, terminates;

(2) all property owned by each of the limited liability companies and other entities that are party to the merger vests in the surviving entity;

(3) all debts, liabilities, and other obligations of each limited liability company and other entity that is party to the merger become the obligations of the surviving entity;

(4) an action or proceeding pending by or against a limited liability company or other party to a merger may be continued as if the merger had not occurred or the surviving entity may be substituted as a party to the action or proceeding; and

(5) except as prohibited by other law, all the rights, privileges, immunities, powers, and purposes of every limited liability company and other entity that is a party to a merger vest in the surviving entity.

(b) The [Secretary of State] is an agent for service of process in an action or proceeding against the surviving foreign entity to enforce an obligation of any party to a merger if the surviving foreign entity fails to appoint or maintain an agent designated for service of process in this State or the agent for service of process cannot with reasonable diligence be found at the designated office. Upon receipt of process, the [Secretary of State] shall send a copy of the process by registered or certified mail, return receipt requested, to the surviving entity at the address set forth in the articles of merger. Service is effected under this subsection at the earliest of:

(1) the date the company receives the process, notice, or demand;

(2) the date shown on the return receipt, if signed on behalf of the company; or

(3) five days after its deposit in the mail, if mailed postpaid and correctly addressed.

(c) A member of the surviving limited liability company is liable for all obligations of a party to the merger for which the member was personally liable before the merger.

(d) Unless otherwise agreed, a merger of a limited liability company that is not the surviving entity in the merger does not require the limited liability company to wind up its business under this [Act] or pay its liabilities and distribute its assets pursuant to this [Act].

(e) Articles of merger serve as articles of dissolution for a limited liability company that is not the surviving entity in the merger.

§ 907. [Article] not exclusive.

This [article] does not preclude an entity from being converted or merged under other law.

ARTICLE 10
FOREIGN LIMITED LIABILITY COMPANIES

§ 1001. Law governing foreign limited liability companies.

(a) The laws of the State or other jurisdiction under which a foreign limited liability company is organized govern its organization and internal affairs and the liability of its managers, members, and their transferees.

(b) A foreign limited liability company may not be denied a certificate of authority by reason of any difference between the laws of another jurisdiction under which the foreign company is organized and the laws of this State.

(c) A certificate of authority does not authorize a foreign limited liability company to engage in any business or exercise any power that a limited liability company may not engage in or exercise in this State.

Comment

The law where a foreign limited liability company is organized, rather than this Act, governs that company's internal affairs and the liability of its owners. Accordingly, any difference between the laws of the foreign jurisdiction and this Act will not constitute grounds for denial of a certificate of authority to transact business in this State. However, a foreign limited liability company transacting business in this State by virtue of a certificate of authority is limited to the business and powers that a limited liability company may lawfully pursue and exercise under Section 112.

§ 1002. Application for certificate of authority.

(a) A foreign limited liability company may apply for a certificate of authority to transact business in this State by delivering an application to the [Secretary of State] for filing. The application must set forth:

(1) the name of the foreign company or, if its name is unavailable for use in this State, a name that satisfies the requirements of Section 1005;

(2) the name of the State or country under whose law it is organized;

(3) the street address of its principal office;

(4) the address of its initial designated office in this State;

(5) the name and street address of its initial agent for service of process in this State;

(6) whether the duration of the company is for a specified term and, if so, the period specified;

(7) whether the company is manager-managed, and, if so, the name and address of each initial manager; and

(8) whether the members of the company are to be liable for its debts and obligations under a provision similar to Section 303(c).

(b) A foreign limited liability company shall deliver with the completed application a certificate of existence or a record of similar import authenticated by the secretary of state or other official having custody of company records in the State or country under whose law it is organized.

Comment

As with articles of organization, the application must be signed and filed with the filing office. See Sections 105, 107 (name registration), 205, 206, 209 (liability for false statements), and 1005.

§ 1003. Activities not constituting transacting business.

(a) Activities of a foreign limited liability company that do not constitute transacting business in this State within the meaning of this [article] include:

(1) maintaining, defending, or settling an action or proceeding;

(2) holding meetings of its members or managers or carrying on any other activity concerning its internal affairs;

(3) maintaining bank accounts;

(4) maintaining offices or agencies for the transfer, exchange, and registration of the foreign company's own securities or maintaining trustees or depositories with respect to those securities;

(5) selling through independent contractors;

(6) soliciting or obtaining orders, whether by mail or through employees or agents or otherwise, if the orders require acceptance outside this State before they become contracts;

(7) creating or acquiring indebtedness, mortgages, or security interests in real or personal property;

(8) securing or collecting debts or enforcing mortgages or other security interests in property securing the debts, and holding, protecting, and maintaining property so acquired;

(9) conducting an isolated transaction that is completed within 30 days and is not one in the course of similar transactions of a like manner; and

(10) transacting business in interstate commerce.

(b) For purposes of this [article], the ownership in this State of income-producing real property or tangible personal property, other than property excluded under subsection (a), constitutes transacting business in this State.

(c) This section does not apply in determining the contacts or activities that may subject a foreign limited liability company to service of process, taxation, or regulation under any other law of this State.

§ 1004. Issuance of certificate of authority.

Unless the [Secretary of State] determines that an application for a certificate of authority fails to comply as to form with the filing requirements of this [Act], the [Secretary of State], upon payment of all filing fees, shall file the application and send a receipt for it and the fees to the limited liability company or its representative.

§ 1005. Name of foreign limited liability company.

(a) If the name of a foreign limited liability company does not satisfy the requirements of Section 105, the company, to obtain or maintain a certificate of authority to transact business in this State, must use a fictitious name to transact business in this State if its real name is unavailable and it delivers to the [Secretary of State] for filing a copy of the resolution of its managers, in the case of a manager-managed company, or of its members, in the case of a member-managed company, adopting the fictitious name.

(b) Except as authorized by subsections (c) and (d), the name, including a fictitious name to be used to transact business in this State, of a foreign limited liability company must be distinguishable upon the records of the [Secretary of State] from:

(1) the name of any corporation, limited partnership, or company incorporated, organized, or authorized to transact business in this State;

(2) a name reserved or registered under Section 106 or 107; and

(3) the fictitious name of another foreign limited liability company authorized to transact business in this State.

(c) A foreign limited liability company may apply to the [Secretary of State] for authority to use in this State a name that is not distinguishable upon the records of the [Secretary of State] from a name described in subsection (b). The [Secretary of State] shall authorize use of the name applied for if:

(1) the present user, registrant, or owner of a reserved name consents to the use in a record and submits an undertaking in form satisfactory to the [Secretary of State] to change its name to a name that is distinguishable upon the records of the [Secretary of State] from the name of the foreign applying limited liability company; or

(2) the applicant delivers to the [Secretary of State] a certified copy of a final judgment of a court establishing the applicant's right to use the name applied for in this State.

(d) A foreign limited liability company may use in this State the name, including the fictitious name, of another domestic or foreign entity that is used in this State if the other entity is incorporated, organized, or authorized to transact business in this State and the foreign limited liability company:

(1) has merged with the other entity;

(2) has been formed by reorganization of the other entity; or

(3) has acquired all or substantially all of the assets, including the name, of the other entity.

(e) If a foreign limited liability company authorized to transact business in this State changes its name to one that does not satisfy the requirements of Section 105, it may not transact business in this State under the name as changed until it adopts a name satisfying the requirements of Section 105 and obtains an amended certificate of authority.

§ 1006. Revocation of certificate of authority.

(a) A certificate of authority of a foreign limited liability company to transact business in this State may be revoked by the [Secretary of State] in the manner provided in subsection (b) if:

(1) the company fails to:

(i) pay any fees, taxes, and penalties owed to this State;

(ii) deliver its annual report required under Section 211 to the [Secretary of State] within 60 days after it is due;

(iii) appoint and maintain an agent for service of process as required by this [article]; or

(iv) file a statement of a change in the name or business address of the agent as required by this [article]; or

(2) a misrepresentation has been made of any material matter in any application, report, affidavit, or other record submitted by the company pursuant to this [article].

(b) The [Secretary of State] may not revoke a certificate of authority of a foreign limited liability company unless the [Secretary of State] sends the company notice of the revocation, at least 60 days before its effective date, by a record addressed to its agent for service of process in this State, or if the company fails to appoint and maintain a proper agent in this State, addressed to the office required to be maintained by Section 108. The notice must specify the cause for the revocation of the certificate of authority. The authority of the company to transact business in this State ceases on the effective date of the revocation unless the foreign limited liability company cures the failure before that date.

§ 1007. Cancellation of authority.

A foreign limited liability company may cancel its authority to transact business in this State by filing in the office of the [Secretary of State] a certificate of cancellation. Cancellation does not terminate the authority of the [Secretary of State] to accept service of process on the company for [claims for relief] arising out of the transactions of business in this State.

§ 1008. Effect of failure to obtain certificate of authority.

(a) A foreign limited liability company transacting business in this State may not maintain an action or proceeding in this State unless it has a certificate of authority to transact business in this State.

(b) The failure of a foreign limited liability company to have a certificate of authority to transact business in this State does not impair the validity of a contract or act of the company or prevent the foreign limited liability company from defending an action or proceeding in this State.

(c) Limitations on personal liability of managers, members, and their transferees are not waived solely by transacting business in this State without a certificate of authority.

(d) If a foreign limited liability company transacts business in this State without a certificate of authority, it appoints the [Secretary of State] as its agent for service of process for [claims for relief] arising out of the transaction of business in this State.

§ 1009. Action by [Attorney General].

The [Attorney General] may maintain an action to restrain a foreign limited liability company from transacting business in this State in violation of this [article].

ARTICLE 11
DERIVATIVE ACTIONS

§ 1101. Right of action.

A member of a limited liability company may maintain an action in the right of the company if the members or managers having authority to do so have refused to commence the action or an effort to cause those members or managers to commence the action is not likely to succeed.

Comment

A member may bring an action on behalf of the company when the members or managers having the authority to pursue the company recovery refuse to do so or an effort to cause them to pursue the recovery is not likely to succeed. *See* Comments to Section 411(a) (personal action of member against company or another member).

§ 1102. Proper plaintiff.

In a derivative action for a limited liability company, the plaintiff must be a member of the company when the action is commenced; and:

(1) must have been a member at the time of the transaction of which the plaintiff complains; or

(2) the plaintiff's status as a member must have devolved upon the plaintiff by operation of law or pursuant to the terms of the operating agreement from a person who was a member at the time of the transaction.

§ 1103. Pleading.

In a derivative action for a limited liability company, the complaint must set forth with particularity the effort of the plaintiff to secure initiation of the action by a member or manager or the reasons for not making the effort.

Comment

There is no obligation of the company or its members or managers to respond to a member demand to bring an action to pursue a company recovery. However, if a company later decides to commence the demanded action or assume control of the derivative litigation, the member's right to commence or control the proceeding ordinarily ends.

§ 1104. Expenses.

If a derivative action for a limited liability company is successful, in whole or in part, or if anything is received by the plaintiff as a result of a judgment, compromise, or settlement of an action or claim, the court may award the plaintiff reasonable expenses, including reasonable attorney's fees, and shall direct the plaintiff to remit to the limited liability company the remainder of the proceeds received.

ARTICLE 12
MISCELLANEOUS PROVISIONS

§ 1201. Uniformity of application and construction.

This [Act] shall be applied and construed to effectuate its general purpose to make uniform the law with respect to the subject of this [Act] among States enacting it.

§ 1202. Short title.

This [Act] may be cited as the Uniform Limited Liability Company Act (1995).

§ 1203. Severability clause.

If any provision of this [Act] or its application to any person or circumstance is held invalid, the invalidity does not affect other provisions or applications of this [Act] which can be given effect without the invalid provision or application, and to this end the provisions of this [Act] are severable.

§ 1204. Effective date.

This [Act] takes effect [_____].

§ 1205. Transitional provisions.

(a) Before January 1, 199___, this [Act] governs only a limited liability company organized:

(1) after the effective date of this [Act], unless the company is continuing the business of a dissolved limited liability company under [Section of the existing Limited Liability Company Act]; and

(2) before the effective date of this [Act], which elects, as provided by subsection (c), to be governed by this [Act].

(b) On and after January 1, 199_____, this [Act] governs all limited liability companies.

(c) Before January 1, 199_____, a limited liability company voluntarily may elect, in the manner provided in its operating agreement or by law for amending the operating agreement, to be governed by this [Act].

Comment

Under subsection (a)(1), the application of the Act is mandatory for all companies formed after the effective date of the Act determined under Section 1204. Under subsection (a)(2), the application of the Act is permissive, by election under subsection (c), for existing companies for a period of time specified in subsection (b) after which application becomes mandatory. This affords existing companies and their members an opportunity to consider the changes effected by this Act and to amend their operating agreements, if appropriate. If no election is made, the Act becomes effective after the period specified in subsection (b). The period specified by adopting States may vary, but a period of five years is a common period in similar cases.

§ 1206. Savings clause.

This [Act] does not affect an action or proceeding commenced or right accrued before the effective date of this [Act].

PART FOUR
SAMPLE AGREEMENT

FORM OF LIMITED LIABILITY COMPANY OPERATING AGREEMENT[*]

Editor's note: This agreement was drafted by Robert R. Keatinge, Esq., of Counsel, Holland & Hart LLP, Denver, Colorado. Mr. Keatinge is a leading figure in the law of unincorporated business organizations. He played a key role in drafting statutes that created the limited liability company form of doing business. He also was a member of the drafting committee for the revised Uniform Partnership Act and for the limited liability partnership amendments to that Act.

The decision to include a lengthy and sophisticated agreement was based on the reasoning that it is useful for the student reader to see a full development of the variations and complexities possible in the LLC operating agreement. Also, it is easier for an attorney drafting an LLC agreement to edit down from a long form than it is to create new provisions without guidance.

MANAGER-MANAGED[1] [LONG FORM]
[OPERATING/LIMITED LIABILITY COMPANY]
AGREEMENT[2] OF
[_____], LLC
A [STATE] LIMITED LIABILITY COMPANY
EFFECTIVE AS OF [_____, ____]

THE INTERESTS DESCRIBED AND REPRESENTED BY THIS [OPERATING/LIMITED LIABILITY COMPANY] AGREEMENT HAVE NOT BEEN REGISTERED UNDER THE SECURITIES ACT OF 1933 OR ANY APPLICABLE STATE SECURITIES LAWS (THE "SECURITIES LAWS") AND MAY BE RESTRICTED SECURITIES AS THAT TERM IS DEFINED IN RULE 144 UNDER THE SECURITIES LAWS. TO THE EXTENT THE INTERESTS CONSTITUTE SECURITIES UNDER THE SECURITIES LAWS, THE SECURITIES MAY NOT BE OFFERED FOR SALE, SOLD, OR OTHERWISE TRANSFERRED EXCEPT PURSUANT TO AN EFFECTIVE REGISTRATION STATEMENT OR QUALIFICATION UNDER THE SECURITIES LAWS OR PURSUANT TO AN EXEMPTION FROM REGISTRATION UNDER THE SECURITIES LAWS, THE AVAILABILITY OF WHICH IS TO BE ESTABLISHED TO THE SATISFACTION OF THE COMPANY.[3]

---

[1] In most states, LLCs can be organized either as "member-managed" LLCs or "manager-managed" LLC. In a member-managed LLC, each member is an agent of the LLC for carrying on the business of the LLC in the usual course. On the other hand, in a manager-managed LLC, members do not have agency authority, and managers do. This is a manager-managed LLC. Some states, such as Colorado, permit an LLC to be manager-managed (i.e., to provide that members do not have agency authority) but do not require that the LLC have a manager. In such case, the members will determine who will exercise authority on behalf of the LLC.

This operating agreement is for a manager-managed LLC with a manager.

[2] The agreement is referred to in different ways in different statutes. The predominant nomenclature is "operating agreement," but it is known in Delaware as a "limited liability company agreement," and elsewhere as "regulations" or a "member control agreement." Delaware acknowledges that an agreement will still constitute a limited liability company agreement under its act even if it is referred to as an "operating agreement." 6 Del. C. § 18-101(7) (" 'Limited liability company agreement' means any agreement (whether referred to as a limited liability company agreement, operating agreement or otherwise). . .").

[3] Many interests in LLCs will be considered securities. If they are considered securities and are intended to be sold pursuant to an exemption from registration based on sales of securities not acquired for resale, the issuer will want to assure itself that the securities are not being sold to "Underwriters" (i.e., persons acquiring the securities for resale). Among the actions that the Company may take to assure that the securities are not being acquired for resale are:

(1) Reasonable inquiry to determine if the purchaser is acquiring the securities for himself or for other persons;

(2) Written disclosure to each purchaser prior to sale that the securities have not been registered under the Act and, therefore, cannot be resold unless they

TABLE OF CONTENTS

ARTICLE 1 DEFINITIONS

---

are registered under the Act or unless an exemption from registration is available; and

(3) Placement of a legend on the certificate or other document that evidences the securities stating that the securities have not been registered under the Act and setting forth or referring to the restrictions on transferability and sale of the securities.

See Regulation D, Rule 502(d), 17CFR230.502(d).

ARTICLE 13 MISCELLANEOUS PROVISIONS

This Agreement[4] is made and entered into this [_____] day of

---

[4] Under most statutes an organization does not qualify as a limited liability company until it has at least one member (*see, e.g.*, 6 Del. C § 18-101(6) (" 'Limited liability company' and 'domestic limited liability company' means a limited liability company formed under the laws of the State of Delaware and having 1 or more members."), but is formed by filing articles of organization or a certificate of formation (*see, e.g.*, 6 Del. C. § 18-201(b) ("A limited liability company is formed at the time of the filing of the initial certificate of formation in the office of the Secretary of State or at any later date or time specified in the certificate of formation if, in either case, there has been substantial compliance with the requirements of this section. A limited liability company formed under this chapter shall be a separate legal entity, the existence of which as a separate legal entity shall continue until

[_____], 20[____], by and among *[the Company and]*[5] each of the Members whose signatures appear on the signature page hereof (the "Initial Members"). In consideration of the mutual covenants contained herein and for other good and valuable consideration, the Members and the Company (and each person who subsequently becomes an Equity Owner) hereby agree as follows:

ARTICLE 1
DEFINITIONS

The following terms used in this Agreement shall have the following meanings (unless otherwise expressly provided herein); certain other capitalized terms have the meanings ascribed to them throughout this Agreement.

1.1. Act. The *[State]* Limited Liability Company Act*[, as amended from time to time]*.[6]

1.2. Adjusted Capital Contributions. An amount equal to the excess of such Equity Owner's Capital Contributions, if any, pursuant to Section 8.1 and Section 8.2, over any Distributions made to such Equity Owner pursuant to Section 9.4(b)(ii).[7]

---

cancellation of the limited liability company's certificate of formation"). As such the effective date of the agreement should be as of or after the effective date of the filed articles. *See, e.g.*, 6 Del. C. § 18-101.

[5] Bracketed and italicized language in this agreement represents optional or alternative provisions that a drafter may want to consider including.

There has been a concern about whether the LLC itself should be a party to the operating agreement (or at least be bound by the operating agreement). *Compare* Bubbles & Bleach, LLC v. Becker, No. 97 C 1320, 1997 WL 285938 (N.D. Ill. May 23, 1997) (holding an arbitration agreement not binding on an LLC because it was not a party to it), *with* Elf Atochem North America, Inc. v. Jaffari, 727 A.2d 286 (Del. 1999) (to the contrary). The Delaware LLC act has addressed this issue in 6 Del. C. § 18-101(7) ("A limited liability company is not required to execute its limited liability company agreement. A limited liability company is bound by its limited liability company agreement whether or not the limited liability company executes the limited liability company agreement.").

[6] This operating agreement is intended to as a generic example. It will need to be adapted to the particular language and limitations of the act under which the LLC is organized. Some amendments to the LLC statute will not be effective as to existing LLCs in order to avoid disturbing contractual relationships. It may be appropriate to include the express reference to the act "as amended" to ensure that such amendments will be used in interpreting the agreement.

[7] This definition is intended to be used when alternative 2 in section 9.4 is used. The "adjusted capital contributions" represents the total value of the contributions by a member reduced by the actual amount of cash distributed to the member (not counting any cash distributed on account of a preferred accrual). Allocations of profits and losses are disregarded in determining the adjusted capital contributions.

1.3. Affiliate. In the case of an individual, the spouse, estate, heirs, devisees, lineal descendants (including adopted children) or the spouse of a lineal descendant of that individual, or a trust or other Entity formed by the individual for the benefit of the individual or his spouse or lineal descendants or the spouse of a lineal descendant of that individual and in which day-to-day voting control is directly or indirectly held by the individual, and in the case of a Person other than an individual, (a) any Person directly or indirectly controlling, controlled by, or under common control with such Person, (b) any Person owning or controlling ten percent (10%) or more of the outstanding voting interests of such Person, (c) any officer, director, manager, or general partner of such Person, or (d) any Person who is an officer, director, manager, general partner, trustee, or holder of ten percent (10%) or more of the voting interests of any Person described in clauses (a) through (c) of this sentence. For purposes of this definition, the term "control," "controls," "controlling," "controlled by," or "under common control with" shall mean the possession, direct or indirect, of the power to direct or cause the direction of the management and policies of a Person, whether through the ownership of voting securities, by contract or otherwise. [8]

1.4. Agreement. This *[Operating/Limited Liability Company]* Agreement as originally executed and as amended from time to time.

1.5. Annual Operating Plan. The business plan designated as such pursuant to Section 5.12. [9]

1.6. Approve or Approval.

(a) With respect to Members, such Members' approval expressed by the Members holding the required number of Voting Interests at a meeting of the Members or expressed by written consent by Members holding the required number of Voting Interests as provided for in Article 7 of this Agreement; and

(b) With respect to Managers, such Managers' approval as required pursuant to Section 5.1.

1.7. [Articles of Organization/Certificate of Formation.] The *[articles of organization/certificate of formation]* of the Company as filed with the Secretary of State as the same may be amended from time to time.

1.8. Available Ownership Interest. The Ownership Interest designated as such in Section 8.5(b)(i).

---

[8] This definition should be used when there are restrictions (or approval requirements) with respect to certain transactions with Equity Owners, Managers, or any of their Affiliates.

[9] This agreement provides for a business plan as a way of anticipating expenditures and other issues which might otherwise require approval. If the Members are willing to expend the effort to maintain an operating plan it can be a useful vehicle for operating the business of the Company.

1.9. <u>Bankruptcy</u>. With respect to a Person, the occurrence of any of the following events:

(a) Such Person makes an assignment for the benefit of creditors;

(b) Such Person files a voluntary petition in bankruptcy;

(c) Such Person is adjudged a bankrupt or insolvent, or has entered against it an order for relief, in any bankruptcy or insolvency proceeding;

(d) Such Person files a petition or answer seeking for itself any reorganization, arrangement, composition, readjustment, liquidation, dissolution, or similar relief under any statute, law or regulation;

(e) Such Person files an answer or other pleading admitting or failing to contest the material allegations of a petition filed against it in any proceeding of this nature;

(f) Such Person seeks, consents to, or acquiesces in the appointment of a trustee, receiver, or liquidator of such Person or of all or any substantial part of its properties; or

(g) One hundred twenty (120) days after the commencement of any proceeding against such Person seeking reorganization, arrangement, composition, readjustment, liquidation, dissolution, or similar relief under any statute, law, or regulation, if the proceeding has not been dismissed, or if within ninety (90) days after the appointment without its consent or acquiescence of a trustee, receiver, or liquidator of such Person or of all or any substantial part of its properties, the appointment is not vacated or stayed, or within ninety (90) days after the expiration of any such stay, the appointment is not vacated.

1.10. <u>Buying Member</u>. A Member exercising the option granted pursuant to Section 10.2(b).

1.11. <u>Buy Notice</u>. The notice given pursuant to Section 10.2(b).

1.12. <u>Buy Option</u>. The option granted pursuant to Section 10.2(b).

1.13. <u>Capital Account</u>. As of any given date, the capital account of each Equity Owner as described in Section 8.3 and maintained to such date in accordance with this Agreement.[10]

1.14. <u>Capital Contribution</u>. Any contribution to the capital of the Company in cash or property by an Equity Owner whenever made. "<u>Initial Capital Contribution</u>" shall mean the initial contribution to the capital of the Company pursuant to this Agreement.

1.15. <u>Code</u>. The Internal Revenue Code of 1986, as amended from time to time.

---

[10] The Capital Account is where the allocation of profits and losses are turned into cash distributions. On the liquidation of the Company, the Capital Accounts will dictate the amounts distributed to each of the Equity Owners.

1.16. Company. [_____] LLC.

1.17. Company Minimum Gain. Partnership minimum gain as determined in accordance with Section 1.704-2(d) of the Regulations.

1.18. Company Property. All assets (real or personal, tangible or intangible, including cash) of the Company.

1.19. CPI Index. The Consumer Price Index for All Items All Urban Consumers (DPI-U) (1982-84 = 100) for the United States, as published by the United States Department of Labor's Bureau of Labor Statistics.

1.20. Default Buyout Price. The price established by Section 8.5(b)(v).

1.21. Defaulting Equity Owner. An Equity Owner designated as such in Section 8.5.

1.22. Default Notice. The notice required by Section 8.5.

1.23. Default Purchase Option. The option granted pursuant to Section 8.5(b).

1.24. Default Purchase Option Notice. The notice required by Section 8.5(b).

1.25. Deficit Capital Account. With respect to any Equity Owner, the deficit balance, if any, in such Equity Owner's Capital Account as of the end of the Fiscal Year, after giving effect to the following adjustments:

(a) Credit to such Capital Account the amount, if any, which such Equity Owner is obligated to restore under Section 1.704-1(b)(2)(ii)(c) of the Regulations, as well as any addition thereto pursuant to the next to last sentence of Sections 1.704-2(g)(1) and (i)(5) of the Regulations, after taking into account thereunder any changes during such year in Company Minimum Gain and in any Equity Owner Minimum Gain; and

(b) Debit to such Capital Account the items described in Sections 1.704-1(b)(2)(ii)(d)(4), (5) and (6) of the Regulations.

This definition of Deficit Capital Account is intended to comply with the provisions of Sections 1.704-1(b)(2)(ii)(d) and 1.704-2 of the Regulations, and shall be interpreted consistently with those provisions.

1.26. Depreciation. For each Fiscal Year, an amount equal to the depreciation, amortization, or other cost recovery deduction allowable with respect to an asset for such Fiscal Year, except that if the Gross Asset Value of an asset differs from its adjusted basis for federal income tax purposes at the beginning of such Fiscal Year, Depreciation shall be an amount which bears the same ratio to such beginning Gross Asset Value as the federal income tax depreciation, amortization, or other cost recovery deduction for such Fiscal Year bears to such beginning adjusted tax basis; provided, however, that if the adjusted basis for federal income tax purposes of an asset at the beginning of such Fiscal Year is zero, Depreciation shall be determined with reference to such beginning Gross Asset Value using any reasonable method selected by the Managers. Notwithstanding the foregoing, if the Company uses the remedial method pursuant to Section 1.704-3(d) of the Regulations with respect to one or more of the Company's assets, Depreciation with respect to such assets shall not be determined in accordance with the preceding sentence of this definition, but shall instead be determined in a manner consistent with tax capital accounting principles and consistent with the treatment of such assets under the remedial method, as determined by the Managers in consultation with the Company's tax advisors.

1.27. Disability or Disabled. With respect to any individual a permanent disability as determined by *[two]* physicians, *[one selected by the Company and one by the authorized agent of such Person,]* who has examined such Person and concluded that such Person is incapable of performing his usual duties for a continuous period of *[two]* months or more.[11]

1.28. Distributable Cash. All cash, whether revenues or other funds received by the Company, less the sum of the following to the extent paid or set aside by the Company: (i) all principal and interest payments on indebtedness of the Company and all other sums paid to lenders; (ii) all cash expenditures incurred incident to the normal operation of the Company's business; and (iii) Reserves. Any funds released from a Reserve shall be considered a cash receipt by the Company for purposes of this definition.

1.29. Distribution. Any Transfer of Company Property from the Company to or for the benefit of an Equity Owner by reason of such Equity Owner's ownership of an Economic Interest.

1.30. Donee. A Person designated as such in Section 10.5.

1.31. Economic Interest. An Equity Owner's share of one or more of the Profits, Losses, and Distributions pursuant to this Agreement and the Act, but not including any right to participate in the management or affairs of the Company, such as the right to Approve or otherwise participate in any decision of the Members or Managers.[12]

1.32. Economic Interest Owner. The owner of an Economic Interest who is not a Member.

---

[11] The definition of "Disability" is used in conjunction with removal of Managers or withdrawals/transfers of Ownership Interests.

[12] Definitions such as "Economic Interest," Economic Interest Owner," and "Equity Owner" are intended to facilitate the distinction between "Members" who are admitted to the LLC either at the outset or by the consent of the other Members and who have both economic rights and rights to participate in management of the Company and "Economic Interest Owners" who are assignees or transferees of an interest but who are not admitted as Members and therefore do not have the right to participate in management or to receive information from the Company.

1.33. Electing Equity Owner. An Equity Owner designated as such in Section 8.5(b)(iii).

1.34. Entity. Any general partnership (including a limited liability partnership), limited partnership (including a limited liability limited partnership), limited liability company, corporation, joint venture, trust, business trust, cooperative, association, foreign trust, or foreign business organization.

1.35. Equity Owner. An Economic Interest Owner or a Member.

1.36. Equity Owner Minimum Gain. Partner nonrecourse debt minimum gain as determined under Section 1.704-2(i)(3) of the Regulations.

1.37. Equity Owner Nonrecourse Debt. Partner nonrecourse debt as defined under Section 1.704-2(b)(4) of the Regulations.

1.38. Exercise Notice. The notice required by Section 8.5(b)(ii).

1.39. Fiscal Year. The taxable year of the Company as determined under the Code.

1.40. Gift. A gift, devise, bequest, or other transfer for no consideration, whether or not by operation of law, except in the case of Bankruptcy.

1.41. Gifting Equity Owner. Any Equity Owner who Gifts all or any part of its Ownership Interest.

1.42. Gross Asset Value.[13] With respect to any asset, the asset's adjusted basis for federal income tax purposes, except as follows:

(a) The initial Gross Asset Value of any asset contributed by an Equity Owner to the Company shall be the gross fair market value of such asset on the date of contribution, *[as determined by the contributing Member and the Managers]*, provided that the initial Gross Asset Values of the assets contributed to the Company pursuant to Section 8.1 hereof shall be as set forth in Exhibit 8.1, and provided further that, if the contributing Member is a Manager, the determination of the fair market value of any other contributed asset shall require the Approval of the other Members owning a Majority Interest (determined without regard to the Voting Interest of such contributing Member);

(b) The Gross Asset Values of all Company assets shall be adjusted to equal their respective gross fair market values (taking into account Section 7701(g) of the Code), as *[reasonably]* determined by the Managers[14] as of the following times: (i) the acquisition of an interest by any

---

[13] As noted in definitions set forth below, the definition of "Gross Asset Value" facilitates several economic transactions, not the least of which is to provide for "book-ups" by which the economic interests of the Equity Owners is adjusted on the admission or redemption of an Equity Owner.

[14] This provision sets forth the rules for a "book-up" of the assets of the Company

new Equity Owner or an additional interest by an existing Equity Owner in exchange for more than a *de minimis* contribution of property (including money); (ii) the Distribution by the Company to an Equity Owner of more than a *de minimis* amount of property as consideration for an Ownership Interest; *[and]* (iii) the liquidation of the Company within the meaning of Section 1.704-1(b)(2)(ii)(g) of the Regulations; *[and (iv) the grant of an Ownership Interest in the Company (other than a de minimis interest) as consideration for the provision of services to or for the benefit of the Company by an existing Equity Owner acting in the capacity of an Equity Owner or by a new Equity Owner acting in the capacity of an Equity Owner or in anticipation of being an Equity Owner;]*[15] provided, however, that adjustments pursuant to clauses (i) and (ii) above shall be made only if the Managers *[reasonably]* determine that such adjustments are necessary or appropriate to reflect the relative economic interests of the Equity Owners in the Company;

(c) The Gross Asset Value of any Company asset Distributed to any Equity Owner shall be adjusted to equal the gross fair market value of such asset on the date of Distribution as **[reasonably]** determined by the distributee and the Managers, provided that, if the distributee is a Manager, the determination of the fair market value of the Distributed asset shall require the Approval of the other Members owning a Majority Interest (determined without regard to the Voting Interest of the distributee Member); and

(d) The Gross Asset Values of Company assets shall be increased (or decreased) to reflect any adjustments to the adjusted basis of such assets pursuant to Section 734(b) or Section 743(b) of the Code, but only to the extent that such adjustments are taken into account in determining Capital Accounts pursuant to Section 1.704-1(b)(2)(iv)(m) of the Regulations and Section 9.2(g) and subparagraph (g) under the definition of Profits and Losses; provided, however, that Gross Asset Values shall not be adjusted pursuant to this subparagraph (d) of this definition to the extent that the Managers **[reasonably]** determine that an adjustment pursuant to subparagraph (b) of this definition is necessary or appropriate in connection with a transaction that would otherwise result in an adjustment pursuant to this subparagraph (d).

---

on certain events. The effect of the book-up is to adjust the value of the Capital Accounts to fair market value on these events by treating the Company as if the assets were sold for fair market value and the resulting profits and losses were allocated in accordance the provisions for sharing profits and losses within the agreement. It is ordinarily done to ensure that on the admission or departure of a member, the historic members get the benefit of unrealized appreciation of the assets that has not yet been allocated to the owners.

[15] This provision allows for a book-up on the grant of a "profits interest." In order for a compensatory interest to constitute a "profits interest" under Rev. Proc. 93-27, it must entitle it holder to an interest that would yield nothing if the LLC were liquidated immediately after it is granted.

If the Gross Asset Value of an asset has been determined or adjusted pursuant to subparagraph (a), (b), or (d) of this definition, then such Gross Asset Value shall thereafter be adjusted by the Depreciation taken into account with respect to such asset for purposes of computing Profits and Losses.

1.43. Hypothecation. A lien, pledge, hypothecation, mortgage, grant of a security interest, or effecting an encumbrance either as security for repayment of a liability or for any other purpose.

1.44. Issuance Items. Any income, gain, loss or deduction realized by the Company as a direct or indirect result of the issuance of an interest in the Company by the Company to an Equity Owner.

1.45. Loan Decision Period. The time period specified in Section 8.5(a).

1.46. Liquidators. The Persons specified as such in Section 12.3(a).

1.47. Majority Interest. One or more Voting Interests of Members which taken together exceed fifty percent (50%) of the aggregate of all Voting Interests.

1.48. Managers. One or more managers designated as provided in Section 5.2.

1.49. Member. Each of the parties who executes a counterpart of this Agreement as a Member (an "Initial Member") and each Person who may hereafter become a Member. If a Person is a Member immediately prior to the purchase or other acquisition by such Person of an Economic Interest, such Person shall have all of the rights of a Member with respect to such purchased or otherwise acquired Economic Interest, as the case may be.

1.50. Membership Interest. A Member's entire interest in the Company, including such Member's Economic Interest and such other rights and privileges that the Member may enjoy by being a Member.

1.51. Non-cash Consideration. The consideration designated as such pursuant to Section 10.2(a).

1.52. Non-Defaulting Equity Owners. The Equity Owners designated as such pursuant to Section 8.5.

1.53. Notice of Sale. The notice provided pursuant to Section 10.2(a).

1.54. Offered Interest. The Ownership Interest offered pursuant to Section 10.2(a).

1.55. Option Period. The period of time provided for pursuant to Section 10.2(b).

1.56. Ownership Interest. In the case of a Member, the Member's Membership Interest; and in the case of an Economic Interest Owner, the Economic Interest Owner's Economic Interest.

1.57. Person. Any individual or Entity, and the heirs, executors, administrators, legal representatives, successors, and assigns of such "Person" where the context so permits.

1.58. Preferred Accrual. The mathematical equivalent of interest at the rate of ten percent simple interest per annum on the balance from time to time of their respective Adjusted Capital Contributions.[16]

1.59. Prime Rate. The prime commercial lending rate in effect from time to time at the principal bank used by the Company for banking and borrowing purposes.

1.60. Profits and Losses. For each Fiscal Year of the Company an amount equal to the Company's net taxable income or loss for such year as determined for federal income tax purposes (including separately stated items) in accordance with the accounting method and rules used by the Company and in accordance with Section 703 of the Code with the following adjustments:

(a) Any items of income, gain, loss and deduction allocated to Equity Owners pursuant to Sections 9.2, 9.3, or 9.12 shall not be taken into account in computing Profits or Losses;

(b) Any income of the Company that is exempt from federal income tax and not otherwise taken into account in computing Profits and Losses (pursuant to this definition) shall be added to such taxable income or loss;

(c) Any expenditure of the Company described in Section 705(a)(2)(B) of the Code or treated as such in Section 1.704-1(b)(2)(iv)(*i*) of the Regulations and not otherwise taken into account in computing Profits and Losses (pursuant to this definition) shall be subtracted from such taxable income or loss;

(d) In the event the Gross Asset Value of any Company asset is adjusted pursuant to subparagraphs (b) or (c) of the definition of Gross Asset Value, the amount of such adjustment shall be taken into account as gain or loss from the disposition of such asset for purposes of computing Profits and Losses;[17]

(e) Gain or loss resulting from any disposition of any Company asset with respect to which gain or loss is recognized for federal income tax purposes shall be computed with reference to the Gross Asset Value of the asset disposed of, notwithstanding that the adjusted tax basis of such asset differs from its Gross Asset Value;

---

[16] This definition is intended to be used when alternative 2 in section 9.4 and, in particular section 9.4(b)(i), is used. The Preferred Accrual sometimes described as a "Preferred Return" is an interest-like amount paid on, and returned in addition to, Adjusted Capital Contributions.

[17] This provision works together with the definition of Gross Asset Value to cause the amount of the adjustment to be credited to, or debited from Capital Accounts in the event of a book-up.

(f) In lieu of the depreciation, amortization, and other cost recovery deductions taken into account in computing such taxable income or loss, there shall be taken into account Depreciation for such Fiscal Year; and

(g) To the extent an adjustment to the adjusted tax basis of any asset pursuant to Section 734(b) or Section 743(b) of the Code is required pursuant to Section 1.704-1(b)(2)(iv)(*m*) of the Regulations in determining Capital Accounts, the amount of such adjustment shall be treated as an item of gain (if the adjustment increases the basis of the asset) or loss (if the adjustment decreases the basis of the asset) from the disposition of the asset and shall be taken into account for purposes of computing Profits or Losses.

1.61. Purchase Price. The price determined pursuant to Section 10.2(a).

1.62. Regulations. The proposed, temporary, and final regulations promulgated under the Code in effect as of the date of filing the *[Articles of Organization/Certificate of Formation]* and the corresponding sections of any regulations subsequently issued that amend or supersede such regulations.

1.63. Regulatory Allocations. The allocations made pursuant to Sections 9.2(a), 9.2(b), 9.2(c), 9.2(d), 9.2(e), 9.2(f), and 9.2(g).

1.64. Remaining Members. The members designated as such pursuant to Section 10.2(a).

1.65. Reorganization. The merger or conversion of the Company, the sale or other disposition of all or substantially all of the assets of the Company, the sale or other disposition of all or substantially all of the Ownership Interests, or any other transaction pursuant to which one or more Persons acquire all or substantially all of the assets of, or Ownership Interests in, the Company in a single or series of related transactions, including a merger or conversion of the Company into a corporation or other Entity, whether or not such corporation or other Entity has the same owners as the Company and whether or not additional capital is contributed to such corporation or other Entity; provided, however, that a Reorganization in no event shall include the merger or conversion of the Company into a general partnership which is not a limited liability partnership or a limited partnership that is not a limited liability limited partnership.[18]

1.66. Reserves. With respect to any fiscal period, funds set aside or amounts allocated during such period to reserves which shall be maintained in amounts *[reasonably]* deemed sufficient by the Managers for working capital and for payment of taxes, insurance, debt service, or other costs or

---

[18] This last clause is intended to exclude the conversion of the Company into an organization in which one or more Equity Owners will undertake liability for the obligations of organization.

expenses incident to the ownership or operation of the Company's business.[19]

1.67. Sale or Sell. A sale, assignment, exchange, Hypothecation, assignment by reason of Bankruptcy, *[or]* other transfer for consideration, *[or change in ownership by reason of the Reorganization or other transformation in the identity or form of business organization of the owner, regardless of whether such change or transformation is characterized by state law as not changing the identity of the owner].*

1.68. Secretary of State. The Secretary of State of **[State]**.

1.69. Securities Laws. Any Federal securities acts and laws as well as the securities acts and laws of any state, including the Securities Act of 1933.

1.70. Seller's Estimate. The estimate made pursuant to Section 10.2(a).

1.71. Selling Equity Owner. Any Equity Owner that Sells all or any portion of its Ownership Interest.

1.72. Sharing Ratio. The percentages in which the Equity Owners share those items making specific references to "Sharing Ratios" in this Agreement.[20] The initial[21] Sharing Ratio shall be:

Equity Owners   **Sharing Ratio**

_____   _____

_____   _____

_____   _____

The Sharing Ratio shall be adjusted from time to time as provided in this Agreement.[22]

---

[19] Reserves, and the determination of Reserves, is important in establishing the amount of Distributable Cash. While the determination of Reserves may be less important where the Managers have discretion in making Distributions, if the Managers are required to Distribute Distributable Cash, "Reserves" provide the one basis on which Managers can retain cash for operations.

[20] Sharing Ratio serves to define the manner in which voting is conducted and the percentages in which Profits and Losses are shared.

[21] Upon transfer of a partial interest or the admission or redemption of Equity Owners the Sharing Ratio will need to be adjusted. If there are to be a lot of transactions of that sort, it may be more efficient to use "Units" to determine the manner in which management and economic results are to be shared. The concern with the use of Units is that it is easy for people to confuse "Units" with shares of stock in a corporation. Like "Sharing Ratios," "Units" serve only as a measure of sharing management and profits, but do not include Capital Accounts, which are determined in the first instance by the initial contributions.

[22] The events that may require the adjustment of the Sharing Ratio include: (1) the admission of a new Member; (2) disproportionate contributions of capital, if the agreement so provides, (3) the redemption of an Equity Owner; (4) disproportionate distributions of capital; or (5) as a consequence of a default under the agreement if the agreement so provides.

1.73. Tax Profits. The amounts designated as such pursuant to Section 9.4(a).

1.74. Tax Rate. The highest marginal federal and [State] income tax rate for individuals then in effect (after taking into account the assumed deductibility of the amount of *[State]* income tax from federal taxable income).

1.75. Third Party Offer. An offer designated as such pursuant to Section 10.2(a).

1.76. Third Party Purchaser. A Person designated as such pursuant to Section 10.2(a).

1.77. TMP. The Tax Matters Partner designated in Section 9.11.

1.78. Transfer. Any Sale or Gift.

1.79. Transferring Equity Owner. Selling Equity Owner or a Gifting Equity Owner.

1.80. Two-Thirds Interest. One or more Voting Interests of Members which taken together exceed 66.67% of the aggregate of all Voting Interests.

1.81. Unrecovered Losses. Amounts designated as such pursuant to Section 9.1(b)(i).

1.82. Voting Interest. The percentages in which the Members are entitled to vote for purposes of those provisions making specific references to "Voting Interest" in this Agreement.[23] The initial Voting Interests shall be:

Members	Voting Interest
_____	_____
_____	_____
_____	_____

The Voting Interest shall be adjusted from time to time as provided in this Agreement.[24]

---

[23] Often the "Voting Interest" is simply the Sharing Ratio adjusted to exclude Economic Interest Owners from the computation.

[24] The events that may require the adjustment of the Voting Interest include: (1) the admission of a new Member; (2) disproportionate contributions of capital, if the agreement so provides, (3) the redemption of an Equity Owner; (4) disproportionate distributions of capital; (5) as a consequence of a default under the agreement if the agreement so provides; or (6) the transfer of an interest to a transferee who is not admitted as a Member.

ARTICLE 2
FORMATION OF COMPANY

2.1. Formation. On [_____], 20[____], [_____] organized a limited liability company pursuant to the Act by *[executing and delivering the Certificate of Formation] [causing the Articles of Organization to be delivered]*[25] to the Secretary of State in accordance with and pursuant to the Act. The Company and the Members hereby forever discharge the organizer, and the organizer shall be indemnified by the Company and the Members from and against any expense or liability actually incurred by the organizer by reason of having been the organizer of the Company.

2.2. Name. The name of the Company is [_____] LLC.

2.3. Principal Place of Business. The principal place of business of the Company shall be *[_____] [as set forth in the Articles of Organization].*[26] The principal place of business may be changed from time to time by filing a notice of change of the address of the principal office with the Secretary of State pursuant to the Act. The Company may locate its places of business and registered office at any other place or places as the Managers may from time to time deem advisable.

2.4. Registered Office and Registered Agent. The Company's initial registered office and the name of the registered agent at such address shall be as set forth in the *[Articles of Organization/Certificate of Formation]*. The registered office and registered agent may be changed from time to time by filing a notice of change in the address of the new registered office or the name of the new registered agent with the Secretary of State pursuant to the Act.

2.5. Term. The Company shall continue in existence until it terminates in accordance with the provisions of this Agreement or the Act.

ARTICLE 3
BUSINESS OF COMPANY

The business of the Company shall be:

---

[25] This language should conform to the language used in the state LLC statute with respect to filing.

[26] Some state statutes require that a principal office or principal place of business [often a mailing address that does not need to be in the state] be listed in the articles of organization. This is an address that may be used to mail notice to the Company if the registered agent cannot be found. If the principal place of business is required to be set forth in the articles, it reduces the possibility of error to refer to that address rather than set it forth again here.

(a) *[To acquire, improve, manage, operate and dispose of real property and to accomplish any lawful business whatsoever, or which shall at any time appear conducive to or expedient for the protection or benefit of the Company and its assets.]*[27]

(b) To exercise all other powers necessary to or reasonably connected with the Company's business that may be legally exercised by limited liability companies under the Act.

(c) To engage in all activities necessary, customary, convenient, or incident to any of the foregoing.

ARTICLE 4
NAMES AND ADDRESSES OF EQUITY OWNERS

4.1. Initial Members. The names and addresses of the Initial Members are as set forth on the attached Exhibit 8.1.[28]

4.2. Other Equity Owners. The names and addresses of other Equity Owners shall be maintained as provided under Sections 13.1 and 13.2.

ARTICLE 5
RIGHTS AND DUTIES OF MANAGERS

5.1. Management. The business and affairs of the Company shall be managed by its Managers. Except for situations in which the Approval of the Members is expressly required by this Agreement or by non-waivable provisions of applicable law, the Managers shall have full and complete authority, power, and discretion to manage and control the business, affairs and Properties of the Company, to make all decisions regarding those matters and to perform any and all other acts and activities customary or incident to the management of the Company's business. At any time when there is more than one Manager, *[any one Manager may take any action permitted to be taken by the Managers, unless the Approval of more than*

---

[27] The business of the Company is important for several reasons. First, what constitutes decisions in the ordinary course of the Company's business will be dictated by what that business is. Second, the business of the company may serve as a limitation on the ability of managers to take the Company in a dramatically different direction without whatever consent is necessary to amend this provision. Third, the business of the Company will be important in determining what constitute opportunities of the Company which need to be offered to it by those who owe fiduciary duties to the Company.

[28] Most statutes require a record of the names and addresses of members as well as the amount of cash and agreed value of contributions. This may be done in the text of the agreement, in an appendix or in a separate record (particularly with respect to the contribution). Because the initial Members need to be parties to the Operating Agreement, it is a good idea to identify them in it and have them sign it.

one of the Managers is expressly required pursuant to this Agreement or the Act or unless a majority of the Managers determine in a writing provided to the remaining Managers prior to such Managers taking a specified action that the Approval of more than one of the Managers is required in order to take such action]. [29] Unless authorized to do so by this Agreement or by the Managers, no attorney-in-fact, employee, or other agent of the Company shall have any power or authority to bind the Company in any way, to pledge its credit, or to render it liable pecuniarily for any purpose.

5.2. Number, Tenure and Qualifications. The number of Managers shall be fixed from time to time by the Approval of Members holding at least a *[Two-Thirds]* Interest, [30] but in no instance shall there be less than one Manager. [31] The Members hereby set the number of Managers at [_____], and the Managers shall be [_____], [_____], and [_____]. Each Manager shall hold office until such Manager resigns pursuant to Section 5.8 or is removed pursuant to Section 5.9. Managers need not be residents of **[State]** or Members.

5.3. Certain Powers of Managers. Without limiting the generality of Section 5.1 but subject to the limitations of Section 5.4, the Managers shall have power and authority, on behalf of the Company, to: [32]

(a) Acquire property from any Person as the Managers may determine (the fact that a Manager or an Equity Owner is directly or indirectly affiliated or connected with any such Person shall not prohibit the Managers from dealing with that Person);

(b) Borrow money for the Company from banks, other lending institutions, the Managers, Equity Owners, or Affiliates of the Managers or Equity Owners on such terms as the Managers deem appropriate and, in connection therewith, to Hypothecate Company Property to secure repayment of the borrowed sums;

---

[29] This provision enables Managers in a multi-Manager Company to take action without having to meet. An alternative to this is to have a "managing Manager" or other officer who is subject to the control of the Managers but may take day-to-day decisions.

[30] In some circumstances, the Members may want the ability for each Member to appoint and remove a Manager. If Managers are effectively serving in representative capacities with their principal obligations to the Member appointing the Manager, that consequences of that should be clear. That arrangement may have a significant impact on the duties of the Managers and a consequence of a Member's default may the removal or suspension of voting rights of the Manager appointed by that Member.

[31] As noted above, some states permit a Manager-managed Company to operate without a Manager and no statute states what the penalty for failing to maintain a Manager is.

[32] The matters set forth in this and subsequent sections should be reviewed so that each decision gets a level of approval that the Members believe to be appropriate in light of the deal and the Members' desires.

(c) Purchase liability and other insurance to protect the Company's property and business;

(d) Hold and own any Company real or personal properties in the name of the Company;

(e) Invest any Company funds (by way of example but not limitation) in time deposits, short-term governmental obligations, commercial paper, or other investments;

(f) Execute on behalf of the Company all instruments and documents, including checks, drafts, notes and other negotiable instruments; mortgages or deeds of trust; security agreements; financing statements; documents providing for the acquisition, mortgage, or disposition of Company Property; assignments; bills of sale; leases; partnership agreements; operating (or limited liability company) agreements of other limited liability companies; and any other instruments or documents necessary, in the *[reasonable]* opinion of the Managers, to the conduct of the business of the Company;

(g) Employ accountants, legal counsel, managing agents, or other experts to perform services for the Company and to compensate them from Company funds;

(h) Enter into any and all other agreements on behalf of the Company, with any other Person for any purpose and in such forms as the Managers may approve;

(i) Execute and file such other instruments, documents, and certificates which may from time to time be required by the laws of *[State]* or any other jurisdiction in which the Company shall determine to do business, or any political subdivision or agency thereof, to effectuate, implement, continue, and defend the valid existence of the Company;

(j) Open bank accounts in the name of the Company and to be the sole signatory thereon unless the Managers determine otherwise;

(k) Cause the Company to be a party to a Reorganization; and

(l) Do and perform all other acts as may be necessary or appropriate to the conduct of the Company's business.

5.4. Limitations on Authority. Notwithstanding any other provision of this Agreement, the Managers shall not cause or commit the Company to do any of the following without the Approval of Members holding a *[Two-Thirds Interest]*:

(a) Sell or otherwise dispose all or substantially all of the Company Property or any Company Property other than in the ordinary course of business;

(b) Hypothecate any Company Property to the extent that the secured indebtedness from such Hypothecation would exceed $_____;[33]

(c) Incur or refinance any indebtedness for money borrowed by the Company, whether secured or unsecured and including any indebtedness for money borrowed from a Member if, after such financing, the aggregate indebtedness of the Company would exceed $_____;[34]

(d) Incur any liability or make any single expenditure or series of related expenditures in an amount exceeding $_____;[35]

(e) Construct any capital improvements, repairs, alterations or changes involving an amount in excess of $_____;[36]

(f) Lend money to or guaranty or become surety for the obligations of any Person;

(g) Compromise or settle any claim against or inuring to the benefit of the Company involving an amount in controversy in excess of $_____; or

(h) Cause the Company to commence a voluntary case as debtor under the United States Bankruptcy Code.

5.5. Liability for Certain Acts.

(a) The Managers do not, in any way, guarantee the return of the Equity Owners' Capital Contributions or a profit for the Equity Owners from the operations of the Company.

(b) No Manager *[and no Affiliate of a Manager]* shall be liable to the Company or to any Equity Owner for any loss or damage sustained by the Company or any Equity Owner (or successor thereto), except to the extent, if any, that the loss or damage shall have been the result of *[negligence,] [gross negligence,]*[37] fraud, deceit, willful misconduct, or

---

[33] If the Company maintains an Annual Operating Plan, these should be tied to that Plan, e.g., exceeding the amount specified in the Annual Operating Plan by more than $_____ or may not be in excess of _____% of the amount specified in the Annual Operating Plan.

[34] If the Company maintains an Annual Operating Plan, these should be tied to that Plan, e.g., exceeding the amount specified in the Annual Operating Plan by more than $_____ or may not be in excess of _____% of the amount specified in the Annual Operating Plan.

[35] If the Company maintains an Annual Operating Plan, these should be tied to that Plan, e.g., exceeding the amount specified in the Annual Operating Plan by more than $_____ or may not be in excess of _____% of the amount specified in the Annual Operating Plan.

[36] If the Company maintains an Annual Operating Plan, these should be tied to that Plan, e.g., exceeding the amount specified in the Annual Operating Plan by more than $_____ or may not be in excess of _____% of the amount specified in the Annual Operating Plan.

[37] The default standard of care under the uniform partnership and LLC statutes is gross negligence.

[intentional][38] breach of this Agreement by such Manager *[or by such Affiliate of a Manager]*.

5.6. Managers and Members Have No Exclusive Duty to Company.

The Managers, Members, *[and their Affiliates]* shall have no exclusive duty to act on behalf of the Company. Each Manager, Member, *[and their Affiliates]* may have other business interests and may engage in other activities in addition to those relating to the Company. Neither the Company nor any Member shall have any right, by virtue of this Agreement, to share or participate in any other investments or activities of any other Member, the Manager, *[or any of their Affiliates]*. Neither any Manager, Member, *[or any of their Affiliates]* shall incur any liability to the Company or to any of the Equity Owners as a result of engaging in any other business or venture.[39]

5.7. Indemnity of the Managers, Employees and Other Agents.

(a) The Company shall indemnify each Manager *[and its Affiliates]* for any loss in connection with its activities (other than solely in its capacity as an Equity Owner, if applicable) in connection with the establishment, management or operations of the Company and make advances for expenses to the maximum extent permitted under the Act, except to the extent the claim for which indemnification is sought results from an act or omission for which the Manager *[or the Affiliates of such Manager]* *[may be]* *[is]* held liable to the Company or to a Member under Section 5.5(b).[40] The Company shall indemnify its employees and other agents

---

[38] Consider as alternatives or in addition, "material" and "repeated."

[39] This provision should be carefully considered in a couple of respects. First, the more specific the waiver of a duty of loyalty is, the more likely it is to enforced by a court. If there are particular types of transactions that can be anticipated, it may be advisable to list them in particular, perhaps using language above followed by something like "Without limiting the generality of the foregoing, the Member expressly agree that a Member or Manager may _____." Second, states differ in the ability to modify duties, particularly the duty of loyalty. The state statute should be carefully review. Finally, the Members should consider whether they want the duty of loyalty reduced to the maximum extent possible. This is one section where the agreement should accurately reflect the expectations of the parties. See, e.g., *McConnell v. Hunt Sport Enterprises*, 725 N.E.2d 1193 (Ohio App. 1999) upholding a provision stating that "Members shall not in any way be prohibited from or restricted in engaging or owning an interest in any other business venture of any nature, including any venture which might be competitive with the business of the Company. . .".

[40] Regardless of how the previous sections address the duty of care and loyalty, the indemnification section should provide for indemnification to the extent that the actions do not violate the standards set forth in those sections so that in the event of any loss, if the loss does not result from the violation of the agreed-upon standard, the Company bears the loss and if it does, the Member or Manager violating the standard bears the loss.

who are not Managers to the fullest extent permitted by law, *[provided that such indemnification in any given situation is Approved by Members owning a Majority Interest]*.

(b) Expenses (including legal fees and expenses) incurred by a Manager *[or by one of its Affiliates]* in defending any claim, demand, action, suit or proceeding subject to subsection (a) above shall be paid by the Company in advance of the final disposition of such claim, demand, action, suit, or proceeding upon receipt of an undertaking (which need not be secured) by or on behalf of the Manager to repay such amount if it shall ultimately be finally determined by a court of competent jurisdiction and not subject to appeal, that the Manager *[or such Affiliate]* is not entitled to be indemnified by the Company as authorized hereunder.

5.8. Resignation. Any Manager may resign at any time by giving written notice to the Members. The resignation of any Manager shall take effect upon receipt of notice thereof or at such later time as shall be specified in such notice; and, unless otherwise specified therein, the acceptance of such resignation shall not be necessary to make it effective. The resignation of a Manager who is also an Equity Owner shall not affect the Manager's rights as an Equity Owner and shall not constitute a withdrawal of an Equity Owner.

5.9. Removal. At a meeting called expressly for that purpose, all or any lesser number of Managers may be removed at any time by Approval of the Members holding a *[Majority Interest]* *[Two-Thirds Interest]* (determined without regard to any Voting Interest held by the Manager who is to be removed and who is also a Member) for *[gross negligence, fraud, deceit or intentional misconduct which had a material adverse effect on the Company, or if the Manager is adjudicated incompetent by a Court of competent jurisdiction/is Disabled] [with or without cause]*. The removal of a Manager who is also an Equity Owner shall not affect the Manager's rights as an Equity Owner and shall not constitute a withdrawal of an Equity Owner.[41]

5.10. Vacancies. Any vacancy occurring for any reason in the number of Managers shall be filled by the Approval of Members holding a *[Majority Interest]* (determined without regard to any Voting Interest owned by a Manager who was removed pursuant to Section 5.9 during the preceding 24-month period). Any Manager's position to be filled by reason of an increase in the number of Managers shall be filled by the Approval of Members holding a Majority Interest.

---

[41] Consider the advisability of including an option in favor of the Company or the other members to purchase the Ownership Interest of a Manager (assuming the Manager has an Ownership Interest) in the event that the Manager is removed for cause pursuant to this Section 5.9. For example, if the Manager commits fraud, the Company will presumably wish it had an option to buy out any Membership Interest owned by the offending Member.

5.11. Compensation, Reimbursement, Organization Expenses.

(a) *[The compensation of the Managers shall be fixed from time to time by Approval of Members holding at least a Majority Interest, and no Manager shall be prevented from receiving such compensation by reason of the fact that he is also a Member.] [No Member shall be entitled to compensation from the Company for services rendered to the Company as such.]* Upon the submission of appropriate documentation, each Manager shall be reimbursed by the Company for reasonable out-of-pocket expenses incurred on behalf, or at the request, of the Company.

(b) The Company shall reimburse _____ and _____ for the legal expenses reasonably incurred by them in connection with the formation, organization and capitalization of the Company, including the legal fees incurred in connection with negotiating and drafting this Agreement and _____.

(c) The Managers shall cause the Company to make an appropriate election to treat the expenses incurred by the Company in connection with the formation and organization of the Company to be amortized over the period allowed by Code Section 709 to the extent that such expenses constitute "organizational expenses" of the Company within the meaning of Code Section 709(b)(2).

(d) *[The Company shall reimburse each Manager for the costs it incurs for legal advice from that Manager's own attorney with respect to the Manager's rights and duties under this Agreement and the Act. The Company and the Members expressly agree that notwithstanding the reimbursement of the Manager's legal expenses, the Manager's attorney shall not be attorney for, nor have an attorney-client relationship with, the Company or for any other Person other than the Manager by reason of the reimbursement.]*[42]

5.12. Annual Operating Plan.[43] The Members have approved the Company's construction budget. The Managers shall prepare for the Approval of the Members each Fiscal Year (no later than thirty (30) days prior to the end of the then current Fiscal Year) a business plan (the "Annual Operating Plan") for the next Fiscal Year, setting forth at a minimum the estimated receipts (including capital calls) and expenditures (capital, operating and other) of the Company in sufficient detail to provide an estimate of cash flow, capital proceeds, and other financial requirements of the Company for such year. Any such Annual Operating Plan shall also

---

[42] In a particularly contentious situation a Manager may want the Company to defer the costs of the Manager's attorney, while affording the Manager the benefit of its own counsel. This provision, if desired, needs to be carefully considered as do the ethical considerations for the attorney for the Manager.

[43] As noted above, if his provision is included. Sections 5.3 and 5.4 should be conformed with the Annual Operating Plan.

include such other information or other matters necessary in order to inform the Members of the Company's business and to enable the Members to make an informed decision with respect to their Approval of such Annual Operating Plan. The Members shall review the proposed Annual Operating Plan and shall offer any revisions thereto within *[30]* days. After the final Annual Operating Plan has been approved by the Members, the Managers shall implement the Annual Operating Plan and shall be authorized to make only the expenditures and incur only the obligations provided for therein (subject to Section 5.4(b)). Notwithstanding the foregoing, the Managers may make any expenditure or incur any obligation, whether or not such expenditure or obligation is provided for in an Annual Operating Plan, which is the legal obligation of the Company and not within the reasonable control of the Managers (e.g., real or personal property taxes). If the Members are not able to agree on an Annual Operating Plan for any year, each line item in the Annual Operating Plan for the prior year shall be increased by the percentage increase in the CPI Index from the first day for which the previous Annual Operating Plan was in effect to the first day for which the new Annual Operating Plan is to be in effect. If the CPI Index is no longer published, published less frequently, or altered in some other manner, then the Managers shall, from time to time, adopt a substitute index or substitute procedure which reasonably reflects and monitors consumer prices, and the resulting plan shall be the Annual Operating Plan for the current year.

5.13. Right to Rely on the Managers. Any Person dealing with the Company may rely (without duty of further inquiry) upon a certificate signed by any Manager as to:

(a) The identity of any Manager or Equity Owner;

(b) The existence or nonexistence of any fact or facts which constitute a condition precedent to acts on behalf of the Company by any Manager or which are in any other manner germane to the affairs of the Company;

(c) The Persons who are authorized to execute and deliver any instrument or document of the Company; or

(d) Any act or failure to act by the Company or any other matter whatsoever involving the Company or any Equity Owner.

ARTICLE 6
RIGHTS AND OBLIGATIONS OF EQUITY OWNERS

6.1. Limitation of Liability. Except as otherwise provided by this Agreement and the non-waivable provisions of the Act, no Equity Owner shall be liable for an obligation of the Company solely by reason of being or acting as an Equity Owner.

6.2. List of Equity Owners. Upon written request of any Member made in good faith and for a purpose reasonably related to the Member's rights as a Member under this Agreement (which reason shall be set forth in the written request), a Manager shall provide a list showing the names, addresses and Ownership Interests of all Equity Owners. Economic Interest Owners shall have no rights to information under this Section 6.2.

6.3. Equity Owners Have No Agency Authority. Except as expressly provided in this Agreement, the Equity Owners (in their capacity as Equity Owners) shall have no agency authority on behalf of the Company.

6.4. Priority and Return of Capital. Except as may be expressly provided in Article 9, no Equity Owner shall have priority over any other Equity Owner, either as to the return of Capital Contributions or as to Profits, Losses or Distributions; provided, however, that this Section 6.4 shall not apply to loans (as distinguished from Capital Contributions) which an Equity Owner has made to the Company.

6.5. Non-Colorado Resident Equity Owners. Equity Owners that are not residents of Colorado agree to sign a completed Colorado Department of Revenue form DR0107 and agree to return the completed form to the Company. Such Equity Owners also agree to file a Colorado income tax return and pay all Colorado taxes with respect to their allocable share of the taxable earnings of the Company each year.[44] All Equity Owners agree to comply with similar provisions imposed on non-resident Equity Owners in any other state in which the Company does business and which imposes similar requirements on non-resident Equity Owners.

ARTICLE 7
ACTIONS OF MEMBERS

7.1. Approval of Members. Unless otherwise required in this Agreement, Approvals of the Members may be communicated or reflected [orally,][45] electronically[,] or in writing, and no action need be taken at a formal meeting. If, however, any Approval is required to be in writing, such Approval shall be evidenced (i) by a written consent, which may be executed in separate written counterparts or (ii) by the Approval of the Members at a meeting, in each case by Members holding the requisite number of Voting Interests required for such Approval. If not done in writing, then (unless such Approval is required to be in writing) any Approval of the Members shall be effective when a sufficient number of Members holding the requisite threshold of Voting Interests required to give such Approval communicate their Approval to the Managers.

---

[44] This provision is obviously based on Colorado law. Some other states have similar provisions and they should be consulted.

[45] While informality can expedite operations, some members may want a written document.

7.2. Members' Meetings. Members may, but are not required to, meet from time to time on at least five days' written notice which may be given by a Manager or by any Member [holding at least a Majority Interest]. Members holding at least a [Majority Interest], represented in person or by proxy, shall constitute a quorum at any meeting of the Members. The foregoing shall constitute the procedure for all meetings of the Members.]

7.3. No Required Meetings. The Members may, but shall not be required to, hold any annual, periodic, or other formal meetings. However, meetings of the Members may be called by any Manager *[who is also a Member]* or by any Member or Members holding at least [_____] percent of the Voting Interests.[46]

7.4. Place of Meetings. The Member or Members calling the meeting may designate any place within *[State]* as the place of meeting for any meeting of the Members; Members holding a Two-Thirds Interest may designate any place outside *[State]* as the place of meeting for any meeting of the Members. If no designation is made, or if a special meeting be otherwise called, the place of meeting shall be the principal executive office of the Company in *[State]*.

7.5. Notice of Meetings. Except as provided in Section 7.6, written notice stating the place, day and hour of the meeting and the purpose or purposes for which the meeting is called shall be delivered not less than ten nor more than 50 days before the date of the meeting, either personally or by mail, by or at the direction of the Member or Members calling the meeting, to each Member entitled to vote at such meeting.

7.6. Meeting of all Members. If all of the Members shall meet at any time and place, either within or outside of *[State]*, and Approve to the holding of a meeting at such time and place, such meeting shall be valid without call or notice, and at such meeting lawful action may be taken.

7.7. Record Date. For the purpose of determining Members entitled to notice of or to vote at any meeting of Members or any adjournment thereof, or Members entitled to receive payment of any Distribution, or in order to make a determination of Members for any other purpose, the date on which notice of the meeting is mailed or the date on which the resolution declaring such Distribution is adopted, as the case may be, shall be the record date for such determination of Members. When a determination of Members entitled to vote at any meeting of Members has been made as provided in this Section 7.7, such determination shall apply to any adjournment thereof.

7.8. Quorum. Members holding at least a *[Two-Thirds Interest]*, represented in person or by proxy, shall constitute a quorum at any meeting of Members. In the absence of a quorum at any such meeting, a majority

---

[46] In some circumstances, such as two-member LLCs, the complex meeting provisions set forth in this and the following sections will be unnecessary and can be dispensed with.

of the Voting Interests so represented may adjourn the meeting from time to time for a period not to exceed 60 days without further notice. However, if the adjournment is for more than 60 days, or if after the adjournment a new record date is fixed for the adjourned meeting, a notice of the adjourned meeting shall be given to each Member of record entitled to vote at the meeting. At such adjourned meeting at which a quorum shall be present or represented, any business may be transacted which might have been transacted at the meeting as originally noticed. The Members present at a duly organized meeting may continue to transact business until adjournment, notwithstanding the withdrawal during such meeting of that number of Voting Interests whose absence would cause less than a quorum.

7.9. Manner of Acting. If a quorum is present, the affirmative vote of Members holding a Majority Interest shall be the act of the Members, unless the vote of a greater or lesser proportion or number is otherwise required by the Act, by the *[Articles of Organization/Certificate of Formation]*, or by this Agreement. Unless otherwise expressly provided herein, Members, who have an interest (economic or otherwise) in the outcome of any particular matter upon which the Members vote, may vote upon any such matter, and their Voting Interest shall be counted in the determination of whether the requisite matter is approved by the Members.

7.10. Proxies. At all meetings of Members, a Member who is qualified to vote may vote in person or by proxy executed in writing by the Member or by a duly authorized attorney-in-fact. Such proxy shall be filed with the Managers before or at the time of the meeting. Such proxy shall expire eleven months from the date of its execution or the date indicated in such proxy, whichever occurs first.

7.11. Action by Members Without a Meeting. Action required or permitted to be taken at a meeting of Members may be taken without a meeting if the action is evidenced by one or more written consents describing the action taken and signed by Members holding sufficient Voting Interests, as the case may be, to Approve such action had such action been properly voted on at a duly called meeting of the Members. Action taken under this Section 7.11 is effective when Members with the requisite Voting Interests have signed the consent, unless the consent specifies a different effective date. The record date for determining the Members who are entitled to take action without a meeting shall be the date the first Member signs a consent.

7.12. Waiver of Notice. When any notice is required to be given to any Member, a waiver thereof in writing signed by the person entitled to such notice, whether before, at, or after the time stated therein, shall be equivalent to the giving of such notice.

ARTICLE 8
CONTRIBUTIONS TO THE COMPANY AND CAPITAL ACCOUNTS

8.1. <u>Members' Capital Contributions</u>. Not later than *[ten days after each of the parties has executed this Agreement and delivered an executed copy of same to the Managers]*, each Equity Owner shall contribute such amount as is set forth in <u>Exhibit 8.1</u> hereto as its share of the Initial Capital Contribution.

8.2. <u>Additional Contributions</u>. *[Each Equity Owner shall be required to make such additional Capital Contributions as shall be determined by the Managers from time to time to be necessary to meet the expenses of the Company; provided, however, that the maximum amount which an Equity Owner shall be required to contribute to the Company pursuant to this Section 8.2 (i.e., in addition to the amount contributed by such Equity Owner pursuant to Section 8.1) shall not exceed the amount set forth corresponding to such Equity Owner's name on <u>Exhibit 8.2</u>. Upon the making of any such determination, the Managers shall give written notice to each Equity Owner of the amount of required additional contribution, and each Equity Owner shall deliver to the Company its pro rata share thereof (in proportion to [Sharing Ratios/other?] of the Member on the date such notice is given) no later than 30 days following the date such notice is given. None of the terms, covenants, obligations or rights contained in this Section 8.2 is or shall be deemed to be for the benefit of any Person other than the Equity Owners and the Company, and no such third person shall under any circumstances have any right to compel any actions or payments by the Managers or the Equity Owners.]*

OR

[Except as set forth in Section 8.1, no Equity Owner shall be required to make any Capital Contributions. To the extent unanimously Approved by the Managers, from time to time, the Equity Owners may be permitted to make additional Capital Contributions if and to the extent that both (i) they so desire and (ii) the Managers determine that such additional Capital Contributions are necessary or appropriate in connection with the conduct of the Company's business (including expansion or diversification). In such event, the Equity Owners shall have the opportunity (but not the obligation) to participate in such additional Capital Contributions proportionate to [their Sharing Ratios]. [At the time such Capital Contributions are made, the Sharing Ratios of the Equity Owners [and Voting Interests of the Members] shall be adjusted in an equitable manner determined by the Managers and the Members in their reasonable discretion.]

8.3. <u>Capital Accounts</u>.

(a) A separate Capital Account shall be maintained for each Equity Owner. Each Equity Owner's Capital Account shall be increased by (i) the amount of money contributed by such Equity Owner to the Company; (ii) the Gross Asset Value of property contributed by such Equity Owner to the Company (net of liabilities secured by such contributed property that the Company is considered to assume or take subject to under Section 752 of the Code); (iii) allocations to such Equity Owner of Profits; and (iv) any items in the nature of income and gain which are specially allocated to the Equity Owner pursuant to Sections 9.2 and 9.3. Each Equity Owner's Capital Account shall be decreased by (1) the amount of money Distributed to such Equity Owner by the Company; (2) the Gross Asset Value of property Distributed to such Equity Owner by the Company (net of liabilities secured by such Distributed property that such Equity Owner is considered to assume or take subject to under Section 752 of the Code); (3) any items in the nature of deduction and loss that are specially allocated to the Equity Owner pursuant to Sections 9.2 and 9.3; and (4) allocations to such Equity Owner of Losses.

(b) Without limiting the other rights and duties of a transferee of an Ownership Interest pursuant to this Agreement, in the event of a permitted sale or exchange of an Ownership Interest in the Company, (i) the Capital Account of the transferor shall become the Capital Account of the transferee to the extent it relates to the transferred Ownership Interest in accordance with Section 1.704-1(b)(2)(iv) of the Regulations, and (ii) the transferee shall be treated as the transferor for purposes of allocations and distributions pursuant to Article 9 to the extent that such allocations and distributions relate to the transferred Ownership Interest.

(c) The manner in which Capital Accounts are to be maintained pursuant to this Section 8.3 is intended to comply with the requirements of Section 704(b) of the Code and the Regulations thereunder. If in the opinion of the Company's accountants the manner in which Capital Accounts are to be maintained pursuant to the preceding provisions of this Section 8.3 should be modified in order to comply with Section 704(b) of the Code and the Regulations thereunder, then, notwithstanding anything to the contrary contained in the preceding provisions of this Section 8.3, the method in which Capital Accounts are maintained shall be so modified; provided, however, that any change in the manner of maintaining Capital Accounts shall not materially alter the economic agreement between or among the Equity Owners.

(d) Upon liquidation of the Company, liquidating Distributions shall be made in accordance with the positive Capital Account balances of the Equity Owners, as determined after taking into account all Capital Account adjustments for the Company's taxable year during which the liquidation occurs. Liquidation proceeds shall be paid in accordance with Section 12.3. The Company may offset damages for breach of this Agreement by any Equity Owner whose interest is liquidated (either upon the withdrawal of the Equity Owner or the liquidation of the Company) against the amount otherwise Distributable to such Equity

Owner. No Equity Owner shall have any obligation to restore all or any portion of a deficit balance in such Equity Owner's Capital Account.

(e) The Managers shall also: (i) make any adjustments that are necessary or appropriate to maintain equality between the Capital Accounts of the Equity Owners and the amount of capital reflected on the Company's balance sheet, as computed for book purposes, in accordance with Section 1.704-1(b)(2)(iv)(q) of the Regulations, and (ii) make any appropriate modifications in the event unanticipated events might otherwise cause this Agreement not to comply with Section 1.704-1(b) of the Regulations; provided that, to the extent that any such adjustment is inconsistent with other provisions of this Agreement and would have a material adverse effect on any Equity Owner, such adjustment shall require the consent of such Equity Owner.

8.4. Withdrawal   or   Reduction   of   Equity   Owners' Contributions to Capital.

(a) A Member may withdraw as a Member at any time. A Member's withdrawal shall cause the Member's Membership Interest to become an Economic Interest, but shall not entitle the former Member or his or her successor to demand that the Economic Interest be liquidated.

(b) An Equity Owner shall not receive a Distribution of any part of its Capital Contribution to the extent such Distribution would violate Section 9.5.

(c) *An Equity Owner, irrespective of the nature of its Capital Contribution, does not have the right to demand and receive property other than cash in return for its Capital Contribution.*

8.5. Remedies for Non-Payment of Capital Contributions.
Failure of any Equity Owner to make full and timely payment to the Company of any additional Capital Contribution properly assessed hereunder shall constitute a breach of this Agreement (and any such Equity Owner shall be hereinafter referred to as a "Defaulting Equity Owner"). Upon such a breach, the Managers shall promptly give notice (the "Default Notice") to all Equity Owners of: (a) the breach and (b) a Special Meeting to discuss the appropriate course of action. The Equity Owners who timely satisfied their obligation to make the required Additional Capital Contributions (the "Non-Defaulting Equity Owners") may, upon the Approval of those Non-Defaulting Equity Owners which are Members holding a majority of the Voting Interests owned by all Non-Defaulting Equity Owners which are Members, pursue the following courses of action:

(a) The Non-Defaulting Equity Owners, shall have an option, but no obligation, to loan to the Company within sixty (60) days after the Default Notice is given (the "Loan Decision Period") the amount which the Defaulting Equity Owners have failed to contribute to the Company (proportionate to the ratio of the interest in Profits held by each respective

Equity Owner electing to loan funds, to the interest in Profits Interests held by all Equity Owners electing to advance funds). The amount that is loaned by any Non-Defaulting Equity Owner shall, at the election of each such Equity Owner (exercised by written notice to the Defaulting Equity Owner and the Company at the time the loan is made), be treated in either of the following manners:

(i) The loan may be treated as a loan to the Company, bearing interest at a floating rate equal to five (5) percentage points higher than the prime commercial lending rate in effect from time to time at the principal bank used by the Company for banking and borrowing purposes Prime Rate, payable out of any funds paid by, or withheld by the Company from, the Defaulting Equity Owner to cure the breach, or at such other time as the Company and the lending Equity Owners may agree. Payments shall be credited first to accrued interest. The promissory note or other loan documentation shall contain such other terms and conditions as mutually agreed by the Company and the lending Equity Owners.

(ii) The loan may be treated as a loan to the Defaulting Equity Owner, followed by a contribution of the borrowed funds to the Company by the Defaulting Equity Owner curing the breach in whole or in part. Such a loan shall be payable on demand and bear interest at the default rate provided above. Until the Defaulting Equity Owner's debt to any Non-Defaulting Equity Owners, together with interest thereon, is paid in full, any funds or property which would otherwise be Distributed to the Defaulting Equity Owner from time to time hereunder shall be paid to such Non-Defaulting Equity Owners, according to their respective shares of loans (which are treated as loans to the Defaulting Equity Owner). Any such payments shall be deemed to be Distributions to the Defaulting Equity Owner by the Company, followed by appropriate payments by the Defaulting Equity Owner to the respective Non-Defaulting Equity Owners. Payments shall be credited first to accrued interest. Payments to Non-Defaulting Equity Owners of loans by them pursuant to either Section 8.5(a)(1) or 8.5(a)(2) shall be made *pari passu*.

(b) If the Non-Defaulting Equity Owners do not make loans pursuant to Section 8.5(a) in an amount at least equal to the amount which the Defaulting Equity Owner failed to contribute (and the Defaulting Equity Owner has not cured said breach prior to the expiration of the Loan Decision Period), then promptly upon the expiration of the Loan Decision Period, the Managers shall give notice (the "Default Purchase Option Notice" as more fully described below) to all of the Equity Owners. The Non-Defaulting Equity Owners shall have the option (but no obligation) for the sixty (60) day period commencing upon the date of the Default Purchase Option Notice to purchase all, but not less than all, of a Defaulting Equity Owner's Interest as provided in this Section 8.5(b). The option granted in this Section 8.5(b) (the "Default Purchase Option") shall be exercisable in the following manner and in accordance with the following terms:

(i) The Default Purchase Option Notice shall notify the Non-Defaulting Equity Owners that they have the opportunity to purchase all, but not less than all, of the Ownership Interest owned by the Defaulting Equity Owner ("Available Ownership Interest").

(ii) A Non-Defaulting Equity Owner wishing to exercise the Default Purchase Option shall so notify (the "Exercise Notice") the Defaulting Equity Owner and the Company within forty-five (45) days after the date that the Default Purchase Option Notice is given.

(iii) Each Non-Defaulting Equity Owner electing to exercise the Default Purchase Option (each an "Electing Equity Owner" and collectively the "Electing Equity Owners") shall be entitled to purchase a portion of the Available Ownership Interest proportionate to the Electing Equity Owner's sharing ratio.

(iv) The closing for any purchase and sale of the Available Ownership Interest pursuant to this Section 8.5(b) shall take place within ninety (90) days after the date that the Default Purchase Option Notice is given. The specific time and place of closing shall be as agreed by the Electing Equity Owners and the Defaulting Member; provided, however, that in the absence of agreement, the closing shall take place at the Company's principal office.

(v) The price for the Defaulting Equity Owner's Ownership Interest (the "Default Buyout Price") shall be equal to *[fifty percent (50%)]* of the Defaulting Equity Owner's Capital Account balance as of the last day of the month preceding the month in which the Exercise Notice is given. For purposes of this Section 8.5(b), the Company's independent certified public accountant shall determine the balance in the Defaulting Equity Owner's Capital Account (without regard to any optional adjustments which may, but are not required, to be made for any purpose, including any optional adjustments that may be made in order to reflect the fair market value of Company Property), and such determination shall be final for purposes of this Agreement.

(vi) Upon any purchase of a Defaulting Equity Owner's Ownership Interest pursuant to this Section 8.5(b), the Default Buyout Price may be paid at closing in immediately available funds, or, in the sole discretion of each Electing Equity Owner, by delivering at closing a note issued by the Electing Members as payment for the portion of the Buyout Price attributable to the portion of the Ownership Interest to be purchased by the Electing Equity Owner. The notes issued as payment for the Default Buyout Price shall be negotiable promissory notes of the Company or of the Electing Equity Owner, as appropriate, bearing interest per annum at a floating rate one percentage point over the prime commercial lending rate in effect from time to time at the principal bank used by the Company for banking and borrowing purposes. Any such notes shall provide for payments of principal and interest in equal consecutive monthly installments over a period of not more than five years from the date of issuance of such note, commencing from the date of issuance of such note. Any such notes shall be prepayable without penalty, in whole or in part, with prepayments applied to the last installment or installments coming due. Such notes shall provide that if any installment of principal or interest is not paid when due or if suit is brought thereon, the maker will pay all costs of collection, including reasonable attorneys' fees.

(vii) After purchasing an Available Ownership Interest, each Electing Equity Owner shall make an additional Capital Contribution to the Company in an amount equal to the proportionate share of the Defaulted Capital Contribution attributable to the portion of the Available Ownership Interest purchased by the Electing Equity Owner.

ARTICLE 9
ALLOCATIONS, INCOME TAX, DISTRIBUTIONS, ELECTIONS AND REPORTS

9.1. Allocations of Profits and Losses from Operations. Except as provided in Sections 9.2 and 9.3, the Profits and Losses for each Fiscal Year shall be allocated as follows:

(a) *[Losses shall be allocated among the Equity Owners in accordance with their relative Sharing Ratios.*

(b) *Profits shall be allocated as follows:*

(i) *First, to each Equity Owner which previously has been allocated Losses pursuant to Section 9.1(a) which have not been fully offset by allocations of Profits pursuant to this Section 9.1(b)(i) ("Unrecovered Losses") until the total amount of Profits allocated to each such Equity Owner pursuant to this Section 9.1(b)(i) is equal to the total amount of Losses which have been allocated to such Equity Owner pursuant to Section 9.1(a). Profits allocated pursuant to this Section 9.1(b)(i) shall be allocated to the Equity Owners in proportion to their respective Unrecovered Losses;*

(ii) *Second, to each Equity Owner an amount equal to the total amount of the Preferred Accrual proportionate with the Preferred Accruals of all Equity Owners until the aggregate amount allocated pursuant to this Section 9.1(b)(ii) equals its Preferred Accrual;*[47]

---

[47] *This section 9.1(b) should be used when section 9.4(b)(i) is used] [consider drafting so that allocations follow cash flow if cash situation may create phantom income problem, but consider risk that income may not be sufficient to follow cash].*

(iii) *Third, to the Equity Owners in proportion to their Sharing Ratios.]*

Notwithstanding the provisions of this Section 9.1, it is the intent of the Equity Owners that Profits and Losses will be allocated in a manner that causes the Capital Accounts of the Equity Owners, in conjunction with all Distributions made in accordance with Section 9.4, to have balances such that the Equity Owners would receive amounts equal to that called for in Section 9.4 on a liquidation pursuant to Article 12 and this Section 9.1 shall be interpreted in a manner to accomplish this result, including special allocations of gross income and gross deductions, by the Managers.

9.2. Special Allocations to Capital Accounts. Notwithstanding Section 9.1 hereof:

(a) In the event that any Equity Owner unexpectedly receives any adjustments, allocations or Distributions described in Sections 1.704-1(b)(2)(ii)(d)(4), (5), or (6) of the Regulations, which create or increase a Deficit Capital Account of such Equity Owner, then items of Company income and gain (consisting of a *pro rata* portion of each item of Company income, including gross income, and gain for such year and, if necessary, for subsequent years) shall be specially allocated to such Equity Owner in an amount and manner sufficient to eliminate, to the extent required by the Regulations, the Deficit Capital Account so created as quickly as possible. It is the intent that this Section 9.2(a) be interpreted to comply with the alternate test for economic effect set forth in Section 1.704-1(b)(2)(ii)(d) of the Regulations.

(b) The Losses allocated pursuant to Section 9.1 hereof shall not exceed the maximum amount of Losses that can be so allocated without causing any Equity Owner to have a Deficit Capital Account at the end of any Fiscal Year. In the event that some, but not all, of the Equity Owners would have Deficit Capital Accounts as a consequence of an allocation of Losses pursuant to Section 9.1 hereof, the limitation set forth in the preceding sentence shall be applied on a Equity Owner by Equity Owner basis so as to allocate the maximum permissible Losses to each Equity Owner under Section 1.704-1(b)(2)(ii)(d) of the Regulations. All Losses in excess of the limitation set forth in this Section 9.2(b) shall be allocated to the Equity Owners in proportion to their respective positive Capital Account balances, if any, and thereafter to the Equity Owners in accordance with their interests in the Company as determined by the Managers in their reasonable discretion. In the event that any Equity Owner would have a Deficit Capital Account at the end of any Fiscal Year, the Capital Account of such Equity Owner shall be specially credited with items of Company income (including gross income) and gain in the amount of such excess as quickly as possible.

(c) Notwithstanding any other provision of this Section 9.2, if there is a net decrease in the Company Minimum Gain during any Fiscal Year, then the Capital Accounts of each Equity Owner shall be specially allocated items of income (including gross income) and gain for such Fiscal

Year (and if necessary for subsequent Fiscal Years) equal to that Equity Owner's share of the net decrease in Company Minimum Gain, determined in accordance with Section 1.704-2(g) of the Regulations. Allocations pursuant to the previous sentence shall be made in proportion to the respective amounts required to be allocated to each Equity Owner pursuant thereto. The items to be so allocated shall be determined in accordance with Sections 1.704-2(f)(6) and 1.704-2(j)(2) of the Regulations. If in any Fiscal Year that the Company has a net decrease in the Company Minimum Gain, if the minimum gain chargeback requirement would cause a distortion in the economic arrangement among the Equity Owners and it is not expected that the Company will have sufficient other income to correct that distortion, the Managers may in their discretion (and shall, if requested to do so by a Equity Owner) seek to have the Internal Revenue Service waive the minimum gain chargeback requirement in accordance with Section 1.704-2(f)(4) of the Regulations.

(d) Notwithstanding any other provision of this Section 9.2 except Section 9.2(c), if there is a net decrease in Equity Owner Minimum Gain attributable to a Equity Owner Nonrecourse Debt during any Fiscal Year, each Equity Owner who has a share of the Equity Owner Minimum Gain as of the beginning of the Fiscal Year shall be specially allocated items of Company income and gain for such Fiscal Year (and, if necessary, subsequent Fiscal Years) equal to such Equity Owner's share of the net decrease in Equity Owner Minimum Gain attributable to such Equity Owner Nonrecourse Debt, determined in accordance with Section 1.704-2(i)(4) of the Regulations. An Equity Owner shall not be subject to this provision to the extent that an exception is provided by Section 1.704-2(i)(4) of the Regulations and any administrative guidance issued by the Internal Revenue Service with respect thereto. Allocations pursuant to the previous sentence shall be made in proportion to the respective amounts required to be allocated to each Equity Owner pursuant thereto. The items to be so allocated shall be determined in accordance with Sections 1.704-2(i)(4) and 1.704-2(j)(2) of the Regulations. Any Equity Owner Minimum Gain allocated pursuant to this provision shall consist of first, gains recognized from the disposition of Company property subject to the Equity Owner Nonrecourse Debt, and, second, if necessary, a *pro rata* portion of the Company's other items of income or gain (including gross income) for that Fiscal Year. This Section 9.2(d) is intended to comply with the minimum gain chargeback requirement in Section 1.704-2(i)(4) of the Regulations and shall be interpreted consistently therewith.

(e) Items of Company loss, deduction and expenditures described in Section 705(a)(2)(B) of the Code which are attributable to any nonrecourse debt of the Company and are characterized as partner nonrecourse deductions under Section 1.704-2(i) of the Regulations shall be allocated to the Equity Owners' Capital Accounts in accordance with said Section 1.704-2(i) of the Regulations.

(f) Beginning in the first taxable year in which there are allocations of "nonrecourse deductions" (as described in Section 1.704-2(b) of the Regulations), such deductions shall be allocated to the Equity Owners in the same manner as Loss is allocated for such period.

(g) To the extent that an adjustment to the adjusted tax basis of any Company asset pursuant to Section 734(b) or 743(b) of the Code is required pursuant to Section 1.704-1(b)(2)(iv)(m)(2) or 1.704-1(b)(2)(iv)(m)(4) of the Regulations, to be taken into account in determining Capital Accounts as the result of a Distribution to an Equity Owner in complete liquidation of its Ownership Interest, the amount of such adjustment to Capital Accounts shall be treated as an item of gain (if the adjustment increases the basis of the asset) or loss (if the adjustment decreases such basis), and such gain or loss shall be specially allocated to the Equity Owners in accordance with their interests in the Company in the event Section 1.704-1(b)(2)(iv)(m)(2) of the Regulations applies, or to the Equity Owner to whom such Distribution was made in the event Section 1.704-1(b)(2)(iv)(m)(4) of the Regulations applies.

(h) The Issuance Items shall be allocated among the Equity Owners so that, to the extent possible, the net amount of such Issuance Items, together with all other allocations under this Agreement to each Equity Owner, shall be equal to the net amount that would have been allocated to each such Equity Owner if the Issuance Items had not been realized.

9.3. Credit or Charge to Capital Accounts. Any credit or charge to the Capital Accounts of the Equity Owners pursuant to the Regulatory Allocations shall be taken into account in computing subsequent allocations of Profits and Losses pursuant to Section 9.1, so that the net amount of any items charged or credited to Capital Accounts pursuant to Section 9.1 and the Regulatory Allocations hereof and this Section 9.3 shall to the extent possible, be equal to the net amount that would have been allocated to the Capital Account of each Equity Owner pursuant to the provisions of this Article 9 if the special allocations required by the Regulatory Allocations hereof had not occurred; provided, however, that no such allocation will be made pursuant to this Section 9.3 if (i) the Regulatory Allocation had the effect of offsetting a prior Regulatory Allocation or (ii) the Regulatory Allocation likely (in the opinion of the Company's accountants) will be offset by another Regulatory Allocation in the future (e.g., Regulatory Allocation of "nonrecourse deductions" under Section 9.2(e) that likely will be subject to a subsequent "minimum gain chargeback" under Section 9.2(c)).

9.4. Distributions. *[ALTERNATIVE 1: Except as provided in Sections 8.3(d) (with respect to liquidating Distributions) and 9.5 (with respect to limitations on Distributions), the Company shall Distribute Distributable Cash [not less frequently than quarterly] to the Equity Owners in accordance with their [Sharing Ratios]. All Distributions which, when made, exceed the recipient Equity Owner's basis in that Equity Owner's Ownership Interest* *shall be considered advances or drawings against the Equity Owner's distributive share of taxable income or gain. To the extent it is determined at the end of the Fiscal Year that the recipient Equity Owner has not been allocated taxable income or gain that equals or exceeds the total of such advances or drawings for such Fiscal Year, such Equity Owner shall be obligated to recontribute any such excess advances or drawings to the Company. Notwithstanding the foregoing sentence, an Equity Owner will not be required to recontribute such advances or drawings to the extent that, on the last day of the Fiscal Year, such Equity Owner's basis in its Ownership Interest in the Company has increased from the time of such advance or drawing. Any advance or drawings which are recontributed by a Equity Owner pursuant to this Section 9.4, shall be redistributed to such Equity Owner either at the option of such Equity Owner or at such time that such distribution will not exceed such Equity Owner's basis in its Ownership Interest.]*

[ALTERNATIVE 2, for illustrative purposes only: Except as provided in Sections 8.3(d) (with respect to liquidating Distributions) and 9.5 (with respect to limitations on Distributions):

(a) The Company shall Distribute Distributable Cash [not less frequently than quarterly] to each Equity Owner in proportion to the federal taxable income of the Company which will be [and has been] allocated to such Equity Owner ("Tax Profits") for the current [and all prior] Fiscal Year[s] as reasonably estimated by the Managers no later than 10 days prior to the dates that federal estimated quarterly taxes are due for individuals an amount equal to the remainder, if any, of: (i) the product of [40%] [the Tax Rate] multiplied times the estimated Tax Profits allocable to such Equity Owner [for the prior years and the] portion of the year ending on the last day of the most recent quarter, minus (ii) the sum of all Distributions made to each such Equity Owner pursuant to this Section 9.4(a) with respect to such Fiscal Year[s], plus the product of [40%] [the Tax Rate] multiplied times any Unrecovered Tax Losses attributable to such Equity Owner as of the first day of the current Fiscal Year. The Unrecovered Tax Losses attributable to an Equity Owner shall mean the positive remainder, if any, of such Equity Owner's share of the Company's federal tax losses for all prior Fiscal Years minus the Equity Owner's share of Tax Profits for all prior Fiscal Years. The objective of this Section 9.4(a) is to make distributions with reference to each Equity Owner's (and such Equity Owner's predecessor's) share of cumulative Company taxable income or loss. Without limiting this objective, for purposes of this Section 9.4(a), an Equity Owner's share of Tax Profits and Unrecovered Tax Losses shall be determined with reference to Sections 704(c), 734, and 743 of the Code. Discretionary Distributions actually made during the calendar year pursuant to Section 9.4(b) shall reduce the Distributions otherwise contemplated by this Section 9.4(a). Distributions made pursuant to this Section 9.4(a) shall be treated as draws upon Distributions to be made pursuant to Sections 9.4(b) and 12.3 such that future Distributions

otherwise contemplated by Sections 9.4(b) and 12.3 shall be reduced by Distributions made pursuant to this Section 9.4(a). [48]

(b) *The Company may Distribute Distributable Cash subject to the Approval in accordance with Section 5.4. All such Distributions shall be made as follows:*

(i) *First, to the Equity Owners in proportion to the Preferred Accruals of all Equity Owners until they have received aggregate Distributions under this Section 9.4(b)(i) equal to Preferred Accrual.*

(ii) *Second, to the Equity Owners proportionate with their Adjusted Capital Contributions until the amount of their respective Adjusted Capital Contributions equals zero.*

(iii) *Third, to the Equity Owners in accordance with their Sharing Ratios.]*

All Distributions which, when made, exceed the recipient Equity Owner's basis in that Equity Owner's Ownership Interest shall be considered advances or drawings against the Equity Owner's distributive share of Profits, or other items of net income or gain. To the extent it is determined at the end of the Fiscal Year that the recipient Equity Owner has not been allocated Profits, or other items of net income or gain, that equals or exceeds the total of such advances or drawings for such year, such Equity Owner shall be obligated to recontribute any such excess advances or drawings to the Company. Notwithstanding the foregoing sentence, an Equity Owner will not be required to recontribute such advances or drawings to the extent that, on the last day of the Fiscal Year, such Equity Owner's basis in its Ownership Interest in the Company has increased from the time of such advance or drawing. Any advance or drawings which are recontributed by a Member pursuant to this Section 9.4, shall be redistributed to such Member either at the option of such Member or at such time that such distribution will not exceed such Member's basis in its Ownership Interest.] [49]

All Distributions to Equity Owners will be subject to withholding if required by the Code or other applicable law. All amounts so withheld nonetheless will be deemed to have been distributed to such Equity Owner.

9.5. Limitation Upon Distributions. No Distribution shall be made if such Distribution would violate the Act. [50]

---

[48] Normally where there is a preferred return it is advisable to have a provision mandating tax distributions. Otherwise, the Member not receiving the preferred return will have taxable income without any distribution to pay the taxes.

[49] Distribution arrangements need to be carefully evaluated (in light of the particular facts of the transaction) under the disguised sale rules. (IRC § 707(a)(2)(b) and Treas. Reg. § 1.707-4 and 1.707-5.

[50] It may be necessary or advisable from a tax standpoint to add special limitations on distributions of appreciated property (or to restrict certain distribution to a member that has contributed appreciated property). See IRC §§ 704(c)(1)(b) and 737.

9.6. Interest on and Return of Capital Contributions. No Member shall be entitled to interest on its Capital Contribution or to return of its Capital Contribution, except as otherwise specifically provided for herein.

9.7. Accounting Period. The Company's accounting period shall be the Fiscal Year.

9.8. Accounting Principles. For financial reporting purposes, the Company shall use accounting principles applied on a consistent basis using the accrual method of accounting determined by the Managers, unless the Company is required to use a different method of accounting for federal income tax purposes, in which case that method of accounting shall be the Company's method of accounting.

9.9. Loans to Company. Nothing in this Agreement shall prevent any Member from making secured or unsecured loans to the Company by agreement with the Company.

9.10. Returns and Other Elections. The Managers shall cause the preparation and timely filing of all tax returns required to be filed by the Company pursuant to the Code and all other tax returns deemed necessary and required in each jurisdiction in which the Company does business. Copies of such returns, or pertinent information therefrom, shall be furnished to the Equity Owners within a reasonable amount of time after the end of the Fiscal Year. All elections permitted to be made by the Company under federal or state laws shall be made by the Managers in their sole discretion; provided, however, that the Managers shall make any tax election requested by Members owning a Majority Interest.

9.11. Tax Matters Partner. Any Manager selected by a vote of the Managers, so long as the Manager so selected is also a Member, is hereby designated the Tax Matters Partner ("TMP") as defined in Section 6231(a)(7) of the Code. The TMP and the other Members shall use their reasonable efforts to comply with the responsibilities outlined in Sections 6221 through 6233 of the Code (including any Regulations promulgated thereunder), and in doing so shall incur no liability to any other Member.

9.12. Certain Allocations for Income Tax (But Not Book Capital Account) Purposes.

(a) In accordance with Section 704(c)(1)(A) of the Code and Section 1.704-1(b)(2)(iv)(d) of the Regulations, if an Equity Owner contributes property with an initial Gross Asset Value that differs from its adjusted basis at the time of contribution, income, gain, loss and deductions with respect to the property shall, solely for federal income tax purposes (and not for Capital Account purposes), be allocated among the Equity Owners so as to take account of any variation between the adjusted basis of such property to the Company and its Gross Asset Value at the time of contribution *[pursuant to the traditional method under Section 1.704-3(b)* *of the Regulations] [in accordance with Section 704(c)(1)(A) of the Code and Section 1.704-1(b)(2)(i)(iv) of the Regulations, if an Equity Owner contributes property with an initial Gross Asset Value that differs from its adjusted basis at the time of contribution, income, gain, loss and deductions with respect to the property shall, <u>solely for federal income tax purposes</u> (and not for Capital Account purposes), be allocated among the Equity Owners so as to take account of any variation between the adjusted basis of such property to the Company and its Gross Asset Value at the time of contribution. Notwithstanding the foregoing sentence, in the event any Equity Owner is limited in recognizing any tax allocations cost recovery deductions or loss with respect to contributed property by the "ceiling rule" as described in Regulation Section 1.704-3(b), then, in addition to the allocation of items with respect to the contributed property allocated pursuant to the previous sentence, all items _____ [51] of the Company other than with respect to the property shall, <u>solely for federal income tax purposes</u> (and not for Capital Account purposes), be allocated among the Equity Owners pursuant to [the traditional method with curative allocations described in Regulation Section 1.704-3(c) so as to offset the effect of the ceiling rule. The allocations described in the previous sentence shall be limited to items of ordinary loss and deduction of the Company other than with respect to the property even if such items do not offset fully the effect of the ceiling rule] [in accordance with the remedial allocation method under Regulation Section 1.704-3(d)].[52] . In the event the Gross Asset Value of any Company asset is adjusted pursuant to Section* **1.42(b)**, *subsequent allocations of income, gain, loss, and deduction with respect to such asset shall take account of any variation between the adjusted basis of such asset for federal income tax purposes and its Gross Asset Value in the same manner as under Code Section 704(c) and the Regulations thereunder.*

(b) All recapture of income tax deductions resulting from sale or disposition of Company Property shall be allocated to the Equity Owners to whom the deduction that gave rise to such recapture was allocated hereunder to the extent that such Equity Owner is allocated any gain from the sale or other disposition of such property.

---

[51] Under the traditional method with curative allocations you can designate the items of income or loss of the Company (other than from the property giving rise to the variation) that will be adjusted, so long as the tax characterization of the item is the same as the property giving rise to the variation.

[52] The selection of the manner in which book-tax differences are recognized can have significant tax consequences and should be considered carefully with the client.

ARTICLE 10
TRANSFERABILITY

10.1. General.

(a) An Equity Owner shall only have the right to Transfer all or any portion of the Equity Owner's Ownership Interests if such Transfer is in full compliance with the provisions herein.

(b) Each Equity Owner hereby acknowledges the reasonableness of the restrictions on Transfer of Ownership Interests imposed by this Agreement in view of the Company's purposes and the relationship of the Equity Owners. Accordingly, the restrictions on Transfer contained herein shall be specifically enforceable.

(c) *[In the event that any Equity Owner Hypothecates any of its Ownership Interest, any such Hypothecation shall be made pursuant to a pledge or hypothecation agreement that requires the pledgee or secured party to be bound by all the terms and conditions of this Article 10, and the pledging Equity Owner shall provide notice of such pledge or encumbrance to the Managers at such time that the Equity Owner first contemplates such Hypothecation.]*

10.2. Right of First Refusal.

(a) A Selling Equity Owner that desires to Sell all or any portion of its Ownership Interest to a third party purchaser *[other than a Member / including a Member (or the Company)]* shall obtain from such third party purchaser ("Third Party Purchaser") a *bona fide* written offer to purchase such interest, stating the terms and conditions upon which the Sale is to be made and the consideration offered therefor ("Third Party Offer"). The Selling Equity Owner shall give written notification ("Notice of Sale") to the Company and the other Equity Owners who are Members (the "Remaining Members"), by certified mail or personal delivery, of its intention to so Sell such Ownership Interest (the "Offered Interest"). The Notice of Sale shall be accompanied by a copy of the Third Party Offer. For purposes of paragraph 10.2(b) and 10.2(c), the purchase price of the Offered Interest (the "Purchase Price") shall be equal to the purchase price offered by such Third Party Purchaser, to the extent such offer consists of cash or a promissory note, plus the fair market value of any consideration other than cash or a promissory note ("Non-cash Consideration"). If any portion of the Purchase Price depends on the value of Non-cash Consideration, then: (i) the Notice of Sale also shall be accompanied by a good faith estimate by the Selling Equity Owner of the fair market value of the Non-cash Consideration ("Seller's Estimate"), and (ii) the fair market value of the Non-cash Consideration shall be equal to either (x) the Seller's Estimate or (y) in the discretion of the Managers, the appraised fair market value of the Non-cash Consideration determined by an independent appraiser selected by the Managers in their sole discretion. The Managers shall have the sole discretion to choose between the amount determined pursuant to clauses (x) and (y) of this subsection 10.2(a). If the appraised fair market value of the Non-cash Consideration is not determined within twenty (20) days after the Notice of Sale, then such fair market value shall be equal to the amount of the Seller's Estimate.

(b) The Remaining Members shall have the option ("Buy Option") to purchase all, but not less than all, of the Offered Interest, on a basis *pro rata* to the Sharing Ratios of the Remaining Members exercising such option pursuant to this Section 10.2(b). The Buy Option may be exercised by one or more of the Remaining Members by giving written notification ("Buy Notice") to the Selling Equity Owner within thirty (30) days after receiving the Notice of Sale (the "Option Period"). Each Remaining Member who timely gives a Buy Notice ("Buying Member") shall purchase such portion of the Offered Interest which is equal to the relative Sharing Ratios of all of the Buying Members. If there are no Buying Members, the Buy Option shall terminate and at any time within ninety (90) days following the expiration of the Option Period, the Selling Equity Owner shall be entitled to consummate the Sale of the Offered Interest to the Third Party Purchaser or one or more of its Affiliates upon terms no less favorable than are set forth in the Third Party Offer.

(c) If there is at least one Buying Member (i) the Buying Members shall designate the time, date and place of closing, provided that the date of closing shall be within thirty (30) days after the receipt of the Buy Notice, and (ii) at the closing, the Buying Members shall purchase, and the Selling Equity Owner shall Sell, the Offered Interest for an amount equal to the Purchase Price and in accordance with such other terms and conditions set forth in the Third Party Offer.

(d) A Sale of an Offered Interest pursuant to this Section 10.2, shall be subject to Sections 10.3 and 10.4.

10.3. Transferee Not Member in Absence of Consent.

(a) Except as provided in this Section 10.3(a), if *[all of the remaining Members / Members holding a Majority Interest / Members Holding a Two-Thirds Interest (inclusive of the Members proposing to sell)]* do not unanimously Approve the proposed Transfer of the Transferring Equity Owner's Ownership Interest to a transferee which is not a Member immediately prior to the Transfer, then the proposed transferee shall have no right to participate in the management of the business and affairs of the Company or to become a Member. Such transferee shall be merely an Economic Interest Owner. No Transfer of a Member's Membership Interest (including any Transfer of the Economic Interest or any other Transfer which has not been approved as provided herein) shall be effective unless and until written notice (including the name and address of the proposed transferee and the date of such Transfer) has been provided to the Company and the non-transferring Members. *[Notwithstanding anything to the contrary herein, any Gift by a Member which is permitted under Section 10.5 and made in accordance with this Section 10.3(a) shall automatically constitute the transferee as a Member.]*

(b) Upon and contemporaneously with any Transfer of an Equity Owner's Ownership Interest, the Transferring Equity Owner shall cease to have any residual rights associated with the Ownership Interest Transferred to the transferee.

10.4. Additional Conditions to Recognition of Transferee.

(a) If a Transferring Equity Owner Transfers an Ownership Interest to a Person who is not already a Member, as a condition to recognizing the effectiveness and binding nature of such Transfer (subject to Section 10.3 above), the remaining Members may require the Transferring Equity Owner and the proposed successor-in-interest to execute, acknowledge and deliver to the Managers such instruments of transfer, assignment and assumption and such other certificates, representations and documents, and to perform all such other acts which the Managers may deem necessary or desirable to accomplish any one or more of the following:

(i) Constitute such successor-in-interest as an Equity Owner;

(ii) Confirm that the proposed successor-in-interest as an Economic Interest Owner, or to be admitted as a Member, has accepted, assumed and agreed to be subject to and bound by all of the terms, obligations and conditions of this Agreement, as the same may have been further amended (whether such Person is to be admitted as a new Member or will merely be an Economic Interest Owner);

(iii) Preserve the Company after the completion of such Transfer under the laws of each jurisdiction in which the Company is qualified, organized or does business;

(iv) *[Prevent a termination of the Company for tax purposes under Section 708(b)(1)(B) of the Code;]*

(v) Maintain the status of the Company as a partnership for federal tax purposes; and

(vi) Assure compliance with any applicable state and federal laws, including Securities Laws and regulations.

(b) Any Transfer of an Ownership Interest and admission of a Member in compliance with this Article 10 shall be deemed effective as of the last day of the calendar month in which the remaining Members' Approval thereto was given *[or, if no such Approval was required pursuant to Section 10.3, then on such date that the successor in interest complies with Section 10.4(a)]*.[53] The Transferring Equity Owner hereby indemnifies

---

[53] This provision should be deleted if last sentence of 10.3 is deleted.

the Company and the remaining Members against any and all loss, damage, or expense (including tax liabilities or loss of tax benefits) arising directly or indirectly as a result of any Transfer or purported Transfer in violation of this Article 10.

(c) Any Equity Owner that Transfers an Ownership Interest shall notify the Company of the Transfer in writing within thirty (30) days of the Transfer, or, if earlier, by March 31 following the Transfer, and must include the names and addresses of the transferor and transferee, the taxpayer identification numbers of the transferor and transferee, if known, and the date of the Transfer.

10.5. Gifts of Ownership Interests. *[A Gifting Equity Owner may Gift all or any portion of its Ownership Interest (without regard to Sections 10.2(a) and 10.2(b)); provided, however, that the successor-in-interest ("Donee") complies with Section 10.4(a) and further provided that the Donee is either the Gifting Equity Owner's spouse, former spouse, lineal descendant (including adopted children) or to an Entity in which day-to-day voting control is directly or indirectly held by one or more of the Gifting Equity Owners, or the Gifting Equity Owner's spouse, former spouse, or lineal descendant (including adopted children). In the event of the Gift of all or any portion of a Gifting Equity Owner's Ownership Interest to one or more Donees who are under twenty-five (25) years of age, one or more trusts shall be established to hold the Gifted Ownership Interests for the benefit of such Donees until the respective Donees reach the age of at least twenty-five (25) years.]*

10.6. Buy-Sell Agreement. [54]

(a) Upon _____ [55] any Member (the "Offeror") [56] may make a buy-sell offer (the "Offer") to any other Equity Owner, (the "Offeree") holding an Ownership Interest by notifying the Offeree and all other Members in writing of the exercise of this right and stating in such notice the Deemed Value and Purchase Price as defined below. The "Deemed Value" is an amount designated by the Offeror to be the value of the Company Property of the Company net of any obligations and liabilities of the Company that would need to be paid or satisfied before a Distribution could be made under Section 12.3(b)(iii)). The "Purchase

---

[54] While the entire agreement is merely intended to assist the drafter in considering issues, this provision merits a great deal of consideration taking into account the ability of parties to pay for the interest, the ability to obtain releases of guarantees, and the viability of the business of the Company on the dissociation of a Member. It may be that on a serious disagreement the only alternative is to dissolve and wind up the Company.

[55] It may be appropriate to condition the buy-sell option on the passage of time or a specific event.

[56] Under this arrangement only Members can be Offerors initiating this process, although the Offeree, who is not necessarily a Member, does have the right to elect to be a purchaser.

Price" with respect to either the Offeree's Ownership Interest or Offeror's Membership Interest[57] in the Company shall be equal to the amount that would have been Distributed to either the Offeror or the Offereee, as the case may be under Section 12.3(b)(iv) on the assumption that the fair market value of the Company's assets available for Distribution under Section 12.3(b)(iv) is the Deemed Value.

(b) Within thirty (30) days after receipt by the Offeree of the Offeror's written notice of the Offer, the Offeree shall send to the Offeror a written notice stating whether the Offeree elects (i) to purchase from the Offeror the Offeror's entire Membership Interest for the Purchase Price of such Interest as provided below (in which case the Offeree shall be the "Purchaser" and the Offeror shall be the "Seller" for purposes of this Section 10.6), or (ii) to sell to the Offeror the Offeror's entire Membership Interest for the Purchase Price of such Interest as provided below (in which case the Offeror shall be the "Purchaser" and the Offeree shall be the "Seller" for purposes of this Section 10.6).

(c) The closing of the sale shall be held at the Company's principal office (or at such other place as the Offeror and the Offeree may in writing agree) no later than fifteen (15) days after the expiration of the notice period specified in subsection (b) above. At the closing the Purchaser shall deliver to the Seller: (i) confirmation of payment of, or a release of the Seller and all Seller's Affiliates from all liabilities of the Company for which the Seller or any Affiliate of the Seller is liable either directly or as a guarantor or with respect to which any asset of the Seller or any Affiliate of the Seller is secured;[58] (ii) payment in cash or immediately available funds of (x) any amount to which the Seller would have been entitled under Section 12.3(b)(iii) on winding up of the Company and (y) the Purchase Price for the Seller's Interest. The Purchaser may reduce the amount due under the foregoing clause by any liquidated and undisputed amounts owed by the Seller to either the Purchaser or the Company.[59] The Purchaser may use assets of the Company to provide some or all of the consideration to be paid to the Seller provided that such use does not violate the Act or otherwise subject the Seller to additional liability to any Person. At the closing Seller shall execute and deliver to the Purchaser a document assigning the Membership Interest to the Purchaser or such other Person as the Purchaser may designate, representing and warranting to the Purchaser, its Affiliates, the Company and the Person to whom the Membership Interest is transferred

---

[57] Note that what is purchased is a Membership Interest not Units, which are just one component of a Membership Interest.

[58] This will require the discharge or release of the Seller from guarantees. This may be difficult and the drafter may want to consider an alternative direct indemnification with respect to guarantees. This can be a particular problem with respect to guarantees with respect to ongoing liabilities such as leases.

[59] The amount owed to the Company may serve as a reduction to the extent that the Purchaser will succeed to the Seller's obligation to the Company.

that the Seller is the sole owner of the Membership Interest being sold, providing for reasonable noncompetition, trade secret, and nondisparagement protection for the Purchaser, its Affiliates, the Company and the Person to whom the Membership Interest is transferred, and agreeing to indemnify the Purchaser, the Company and the Person to whom the Membership Interest is transferred against any liabilities of the Company that were incurred by the Seller or its Affiliate but only if at the time of closing the Purchaser is not aware and has no reason to be aware of such liability. At the closing Purchaser shall execute and deliver to the Seller a document providing reasonable nondisparagement protection for the Seller and its Affiliates and agreeing to indemnify the Seller and its Affiliates against any liabilities of the Company excepting only liabilities that were incurred by the Seller or its Affiliate with respect to which at the time of closing the Purchaser is not aware and has no reason to be aware of such liability.

(d) Each of the Equity Owners agrees that in connection with the exercise of that Member's rights under this Section 10.6, that Member will act in good faith and that in connection with the Offer and the response each Equity Owner shall have the obligation to disclose to the other Member all material facts with respect to the Company and its business. Further the Purchaser shall act in good faith in the preparation of all tax returns and reports of the Company affecting the rights of the Seller or any of its Affiliates.[60]

Except with respect to the obligations of the Members set forth in this Paragraph 10.6, upon the closing described herein, the Seller and its Affiliates shall be released from all obligations of any sort to the Purchaser or the Company by reason of the Seller's having been a Member of the Company or a Party to this LLC Agreement; and the Purchaser, its Affiliates, the Company, and the Person to whom the Interest is Transferred shall be released from all obligations of any sort to the Seller or its Affiliates by reason of Seller's having been a Member of the Company or a Party to this Agreement.

---

[60] This clause should be considered carefully. On the one hand it will make the process fairer. On the other, it will give an Equity Owner who feels misused by the process an easier access to court, particularly where there is the allegation that either the price was not suggested in good faith or that there was information not made available to the Offeree. It should further be noted that many believe that no fiduciary duties are owed to Economic Interest owners who are not Members and such persons are certainly not entitled to the information rights owed to Members. This section would entitle such a person a right to information in connection with the Offer.

ARTICLE 11
ISSUANCE OF MEMBERSHIP INTERESTS

11.1. Issuance of Additional Membership Interests to New Members. From the date of the formation of the Company, any Person acceptable to [_____][61] may become a Member in the Company by the issuance by the Company of Membership Interests for such consideration as the Members *[by their unanimous Approval/holding a Two-Thirds Interest]* shall determine, subject to the terms and conditions of this Agreement.

11.2. Issuance of Additional Membership Interests to Existing Members. From the date of the formation of the Company, the Company may issue additional Ownership Interests to one or more existing Members for such consideration as the Members *[by their unanimous Approval/holding a Two-Thirds Interest]* shall determine, subject to the terms and conditions of this Agreement.

11.3. Part Year Allocations With Respect to New Members. No new Members shall be entitled to any retroactive allocation of losses, income, or expense deductions incurred by the Company. At the time a Member is admitted and in accordance with the provisions of Section 706(d) of the Code and the Regulations thereunder, the Managers may, at their option, close the Company books (as though the Company's Fiscal Year had ended) or make *pro rata* allocations of loss, income, and expense deductions to a new Equity Owner for that portion of the Company's Fiscal Year in which a Person became an Equity Owner.

ARTICLE 12
DISSOLUTION AND TERMINATION

12.1. Dissolution.

(a) The Company shall be dissolved only upon the occurrence of any of the following events:

(i) by the *[unanimous Approval of the Members]/[the Approval of [Members holding a Two-Thirds Interest]*;[62]

(ii) *[by an order of a court of competent jurisdiction in an action commenced by any Member in which the Member can show that:*

(1) *The Members are deadlocked in the management of the Company's affairs with respect to material matters over which they have a vote, and irreparable injury to the Company is threatened or being*

---

[61] Presumably the same Member or Members entitled to Approve the admission of a transferee as a Member must approve this.

[62] In a family LLC carefully consider the potential impact of IRC § 2704(a).

suffered, or the business and affairs of the Company can no longer be conducted, because of the deadlock;

(2) The Managers or other Members in control of the Company have acted, are acting, or will act in a manner that is illegal, oppressive, or fraudulent;

(3) There have been repeated, material breaches of the Agreement by the Company or by other Members or Managers; or

(4) The assets of the Company are being misapplied or wasted,][63] or

(iii) *[upon the expiration of the term, if any, specified in Section 2.5 of this Agreement].*

Notwithstanding anything to the contrary in the Act, the Company shall not be dissolved upon the death, retirement, resignation, expulsion, Bankruptcy or dissolution of an Equity Owner.[64]

(b) As soon as possible following the occurrence of any of the events specified in Section 12.1(a) effecting the dissolution of the Company, the appropriate representative of the Company shall execute all documents required by the Act at the time of dissolution and file or record such statements with the appropriate officials.[65]

12.2. Effect of Dissolution.

Upon dissolution, the Company shall cease to carry on its business, except insofar as may be necessary for the winding up of its business, but its separate existence shall continue until winding up and Distribution is completed.

12.3. Winding Up, Liquidation and Distribution of Assets.

(a) Upon dissolution, an accounting shall be made by the Company's *[Managers] [independent accountants (the "Liquidators")]* of the accounts of the Company and of the Company's assets, liabilities, and results of operations from the date of the last previous accounting until the date of dissolution. The *[Managers] [Liquidators]* shall immediately proceed to wind up the affairs of the Company.

(b) If the Company is dissolved and its affairs are to be wound up, the *[Managers] [Liquidators]* shall:

---

[63] Under some LLC statutes there is not a provision for judicial dissolution even for breach of the agreement, fraud, or conversion. It may be worth considering a provision of this sort in an agreement to protect minority members.

[64] Some statutes still have a default rule under which the LLC will dissolve on the dissociation of a member but allow the modification of that rules in the operating agreement. This language is intended to make clear that such an amendment is appropriate.

[65] If the LLC is not a Colorado LLC, the resignation of a member may need to be specifically addressed. In Colorado, the default rule under the Colorado LLC act is that the resigning member has no right to demand the liquidation of his interest by the LLC and that after resigning he becomes a mere economic interest owner.

(i) Sell or otherwise liquidate all of the Company Property as promptly as practicable (except to the extent that the *[Managers] [Liquidators]* may determine to Distribute in kind any assets to the Equity Owners);

(ii) Allocate any Profit or Loss resulting from such sales to the Equity Owners' Capital Accounts in accordance with Article 9 hereof;

(iii) Discharge all liabilities of the Company, including liabilities to Equity Owners who are also creditors, to the extent otherwise permitted by law, other than liabilities to Equity Owners for Distributions and the return of capital, and establish such Reserves as may be reasonably necessary to provide for contingent liabilities of the Company (for purposes of determining the Capital Accounts of the Equity Owners, the amounts of such Reserves shall be deemed to be an expense of the Company); and

(iv) Distribute the remaining assets to the Equity Owners in accordance with their positive Capital Account balances, as follows:

(1) The positive balance (if any) of each Equity Owner's Capital Account (as determined after taking into account all Capital Account adjustments for the Company's Fiscal Year during which the liquidation occurs) shall be Distributed to the Equity Owners, either in cash or in kind, as determined by the *[Managers] [Liquidators]*, with any Company Property Distributed in kind being valued for this purpose at their fair market value. Any such Distributions to the Equity Owners in respect of their Capital Accounts shall be made in accordance with the time requirements set forth in Section 1.704-1(b)(2)(ii)(b)(2) of the Regulations; and

(2) If any Company Property is to be Distributed in kind, the net fair market value of such Company Property as of the date of dissolution shall be determined by agreement of the Members, or, if the Members do not agree, by an appraiser selected by the *[Managers] [Liquidators]*. Such Company Property shall be deemed to have been sold as of the date of dissolution for their fair market value, and the Capital Accounts of the Equity Owners shall be adjusted pursuant to the provisions of Article 9 and Section 8.3 of this Agreement to reflect such deemed sale.

It is intended that the amount to be Distributed to each Equity Owner pursuant to Section 12.3(b)(iv) (the "Liquidating Distribution") would equal the amount such Equity Owner would receive if liquidation proceeds were instead Distributed in accordance with the provisions set forth in Section 9.4 (the "Targeted Distribution Amounts"). Notwithstanding any provision of this Agreement to the contrary, if any Equity Owner's ending Capital Account balance immediately prior to the Liquidating Distribution otherwise would be less than the balance required to ensure that such Equity Owner receives its Targeted Distribution Amount, then, for such Fiscal Year of liquidation and dissolution and, to the extent amended tax returns can be filed, for prior Fiscal Years of the Company (if necessary), such Equity Owner shall be specially allocated items of income or gain for such current or prior years, and items of loss or deduction for such current or prior years shall be specially allocated to the other Equity Owners, until Profits or Losses for the year of liquidation and dissolution of the Company can be allocated so as to cause such Equity Owner's Liquidating Distribution to equal (or, if not equal to, as close as possible to) the Targeted Distribution Amount for such Equity Owner.[66]

(c) Notwithstanding anything to the contrary in this Agreement, upon a liquidation within the meaning of Section 1.704-1(b)(2)(ii)(g) of the Regulations, if any Equity Owner has a Deficit Capital Account (after giving effect to all contributions, Distributions, allocations and other Capital Account adjustments for all Fiscal Years, including the year during which such liquidation occurs), such Equity Owner shall have no obligation to make any Capital Contribution so as to restore its Capital Account to zero, and the negative balance of such Equity Owner's Capital Account shall not be considered a debt owed by such Equity Owner to the Company, to the other Equity Owners, or to any other Person for any purpose whatsoever.

(d) Upon completion of the winding up, liquidation, and Distribution of the assets, the Company shall be deemed terminated.

(e) The *[Managers] [Liquidators]* shall comply with any requirements of applicable law pertaining to the winding up of the affairs of the Company and the final Distribution of its assets.

12.4. Filing or Recording Statements. Upon the conclusion of winding up, the appropriate representative of the Company shall execute all documents required by the Act at the time of completion of winding up and file or record such documents with the appropriate officials.

12.5. Return of Contribution Nonrecourse to Other Equity Owners. Except as provided by law or as expressly provided in this Agreement, upon dissolution, each Equity Owner shall look solely to the assets of the Company for the return of its Capital Contribution. If the Company Property remaining after the payment or discharge of the debts and liabilities of the Company is insufficient to return the cash contribution of one or more Equity Owners, such Equity Owners shall have no recourse against any other Equity Owner.

---

[66] In the context of the particular deal, think about the possible need for distributions of certain LLC assets to certain members. For example, in strategic ventures, it is often important to carefully address the exit strategy (*i.e.*, and who gets what if the LLC dissolves). The ability of one or more of the members to receive or have the option to receive (or by distribution or purchase) specified assets may be important. It also may be advisable for the operating agreement to require the LLC or members who receive intellectual property assets from the LLC to license those assets to the other members. Also, remember to conform this provision to 8.4.

ARTICLE 13
MISCELLANEOUS PROVISIONS

13.1. Notices. Any notice, demand, or communication required or permitted to be given by any provision of this Agreement shall be deemed to have been sufficiently given or served if sent by facsimile or electronic mail transmission, delivered by messenger, overnight courier, or mailed, certified first class mail, postage prepaid, return receipt requested, and addressed or sent to the Equity Owner's or the Company's address, as set forth on <u>Exhibit 8.1</u> and, if applicable, <u>Exhibit 13.1</u>. Such notice shall be effective, (a) if delivered by messenger or by overnight courier, upon actual receipt (or if the date of actual receipt is not a business day, upon the next business day); (b) if sent by facsimile or electronic mail transmission, upon electronic confirmation of receipt (or if the date of such electronic confirmation of receipt is not a business day, upon the next business day); or (c) if mailed, upon the earlier of (i) three (3) business days after deposit in the mail and (ii) the delivery as shown by return receipt therefor. Any Equity Owner or the Company may change its address by giving notice in writing to the Company and the other Equity Owners of its new address.

13.2. Liquidation Safe Harbor Valuation.[67] This Section 13.2 shall apply after the effective date of any final Regulations or of final guidance by the Internal Revenue Service with respect to the Transfer of a Membership Interest to a new or existing Member of the Company in connection with the performance of services for the Company or otherwise under which the Company may make an election (a *"Safe Harbor Election"*) to treat the liquidation value of Membership Interest so Transferred as being the fair market value of those Membership Interest for purposes of Section 83 of the Code. From and after the effective date of any final Regulations or of final guidance by the Internal Revenue Service, each Member and each Person (including any Person to whom any Units are Transferred in connection with the performance of services for the Company or otherwise) and each assignee and Transferee of a Member who acquires Units agrees that that (a) the Company is authorized and directed to make the Safe Harbor Election, and (b) each such Person agrees to comply with all requirements of such Regulations or guidance with respect to all Units so Transferred while the Safe Harbor Election remains effective. The Safe Harbor Election may be revoked by the consent of *[Members holding a Majority Interest] [all of the Members]*.

13.3. Books of Account and Records. At the expense of the Company, proper and complete records, books of account and other relevant Company documents shall be maintained and preserved, during the term

---

[67] As should be clear from the explanation, this section is intended to anticipate the proposed tax guidance on the issuance of an interest for services. This election will facilitate the issuance of profits interests but will generally be disadvantageous to recipients of capital interests.

of the Company, and for five years *[thereafter] [after dissolution]*, by the Managers, in which shall be entered fully and accurately all transactions and other matters relating to the Company's business in such detail and completeness as is customary and usual for businesses of the type engaged in by the Company. The books and records shall be open to the reasonable inspection and examination of the Equity Owners or their duly authorized representatives, upon reasonable request, during ordinary business hours at the requesting Member's expense. At a minimum the Company shall keep at its principal place of business the following records:

(a) A current list of the full name and last known business, residence, or mailing address of each Equity Owner and Manager, both past and present;

(b) A copy of the Articles of Organization and all amendments thereto, together with executed copies of any powers of attorney pursuant to which any amendment has been executed;

(c) Copies of the Company's federal, state, and local income tax returns and reports, if any, for the four most recent Fiscal Years;

(d) Copies of the Company's currently effective written Agreement, copies of any writings permitted or required with respect to an Equity Owner's obligation to contribute cash, property or services, and copies of any financial statements of the Company for the three most recent Fiscal Years;

(e) Minutes of every annual, special, and court-ordered meeting of the Members and Managers, if any; and

(f) Any written Approvals obtained from Members for actions taken by Members without a meeting.

13.4. Application of [State] Law. This agreement shall be construed and enforced in accordance with and governed by the laws of the state of *[State]* applicable to agreements made and to be performed entirely within such state other than such laws, rules, regulations and case law that would result in the application of the laws of a jurisdiction other than the state of **[State]**.

13.5. Waiver of Action for Partition. During the term of the Company, each Equity Owner irrevocably waives any right that it may have to maintain any action for partition with respect to the Company Property.

13.6. Amendments. *[This Agreement may not be amended except by the unanimous Approval of all of the Members.]*

OR

[This Agreement may be amended only with the Approval of Members holding a [Two-Thirds Interest]. No amendment which has been agreed to in accordance with the preceding sentence shall be effective to the extent that

such amendment has a Material Adverse Effect upon one or more Equity Owners who did not agree in writing to such amendment. For purposes of the preceding sentence, "Material Adverse Effect" shall mean any modification of the relative rights to Distributions by the Company (including allocations of Profits and Losses which are reflected in the Capital Accounts). Without limiting the generality of the foregoing, an amendment which has a proportionate effect on all Equity Owners (or in the case of a redemption of Ownership Interests or issuance of additional Ownership Interests, an amendment which has a proportionate effect on all Equity Owners immediately after such redemption or issuance) with respect to their rights to Distributions shall be deemed to not have a Material Adverse Effect on Equity Owners who do not agree in writing to such amendment. In addition, an amendment made to ensure that Distributions are made in accordance with Section 9.4 shall be deemed to not have a Material Adverse Effect on Equity Owners who do not agree in writing to such amendment. Notwithstanding the foregoing provisions of this Section 13.6, no amendment shall be made to a provision herein which requires the Approval of the Members holding more than a [Two-Thirds Interest], unless Members holding such greater Voting Interests Approve of such amendment.][68]

13.7. <u>Execution of Additional Instruments</u>. Each Equity Owner hereby agrees to execute such other and further statements of interest and holdings, designations, powers of attorney, and other instruments necessary to comply with any laws, rules, or regulations.

13.8. <u>Construction</u>. Whenever the singular number is used in this Agreement and when required by the context, the same shall include the plural and *vice versa*, and the masculine gender shall include the feminine and neuter genders and *vice versa*. The words "including" and "or" shall be ascribed non-exclusive meanings unless the context clearly requires otherwise.

13.9. <u>Effect of Inconsistencies with the Act</u>. It is the express intention of the Equity Owners and the Company that this Agreement shall be the sole source of agreement among them, and, except to the extent that a provision of this Agreement expressly incorporates federal income tax rules by reference to sections of the Code or Regulations or is expressly prohibited or ineffective under the Act, this Agreement shall govern, even when inconsistent with, or different than, the provisions of the Act or any other law or rule. In the event that the Act is subsequently amended or interpreted in such a way to make valid any provision of this Agreement

---

[68] In many respects the amendment provision is the most important provision in the agreement. As a result of the flexibility of LLC statutes, an amendment can make profound changes in the LLC. If fewer than all of the members are needed to amend an agreement, minority members should consider appropriate protections in the even of an unacceptable amendment. Such a provision might include a right to withdraw or a limitation on the ability to amend some provisions of the agreement. Unanimous consent should be required to amend any provision of the agreement which requires a unanimous vote to approve an action.

that was formerly invalid, such provision shall be considered to be valid from the effective date of such interpretation or amendment. The Members and the Company hereby agree that the duties and obligations imposed on the Members as such shall be those set forth in this Agreement, which is intended to govern the relationship among the Company and the Equity Owners, notwithstanding any provision of the Act or common law to the contrary.

13.10. Waivers. The failure of any party to seek redress for violation of or to insist upon the strict performance of any covenant or condition of this Agreement shall not prevent a subsequent act, which would have originally constituted a violation, from having the effect of an original violation.

13.11. Rights and Remedies Cumulative. The rights and remedies provided by this Agreement are cumulative and the use of any one right or remedy by any party shall not preclude or waive the right to use any or all other remedies. Said rights and remedies are given in addition to any other rights the parties may have by law, statute, ordinance, or otherwise.

13.12. Attorneys' Fees. Should the Company or any party to this Agreement reasonably retain counsel for the purpose of enforcing or preventing breach of any provision of this Agreement, including instituting any action or proceeding to enforce any provision of this Agreement, for damages by reason of any alleged breach of any provision of this Agreement, for a declaration of such party's rights or obligations under this Agreement, or for any other judicial remedy, then, if the matter is settled by judicial determination or arbitration, the prevailing party (whether at trial, on appeal, or arbitration) shall be entitled, in addition to such other relief as may be granted, to be reimbursed by the losing party for all costs and expenses incurred, including reasonable attorneys' fees and costs for services rendered to the prevailing party or parties.

13.13. Severability. If any provision of this Agreement or the application thereof to any person or circumstance shall be invalid, illegal, or unenforceable to any extent, the remainder of this Agreement and the application thereof shall not be affected and shall be enforceable to the fullest extent permitted by law. Without limiting the generality of the foregoing sentence, to the extent that any provision of this Agreement is prohibited or ineffective under the Act or common law, this Agreement shall be considered amended to the smallest degree possible in order to make the Agreement effective under the Act or common law.

13.14. Heirs, Successors, and Assigns. Each and all of the covenants, terms, provisions, and agreements herein contained shall be binding upon and inure to the benefit of the parties hereto and, to the extent permitted by this Agreement, their respective heirs, legal representatives, successors, and assigns.

13.15. Creditors. None of the provisions of this Agreement shall be for the benefit of or enforceable by any creditors of the Company.

13.16. Counterparts; Facsimile. This Agreement may be delivered by facsimile and executed in counterparts, each of which shall be deemed an original but all of which shall constitute one and the same instrument.

13.17. Entire Agreement. This Agreement contains the entire agreement of the Company and the Equity Owners relating to the rights granted and obligations assumed under this Agreement. Any oral representations or modifications concerning this Agreement shall be of no force or effect unless contained in a subsequent written modification signed by the Equity Owner to be charged.

13.18. Rule Against Perpetuities. The parties hereto intend that the Rule Against Perpetuities (and any similar rule of law) not be applicable to any provisions of this Agreement. However, notwithstanding anything to the contrary in this Agreement, if any provision in this Agreement would be invalid or unenforceable because of the Rule Against Perpetuities or any similar rule of law but for this Section 13.18, the parties hereto hereby agree that any future interest which is created pursuant to said provision shall cease if it is not vested within twenty-one (21) years after the death of the survivor of the group composed of *[the undersigned individuals]* and their issue who are living on the effective date of this Agreement.[69]

13.19. Power of Attorney.[70] Each Equity Owner hereby irrevocably makes, constitutes, and appoints the Managers, with full power of substitution, so long as such Managers are acting in such a capacity (and any successor Manager thereof so long as such Manager is acting in such capacity), its true and lawful attorney, in such Equity Owner's name, place, and stead (it being expressly understood and intended that the grant of such power of attorney is coupled with an interest) to make, execute, sign, acknowledge, swear, and file with respect to the Company:

(a) *[All amendments of this Agreement adopted in accordance with the terms of Section 13.6]*;

(b) All documents which the Managers deem necessary or desirable to effect the dissolution and termination of the Company;

(c) All bills of sale, assignment forms or other appropriate transfer documents necessary to effectuate Transfers of an Equity Owner's Ownership Interest pursuant to Article 10;

(d) All such other instruments, documents, and certificates which may from time to time be required by the laws of *[State]* or any other jurisdiction in which the Company shall determine to do business, or any

---

[69] While this seems an unnecessary provision, it is included as a protective measure.

[70] It is not clear that this section is necessary or even helpful. To some extent it is a vestige of the Uniform Limited Partnership Act (1916) which required all the limited partners to sign the certificate of limited partnership.

political subdivision or agency thereof, to effectuate, implement, continue, and defend the valid existence of the Company; and

(e) All instruments, documents, and certificates which the Managers deem necessary or desirable in connection with a Reorganization or the dissolution and termination of the Company, either of which has been authorized in accordance with the terms of this Agreement.[71]

This power of attorney shall not be affected by and shall survive the Bankruptcy, insolvency, death, incompetency, or dissolution of an Equity Owner and shall survive the delivery of any assignment by the Equity Owner of the whole or any portion of its Ownership Interest. Each Equity Owner hereby releases each Manager from any liability or claim in connection with the exercise of the authority granted pursuant to this power of attorney, and in connection with any other action taken by such Manager pursuant to which such Manager purports to act as the attorney-in-fact for one or more Equity Owners, if the Manager believed in good faith that such action taken was consistent with the authority granted to it pursuant to this Section 13.19.

13.20. <u>Investment Representations.</u> The undersigned Equity Owners understand (a) that the Ownership Interests evidenced by this Agreement have not been registered under the Securities Laws because the Company is issuing these Ownership Interests in reliance upon the exemptions from the registration requirements of the Securities Laws providing for issuance of securities not involving a public offering, (b) that the Company has relied upon the fact that the Ownership Interests are to be held by each Equity Owner for investment, and (c) that exemption from registrations under the Securities Laws would not be available if the Ownership Interests were acquired by an Equity Owner with a view to distribution.

Accordingly, each Equity Owner hereby confirms to the Company that such Equity Owner is acquiring the Ownership Interests for such own Equity Owner's account, for investment, and not with a view to the resale or distribution thereof. Each Equity Owner agrees not to transfer, sell, or offer for sale any portion of the Ownership Interests unless there is an effective registration relating thereto under the Securities Laws or unless the holder of Ownership Interests delivers to the Company an opinion of counsel, satisfactory to the Company, that such registration or other qualification under applicable Securities Laws is not required in connection with such transfer, offer, or sale. Each Equity Owner understands that the Company is under no obligation to register the Ownership Interests or to assist such Equity Owner in complying with any exemption from registration under

---

[71] The drafter should consider other provisions. For example, if the agreement provides for a forfeiture of equity interest in the event of certain events (*e.g.* termination of employment, breach of the agreement, etc., then you may want to give the Managers a Power of Attorney to effectuate any forfeiture of the ownership interest of the likely uncooperative departing Equity Owner.

the Securities Laws if such Equity Owner should, at a later date, wish to dispose of the Ownership Interest. Furthermore, each Equity Owner realizes that the Ownership Interests are unlikely to qualify for disposition under Rule 144 of the Securities and Exchange Commission unless such Equity Owner is not an "affiliate" of the Company and the Ownership Interest has been beneficially owned and fully paid for by such Equity Owner for at least two years.

Each Equity Owner, prior to acquiring an Ownership Interest, has made an investigation of the Company and its business, and the Company has made available to each Equity Owner all information with respect to the Company which such Equity Owner needs in order to make an informed decision to acquire the Ownership Interest. Each Equity Owner has relied on its own tax and legal advisors in connection with such Equity Owner's decision to acquire an Ownership Interest. Each Equity Owner considers itself to be a Person possessing experience and sophistication as an investor which are adequate for the evaluation of the merits and risks of such Equity Owner's investment in the Ownership Interest.[72]

13.21. Representations and Warranties.

(a) In General. As of the date hereof, each of the Equity Owners hereby makes each of the representations and warranties applicable to such Equity Owner as set forth in Section 13.20 hereof, and such warranties and representations shall survive the execution of this Agreement.

(b) Representations and Warranties. Each Equity Owner represents and warrants that:

(i) Due Incorporation or Formation; Authorization of Agreement. Such Equity Owner, if an Entity, is duly organized (if a corporation) or duly formed (if a partnership or limited liability company), validly existing, and in good standing under the laws of the jurisdiction of its incorporation or formation and has the corporate, partnership, or limited liability company power and authority to own its property and carry on its business as owned and carried on at the date hereof and as contemplated hereby. Such Equity Owner is duly licensed or qualified to do business and in good standing in each of the jurisdictions in which the failure to be so licensed or qualified would have a material adverse effect on its financial condition or its ability to perform its obligations hereunder. Such Equity Owner has the corporate, partnership, or limited liability company power and

---

[72] As noted with respect to the legend on the cover of the agreement, many Membership Interests may be "securities" under the federal and state securities laws. It is probably not a good idea to include this provision unless you conclude, after consulting a securities lawyer, that the Membership Interests are securities and therefore that steps will have to be taken to comply with the securities laws. If a subscription agreement is used and a provision like the foregoing is used in the operating agreement, make sure that the securities lawyer on the deal conforms this provision to the language in the subscription agreement.

authority to execute and deliver this Agreement and to perform its obligations hereunder and the execution, delivery, and performance of this Agreement has been duly authorized by all necessary corporate, partnership or limited liability company action. This Agreement constitutes the legal, valid, and binding obligation of such Equity Owner.

(ii) <u>No Conflict with Restrictions; No Default</u>. Neither the execution, delivery, and performance of this Agreement nor the consummation by such Equity Owner of the transactions contemplated hereby (1) will conflict with, violate, or result in a breach of any of the terms, conditions, or provisions of any law, regulation, order, writ, injunction, decree, determination, or award of any court, any governmental department, board, agency, or instrumentality, domestic or foreign, or any arbitrator, applicable to such Equity Owner or any of its Affiliates, (2) if such Equity Owner is an Entity, will conflict with, violate, result in a breach of, or constitute a default under any of the terms, conditions, or provisions of the articles of incorporation, bylaws, partnership agreement, limited liability company agreement, or operating agreement of such Equity Owner or any of its Affiliates or of any material agreement or instrument to which such Equity Owner or any of its Affiliates is a party or by which such Equity Owner, or any of its Affiliates is or may be bound or to which any of its material properties or assets is subject, (3) will conflict with, violate, result in a breach of, constitute a default under (whether with notice or lapse of time or both), accelerate or permit the acceleration of the performance required by, give to others any material interests or rights, or require any approval under any indenture, mortgage, lease agreement, or instrument to which such Equity Owner or any of its Affiliates is a party or by which such Equity Owner or any of its Affiliates is or may be bound, or (4) will result in the creation or imposition of any lien upon any of the material properties or assets of such Equity Owner or any of its Affiliates.

(iii) <u>Government Authorizations</u>. Any registration, declaration, or filing with, or consent, approval, license, permit, or other authorization or order by, any government or regulatory authority, domestic or foreign, that is required in connection with the valid execution, delivery, acceptance, and performance by such Equity Owner under this Agreement or the consummation by such Equity Owner of any transaction contemplated hereby has been completed, made, or obtained on or before the effective date of this Agreement.

(iv) <u>Litigation</u>. There are no actions, suits, proceedings, or investigations pending or, to the knowledge of such Equity Owner or any of its Affiliates, threatened against or affecting such Equity Owner or any of its Affiliates or any of their properties, assets, or businesses in any court or before or by any governmental department, board, agency, or instrumentality, domestic or foreign, or any arbitrator which could, if adversely determined (or, in the case of an investigation could lead to any action, suit, or proceeding, which if adversely determined could) reasonably be expected to materially impair such Equity Owner's ability to perform its obligations under this Agreement or to have a material adverse effect on the consolidated financial condition of such member; and such Equity Owner or any of its Affiliates has not received any currently effective notice of any default, and such Equity Owner or any of its Affiliates is not in default, under any applicable order, writ, injunction, decree, permit, determination, or award of any court, any governmental department, board, agency, or instrumentality, domestic or foreign, or any arbitrator which could reasonably be expected to materially impair such Equity Owner's ability to perform its obligations under this Agreement or to have a material adverse effect on the consolidated financial condition of such Equity Owner.

(v) <u>Investment Company Act; Public Utility Holding Company Act</u>. Neither such Equity Owner nor any of its Affiliates is, nor will the Company as a result of such Equity Owner holding an Ownership Interest be, an "investment company" as defined in, or subject to regulation under, the Investment Company Act of 1940. Neither such Equity Owner nor any of its Affiliates is, nor will the Company as a result of such Equity Owner holding an Ownership Interest be, a "holding company," "an affiliate of a holding company," or a "subsidiary of a holding company," as defined in, or subject to regulation under, the Public Utility Holding Company Act of 1935.

(vi) <u>Subsidiary</u>. All of the outstanding capital stock or ownership interests in the capital and profits of such Equity Owner is owned, directly or indirectly, by [_____].

(c) <u>Confidentiality</u>. Except as contemplated hereby or required by a court of competent authority, each Equity Owner shall keep confidential and shall not disclose to others and shall use its reasonable efforts to prevent its Affiliates and any of its, or its Affiliates' present or former employees, agents, and representatives from disclosing to others without the prior written Approval of the Managers any information which (x) pertains to this Agreement, any negotiations pertaining thereto, any of the transactions contemplated hereby, or the business of the Company, or (y) pertains to confidential or proprietary information of any Member or the Company or which any Equity Owner has labeled in writing as confidential or proprietary; provided that any Equity Owner may disclose to its and its Affiliates' employees, agents, and representatives any information made available to such Equity Owner. No Equity Owner shall use, and each Equity Owner shall use its best efforts to prevent any Affiliate of such Equity Owner from using, any information which (1) pertains to this Agreement, any negotiations pertaining hereto, any of the transactions contemplated hereby, or the business of the Company, or (2) pertains to the confidential or proprietary information of any Equity Owner or the Company or which any Equity Owner has labeled in writing as confidential or proprietary, except in connection with the transactions contemplated hereby. Notwithstanding the foregoing provisions of this Section 13.21(c), the Equity Owners (and each employee, representative, or other agent of the Equity Owners) may disclose to any and all Persons, without limitation of any kind, the tax treatment and tax structure of the transactions contemplated hereby and all materials of any kind (including opinions or other tax analyses) that are provided to the Equity Owners relating to such tax treatment and tax structure.

CERTIFICATE

The undersigned hereby agree, acknowledge, and certify that the foregoing Agreement, consisting of _____ pages, excluding the Table of Contents and attached Exhibits, constitutes the Agreement of [_____] LLC adopted by the Equity Owners as of [_____].

[_____], *LLC*

By: _____

Its: _____

MEMBERS

_____

_____

_____

_____

_____

PART FIVE
SAMPLE PARTNERSHIP AGREEMENT

SAMPLE GENERAL PARTNERSHIP AGREEMENT[*]

THIS GENERAL PARTNERSHIP AGREEMENT of [*Name of Partnership*], effective as of _____, 20____, by and between [*Name of Partner*], a _____ ("_____"), and [*Name of Partner*], a _____ ("_____").[1]

[ARTICLE I]
CERTAIN DEFINITIONS

The following terms used in this Agreement shall (unless otherwise expressly provided herein or unless the context otherwise requires) have the following respective meanings:

1.1 *Act.* The Revised Uniform Partnership Act (1997), as may be amended from time to time.

1.2 *Affiliate.* An Affiliate of a specified Person is (i) any Person that directly or indirectly through one or more intermediaries controls or is controlled by or is under common control with such specified person, (ii) any Person which is an officer, director, partner (other than a partner as a result of this Agreement) or trustee of, or serves in a similar capacity with respect to, such specified Person, (iii) any Person which is directly or indirectly the owner of more than ten percent (10%) of any class of equity securities of such specified Person and (iv) the parents, siblings, children or spouse of such specified Person.

1.3 *Agreement.* This General Partnership Agreement as the same may be amended from time to time.

1.4 *Available Cash.* That sum of cash resulting from normal business operations of the Partnership, and from any other income or funds derived from Partnership property which the Partners [Managing Partner] reasonably determine[s] to be available for distribution to the

---

[*] This form of partnership agreement is contained in Robert W. Hillman, Allan W. Vestal & Donald J. Weidner, THE REVISED UNIFORM PARTNERSHIP ACT 399–421 (1999) and is reproduced here by permission of the co-authors and West Group. It was drafted by Stearns Weaver Miller Weissler Alhadeff & Sitterson, P.A., of Miami, Florida. The Stearns law firm also has given permission to reprint.

[1] In this form, it is assumed that the partners are entities rather than individuals.

Partners after payment of all cash expenditures, including to the extent applicable, but not limited to, taxes, principal and interest payments on all Partnership indebtedness (including loans from any of the Partners and their Affiliates to the Partnership), insurance, brokerage fees, accounting and legal fees, supplies, ordinary and necessary business expenses and the setting aside of any amounts which the Partners [Managing Partner] reasonably determine[s] are necessary as a reserve for (to the extent applicable) operating expenses, contingencies and anticipated obligations.

1.5 *Capital Accounts.* A separate Capital Account shall be maintained for each Partner in accordance with the following provisions:

1.5.1 To each Partner's Capital Account there shall be credited such Partner's Capital Contributions, such Partner's distributive share of Profits, and any items of income, gain, loss deduction or credit that are specially allocated pursuant to Article VIII hereof, and the amount of any Partnership liabilities that are assumed by such Partner or that are secured by any Partnership property distributed to such Partner.

1.5.2 To each Partner's Capital Account there shall be debited the amount of cash and the fair market value of any Partnership property distributed to such Partner pursuant to any provisions of this Agreement, such Partner's distributive share of Losses, and any items in the nature of expenses or losses that are specially allocated pursuant to Article VIII hereof, and the amount of any liabilities of such Partner that are assumed by the Partnership or that are secured by any property contributed by such Partner to the Partnership.

1.5.3 In the event that the book value of the Partnership assets is adjusted pursuant to the Code, the Capital Accounts of all Partners shall be adjusted simultaneously to reflect the aggregate net adjustments as if the Partnership recognized Profit or Loss equal to the respective amounts of such aggregate net adjustments immediately before the event causing the adjustment to book value.

The foregoing provisions and the other provisions of this Agreement relating to the maintenance of Capital Accounts are intended to comply with Treasury Regulations Section 1.704-1(b), and shall be interpreted and applied in a manner consistent with such Treasury Regulations. In the event the Partners [Managing Partner] reasonably determine[s] that it is prudent to modify the manner in which the Capital Accounts, or any debits or credits thereto, are computed in order to comply with such Treasury Regulations, the Partners [Managing Partner] may make such modification. The Partners [Managing Partner] shall adjust the amounts debited or credited to Capital Accounts with respect to (i) any property contributed to the Partnership or distributed to a Partner, and (ii) any liabilities that are secured by such contributed or distributed property or that are assumed by the Partnership or a Partner, in the event the Partners [Managing Partner] reasonably determine[s] that such adjustments are necessary or appropriate pursuant to Treasury Regulations Section 1.704-1(b)(2)(iv). The Partners [Managing Partner] also shall make any appropriate modifications in the event unanticipated events might otherwise cause this Agreement not to comply with Treasury Regulations Section 1.704-1(b).

1.6 *Capital Contribution.* The amount in cash and the value of property contributed by the Partners to the equity of the Partnership, whether initial Capital Contributions in accordance with Section 6.2 hereof or additional Capital Contributions in accordance with Section 6.3 hereof. Any reference in this Agreement to the Capital Contribution of either a Partner or any permitted assignee of a Partner includes any Capital Contribution previously made by any prior Partner to whose Partnership Interest the then existing Partner or assignee succeeded.

1.7 *Cash from Sales, Financing or Condemnation.* The net cash realized by the Partnership by virtue of the sale, financing, refinancing, condemnation or disposition of the Partnership's property, in whole or in part, after repayment of applicable debt and the payment of all expenses and amounts required to be paid under the instruments evidencing or relating to such debt and all expenses related to the transaction and the retention of such amounts as the Partners [Managing Partner] may reasonably determine to be necessary as a reserve for (to the extent applicable) operating expenses, contingencies and anticipated obligations.

1.8 *Code.* The Internal Revenue Code of 1986, as amended, or corresponding provisions of subsequent revenue laws.

1.9 *Distributions.* Any cash or other property distributed to a Partner as a result of its ownership of Partnership Interests (or the assignee of a Partner's Transferable Interest as a result of its ownership of the Transferable Interest), including but not limited to distribution of Available Cash and distribution of Cash from Sales, Financing or Condemnation and distributions in complete or partial liquidation of the Partnership.

1.10 *Managing Partner.* [*Name of Managing Partner*].

1.11 *Partner or Partners.* [*Name of Partner*], [*Name of Partner*], and any substitute, successor or additional partners as provided herein.

1.12 *Partnership.* [*Name of Partnership*], a [*Name of State*] general partnership.

1.13 *Partnership Interest.* All of a Partner's interest in the Partnership, including the Partner's Transferable Interest and all management and other rights.

1.14 *Percentage Interest.* The percentage interest of a Partner in the Partnership's allocation of Profits, Losses, Available Cash, Cash From Sales, Financing or Condemnation and capital of the Partnership, subject to the terms and conditions of this Agreement, and as set forth opposite its name on Schedule "A" attached hereto and incorporated herein by reference.

1.15 *Person.* Any individual, corporation, business trust, estate, trust, partnership, limited partnership, association, joint venture, limited liability company, governmental subdivision, agency or instrumentality or any other legal or commercial entity.

1.16 *Profits or Losses.* For each fiscal year, an amount equal to the Partnership's taxable income or loss for such fiscal year, determined in accordance with Code Section 703(a) (for this purpose, all items of income, gain, loss or deduction required to be stated separately pursuant to Code Section 703(a)(1) shall be included in taxable income or loss), with the following adjustments:

1.16.1 Any income of the Partnership that is exempt from federal income tax and not otherwise taken into account in computing Profits or Losses pursuant to this Section shall be added to such taxable income or loss;

1.16.2 Any expenditures of the Partnership described in Code Section 705(a)(2)(B) or treated as Code Section 705(a)(2)(B) expenditures pursuant to Treasury Regulations Section 1.704-1(b)(2)(iv), and not otherwise taken into account in computing Profits or Losses pursuant to this Section, shall be subtracted from such taxable income or loss;

1.16.3 To the extent an adjustment to the adjusted tax basis of any Partnership asset pursuant to Code Section 734(b) or Code Section 743(b) is required pursuant to Treasury Regulations Section 1.704-1(b)(2)(iv)(m)(4) to be taken into account in determining Capital Accounts as a result of a distribution other than in liquidation of a Partner's interest, the amount of such adjustment shall be treated as an item of gain (if the adjustment increases the basis of the asset) or loss (if the adjustment decreases the basis of the asset) from the disposition of the asset and shall be taken into account for purposes of computing Profits or Losses; and

1.16.4 Notwithstanding any other provisions of this Section, any items which are specially allocated pursuant to Section 8.3 hereof shall not be taken into account in computing Profits or Losses.

The amounts of the items of Partnership income, gain, loss, or deduction available to be specially allocated pursuant to Section 8.3 hereof shall be determined by applying rules analogous to those set forth in this Section.

1.17 *Treasury Regulations.* Regulations of the United States Treasury Department pertaining to the income tax, as amended, and any successor provisions thereto.

1.18 *Substitute Partner.* A Person who succeeds to the Partnership Interest of any Partner, by sale, exchange, assignment or otherwise, and who has been substituted for such Partner, as provided herein but does not include the transferee of a Partner's Transferable Interest.

1.19 *Transferable Interest.* Only the Partner's share of Profits and Losses of the Partnership and right to receive Distributions.

[ARTICLE II]
FORMATION OF PARTNERSHIP

2.1 *Formation and Name.* By this Agreement and pursuant to the Revised Uniform Partnership Act (1997), the Partners hereby agree to form a general partnership designated [*Name of Partnership*] or such other name as is approved by the Partners and such name shall be used at all times in connection with the Partnership's business and affairs. The Partners shall execute such assumed or fictitious name certificates as may be desirable or required by law to be filed in connection with the formation of the Partnership and shall cause such certificates to be filed in all appropriate public records.

2.2 *Term.* The term of the Partnership shall commence on the date hereof and shall continue in existence until _____, 20____, unless sooner terminated as provided herein or by law.

2.3 *Partnership Registration Statement.* The Partners shall execute and file with the Department of State of the State of [non-uniform State] a "Partnership Registration Statement" in the name of the Partnership in accordance with [a non-uniform statute] and amend and cancel such Partnership Registration Statement from time to time consistent with this Agreement.][2]

[ARTICLE III]
BUSINESS OF THE PARTNERSHIP

The purpose and character of the business of the Partnership shall be to _____ and to engage in any and all activities related or incidental to carrying out the foregoing, and to conduct and engage in any and all activities permitted by law in furtherance of the business of the Partnership.

---

[2] A partnership registration statement is not required by RUPA. However, particular states may have provisions that supplement the Act. In Florida, for example, a non-uniform statute provides that a partnership registration statement must be filed before a certificate of partnership authority can be filed. *See* F.S.A. § 620.8105.

[ARTICLE IV]
ADDRESS OF THE PARTIES

4.1 *Principal Place of Business.* The chief executive office and principal place of business of the Partnership shall be maintained at _____. The Partners may from time to time change such office and principal place of business. The Partners may establish additional places of business of the Partnership when and where required by the Partnership's business.

4.2 *Partners' Addresses.* The addresses of the Partners shall be those stated on Schedule "A" attached hereto and incorporated herein by reference. A Partner may change such address by written notice to the other Partners, which notice shall become effective upon receipt.

[ARTICLE V]
TITLE

Title to all Partnership assets shall be in the name of the Partnership.

[ARTICLE VI]
CONTRIBUTION TO CAPITAL AND STATUS OF PARTNERS

6.1 *Amount of Capital.* The capital of the Partnership shall be the total amount of Capital Contributions to the Partnership by the Partners.

6.2 *Initial Capital Contribution by the Partners.* Simultaneous with the execution of this Agreement, the Partners shall make the following contributions to the capital of the Partnership:

6.2.1 _____ — \$_____; and

6.2.2 _____ — \$_____.

6.3 *Additional Capital Contributions.* Each Partner hereby agrees that, in addition to its initial Capital Contribution under Section 6.2 hereof, it will contribute additional capital to the Partnership if the Partners determine, in their reasonable discretion, that such contributions are required to enable the Partnership to _____ as follows:

[Insert Applicable Provision Regarding Additional Capital Contributions]

Such additional capital contributions shall be made by the Partners within twenty (20) business days after written notice is received by such Partners setting forth the amount of additional capital required.

6.4 *Default in Obligations to Make Additional Capital Contributions.*

*[Insert Applicable Default Provision Regarding
Failure To Make Additional Capital Contributions]* [3]

6.5 *No Assessment on Partners.* No Partner shall be assessed or be liable for additional Capital Contributions in excess of its stated initial Capital Contribution specified in Section 6.2 and any additional Capital Contributions required pursuant to Section 6.3.

6.6 *Withdrawal and Return of Capital.* No Partner shall have the right to withdraw any of its capital without the consent of all the Partners, except upon dissolution and liquidation of the Partnership. Upon circumstances requiring a return of any Capital Contribution, no Partner shall have the right to receive property other than cash except as may be specifically provided herein.

6.7 *Capital Accounts.* There shall be established on the books and records of the Partnership a Capital Account for each Partner. The Capital Account for each Partner shall at all times be maintained and adjusted according to the rules set forth in Section 1.704-1(b)(2)(iv) of the Treasury Regulations.

6.8 *Representations and Warranties of Partners.* Each of the Partners hereby represents and warrants to the other Partners that it (a) is duly organized, validly existing and in good standing under the laws of the state of its organization; (b) has duly executed and delivered this Agreement; and (c) has full right, power and authority to execute and deliver this Agreement and to perform each of its obligations hereunder.

**[ARTICLE VII]
DISTRIBUTIONS**

7.1 *Distributions of Available Cash and Cash from Sales, Financing or Condemnation.* Distributions of Available Cash and Cash from Sales, Financing or Condemnation shall be made periodically at such intervals as shall be determined in the absolute discretion of the Partners [Managing Partner]. Subject to the foregoing, such Distributions shall be allocated to the Partners in the following order of priority:

---

[3] Some possible default provisions include (i) each partner granting to the partnership a security interest in its Partnership Interest to secure the obligation to make additional capital contributions, which security interest may be foreclosed upon the partner's failure to make required capital contributions and (ii) the right (but not the obligation) of the non-defaulting partner to fund the capital contribution not made by the defaulting partner either in the form of an additional capital contribution or interest bearing loan to the partnership and, if it is made in the form of a capital contribution, the percentage interests of the defaulting partner and non-defaulting partner are readjusted accordingly.

[Insert Applicable Provision for Distributions]

[ARTICLE VIII]
ALLOCATION OF PROFITS AND LOSSES FOR INCOME
TAX AND ACCOUNTING PURPOSES[4]

8.1 *Allocation of Profits.* All Profits for accounting purposes, taxable income and gains from sales or exchanges of property (net of losses) for each fiscal year, shall be allocated, on an annual or more frequent basis as determined by the Code and Treasury Regulations promulgated thereunder, to each Partner, in the following order of priority:

[Insert Applicable Provision for Allocation of Profits]

8.2 *Allocation of Losses.* All Losses, losses for accounting purposes, taxable loss and losses from sales or exchanges of property (net of gains) for each fiscal year shall be allocated, on an annual or more frequent basis as determined by the Code and Treasury Regulations promulgated thereunder, to each Partner in the following order of priority:

[Insert Applicable Provision for Allocation of Losses]

Notwithstanding the foregoing, the Losses shall be allocated among the Partners such that the Losses allocated to any Partner pursuant to this Section shall, to the extent possible, not exceed the maximum amount of Losses that can be allocated without causing such Partner to have a negative Capital Account at the end of the fiscal year.

8.3 *Special Allocations.*

[Insert Any Applicable Provisions for Special Allocations of Profits and Losses and Items Thereof]

8.4 *704(c) Allocations.* Any income, gain, loss or deduction with respect to property contributed to the Partnership by a Partner (as required under Code Section 704(c)) will, solely for tax purposes, be allocated among the Partners to take into account the variations between the basis of property contributed to the Partnership and the fair market value of such property in the manner provided in Code Section 704(c). Any elections or other decisions relating to such allocations shall be made by the Partners [Managing Partner] in any manner which reasonably reflects the purpose and intent of this Agreement. Allocations pursuant to this Section 8.4 shall be solely for purposes of federal, state and local taxes and shall not affect, or in any way be taken into account, in computing a Partner's Capital Account or share of Profits, Losses or other items or Distributions pursuant to any provision of this Agreement.

---

[4] *See* Code § 704(b) and Treasury Regulations Section 1.704-1(b).

[ARTICLE IX]
MANAGEMENT OF THE PARTNERSHIP

9.1 *Managing Partner; Rights, Power and Authority.* Subject to the limitations and provisions set forth herein, the Managing Partner shall have full, exclusive and complete authority and discretion in the management and control of the Partnership business for the purposes herein stated and shall make all decisions affecting the business of the Partnership. No other Partner shall have the rights, power or authority granted in this Section 9.1. Persons dealing with the Partnership are entitled to rely conclusively on the power and authority of the Managing Partner. Subject to the limitations and provisions set forth herein, the Managing Partner is hereby granted the right, power and authority to do on behalf of the Partnership all things which, in the Managing Partner's sole judgment and discretion, are necessary, proper, or desirable in connection with its role and function as Managing Partner of the Partnership. Further, the Managing Partner shall have all of the rights and powers of a general partner as provided in the Act and as otherwise provided by law, and any action taken by the Managing Partner permitted by this Agreement shall constitute an act of and serve to bind the Partnership.

9.2 *Matters Requiring Joint Decision of the Partners.* Notwithstanding the rights, power and authority given to the Managing Partner pursuant to Section 9.1 hereof, the rights, power and authority of the Managing Partner shall not include the activities set forth in this Section 9.2 or any other provision of this Agreement requiring the consent or approval of each Partner, which shall be expressly retained for the [unanimous] decision of the Partners and shall be subject to the [unanimous] written approval of the Partners:

[*Insert Any Provision Restricting Authority of Managing Partner*][5]

9.3 *Vote of Partners.* Each Partner shall have an equal vote with respect to the matters set forth in Section 9.2 hereof and all other matters requiring the approval, consent or other determination of the Partners, irrespective of the Partners' respective Percentage Interests.

9.4 *Removal of Managing Partner.* _____ may be removed as the Managing Partner and _____ substituted as the Managing Partner upon _____.

---

[5] The unanimous approval of the partners may be required to, among other things: (i) sell all or substantially all of the partnership's assets, (ii) acquire additional assets, (iii) enter into material agreements, (iv) borrow money or encumber assets, (v) admit additional partners, (vi) engage in transactions with affiliates, (vii) change the business or purpose of the partnership or (viii) confess a judgment.

*[Insert Events or Conditions Requiring
Removal of Managing Partner]*

9.5 *Duties and Obligations of the Partners.* 9.5.1 The Partners shall take all actions which may be necessary or appropriate for the continuation of the Partnership's valid existence as a general partnership under the laws of the State of *[Name of State]*.

9.5.2 Each of the Partners shall devote to the Partnership such time as may be necessary for the proper performance of its duties hereunder. Nothing herein shall prohibit the Partners and their respective Affiliates from engaging in any other business activities during the term of the Partnership, including activities which may be competitive with the Partnership, and nothing shall give the other Partners any interest in any such competitive activities.[6]

9.5.3 The Partners shall, in connection with the performance of their duties hereunder, comply, and shall cause the Partnership to comply, in all respects with the laws of the United States, the State of *[Name of State]* and any other applicable jurisdiction, and with the rules and regulations of any governmental Person promulgated thereunder.

9.6 *A Partner's Duty of Loyalty.* Each Partner agrees: (a) to account to the Partnership and hold as trustee for the Partnership any property, profit or benefit derived by such Partner in the conduct and winding up of the Partnership business or derived from a use by the Partner of Partnership property, including the appropriation of a Partnership opportunity, and (b) to refrain from dealing with the Partnership in the conduct or winding up of the Partnership business as or on behalf of a party having an interest adverse to the Partnership.[7]

9.7 *Indemnification of the Partners.* Neither of the Partners nor any of their respective Affiliates shall be liable to the Partnership or any Partner for any loss or liability incurred in connection with any act performed or omitted in accordance with the terms of this Agreement, nor for negligence, except for any loss or liability incurred in connection with the fraud, gross negligence or reckless conduct, intentional misconduct or knowing violation of the law or this Agreement of such Partner. The Partnership shall, to the fullest extent permitted by law, but only to the extent of the assets of the Partnership, and without recourse to the separate assets of the Partners, indemnify and save harmless each of the

---

[6] Section 103(b)(3) of RUPA restricts the partnership agreement from eliminating the duty of loyalty under Sections 404(b) or 603(b)(3), but provides that the partnership agreement may identify specific types or categories of activities that do not violate the duty of loyalty, if not manifestly unreasonable. All of the partners or a number or percentage specified in the partnership agreement may authorize or ratify, after full disclosure of all material facts, a specific act or transaction that otherwise would violate the duty of loyalty.

[7] *Id.*

Partners from and against any and all liability, loss, cost, expense or damage incurred or sustained by reason of any act or omission in the conduct of the business of the Partnership, regardless of whether acting pursuant to its discretionary or explicit authority hereunder, except any incurred in connection with its fraud, gross negligence or reckless conduct, intentional misconduct or knowing violation of the law or this Agreement. In particular, and without limitation of the foregoing, each of the Partners shall be entitled to indemnification by the Partnership against the reasonable expenses, including attorneys' fees actually and necessarily incurred by such Partner or Affiliates, in connection with the defense of any suit or action to which such Partner or its Affiliates are made a party by reason of its position as a Partner or an affiliate of such Partner herein, to the fullest extent permitted under the provisions of this Agreement, the Act or any other applicable statute. Nothing herein shall make any affiliate of a Partner liable in any way for the acts, omissions, obligations or liabilities of a Partner.

9.8 *Statement of Partnership Authority.* The Partners shall execute and file a "Statement of Partnership Authority" in the name of the Partnership pursuant to Section 303 of the Act which shall state (a) the names of the Partners authorized to execute an instrument transferring real property in the name of the Partnership, if any, and (b) the authority, or limitations on the authority of some or all of the Partners to enter into other transactions on behalf of the Partnership pursuant to Article IX of this Agreement, and any other matter. The Statement of Partnership Authority shall be filed with the Department of State of the State of [*Name of State*] and in the office for recording transfers of real property in each county in which the Partnership owns real property, if any. The Partners shall amend or cancel such Statement of Partnership Authority from time to time consistent with this Agreement. Each Partner hereby agrees not to file a "Statement of Denial" pursuant to Section 304 of the Act denying any fact which would be inconsistent with the authority granted to a Partner pursuant to this Agreement.

[ARTICLE X]
DISPOSITION OF PARTNERSHIP INTERESTS

10.1 *Restrictions.*

10.1.1 No Partner may sell, hypothecate, pledge, transfer, assign or otherwise dispose of its Partnership Interest without the prior written consent of the other Partner, which consent may be withheld in the other Partner's absolute discretion. For the purposes of this Agreement, the transfer, directly or indirectly, of fifty percent (50%) or more of the stock or other ownership interest in a Partner shall be a prohibited disposition. Notwithstanding the foregoing provisions of this Subsection 10.1.1, a Partner shall be permitted to transfer its Partnership Interest or the stock or other ownership interest in such

Partner to an Affiliate of such Partner for estate planning purposes without the consent of the other Partner.

10.1.2 No offer, sale, hypothecation pledge, transfer, assignment, or other disposition of any Partnership Interest may be made unless the Partners shall have received an opinion of counsel satisfactory to them that such proposed disposition (i) may be effected without registration of the Partnership Interest under the Securities Act of 1933, as amended, (ii) would not be in violation of any securities laws (including investment suitability standards) of any jurisdiction applicable to the Partnership, and (iii) would not result in the termination of the Partnership under Code Section 708.

10.1.3 Nothing contained in this Article X shall be deemed to prohibit any Partner from transferring to any Person its Transferable Interest; provided that no such assignment of a Partner's Transferable Interest shall entitle the transferee to become a Partner, to interfere or otherwise participate in the management or conduct of the affairs or business of the Partnership, to require access to any information on account of Partnership transactions or to inspect the books and records of the Partnership. The transferee Partner's sole connection with or rights against the Partnership or any other Partner is (i) to receive, in accordance with the transfer, Distributions to which the transferor would otherwise be entitled and (ii) to receive, upon dissolution and winding up of the Partnership business, in accordance with the transfer, an account of Partnership transactions only from the date of the latest account agreed to by all of the Partners and the net amount otherwise distributable to the transferor. The transferor Partner retains the rights and duties of a Partner other than with respect to the Transferable Interest so transferred and is not relieved of its liability as a Partner under this Agreement or the Act. The Partnership shall, upon receipt of written notice of transfer of the Partner's Transferable Interest, allocate all further Profits and Losses and make all further Distributions so transferred to the transferee for such times as the Transferable Interest is transferred on the Partnership's books in accordance with this provision. The Partnership shall not give effect to the transfer of a Partner's Transferable Interest until it has received written notice of such transfer which notice shall include the name and address of the transferee and the effective date of the transfer.

10.2 *Admission of Substitute Partner.*

10.2.1 Subject to the other provisions of this Article X, an assignee of the Partnership Interest of a Partner (which shall be understood to include any purchaser, transferee, donee, or other recipient of any disposition of such Partnership Interest) shall be deemed admitted as a Substitute Partner of the Partnership only upon the satisfactory completion of the following:

10.2.1.1 Consent of the other Partners (which may be given or withheld in the other Partner's sole discretion) shall have been given, which consent may be evidenced by the execution by the other Partners of a certificate evidencing the admission of such person as a Partner.

10.2.1.2 The assignee shall have accepted and agreed to be bound by the terms and provisions of this Agreement by executing a counterpart thereof, and such other documents or instruments as the Partners may reasonably require in order to accomplish the admission of such person as a Partner.

10.2.1.3 If the assignee is not an individual, the assignee shall have provided the Partners with evidence satisfactory to counsel for the Partnership of its authority to become a Partner under the terms and provisions of this Agreement.

10.2.1.4 The assignee shall have paid all reasonable legal fees and administrative costs of the Partnership and the Partners and filing and publication costs in connection with its substitution as a Partner.

10.2.2 Upon the satisfactory completion of the requirements described in Section 10.2.1 for the admission of a Substitute Partner, as determined by the Partners in their reasonable discretion, a Substitute Partner shall be treated as a Partner for all purposes of this Agreement commencing the first day of the next following calendar month. Any Person so admitted to the Partnership as a Partner shall be subject to all provisions of this Agreement as if originally a party hereto but such Substitute Partner's liabilities hereunder shall commence to accrue as of the date such Substitute Partner is admitted to the Partnership. The Partnership shall, upon substitution of a Partner, pursuant to the provisions of this Section 10.2, thereafter allocate all further Profits and Losses and make all further Distributions on account of the Partnership Interest so assigned to the assignee for such time as the interest is transferred on the Partnership books in accordance with the above provisions.

10.3 *Rights of Assignee of Partnership Interest of a Partner.*

10.3.1 Subject to the provisions of Section 10.1 hereof, and except as required by operation of law, the Partnership shall not be obligated for any purposes whatsoever to recognize the assignment by any Partner of its Partnership Interest until the Partnership has received notice thereof, which notice must include such information and documentation with respect to the assignment as the Partners may require.

10.3.2 Any person who is the assignee of all or any portion of a Partner's Partnership Interest, but does not become a Substitute Partner, and desires to make a further assignment of such Partnership

Interest, shall be subject to all the provisions of this Article X to the same extent and in the same manner as any Partner desiring to make an assignment of its Partnership Interest.

10.3.3 An assignee who has not been substituted as a Partner shall not be counted for purposes of any matter requiring the consent of the Partners.

10.4 *Contravention Voids Assignment.* Any sale, hypothecation, pledge, transfer, assignment or other disposition in contravention of this Agreement shall be void and ineffective and shall not bind or be recognized by the Partnership.

[ARTICLE XI]
DISSOCIATION OF A PARTNER

11.1 *Dissociation.* A Partner is dissociated from the Partnership upon the occurrence of any of the following events: [8]

11.1.1 The Partnership having received written notice of the Partner's express will to immediately withdraw as a partner or withdraw on a later date specified by the Partner; [9]

11.1.2 The Partner's expulsion by a unanimous vote of the other partners if:

11.1.2.1 It is unlawful to carry on the Partnership business with such Partner;

11.1.2.2 There has been a transfer of all or substantially all of such Partner's Transferable Interest in the Partnership other than a permitted transfer for security purposes, or a court order charging the Partner's Partnership Interest, which has not been foreclosed;

11.1.2.3 Within 90 days after the Partnership notifies a corporate Partner that it will be expelled because it has filed a certificate of dissolution or the equivalent, its charter has been revoked, or its right to conduct business has been suspended by the jurisdiction of its incorporation, there is no revocation of the certificate of dissolution or no reinstatement of the corporate Partner's charter or the corporate Partner's right to conduct business; or

11.1.2.4 A partnership that is a Partner has been dissolved and its business is being wound up;

---

[8] In addition to the events causing dissociation listed herein, a partner may be dissociated upon the occurrence of (i) an event agreed to in the partnership agreement or (ii) a partner's expulsion pursuant to the partnership agreement.

[9] Section 103(b)(6) of RUPA prohibits the partnership agreement from denying this power of a partner to dissociate.

11.1.3 On application by the Partnership or another Partner, the Partner's expulsion by judicial determination because:

11.1.3.1 The Partner engaged in wrongful conduct that adversely and materially affected the Partnership's business;

11.1.3.2 The Partner willfully or persistently committed a material breach of the Agreement or of a duty owed to the Partnership or the other Partners under Sections 9.6 or 14.5 hereof;

11.1.3.3 The Partner engaged in conduct relating to the Partnership's business which makes it not reasonably practicable to carry on the business in partnership with the Partner;

11.1.4 The Partner's:

11.1.4.1 Becoming a debtor in bankruptcy;

11.1.4.2 Executing an assignment for the benefit of creditors;

11.1.4.3 Seeking, consenting to, or acquiescing in the appointment of a trustee, receiver, or liquidator of such Partner or of all or substantially all of such Partner's property; or

11.1.4.4 Failing, within 90 days after appointment, to have vacated or have stayed the appointment of a trustee, receiver or liquidator of the Partner or of all or substantially all of the Partner's property obtained without the Partner's consent or acquiescence, or failing within 90 days after the expiration of a stay to have the appointment vacated;

11.1.5 In the case of a Partner who is an individual:

11.1.5.1 The Partner's death;

11.1.5.2 The appointment of a guardian or general conservator for the Partner; or

11.1.5.3 A judicial determination that the Partner has otherwise become incapable of performing the Partner's duties under the Agreement;

11.1.6 In the case of a Partner that is a trust or is acting as a Partner by virtue of being a trustee of a trust, distribution of the trust's entire Transferable Interest in the Partnership, but not merely by reason of the substitution of a successor trustee;

11.1.7 In the case of a Partner that is an estate or is acting as a Partner by virtue of being a personal representative of an estate, distribution of the estate's entire Transferable Interest in the Partnership, but not merely by reason of the substitution of a successor personal representative;

11.1.8 Termination of a Partner who is not an individual, partnership, corporation, trust, or estate; or

11.1.9 The Partner's direct or indirect transfer of all or any portion of its Partnership Interest in violation of Section 10.1 hereof.

11.2 *Purchase of Dissociated Partner's Partnership Interest.* [10]

11.2.1 If a Partner is dissociated from the Partnership without resulting in a dissolution and winding up of the Partnership business under Section 11.1 hereof, the Partnership shall cause the dissociated Partner's Partnership Interest to be purchased for a "Buyout Price" determined pursuant to Section 11.2.2 hereof.

11.2.2 The Buyout Price of a dissociated Partner's Partnership Interest is the amount that would have been distributable to the dissociating Partner under Section 12.3.3 hereof if, on the date of dissociation, the assets of the Partnership were sold at a price equal to the greater of the liquidation value of the assets or the value of the assets based upon a sale of the entire business as a going concern without the dissociated Partner, and the Partnership was wound up as of such date. Interest shall be paid from the date of the Partner's dissociation to the date of payment of the Buyout Price.

11.2.3 Damages for wrongful dissociation under Section 11.3 hereof, and all other amounts owing, whether or not presently due, from the dissociated Partner to the Partnership, shall be offset against the Buyout Price. Interest shall be paid from the date the amount owed by the dissociated Partner becomes due to the date of payment.

11.2.4 A Partnership shall indemnify a dissociated Partner whose interest is being purchased against all Partnership liabilities, whether incurred before or after the dissociation, except liabilities incurred by an act of the dissociated Partner.

11.2.5 If no agreement for the Buyout Price to be paid for the purchase of a dissociated Partner's Partnership Interest is reached within 120 days after a written demand for payment, the Partnership shall pay, or cause to be paid, in cash to the dissociated Partner the amount the Partnership estimates to be the Buyout Price and accrued interest, reduced by any offsets and accrued interest under Section 11.2.3 hereof.

---

[10] This section tracks Section 701 of RUPA. The obligation of the partnership to purchase, or cause to be purchased, the partnership interest of a dissociated partner may be varied in the partnership agreement. The partnership agreement may, for example, fix the method or formula for determining the buyout price and all of the other terms and conditions of the buyout right. A provision providing for a complete forfeiture of the dissociated partner's partnership interest would probably be unenforceable.

11.2.6 If a deferred payment is authorized under Section 11.2.8 hereof, the Partnership may tender a written offer to pay the amount it estimates to be the Buyout Price and accrued interest, reduced by any offsets under Section 11.2.3 hereof, stating the time of payment, the amount and type of security for payment, and the other terms and conditions of the obligation.

11.2.7 The payment or tender required by Sections 11.2.5 or 11.2.6 hereof must be accompanied by the following:

11.2.7.1 A statement of Partnership assets and liabilities as of the date of dissociation;

11.2.7.2 The latest available Partnership balance sheet and income statement, if any;

11.2.7.3 An explanation of how the estimated amount of the payment was calculated; and

11.2.7.4 Written notice that the payment is in full satisfaction of the obligation to purchase unless, within 120 days after the written notice, the dissociated Partner commences an action to determine the Buyout Price, any offsets under Section 11.2.3 hereof, or other terms of the obligation to purchase.

11.2.8 A Partner who wrongfully dissociates is not entitled to payment of any portion of the Buyout Price until the expiration of the term of the Partnership or completion of the undertaking, unless the Partner establishes to the satisfaction of the court that earlier payment will not cause undue hardship to the business of the Partnership. A deferred payment must be adequately secured and shall bear interest.

11.2.9 A dissociated Partner may maintain an action against the Partnership to determine the Buyout Price of its Partnership Interest, any offsets under Section 11.2.3 hereof, or other terms of the obligation to purchase. The action must be commenced within 120 days after the Partnership has tendered payment or an offer to pay or within 1 year after written demand for payment if no payment or offer to pay is tendered. The court shall determine the Buyout Price of the dissociated Partner's Partnership Interest, any offset due under Section 11.2.3 hereof, and accrued interest, and enter judgment for any additional payment or refund. If deferred payment is authorized under Section 11.2.8 hereof, the court shall also determine the security for payment and other terms of the obligation to purchase. The court may assess reasonable attorney's fees and the fees and expenses of appraisers or other experts for a party to the action, in amounts the court finds equitable, against a party that the court finds acted arbitrarily, vexatiously, or not in good faith. The finding may be based on the Partnership's failure to tender payment or an offer to pay or to comply with Section 11.2.7.

11.3 *Wrongful Dissociation.*

11.3.1 Each Partner hereby agrees not to voluntarily dissociate without the consent of all of the other Partners. Accordingly, a Partner's dissociation is wrongful if, before the expiration of the term of this Agreement, the Partner:[11]

11.3.1.1 Withdraws by express will, unless the withdrawal follows within 90 days after another Partner's dissociation under Sections 11.1.4 through 11.1.8 hereof or wrongful dissociation under this Section;

11.3.1.2 Is expelled by judicial determination under Section 11.1.3 hereof; or

11.3.1.3 Directly or indirectly transfers all or any portion of its Partnership Interest in violation of Section 10.1 hereof.

11.3.2 A Partner who wrongfully dissociates is liable to the Partnership and to the other Partners for damages caused by dissociation. This liability is in addition to any other obligation of such Partner to the Partnership or the other Partners.

11.4 *Effect of Dissolution.* A Partner's right to participate in the management and conduct of the Partnership terminates upon its dissociation with the Partnership except that a Partner who has not wrongfully dissociated may, after dissolution of the Partnership, participate in winding up the Partnership's business.

11.5 *Statement of Dissociation.* The Partnership shall file a "Statement of Dissociation" under Section 704 of the Act after the dissociation of a Partner. The Statement of Dissociation shall be filed with the Department of State of the State of [*Name of State*] and in the Office for recording transfers of real property in each county in which the Partnership owns real property, if any.

[ARTICLE XII]
DISSOLUTION

12.1 *Dissolution.* The Partnership shall be dissolved and terminated upon the earliest to occur of the following:

12.1.1 The expiration of ninety (90) days after a Partner's dissociation under Sections 11.1.4 through 11.1.8 or by wrongful dissociation under Section 11.3, unless before such time a majority in interest of the remaining Partners agree to continue the Partnership.

---

[11] A partner's dissociation is also wrongful if the actions specified in partnership agreement Section 11.3 occur before the completion of an undertaking specified in the partnership agreement.

12.1.2 The Partners mutually agree in writing to terminate the Partnership;

12.1.3 The expiration of the term of the Partnership;

12.1.4 The sale or other disposition of all or substantially all of the Partnership assets by the Partnership;

12.1.5 An event which makes it unlawful for all or substantially all of the business of the Partnership to be continued which is not cured within ninety (90) days after notice to the Partnership of such event; or

12.1.6 Entry of a decree of judicial determination of dissolution under the Act.

12.2 *Effective Date of Dissolution.* Dissolution of the Partnership shall be effective on the earlier of _____, 20____, or the day on which the event occurs giving rise to the dissolution, but the Partnership shall not terminate until the assets of the Partnership shall have been distributed as provided in Section 12.3.3 below. Notwithstanding the dissolution of the Partnership, prior to the termination of the Partnership, as aforesaid, the business of the Partnership and the affairs of the Partners, as such, shall continue to be governed by this Agreement.

12.3 *Procedure in Dissolution and Liquidation.*

12.3.1 *Winding up.* Upon dissolution of the Partnership pursuant to Section 12.1 hereof, the Partnership shall immediately commence to wind up its affairs and the Partners shall proceed with reasonable promptness to liquidate the business of the Partnership.

12.3.2 *Management Rights During Winding up.* During the period of the winding up of the affairs of the Partnership, the rights and obligations of the Partners, except a Partner who has wrongfully dissociated, set forth herein with respect to the management of the Partnership shall continue. For purposes of winding up, the Partners shall continue to act as such and shall make all decisions relating to the conduct of any business or operations during the winding up period and to the sale or other disposition of Partnership assets in accordance with the terms of this Agreement.

12.3.3 *Liquidation.* Upon dissolution of the Partnership, the Partners, other than a Partner who has wrongfully dissociated, shall wind up the affairs of the Partnership and apply and distribute its assets or the proceeds thereof as contemplated by this Agreement. As soon as possible after the dissolution of the Partnership, a full account of the assets and liabilities of the Partnership shall be taken, and a statement shall be prepared by the independent certified public accountants then acting for the Partnership, setting forth the assets and liabilities of the Partnership. A copy of such statement shall be furnished to each of the Partners within thirty (30) days after such dissolution. Thereafter, the Partners, other than a Partner who has wrongfully dissociated, shall, in their sole and absolute discretion, either liquidate the Partnership's assets as promptly as is consistent with obtaining, insofar as possible, the fair market value thereof or determine to distribute all or part of the assets in kind. Any proceeds from liquidation, together with any assets which the Partners, other than a Partner who has wrongfully dissociated, determine to distribute in kind, shall be applied in the following order:

12.3.3.1 First, the expenses of liquidation and the debts of the Partnership. Any reserves shall be established or continued which the Partners may deem reasonably necessary for any contingent or unforeseen liabilities or obligations of the Partnership arising out of or in connection with the Partnership or its liquidation. Such reserves shall be held by the Partnership for the purpose of disbursement in payment of any of the aforementioned contingencies, and at the expiration of such period as the Partners shall deem advisable, the Partnership shall distribute the balance thereafter remaining in the manner provided in the following subdivisions of this Article; and

12.3.3.2 Then, to the Partners pro rata in accordance with the positive Capital Account balances of the Partners.

Any assets of the Partnership to be distributed in kind shall be distributed on the basis of the fair market value thereof and may be distributed to any Partner entitled to any interest in such assets as a tenant-in-common with all other Partners so entitled.

In addition, no Partner shall be required to contribute any amounts to the Partnership solely by reason of a deficit balance in such Partner's Capital Account upon liquidation of such Partner's Interest in the Partnership.

12.4 *Statement of Dissolution.* After dissolution, Partners, other than a Partner who has wrongfully dissociated, shall file a Statement of Dissolution pursuant to Section 805(a) of the Act.

12.5 *Termination.* Upon the completion of the distribution of Partnership assets as provided in this Section 12.4, the Partners shall take such other actions as may be necessary to terminate completely the Partnership.

[ARTICLE XIII]
BOOKS AND RECORDS: REPORTS

13.1 *Books and Records.* The Managing Partner shall maintain on behalf of the Partnership adequate books and records of the Partnership at the chief executive office of the Partnership, setting forth a true and accurate account of all business transactions arising out of and in connection with the conduct of the Partnership. Any Partner or its designated representative shall have the right during ordinary business hours of the Partnership to have access to and inspect and copy the contents of said books or records.[12]

The Partnership may impose a reasonable charge, covering the costs of labor and material, for copies of documents furnished.

13.2 *Reports.* Each Partner shall be furnished quarterly by the Partnership with (i) [annual] [unaudited] financial statements for the [fiscal year] then ended within (_____) days of such [fiscal year-end], which shall be prepared in accordance with generally accepted accounting principles by an independent certified public accountant, and (ii) a report of the activities of the Partnership during the period covered by the report.

13.3 *Tax Information.* Necessary tax information for the preparation of the Partners' federal income tax returns shall be delivered to the Partners on an annual basis. Every reasonable effort shall be made by the Partners to cause the Partnership to furnish such information within [90] days after the end of the Partnership's fiscal year. The tax returns of the Partnership shall be approved by the Partners.

13.4 *Tax Election.* All tax elections on behalf of the Partnership may be made or rescinded in the discretion of the Partners, including, but not limited to, election under Section 754 of the Code on behalf of the Partnership. Adjustments available under Section 743 of the Code as a result of such election shall be taken into account by the Partners affected thereby on their individual Federal income tax returns and by the Partnership and shall not be taken into account in computing the Profits and Losses of the Partnership for purposes of this Agreement.

13.5 *Tax Controversies.* Should there be any controversy with the Internal Revenue Service or any other taxing authority involving the Partnership or an individual Partner or Partners as a result of being a Partner in the Partnership, the outcome of which may adversely affect the Partnership either directly or indirectly, the Partnership may incur expenses it deems necessary and advisable in the interest of the Partnership to oppose such proposed deficiency, including, without limitation, attorneys' and accountants' fees. The Managing Partner shall act as the "Tax Matters Partner" as defined under Section 6231(a)(7) of the Code; provided, however, that all decisions relating to settling or refusing to settle any controversy with the Internal Revenue Service shall be approved by the Partners.

---

[12] Section 103(b)(2) of RUPA prohibits the partnership agreement from unreasonably restricting a partner's right of access to books and records pursuant to Section 403(b).

13.6 *Fiscal Year.* The fiscal year of the Partnership for both accounting and federal income tax purposes shall be the calendar year. For accounting and federal income tax purposes, the Partnership shall report its operations and profits and losses in accordance with the method determined by the Partners.

[ARTICLE XIV]
GENERAL PROVISIONS

14.1 *Notices.* Any notice to be given under this Agreement shall be made in writing and shall be deemed to be given when delivered by U.S. registered or certified mail, return receipt requested, or hand delivery or overnight delivery service to the party at its address. Notice may be given by telecopy provided a hard copy of such notice is mailed in accordance with this Section on the next business day following such telecopy delivery. The addresses of the Partners for this purpose shall be those stated on Schedule "A" attached hereto and incorporated herein by reference (or such other address as they shall supply for such purposes to the other parties hereto).

14.2 *Governing Law; Venue.* This Agreement shall be governed and construed in accordance with the laws of the State of [*Name of State*], both substantive and remedial.

14.3 *Conflict with the Act.* Except as otherwise provided in Section 103(b) of the Act, in the event of any conflict between the terms of this Agreement and the Act, the terms of this Agreement shall control.

14.4 *Survival of Rights.* Except as otherwise provided herein, this Agreement shall be binding upon and inure to the benefit of the Partners and their personal representative, successors and assigns.

14.5 *Dealings in Good Faith; Best Efforts.* Each Partner hereby agrees to discharge its duties to the Partnership and the other Partners under this Agreement and the Act and exercise any rights consistently with the obligation of good faith and fair dealing.[13]

Each Partner further agrees to use its best efforts to ensure that the purposes of this Agreement are realized and to take all steps as are reasonable in order to implement the operational provisions of this Agreement. Each Partner agrees to execute, deliver and file any document or instrument necessary or advisable to realize the purposes of this Agreement.

---

[13] Section 103(b)(5) restricts the partnership agreement from eliminating the obligation of good faith and fair dealing except to provide that the partnership agreement may prescribe the standards by which the performance of the obligation is to be measured if the standards are not manifestly unreasonable.

14.6 *Additional Partners.* Each substitute, additional or successor Partner shall become a signatory hereof by signing such number of counterparts of this Agreement and such other instrument or instruments, and in such manner, as the Managing Partner shall determine. By so signing, each substitute, additional or successor Partner, as the case may be, shall be deemed to have adopted and to have agreed to be bound by all the provisions of this Agreement; provided, however, that no such counterpart shall be binding until the provisions of Article X hereof, as applicable, shall have been satisfied.

14.7 *Validity.* In the event that any provision of this Agreement shall be held to be invalid, the same shall not affect in any respect whatsoever the validity of the remainder of this Agreement.

14.8 *Integrated Agreement.* This Agreement constitutes the entire understanding and agreement among the parties hereto with respect to the subject matter hereof, and there are no agreements, understandings, restrictions, representations or warranties among the parties other than those set forth herein or herein provided for.

14.9 *Agreements in Counterparts.* This Agreement may be executed in several counterparts, and as executed shall constitute one Agreement, binding on all the parties hereto, notwithstanding that all the parties are not signatory to the original or to the same counterpart.

14.10 *Headings.* The headings, titles and subtitles used in this Agreement are inserted only for convenience of reference and shall not control or affect the meaning or construction of any of the provisions hereof.

14.11 *Gender.* Words of the masculine or neuter gender shall be deemed and construed to include correlative words of the masculine, feminine and neuter genders.

14.12 *Attorneys' Fees.* In the event any Partner institutes legal proceedings in connection with, or for the enforcement of, this Agreement, the prevailing party shall be entitled to recover and be reimbursed its cost of arbitration and suit, including reasonable costs associated with the arbitration, attorneys' fees, paralegals' fees and legal assistants' fees, at both trial and appellate levels, from the non-prevailing party.

14.13 *No Third Party Beneficiary.* Nothing expressed or implied in this Agreement is intended, or shall be construed, to confer upon or give any person, firm, corporation, Partnership, association or other entity, other than the parties hereto and their respective legal representatives and permitted successors and assigns, any rights or remedies under or by reason of this Agreement.

IN WITNESS WHEREOF, the parties have executed this General Partnership Agreement on the date first above written.

PARTNERS:

_____

_____

SCHEDULE A
PARTNERS' NAMES, ADDRESSES AND
PERCENTAGE INTERESTS

Name	Address	Percentage Interest

PART SIX
STATUTORY SHORT FORM POWER OF ATTORNEY

UNIFORM STATUTORY FORM POWER OF ATTORNEY ACT*

Editor's note: This uniform act is set forth in volume 8B of UNIFORM LAWS ANNOTATED. It has been adopted in Arkansas, California, Colorado, District of Columbia, Montana, New Mexico, Oklahoma, and Wisconsin (*see* www.nccusl.org). In addition, other states, e.g., Minnesota and New York among others, have legislation similar to that contained here, setting forth by statute a short form power of attorney with provisions describing the powers granted in the short form. The statutory short form power of attorney is included in these materials because it is a convenient, comprehensive, and reliable method of creating a power of attorney. Also, the form included here can be used as a common law power of attorney in a state that does not have an enabling statute and as a source of ideas and provisions for one drafting a power of attorney.

The statutory short form power of attorney is different from the durable power of attorney that is authorized by statute in many states largely as a result of the widespread adoption of the model probate code. The statutory short form can be made durable in nature, however, as authorized by Section 2 contained below.

PREFATORY NOTE

The Uniform Statutory Power of Attorney Act, when adopted by a state, will give legislative sanction to a statutory form that can be used in whole or part instead of individually drafted forms or forms adapted from a form book. Use of the statutory form will be supported by the expressed authority of the state and have the statutory construction provided by Sections 3 through 17. It is hoped that the form will become familiar and be readily accepted by persons who see it. Acts of this kind have been adopted by several states, including California, Illinois, Minnesota, and New York. This proposed Act is based in part of those examples.

Section 1 is the form itself. It is a list of powers. The items relate to various separate classes of activities, except the last, which is inclusive. Health care matters are not included. Since they involve intensely controversial personal as well as economic considerations, they are left to other legislation. Space is provided for special provisions. After the introductory phrase, the term "agent" is used throughout the Act in place of the longer and less familiar, "attorney-in-fact." Special effort is made throughout the

Act to make the language as informal as possible without impairing its effectiveness.

Section 2 and the form itself permit the power of attorney to remain in effect after the disability of the principal if that is permitted by other law of the state. It does not by itself authorize the creation of a durable power. It is included because of the growing interest in durable powers and the fact that they are recommended by other acts proposed by the National Conference of Commissioners on Uniform State Laws.

Section 3 is the legislative construction of the authority that may be incidentally necessary for the exercise of a power vested in the form.

Sections 4 through 16 are the legislative construction of the list of brief topics in the form. Each section identifies actions that are permitted as appropriate to the particular grant of power. The statements, without being exhaustive, attempt to be amply illustrative.

The Act as a whole provides a practical method of granting powers of whatever scope may be appropriate for people in a wide variety of circumstances.

§ 1. Statutory form of power of attorney

(a) Form. The following statutory form of power of attorney is legally sufficient:

STATUTORY POWER OF ATTORNEY

NOTICE: THE POWERS GRANTED BY THIS DOCUMENT ARE BROAD AND SWEEPING. THEY ARE EXPLAINED IN THE UNIFORM STATUTORY FORM POWER OF ATTORNEY ACT. IF YOU HAVE ANY QUESTIONS ABOUT THESE POWERS, OBTAIN COMPETENT LEGAL ADVICE. THIS DOCUMENT DOES NOT AUTHORIZE ANYONE TO MAKE MEDICAL OR OTHER HEALTH-CARE DECISIONS FOR YOU. YOU MAY REVOKE THIS POWER OF ATTORNEY IF YOU LATER WISH TO DO SO.

I, _____, (insert your name and address), appoint _____ (insert the name and address of the person appointed) as my agent (attorney-in-fact) to act for me in any lawful way with respect to the following initialed subjects:

TO GRANT ALL OF THE FOLLOWING POWERS, INITIAL THE LINE IN FRONT OF (N) AND IGNORE THE LINES IN FRONT OF THE OTHER POWERS. TO GRANT ONE OR MORE, BUT FEWER THAN ALL OF THE FOLLOWING POWERS, INITIAL THE LINE IN FRONT OF EACH POWER YOU ARE GRANTING. TO WITHHOLD A POWER, DO NOT INITIAL THE LINE IN FRONT OF IT. YOU MAY, BUT NEED NOT, CROSS OUT EACH POWER WITHHELD.

INITIAL

_____ (A) Real property transactions.

_____ (B) Tangible personal property transactions.

_____ (C) Stock and bond transactions.

_____ (D) Commodity and option transactions.

_____ (E) Banking and other financial institution transactions.

_____ (F) Business operating transactions.

_____ (G) Insurance and annuity transactions.

_____ (H) Estate, trust, and other beneficiary transactions.

_____ (I) Claims and litigation.

_____ (J) Personal and family maintenance.

_____ (K) Benefits from social security, medicare, medicaid, or other governmental programs or military service.

_____ (L) Retirement plan transactions.

_____ (M) Tax matters.

_____ (N) ALL OF THE POWERS LISTED ABOVE. YOU NEED NOT INITIAL ANY OTHER LINES IF YOU INITIAL LINE (N).

SPECIAL INSTRUCTIONS:

ON THE FOLLOWING LINES YOU MAY GIVE SPECIAL INSTRUCTIONS LIMITING OR EXTENDING THE POWERS GRANTED TO YOUR AGENT:

_____

_____

_____

UNLESS YOU DIRECT OTHERWISE, THIS POWER OF ATTORNEY IS EFFECTIVE IMMEDIATELY AND WILL CONTINUE UNTIL IT IS REVOKED.

This power of attorney will continue to be effective even though I become disabled, incapacitated, or incompetent.

STRIKE THE PRECEDING SENTENCE IF YOU DO NOT WANT THIS POWER OF ATTORNEY TO CONTINUE IF YOU BECOME DISABLED, INCAPACITATED, OR INCOMPETENT.

I agree that any third party who receives a copy of this document may act under it. Revocation of the power of attorney is not effective as to a third party until the third party learns of the revocation. I agree to indemnify the third party for any claims that arise against the third party because of reliance on this power of attorney.

Signed on _____, 20_____.

(Your Signature)

(Your Social Security Number)

STATE OF _____

COUNTY OF _____

This document was acknowledged before me on _____ (date) by _____ (name of principal). My commission expires: _____ .

Notary Public

[Seal]

(b) **Requirements.** A statutory power of attorney is legally sufficient under this act if the wording of the form complies substantially with subsection (a), the form is properly completed, and the signature of the principal is acknowledged.

(c) **Grant of all listed powers.** If the line in front of (N) of the form under subsection (a) is initialed, an initial on the line in front of any other power does not limit the powers granted by line (N).

Comment

Section 1 provides the form that is sufficient and necessary to bring the Act into operation. A form used to create a power of attorney subject to the Act should use the language provided in Section 1. Minor variances in wording will not take it out of the scope of the Act.

Neither Section 1 nor the Act as a whole attempts to provide an exclusive method for creating a power of attorney. Other forms may be used and other law employed to create powers of attorney. However, it is hoped that this Act will be sufficient for most purposes.

If the law of an enacting state requires additional witnesses for real property transactions or any other class of powers, the form should be varied to provide a place for them. If necessary, the form of the acknowledgment should also be varied to conform to the law that governs acknowledgments in the enacting state.

Neigher the form in Section 1 nor the construction of the form provided by Sections 3 through 16 attempts to allow the grant of the power to make a will, although several of the powers, especially (I), could be used in planning the disposition of an estate.

§ 2. Durable power of attorney

A power of attorney legally sufficient under this [Act] is durable to the extent that durable powers are permitted by any other law of this state and the power of attorney contains language, such as "this power of attorney will continue to be effective even though I become disabled, incapacitated, or incompetent", showing the intent of the principal that the power granted may be exercised notwithstanding later disability, incapacity, or incompetency.

Comment

Section 2 makes it explicit that, subject to the law of the enacting state, a power of attorney may continue when the principal is disabled, incapacitated, or becomes incompetent. The form in Section 1 includes a provision for continuance under those circumstances. That provision may be used or stricken at the discretion of the principal.

§ 3. Construction of powers generally

By executing a statutory power of attorney with respect to a subject listed in section 1(a), the principal, except as limited or extended by the principal in the power of attorney, empowers the agent, for that subject to:

(1) demand, receive, and obtain by litigation or otherwise, money or other thing of value to which the principal is, may become, or claims to be entitled; and conserve, invest, disburse, or use anything so received for the purposes intended;

(2) contract in any manner with any person, on terms agreeable to the agent, to accomplish a purpose of a transaction, and perform, rescind, reform, release, or modify the contract or another contract made by or on behalf of the principal;

(3) execute, acknowledge, seal, and deliver a deed, revocation, mortgage, lease, notice, check, release, or other instrument the agent considers desirable to accomplish a purpose of a transaction;

(4) prosecute, defend, submit to arbitration, settle, and propose or accept a compromise with respect to, a claim existing in favor of or against the principal or intervene in litigation relating to the claim;

(5) seek on the principal's behalf the assistance of a court to carry out an act authorized by the power of attorney;

(6) engage, compensate, and discharge an attorney, accountant, expert witness, or other assistant;

(7) keep appropriate records of each transaction, including an accounting of receipts and disbursements;

(8) prepare, execute, and file a record, report, or other document the agent considers desirable to safeguard or promote the principal's interest under a statute or governmental regulation;

(9) reimburse the agent for expenditures properly made by the agent in exercising the powers granted by the power of attorney; and

(10) in general, do any other lawful act with respect to the subject.

§ 4. Construction of power relating to real property transactions

In a statutory power of attorney, when properly recorded, the language granting power with respect to real property transactions empowers the agent to:

(1) accept as a gift or as security for a loan, reject, demand, buy, lease, receive, or otherwise acquire, an interest in real property or a right incident to real property;

(2) sell, exchange, convey with or without covenants, quitclaim, release, surrender, mortgage, encumber, partition, consent to partitioning, subdivide, apply for zoning, rezoning, or other governmental permits, plat or consent to platting, develop, grant options concerning, lease, sublease, or otherwise dispose of, an interest in real property or a right incident to real property;

(3) release, assign, satisfy, and enforce by litigation or otherwise, a mortgage, deed of trust, encumbrance, lien, or other claim to real property which exists or is asserted;

(4) do any act of management or of conservation with respect to an interest in real property, or a right incident to real property, owned, or claimed to be owned, by the principal, including:

(i) insuring against a casualty, liability, or loss;

(ii) obtaining or regaining possession, or protecting the interest or right, by litigation or otherwise;

(iii) paying, compromising, or contesting taxes or assessments, or applying for and receiving refunds in connection with them; and

(iv) purchasing supplies, hiring assistance or labor, and making repairs or alterations in the real property;

(5) use, develop, alter, replace, remove, erect, or install structures or other improvements upon real property in or incident to which the principal has, or claims to have, an interest or right;

(6) participate in a reorganization with respect to real property or a legal entity that owns an interest in or right incident to real property and receive and hold shares of stock or obligations received in a plan of reorganization, and act with respect to them, including:

(i) selling or otherwise disposing of them;

(ii) exercising or selling an option, conversion, or similar right with respect to them; and

(iii) voting them in person or by proxy;

(7) change the form of title of an interest in or right incident to real property;

(8) dedicate to public use, with or without consideration, easements or other real property in which the principal has, or claims to have, an interest.

§ 5. Construction of power relating to tangible personal property transactions

In a statutory power of attorney, the language granting power with respect to tangible personal property transactions empowers the agent to:

(1) accept as a gift or as security for a loan, reject, demand, buy, receive, or otherwise acquire ownership or possession of tangible personal property or an interest in tangible personal property;

(2) sell, exchange, convey with or without covenants, release, surrender, mortgage, encumber, pledge, hypothecate, create a security interest in, pawn, grant options concerning, lease, sublease to others, or otherwise dispose of tangible personal property or an interest in tangible personal property;

(3) release, assign, satisfy, or enforce by litigation or otherwise, a mortgage, security interest, encumbrance, lien, or other claim on behalf of the principal, with respect to tangible personal property or an interest in tangible personal property; and

(4) do an act of management or conservation with respect to tangible personal property or an interest in tangible personal property on behalf of the principal, including:

(i) insuring against casualty, liability, or loss;

(ii) obtaining or regaining possession, or protecting the property or interest, by litigation or otherwise;

(iii) paying, compromising, or contesting taxes or assessments or applying for and receiving refunds in connection with taxes or assessments;

(iv) moving from place to place;

(v) storing for hire or on a gratuitous bailment; and

(vi) using, altering, and making repairs or alterations.

§ 6. Construction of power relating to stock and bond transactions

In a statutory power of attorney, the language granting power with respect to stock and bond transactions empowers the agent to buy, sell, and exchange stocks, bonds, mutual funds, and all other types of securities and financial instruments except commodity futures contracts and call and put options on stocks and stock indexes, receive certificates and other evidences of ownership with respect to securities, exercise voting rights with respect to securities in person or by proxy, enter into voting trusts, and consent to limitations on the right to vote.

§ 7. Construction of power relating to commodity and option transactions

In a statutory power of attorney, the language granting power with respect to commodity and option transactions empowers the agent to buy, sell, exchange, assign, settle, and exercise commodity futures contracts and call and put options on stocks and stock indexes traded on a regulated option exchange, and establish, continue, modify, and terminate option accounts with a broker.

§ 8. Construction of power relating to banking and other financial institution transactions

In a statutory power of attorney, the language granting power with respect to banking and other financial institution transactions empowers the agent to:

(1) continue, modify, and terminate an account or other banking arrangement made by or on behalf of the principal;

(2) establish, modify, and terminate an account or other banking arrangement with a bank, trust company, savings and loan association, credit union, thrift company, brokerage firm, or other financial institution selected by the agent;

(3) hire a safe deposit box or space in a vault;

(4) contract to procure other services available from a financial institution as the agent considers desirable;

(5) withdraw by check, order, or otherwise money or property of the principal deposited with or left in the custody of a financial institution;

(6) receive bank statements, vouchers, notices, and similar documents from a financial institution and act with respect to them;

(7) enter a safe deposit box or vault and withdraw or add to the contents;

(8) borrow money at an interest rate agreeable to the agent and pledge as security personal property of the principal necessary in order to borrow, pay, renew, or extend the time of payment of a debt of the principal;

(9) make, assign, draw, endorse, discount, guarantee, and negotiate promissory notes, checks, drafts, and other negotiable or nonnegotiable paper of the principal, or payable to the principal or the principal's order, receive the cash or other proceeds of those transactions, accept a draft drawn by a person upon the principal, and pay it when due;

(10) receive for the principal and act upon a sight draft, warehouse receipt, or other negotiable or nonnegotiable instrument;

(11) apply for and receive letters of credit, credit cards, and traveler's checks from a financial institution, and give an indemnity or other agreement in connection with letters of credit; and

(12) consent to an extension of the time of payment with respect to commercial paper or a financial transaction with a financial institution.

§ 9. Construction of power relating to business operating transactions

In a statutory power of attorney, the language granting power with respect to business operating transactions empowers the agent to:

(1) operate, buy, sell, enlarge, reduce, and terminate a business interest;

(2) to the extent that an agent is permitted by law to act for a principal and subject to the terms of the partnership agreement to:

(i) perform a duty or discharge a liability and exercise a right, power, privilege, or option that the principal has, may have, or claims to have, under a partnership agreement, whether or not the principal is a partner;

(ii) enforce the terms of a partnership agreement by litigation or otherwise; and

(iii) defend, submit to arbitration, settle, or compromise litigation to which the principal is a party because of membership in the partnership;

(3) exercise in person or by proxy, or enforce by litigation or otherwise, a right, power, privilege, or option the principal has or claims to have as the holder of a bond, share, or other instrument of similar character and defend, submit to arbitration, settle, or compromise litigation to which the principal is a party because of a bond, share, or similar instrument;

(4) with respect to a business owned solely by the principal:

(i) continue, modify, renegotiate, extend, and terminate a contract made with an individual or a legal entity, firm, association, or corporation by or on behalf of the principal with respect to the business before execution of the power of attorney;

(ii) determine:

(A) the location of its operation;

(B) the nature and extent of its business;

(C) the methods of manufacturing, selling, merchandising, financing, accounting, and advertising employed in its operation;

(D) the amount and types of insurance carried;

(E) the mode of engaging, compensating, and dealing with its accountants, attorneys, and other agents and employees;

(iii) change the name or form of organization under which the business is operated and enter into a partnership agreement with other persons or organize a corporation to take over all or part of the operation of the business; and

(iv) demand and receive money due or claimed by the principal or on the principal's behalf in the operation of the business, and control and disburse the money in the operation of the business;

(5) put additional capital into a business in which the principal has an interest;

(6) join in a plan of reorganization, consolidation, or merger of the business;

(7) sell or liquidate a business or part of it at the time and upon the terms the agent considers desirable;

(8) establish the value of a business under a buy-out agreement to which the principal is a party;

(9) prepare, sign, file, and deliver reports, compilations of information, returns, or other papers with respect to a business which are required by a governmental agency or instrumentality or which the agent considers desirable, and make related payments; and

(10) pay, compromise, or contest taxes or assessments and do any other act which the agent considers desirable to protect the principal from illegal or unnecessary taxation, fines, penalties, or assessments with respect to a business, including attempts to recover, in any manner permitted by law, money paid before or after the execution of the power of attorney.

§ 10. Construction of power relating to insurance transactions

In a statutory power of attorney, the language granting power with respect to insurance and annuity transactions empowers the agent to:

(1) continue, pay the premium or assessment on, modify, rescind, release, or terminate a contract procured by or on behalf of the principal which insures or provides an annuity to either the principal or another person, whether or not the principal is a beneficiary under the contract;

(2) procure new, different, and additional contracts of insurance and annuities for the principal and the principal's spouse, children, and other dependents; and select the amount, type of insurance or annuity, and mode of payment;

(3) pay the premium or assessment on, modify, rescind, release, or terminate a contract of insurance or annuity procured by the agent;

(4) designate the beneficiary of the contract, but an agent may be named a beneficiary of the contract, or an extension, renewal, or substitute for it, only to the extent the agent was named as a beneficiary under a contract procured by the principal before executing the power of attorney;

(5) apply for and receive a loan on the security of the contract of insurance or annuity;

(6) surrender and receive the cash surrender value;

(7) exercise an election;

(8) change the manner of paying premiums;

(9) change or convert the type of insurance contract or annuity, with respect to which the principal has or claims to have a power described in this section;

(10) change the beneficiary of a contract of insurance or annuity, but the agent may not be designated a beneficiary except to the extent permitted by paragraph (4);

(11) apply for and procure government aid to guarantee or pay premiums of a contract of insurance on the life of the principal;

(12) collect, sell, assign, hypothecate, borrow upon, or pledge the interest of the principal in a contract of insurance or annuity; and

(13) pay from proceeds or otherwise, compromise or contest, and apply for refunds in connection with, a tax or assessment levied by a taxing authority with respect to a contract of insurance or annuity or its proceeds or liability accruing by reason of the tax or assessment.

§ 11. Construction of power relating to estate, trust, and other beneficiary transactions

In a statutory power of attorney, the language granting power with respect to estate, trust, and other beneficiary transactions, empowers the agent to act for the principal in all matters that affect a trust, probate estate, guardianship, conservatorship, escrow, custodianship, or other fund from which the principal is, may become, or claims to be entitled, as a beneficiary, to a share or payment, including to:

(1) accept, reject, disclaim, receive, receipt for, sell, assign, release, pledge, exchange, or consent to a reduction in or modification of a share in or payment from the fund;

(2) demand or obtain by litigation or otherwise money or other thing of value to which the principal is, may become, or claims to be entitled by reason of the fund;

(3) initiate, participate in, and oppose litigation to ascertain the meaning, validity, or effect of a deed, will, declaration of trust, or other instrument or transaction affecting the interest of the principal;

(4) initiate, participate in, and oppose litigation to remove, substitute, or surcharge a fiduciary;

(5) conserve, invest, disburse, and use anything received for an authorized purpose; and

(6) transfer an interest of the principal in real property, stocks, bonds, accounts with financial institutions, insurance, and other property, to the trustee of a revocable trust created by the principal as settlor.

§ 12. Construction of power relating to claims and litigation

In a statutory power of attorney, the language with respect to claims and litigation empowers the agent to:

(1) assert and prosecute before a court or administrative agency a claim, claim for relief, cause of action, counterclaim, offset, and defend against an individual, a legal entity, or government, including suits to recover property or other thing of value, to recover damages sustained by the principal, to eliminate or modify tax liability, or to seek an injunction, specific performance, or other relief;

(2) bring an action to determine adverse claims, intervene in litigation, and act as amicus curiae;

(3) in connection with litigation, procure an attachment, garnishment, libel, order of arrest, or other preliminary, provisional, or intermediate relief and use an available procedure to effect or satisfy a judgment, order, or decree;

(4) in connection with litigation, perform any lawful act, including acceptance of tender, offer of judgment, admission of facts, submission of a controversy on an agreed statement of facts, consent to examination before trial, and binding the principal in litigation;

(5) submit to arbitration, settle, and propose or accept a compromise with respect to a claim or litigation;

(6) waive the issuance and service of process upon the principal, accept service of process, appear for the principal, designate persons upon whom process directed to the principal may be served, execute and file or deliver stipulations on the principal's behalf, verify pleadings, seek appellate review, procure and give surety and indemnity bonds, contract and pay for the preparation and printing of records and briefs, receive and execute and file or deliver a consent, waiver, release, confession of judgment, satisfaction of judgment, notice, agreement, or other instrument in connection with the prosecution, settlement, or defense of a claim or litigation;

(7) act for the principal with respect to bankruptcy or insolvency proceedings, whether voluntary or involuntary, concerning the principal or some other person, with respect to a reorganization proceeding, or a receivership or application for the appointment of a receiver or trustee which affects an interest of the principal in property or other thing of value; and

(8) pay a judgment against the principal or a settlement made in connection with litigation and receive and conserve money, or other thing of value paid in settlement of or as proceeds of a claim or litigation.

§ 13. Construction of power relating to personal and family maintenance

In a statutory power of attorney, the language granting power with respect to personal and family maintenance empowers the agent to:

(1) do the acts necessary to maintain the customary standard of living of the principal, the principal's spouse, children, and other individuals customarily or legally entitled to be supported by the principal, including providing living quarters by purchase, lease, or other contract, or paying the operating costs, including interest, amortization payments, repairs, and taxes on premises owned by the principal and occupied by those individuals;

(2) provide for the individuals described in paragraph (1) normal domestic help; usual vacations and travel expenses; and funds for shelter, clothing, food, appropriate education, and other current living costs;

(3) pay for the individuals described in paragraph (1) necessary medical, dental, and surgical care, hospitalization, and custodial care;

(4) continue any provision made by the principal, for the individuals described in paragraph (1), for automobiles or other means of transportation, including registering, licensing, insuring, and replacing them;

(5) maintain or open charge accounts for the convenience of the individuals described in paragraph (1) and open new accounts the agent considers desirable to accomplish a lawful purpose; and

(6) continue payments incidental to the membership or affiliation of the principal in a church, club, society, order, or other organization or to continue contributions to those organizations.

§ 14. Construction of power relating to benefits from social security, medicare, medicaid, or other governmental programs, or military service

In a statutory power of attorney, the language granting power with respect to benefits from social security, medicare, medicaid or other governmental programs, or civil or military service, empowers the agent to:

(1) execute vouchers in the name of the principal for allowances and reimbursements payable by the United States or a foreign government or by a state or subdivision of a state to the principal, including allowances and reimbursements for transportation of the individuals described in section 13(1), and for shipment of their household effects;

(2) take possession and order the removal and shipment of property of the principal from a post, warehouse, depot, dock, or other place of storage or safekeeping, either governmental or private, and execute and deliver a release, voucher, receipt, bill of lading, shipping ticket, certificate, or other instrument for that purpose;

(3) prepare, file, and prosecute a claim of the principal to a benefit or assistance, financial or otherwise, to which the principal claims to be entitled, under a statute or governmental regulation;

(4) prosecute, defend, submit to arbitration, settle, and propose or accept a compromise with respect to any benefits the principal may be entitled to receive; and

(5) receive the financial proceeds of a claim of the type described in this section, conserve, invest, disburse, or use anything received for a lawful purpose.

§ 15. Construction of power relating to retirement plan transactions

In a statutory power of attorney, the language granting power with respect to retirement plan transactions empowers the agent to:

(1) select payment options under any retirement plan in which the principal participates, including plans for self-employed individuals;

(2) designate beneficiaries under those plans and change existing designations;

(3) make voluntary contributions to those plans;

(4) exercise the investment powers available under any self-directed retirement plan;

(5) make "rollovers" of plan benefits into other retirement plans;

(6) if authorized by the plan, borrow from, sell assets to, and purchase assets from the plan; and

(7) waive the right of the principal to be a beneficiary of a joint or survivor annuity if the principal is a spouse who is not employed.

§ 16. Construction of power relating to tax matters

In a statutory power of attorney, the language granting power with respect to tax matters empowers the agent to:

(1) Prepare, sign, and file federal, state, local, and foreign income, gift, payroll, federal insurance contributions act returns, and other tax returns, claims for refunds, requests for extension of time, petitions regarding tax matters, and any other tax-related documents, including receipts, offers, waivers, consents (including consents and agreements under internal revenue code section 2032A or any successor section), closing agreements, and any power of attorney required by the internal revenue service or other taxing authority with respect to a tax year upon which the statute of limitations has not run and the following 25 tax years;

(2) pay taxes due, collect refunds, post bonds, receive confidential information, and contest deficiencies determined by the internal revenue service or other taxing authority;

(3) exercise any election available to the principal under federal, state, local, or foreign tax law; and

(4) act for the principal in all tax matters for all periods before the internal revenue service, and any other taxing authority.

Comment

Sections 3 through 16 explain the several powers listed in the form in Section 1. Section 3 provides general powers that apply to all of the defined classes of authority listed in (A) through (M) of the form, subject to any conditions set by the principal. The powers listed in Sections 3 through 16 are equivalent to those that the principal might exercise himself or herself and also state those necessary for the agent to act.

The language in Sections 4 through 16 makes explicit reference to authority that would be appropriate for each class of transaction. The language in those subsections identifies activities that are typical responsibilities for the particular class of transaction.

Any of Sections 4 through 16, together with the general authority in Section 3, gives the agent or attorney-in-fact complete power for the class of transactions. The recitation of particular powers in each subsection explains the scope of the individual subsection and assures the user of the Act and the form that the matters that are the users' particular concern are covered by the Act.

A general effect of Sections 3 through 16 is that the agent or attorney-in-fact can exercise authority subject to the same conditions and limitations as the principal. In a few instances the limiting conditions are made explicit. For example in Section 9 it is stated that partnership powers are subject to the terms of the partnership agreement. But all authority is subject to conditions of fact and law that exist outside the Act. A collection agency could not escape regulation by acting under this power of attorney or a trust could not be created that violated a rule against perpetuities and so forth.

§ 17. Existing interests; foreign interests

The powers described in sections 3 through 16 are exercisable equally with respect to an interest the principal has when the power of attorney is executed or acquires later, whether or not the property is located in this state, and whether or not the powers are exercised or the power of attorney is executed in this state.

Comment

Section 17 makes the power of attorney explicitly effective for property and in places that might otherwise be subject to dispute.

§ 18. Uniformity of application and construction

This [Act] shall be applied and construed to effectuate its general purpose to make uniform the law with respect to the subject of this [Act] among states enacting it.

§ 19. Short title

This [Act] may be cited as the Uniform Statutory Form Power of Attorney Act.

§ 20. Severability clause

If any provision of this [Act] or its application to any person or circumstance is held invalid, the invalidity does not effect other provisions or applications of this [Act] which can be given effect without the invalid provision or application, and to this end the provisions of this [Act] are severable.

§ 21. Effective date

This [Act] takes effect. . . .

PART SEVEN
THE RESTATEMENT OF AGENCY

SELECTED EXCERPTS FROM THE RESTATEMENT (SECOND) OF AGENCY[*]

§ 1. Agency; Principal; Agent

(1) Agency is the fiduciary relation which results from the manifestation of consent by one person to another that the other shall act on his behalf and subject to his control, and consent by the other so to act.

---

(2) The one for whom action is to be taken is the principal.

(3) The one who is to act is the agent.

§ 2. Master; Servant; Independent Contractor

(1) A master is a principal who employs an agent to perform service in his affairs and who controls or has the right to control the physical conduct of the other in the performance of the service.

(2) A servant is an agent employed by a master to perform service in his affairs whose physical conduct in the performance of the service is controlled or is subject to the right of control by the master.

(3) An independent contractor is a person who contracts with another to do something for him but who is not controlled by the other nor subject to the other's right to control with respect to his physical conduct in the performance of the undertaking. He may or may not be an agent.

§ 4. Disclosed   principal;   partially   disclosed   principal; undisclosed principal

(1) If, at the time of a transaction conducted by an agent, the other party thereto has notice that the agent is acting for a principal and of the principal's identity, the principal is a disclosed principal.

(2) If the other party has notice that the agent is or may be acting for a principal but has no notice of the principal's identity, the principal for whom the agent is acting is a partially disclosed principal.

(3) If the other party has no notice that the agent is acting for a principal, the one for whom he acts is an undisclosed principal.

§ 6. Power

A power is an ability on the part of a person to produce a change in a given legal relation by doing or not doing a given act.

Comment

a. The word "power" denotes not a physical or mental quality but a legal attribute, the ability to change legal relations. This ability may be rightfully exercised, as where an agent makes an authorized contract; or it may be wrongfully exercised, as where an agent, having apparent authority so to do, makes an unauthorized contract.

§ 7. Authority

Authority is the power of the agent to affect the legal relations of the principal by acts done in accordance with the principal's manifestations of consent to him.

§ 8. Apparent authority

Apparent authority is the power to affect the legal relations of another person by transactions with third persons, professedly as agent for the other, arising from and in accordance with the other's manifestations to such third persons.

§ 8A. Inherent agency power

Inherent agency power is a term used in the restatement of this subject to indicate the power of an agent which is derived not from authority, apparent authority or estoppel, but solely from the agency relation and exists for the protection of persons harmed by or dealing with a servant or other agent.

§ 8B. Estoppel; change of position

(1) A person who is not otherwise liable as a party to a transaction purported to be done on his account, is nevertheless subject to liability to persons who have changed their positions because of their belief that the transaction was entered into by or for him, if

(a) he intentionally or carelessly caused such belief, or

(b) knowing of such belief and that others might change their positions because of it, he did not take reasonable steps to notify them of the facts.

(2) An owner of property who represents to third persons that another is the owner of the property or who permits the other so to represent, or who realizes that third persons believe that another is the owner of the property, and that he could easily inform the third persons of the facts, is subject to the loss of the property if the other disposes of it to third persons who, in ignorance of the facts, purchase the property or otherwise change their position with reference to it.

(3) Change of position, as the phrase is used in the restatement of this subject, indicates payment of money, expenditure of labor, suffering a loss or subjection to legal liability.

§ 12. Agent is a holder of a power

An agent or apparent agent holds a power to alter the legal relations between the principal and third persons and between the principal and himself.

§ 13. Agent as a fiduciary

An agent is a fiduciary with respect to matters within the scope of the agency.

Comment

a. The agreement to act on behalf of the principal causes the agent to be a fiduciary, that is, a person having a duty, created by his undertaking, to act primarily for the benefit of another in matters connected with his undertaking. Among the agent's fiduciary duties to the principal is the duty to account for profits arising out of the employment, the duty not to act as, or on account of, an adverse party without the principal's consent, the duty not to compete with the principal on his own account or for another in matters relating to the subject matter of the agency, and the duty to deal fairly with the principal in all transactions between them.

§ 14. Control by principal

A principal has the right to control the conduct of the agent with respect to matters entrusted to him.

Comment

a. The right of control by the principal may be exercised by prescribing what the agent shall or shall not do before the agent acts, or at the time when he acts, or at both times. The principal's right of control is continuous and continues as long as the agency relation exists, even though the principal agreed that he would not exercise it. Thus, the agent is subject to a duty not to act contrary to the principal's directions, although the principal has agreed not to give such directions.

§ 26. Creation of authority; general rule

Except for the execution of instruments under seal or for the performance of transactions required by statute to be authorized in a particular way, authority to do an act can be created by written or spoken words or other conduct of the principal which, reasonably interpreted, causes the agent to believe that the principal desires him to so act on the principal's account.

§ 27. Creation of apparent authority; general rule

Except for the execution of instruments under seal or for the conduct of transactions required by statute to be authorized in a particular way, apparent authority to do an act is created as to a third person by written or spoken words or any other conduct of the principal which, reasonably interpreted, causes the third person to believe that the principal consents to have the act done on his behalf by the person purporting to act for him.

§ 43. Acquiescence by principal in agent's conduct

(1) Acquiescence by the principal in conduct of an agent whose previously conferred authorization reasonably might include it, indicates that the conduct was authorized; if clearly not included in the authorization, acquiescence in it indicates affirmance.

(2) Acquiescence by the principal in a series of acts by the agent indicates authorization to perform similar acts in the future.

§ 82. Ratification

Ratification is the affirmance by a person of a prior act which did not bind him but which was done or professedly done on his account, whereby the act, as to some or all persons, is given effect as if originally authorized by him.

§ 83. Affirmance

Affirmance is either

(a) a manifestation of an election by one on whose account an unauthorized act has been done to treat the act as authorized, or

(b) conduct by him justifiable only is there were such an election.

§ 219. When master is liable for torts of his servants

(1) A master is subject to liability for the torts of his servants committed while acting in the scope of their employment.

(2) A master is not subject to liability for the torts of his servants acting outside the scope of their employment, unless:

(a) the master intended the conduct or the consequences, or

(b) the master was negligent or reckless, or

(c) the conduct violated a non-delegable duty of the master, or

(d) the servant purported to act or to speak on behalf of the principal and there was reliance upon apparent authority, or he was aided in accomplishing the tort by the existence of the agency relation.

§ 220. Definition of servant

(1) A servant is a person employed to perform services in the affairs of another and who with respect to the physical conduct in the performance of the services is subject to the other's control or right to control.

(2) In determining whether one acting for another is a servant or an independent contractor, the following matters of fact, among others, are considered:

(a) the extent of control which, by the agreement, the master may exercise over the details of the work;

(b) whether or not the one employed is engaged in a distinct occupation or business;

(c) the kind of occupation, with reference to whether, in the locality, the work is usually done under the direction of the employer or by a specialist without supervision;

(d) the skill required in the particular occupation;

(e) whether the employer or the workman supplies the instrumentalities, tools, and the place of work for the person doing the work;

(f) the length of time for which the person is employed;

(g) the method of payment, whether by the time or by the job;

(h) whether or not the work is part of the regular business of the employer;

(i) whether or not the parties believe they are creating the relation of master and servant; and

(j) whether the principal is or is not in business.

§ 228. General statement of scope of employment

(1) Conduct of a servant is within the scope of employment if, but only if:

(a) it is of the kind he is employed to perform;

(b) it occurs substantially within the authorized time and space limits;

(c) it is actuated, at least in part, by a purpose to serve the master, and

(d) if force is intentionally used by the servant against another, the use of force is not unexpectable by the master.

(2) Conduct of a servant is not within the scope of employment if it is different in kind from that authorized, far beyond the authorized time or space limits, or too little actuated by a purpose to serve the master.

§ 235. Conduct not for purpose of serving master

An act of a servant is not within the scope of employment if it is done with no intention to perform it as a part of or incident to a service on account of which he is employed.

§ 261. Agent's position enables him to deceive

A principal who puts a servant or other agent in a position which enables the agent, while apparently acting within his authority, to commit a fraud upon third persons is subject to liability to such third persons for the fraud.

§ 388. Duty to account for profits arising out of employment

Unless otherwise agreed, an agent who makes a profit in connection with transactions conducted by him on behalf of the principal is under a duty to give such profit to the principal.

§ 389. Acting as adverse party without principal's consent

Unless otherwise agreed, an agent is subject to a duty not to deal with his principal as an adverse party in a transaction connected with his agency without the principal's knowledge.

Comment

c. The rule stated in this Section is not based upon the existence of harm to the principal in the particular case. It exists to prevent a conflict of opposing interests in the minds of agents whose duty it is to act solely for the benefit of their principals. The rule applies, therefore, even though the transaction between the principal and the agent is beneficial to the principal.

§ 390. Acting as adverse party with principal's consent

An agent who, to the knowledge of the principal, acts on his own account in a transaction in which he is employed has a duty to deal fairly with the principal and to disclose to him all facts which the agent knows or should know would reasonably affect the principal's judgment. unless the principal has manifested that he knows such facts or that he does not care to know them.

Comment

c. . . . If the agent is one upon whom the principal naturally would rely for advice, the fact that the agent discloses that he is acting as an adverse party does not relieve him from the duty of giving the principal impartial advice based upon a carefully formed judgment as to the principal's interests. If he cannot or does not wish to do so, he has a duty to see that the principal secures the advice of a competent and disinterested third person.

§ 392. Acting for adverse party with principal's consent

An agent who, to the knowledge of two principals, acts for both of them in a transaction between them, has a duty to act with fairness to each and to disclose to each all facts which he knows or should know would reasonably affect the judgment of each in permitting such dual agency, except as to a principal who has manifested that he knows such facts or does not care to know them.

§ 395. Using or disclosing confidential information

Unless otherwise agreed, an agent is subject to a duty to the principal not to use or to communicate information confidentially given him by the principal or acquired by him during the course of or on account of his agency or in violation of his duties as agent, in competition with or to the injury of the principal, on his own account or on behalf of another, although such information does not relate to the transaction in which he is then employed, unless the information is a matter of general knowledge.

Comment

b. The rule stated in this Section applies not only to those communications which are stated to be confidential, but also to information which the agent should know his principal would not care to have revealed to others or used in competition with him.

§ 396. Using confidential information after termination of agency

Unless otherwise agreed, after the termination of the agency, the agent:

(a) has no duty not to compete with the principal;

(b) has a duty to the principal not to use or to disclose to third persons, on his own account or on account of others, in competition with the principal or to his injury, trade secrets, written lists of names, or other similar confidential matters given to him only for the principal's use or acquired by the agent in violation of duty. The agent is entitled to use general information concerning the method of business of the principal and the names of the customers retained in his memory, if not acquired in violation of his duty as agent;

(c) has a duty to account for his profits made by the sale or use of trade secrets and other confidential information, whether or not in competition with the principal;

(d) has a duty to the principal not to take advantage of a still subsisting confidential relation created during the prior agency relation.

SELECTED EXCERPTS FROM THE RESTATEMENT (THIRD) OF AGENCY[*]

§ 1.01. Agency Defined

Agency is the fiduciary relationship that arises when one person (a "principal")manifests assent to another person (an "agent")that the agent shall act on the principal's behalf and subject to the principal's control, and the agent manifests assent or otherwise consents so to act.

§ 1.04. Terminology

(1) *Coagents.* Coagents have agency relationships with the same principal. A coagent may be appointed by the principal or by another agent actually or apparently authorized by the principal to do so.

(2) *Disclosed, undisclosed, and unidentified principals.* (a) *Disclosed principal.* A principal is disclosed if, when an agent and a third party interact, the third party has notice that the agent is acting for a principal and has notice of the principal's identity.

   (b) *Undisclosed principal.* A principal is undisclosed if, when an agent and a third party interact, the third party has no notice that the agent is acting for a principal.

   (c) *Unidentified principal.* A principal is unidentified if, when an agent and a third party interact, the third party has notice that the agent is acting for a principal but does not have notice of the principal's identity.

(3) *Gratuitous agent.* A gratuitous agent acts without a right to compensation.

(4) *Notice.* A person has notice of a fact if the person knows the fact, has reason to know the fact, has received an effective notification of the fact, or should know the fact to fulfill a duty owed to another person. Notice of a fact that an agent knows or has reason to know is imputed to the principal as stated in §§ 5.03 and 5.04. A notification given to or by an agent is effective as notice to or by the principal as stated in § 5.02.

(5) *Person.* A person is (a) an individual; (b) an organization or association that has legal capacity to possess rights and incur obligations; (c)

a government, political subdivision, or instrumentality or entity created by government; or (d) any other entity that has legal capacity to possess rights and incur obligations.

(6) *Power given as security.* A power given as security is a power to affect the legal relations of its creator that is created in the form of a manifestation of actual authority and held for the benefit of the holder or a third person. It is given to protect a legal or equitable title or to secure the performance of a duty apart from any duties owed the holder of the power by its creator that are incident to a relationship of agency under § 1.01.

(7) *Power of attorney.* A power of attorney is an instrument that states an agent's authority.

(8) *Subagent.* A subagent is a person appointed by an agent to perform functions that the agent has consented to perform on behalf of the agent's principal and for whose conduct the appointing agent is responsible to the principal. The relationship between an appointing agent and a subagent is one of agency, created as stated in § 1.01.

(9) *Superior and subordinate coagents.* A superior coagent has the right, conferred by the principal, to direct a subordinate coagent.

(10) *Trustee and agent-trustee.* A trustee is a holder of property who is subject to fiduciary duties to deal with the property for the benefit of charity or for one or more persons, at least one of whom is not the sole trustee. An agent-trustee is a trustee subject to the control of the settlor or of one or more beneficiaries.

§ 2.01. Actual Authority

An agent acts with actual authority when, at the time of taking action that has legal consequences for the principal, the agent reasonably believes, in accordance with the principal's manifestations to the agent, that the principal wishes the agent so to act.

§ 2.02. Scope Of Actual Authority

(1) An agent has actual authority to take action designated or implied in the principal's manifestations to the agent and acts necessary or incidental to achieving the principal's objectives, as the agent reasonably understands the principal's manifestations and objectives when the agent determines how to act.

(2) An agent's interpretation of the principal's manifestations is reasonable if it reflects any meaning known by the agent to be ascribed by the principal and, in the absence of any meaning known to the agent, as a reasonable person in the agent's position would interpret the manifestations in light of the context, including circumstances of which the agent has notice and the agent's fiduciary duty to the principal.

(3) An agent's understanding of the principal's objectives is reasonable if it accords with the principal's manifestations and the inferences that a reasonable person in the agent's position would draw from the circumstances creating the agency.

§ 2.03. Apparent Authority

Apparent authority is the power held by an agent or other actor to affect a principal's legal relations with third parties when a third party reasonably believes the actor has authority to act on behalf of the principal and that belief is traceable to the principal's manifestations.

§ 2.04. Respondeat Superior

An employer is subject to liability for torts committed by employees while acting within the scope of their employment.

§ 2.05. Estoppel To Deny Existence Of Agency Relationship

A person who has not made a manifestation that an actor has authority as an agent and who is not otherwise liable as a party to a transaction purportedly done by the actor on that person's account is subject to liability to a third party who justifiably is induced to make a detrimental change in position because the transaction is believed to be on the person's account, if

(1) the person intentionally or carelessly caused such belief, or

(2) having notice of such belief and that it might induce others to change their positions, the person did not take reasonable steps to notify them of the facts.

§ 2.06. Liability Of Undisclosed Principal

(1) An undisclosed principal is subject to liability to a third party who is justifiably induced to make a detrimental change in position by an agent acting on the principal's behalf and without actual authority if the principal, having notice of the agent's conduct and that it might induce others to change their positions, did not take reasonable steps to notify them of the facts.

(2) An undisclosed principal may not rely on instructions given an agent that qualify or reduce the agent's authority to less than the authority a third party would reasonably believe the agent to have under the same circumstances if the principal had been disclosed.

§ 3.01. Creation Of Actual Authority

Actual authority, as defined in § 2.01, is created by a principal's manifestation to an agent that, as reasonably understood by the agent, expresses the principal's assent that the agent take action on the principal's behalf.

§ 3.02. Formal Requirements

If the law requires a writing or record signed by the principal to evidence an agent's authority to bind a principal to a contract or other transaction, the principal is not bound in the absence of such a writing or record. A principal may be estopped to assert the lack of such a writing or record when a third party has been induced to make a detrimental change in position by the reasonable belief that an agent has authority to bind the principal that is traceable to a manifestation made by the principal.

§ 3.03. Creation Of Apparent Authority

Apparent authority, as defined in § 2.03, is created by a person's manifestation that another has authority to act with legal consequences for the person who makes the manifestation, when a third party reasonably believes the actor to be authorized and the belief is traceable to the manifestation.

§ 3.06. Termination Of Actual Authority—In General

An agent's actual authority may be terminated by:

(1) the agent's death, cessation of existence, or suspension of powers as stated in § 3.07(1) and (3); or

(2) the principal's death, cessation of existence, or suspension of powers as stated in § 3.07(2) and (4); or

(3) the principal's loss of capacity, as stated in § 3.08(1) and (3); or

(4) an agreement between the agent and the principal or the occurrence of circumstances on the basis of which the agent should reasonably conclude that the principal no longer would assent to the agent's taking action on the principal's behalf, as stated in § 3.09; or

(5) a manifestation of revocation by the principal to the agent, or of renunciation by the agent to the principal, as stated in § 3.10(1); or

(6) the occurrence of circumstances specified by statute.

§ 3.07. Death, Cessation Of Existence, And Suspension Of Powers

(1) The death of an individual agent terminates the agent's actual authority.

(2) The death of an individual principal terminates the agent's actual authority. The termination is effective only when the agent has notice of the principal's death. The termination is also effective as against a third party with whom the agent deals when the third party has notice of the principal's death.

(3) When an agent that is not an individual ceases to exist or commences a process that will lead to cessation of existence or when its powers are suspended, the agent's actual authority terminates except as provided by law.

(4) When a principal that is not an individual ceases to exist or commences a process that will lead to cessation of its existence or when

its powers are suspended, the agent's actual authority terminates except as provided by law.

§ 3.08. Loss Of Capacity

(1) An individual principal's loss of capacity to do an act terminates the agent's actual authority to do the act. The termination is effective only when the agent has notice that the principal's loss of capacity is permanent or that the principal has been adjudicated to lack capacity. The termination is also effective as against a third party with whom the agent deals when the third party has notice that the principal's loss of capacity is permanent or that the principal has been adjudicated to lack capacity.

(2) A written instrument may make an agent's actual authority effective upon a principal's loss of capacity, or confer it irrevocably regardless of such loss.

(3) If a principal that is not an individual loses capacity to do an act, its agent's actual authority to do the act is terminated.

§ 3.11. Termination Of Apparent Authority

(1) The termination of actual authority does not by itself end any apparent authority held by an agent.

(2) Apparent authority ends when it is no longer reasonable for the third party with whom an agent deals to believe that the agent continues to act with actual authority.

§ 3.14. Agents With Multiple Principals

An agent acting in the same transaction or matter on behalf of more than one principal may be one or both of the following:

(a) a subagent, as stated in § 3.15; or

(b) an agent for coprincipals, as stated in § 3.16.

§ 3.15. Subagency

(1) A subagent is a person appointed by an agent to perform functions that the agent has consented to perform on behalf of the agent's principal and for whose conduct the appointing agent is responsible to the principal. The relationships between a subagent and the appointing agent and between the subagent and the appointing agent's principal are relationships of agency as stated in § 1.01.

(2) An agent may appoint a subagent only if the agent has actual or apparent authority to do so.

§ 3.16. Agent For Coprincipals

Two or more persons may as coprincipals appoint an agent to act for them in the same transaction or matter.

§ 4.01. Ratification Defined

(1) Ratification is the affirmance of a prior act done by another, whereby the act is given effect as if done by an agent acting with actual authority.

(2) A person ratifies an act by

(a) manifesting assent that the act shall affect the person's legal relations, or

(b) conduct that justifies a reasonable assumption that the person so consents.

(3) Ratification does not occur unless

(a) the act is ratifiable as stated in § 4.03,

(b) the person ratifying has capacity as stated in § 4.04,

(c) the ratification is timely as stated in § 4.05, and

(d) the ratification encompasses the act in its entirety as stated in § 4.07.

§ 5.01. Notifications And Notice—In General

(1) A notification is a manifestation that is made in the form required by agreement among parties or by applicable law, or in a reasonable manner in the absence of an agreement or an applicable law, with the intention of affecting the legal rights and duties of the notifier in relation to rights and duties of persons to whom the notification is given.

(2) A notification given to or by an agent is effective as notification to or by the principal as stated in § 5.02.

(3) A person has notice of a fact if the person knows the fact, has reason to know the fact, has received an effective notification of the fact, or should know the fact to fulfill a duty owed to another person.

(4) Notice of a fact that an agent knows or has reason to know is imputed to the principal as stated in §§ 5.03 and 5.04.

§ 5.02. Notification Given By Or To An Agent

(1) A notification given to an agent is effective as notice to the principal if the agent has actual or apparent authority to receive the notification, unless the person who gives the notification knows or has reason to know that the agent is acting adversely to the principal as stated in § 5.04.

(2) A notification given by an agent is effective as notification given by the principal if the agent has actual or apparent authority to give the notification, unless the person who receives the notification knows or has reason to know that the agent is acting adversely to the principal as stated in § 5.04.

§ 5.03. Imputation Of Notice Of Fact To Principal

For purposes of determining a principal's legal relations with a third party, notice of a fact that an agent knows or has reason to know is imputed to the principal if knowledge of the fact is material to the agent's duties to the principal, unless the agent

(a) acts adversely to the principal as stated in § 5.04, or

(b) is subject to a duty to another not to disclose the fact to the principal.

§ 5.04. An Agent Who Acts Adversely To A Principal

For purposes of determining a principal's legal relations with a third party, notice of a fact that an agent knows or has reason to know is not imputed to the principal if the agent acts adversely to the principal in a transaction or matter, intending to act solely for the agent's own purposes or those of another person. Nevertheless, notice is imputed

(a) when necessary to protect the rights of a third party who dealt with the principal in good faith; or

(b) when the principal has ratified or knowingly retained a benefit from the agent's action.

A third party who deals with a principal through an agent, knowing or having reason to know that the agent acts adversely to the principal, does not deal in good faith for this purpose.

§ 6.01. Agent For Disclosed Principal

When an agent acting with actual or apparent authority makes a contract on behalf of a disclosed principal,

(1) the principal and the third party are parties to the contract; and

(2) the agent is not a party to the contract unless the agent and third party agree otherwise.

§ 6.02. Agent For Unidentified Principal

When an agent acting with actual or apparent authority makes a contract on behalf of an unidentified principal,

(1) the principal and the third party are parties to the contract; and

(2) the agent is a party to the contract unless the agent and the third party agree otherwise.

§ 6.03. Agent For Undisclosed Principal

When an agent acting with actual authority makes a contract on behalf of an undisclosed principal,

(1) unless excluded by the contract, the principal is a party to the contract;

(2) the agent and the third party are parties to the contract; and

(3) the principal, if a party to the contract, and the third party have the same rights, liabilities, and defenses against each other as if the principal made the contract personally, subject to §§ 6.05–6.09.

§ 6.06. Setoff

(1) When an agent makes a contract on behalf of a disclosed or unidentified principal, unless the principal and the third party agree otherwise,

(a) the third party may not set off any amount that the agent independently owes the third party against an amount the third party owes the principal under the contract; and

(b) the principal may not set off any amount that the third party independently owes the agent against an amount the principal owes the third party under the contract.

(2) When an agent makes a contract on behalf of an undisclosed principal,

(a) the third party may set off

(i) any amount that the agent independently owed the third party at the time the agent made the contract and

(ii) any amount that the agent thereafter independently comes to owe the third party until the third party has notice that the agent acts on behalf of a principal against an amount the third party owes the principal under the contract;

(b) after the third party has notice that the agent acts on behalf of a principal, the third party may not set off any amount that the agent thereafter independently comes to owe the third party against an amount the third party owes the principal under the contract unless the principal consents; and

(c) the principal may not set off any amount that the third party independently owes the agent against an amount that the principal owes the third party under the contract, unless the principal and the third party agree otherwise.

(3) Unless otherwise agreed, an agent who is a party to a contract may not set off any amount that the principal independently owes the agent against an amount that the agent owes the third party under the contract. However, with the principal's consent, the agent may set off any amount that the principal could set off against an amount that the principal owes the third party under the contract.

§ 6.07. Settlement With Agent By Principal Or Third Party

(1) A principal's payment to or settlement of accounts with an agent discharges the principal's liability to a third party with whom the agent

has made a contract on the principal's behalf only when the principal acts in reasonable reliance on a manifestation by the third party, not induced by misrepresentation by the agent, that the agent has settled the account with the third party.

(2) A third party's payment to or settlement of accounts with an agent discharges the third party's liability to the principal if the agent acts with actual or apparent authority in accepting the payment or settlement.

(3) When an agent has made a contract on behalf of an undisclosed principal,

(a) until the third party has notice of the principal's existence, the third party's payment to or settlement of accounts with the agent discharges the third party's liability to the principal;

(b) after the third party has notice of the principal's existence, the third party's payment to or settlement of accounts with the agent discharges the third party's liability to the principal if the agent acts with actual or apparent authority in accepting the payment or settlement; and

(c) after receiving notice of the principal's existence, the third party may demand reasonable proof of the principal's identity and relationship to the agent. Until such proof is received, the third party's payment to or settlement of accounts in good faith with the agent discharges the third party's liability to the principal.

§ 6.08. Other Subsequent Dealings Between Third Party And Agent

(1) When an agent has made a contract with a third party on behalf of a disclosed or unidentified principal, subsequent dealings between the agent and the third party may increase or diminish the principal's rights or liabilities to the third party if the agent acts with actual or apparent authority or the principal ratifies the agent's action.

(2) When an agent has made a contract with a third party on behalf of an undisclosed principal,

(a) until the third party has notice of the principal's existence, subsequent dealings between the third party and the agent may increase or diminish the rights or liabilities of the principal to the third party if the agent acts with actual authority, or the principal ratifies the agent's action; and

(b) after the third party has notice of the principal's existence, subsequent dealings between the third party and the agent may increase or diminish the principal's rights or liabilities to the third party if the agent acts with actual or apparent authority or the principal ratifies the agent's action.

§ 6.09. Effect Of Judgment Against Agent Or Principal

When an agent has made a contract with a third party on behalf of a principal, unless the contract provides otherwise,

(1) the liability, if any, of the principal or the agent to the third party is not discharged if the third party obtains a judgment against the other; and

(2) the liability, if any, of the principal or the agent to the third party is discharged to the extent a judgment against the other is satisfied.

§ 7.01. Agent's Liability To Third Party

An agent is subject to liability to a third party harmed by the agent's tortious conduct. Unless an applicable statute provides otherwise, an actor remains subject to liability although the actor acts as an agent or an employee, with actual or apparent authority, or within the scope of employment.

§ 7.02. Duty To Principal; Duty To Third Party

An agent's breach of a duty owed to the principal is not an independent basis for the agent's tort liability to a third party. An agent is subject to tort liability to a third party harmed by the agent's conduct only when the agent's conduct breaches a duty that the agent owes to the third party.

§ 7.07. Employee Acting Within Scope Of Employment

(1) An employer is subject to vicarious liability for a tort committed by its employee acting within the scope of employment.

(2) An employee acts within the scope of employment when performing work assigned by the employer or engaging in a course of conduct subject to the employer's control. An employee's act is not within the scope of employment when it occurs within an independent course of conduct not intended by the employee to serve any purpose of the employer.

(3) For purposes of this section,

(a) an employee is an agent whose principal controls or has the right to control the manner and means of the agent's performance of work, and

(b) the fact that work is performed gratuitously does not relieve a principal of liability.

§ 7.08. Agent Acts With Apparent Authority

A principal is subject to vicarious liability for a tort committed by an agent in dealing or communicating with a third party on or purportedly on behalf of the principal when actions taken by the agent with apparent authority constitute the tort or enable the agent to conceal its commission.

§ 8.01. General Fiduciary Principle

An agent has a fiduciary duty to act loyally for the principal's benefit in all matters connected with the agency relationship.

§ 8.08. Duties Of Care, Competence, And Diligence

Subject to any agreement with the principal, an agent has a duty to the principal to act with the care, competence, and diligence normally exercised by agents in similar circumstances. Special skills or knowledge possessed by an agent are circumstances to be taken into account in determining whether the agent acted with due care and diligence. If an agent claims to possess special skills or knowledge, the agent has a duty to the principal to act with the care, competence, and diligence normally exercised by agents with such skills or knowledge.

§ 8.14. Duty To Indemnify

A principal has a duty to indemnify an agent

(1) in accordance with the terms of any contract between them; and

(2) unless otherwise agreed,

    (a) when the agent makes a payment

        (i) within the scope of the agent's actual authority, or

        (ii) that is beneficial to the principal, unless the agent acts officiously in making the payment; or

    (b) when the agent suffers a loss that fairly should be borne by the principal in light of their relationship.

§ 8.15. Principal's Duty To Deal Fairly And In Good Faith

A principal has a duty to deal with the agent fairly and in good faith, including a duty to provide the agent with information about risks of physical harm or pecuniary loss that the principal knows, has reason to know, or should know are present in the agent's work but unknown to the agent.